THE BURIED MAN

STEPHEN COAN

The Buried Man

A Life of H. Rider Haggard

HURST & COMPANY, LONDON

First published in the United Kingdom in 2025 by
C. Hurst & Co. (Publishers) Ltd.,
New Wing, Somerset House, Strand, London, WC2R 1LA
© Stephen Coan, 2025
All rights reserved.

A Cataloguing-in-Publication data record for this book
is available from the British Library.

ISBN: 9781911723752

www.hurstpublishers.com

Printed and bound in Great Britain by Bell & Bain Ltd, Glasgow

For Antoaneta,
Tzvetelina, Nicholas and Alexandra
and in memory of my parents
Donovan Walter Coan (1919–1993)
&
Eileen Mary Coan (née Wrangle) (1926–2012)

CONTENTS

Map ix

Acknowledgments xi

Note on orthography xv

List of Illustrations xvii

Introduction 1

Prologue 7

1   'I too must die' 13

2   'Love's sweet dream' 27

3   'A mass of contradictory evidence' 45

4   'The first thing I ever wrote' 61

5   'A stranger in strange lands' 73

6   'One of the hardest journeys imaginable' 85

7   'Pleasant recollections' 107

8   'A crushing blow' 117

9   'Disaster in Zululand' 133

10   'My own sweet love' 147

11   'Land of murder and sudden death' 167

12   'Write a bit, don't you?' 187

13   'The most amazing story ever written' 207

14   'Immortal love' 225

15   'The literature of another planet' 239

16   'Between success and attacks' 249

17   'Passionate and poetic' 263

18 'I descended into hell' 279

19 'Oceans of gore' 291

20 'Speculative and nerve-racking' 301

21 'Accurate observation' 317

22 'Higher aims' 333

23 'Sadness of the world' 347

24 'Recognition – with a vengeance' 361

25 'Land of troubles' 375

26 'Returned from the dead' 385

27 '400 miles through Zululand' 397

28 'Armageddon has fallen' 409

29 'A second St. Paul' 421

30 'One of the hells' 431

31 'I sink into old age' 445

32 'Old pharaoh' 459

Appendix: Mhlopekazi 473

Notes 475

Bibliography 605

Index 621

Southern Africa 1875–1916

© S.Ballard (2024)

ACKNOWLEDGMENTS

When it comes to researching and writing about Henry Rider Haggard all roads lead to Ditchingham Lodge on the Haggard estate close to the village of Ditchingham in Norfolk, England. A long journey from my home in South Africa.

My first visit there was in November 1997. Sitting beside the flame and crackle of a welcoming fireside I outlined my intentions to Mark and Nada Cheyne, descendants of Haggard and custodians of the Cheyne Collection of Haggard material. Not only did they give their blessing to my biographical project but they also presented me with the manuscript of Haggard's account of his 1914 visit to South Africa and bade me find a publisher. The result was *Diary of an African Journey* (2000). In due course further manuscripts came to light which led to the publication of *Mameena and Other Plays, the Complete Dramatic works of H. Rider Haggard* (2008).

I visited Ditchingham Lodge many times thereafter to do further research and enjoy Mark and Nada's hospitality, which by then had evolved into friendship. That they are not alive to see this biography is a source of great regret. Sadly, I can now only record my gratitude and affection.

My connection with the family continued as Mark and Nada's daughter Dorothy took on responsibility for the collection, her assistance with specific items is noted in the text, and I thank her for her warm hospitality over the years and a memorable visit to Bradenham Hall where Haggard grew up. Dorothy's sister Judy and their brother Jonathan have also played a role in this book, as has their elder brother Rider Cheyne, named after his great-grandfather and long resident in Canada. Rider was happily forthcoming with information and a wonderful companion on two visits to South Africa, one with his wife Donna-Marie, when we stayed at Haggard's farm Hilldrop (now a hotel) near Newcastle in northern KwaZulu-Natal.

Move on a generation to Richard Stearn, current copyright holder of the unpublished material in the Cheyne Collection, I thank him wholeheartedly for his permission to use material from the collection.

While researching and writing this book I have received assistance from many people to whom I now extend my thanks and make due acknowledgment:

The late Roger Allen, founder of the Rider Haggard Society, was always eager to assist, as has been his successor Shirley Addy whose own writing on Haggard and Egypt has been made use of in this book. The late John Blatchly, former headmaster

ACKNOWLEDGMENTS

and subsequently archivist of Ipswich School, who enthusiastically joined several dots and provided background information for Haggard's attendance at the school. As did the school's current archivist Caleb Howgego. Most biographers owe a debt to those who wrote before and I have had the privilege of contact and consequent perspectives from five of Haggard's previous biographers, the late Morton Cohen, Peter Berresford-Ellis, Norman Etherington, D.S. Higgins, and Victoria Manthorpe. John Conyngham, author, friend, colleague, and former editor at the *Witness* newspaper in Pietermaritzburg, for pertinent conversation and encouragement. Haggard scholar Patricia Crouan-Véron, with whom I have had much enjoyable discussion during her visits to South Africa from her native France. The late Stephen Gray, author, poet and critic, generously shared information on Haggard, spotted many a reference, and handed on several books. I regret he did not live to see the outcome. A similar regret applies to the eminent historian, the late Jeff Guy, from whom many a gruff observation while in the queue of our local supermarket resulted in several course corrections during my research. Jeff was just one of a cohort of South African historians from whom I have benefitted via both personal interaction and reading, as reflected in the bibliography. Two I would like to single out are John Laband, for his writing on the Zulus and their history; and John Wright, co-editor of the *James Stuart Archives*, that extraordinary window into nineteenth and early twentieth century South African history. Ian Knight, Anglo-Zulu War historian, has long supported my interest in Haggard. I thank him for a personal tour of the battlefields of Isandlwana and Rorke's Drift in the 1990s, and for much conversation and correspondence. Anne Lehmkuhl, who unlocked the door to the Lehmkuhl family history and who also put me in touch with the late Peter Smits who was able to do the same for the Ford family and so round out background on Haggard's life in the Pretoria of the 1870s. My friend and former colleague on the *Witness*, Christopher Merrett, author, critic and sharp social and political analyst, for the index. A special debt of gratitude is owed to Haggard scholar Lindy Stiebel who I first 'met' when the arrival of a letter from her to Mark Cheyne coincided with my first visit to Ditchingham in 1997. We later met in person in Durban and have since enjoyed copious discussion on Haggard as well as collaborating on the *Rider Haggard Trail* pamphlet, a contribution to literary tourism in KwaZulu-Natal, and I thank her for happily sharing with me her extensive knowledge of Haggard and his work. The late Alfred Tella, Haggard collector and my co-editor on *Mameena, the Collected Plays of H. Rider Haggard*, who kindly sent me copies of his privately published Haggard items. Though we never met in person (he lived in the United States) we participated in a long and lively correspondence. Gavin Whitelaw, archaeologist at the KwaZulu-Natal Museum, Pietermaritzburg, who helped to locate Pagadi's Kop; and Rauri Alcock who drove me there. Dumisani Zondi for his translation from isiZulu to English of John Dube's preface to the Zulu version of *Nada the Lily*.

ACKNOWLEDGMENTS

Many people have assisted me with Haggard books, newspaper cuttings, photographs, quotes, anecdotes, made connections and comments, which influenced my research and found their way into this book: Jennifer Aitchison, Chris Allhusen (owner of Bradenham Hall, for allowing myself and Dorothy Cheyne to visit the hall and its environs); Carlo Alves (for sight of Haggard's briefcase sporting the initials HRH), David Attwell, the late Maria Bambus, Penelope Bernard, Marius Brits, Terri Broll, Creina Alcock, Barbara Benson, Neil Bloy, Ian Carbutt, Grant Christison, Lindsay Christison, Jane and Vincent Carruthers, the late Laura Chrisman, the late Connol 'Pip' Coan, Gwilym Colenso, the late Tim Couzens, Neil Curry, Raphael de Kadt, Philip Daniel, John Deare, Nicholas Dennys, John Dickie, Malcolm Draper, Anne and Graham Dominy, Helena Drysdale, Mark Fricker, the late Robin Fryde, Mary Gardner, Susan Geisel, the late Betty Gilderdale, David Goldthorpe (of Sotheby's, for relevant sales catalogues); Robin Griffiths, the late Anne Harcombe, Louise Hall, Judy Hickey, Justin Gordon, Reg and Bea Gush, Andre and Lelani Joubert (who run Haggards on Hilldrop, once Haggard's home and now a National Monument); Gordon Key, Regi Khumalo, Adrian Koopman, the late Clive Lawrance, David Livingstone, Jean McNeil, Thokozani Mdluli (who took me to the top of Tshaneni, Ghost Mountain), the late Rosemary Metcalf, Julia Meintjes, Wayne Mills, Alastair Mitchell, Martin Plaut, the late David Rattray, Christoph Rippe, Maureen and Roy Rutherfoord (owners of the Ghost Mountain Inn), Cedric Sissing, Jabulani Sithole, Norma Shepstone, the late Margaret and Brian Smith (an aunt and uncle who encouraged my reading), Shelagh O'Byrne Spencer, Anthony Stidolph, Paul Stidolph, Dom Theobald (tenant at Ditchingham House, for allowing access to his flat wherein lies Haggard's study); the late Paul Thompson; the late Gilbert Torlage; Tania Zulli, Margaret von Klemperer, the late Denys Whatmore and John Young.

A book such is this is also the result of the skills and acumen of the staff of various archives and libraries holding Haggard material. I thank them for their assistance.

In South Africa: Brenthurst Library, Johannesburg, especially to director Sally MacRoberts for permission to quote from the unpublished Haggard manuscript 'Camp Life in Pretoria'; library director Jennifer Platt who not only drew requested items but selected others of relevance; and librarian Desre Stead. Bessie Head Municipal Library (formerly the Natal Society Library), Pietermaritzburg, especially the director, the late John Morrison, and special collections librarian, the late David Buckley. Campbell Collections, University of KwaZulu-Natal, Durban, especially Special Collections librarian Mbalenhle Zulu; Cape Town Archives Repository; Cecil Renaud Library, Pietermaritzburg, University of KwaZulu-Natal, Pietermaritzburg; Archives Repository, especially Pieter Nel and Thabani Mdladla. Transvaal Archives, Pretoria; and Wits Historical Papers Research Archive, William Cullen Library, University of the Witwatersrand, Johannesburg.

ACKNOWLEDGMENTS

In the United Kingdom: British Library, London; Caird Library, National Maritime Museum, Greenwich; Cambridge University Library; Norfolk Record Office, Norwich; Weston Library, Bodleian Libraries' special collections, Oxford.

In the United States: Columbia University, Rare Book and Manuscript Library, New York; Huntington Library, San Marino, California; Lockwood Collection, State University of New York, Buffalo; Cushing Memorial Library and Archives, Texas A&M University.

Finally, my thanks to Michael Dwyer, publisher at Hurst, for his faith in this book; Kathleen May, associate publisher and director of sales and marketing; editor Russell Martin, Daisy Leitch, production director, Niamh Drennan, production assistant, proofreader Geraldine Klumb; Mei Jayne Yew, assistant editor.

Of the many companions on this journey, none have been more constant and supportive than my partner Antoaneta Slavova to whom I dedicate this book.

Stephen Coan
Johannesburg
South Africa

NOTE ON ORTHOGRAPHY

Current orthography has been used in the text for names and words in isiZulu. Contemporary spellings have been used in quotations and any italicised words are as per the originals.

Some sections in Chapter 14, 'Immortal love', dealing with *She*, are revised from my essay '"The Most Extraordinary Romance", H. Rider Haggard and the writing of *She*' from Zulli, Tania (ed.), *She: Explorations into a Romance*, Rome: Aracne, 2009.

LIST OF ILLUSTRATIONS

1. Theophilus Shepstone and William Sargeaunt with staff in Pretoria, 1877. Standing, from left to right, John Sargeaunt, Arthur Cochrane, Captain James Fencott 'Jumbo' James, Captain Robert Patterson. Seated (l-r) Melmoth Osborn, Sargeaunt, Shepstone, H. Rider Haggard and Vacy Lyle. Captain Patterson and John Sargeaunt would be murdered on their expedition to the Victoria Falls, an event Haggard drew on for *King Solomon's Mines*. Campbell Collections, University of KwaZulu-Natal.

2. Autographed portrait photograph presented by Haggard to Theophilus Shepstone in 1881. Reproduced from C.J. Uys, *In the Era of Shepstone*.

3. Ida Hector, Haggard's secretary. *Ladies' Home Journal*, February, 1894.

4. Haggard and Masuku during Haggard's 1914 visit to South Africa. *The Pictorial*, 3 April 1914. Pietermaritzburg Archive Repositories.

5. Francis La Monaca at work on his bust of Haggard in 1922. Cushing Memorial Library and Archives, Texas A&M University.

6. Pencil sketch of H. Rider Haggard in his youth. Artist unknown. Reproduced from *The Days of My Life*, Vol.1.

7. Ella Haggard, Haggard's mother. Reproduced from *The Days of My Life*, Vol.1.

8. William Meybohm Haggard, Haggard's father. Cheyne Collection.

9. Elizabeth 'Lilly' Jackson. Cheyne Collection.

10. Theophilus Shepstone and his staff on the day of the Annexation of the Transvaal, 12 April 1877. The flag on the left would not be raised until 24 May 1877, Queen Victoria's official birthday. From left to right (standing), Sub-Inspector Frederick L. Phillips, Melmoth Osborn, Colonel Edward Brooke, Captain James Fencott 'Jumbo' James; (seated) Joseph Henderson, Shepstone, Vacy Lyle, Frederick Fynney. Haggard is seated on the ground. Author collection.

11. Lewis and Johanna Ford. Author collection.

12. Arthur Cochrane. Cheyne Collection.

13. Masuku in 1914. Cheyne Collection.

14. Mhlopekazi in the 1870s, on the staff of Theophilus Shepstone. He would later become famous as the fictional character Umslopogaas. Cheyne Collection.

15. Mhlopekazi in old age. Cheyne Collection.

16. Louise Margitson and Haggard with his sister Mary behind them. The photograph was taken during their engagement. Cheyne Collection.

17. Haggard (seated) and Arthur Cochrane shortly after their return from Natal in 1881. The knobkerrie that Masuku gave Haggard is planted in the flowerbed. Cheyne Collection.

18. Haggard's son, Jock. Cheyne Collection.

19. Charles Longman, Haggard's friend and publisher. Cheyne Collection.

20. The Haggard brothers. Left to right, Alfred, Andrew, Rider, William and Jack. Cheyne Collection.

21. Haggard in the early 1890s. Cheyne Collection.

22. Haggard in the late 1890s. Wikipedia Commons.

23. Haggard and Lilias, his youngest daughter and first biographer. Cheyne Collection.

24. Haggard (far right) and his daughter Angela with friend and dragoman at the temple of Karnak, Egypt, 1904. From *Rider Haggard and Egypt* by Shirley M. Addy.

25. Haggard (left foreground) contemplating the memorial to the 24th Regiment (South Wales Borderers) at Isandlwana a few weeks after its unveiling in March 1914. J.Y. Gibson is standing to his right and the driver, H.M. Edwardes, is behind him. *Windsor Magazine*, Bodleian Library, University of Oxford.

26. The Overland stuck fast in the uMhlathuze River during the 1914 trip to Zululand. From left to right, Haggard, Sikouyana and Nombi. The latter would become a major character in *Finished*. *Windsor Magazine*, Bodleian Library, University of Oxford.

27. John Langalibalele Dube, founding president of the African National Congress who Haggard interviewed in 1914. John and Angelina Dube with their children in the mid-1930s: from left) Nomagugu, Joan Lulu, James Sipho and Douglas Sobantu. Campbell Collections, University of KwaZulu-Natal.

28. John Langalibalele Dube. Campbell Collections, University of KwaZulu-Natal.

29. Haggard in Egypt, at the temple in Abydos in 1924. 'Surely such a spot should be holy if there is aught so upon the earth.' Cheyne Collection.

30. Bradenham Hall, Norfolk, where Haggard grew up. Photo Stephen Coan.

31. Government House, Pietermaritzburg, where Haggard lived and worked when on the staff of the Lieutenant-Governor of Natal in the 1870s, as it is today. Photo Ian Carbutt.

32. 'The Palatial', the dwelling built by Haggard and Cochrane in Pretoria in the late 1870s, as it was in 1914. Later known as 'Jess's Cottage'. Cheyne Collection.

33. Hilldrop farmhouse depicted in the lower right corner of the Haggard memorial window at St Mary's, Ditchingham. Photo Stephen Coan.

34. Hilldrop today. Photo Stephen Coan.

35. Ditchingham House. Photo Stephen Coan.

36. Rear of Ditchingham House. Haggard's study is above the garden seat and the shrubbery. Photo Stephen Coan.

37. 1 Fairholme Road (to the right) at the corner with Gledstanes Road, West Kensington, where Haggard wrote *King Solomon's Mines*. Photo Alastair Mitchell.

38. Exterior of 56 Gunterstone Road in West Kensington, showing the front room wherein Haggard wrote *She* and the incident with the mummy occurred. Photo Alastair Mitchell.

INTRODUCTION

Henry Rider Haggard's adventure novel *King Solomon's Mines*, set in sub-Saharan Africa, was one of the most widely read books of the late-Victorian era. Its publication in 1885 effectively inaugurated the era of the bestseller, its subject matter tapping into the British reading public's fascination with Africa and satisfying a curiosity hitherto largely catered for by travellers' journals and tales of exploration. As a consequence of its huge success Haggard was to remain best known as a writer of adventure stories, but there was another side to Haggard born of a desire to be of service to his country and its empire. Haggard travelled the world in this weightier guise, writing extensively about agriculture, social issues, and events in Africa.

King Solomon's Mines was advertised by its publisher as 'the most amazing story ever written' but, when thumping down the manuscript of *She* on the desk of his literary agent's desk in 1887, Haggard declared: 'There is what I shall be remembered by.'[1] At the time of writing this biography, both titles remain in print in critical and popular editions. *Allan Quatermain* (1887), the sequel to *King Solomon's Mines*, occasionally joins them. In total Haggard wrote seventy books, including adventure stories – or 'romances' as they were then styled – as well as contemporary novels and non-fiction works.

Haggard retained his bestselling status well into the second half of the twentieth century. In 1949 Macdonald began issuing 'The Romances of Sir Henry Rider Haggard' in what became a 22-volume edition. The most popular titles were reprinted several times and the entire series reissued with new dustjacket illustrations in the early 1970s. When Pulp Fictions launched their reprints of 'Ripping Yarns & Thrilling Tales' in the late 1990s, the Haggard titles 'proved to be the most popular'.[2] The four-novel sequence featuring Ayesha, She-Who-Must-Be-Obeyed, was recently republished with mildly erotic covers to chime with the success of E.L. James's *Fifty Shades of Grey*.

Once upon a time there was a period when Haggard's surname was synonymous with a continent. 'Haggard's Africa' was a familiar phrase in tourist and safari publicity brochures, including their internet incarnations, but this has become less frequent. Haggard's books are inescapably of their time: they draw charges of racism and promoting British imperialism; and the hunting scenes are no longer acceptable to modern tastes. The generations of readers who grew up reading Rider Haggard are fading away. That he continues to be read – by academics, scholars and attentive readers – is because his books open a unique window into the late-Victorian Age. When reviewing Morton Cohen's *Rider Haggard: His Life and Works* (1960), the writer and critic V.S. Pritchett recalled E.M. Forster talking of novelists 'sending down a bucket into the unconscious', and concluded, if that was the case, then 'the author of *She* installed a suction pump' draining 'the whole reservoir of the public's secret desires'.[3] Haggard's work, especially *She*, attracted the attention of Sigmund Freud and Carl Jung, who saw his writing as an expression of the human unconscious and Ayesha or She a feminine archetype, especially as *She*, according to Haggard, was written in 'white heat' bypassing the mediation of the intellect.[4]

Haggard's awareness of his feminine side is well attested: the majority of his books feature strong female characters and twenty-eight of his fiction titles – well over half – use female names while at least two others began life in manuscript with feminine titles, only to be changed later owing to their prior use by other authors.[5] On reading Haggard's first novel, *Dawn*, Olive Schreiner thought the author's name was a pseudonym: the writer 'must be a woman. I can't make out what *type* of man would have written such a book.'[6]

While the popular readership for Haggard may have declined, the many annotated editions of Haggard's key texts signal the boom in academic and scholarly interest. This began in the 1980s and now embraces an ever growing body of scholarship, comprising books, theses and papers, emanating from many countries around the globe, including Argentina, Brazil, France, Italy, South Africa, Turkey, the United Kingdom and the United States.

* * *

Henry Rider Haggard was born on 22 June in 1856, the eighth child of a family of ten – seven sons and three daughters. His father William Meybohm Haggard, the local squire, was the owner of Bradenham Hall standing on the gentle rise above the village of West Bradenham in Norfolk. In 1875, after a rather chaotic education, Haggard found himself in southern Africa in the British colony of Natal, an intern on the staff of Lieutenant Governor Henry Bulwer. Haggard would subsequently be involved as a minor player in the annexation of the Transvaal and stood on the sidelines of the Anglo-Zulu War. He married during a visit to England and finally left southern Africa in 1881. He embarked on a legal career while writing on the side until *King Solomon's Mines* changed his fortunes and he began writing full-time. Though he failed to obtain a seat in parliament, he was ever keen to be of service to his country and its empire. A capable farmer, he became an agricultural expert and reformer, serving on various government commissions. Haggard's knighthood, bestowed in 1912, was in recognition of his public service and not his writing. By the time of his death in May 1925, Haggard had produced forty-eight adventure stories, many of them set in Africa, twelve contemporary novels, and ten works of non-fiction, including his autobiography, *The Days of My Life*, published posthumously in 1926. Then silence: no authorised biography, no collected letters, no volumes of appreciation or reminiscence. Nevertheless Haggard's titles enjoyed frequent reprinting, and his two most famous books, *King Solomon's Mines* and *She*, as mentioned above, remain in print nearly 140 years after they were written.

The biographical silence was first broken in 1951 with the publication of *The Cloak That I Left* written by his daughter Lilias Rider Haggard. Understandably sympathetic to its subject, it is also unflinchingly forthright as to her father's flaws, the constraints of his marriage, and his depressive temperament. Lilias's memoir was followed in 1960 by Cohen's *Rider Haggard: His Life and Works*, and while subsequent biographies have each in their turn thrown new light on Haggard's life, Cohen's elegant and scholarly work remains pre-eminent. In 1965 Cohen published *Rudyard Kipling to Rider Haggard: The Record of a Friendship*, constructed upon the correspondence between the two writers.

Peter Berresford Ellis's biography *H. Rider Haggard: A Voice from the Infinite* (1978) sought to establish – or re-establish – Haggard in the English literary canon.

Haggard's own silence was broken in 1980 by *The Private Diaries of Sir H. Rider Haggard*, edited by D.S. Higgins from the twenty-six volumes of diaries begun by Haggard in 1914 and continued until his death in 1925. The title is something of a misnomer, as there is nothing within its pages of the nature suggested: no personal revelations, no intimate confessions – unless they be those of religious faith and belief – and, in any case, Haggard always intended his diaries for publication and had discussed the matter with Kipling.

Higgins's coup in his subsequent biography *Rider Haggard: The Great Storyteller* (1981) was the identification of Haggard's first and lost love with whom Haggard believed he would be reunited eternally in the hereafter. Despite being a key figure in Haggard's life, she had remained unidentified. Haggard referred to her but didn't name her in his autobiography and Lilias refers to her simply as 'Lilith'.[7] Higgins was the first to identify her as Mary Elizabeth Jackson, sister of the East African colonial official Frederick Jackson, who was called Lilly by her friends and family.

Tom Pocock's biography *Rider Haggard and the Lost Empire* (1993) placed an emphasis on Haggard's public service, which Haggard regarded as more important than his writing. Victoria Manthorpe's composite biography of the Haggard siblings, *Children of the Empire: The Victorian Haggards* (1996), exposed for the first time the affair Haggard had in Pretoria with a 'Mrs Ford' as well as the subsequent birth (and death) of their child.

Though not a biography, mention should be made of Norman Etherington's literary study *Rider Haggard* (1984). Other volumes aimed primarily at an academic audience include Wendy Katz's *Rider Haggard and the Fiction of Empire* (1987); Shirley Addy's *Rider Haggard and Egypt* (1998); Laura Chrisman's *Rereading the Imperial Romance* (2000); Lindy Stiebel's *Imagining Africa: Landscape in H. Rider*

Haggard's African Romances (2001); Gerald Monsman's *Rider Haggard on the Imperial Frontier* (2006); *She: Explorations into a Romance*, edited by Tania Zulli (2009); Zulli's *Colonial Transitions: Literature and Culture in the Late Victorian Age* (2012); and Richard Reeves, *The Sexual Imperative in the Novels of Sir Henry Rider Haggard* (2018).

The year 2000 saw the first publication of Haggard's *Diary of an African Journey*, the product of his 1914 visit to South Africa as a member of the Dominions Royal Commission. This marked his return to the subcontinent that had inspired the romances to which he owed his fame. A product of Haggard's middle age, the diary is a contrasting mirror to the younger Haggard and the historical events that formed the backdrop to his life in southern Africa from 1875 to 1881. The diary also gives an indication of how Haggard's views, opinions and sympathies had changed in the intervening years.

By and large Haggard took the establishment line when it came to matters of governance, but he was untypically sympathetic to the plight of the indigenous peoples, particularly the Zulu of south-eastern Africa, for whom he had a keen regard and empathy. In 1914 Haggard was alert to the political and social implications of a small white settler society dominating an overwhelmingly black population and keen to canvass the opinions of all involved. So it was not surprising that John Dube, president of the African National Congress, should come to his notice and typical of Haggard that he should seek him out for interview.

The Dube interview (unrecorded by previous Haggard biographers) along with Haggard's observations on racial tensions, migrant labour and prevailing conditions in Zululand, in addition to those on South Africa's political future recorded in his diary, serves to cut against the grain of academic and popular perceptions of Haggard and his writing. As Tania Zulli states, 'categorising his prose under the label of imperialist fiction would be both reductive and hazardous'.[8] Apart from his 'nationalistic attitudes, his work discloses a deep understanding of the brutality of colonial rule, together with a romantic nostalgia for an uncontaminated romantic past'.[9]

To return to the biographies. None are to be discounted, but their perspective is mainly that of the Global North, and South African scholarship and historiography of the last fifty years is rarely taken into account. For example, Haggard's views on nineteenth-century South African history, as expressed in his first book, the non-fiction work *Cetywayo and His White Neighbours*, and in his autobiography are those of his mentor, the Natal civil servant Theophilus Shepstone, and represent an 'establishment' position, a point of vantage long since revised by South African historians. Despite this, Haggard's version of South African history has largely been left unquestioned and replicated by biographers and in academic papers dealing with his work. *The Buried Man* seeks to amend this and has dealt with Haggard's years in southern Africa and his lifelong connection with the subcontinent in greater detail than before as well as incorporating recent historiography.

INTRODUCTION

Neil Hultgren has pointed out that 'Haggard criticism has evinced a continued interest in issues of gender and imperialism. This fascination was to a great extent influenced by the popularity of postcolonial criticism after 1985.' However, since 2000, critics have had to 'contend with a field saturated by postcolonial approaches to Haggard. Rather than return to the issues of imperialism and gender, recent critics of Haggard rely on approaches from textual studies and cultural history to explore newer, more specific aspects of Haggard's work.'[10]

I confess to having some sympathy for the late South African historian Jeff Guy's frustration at the 'obsessive attention paid to Haggard's African novels by literary scholars,'[11] while acknowledging *The Buried Man* constitutes a response to that attention and is, hopefully, something of a corrective and an inspiration.

***

A few words on the title *The Buried Man*, a phrase taken from Graham Greene's essay, 'Rider Haggard's Secret'. In Greene's estimation, Haggard's 'secret' was revealed when in conversation with Kipling he let slip that he 'thought this world was one of the hells.'[12] The comment 'starts shockingly from the page in its very casualness,' writes Greene, 'and then we begin to remember the passages we skated so lightly over in the adventure stories when we were young and the world held promise ... We did not notice the melancholy end of every adventure.'[13]

Haggard's existential fatalism permeates his work, often articulated by his hero Allan Quatermain who, as Haggard admits, is 'only myself set in a variety of imagined situations, thinking my thoughts and looking at life through my eyes.'[14] Much of Haggard's fiction, especially the contemporary Victorian and Edwardian novels, can be read as autobiographical psycho-dramas: variations on the theme of triangular love, reinventions and reimaginings of his relationships with Lilly and Louie. Haggard 'was a public author', observes Greene, 'and the private life remained the private life in so far as he could control it'.[15] It is in his books that can be found 'the emergence of the buried man'.[16]

PROLOGUE

IMPI YABANTWANA: THE WAR OF THE CHILDREN

On 2 December 1856, when Theophilus Shepstone, Natal's Secretary for Native Affairs, arrived on the southern bank of the Thukela River around midday, the battle he hoped to prevent was already over. 'The loss of life has been awful,' he reported in a dispatch to his superior, the Lieutenant Governor of Natal, Sir John Scott. 'The sandbanks in the river were strewn with dead bodies and many were floating in the eddies of the streams. From the field of battle to the river, the country is filled with dead and dying.'[1]

In the second half of the nineteenth century the Thukela River constituted the northern border between Natal and the kingdom of the Zulu, 'the people of heaven'. The battle of Ndondakusuka, 'one of the greatest battles ever fought on the soil of Zululand,'[2] was named after the highest hill in the area, Ndondakusuka (in isiZulu, 'slow to move'), and furnished the decisive climax to *Impi yabaNtwana* – the War of the Children – finally settling the question of who of the two half-brothers, Cetshwayo and Mbuyazi, sons of King Mpande kaSenzangakhona, would accede to the Zulu throne on the death of their father. Death due to natural causes was an unlikely end for a Zulu king: Shaka kaSenzangakhona, who established the Zulu as a people to be reckoned with in south-east Africa during the early nineteenth century, had been assassinated in 1828 by his brother Dingane, who in turn was deposed and replaced by his brother Mpande.[3]

The lack of an agreed principle of succession was especially problematic in a polygamous society. In theory at least, the heir was considered to be the eldest son of the *inkosikazi* or great wife, often married or named late in life to minimise the risk of the king's assassination by an adult son. Breaking from convention, Mpande designated Cetshwayo his heir early in his reign. In 1839 Mpande travelled south with seven-year-old Cetshwayo to Pietermaritzburg, then capital of the Boer republic of Natalia, to seek aid from the Boers in his struggle against King Dingane. Mpande presented Cetshwayo to the Volksraad (parliament) as the son of his *inkosikazi*, Ngqumbazi.[4] This politically expedient move on Mpande's part laid the foundations for future troubles when Cetshwayo grew to maturity, 'confident of his grand destiny as the next king'[5] and attracting a substantial following eager to attach themselves to a rising royal star.

In the early 1850s the ageing Mpande feared his grip on authority was weakening and manoeuvred to prevent the emergence of Cetshwayo as his unchallenged heir and potential assassin by supporting the claim to the throne of another son, Mbuyazi. By way of justification Mpande said that he had identified Cetshwayo as heir before becoming king but that Mbuyazi, born to a different mother a few months after Cetshwayo (both were born in 1832), had a better claim to the throne as his mother Monase had been specially chosen by the childless King Shaka from his *isigodlo* (women's quarters) to be the bride of Mpande and to breed sons and heirs in his stead.

Genealogical sleight of hand aside, Mpande feared and disliked the vigorous Cetshwayo but 'deeply loved Mbuyazi'.[6] In 1850 or 1851 both princes, now in their late teens, were inducted into the newly formed uThulwana *ibutho* or age-group regiment. Cetshwayo quickly gained a reputation as a brave and resourceful warrior and a clique formed around him, calling themselves the uSuthu – 'with the long horns' – a name derived from the Sotho-type cattle Cetshwayo's supporters had captured from the Pedi during a raid in 1851. Mbuyazi's faction was known as the iziGqoza, from the word meaning 'to drop down like drops of water from a roof', a reference to the steady trickle of followers willing to acknowledge Mbuyazi's claim to the throne, albeit one not constant enough to counter the growing support for Cetshwayo. By the mid-1850s Cetshwayo had mustered strong support in the northern and southern regions of the kingdom and could rely on the allegiance of several leading chiefs whereas Mbuyazi had alienated the king's council when he blatantly advertised his aspirations by creating his own *inkatha*, a plaited coil of grass symbolic of kingship.

A request by Cetshwayo to discuss the disputed succession was rejected by Mpande, who instead allocated a tract of land to Mbuyazi in the south-east of Zululand, an area owing allegiance to Cetshwayo where he grazed some of his cattle herds. Provocatively Mbuyazi began appropriating cattle belonging to Cetshwayo, eliminating opponents, establishing homesteads, and demanding tribute. Advised by senior members of the uSuthu to act immediately, Cetshwayo advanced south with a considerable force, attracting further adherents along the way.

Mbuyazi retreated south towards the Thukela and Natal, mindful of his father's advice that when all else failed 'go to the country of the whites. I too was brought to power by them.'[7] He was accompanied by all his followers, including women, children and the elderly, and their cattle herds. The iziGqoza encamped in and around an abandoned homestead known as Ndondakusuka on the hill of the same name overlooking the Lower Drift of the Thukela River. From this vantage point Mbuyazi attempted to enlist the support of local white settlers with offers of land. His approach was rejected, but Mbuyazi's appeal for assistance was passed on to

'Shepstone's eyes and ears on the Zulu frontier', Captain Joshua Walmsley, Natal's Zulu border agent on the southern bank of the Thukela.[8] Walmsley sent a rider to Pietermaritzburg, one hundred miles away and now capital of an English colony, for orders from Shepstone. Shepstone left for the border immediately on receiving the news, presumably in the hope of using his influence over the Zulu, both real and imagined, to avert bloodshed.

Meanwhile Walmsley allowed his assistant John Dunn, 'a forceful and adventurous frontiersman with a preference for Zulu over European ways', to cross the Thukela with thirty-five African policemen he had 'trained in the use of firearms and horses, and a hundred of his African hunters', ostensibly to negotiate a peace settlement; in reality it was a thinly disguised excuse for Dunn to exploit the situation and share in the spoils of war. In Zululand Dunn and his men were joined by a handful of white settlers, and the combined force became known as the iziNqobo, or 'the Crushers', thanks to their firepower.[9]

Realising battle between Cetshwayo and Mbuyazi was imminent, white traders, settlers and their families in Zululand took to their waggons and fled south to Natal with their cattle and belongings. The Thukela, in flood from summer rains, proved a formidable barrier. Many abandoned their waggons on the north bank and, driving their livestock before them across the Lower Drift, made for a sandbank close to the Natal side of the river where the depth of a final channel barred any further progress. Most remained stranded on the sandbank with their families and cattle.

Perversely, a lone white man was heading the other way: Melmoth Osborn, an interpreter in the employ of the Natal Native Affairs department at the small town of Verulam fifty miles south of the border. On 1 December the 22-year-old Osborn, hearing the battle 'was to take place on the morrow' and 'being young and enterprising, swam his horse across the Tugela River, taking his chance of the [crocodiles], and under the cover of darkness hid in some bushes upon a kopje, tying his coat over the horse's head to keep it from neighing'.[10]

When the uSuthu began their advance late in the afternoon of 1 December, the iziGqoza immediately responded, burning a firebreak in the grass along the ridge – the black stubble and ash marking their line of last retreat – and advanced to meet the enemy. After some brief skirmishing, both sides retired for the night, taking up their positions on hills on opposite sides of the grassy, bush-dotted Mandeni valley: the uSuthu to the west, the iziGqoza to the east. Below the heights, swollen by summer rains, the Thukela thrummed swift, strong and wide between banks littered with crocodiles inert as fossils.

After a night of thunder and drenching rain the warriors of both armies – estimated at between 22,000 and 27,000 men – sleepless, tired and wet, took up their positions readying themselves for the battle they knew must be fought that day. It was the sixth day of the fifth month in the Zulu lunar calendar, *uZibandlela*, the name indicating summer was well under way and rich green grass covered the footpaths; more prosaically 2 December 1856. They formed up in the traditional Zulu fighting formation of chest and horns, '*impondo zankomo* – literally "the beast's horns", after a symbolic resemblance to a charging bull', the central chest advancing to the attack and occupying the enemy's attention while the horns outflanked and encircled them.[11]

Mbuyazi was standing on the hillside with his commanders when a gust of wind blew an ostrich plume from his headdress, a chance occurrence immediately interpreted as an evil omen. Meanwhile, in the opposing camp, Cetshwayo fell to his knees, crushing a shield belonging to Mbuyazi. Cetshwayo planned to send out the right horn of the uSuthu at speed to prevent any escape of the iziGqoza south across the Thukela, then envelop them with both horns and send in the chest to crush all resistance. The right horn advanced, booming their battle cry '*uSuthu!*' The iziGqoza responded with theirs: '*Laba, laba, laba, ba yoze ba si bone!*' (Those people are really going to see who we are!)[12] Dunn and his Crushers in Mbuyazi's left horn frustrated the uSuthu right, repulsing two charges. The uSuthu changed tactics accordingly and, applying pressure on the iziGqoza right, broke it. Seeing this, the left horn lost its nerve and fell back, and the entire uSuthu force surged forward.

Melmoth Osborn watching from his hiding place told of what he saw:

> Umbelazi's host was placed with its rear to the Tugela, towards which by degrees it was pressed back by the great impi of Cetywayo. Now Panda had sent one of his own favourite regiments to assist Umbelazi, whom he loved, with orders that it was not to join in the fight unless the battle turned against him. Seeing that the prince was being worsted, this veteran regiment, nearly three thousand strong, moved out in a triple line to his assistance. As they charged forward Cetywayo sent a regiment of young men to meet them ... the roar of their meeting shields as like to the roar of an angry sea. For a minute the air seemed to be alight with their shimmering spears; then there came ... a long, slow heave, such as is the heave of wave above a sunken rock, as Panda's regiment passed over their opponents, utterly wiping them out. A third of their number were dead, but they charged on to meet a second regiment dispatched against them by Cetywayo. After a fearful fight this regiment they destroyed also; but now only six hundred of their number were left alive, and as these were too weak to charge a third time they formed a circle round a little hill. Here Cetywayo poured his power on them, here they fought furiously till not a man of them remained, for here they fell buried beneath the bodies of their foes.[13]

The seared line of last retreat was left far behind as the iziGqoza fled. Retreat became rout then massacre as the uSuthu relentlessly pursued their enemy down the slopes to the bank of the Thukela, flushing out non-combatants hiding in the wooded valleys and kloofs along the way.

Around ten o'clock the traders and their families stranded on the sandbank in the Thukela saw the iziGqoza come into view, Dunn among them with frantic fugitives trying to grab a ride on his horse. Dunn abandoned his mount and swam to safety through 'a drowning mass of bodies in a wild and higgledy-piggledy confusion of heads, arms and legs, whilst the yelling was something awful.'[14]

On the banks of the Thukela and in the river itself the uSuthu 'exacted a heavy toll, slaughtering everyone regardless of sex or age'.[15] Aroused from their prehistoric lethargy, crocodiles slid into the water and took advantage of the unexpected bounty. Surrounded by horrific scenes of carnage, the settlers looked on helplessly but were otherwise left unscathed. Cetshwayo had ordered no white person be harmed. Cattle and waggons were another matter: the former were run off by the uSuthu and the waggons plundered.

The slaughter witnessed by the settlers was immense; even conservative sources suggest the iziGqoza lost as many as 5,000 warriors and two or three times that amount of non-combatants. The total number of lives lost is thought to have exceeded 20,000.[16] With Mbuyazi and five of his brothers among the dead, Cetshwayo's succession was assured.

Six months prior to the battle of Ndondakusuka, Henry Rider Haggard was born in the northern hemisphere's midsummer on 22 June 1856 at Bradenham, Norfolk. In Zululand his birth coincided with the first month of the year, *uNcwaba*, the name derived from *ncwaba*, meaning 'glossy, fresh, clean, attractive', in reference to the time 'when the first grass appears after veld-burning.'[17] In 1875 the 19-year-old Haggard would travel to Natal on the staff of a family friend, Sir Henry Bulwer, newly appointed Lieutenant Governor of Natal, and the first of a fraternal network of imperial officials, civil servants, soldiers and diplomats that Haggard would become part of for the rest of his days, some of whom would play pivotal roles in Haggard's life. In Pietermaritzburg Haggard would meet Theophilus Shepstone and Melmoth Osborn. Shepstone would become a surrogate father-figure and mentor, Osborn a colleague and friend. The battle of Ndondakusuka, as described to Haggard by Osborn, would become the template for the epic battle featuring the 'last stand of the Greys' in *King Solomon's Mines*, which, like its historical counterpart, was also fought to decide a question of royal succession and issues of inheritance.

The 'wars of children' royal and civil, the advent of rightful heirs determined to claim thrones or fortunes, populate Haggard's fiction, both the adventure stories for which he is best known and the contemporary novels set in Victorian and Edwardian England. Scenes of epic slaughter and Homeric combat are a distinctive hallmark of Haggard's work and Ndondakusuka is the blueprint for them all.

The struggle between Cetshwayo and Mbuyazi was subjected to closer scrutiny in *Child of Storm* with Allan Quatermain, hero of *King Solomon's Mines*, as a witness and participant. In 1914, in the early months of the First World War as the British Expeditionary Force fought its bloody way back and forth through Picardy, Artois and Flanders, the battle of Ndondakusuka played out nightly across the stage of the Globe Theatre on London's Shaftesbury Avenue in *Mameena*, a spectacular and innovative stage adaptation of *Child of Storm*, produced by the famous impresario and actor-manager Oscar Asche, retitled with the name of the book's Zulu heroine.

The confluence of life and fate that saw Haggard born in the same year as the culmination of the 'war of the children' would undoubtedly have appealed to the romantic in him. The dispositions of nature and nurture aside, the trajectory of Haggard's life and work, the personal and the political, the writing and the public service, was foreshadowed and, to a great extent, determined by these dramatic events and the actors involved therein on the south-eastern seaboard of South Africa.

1

'I TOO MUST DIE'

Henry Rider Haggard's family had deep roots in the English countryside, yet neither of his parents was born in England. His father William's birthplace (as we shall see) was St Petersburg, while his mother Ella Doveton was born on 16 June 1819 in Bombay, India's thriving western port and administrative capital of the East India Company's Bombay Presidency.[1] Ella was the first child of Bazett Doveton, a lawyer in the Indian Civil Service, and his wife Sarah Bazett.[2] Young Ella's 'Mama', enfeebled by Bombay's tropical heat, spent most of her time in a near-permanent state of decline. In 1822 at the recommendation of her doctors, Sarah Doveton returned to England with Ella, now nearly three, and her younger brother Bazett, just turned two. In January 1823 the two children were left in the care of an aunt and Sarah returned to Bombay where ill health continued to lay her low and contrived her return to England at the end of 1826 with a new addition to the family, daughter Caroline.

In England Ella and Bazett were educated by governesses until 1829 when Ella was sent to school at Gough House in Chelsea and Bazett, after attending a preparatory school for boys in Clapham, went on to Rottingdean School.[3] Ella proved a good scholar though not always a happy one. In her diary she records being tormented by the other girls, and during the holidays, she threw herself 'at Mama's feet and entreated her to take me from this prison house' where she was 'ill-treated and abused by all'.[4] One should allow for a degree of adolescent self-pity, as Ella later recalled Gough House with affection as that 'dear old place'.[5] Bazett, her 'poor, beautiful, little brother!',[6] had real cause for complaint. He was bullied to death at Rottingdean.

In 1837 Ella returned to India and was reunited with her parents (her mother having preceded her) and in the tight-knit British circle of civil servants and soldiers in Bombay soon became a star attraction, 'as was natural in the case of one of her charm who was known also to be a considerable heiress'.[7] There was a queue of hopeful candidates for Ella's hand – a Mr Smith was particularly tiresome, proposing once in person then using mutual friends to act as go-betweens. Ella also had Indian admirers, including Aga Mahomed Jaffer, met at a dinner hosted by the prominent

Bombay merchant Cursetjee Cowasjee, who subsequently called to pay Ella 'fine compliments'.[8]

While such dalliances, *faux naïf* or otherwise, played out amidst the enervating heat of Bombay, the British looked forward to their annual migration to 'the Hills' and pressure mounted for romances to be brought to proper and preferably happy conclusions. At a fancy dress party on 27 September, shortly before the Dovetons' departure for cooler climes, Ella 'was tormented after supper with five applications for my *fair* hand, 4 of whom were extremely pertinacious, one actually twice throwing himself on his knees! To my great horror.'[9] This despite Ella having made abundantly clear she 'did not intend to marry in India'.[10]

Ella and her family left for the Hills on 3 October 1838. Thereafter Ella and her mother planned to return to England in January 1839, to be joined there by her father on his retirement from the Indian Civil Service in 1840. At a dinner party held a month before their departure Ella had her future predicted by an Indian fortune-teller: she would 'remain long indifferent' to love but 'was loved' and in due course 'should have a son, "an honour to his family and the admiration of the world"'.[11]

Ella and her mother travelled to England from India in 1839, sailing to Aden, and then making their way overland through Egypt, where they visited the ancient sites of Thebes and Luxor, instilling in Ella a lifelong interest in ancient Egypt, which she would pass on to her son.

Ella managed to remain indifferent to matters of the heart until the age of 25 when she married William Meybohm Rider Haggard, squire, lawyer, landowner and proprietor of Bradenham Hall in west Norfolk. How their match came about is unknown, but it was certainly a good one for the 35-year-old William, for Ella was co-heiress to her father's fortune. Shortly after their marriage in May 1844 William's younger brother James married Ella's younger sister Caroline, and thus the entire Doveton inheritance came to the Haggards.

The Haggard family owned Bradenham Hall, 'a beautifully situated and comfortable red-brick house'[12] built in 1772 with 'long windows and irregularly shaped sunny rooms' standing 'upon some of the highest and best timbered land in Norfolk' contemplating 'a small, well-wooded park which fell away in a gentle slope to a stream, and the village and church of West Bradenham'. At the rear of the Hall – one of two gravelled drives led there – were the stables, the coach house, two walled kitchen gardens and apple orchards. Threading the Long Plantation 'were various shrubbery walks leading to a deep pond of sinister aspect, a summer house where generations of the family had carved their names, and finally to the white gate of the drive which opened to a by-road known as Haggard's Hill', down which thundered an invisible coach and four, the ghost of Bradenham Hall according to local tradition.[13]

Ghosts would have felt at home amidst the Haggards' sturdy Jacobean and Georgian furniture, now complemented by Ella's family artefacts, the walls hung with family portraits. One of the ghosts was said to be that of Emma, Lady Hamilton, the beloved of Admiral Lord Nelson, who visited Bradenham Hall several times after Nelson's death at Trafalgar during the tenancy of Thomas Bolton, husband of Emma's close friend Susannah, Nelson's sister. Lady Hamilton's occasional presence at Bradenham was still vivid in local memory, and as a child Haggard knew an old man in the village who had been a pageboy at the Hall and remembered Lady Hamilton well, and 'when I asked him to describe her, said "She waur a rare fine opstanding (here followed an outspoken and opprobrious term), she waur!"'[14]

The Haggards were relative newcomers to the area, having taken up residence at Bradenham Hall in 1818, which is perhaps why they, especially Rider, played up their ancestral past. According to a nephew, Haggard possessed 'the dynastic sense'.[15] That this would be tragically frustrated only increased the adult Haggard's awareness of the silent generations who preceded him. Born 'of the class of landed gentry or "squires"',[16] the Haggard line was gilded by family tradition with an illustrious predecessor: 'a Danish gentleman of the famous Guildenstjerne family whose seat was at Aagaard in Jutland'.[17] Anders Pedersen Gylderstjerne, a Danish mercenary knighted for his services to the English Crown in 1433, anglicised his name to Andrew and took the surname Ogard or Agard after his place of birth, living out the rest of his life at Bradenham, and dying there in 1454.[18] Haggard casts Sir Andrew in heroic mould: a 'very remarkable man' who distinguished himself 'greatly in the French wars of the time of Henry VI'.[19] There was no proof 'of the descent of my family from this Sir Andrew'; nonetheless the Haggards 'cherish their traditional ancestor to this day, and still carry his golden star'.[20]

According to *Burke's Landed Gentry*, the direct Haggard line of descent begins with David Haggard of Ware in Hertfordshire, whose will was proved in 1534. The Haggard family remained at Ware for 150 years, subsequently moving to Old Ford House, St Mary Stratford-le-Bow, in the City of London. Haggard's father told a story of how 'John Haggard who died in 1776',[21] fearful after a burglary, sold the Bow property and moved to Benington in Hertfordshire.

Earlier, in 1760, John's son William Henry Haggard had married Susan Rebecca Barnham, daughter of the Sheriff of Norwich, the county town of Norfolk, where the couple settled. In 1818 William's eldest son, William Henry, Rider's great-grandfather, bought Bradenham Hall in order to be close to his friend William Mason, who lived in nearby Necton Hall near Swaffham, 'with whom he had shared rooms at Emmanuel College, Cambridge'.[22] Here matters come full circle as Haggard happily notes that 'oddly enough' Bradenham Hall once belonged 'to old Sir Andrew Ogard, or Agard, in right of his wife'.[23]

Great-grandfather William studied law at Lincoln's Inn but, preferring literature to law, built up an impressive library. When called to the Bar 'he refused to practise and retired to Bradenham to enjoy the life of a Squire on an exceedingly comfortable income, the product of his ancestors' industry'.[24] A 'very handsome man with charming manners', in 1781 William married Frances Amyand, daughter of the

Reverend Thomas Amyand and Frances Rider, granddaughter of Claudius Amyand, a French Huguenot who fled persecution in France and became Surgeon to George II. Thus were the names Rider and Amyand introduced into the Haggard family, the latter bringing with it 'that accursed Amyand blood',[25] frequently blamed for the excesses of the Haggard male line:

> Wayward, wild, excitable and brilliant, with more than a hint of mental instability, the Amyand blood took possession of the Haggard stock, kept their noses and a portion of their common sense, but drowned their business ability; bestowed on most of them courage without endurance, and enterprise without perseverance. It gave them also long, fine-boned bodies, which at fifty and sixty (they seldom lived longer than that) were as slim as in their youth, red and yellow heads, brilliant blue eyes, and a fatal charm of manner.[26]

Lilias Rider Haggard credits the 'Amyand blood' with bequeathing 'a passion for wandering ... inconveniently wedded' to 'an equally passionate love of their home acres'. The consequent restlessness saw them scatter across the globe and 'instead of banking and trade they took to the Army, the Navy, the Indian services – anything which promised adventure, excitement, change, to ease the fret of their restless minds. And as they did, so did their children. Tales of their scrapes and escapes, their eccentricities and extravagances, their dare-devil pranks, and far from reputable love affairs, persist until this day.' [27]

The Amyand family had extensive business interests and were active in St Petersburg, capital of imperial Russia and home to a sizeable British commercial community, where William Henry's eldest son, another William, joined the firm and in 1816 married Elizabeth Meybohm, a German Jew, eldest daughter and co-heiress of Jacob Jeremiah Meybohm whose father had become a naturalised British subject in 1752.[28] William and Elizabeth's first child, Haggard's father, William Meybohm Rider Haggard, was born in St Petersburg on 19 April 1817. Another son, James, who died in infancy, was followed in 1821 by a daughter, Frances (known as Fanny), who was born at Bradenham Hall, where the family had settled after Napoleon's invasion of Russia in 1812 and upheavals thereafter 'nearly ruined the Amyand business', bringing William and his Russian wife 'home in a hurry to Bradenham'.[29] Another son, also christened James, was born at Bradenham in 1824. On the death of his father in 1843 William inherited the Bradenham estate and a year later married Ella Doveton.

If the Haggards looked askance at traits bestowed by the 'accursed Amyand blood', they were positively tight-lipped about transfusions via the Dovetons. According to Victoria Manthorpe, 'a man named Torlassi (or Torlesse) married a begum (a well-born Moslem woman) and their daughter Eleanor married a Colonel Bond. [Their] daughter, Ellen Maria Bond, married Bazett Doveton and was Mrs Haggard's mother.'[30] Genealogical lines now available appear to contradict some of this. Ella's maternal grandfather, Lieutenant Colonel Charles John Bond, married Mary Barton Torlesse in 1800. Their daughter Ellen Maria Bond married Bazett Doveton and was Ella Doveton's mother.[31] Whatever the truth of the matter, the Haggards were certain there was Indian blood in the family, and as times grew more conservative the subject became taboo. The subject of 'the Begum' was studiously avoided among the Doveton and Haggard families, and decades later in 1917 Ellen Haggard, daughter of James Haggard and his wife Caroline, learnt of the matter through Haggard's eldest brother, Will. Writing to her cousin Ella, Haggard's older sister, Ellen said the truth of what Will had told her was confirmed by her mother. 'She naturally did not care to speak about her grandmother's unedifying past, nor the taint of black blood she imported into the family, but she could not deny the facts.'[32]

Genetic inheritance notwithstanding, William and Ella soon set about creating a large family. Their first child, Ella Doveton, was born in Rome on 10 March 1845 when the couple 'were still upon a marriage tour'.[33] As was the Victorian custom, the first daughter was named after her mother. The first son would take his father's name, and Ella was followed in 1846 by William Henry, Bazett Michael in 1847, Alfred Hinuber in 1849, John George in 1850, Elizabeth Cecilia in 1852 and Andrew Charles in 1854.

William and Ella and their growing family settled easily into the rhythms of East Anglian county life. In the first half of the nineteenth century Norfolk was 'England's foremost agricultural county'.[34] The industrial revolution and the resultant growth of cities had created an ever-increasing urban population requiring to be fed. Improvements in agricultural methods, machinery and, vitally, transport by means of the new railway system saw Norfolk, well known for quality wheat and barley, perfectly placed to profit from the 'Golden Age of English Farming', which lasted from the 1830s to the 1870s, when cheap grain imports from the United States and Canada undercut English farmers and led to an agricultural depression.

The mid-nineteenth-century profits from farming were sufficient to maintain the comfortable lifestyle of the country gentry enjoyed by Haggard's great-grandfather in the preceding century. The flavour of East Anglian life in this time of plenty is captured in the diaries of a friend of William Haggard, the Reverend Benjamin Armstrong, vicar of St Nicholas's Church in East Dereham, the nearest town to Bradenham Hall. On 26 October 1853 Armstrong attended a 'regular country party' and those present consisted

> of the Vicar, the Curate, the lawyer, the Doctor, and some wealthy yeomen like the host. The eating and drinking began at 7 and continued without intermission until 1 in the morning. First there was wine & dessert, then tea, accompanied by innumerable cakes, then wine and spirits with a pipe, then supper, of an excellent but heavy kind, & finally spirits and tobacco again. The conversation was about farming & local matters, & the only two things I heard, which are worth remembering, are that 6,000 wild

ducks had been taken at a neighbouring decoy, and, that more opium was consumed between Boston & York than in any other part of the country.[35]

In January 1855 Armstrong recorded William Haggard's enlistment as a captain in the East Norfolk Regiment of Militia when an outburst of patriotic fervour – the Crimean War was in its second year – saw a significant rise in recruitment among the local militias.

To William's wife Ella fell the responsibility of running Bradenham Hall, a responsibility entailing 'perpetual sacrifice of one's feelings and inclinations', according to another contemporary lady of the house.[36] Ella's 'very considerable capacity for a literary career' was her primary sacrifice; 'the anxieties of a large family, with the home and local duties to which she earnestly devoted herself, and in her later years ever increasing ill-health, effectively put a stop to such ambitions'.[37]

Towards the end of 1855, patriotic ardour spent, William succumbed to 'one of the restless, nomadic fits which frequently seized him' and took 'the whole family abroad for the winter'.[38] When 'economy was the order of the day', the Haggard patriarch would let the Hall and decamp en famille to other quarters either in England or abroad, though 'what economy my father can have found in dragging a tumultuous family about the Continent I cannot conceive'.[39]

The Haggards spent the winter of 1855 and 1856 in France, returning in May to prepare for the birth of their eighth child. The Hall required some refurbishment after the tenancy and Ella decided to stay at Wood Farm for her confinement, 'a pleasant, thatched house' on the Bradenham estate 'surrounded by barns and cattle sheds, to the north of Bradenham Wood and approached by a field path and a green lane from the Hall'.[40] There, on 22 June 1856, a few days after her thirty-seventh birthday, Ella gave birth to a boy. 'He was a delicate baby, yellow with jaundice, but slowly he gained strength.'[41] The birth was registered on 30 July, the baby's name recorded as Henry Constantine.

By early August mother and child had joined the rest of the family at the Hall where 'the baby developed some internal trouble, with a return of the jaundice with which he was born'.[42] The condition was life-threatening and the vicar of St Andrew's, West Bradenham, was urgently summoned to baptise the infant, doing so in a large Lowestoft porcelain china bowl and bestowing the names Henry Rider. Rider, as he was known thereafter, recalled his mother often telling him of how 'old Clouting', the local doctor, had despaired and 'gone away saying that there was no hope for me' and how 'she took me in hand herself, dosing me with brandy and wrapping me in boiling flannels, with the result that I did not die after all'.[43]

Haggard was the 'eighth child of the family of ten – seven sons and three daughters'. He was followed by Eleanora Mary, born on 1 June 1858, and 'the last of us, my brother Arthur, appeared in November 1860 ... This allows nearly sixteen years between the eldest and the youngest, including one who came into the world still-born. Although she had ten children living, my mother never ceased to regret this boy, and I remember her crying, when she pointed out to me where he was buried in Bradenham churchyard.'[44]

In the fields and woods surrounding Bradenham Hall, Haggard enjoyed the childhood of his class: 'mostly of a sporting character. Like the majority of country-bred boys I adored a gun.'[45] Armed with an ancient single-barrelled muzzle-loader, Haggard came close to shooting his brother Andrew while hunting rabbits and on another occasion 'went within an ace of putting an end to my mortal career, contriving in some mysterious way to let it off so that the charge just grazed my face'.[46] Nor was he stranger to the casual cruelties of childhood: 'I did terrible deeds with that gun': once, finding no other game available, he shot a nesting mistle thrush, 'a crime that has haunted me ever since'. His depredations extended to poaching pheasant and the killing of a local farmer's best-laying duck 'with results almost as painful to me as to the duck, which was demonstrated to have about a dozen eggs inside it'.[47]

Haggard rode to hounds from a young age and his father was a frequent riding companion. Haggard described his father as 'a typical squire of the old sort, a kind of Sir Roger de Coverley.'[48] He reigned at Bradenham like a king, blowing everybody up and making rows innumerable. Yet I do not think there was a more popular man in the county of Norfolk.'[49] Tales of Haggard senior's ebullient character entered both family and local folklore. William Haggard was a practising barrister and on one occasion, when 'prosecuting a man for stealing twelve hogs', he addressed the jury in a manner 'to bring home to them the enormity of the defendant's crime'.

> 'Gentlemen of the Jury,' he said, 'think what this man has done. He stole not one hog but twelve hogs, and not only twelve hogs but twelve fat hogs, exactly the same number, Gentlemen of the Jury, as I see in the box before me!'
> The story adds that the defendant was acquitted![50]

As Justice of the Peace and Master of the Quarter Sessions for Norfolk, William Haggard acquitted himself with 'great dignity, to which his appearance – for he was a very handsome man, better looking indeed than any of his sons – and his splendid voice added not a little'.[51] A voice so loud, it was said that if you wished to discover his whereabouts in Norwich all you 'needed to do was to stand in the market-place for a while to listen'.[52] In his Norfolk-set novel *Colonel Quaritch, V.C.*, Haggard's father is the model for Squire de la Molle, gifted with 'a voice that made the walls shake'.[53]

Haggard and his siblings inherited their father's voice, 'though not to the same degree'.[54] Rider inherited the volume accompanied by a pronounced lisp. According to his nephew Godfrey Haggard, 'he pronounced his Rs like Ws, and a TH was beyond him; so that a Very Thorough Rogue would sound like a Vewy Forough Wogue'.[55] Another nephew, Andrew Haggard, says his uncle also 'had a habit of concluding every remark with the expression "wha' hey"' and remembered as a boy his aunt Lilias asking her father, '"Daddy, what rhymes with trumpet?" And him replying "Wimes wiv twumpet? Why, cwumpet or stwumpet wha' hey?'"[56] Nonetheless Haggard became a respected and oft-requested public speaker.

William Haggard's booming voice was paired with a volatile temper: 'Nobody could be more absolutely delightful than my father when he chose, and, *per contra*, I am bound to add that nobody could be more disagreeable.'[57] When angered by one of his sons he would 'thunder "Out of the house, sir ... Out of the house!" pointing to the front door'.[58] Alternatively 'he would rise majestically' from the table and announce solemnly that 'he refused to be insulted in his own house, and depart', banging doors behind him prior to exiting into the garden, then banging his way back inside again to take his seat in a 'sweet temper, the exercise having relieved his feelings'.[59]

This behaviour extended to the family retainers, who, despite being treated 'in a fashion that no servant would put up with nowadays', remained fond of their master. 'It was "only the Squire's way", they said.'[60] One employee had the measure of his employer, his indispensable factotum Samuel Adcock, 'a stout, humorous person whose face was marked all over with small-pox pits'.[61] Once a week

> Samuel was had in to the vestibule and abused in a most straightforward fashion, but he never seemed to mind.
>
> 'I believe, Samuel,' roared my father at him in my hearing, 'donkey as you are, you think that no one can do anything except yourself.'
>
> 'Nor they can't, Squire,' replied Samuel calmly, which closed the conversation.[62]

Adcock appears as Squire de la Molle's factotum George in *Colonel Quaritch, V.C.*

William Haggard's fiefdom included St Andrew's Church, and local legend recalls Sunday being 'almost as much the Squire's day as it was God's'.[63] The Haggards sat in the chancel and latecomers would be greeted by the sight of William stepping into the central aisle and pointedly consulting his fob watch prior to holding 'it aloft that the sinners as they walked up the church might become aware of the enormity of their offence', oblivious to the fact he was often late himself. The service over, no one stirred until the squire had paced slowly down the aisle and taken up his position in the porch. 'Here he stood and watched the congregation emerge, counting them like sheep.'[64]

Given William Haggard's conduct it is not surprising his friend and neighbour Colonel George Blomefield at Necton Hall dubbed the Haggards 'harum scarum', but did Haggard's lord of the manor eccentricities extend further to the exercising of *droit de seigneur*? Alfred Thacker, a stable boy at Bradenham, was born in 1858, but his parents Samuel and Martha Thacker only had him baptised ten years later. 'When he grew up to resemble Andrew Haggard it made some people wonder,' writes Victoria Manthorpe, and Thacker's paternity 'was attributed to William or to his brother James'.[65] The sexual abuse of female servants was not uncommon and Norfolk had one of the highest bastardy rates in the country during the nineteenth century; irregular relationships and their offspring were open secrets among the landed gentry.[66] In 1881 when Haggard was farming outside Newcastle in Natal, he would go into partnership with George Blomefield, 'alias George Mayes, the illegitimate child of old Colonel Blomefield of Necton Hall, Norfolk'.[67]

In comparison with his unpredictable father, Haggard's mother was a benign presence. 'No night goes by that I do not think of her and pray that we may meet again to part no more.'[68] Haggard idolised her: 'she was perhaps the ablest woman whom I have known, though she had no iron background to her character; for that she was too gentle'.[69] All but submerged in the role of a Victorian wife and mother, the softly spoken Ella Haggard was a resilient woman who developed her own tactics in dealing with the Haggard family's exhausting high spirits: 'In the midst of all this hubbub sat my dearest mother – like an angel that had lost her way and found herself in pandemonium.' Once asked 'how on earth she made herself heard in the midst of so much noise at table', she replied, 'I whisper! When I whisper they all stop talking, because they wonder what is the matter. Then I get my chance.'[70]

Haggard acknowledged life at Bradenham must have been 'very dull' for his mother, and her descriptions of the 'wearisome and interminable local dinner-parties to which she was obliged to attend in her early married life' reflect those the Reverend Benjamin Armstrong committed to his diary. 'The men she met at them talked, she said, chiefly about "roots", and for a long while she could not imagine what these roots might be and why they were so interested in them, until at length she discovered that they referred to mangold-wurzel and to turnips, both as crops and as a shelter for the birds which they loved to shoot.'[71]

Ella's 'various duties' at Bradenham Hall 'left her scarcely an hour to follow her own literary and artistic tastes. All she could do was to give a little attention to gardening, to which she was devoted.'[72] But she also carved out gaps of time in which to write poetry. Her epic poem *Myra; or the Rose of the East: A Tale of the Afghan War*, 'illustrative of the Cabul Campaign of 1842', was likely written at Wood Farm prior to the birth of Rider in 1856. Published the following year, it unfortunately appeared 'when all England was aghast at the horrors of the Indian Mutiny, and had little taste for peaceful poems connected with the continent, and for praise of the fidelity of the Sepoy'.[73] Good reviews did not translate into sales.

Haggard always credited his literary talents to his mother; from whom he also inherited a love of gardening and a fascination for ancient Egypt, an interest further encouraged in childhood by Norfolk neighbours, the Tyssen-Amhersts. The High Sheriff of Norfolk, Lord William Amherst Tyssen-Amherst owned one of the county's great estates, 'where ten thousand acres of farmland and fifteen hundred of parkland surrounded a mansion overlooking a vast lake scattered with islands'.[74] The mansion was Didlington Hall where Amherst and his wife Margaret, who shared his passion for Egyptology, amassed a vast library and what was then the 'greatest collection of Egyptian sculpture and some important papyri in Britain' as well as several mummies.[75] A wooden *ushabti*[76] was said to have 'a charming expression', which inspired Haggard's creation of Ayesha, something he always denied.[77] Tyssen-Amherst built a museum to house the collection attached to the Hall, its exterior approach guarded by seven huge black granite sculptures of the warrior goddess Sekhmet.

At Didlington, Haggard met the Tyssen-Amherst's eldest daughter, Mary, and was equally captivated by her father's collection.[78] Another child whose sense of wonder was ignited by exposure to the Amherst Egyptian artefacts was Howard Carter, future discoverer of the tomb of Tutankhamun, who lived with his family in nearby Swaffham. His father, the artist Samuel Carter, had a loyal clientele in the local gentry, for whom he painted portraits, family groups and award-winning livestock. William Tyssen-Amherst was a regular client.[79]

Haggard's childhood was not entirely spent in Norfolk. When economy dictated, Bradenham Hall was let and the Haggards resided for lengthy periods either on the Continent or elsewhere in England. Leamington Spa in Warwickshire was a favourite spot for temporary relocation and it was there Haggard's eldest sister, Ella, met the Reverend Charles Maddison Green, whom she would marry in 1869, and where Haggard's younger brother, Arthur, struck up a friendship with a boy named Frederick Jackson, the two boys subsequently going to the same public school, Shrewsbury in Shropshire, and on to Cambridge University.[80]

The exact sequence of the Haggard continental expeditions is uncertain. One trip, possibly commencing in 1861 when Bradenham Hall was let for two years, included a visit to Germany and a tour down the Rhine, during which the five-year-old Rider was thrown into the river by his brothers: 'After nearly drowning I learned to swim.'[81] On another occasion, leaving his family to admire the scenery, Rider sneaked off to his cabin to read a book. His father soon descended and 'dragged me out by the scruff of the neck, exclaiming loudly, to the vast amusement of the other passengers: "I have paid five thalers for you to improve your mind by absorbing the beauties of nature, and absorb them you shall!"'[82]

Haggard had been taught to read by his eldest sister, Ella, to whom he dedicated his novel of the Crusades, *The Brethren*, crediting her with opening to his 'childish eyes that gate of ivory and pearl which leads to the blessed kingdom of Romance'. As a boy Haggard 'loved those books that other boys love, and I love them still'.[83] A popular children's title of the time read by Haggard was Thomas Day's *The History of Sandford and Merton*, initially published in instalments in the 1780s, chronicling the transformation of Tommy Merton from spoilt brat to honourable hard-working gentleman thanks to the example of his straight-as-a-die friend Henry Sandford. Other favourites included tales from the *Arabian Nights*, Alexandre Dumas's *The Three Musketeers*, the poetry of Edgar Allan Poe, and Thomas Babington Macaulay's *Lays of Ancient Rome*.

An especial favourite was Daniel Defoe's *Robinson Crusoe*, a birthday present from the Barkers, Norfolk neighbours at Shipdham Hall. One Sunday morning when Haggard was expected to go to church with the rest of the family, he hid beneath a bed with the book; discovered there by his sister Ella and a governess, he refused to come out and they resorted to force. 'The two ladies tugged as best they might but I clung to Crusoe and the legs of the bed, and kicked till, perfectly exhausted, they took their departure in no very Christian frame of mind, leaving me panting indeed, but triumphant.'[84]

On the same trip to Germany featuring the impromptu swimming lesson, the Haggard family stayed in Cologne where they held a supper party, 'a considerable affair', for members of the Amyand and Meybohm families. When the guests 'trooped in to supper, they were astonished to find a single small boy, to wit myself, seated at the end of the table and just finishing an excellent meal. "Rider," said my father in tones of thunder, "what are you doing here? Explain, sir! Explain!"' Haggard obliged: '"I knew that when you all came in there would be no room for me, so I had my supper first."'[85]

Dunkerque on the northern French coast was another temporary domicile 'where we used to have lively times'.[86] Haggard and his elder brothers Jack and Andrew formed a gang of English boys to fight the French *garçons* from a local school who 'outnumbered us by far, but what we lacked in numbers we made up for by the ferocity of our attack'. This included stretching a rope across the street 'over which the little Frenchmen, as they gambolled joyously out of school, tripped and tumbled'. Then 'we raised our British war-cry and fell upon them'.[87] Blows and insults were exchanged – 'yells of "*Cochons d'Anglais!*" and the answering shouts of "*Yah! Froggie, allez a votre maman!*" as we hit and kicked and wallowed in the mire'. Complaints to the local gendarmerie saw the Haggard-led gang 'deprived of this particular joy'.[88]

Another 'foreign adventure' took place when Haggard was older at the seaside resort of Le Tréport in Normandy. Notices forbade swimming because of the dangerous currents. 'Was a British boy to be deterred from bathing by French notices? Never!' With younger brother Arthur in tow, Rider found a place where they could swim unobserved. Telling Arthur not to get out of his depth, Rider swam out beyond the breakers only to get into difficulties when swimming back. His return was a close-run thing and, while he lay panting on the beach, some coastguards 'arrived at a run and very properly expressed their views in the most strenuous language'. Having caught his breath, Haggard sat up. '"Si je noye, qu'est ce que cela vous fait?" (if I drown, what has it to do with you?)" ... my individual fate did not matter twopence to them, but "how about the reputation of Tréport as a bathing-place?"'[89] Haggard kept this escapade a secret from his parents.

Beyond the bounds of parental control and in the company of his peers, Haggard was an assertive, boisterous child, but there was also an introspective side to his nature, coloured by morbid thoughts of death and dying. In 'Childhood

Reminiscences', Haggard says his earliest recorded memory was of being taken to church in December 1861 where he 'heard some music that struck me'. On being informed it was Handel's 'Dead March' from *Saul* and being played because Albert, the Prince Consort had died, 'I remember my astonishment, for I had not previously understood that Princes were subject to the accident of death.'[90]

Haggard records that 'most of my earliest reminiscences are connected with religious matters'. Told of the omnipresence of God by his sister Ella, he undertook a search for the deity, 'beginning under the school room table and ending in the cupboards.'[91] Soon after this incident he 'first looked on death. An old man had died in the village, and I persuaded the carpenter who had charge of his obsequies to show me the body. I can see it now, the coffined remains of a man pale and stern and beautiful, dressed in a white robe, and with a pillow stuffed with shavings beneath his head. I do not remember that the sight frightened me at all, but it made me think.'[92]

Haggard's 'most terrible reminiscence of childhood' occurred 'a year or two later. I went to bed one night and instead of undressing sat down and began to think. As I thought, suddenly and for the first time, I realised that I myself must die, must cease to play and eat and sleep, to pass away into the dark of nothingness.'[93] In his autobiography Haggard describes this experience as taking place in the Sandwich Room, a small dressing room on the second floor of Bradenham Hall 'sandwiched' between a larger bedroom and the library. He was 'about nine years old' and unable to fall asleep when

> It came home to me that I too must die; that my body must be buried in the ground and my spirit be hurried off to a terrible, unfamiliar land which to most people was known as Hell. In those days it was common for clergymen to talk a great deal about Hell, especially to the young. It was an awful hour. I shivered, I prayed, I wept. I thought I saw Death waiting for me by the library door. At last I went to sleep to dream that I was already in this hell and that the peculiar form of punishment allotted to me was to be continually eaten alive by rats![94]

Drawing on what she was told by her father, his youngest daughter, Lilias, records this incident as having occurred on the night of 21 July 1869 after the wedding of his eldest sister, Ella, to the Reverend Charles Green, a month after Haggard turned 13. The wedding took place in the morning and, according to the Reverend Benjamin Armstrong, the 'whole neighbourhood was there. The entire poor of the village were feasted & there was a grand supper for the guests.'[95]

To accommodate the influx of family, friends and new in-laws, Haggard was moved from the attic room where he shared a four-poster bed with his brother Andrew to the Sandwich Room. 'No one liked the Sandwich,' writes Lilias. 'It was lined with books to the ceiling which made it dark and shut-in and stuffy.' The sounds of celebration gradually faded, the guests left in their carriages, Haggard's father called in the dogs and locked the doors. 'The clock on the landing struck midnight

... and the house grew silent except for creaks and cracks and sighing noises.' Haggard lay wide awake and frightened. 'There seemed to be something else in the room, and once he thought he heard the swish of a silk skirt.' Stories of Lady Hamilton and her visits to the hall, 'of the stiff brocades and silks she loved to wear ... came back unbidden to his mind'. Pulling the bedclothes over his head, he fell 'into an uneasy doze, in which he dreamed he was a rat and an enormous ferret with flaming eyes was chasing him down a tunnel, which grew narrower and narrower, until he could feel its hot breath blowing on his neck'. He woke up:

> The moon was shining through the window so brilliantly that he could see every detail in the room. A little breeze rattled the stiff magnolia branches outside, and the shifting shadow of the leaves danced over the bed. He put out his hand and let them flicker over it – how odd it seemed in the moonlight, dead – dead. Then it happened. He realised that one day that hand would be limp also, that he could not lift it anymore – it would be dead – he would be dead.[96]

Lilias also records a memory from her father's childhood of a 'disreputable rag doll of particularly hideous aspect, with boot button eyes, hair of black wool and a sinister leer upon its face'. The young Rider was terrified of it and, on discovering this, an 'unscrupulous nurse' used it to 'frighten him into obedience'. The doll was named She-Who-Must-Be-Obeyed.[97]

Haggard also told Lilias of the time when he had grown too old for the nursery and began sharing the four-poster in the attic with Andrew. While hunting mice with a dog on the lower landing, the two boys knocked down and 'decapitated a scantily clad draped marble female which stood on a table in the window'. Their father emerged at that precise moment, and his customary roar was given added impetus by the fact the statue had been a present from his wife on their honeymoon in Rome.

The two miscreants were sent 'supperless to bed', where Haggard relieved his boredom by outlining his initials 'with rusty pin heads'.[98] This was the first recorded application of his initials H.R.H., which, as he was well aware, also stood for 'His Royal Highness'. These illustrious capitals would later be inscribed by him on a variety of tempting surfaces at school, his homes and greenhouses, as well as engraved on briefcases and luggage and, most memorably, planted out in daffodils on a bank in the garden of Ditchingham House, his future Norfolk home, where they continue to bloom every spring.[99] The act of inscription must have been especially empowering for a melancholic and frightened boy who would recollect 'that on the whole I was rather a quiet youth, at any rate by comparison. Certainly I was very imaginative, although I kept my thoughts to myself, which I dare say had a good deal to do with my reputation for stupidity. I believe I was considered the dull boy of the family.'[100]

Assorted governesses, 'foreign and otherwise',[101] were employed at Bradenham Hall to educate Rider and his younger siblings, Mary and Arthur. 'I fear that I was more or less of a dunderhead at lessons.'[102] Even his beloved mother shared the family consensus that Haggard was a dull child, 'although she always indignantly denied the story in after years, I remember when I was about seven my dear mother declaring that I was as heavy as lead in body and mind'.[103]

2

'LOVE'S SWEET DREAM'

Haggard was 9 years old in 1865 when his family moved to London to take up residence at 24 Leinster Square, a fashionable address on the border of Notting Hill and Bayswater, north of Hyde Park and Kensington Gardens, where 'impressive Regency-style terraces ... were arranged around squares almost as grand as those of Mayfair'.[1]

Haggard was sent to a day-school 'managed by the head master and an usher [junior teacher] ... a lanky, red-haired, pale-faced man' hated by all the boys 'because of his violent temper and injustice'.[2] One day when the usher's back was turned, Haggard shook his fists at him, causing the other boys to laugh. Identified as the culprit, Haggard was called by the usher to the front. '"You young brute!" he said. "I'll see you in your grave before you shake your fists at me again." Then he doubled his own and, striking me first on one side of the head and then on the other, knocked me all the way down the long room and finally over a chair into a heap of slates in a corner, where I lay a while almost senseless. I recovered and went home.' His eldest sister, Ella, 'noticing my bruised and dazed condition, cross-examined me until I told her the truth'.[3] The incident must have shocked Haggard's mother, inevitably recalling the bullying to death of her brother. A meeting between Haggard's father and the headmaster resulted in the dismissal of the usher and Haggard's departure to another school where pupils 'were supposed to receive a sound business education'.[4] Haggard's dread of the usher remained: 'so great was my fear of him' that on encountering him in Hyde Park near Rotten Row, 'I never stopped running till I reached the Marble Arch' on the opposite side of the park.[5]

Around this time Haggard was subjected to an examination by his future brother-in-law the Reverend Charles Maddison Green in order to ascertain 'what amount of knowledge I had acquired'.[6] So appalling was the outcome that when informed of the result, 'my indignant father burst into the room where I sat resigned to fate, and, in a voice like to that of an angry bull, roared out at me that I was "only fit to be a greengrocer"'. The humiliated child went for a walk with his older brother Andrew, who had eavesdropped behind the door. In doleful silence the two boys paced the pavements to Westbourne Grove and 'a fruit and vegetable store ... My brother stood contemplating it for a long while. At last he said: "I say, old fellow, when you become a greengrocer, I hope you'll let me have oranges cheap!" To this day I have never quite forgiven Andrew for that most heartless remark.'[7]

As a consequence of his examination by Ella's fiancé, Haggard's education was placed in the hands of the Reverend Henry Graham, 'who took in two or three small boys' at his rectory in Garsington, near Oxford.[8] Graham and his wife were friends of the Haggard family and Rider had previously stayed with them to convalesce after a childhood illness and been 'very happy there'.[9] Garsington was, and remains, a 'straggling hamlet'[10] of sturdy limestone cottages strung along a lane meandering up a steep hill to St Mary's Church perched on an outcrop above a wide valley – source of hot thermals in summer and cold winds in winter – with the Chilterns on the far side.

The seventeenth-century vicarage, built as a refuge for scholars 'when plague raged in Oxford', was 'long, and low, and grey'. In the garden stood a 'great square pigeon house' where the boys would go at night to catch the roosting birds 'which we afterwards ate in pies'. A pollarded willow smothered in ivy bore 'the biggest and blackest berries possible', annually appropriated for Christmas decorations, and in a local orchard the young Haggard had a 'violent collision' with an apple tree while riding a pony, 'but the head was the harder, and the bough "carried away"'.[11]

The hollow trunk of an ancient elm provided 'ample room to sit' and a suitably discreet location for Haggard and a 'little fair-haired girl' to teach 'each other the rudiments of flirtation'.[12] The girl was 'Mrs. Graham's little sister Blanche, who was as fair in colouring as one of her name should be'.[13] Blanche appears as Stella Carson in *Allan's Wife*, a prequel to *King Solomon's Mines*. Garsington becomes Garsingham in the book and the drawing room of the vicarage the setting for a strange, possibly autobiographical scene. At a Christmas party the shy young Quatermain hides himself behind a chair and watches 'little Stella Carson ... giving the children presents off the tree. She was dressed as Father Christmas, with some soft white stuff round her lovely little face, and she had large dark eyes.' Come Quatermain's turn to receive a present, 'Stella reached it down from one of the lower boughs of the tree and handed it to me, saying – "Dat is my Christmas present to you, little Allan Quatermain."' As she gave him the present, Stella's sleeve 'touched one of the tapers and caught fire', the flames running her arm towards her throat.

> She stood quite still. I suppose that she was paralysed with fear; and the ladies who were near screamed very loud, but did nothing. Then some impulse seized me – perhaps instinct would be a better word to use, considering my age. I threw myself upon the child, and, beating at the fire with my hands, mercifully succeeded in extinguishing it before it really got hold. My wrists were so badly scorched that they had to be wrapped up in wool for a long time afterwards, but with the exception of a single burn upon her throat, little Stella Carson was not much hurt.[14]

The origins of Allan Quatermain, Haggard's most famous hero, can be traced to Garsington, where Haggard came to know a local pig farmer, William Quartermaine, 'a fine handsome man of about fifty, with grey hair and aristocratic features [who] always wore a beautiful smock-frock'. Quartermaine and his wife Jayne were kind to the youngster. Quartermaine gave him 'the largest walnuts I ever saw' from a tree in his meadow and 'I made boats out of their shells'.[15] Quartermaine's 'genial-hearted' wife supplied 'unlimited milk' to drink.[16] On a nostalgic visit to Garsington in 1887, Haggard found 'a good many new gravestones' in St Mary's churchyard, among them two 'erected to the memory of William Quartermaine and his "beloved wife"'.[17] Why Haggard changed the spelling of the surname to Quatermain when naming his hero remains a mystery.[18]

Life at Garsington was not all bucolic idyll with occasional lessons. Mr Graham's was a working vicarage and his pupils were required to assist him in his religious duties. One dank November afternoon Haggard accompanied Graham 'to administer the last sacrament to a dying parishioner', walking along a lane 'ankle-deep in mud, so deep that it was necessary to walk upon the sodden bank of the hedgerow'.[19] Thereafter came the funeral: 'beneath the lych-gate stands the clergyman in white and fluttering robes, while down the path, followed by the black-robed mourners, comes the slow procession of the dead'.[20]

There were lighter moments, such as the 'hot summer afternoon' when a donkey put his head through the open chancel door of St Mary's and 'inopportunely brayed'.[21] Haggard was seated among the choir in the chancel until, to his 'intense and bitter mortification', he was removed as being 'really too weak in the qualities necessary to vocal music'.[22]

Haggard drew on his time at Garsington for his novel *Love Eternal*, where the vicarage is referred to as Monk's Acre and Mr Graham and Blanche are the models for Mr Knight and his daughter Isobel. Knight opens a school at Garsingham 'and after an exchange of the "highest references", two little boys appeared at Monk's Acre, both of them rather delicate in health'.[23] One of them, the book's hero Godfrey, returns to the school as an adult and, tired from his long journey, sits 'himself down in that same chair in which Isobel had kissed him when he was a little boy'.[24]

Happy days at Garsington came to an end and 'the question arose as to where I should be sent to [secondary] school'.[25] Haggard's elder brothers, with the exception of Jack who entered Dartmouth Naval College in 1864 at the age of 14, had all enjoyed 'the advantage of a public school education'.[26] William and Bazett went to Winchester College, Alfred to Haileybury, Andrew to Westminster, and Rider's younger brother, Arthur, thanks to a legacy, attended Shrewsbury. The Haggard girls, sisters Ella, Mary and Cecilia, were tutored at Bradenham and local finishing schools, but when it came to Rider 'funds were running short ... Also, as I was supposed to be not very bright, I dare say it was thought that to send me to a public school would be to waste money.' So it was decreed Haggard should attend Ipswich

Grammar School, 'which had the advantages of being cheap and near at hand'.[27] Dwindling family finances reflected the falling fortunes of British agriculture, in addition to which Haggard's father, 'who had the passion of his generation for land', had invested most of his wife's fortune 'in that security just at the commencement of its great fall in value'.[28]

Much has been made of Haggard being disadvantaged by being dispatched to a grammar school as opposed to a public school, but is the fuss really warranted?[29] True, the pupils at Ipswich Grammar School in the Suffolk county capital came from 'gentle, but not wealthy'[30] families, but the school boasts a long tradition, tracing its origins back to 1399, making it the fourth oldest school in Britain. The school coalesced into its present form when older educational institutions in Ipswich, such as St Mary's College, were incorporated into the model grammar school founded by Cardinal Thomas Wolsey in 1528. Ipswich Grammar may have fallen from favour in subsequent centuries, but during the latter half of the nineteenth the school enjoyed a renaissance under the headmaster Hubert Ashton Holden. Haggard boarded at Ipswich from 1869 to 1872, in the middle of Holden's twenty-five-year tenure from 1858 to 1883, and thought him the 'best thing about the school ... a charming and a kindly gentleman, also one of the best scholars of his age'.[31] According to John Blatchly, a later Ipswich Grammar headmaster and school historian, Holden 'was certainly the greatest scholar in the school's history'.[32] Holden was educated at King Edward's School, Edgbaston, and was 'successively scholar, fellow, tutor and classical lecturer at Trinity College, Cambridge'.[33] Prior to taking up the post at Ipswich Grammar, Holden had been vice principal of Cheltenham College. He and his wife Laetitia had three sons and seven daughters.

On installation as headmaster Holden set about rectifying the 'low standard of scholarship in the boys' and the 'professional insufficiency in the staff'.[34] Average pupil numbers were just below a hundred during Holden's headmastership, in spite of which they managed to achieve '133 distinctions won at the universities and elsewhere, including six fellowships, 54 scholarships, forty honours in the class lists, nine university prizes'.[35] None of these honours accrued to Haggard, however, whose time at Ipswich Grammar was undistinguished: 'I did not care for school, and found it monotonous', though he did recall being popular among his schoolmates, who 'showed their affection by naming me "Nosey" in allusion to the prominence of that organ on my undeveloped face'.[36]

Haggard attracted unwelcome attention on his first day at Ipswich Grammar in 1869 after being deposited there by his father, who had selected a hat for his son 'such as is generally worn by a curate, being of the ordinary clerical black felt and shape'.[37] Topped with this inappropriate head-gear, Haggard was sent to the playground where he stood alone, 'a forlorn and lanky figure. Presently a boy came up and hit me in the face, saying: "Phillips ... sends this to the new fellow in a parson's hat."'[38] Haggard was outraged: '"Show me Phillips," I said, and a very big boy was pointed out to me.' Haggard walked up to him and, notwithstanding the daunting size of Edward Phillips, a Shropshire lad from Ludlow, punched him in the face. A fight ensued in which 'of course I got the worst'. But Haggard gained the respect of his schoolfellows, who tolerated his clergyman's hat 'until I managed to procure another'.[39]

As well as the melancholy introvert that Haggard portrays himself as being in childhood and youth, he was also a boy perfectly willing and able to fight his corner with words and fists. He needed to be. Ipswich Grammar was 'a rough place, and there was much bullying of which the masters were not aware'.[40] One 'fine young man', one of the biggest boys in the school, 'was a great bully and, unknown to the masters, used to cruelly maltreat those who were smaller and weaker than himself. This lad became a clergyman, and, as it happened, in after years I struck his spoor in a very remote part of the world.'[41]

Haggard does not name the bully, but he can be identified as Armine Francis King, who attended Ipswich Grammar from 1867 to 1875 and was the son of the Reverend Richard Henry King of Little Glemham in Suffolk. A seemingly model pupil, he was captain of football in 1874, of cricket in 1875, and in the same year head of school. An Albert Scholar at Keble College, Oxford, he was subsequently ordained an Anglican priest and went to Japan where he became chaplain at St Andrew's Church at Shiba-koen, Tokyo, serving the British expatriate community. There he met Haggard's sister Mary, by then Baroness d'Anethan, wife of the Belgian ambassador to Japan, who provided evidence of King's 'spoor' to her brother.[42]

Meanwhile the fisticuffs at Ipswich Grammar continued and Haggard piled in. In 1896 an anonymous contemporary at Ipswich Grammar rendered a striking pen portrait of the young Haggard:

> [Haggard was] a tall lad, who was evidently growing out of his clothes, with loosely-hung frame, features thin almost to gauntness but lighted up by bright eyes, which revealed an innate kindliness of disposition, and a shock of rather rebellious hair. His manner was remarkably diffident, and he had the aspect of one who had been startled, but not frightened. At that time he certainly gave no indication of his future fame, save that I seem to recall a certain dormitory reputation for yarn-spinning. His ascent of Parnassus was made with toil and difficulty, and after three terms in the same Form he was 'shoved up' – the phrase is ugly but singularly expressive – to the Upper Fourth, where he passed four more terms, and finally he got a move to the Lower Fifth, which was just before he left. He was almost invariably nearer the bottom of the form than the top, and the extent of his classical attainments that his books reveal is a source of wonder to his old schoolfellows.[43]

As will be seen, there was a good reason for the extent of Haggard's proficiency in Latin and Greek exhibited in his books, but while at Ipswich Grammar he did excel at least once in classics when 'by some accident I wrote a really fine set of Latin verses'[44] for master 'Guts' Sanderson, like Holden a notable classical scholar. Sanderson was one of Holden's first appointments and he remained at the school until Holden's resignation in 1883. The two men complemented each other: Holden 'always precise and dapper', holding himself 'aloof from the town, its magnates and its affairs'; Sanderson boasting 'a Herculean frame, carelessly dressed' and throwing himself 'into various aspects of Ipswich life'.[45] He was idolised by the boys, who nicknamed him 'Guts', a tribute to his Falstaffian dimensions.

When Haggard presented his 'fine set of verses', Sanderson accused him of cribbing. Haggard denied the charge and Sanderson called him a liar, 'for he was sure that there was no one in the school who could write such verses'.[46] When Sanderson discovered he had falsely accused the boy, 'he summoned the whole school and offered me a public apology'.[47]

Haggard achieved one other academic distinction. 'Guts' offered 'a special prize' to the pupil who could write the best descriptive essay on a subject of their choice. Haggard chose a surgical operation, despite never having been 'in a hospital or seen an operation, so any information I had upon the matter must have come from reading. Still I beat all the other essayists hollow and won the prize'.[48] This essay and the Latin verses aside, Haggard's academic career was unremarkable. Haggard admitted he 'was slow' at his lessons and that 'to this day there are subjects at which I am extremely stupid ... all mathematics are absolutely abhorrent to me, while as for Euclid it bored me so intensely that I do not think I ever mastered the meaning of the stuff'.[49] Lack of academic prowess was no bar to further study, however, and Haggard's name was entered at St John's College, Cambridge, by the classical scholar Sir John Edwin Sandys, a friend of his father.[50] Haggard fared better on the sports fields, being 'elected captain of the second football team, but did not stay long enough at Ipswich to get into the first'.[51]

Haggard spent the midwinter holidays of 1871 at Bradenham Hall. Amateur dramatics were a staple of the Victorian festive season and Rider, his brothers and sisters Bazett, Alfred, Andrew, Arthur and Mary, with friends Julia Barker (Bazett's future wife) and a Miss Wilson presented a double bill: *Dearest Mamma: A Commedietta in One Act* by Walter Gordon (Rider took the role of Brown 'The Footman') followed by *Count Fosco, or, The Brotherhood* (adapted from Wilkie Collins's *The Woman in White*) in which Haggard was promoted to servant. The entertainment ended with the singing of 'God Save the Queen'.

This was the last occasion so many of the Haggard siblings would gather in the family home. For Haggard's older brothers, at least, their careers were taking them to various corners of the world. Will had already begun a diplomatic career and was now in Berne, Switzerland, and Jack, a sub-lieutenant in the Royal Navy, was serving in the Mediterranean after suppressing pirates in the Pacific and playing a part in the naval support of the Magdala campaign to dethrone Emperor Tewodros II of Ethiopia. In the summer Alfred would head for the Bengal Presidency to embark on a career in the Indian Civil Service; Andrew would soon be joining his regiment, the King's Own Scottish Borderers, which would take him to India, Egypt and the Sudan.[52] Bazett remained closer to home, a barrister in Norwich.

The summer holidays of 1872 were spent in Switzerland where Rider initially lodged 'with a foreign family in order to improve my French' and, thanks to 'the able assistance of the young ladies of the house', acquired 'a good colloquial knowledge of that language in quite a short time'.[53] Thereafter he joined the rest of his family staying in the village of Flüelen on Lake Lucerne, from where he and Andrew took a two-day walking trip to the St Gotthard Pass. Here they planned to meet and bid farewell to Alfred, who was taking the coach to Brindisi on the heel of Italy from where he would sail via the Suez Canal to India.

Before Alfred's final farewell, Rider and Andrew overnighted at a wayside inn. The next morning 'the pretty Swiss chambermaid', with whom they had made friends, took them to a nearby mortuary 'and, among a number of other such gruesome relics, showed us the skull of her own father, which she polished up affectionately with her apron'.[54] After this macabre flirtation, the two brothers stepped out to the top of the pass to meet Alfred's coach. Rider, Andrew and their father, who had accompanied Alfred thus far, shouted their goodbyes as the coach departed, with William Haggard 'waving a tall white hat out of which, to the amazement of the travellers, fell two towels and an assortment of cabbage leaves and other greenery. It was like a conjuring trick.' The day was hot and he 'feared sunstroke'.[55]

Once the careers of his elder brothers were set in motion, attention turned to Rider. With 'characteristic suddenness my father made up his mind that I was to leave, so Ipswich knew me no more'.[56] William Haggard determined his son should have a career in the Foreign Office, and to prepare for the necessary examination, he was sent to a Mr Bernard, a private tutor in South Kensington, London, 'a French professor who had married one of my sister's school-mistresses'.[57] Haggard's brother Will was also there studying for some examinations in furtherance of his diplomatic career. On passing, he was posted to Washington.

Haggard remained in London with the French professor and his wife: both were 'charming' but, 'having married late in life, they did not in the least assimilate'.[58] The professor's religious views were 'broad', whereas those of his wife, a member of the Society of Plymouth Brethren, were 'narrow'. Informed by her that he would go to hell, the professor indicated that, 'if she were not there, that fate would have its consolations'. Their 'rows were awful. I never knew a more ill-assorted pair.'[59] Haggard remained with them for most of 1873 'imbibing some knowledge of French literature, and incidentally of the tenets of the Plymouth Brethren'. Then came another sudden intervention on the part of Haggard's father: 'I was to go to Scoones, the great crammer, and there make ready to face the Foreign Office examination.'[60]

Scoones, an educational forcing house coaching candidates for the Foreign Office and Diplomatic Service examinations as well as those of the Indian Civil Service, was owned and managed by William Baptiste Wordsworth Scoones, a British national born in Paris in 1838. Scoones himself was a cultured 'kindly, keen, white-haired man'[61] with literary and artistic interests (he was a serious collector and patron of James McNeill Whistler), author of several works on education and the civil service, and editor of *Four Centuries of English Letters*. Scoones the institution was the most famous crammer of the day, enjoying 'a complete monopoly as regards candidates for the FO, Diplomatic and Consular Services',[62] and was located in Covent Garden at Garrick Chambers, 19 Garrick Street, next to the Garrick Club.

The Scoones curriculum was overseen by its French-born director, André Turquet, and many of the teachers were prominent in other fields. Pupils at Scoones were 'tutored hard in recommended texts for the entrance exam including Smith's *Wealth of Nations*, Mill's *Principles of Political Economy* as well as German, French and Latin and how to answer the infamous "Catch" questions that the FO examiners famously set'.[63] They also 'lived rather wild lives with drinks at The Fielding Club, regular trips to the Gaiety and Savoy theatres as well as indulging in séances!'[64]

Scoones, distantly related to the Haggards through his wife Henrietta, 'tutored two generations of the family' and 'liked to say that the Haggards developed slowly and late'.[65] Haggard began cramming at Scoones shortly after his eighteenth birthday in June 1874 when, after a brief holiday at Bradenham, he was 'put in lodgings alone in London, entirely uncontrolled in any way'.[66] Haggard compared the experience to that of being thrown into the Rhine by his brothers: 'After nearly drowning I learned to swim, and in a sense the same may be said of my London life'.[67] His first London address was 'somewhere near Westbourne Grove and kept by a young widow. As they did not turn out respectable I was moved to others in Davies Street' near Berkeley Square, 'an excellent situation for a young gentleman about town'.[68]

The nineteenth century was 'London's explosive century':[69] a population of just under a million people in 1801 rose by about a fifth each decade, and by the end of the century London's population was six and a half million, 'about the same as the combined populations of Europe's four greatest cities, Paris, Berlin, Vienna and St Petersburg'.[70] In the mid-1840s London was already 'the greatest city on the earth, the capital of empire, the centre of international trade and finance, a vast world market into which the world poured'.[71] By the 1870s the city was the driving engine of a colossal global commercial and trading empire underpinned by military and naval might; an empire accounting for nearly a quarter of the world's surface and over a fifth of its population. Living in London, Haggard was at its nerve centre, the departure point into a wider world in which Englishmen felt it part of the natural order, if not the divine, that they were ordained to play the commanding role.

At Scoones Haggard made several friends, identified in his autobiography as Arthur L., Walsh, Norris, and Justin Sheil. Another London acquaintance was Thomas Gibson Bowles, editor of the magazine *Vanity Fair*, which he had founded in 1868. Haggard met Bowles, then in his thirties, 'at the house of some friends and had many talks with him'.[72] Haggard remembered how he met Bowles but hadn't 'the faintest recollection' of how he managed an entrée into spiritualism's select inner circle and became 'a frequent visitor' at the house of Lady Poulett in Mayfair's fashionable Hanover Square.[73]

Spiritualism was the craze of the decade: part parlour game, part erotic cabaret, part pushing the boundaries of knowledge, part reaction against the determinism arising from Charles Darwin's evolutionary theories – a scientific religion for a scientific age. Darwin's co-evolutionist Alfred Russel Wallace was an avid spiritualist, and matters psychic attracted some of the finest minds of the century, including the American psychologist and philosopher William James, the philosopher Henry Sidgwick and the physicist Oliver Lodge. But, as Alex Owen remarks, an 'important and often overlooked aspect of Victorian mediumship was that it could be enormous fun':[74] many of its devotees were willing dupes of what was often a skilful conjuring display.[75]

Spiritualism had thrived in Britain since its importation from the United States, where in the early 1850s two sisters, Margaret and Kate Fox, 'began channelling ghosts in a house near Rochester in New York State'.[76] In the Britain of the time 'table-tilting had become the fashionable social pastime, even in the Royal residence at Osborne, where the table moved for Victoria and Albert'.[77] Séances were attended by leading figures of the day – Thomas Macaulay, John Ruskin, Bishop Samuel Wilberforce, William Ewart Gladstone and Lewis Carroll – seated at tables around the country eager to be impressed and entertained by spirit writing, the sound of disembodied voices, or the sudden appearance of solid objects or 'apports'. Inevitably the spectre of fraud and trickery cast a shadow over the enterprise, and in order to demonstrate the seriousness of their endeavour, British spiritualists were intent on producing a visible, corporeal spirit form. The Fox sisters had managed this in the United States, but such manifestations had so far eluded English mediums and would not occur until the 1870s.

Lady Poulett introduced Haggard 'to the spiritualistic society of the day', some of whom entertained hopes he 'might develop into a first-class medium'.[78] Haggard does not elaborate further, but in *Love Eternal* Godfrey (who also attends Scoones) exhibits psychic powers though he eventually rejects and suppresses them. Haggard attended séances at 20 Hanover Square together with 'other habitués of the "circle"',[79] which included Lady Caithness, second wife of the Fourteenth Earl of Caithness; she and Lady Poulett were founding council members of the British National Association of Spiritualists in 1874 and both knew the Theosophist Madame Blavatsky.[80]

The reigning king of spiritualism during Haggard's residence in London was Daniel Dunglas Home, the most famous medium of the time who 'gave séances for the royalty and aristocracy of Russia, France, and Holland, and was eagerly sought after by the wealthy and titled in Britain'.[81] This didn't save him from being mercilessly satirised by Robert Browning in his poem 'Mr Sludge, "The Medium"'. Haggard never saw Home in action, but he did encounter another famous medium, the matronly Agnes Guppy-Volckman, better known as Mrs Guppy, who 'perfected the production of spirit "apports", usually flowers or pretty gifts, which showered down on the surprised and delighted sitters'.[82] When Alfred Russel Wallace requested 'a sunflower at one séance a six-foot specimen complete with clods of earth fell at his feet'.[83] Haggard attended a séance with Mrs Guppy where 'the table suddenly became covered with great quantities of roses covered with dew'.[84]

Haggard and a friend, probably Norris, were given to playing jokes at these séances, and Mrs Guppy's roses afforded a golden opportunity: 'my friend and I, having unlinked our hands, broke a number of fat, hard buds and, knowing where she was sitting, discharged them through the darkness with all our strength straight at the head of Mrs. Guppy. Little wonder that presently we heard that poor lady exclaim: "Oh! the spirits are hurting me so."'[85]

A similar response was drawn from Lady Caithness when Haggard 'in the course of my investigation of certain phenomena that were happening underneath the table ... landed her a most severe kick upon the shins'.[86] Haggard thought it 'all very amusing, and would have done no harm had the business stopped there. But it did not.'[87] Haggard doesn't elaborate, but it is probable he is referring to the materialisation of spirit forms.

In the 1870s the talents of Mrs Guppy and her peers were gradually overshadowed by the arrival of younger and more attractive female mediums able to conjure up spirit manifestations – 'the two princesses of the spiritualist world during the 1870s were Florence Cook and Mary Rosina Showers'.[88] By 1873 Florence Cook was able to produce 'full figure manifestations' of a spirit named Katie King, thus presenting 'for confirmed spiritualists the final empirical evidence for the reality of spirit life and the existence of an unseen world' and had 'believers and non-believers alike clamouring for entrance to her séances'.[89]

Haggard doesn't record meeting Cook, but he did attend a session with Mary Rosina Showers at the house of Mrs Makdougall Gregory, widow of William Gregory, a professor of chemistry at the University of Edinburgh who had been fascinated by mesmerism, spiritualism's precursor. At 21 Green Street, Mayfair, 'I witnessed remarkable things', writes Haggard. Mary Showers, 'plump, attractive and fair, with a "large mop of hair falling down to her waist" and a dreamy look in her eyes',[90] was able to manifest more than one spirit and Florence, Maple, Lenore, Sally and Peter '(who spoke with a deep sonorous voice from within the cabinet) were all familiar to Miss Showers's friends and supporters'.[91] At Green Street, Haggard met Florence and Lenore when Showers 'sank into a trance', and after some minor manifestations

> two young women of great beauty – or perhaps I should say young spirits – one dark and the other fair, appeared in the lighted room. I conversed with and touched them both, and noted that their flesh seemed to be firm but cold ... being a forward youth

of inquiring mind, I even asked the prettier of the two to allow me to give her a kiss. She smiled but did not seem to be at all annoyed, but I never got the kiss. I think she remarked that it was not permissible.[92]

On another occasion Haggard and some of his friends from Scoones arranged a séance at the house of Norris's uncle in St James's Place. It would be the last séance Haggard attended. The medium, 'a feeble little man ... was pounced upon by two of the strongest young men present, who never let go of him until the end of the proceedings', which were 'various and tumultuous'. In a darkened dining room, the table skipped, lights floated in the air, cold little hands picked the sitters' shirt fronts, feather fans flew off the mantelpiece and fanned perspiring faces, objects were swirling through the air; when 'heavy articles' were heard moving around the room, the lamps were lit 'and there, in the centre of the dining-table, one upon the other ... were the two massive dining-room arm-chairs, and on the top of these, reaching nearly to the ceiling, appeared Mr. Norris's priceless china candelabra'. How could this have been done? The medium had been restrained and, even if he wasn't, he 'could never have lifted those chairs'.[93]

Haggard could not provide an answer either then or when writing his autobiography, though he was inclined 'to think that certain forces with which we are at present unacquainted were set loose that produced phenomena which, perhaps, had their real origin in our own minds, but nevertheless were true phenomena'.[94] Whatever the explanation, he was 'quite sure' spiritualism was 'mischievous and to be discouraged. Bearing in mind its effect upon my own nerves, never would I allow any young person over whom I had control to attend a séance.'[95]

Much as he later condemned it, Haggard's encounter with spiritualism stimulated and enlarged his religious landscape, and throughout his life he avidly explored theological and esoteric literature and enthusiastically discussed questions of life and death with others, especially Anglican clergymen. He kept abreast of the psychical research of 'wise scientists like Sir Oliver Lodge', but otherwise felt such matters should be left to 'the expert and earnest investigator, or become the secret comfort of such few hearts as can rise now and again beyond the world, making as it were their trial flights towards that place where, as we hope, their rest remaineth'.[96]

The erotic charge in Haggard's description of the séance featuring the two 'young women of great beauty' is inescapable; the object of Haggard's desire was now to manifest herself in less elusive form. During the time Haggard attended Scoones, 'a great event happened. I fell truly and earnestly in love.'[97] In the spring of 1875 at a ball in Richmond the 18-year-old Haggard encountered 'a very beautiful young lady a few years older than myself to whom I was instantly and overwhelmingly attracted'.[98] By the end of the evening Haggard had fallen 'headlong and violently in love'.[99]

When the ball was over, Haggard escorted his newly beloved to her carriage. 'The house where the ball took place had a garden in front, down which garden ran a carpeted path. At the end of the path a great arch had been erected for the occasion, and through this arch I followed the young lady.'[100] Under the arch she 'hesitated a moment, turning to smile at him, the light shining down on her hair'. Haggard, who had intended asking her where she lived, was so smitten that he 'let her get into her waiting carriage with never a word, and drive away into the night'.[101] Haggard was quick to remedy his omission: 'even goddesses must eat' and, as he knew the neighbourhood in which she lived, 'a well-directed inquiry'[102] at a local butcher's shop produced the desired information.

Haggard's first love became the dominant love of his life both in reality and, more enduringly, as a fixed component of his psychological make-up, kindled and rekindled by chance circumstances of the years to come; re-evaluated and reimagined in his fiction. Reflecting on his first experience of love, Haggard wrote:

> If all goes well, this, I suppose, is one of the best things that can happen to a young fellow. It steadies him and gives him an object in life: someone for whom to work. If all goes ill, it is one of the worst, for then the reverse is apt to come about. It unsteadies him, makes him reckless, and perhaps throws him in the way of undesirable adventures. In my case, in the end all went wrong, or seemed to do so at the time.[103]

Haggard never committed the name of his beloved to print. Her name, or at least *a* name, was first given in *The Cloak That I Left* in which Lilias writes of her father seeing 'Lilith' for the first time 'in the full beauty of her youth – perhaps twenty-one, with a rather heavy, placid face, blue eyes, and a mass of golden-brown, curling hair'.[104] The name used by Lilias is a telling one; in Jewish mythology Lilith is a sexually assertive woman, the first woman and wife of the first man, Adam, whom she leaves behind in the Garden of Eden after having sexual intercourse with an archangel. Lilith's identity was finally revealed in 1981 after considerable detective work on the part of Haggard's biographer D.S. Higgins. 'Lilith' was Mary Elizabeth Jackson, known to her family and friends as Lilly.[105] We have already encountered her surname at Leamington Spa, where Haggard's younger brother, Arthur, struck up a friendship with Frederick Jackson during one of the Haggard family's periodic relocations. Lilly was Frederick's sister. Their father John Jackson came from a long line of successful Yorkshire farmers and was known as 'Jack of Oran', courtesy of living at Oran House near Catterick. An 'expert on bloodstock', he 'amassed a fortune on the turf'.[106] He married twice, first to Charlotte Goodricke by whom he had four daughters: Eliza, Alice, Laura and Lilly, who was born on 19 October 1854. After Charlotte's death he married Jane Outhwaite, who gave birth to Frederick on 14 February 1860. When John Jackson died of tuberculosis in 1869 at the age of 43, his Yorkshire estate was sold and his fortune placed in trust. Jane and the five children moved south, 'eventually taking up residence at Aston Lodge, Leamington'.[107]

In the spring and early summer of 1875 all went well. Lilly and Rider enjoyed a rose-tinted romance akin to that of the characters Arthur and Angela in Haggard's first novel, *Dawn*:

> For them, the long June days were golden, but all too short. Every morning found their mutual love more perfect, but when the flakes of crimson light faded from the skies, and night dropped her veil over the tall trees and peaceful lake, by some miracle it had grown deeper and more perfect still ... And, the more he saw of her, the prouder he was to think that such a perfect creature should so dearly love himself; and with the greater joy did he look forward to that supreme and happy hour when he should call her his.[108]

Haggard's second novel, *The Witch's Head*, contains several autobiographical elements, including the first meeting at a ball of the main character Ernest Kershaw and the 'radiant creature' Eva Ceswick, her forename kin to that of the first woman in the Bible, who makes a grand entrance: 'dressed in white *soie de chine*, in the bosom of which was fixed a single rose. The dress was cut low, and her splendid neck and arms were entirely without ornament.' From Eva's 'dark eyes there shone a light that few men could look upon and forget, and yet there was nothing bold about it ... her eyes met his own, and something passed from them into his heart that remained there all his life.'[109]

Lilias suggests Lilly Jackson was more worldly-wise than Haggard and initially didn't take his avowals of love seriously. This behaviour is reflected in *The Witch's Head* where Eva's initial coquettishness with Ernest evolves, to her surprise, into something deeper. Haggard and Lilly became secretly engaged, as do Ernest and Eva in *The Witch's Head*, though somewhat reluctantly on Eva's part: 'am *I* not worth a little patience? There is not the slightest possibility, so far as I can see, of our getting married at present; so the question is, if it is of any use to trumpet out an engagement that will only make us the object of a great deal of gossip?'[110]

The couple met frequently during the two months before Haggard left for France to join his family for the summer holidays, where in the course 'of one of his continual expeditions, my father had settled for a while at Tours'[111] in the Loire Valley, a longstanding British expatriate outpost in France, 'an oasis of Anglo-Saxondom in a desert of continentalism' where the natives were said to speak the best French on the planet.[112] Haggard resided separately from the rest of his family at 25 rue Bretonneau with an elderly Professor Demeste and his wife, 'in order that I might pursue my studies of the language'.[113] The Haggard family occupied 23 rue de Bordeaux near the Place Jean Jaurès, where Haggard would meet them before setting off on sightseeing expeditions.

Perhaps it was at Tours that Haggard made 'a discreditable exhibition of feeling over a book' while reading Edward Bulwer-Lytton's novel *Kenelm Chillingly* 'until the small hours', when he 'wept over the death of Lilly'.[114] Certainly it was at Tours shortly before his nineteenth birthday in June 1875 that a decision was made, irrevocably changing the course of Haggard's life: 'my father saw in *The Times*, or heard otherwise, that Sir Henry Bulwer ... had been appointed to the Lieutenant-Governorship of Natal. Now my father was a man of ideas who never lost a chance of finding an opening for one of his sons, and the Bulwers of Heydon in Norfolk were, as it happened, old friends of our family.'[115] Haggard's mother Ella took the initiative and wrote to Bulwer requesting he consider taking her son to Natal on his staff, possibly as private secretary. Bulwer replied saying he would consider the matter but was not in a position to give any guarantees as his appointment was not yet official. Bulwer said his own mother spoke 'very highly' of young Haggard 'and I should be happy if I could do anything which would help him in his object of entering the Colonial Service', but not as Bulwer's private secretary, as someone with experience was required. Nevertheless it would be 'worth his while to come with me as an unpaid assistant',[116] as a suitable position might well arise later.

A mutual friend of Haggard and Lilly named Scycester somehow got wind of all this and informed Lilly in a letter. She replied to Scycester saying she 'considered it extremely foolish' of Haggard 'to change [his] mind so often'. Scycester passed on Lilly's scathing comment to Haggard, who immediately wrote to her in an attempt to disabuse her of his inconstancy and played down the likelihood of a Natal appointment: 'to begin with it seems improbable that I shall ever go to Natal & if I do it will not be in pursuit of amusement or fantasy, but of solid advantage. I have as my object to make a sufficient income in a limited time and by this means I should get two years start.'[117] Haggard hoped Lilly was 'thoroughly enjoying the season', adding that 'I often think of you all as I sit here of an evening and smoke my solitary pipe. My hosts are worthy people but not companions and I do not go down to see my own people very often ... as I wish to avoid speaking English so between the two I find myself lonesome at times.'[118] The letter is a surprising one in tone and content: no suggestion of a passionate romance, no evidence of love or even love unrequited, and the sign-off is strikingly formal: 'I have no right to bother you with my grumbling, so believe me my dear Miss Jackson, with love to your sisters and Mrs David ever very sincerely yours, H. Rider Haggard'.[119] That this undated letter remains in the Cheyne Collection raises the question: was it actually sent? No other letters to or from Lilly remain extant.

While the lonely youth wreathed himself in tobacco smoke, his brother Jack, currently on leave from the navy and also at Tours, became enamoured of Etta White, one of two English sisters. His mother was singularly unimpressed and wished the two young women would go to India, 'where no doubt their fine faces and figures would soon find them a husband!'[120]

Ella Haggard continued her epistolary bombardment of Sir Henry Bulwer, referring to the friendship between the two families to strengthen her case and reiterating Rider's keenness to qualify himself for any 'opportunity the future may afford'.[121] Bulwer's reply repeated that appointing Rider as private secretary was not a good idea. 'If he comes ... the only certain advantages he would have would be the opportunity of seeing a fine country and the opportunity of learning something of official life and work which might be useful to him,'[122] and not as an entrée to the Colonial Service. Bulwer's letter has all the hallmarks of someone saying 'no' without actually saying it in the hope that the letter's recipient will get the message. The recipient didn't and, as Haggard records, 'Sir Henry assented, which was extremely kind of him, as I do not remember that he had ever set eyes on me.' Accordingly, 'in a week or two Scoones and the Foreign Office had faded into the past'.[123] Haggard reported 'to my future chief in London, where he set me to work at once ordering wine and other stores to be consumed at Government House in Natal'.[124]

The 38-year-old Bulwer (a nephew of the novelist Edward Bulwer-Lytton) was set to replace the acting Governor of Natal, Sir Garnet Wolseley, currently serving an interim term after the recall of Sir Benjamin Pine. Educated at Charterhouse and Trinity College, Cambridge, Bulwer had served his first colonial appointment as private secretary to the Lieutenant Governor of Prince Edward Island. Subsequent postings took him to the Ionian Islands and Constantinople, from where he moved up the ranks via Trinidad, Dominica and the Leeward Islands to become Governor of Labuan in Malaysia and British Consul General for Borneo. Portly, ginger-thatched with matching moustache and goatee, Sir Henry was fastidious, fussy, finicky and a stickler for the proprieties but a 'thorough gentleman withal and an experienced imperial administrator'.[125]

While Haggard was kept busy organising supplies, his brother Bazett was recruited to buy firearms: a breech-loading Martini-Henry rifle and a Westley Richards falling block rifle, 'a very useful rifle for a youth, being light and yet a good killing rifle'.[126] In between kitting himself out and making his farewells, Haggard paid court to Lilly. Perhaps this was when the two came to some kind of understanding – the unofficial engagement mentioned earlier – and though both agreed not to make it public, 'he carried away in his heart the most precious thing in the world – first love, and the undimmed hopes of youth, to whom heaven and earth is not impossible'.[127]

In Tours Ella wrote a farewell letter to her 19-year-old son packed full with well-meant advice:

> I hope you have managed the wine well. Your father begs me to tell you, for your consolation, that you will get into nice trouble if you have not! Be careful always to get a very clear understanding of Sir Henry's directions so as to make no mistakes which might reflect on you. Make him repeat anything you are in doubt about – if you can! This I give you as a general hint only, which may be useful, and do not forget what I said about order and punctuality, etc.[128]

A family letter, it was signed by the other Haggards at Tours and included messages from his father and his brother Jack. His mother enclosed a seven-stanza poem, of which four follow:

To my son Rider (on leaving home. July 1875)

> Nineteen short summers o'er thy youthful head
> Have shone and ripened as they flitted by:
> May their rich fruit o'er coming years be shed,
> And make God's gift of life, a treasury.
>
> That life is granted, not in Pleasure's round
> Or even Love's sweet dream, to lapse, content:
> Duty and Faith are words of solemn sound,
> And to their echoes must thy soul be bent.[129]
>
> * * *
>
> But a few days: and far across the flood,
> To stranger lands with strangers wilt thou roam;
> Yet shall not absence loose the bonds of blood,
> Or still the voices of thy distant home.
>
> So, go thy way, my Child! I love thee well:
> *How* well, no heart but Mother's heart may know
> Yet One loves better, – more than words can tell, –
> Then trust Him, now and evermore; and go![130]

On the brink of departure to 'where the real business of my life began',[131] Haggard described himself as being 'a tall young fellow, quite six feet, and slight; blue-eyed, brown-haired, fresh complexioned, and not at all bad looking ... Mentally I was impressionable, quick to observe and learn whatever interested me, and could already hold my own in conversation. Also, if necessary, I could make a public speech.'[132]

The confidence of youth masked his darker side and Haggard confesses to being 'subject to fits of depression and liable to take views of things too serious and gloomy for my age – failings I may add, that I have never been able to shake off'.[133] By the time Haggard began writing his autobiography in 1911, his depression was chronic; quite apart from a depressive predisposition, the events of his life had served to reinforce the morbid, fatalistic predilections which had their origins in his childhood and adolescent years.

In late July 1875 Haggard travelled by train from London's Paddington station to Dartmouth on the coast of Devon, where he boarded the *Windsor Castle*. The ship's departure is described in Haggard's first novel, *Dawn*, the vessel renamed the *Warwick Castle*. For the characters Arthur and Angela substitute Rider and Lilly. Beneath the 'penetrating drizzle that is generally to be met with off the English coast', Arthur stands alone 'on the heaving deck' surrounded by a 'grey waste of tossing waters' and in the far distance the fading English coastline.

> Faint it grew, and fainter yet, and, as it disappeared, he thought of Angela, and a yearning sorrow fell upon him. When, he wondered sadly, should he again look into her eyes, and hold that proud beauty in his arms; what fate awaited them in the future that stretched before them, dim as the darkening ocean, and more uncertain. Alas! he could not tell, he only felt that it was very bitter to be parted thus from her to whom had been given his whole heart's love, to know that every fleeting moment widened a breach already far too wide, and not to know if it would again be narrowed, or if this farewell would be the last.[134]

3

'A MASS OF CONTRADICTORY EVIDENCE'

Haggard's first sight of land after leaving England was the Portuguese island of Madeira. In 1875 this was the last point of direct telegraphic communication with London, thereafter telegrams headed south by ship to Cape Town. Consequently, official dispatches and mail took between three and four weeks between London and Cape Town, plus another week to Haggard's final destination, Pietermaritzburg in Natal.[1]

The subtropical heat of Madeira was 'something tremendous', but once the *Windsor Castle* was south of the equator temperatures cooled to the milder degrees typical of the southern hemisphere in winter. The monotony of the voyage was offset by the 'pleasant lot of people on board and [we] amused ourselves very fairly well ... Among other things we got up a sort of penny reading',[2] for which Haggard wrote the prologue.

Haggard made a friend in William Beaumont, 'an excessively nice fellow ... we are great allies'.[3] The 24-year-old Beaumont had first come to Natal in 1871 after being gazetted to the 75th Regiment following his training at the Royal Military Academy, Sandhurst. He resigned from the army in 1873 to become private secretary to Natal's Lieutenant Governor, Benjamin Pine, whom Bulwer was replacing following Sir Garnet Wolseley's interim appointment. Beaumont was returning to South Africa after a spell of home leave to take up his new post as clerk under Natal's Colonial Secretary, Frederick Broome.

Entertainment and friendship aside, Haggard found himself in the role of acting private secretary to Bulwer and was kept busy poring over official reports and blue books in order to familiarise himself with the situation awaiting him in Natal, in particular 'getting up all the Langalibalele case and extracting the pith from a mass of blue books'.[4] The 1873 rebellion of the Hlubi chief Langalibalele and his subsequent trial had dramatically exposed the fault lines of Natal settler society, forcing the British government to intervene, an intervention leading directly to the appointment of Sir Henry Bulwer as the new Lieutenant Governor and facilitating Haggard's coming to southern Africa.

At the end of his four-week voyage aboard the *Windsor Castle* lay southern Africa, a patchwork of British colonies, Boer republics and African kingdoms. In the British colonies of the Cape and Natal and the Boer republics of the Orange Free State and the Transvaal (Zuid-Afrikaansche Republiek), white settlers lived alongside the indigenous peoples they had either dispossessed or displaced. North of Natal lay the kingdoms of the Zulu and the Swazi, and on the ill-defined border of the north-east Transvaal the Pedi polity was a formidable presence. North of the Limpopo River were the kingdoms of the Mashona and the Ndebele, migrant offshoot of the Zulus, and to their west the land of the Tswana.

At the time of Haggard's arrival, southern Africa was undergoing a major economic and social transformation, powered by the discovery of diamonds at Kimberley in the northern Cape and then of gold. In 1867 the German explorer and geologist Carl Mauch discovered gold-bearing reefs in Mashonaland, north of the Limpopo, which he and others claimed was the biblical land of Ophir from where King Solomon had obtained his gold. Although the gold rush that followed 'produced only disappointing results,'[5] nevertheless the existence of a fabulous El Dorado in the north became an *idée fixe*. Alluvial gold was subsequently discovered in the early 1870s in areas around Lydenburg and Pilgrim's Rest in the Transvaal, and diggers came from around the world to exploit the fields. By the time of Haggard's arrival in southern Africa in 1875, 'it was a commonplace that the Transvaal, undeveloped though it was, was potentially the richest part of South Africa.'[6] As a consequence, the British government began to reassess the economic potential of its otherwise troublesome African interests and consider ways of bringing the region under its control the better to exploit its resources.

In the 1870s, the weak point through which the British sought to gain entry was the Transvaal – like its neighbour the Orange Free State, a ramshackle affair with poor governance and a limited ability to raise taxes. Its population of Boer settlers was dwarfed in numbers by the indigenous peoples including the Bapedi, with whom the Boers lived in constant friction, raiding and counter-raiding. In the late 1870s a scheme was hatched by the British government to bring about a confederation of states in southern Africa under British suzerainty and the first step in its achievement involved a brazen takeover of the Transvaal by a small British party, which proceeded to raise the Union Jack in Pretoria. As we shall see, Haggard would play a prominent role in this.

When the *Windsor Castle* docked at Cape Town on 18 August 1875, disembarking passengers were greeted by the Cape's famous south-easter – 'a tremendous wind which blew the dust in your eyes and made everything uncomfortable'[7] – dubbed the 'Cape Doctor' thanks to blowing away 'insects, miasmas, smogs and pollution from the atmosphere of the Cape'.[8] Bulwer and Haggard put up at Government House the official residence of the Cape Governor, Sir Henry Barkly.[9] Barkly was away at the

Kimberley diamond fields, and his absence was a frustration for Bulwer, who had expected a briefing and exchange of views with the Governor. He had also hoped to meet General Wolseley on his way home from Natal. But Wolseley was still in Durban, 'which is very awkward, as we do not know whether to wait for him or to go on and meet him there', according to Haggard. 'Altogether the thing has been muffed.'[10]

The Cape Doctor having ceased its ministrations, the next day was 'one of the most perfect days I ever saw', resembling the 'heat of our May Days only finer. Table Mountain stands out sharp and clear.' Haggard found it 'very queer' to find himself in the southern hemisphere's spring.[11] Taking advantage of the good weather, he strolled into town – 'not a pretty one, it has an unfinished, straggling look, but is all the same an active and progressing place, especially since the discovery of the diamond fields'.[12] Haggard was looking forward to a ball given by the 'Merchants of Cape Town ... It will be a good opportunity of studying the Cape Town aristocracy.'[13] Meanwhile he and Bulwer called on the Bishop of Cape Town, William West Jones, at his Bishopscourt residence on the eastern side of Table Mountain. 'The Barklys have a first rate four in hand and we drove through a beautiful country, so our drive was a pleasant one.' Haggard warmed to the bishop, finding him 'a thorough specimen of muscular Christianity'.[14]

During what turned out to be a week in Cape Town, Haggard got a taste of what lay ahead in Natal: 'I find myself responsible for everything, and everybody comes and bothers me ... I expect I shall have a tremendous lot of work at Natal as the Chief told me that he was going to entertain a good deal, and all that will fall on my shoulders in addition to business. We are very good friends and shall, I think, continue to be so, as he is not a captious or changeable man.'[15] As Haggard would soon discover, Bulwer was well endowed with both qualities.

Sailing to Natal aboard the *Florence*, a coastal steamer, there were brief stopovers to disembark passengers at Port Elizabeth and East London, and 'four or five days' steaming along the green and beautiful coasts of south-eastern Africa, on which the great rollers break continually, brought us to Port Natal [Durban]'.[16]

The first white – and English – settlement was established in Natal in 1824 on the shores of a huge bay where a band of British adventurers set up shop as the trading settlement of Port Natal (later Durban). One of the traders, Henry Fynn, befriended the Zulu king Shaka kaSenzangakhona and obtained permission for them to occupy land for trading purposes. Shaka's usurper and successor, his half-brother Dingane, faced a larger threat to Zulu sovereignty when a group of Dutch-speaking Boer pastoralists from the Cape Colony, the Voortrekkers, arrived in what is now Natal on their so-called Great Trek and sought to obtain land for settlement. When a Boer party, led by Piet Retief, came to ratify a treaty with the king, they were murdered at the royal homestead of uMgungundlovu on 6 February 1838 and Zulu impis were sent out to attack and destroy the trekker waggon encampments along the Bloukrans and Bushman's rivers. Over six hundred men, women and children were killed and thereafter the area was known as Weenen – the place of weeping. Eventually a Boer force was sent in retaliation and on 16 December the Zulu army was defeated on the banks of the Ncome River. The river was renamed the Blood River as it is said the water turned red with blood. After this defeat Dingane's power evaporated and he was trounced by his brother Mpande, who succeeded him as Zulu king.

The Boers secured a treaty with Mpande ceding the land initially requested by Retief, bordered by the Thukela river to the north and the Mzimvubu to the south. The trekkers named this new state the Republic of Natalia with Pietermaritzburg as its seat of government. However, Boer raiding south of the Mzimvubu created unstable conditions on the northern borders of the Cape Colony and the British government there decided to intervene. A small force of British troops occupied Port Natal, where the Union Jack was raised on 4 May 1842. On 31 May 1844 Natal was formally annexed as an autonomous district of the Cape Colony, and a full colonial administration was set in place, headed by a Lieutenant Governor assisted by a Colonial Secretary, a Crown Prosecutor and a Diplomatic Agent to the Native Tribes. The majority of Boers, resentful at finding themselves again under British rule, trekked off into the interior but their numbers were soon replaced by British settlers.

In time, growing white settlement and economic prosperity led to aspirations of self-government. A step was made along the road to greater autonomy in 1856 when Natal was granted its first representative institutions in terms of the Charter of Natal, which separated it from the Cape and 'endowed it with an independent administrative structure'[17] consisting of a Governor or Lieutenant Governor assisted by an executive council. Twelve of its sixteen members were elected and four were Crown appointments: the Colonial Secretary, the Colonial Treasurer, the Attorney General, and the Diplomatic Agent to the Native Tribes, now dubbed the Secretary for Native Affairs, a post held by Theophilus Shepstone since its creation in 1846.

We first encountered Shepstone in 1856 on the southern bank of the Thukela contemplating the horrific aftermath of the battle of Ndondakusuka in which Cetshwayo asserted his right to inherit the Zulu throne. Born in England in 1817, Shepstone came to southern Africa as the youngest member of one of the many families that made up the 1820 British settlers in the Eastern Cape. Shepstone's father, a stonemason by trade, turned to missionary work as a Wesleyan lay preacher and, as his family moved around the Cape frontier, young Shepstone acquired fluency in isiXhosa, an Nguni language closely related to isiZulu, while building up his knowledge of the indigenous people, their forms of governance and ways of life. In 1834, when war broke out with the Xhosa, Shepstone's proficiency in the language brought him an appointment as government interpreter on the staff of Colonel (later, Sir) Harry Smith, a hero of the Peninsular War. Smith became Shepstone's mentor on all matters African. In correspondence Smith always addressed Shepstone by his Xhosa name Somtseu (now rendered Somtsewu or Somsewu). According to Ruth Gordon, Shepstone thought the Xhosa-Zulu-Sesotho name translated as 'great white father', though she also acknowledged another meaning, 'the great hunter'. Haggard refers to Shepstone as 'Mighty Hunter'.[18] More recently the historian Jeff Guy translated the name as 'father of whiteness'.[19]

In 1846, after ten years as Resident Agent on the Cape eastern frontier, Shepstone was appointed Diplomatic Agent to the Native Tribes of Natal. This role would see him become one of the most powerful and influential men in the colony. The idea of the chief, the *inkosi*, was central to Shepstone's view of how the indigenous peoples of southern African should be governed in a manner that would both serve the white settler community's need for labour and ensure their safety and security. Shepstone envisioned himself as the ultimate chief: the Great White King ruling over the African people of Natal, living in his idea of a traditional tribal society. To this end Shepstone created a system of administering the African populations of Natal through resettlement in reserves where customary or native law was recognised unless it was considered 'repugnant to the general principles of humanity'. In this system lie the origins of the segregationist policies that culminated in 'separate development' or apartheid.[20]

In implementing this system of indirect rule, of controlling African communities through the power of their chiefs, Shepstone ensured that non-compliant chiefs were either marginalised or, as in the case of the Hlubi leader Langalibalele kaMthimkhulu, designated rebels and ruthlessly subjugated.

As well as a 'system', Shepstone also created what could be termed the 'Shepstone bureau', which included family members – his brother John Shepstone and, in due course, his son Henrique – as well as friends and associates such as Melmoth Osborn and Frederick Fynney, men who had an intimate knowledge of the local people, their language and customs, and who used their knowledge to better implement colonial rule.

Indirect rule maintained control over Natal's African population, but ever present in Shepstone's mind was the powerful Zulu kingdom north of the Thukela, which he sought to bring if not under his direct control, then at least under his direct influence. To that end he cultivated a relationship with the Zulu throne. Shepstone also extended his sphere of interest to include the Ndebele under Lobengula, the heir to Mzilikazi, as well as forging close links with the Swazi royal family. In all three instances – Zulu, Ndebele and Swazi – his aim was to manipulate the line of succession to the throne and bring them into his orbit of control.[21]

After the death of the Mpande in 1872, the crown prince Cetshwayo was recognised by the Zulu as the late king's rightful heir. When Cetshwayo informed the Natal government of his father's death, he invited Shepstone to visit Zululand after the traditional year of mourning was over. In early August 1873 Shepstone set out from Pietermaritzburg with an armed escort of officers and men of the Natal Volunteer Corps in order to 'impress the Zulu with their military effectiveness'.[22]

Both men were playing a political game. Cetshwayo wanted Shepstone's support in the Zulu's long-standing territorial dispute with Transvaal while Shepstone's blessing on his kingship would also deter ambitious *amakosi* (chiefs or kings) eyeing the Zulu throne. For Shepstone this was a golden opportunity to extend British influence into the Zulu kingdom and to assert his authority as 'the Great White Chief' and crown Cetshwayo himself. His plan was thwarted; on arrival, Shepstone learned Cetshwayo had been crowned according to Zulu custom. Not to be outdone, Shepstone went ahead with his own 'coronation' in which Cetshwayo was invested with a scarlet and gold mantle and a pantomime crown run up by a military tailor. He was then taken to a chair of state in front of the marquee and, after a seventeen-gun salute, Shepstone declared Cetshwayo king.

In same year Natal was shaken by the so-called Langalibalele Rebellion, which laid bare the shaky foundations of indirect rule and illustrated, as Haggard told his father, 'the tremendous state of ferment and excitement the Colony was and still is in'.[23] Langalibalele kaMthimkhulu was the Hlubi *inkosi*. When he failed to answer a summons by Shepstone to travel to Pietermaritzburg and account for the lack of registration of firearms among his followers, a military expedition was sent after him. In a skirmish high in the Drakensberg a colonial force led by Major Anthony Durnford was routed by the Hlubi and five men were killed, three of them white troopers.[24] Eventually, Langalibalele was caught and arrested and sentenced to banishment after a trial according to 'native law' that was stage-managed by Shepstone.

A lone voice spoke up against this legal and humanitarian outrage – John Colenso, Bishop of Natal. In a tragic irony Shepstone and Colenso were the best of friends, and even his excommunication for his controversial theological views by the Anglican Church, which appointed another bishop, William K. Macrorie, in his place, didn't affect their friendship. What did drive a rift between the two men was the trial of Langalibalele. Colenso believed that a fellow human being had been unfairly tried and his people cruelly treated, and that Shepstone, his closest friend and ally, was deeply implicated. 'It must be the war to the knife between us,' declared Colenso.[25]

Colenso embarked on a protracted legal battle that took both men to London to give evidence at the Colonial Office. With a dutiful nod to justice, the result was a compromise designed to appease conservative white settler sentiment (firmly behind Shepstone) and, from a strategic point of view, to further the confederation plans of the Colonial Secretary, Lord Carnarvon. During his first appointment he had introduced the British North America Act of 1867 conferring self-government and Dominion status on Canada by means of a confederal arrangement. Now in 1874, once again Colonial Secretary, Carnarvon wondered whether the solution he had pioneered for Canada could be imposed on the 'chaotic character of the interior of southern Africa', where continuing instability threatened long-term British interests.[26] A secure South Africa was not only a strategic necessity but the revelation of its vast mineral wealth made it a highly desirable addition to the British Empire. Those inconvenient independent and sovereign African states were simply obstructive anachronisms (as well as potential sources of labour). A stable (and assuredly British) South Africa would require a final reckoning with the Xhosa, the Pedi and the Zulu. And there were those pesky Boer republics too.

The Langalibalele fiasco played straight into Carnarvon's hands. He considered the evidence, interviewed Colenso and Shepstone, and pronounced judgment. The Natal Governor, Benjamin Pine, was held responsible, recalled and retired on pension. There were also to be 'substantial changes in Natal's constitutional composition',[27] which would give Carnarvon 'more effective control over at least one of the variables in the complex southern African equation'.[28] Shepstone, for his part, emerged unscathed, successfully ingratiating himself with Carnarvon and the Colonial Office as a valuable ally and the go-to expert on all matters Zulu. Not for nothing was he described as an 'Africander Talleyrand'.[29]

Queen Victoria's favourite general, the thrusting, egotistical Major General Sir Garnet Wolseley, was appointed Special Commissioner to Natal to implement Carnarvon's plan. Wolseley, 'Our Only General', as the press would have it, was the most famous military figure of the day. He had fought in the Crimea, India, China and Canada. Once in Natal, Wolseley embarked on a campaign of spin-doctoring, hectoring and plain bullying. His staff, most of whom had served with him before, were 'instructed to dance special attendance upon the most influential wives in the colony' and he had both bishops – Colenso and Macrorie – to dine. Wolseley also pushed through the amendment to Natal's constitution against vigorous opposition both in the legislature and in the city's leading newspaper, the *Natal Witness*.[30] The Act secured the assent of the British government on 24 September. By then Haggard had been in Natal for nearly a month.

Wolseley was at his desk in Government House in Pietermaritzburg when he heard the signal gun on the nearby heights of Fort Napier announce 'the arrival of the steamer carrying Sir H. Bulwer to relieve me – Hurrah – I feel like a schoolboy just told that I may go for some holidays.'[31] Wolseley left the next day for Durban, where he put up at St George's Hotel, 'a tidy little Inn'.[32] That afternoon Bulwer and Haggard, staying in a suite at the Royal Hotel, called upon Wolseley and 'had about three hours' conversation upon public matters'.[33] Wolseley was unimpressed by Haggard: '[Bulwer's] only staff consists of a leggy-looking youth not long I should say from school who seems the picture of weakness and dullness ... [Bulwer] little knows what is before him if he thinks he can get on in Natal with such help alone.'[34] Over the next few days Bulwer was briefed by Wolseley on the situation in Natal – 'I do not envy his position under existing circumstances'.[35]

Bulwer and his staff departed from Durban on the morning of Wednesday, 1 September, coming up 'the fifty-four miles to Pietermaritzburg over most tremendous hills in five and a half hours, going at full gallop all the way in a four-horse wagonette' occupied by Bulwer, Theophilus Shepstone, Broome, Beaumont and Haggard. 'Some of the scenery was very fine, but we were so choked by the dust, which was so thick that you could not see the road beneath you, that we did not much enjoy it.' The guard of honour, a mounted troop of Maritzburg's volunteer regiment, the Natal Carbineers, 'did not improve matters'.[36]

Whatever the direction, the approach to Pietermaritzburg involves a descent, often steep, from the surrounding hills to the city cradled in a valley bowl through which flows the Msunduzi River. Laid out in a typical grid street plan in 1838 by Voortrekkers from the Cape, the city was named after two of the trek leaders, Pieter Retief and Gerrit Maritz.[37] Following the British annexation in 1843, Pietermaritzburg became the seat of the colony's administration. British troops planted the Union Jack on a vantage point to the west of the town, pitching their camp on the site of what would become Fort Napier, named after the Cape Governor, Sir George Napier. The garrison, though never large in terms of numbers, was a potent symbol of British imperial might projected at Boer and Zulu alike. Its presence, particularly the officer class, also bestowed a degree of respectability on Pietermaritzburg. If 'Victorian British society was attempting to replicate itself on African soil',[38] the garrison provided a handy reference point, one embedded in the city's social life with balls, amateur theatricals, sporting events, and the ubiquitous brass band, crucial factors 'in the development of the political and cultural consciousness of settler society'.[39] But the British society replicated in Natal lacked an upper class of titled landed gentry, and the colonial elite were mainly occupied in trade. This was Victorian England-lite, populated by a middle class acidly derided by the snobbish Wolseley in his diary.

The middling classes of Maritzburg (as it is frequently abbreviated) were preparing to welcome their new Governor: 'the immense amount of bunting displayed in all parts of the city' indicated 'an event of unusual importance was expected to take place during the day', reported the *Natal Witness*.[40] According to Haggard, 'we entered in grand style amidst loud hurrahs. We galloped up to Government House, where the regiment was drawn up on the lawn, and as soon as the carriage stopped the band struck up "God Save the Queen" and salutes were fired from the fort. Then all the grandees of Maritzburg came forward and paid their respects to the Governor, and at last we were left alone to clean ourselves as best we could.'[41]

A 'charming town of the ordinary Dutch character' was Haggard's initial impression of the city, 'with wide streets bordered by sluits [channels or ditches] of running water and planted with gum trees'.[42] He thought Government House a 'very pretty building' and, though not on the scale of Cape Town's Government House, 'far from small. I, who have to look after it, find it too large.' Haggard was assigned 'a large bedroom upstairs' and an office 'in the Executive Council chamber'.[43]

On Thursday Bulwer was sworn into office, and 'the day being brilliantly fine, there was a very large attendance at the Court House, particularly of the fair sex'.[44] Bulwer's commission and proclamation were read out by the city's mayor during a 'very swell ceremony indeed', involving Haggard in 'an extraordinary amount of scraping and bowing, presenting and pocketing, or trying to pocket, enormous addresses, commissions, etc., etc.'[45] At a reception held after the ceremony the guests came 'so thick and fast' that Haggard 'had no time to decipher their, for the most part, infamously written cards, so I had to shout out their names at haphazard'.[46]

Business in the city 'was almost entirely suspended' during the swearing-in and the reception; 'however by one o'clock all was over, the crowd cleared away, and matters were allowed to resume their usual course. One or two flags were allowed to remain waving in the breeze for the remainder of the day, in honour of the auspicious event.'[47] Thus ended the faintly ironic account in the *Natal Witness*, which referred to Haggard, without naming him, as Bulwer's private secretary.[48] The report was incorrect: Bulwer had appointed Beaumont in that role and, though Bulwer had 'a very good opinion' of Haggard, 'he *always intended* to have an older man help him *at first* ... I am not in the least disappointed; indeed now that I see something of the place, and of the turbulent character of its inhabitants, I should have much wondered if he had made a fellow young as I am private secretary.'[49]

Stiff upper lip to the fore, Haggard nevertheless regretted the lost opportunity to stand on his own two feet financially: 'I am sorry, very sorry, still to be dependent on my Father, but you may be sure my dear Mother that I will be as moderate as I can. At any rate I will cost less than if I had been at home.'[50] Haggard was confident enough to boost his future prospects, and 'pretty well convinced' he would be Bulwer's private secretary 'sooner or later' and then have all Bulwer's 'powerful interests to back me ... several times he has said quite seriously, "When you become a Colonial Governor you will find &c. &c." I continue to get on very well with him, indeed we are the best of friends, and I have many friendly jaws with him.'[51]

Affable chats aside, young Haggard was highly stressed supervising the entertainments at Government House. Bulwer being a bachelor, Haggard was cast in the role of dutiful wife. 'I have all this large house entirely under me, and being new to it find it difficult work. I have often seen with amusement the look of anxiety on a hostess's face at a dinner-party, but, by Jove, I find it far from amusing now. Dinner days are black Mondays to me.'[52]

Haggard acquired his own personal servant, Masuku, 'a member of the Buthelezi tribe ... to which many notables in Zulu history belonged'. Masuku had been born in 1854, two years before the battle of Ndondakusuka in which his father fought 'on the side of Cetshwayo ... but owing to the induna [councillor] under whom he served being suspected of disloyalty, the said induna, with Masuku's father and others, was obliged to take refuge in Natal'.[53] Masuku is a major character (as Mazooku) in Haggard's second novel, *The Witch's Head*.[54]

Familiarity bred affection and on closer acquaintance with the city Haggard decided Pietermaritzburg was 'very pretty, surrounded on every side with hills, some of which, such as Table Mountain, are very fine.'[55] This was perhaps his only point of agreement with Bishop Colenso, who had so positioned his study desk to ensure the mountain would be the first thing he saw on looking up from his work. When mugging up on the Langalibalele Rebellion, Haggard concluded the bishop did not 'come out of the affair very well', and after reading Colenso's account of events, he thought Colenso 'must be either a knave or a fool and he certainly isn't a fool'.[56] This judgement seems to indicate Haggard had quickly adopted the conservative settler-colonial perspective while en route to Natal, probably taking the cue from his friend Beaumont. 'The fact of the matter is that it is perfectly easy for people to sit in their armchairs at home and to talk about your black brethren and all that sort of thing but those who live on the spot cannot afford to risk their own lives and the lives of their wives and children by allowing the Kafirs, who are 20 to one, to get the upper hand.'[57]

Haggard met Colenso during his first few days in Pietermaritzburg and, thanks to their Norfolk connections, Colenso 'recognised my name the first time I saw him'.[58] In his youth Haggard shared the white settler prejudices against Colenso; a generation later, his sentiments were closer to those of the bishop, writing that Colenso was unpopular among Natal colonists not for his religious views but 'because he was such a strong advocate of the rights of natives'. By 1914 Haggard was more or less in sympathy with him.

> White settlers, especially if they be not of the highest order, are too apt to hate, despise, and revile the aboriginal inhabitants among whom they find themselves. Often this is because they fear them, even more frequently because the coloured people, not needing to do so, will not work for them at a low rate of wage. For example, they cannot understand why these blacks should object to spend weeks and months hundreds of feet underground, employed in the digging of ore, and, in their hearts, often enough would like to compel them by force to do their will. Yet surely the Kaffir whose land we have taken has a right to follow his own opinions and convenience on the subject.[59]

In 1875 Haggard was also introduced to 'the other bishop',[60] William Macrorie, but he had yet to encounter Maritzburg's less elevated citizenry: 'from what I have seen of them I think that I shall like them very well if they weren't such awful gossips. One morning when I walked down street at about half-past eight, two days afterwards I heard what sort of coat I was wearing, the shape of my cape, who I spoke to, and what shops I went into.'[61]

Haggard enjoyed life in the Natal capital: 'the climate is magnificent, the scenery very fine. We are now just entering on the rainy season which lasts all the spring and early summer, but it does not rain continuously, only comes on every now and then. Altogether the weather is very like an English September.'[62] He had yet to endure the hot and humid midsummer months, which took him by surprise and saw him order 'a couple of suits of light clothes' from London. 'I made a great mistake in bringing out such heavy things, one of my coats I have not been able to wear. It is a great mistake getting clothes here they are very expensive and very bad.'[63] High temperatures hindered social activities, such as the ball held at Government House on 8 December: 'It was understood that about 250 had been invited', reported the *Natal Witness*, but far less turned up. 'Our readers will be aware that the weather was hot and the host and his aide de camp were courteous. It only remains to add that the music, played by the band of 1-13th was good, the company was mixed, the dresses very good for a place where materials are hard to get, and the dancing somewhat provincial.'[64]

Haggard was getting the measure of colonial life and assertive in his opinions: 'Whatever be the ultimate end of this Colony for the next twenty years it must go ahead and anybody with his wits about him must get on.'[65] He comically posed as an old Africa hand when writing to the Demestes, his hosts in Tours, informing them he was off 'up country to have a hand to hand fight with a lion'.[66] Lions around Maritzburg had been shot out long ago, but there remained 'a variety of small antelope which, with jackal and hill leopards', enough to make the county of Pietermaritzburg 'the hunting shire of Natal'.[67] Colonial Natal recreated the English country scene by hunting with hounds – 'we run buck with them', Haggard told his mother. 'I borrowed an animal who was a good jumper and willing but rather shaky in the forelegs, so I came down twice, horse and all, without hurting myself, however. The sport is not good for even when you get your Buck well away there is as a rule nothing to jump, so your chief excitement is to avoid the holes which abound.'[68]

Throughout December Haggard was hard at work on the arrangements for the turning of the first sod of the Natal Government Railways line from Durban to Pietermaritzburg on New Year's Day. A line from Durban to the capital was vital as 'the absence of navigable rivers' meant the 'only means of transport for freight and passengers from Durban to the vast hinterland was by ox-wagon and stagecoach',[69] but in view of the successive waves of hills and valleys rising from the coastal plain, animal-drawn transport 'was expensive and slow, taking some three or more days from the port to Pietermaritzburg'.[70] The only direct road between Durban and Pietermaritzburg was the 'old Dutch road', a well-worn 56-mile dirt road, a six- hour journey by stagecoach.

In 1875 the contract for a railway was drawn up with the construction company Wythes and Jackson, the articles of which were signed by the Crown Agents of the colonies, the chief financial officers of empire, one of whom was William Sargeaunt, representing the Governor of Natal. A good friend of Shepstone's, Sargeaunt had been Colonial Secretary of Natal in the 1850s and, as clerk to both the executive and legislative councils, his 'financial acumen was of much assistance' in putting 'the economy of Natal upon a sound basis'. He left Natal in 1859 to become Lieutenant

Governor of St Vincent and the Grenadines in the Caribbean and was appointed a Crown Agent in 1862.[71]

Once the contract was signed came the ceremonial of 'turning of the first sod', the 'gayest, brightest and most joyful day Natal ever witnessed'.[72]

> Visitors from all parts came pouring into the town, every hotel and boarding house being besieged and the life and activity which prevailed in West Street [Durban's main thoroughfare at the time] reminded one of a principal street in London ... Banners and flags were flying from nearly all of the houses in West Street, pieces of ornamental drapery were hung on lines at intervals across the street, and the houses were more or less decorated, notably the Town Office, from which a large Union Jack, together with other flags, were flying, and which, having been gorgeously decorated, presented a gay and festive appearance. During the morning the excitement of the town became considerable. Bugle calls were sounding, volunteers were mustering, crowds of people were wending their way to the Market House Square – the place of assembly of the procession – and the whole town seemed radiant under the brightening influence of the time.[73]

In keeping with the formality of the occasion, the Colonial Secretary, Frederick Broome, 'got himself into his gold-laced coat' and, à la Haggard senior, 'lined the inside of his cocked hat with plantain-leaves', groaning as much 'at the idea of substituting this futile head-gear for his hideous but convenient pith helmet'.[74] His wife Lady Barker was wearing her 'best gown' but was

> horrified to find how much a smart bonnet ... sets off and brings out the shades of tan in a sun-browned face; and for a moment I too entertain the idea of retreating once more to the protecting depths of my old shady hat. But a strong conviction of the duty one owes to a 'first sod', and the consoling reflection that, after all, everybody will be equally brown (a fallacy, by the way: the D'Urban beauties looked very blanched by this summer weather), supported me, and I followed F[rederick] and his cocked hat into the waiting carriage.[75]

Haggard had come to know Lady Barker and her husband well, and they were his first literary mentors. The poet Robert Browning, a close friend of Broome, described him as 'one of the handsomest men I ever saw'.[76] He had married Lady Anne Barker, eleven years his senior, in 1865 (she retained her title as it was a requirement of her receiving the pension due to her as the widow of Colonel Sir George Barker, who died in India in 1861). After a few years of sheep farming in New Zealand, the couple returned to England and embarked on writing careers, Broome becoming a book reviewer and a special correspondent for *The Times*. His circle at the Garrick Club included Anthony Trollope, Matthew Arnold and George Grove, editor of *Macmillan's Magazine*.

In February 1875, Lord Carnarvon, another Garrick acquaintance, suggested Broome go to Natal as Colonial Secretary to Wolseley. Her husband's sudden overseas appointment came as a shock to Lady Barker, herself an established writer and a fixture of London's literary scene and pregnant with her fifth child. Pragmatic considerations won the day: a career in the Colonial Service would offer a 'chance of adventure as well as a secure income'.[77]

Wolseley protested vehemently against Carnarvon's insistence on a civilian being appointed Colonial Secretary instead of Wolseley's preferred candidate. Why Carnarvon insisted on Broome is not clear, but Adrian Preston, editor of Wolseley's diaries, suggests it was because Carnarvon thought a civilian would check Wolseley's 'more extreme inclinations' and by 'breaking the solidly military complexion of the mission make it more acceptable to the Natalians'. As it turned out, Broome 'proved a troublesome irritant who had eventually to be muzzled'.[78] Broome had a volatile temper and a tendency to be quarrelsome. His article 'Literature and Art in London in the Present Day', which ranged 'fearlessly over the London literary and artistic scene', published in the April 1875 edition of *Evening Hours*,[79] effectively burned his London literary bridges, though by then Broome was safely in Pietermaritzburg and featuring frequently in Wolseley's diaries: 'From all quarters I hear complaints against Broome: he has no tact and is very indiscreet. The more I see of him the more I feel convinced of how injurious to the public interests it was sending him out here with me.'

Wolseley comforted himself with the thought that Broome's boorish behaviour and 'his want of manners is useful to me, as it throws out my suavity!! and bonnehommie!! [*sic*] in better relief – men are glad to come from him to me'.[80] Broome was singularly unloved. Found guilty of assaulting his butler, he was blackballed from Pietermaritzburg's exclusive Victoria Club, where he was staying prior to Lady Barker's arrival, and when he 'applied to get into the Royal Hotel the owner would not allow him as he said that he had made himself so unpopular already, that if he was allowed to live there, others would leave the house'.[81]

Lady Barker joined her husband in late October 1875. As well as five children, Lady Barker had twelve books to her name. Her first was the result of Alexander Macmillan (he had published Frederick's poetry) suggesting she 'might think of writing down a feminine point of view of their time in New Zealand'.[82] *Station Life in New Zealand* became an instant bestseller on publication in 1870. Thanks to her husband's connections Lady Barker was invited to become the founding editor of a Church of England magazine, *Evening Hours*, a 'high class literary and social magazine'.[83] As editor and contributor, she effectively invented the women's magazine. The books kept on coming: children's stories, advice on housekeeping, further reminiscences of New Zealand, and *Sybil's Book*, an English response to Louisa M. Alcott's *Little Women* and Susan Coolidge's *What Katy Did*. When her husband went to Natal, Lady Barker remained in London and, being delivered of a baby boy in April, stood down as editor of *Evening Hours*. In September, accompanied by a French cook and a butler plus a nanny for 5-year-old Guy and

7-month-old Louis, Lady Barker sailed south, having arranged to send 'Letters from Africa' to *Evening Hours*.[84]

The turning of the first sod in Durban was an ideal subject for one of these monthly 'letters', and Lady Barker stepped eagerly into the open carriage with her husband to join Durban's mayor Benjamin Greenacre, Bulwer, Captain William Cox, his military aide-de-camp, and Haggard.[85] At the stroke of noon – band playing, crowds cheering – the assembled procession moved off, headed by mounted troopers from the Natal Carbineers – 'a plucky little handful of light horse clad in blue and silver, who have marched, at their own charges, all the way down from Maritzburg'.[86] These were followed by troopers of the Durban volunteer regiment, the Victoria Mounted Rifles, who preceded a 'strong body of Kafir police, trudging along through the dust with odd shuffling gait, bended knees, bare legs, bodies leaning forward, and keeping step and time by means of a queer sort of barbaric hum and grunt'.[87] Behind them trailed the fife and drum band of the Royal Durban Rifles, hundreds of schoolchildren, members of the Ancient Order of Forests, Independent Order of Oddfellows, Independent Order of Templars, a brass band, artillery, town councillors, heads of department, magistrates, consuls, Government Railways Engineer's staff, members of the legislative and executive councils, and, finally, bringing up the rear, the VIP carriage bearing Sir Henry Bulwer et al.

The half-mile procession headed towards a specially erected triumphal arch bearing the words 'God Save the Queen', beneath which lay the famous sod 'looking very faded and depressed, with a little sunburned grass growing feebly on it, but still a genuine sod and no mistake'.[88] Beside it were a spade and a wheelbarrow. The dignitaries took up their allotted places around the arch, hemmed in by dense crowds. 'Never had such a sight been seen in Natal before; never had there been such masses of people congregated together in triumph of an undertaking which had attracted thousands – the young, the old, and the black as well as white to the spot.'[89] There were prayers, there were speeches, then His Excellency 'dexterously cut the turf, placed it in [the] wheelbarrow and wheeled it running for some distance',[90] the cue for the firing of a royal salute of twenty-one guns and a children's choir singing 'God Bless the Prince of Wales', crowned with 'hearty cheers' from the assembled thousands.[91] And so to lunch.

Durban's Market House was hung with coats of arms, crimson drapery and 'two large allegorical pictures', one representing railway construction 'in the shape of a deep cutting, with the word "Labour" underneath; the other represented the line as finished; a train crossing a high viaduct, situated amidst a picturesque country. Beneath this was the legend "Railways". Between the paintings were set 'on a bold scale ... the conjoined arms of Great Britain and Natal, in a semi-circular shield, surrounded by the familiar words, *The Earth is the Lord's, and the fullness thereof*".[92]

The assembled company enjoyed a 'very abundant bill of fare' that included 'turkeys, geese, ducks, fowls, sucking pigs, hams, tongues, lamb, corned beef, roast beef, roast mutton, sheep's tongues, beef steak pies, potatoes, cucumbers, apple and mint sauce', followed by 'fruit tarts, tartlets, custards, jellies, sponge cakes, Christmas cakes, biscuits, Victoria sandwiches'.[93] Lady Barker was 'much amused at the substantial and homely character of the menu', which included a 'favourite specimen of the confectioner's art ... a sort of solid brick of plum pudding, with, for legend, "The First Sod" tastefully picked out in white almonds on its dark surface'.[94]

By mid-February 1876 temperatures were beginning to cool, and Haggard was 'getting on all right' and liked 'the place on the whole, though the people are a queer lot', Haggard told his mother. 'We had our weekly big dinner last night and it went off very well. It would amuse you to see me doing the honours at the top of that big table. I assure you I am getting quite a proficient at it.'

Despite reservations about the locals, there is no doubt Haggard had entered into the spirit of colonial life and become part of Maritzburg's social fabric. He bought himself a horse and had since 'quite got over all signs of liver ... This place, if only you take exercise, is as healthy as England.'[95] Exercise meant riding. 'I got out for a day's buck-hunting the other day to a place about twelve miles off, a farm of fertile plain (about 12,000 acres). The owner of it, a very good fellow, is one of the few people who preserve their buck.'[96] This was Malvern Farm, owned by Charles Woodroffe and his wife Marina, who mentions Haggard coming 'to the farm for shooting parties' in her memoir *Sunrise to Evening Star*.[97] Bulwer was also a 'great friend' of the Woodroffes and they attended 'many dinners and balls at Government House'.[98]

On 9 March 1876 Bulwer presided over the opening of the Alexandra Bridge over the Msunduzi in Alexandra Park, a short walk from the centre of Maritzburg. Haggard was in charge of the catering and also had a speaking role. The baptism of the bridge was to be followed by tiffin, and 'after a pleasant walk of a few minutes, the party found themselves at a marquee ... where a sumptuous repast was provided', according to the *Natal Witness*. 'The party sat down, to the number of over 80, to a table well laid out in a tent decorated throughout with evergreens and flowers.' Various dignitaries, among them Theophilus Shepstone, made speeches and proposed toasts, including one to 'The Ladies' on 'behalf of whom Mr Haggart [*sic*] replied, and kept the company in constant laughter'.[99] The *Witness* consistently misspelt Haggard's surname as Haggart, an improvement nonetheless on the Cape Town newspapers, who had referred to him as Waggart.

4

'THE FIRST THING I EVER WROTE'

Writing to his mother on Easter Sunday, 16 April 1876, Haggard was at a loss for words: 'I saw a curious sight the other day, a witch dance. I cannot attempt to describe it, it is a weird sort of thing.'[1] To remedy his inadequacy Haggard recommended his mother buy a copy of *Evening Hours* the month after she received his letter, where she would find 'a very good description' written by Lady Barker.[2] The 'witch dance' was hosted by Barker at her home on Mountain Rise to the north of Pietermaritzburg, looking out over the city to the Edendale valley beyond. Apart from its red-tiled roof, Lady Barker disliked the squat and square red-brick single-storey house rented from the city's chief baker, christening it the 'Cottage Loaf'.[3]

Barker's invitation cards were headed 'Tea and Witches', and on the afternoon of Wednesday, 29 March, guests began assembling in the garden and on the verandah of the Cottage Loaf. Tea was at five. As well as invited guests, others turned up to satisfy their curiosity, the objects of which arrived at two in the afternoon, 'escorted by nearly the whole black population of Maritzburg' shouting and singing outside the garden fence. There were five 'witches', who, as Barker was at pains to point out, were not witches at all, but 'witch finders' or 'witch-doctors', which she rendered in isiZulu as *abangoma* (that is, *izangoma* or, more commonly in English, sangomas) or *izinyanga*, the former diviners, the latter herbalists. The presence of the five women, Nozinyanga, Nozilwane, Nomaruso, Umgiteni and Umanonjazzla, aroused 'a strong undercurrent of interest and excitement beneath the light laughter and frolic of our summer-afternoon tea-party'.[4]

Barker told her readers that the 'terrible interest attaching to these women' related to their role in Zulu society, where it was 'the custom whenever anything went wrong, either politically or socially ... to attribute the shortcomings to witch-agency'. The next step was 'to seek out and destroy the witch or witches', for which purpose a 'great meeting would be summoned by order of the king and under his superintendence, and a large ring of natives would sit trembling and in fear of their lives on the ground'. In the centre danced the *izangoma* and 'as they gradually lashed themselves up to a frantic state of frenzy – bordering, in fact, on demoniacal possession – they lightly switched with their quagga [zebra] tail on one or other of the quivering spectators'. Thus identified, the victim was 'dragged away and butchered on the spot'.[5]

Grand Guignol expectations aside, there was another element to the guests' anticipation. Africans in colonial Natal were forbidden to consult 'witch-doctors' and consequently Lady Barker's tea party was breaking the law, something which made her husband Frederick Broome, a senior civil servant, distinctly uneasy, 'observing from time to time that my proceedings were at once illegal and improper'.[6]

The appointed hour of five brought with it 'a regiment of riders, thirsting for tea and clamorous to see the witches'. Among them were Haggard, Shepstone and the chief interpreter for the Natal government, Frederick Fynney, who was to be master of ceremonies. While the others tucked into their tea, Fynney went off to fetch the 'witch finders', who appeared wearing 'full official dress, walking along in a measured, stately step, keeping time and tune to the chanting of a body-guard of girls and women'. Walking past the verandah, they raised their right hands 'with the low cry of "Inkosi!" in salutation'.[7] The guests took up their position 'at one side of the little semi-circular lawn, where the dance-crescent was already formed, supplying ourselves the place of the supposed ring of spectators and victims'.[8]

Proceedings were opened by Nozilwane, 'a small, lithe woman with a wonderfully pathetic, wistful face ... who in her day must doubtless have brushed away many a man's life with the quagga's tail she brandished so lightly'.[9] Wearing lynx skins 'folded over and over from waist to knee', she had covered her upper body with 'strings of wild beasts' teeth and fangs, skeins of brilliantly-hued yarn, beads, strips of snake skin and fringes of Angora goat fleece'. Lynx tails 'hung down like lappets on each side of her face, which was overshadowed, almost hidden, by the profusion of sakabula feathers,[10] in which small bladders 'were interspersed, and skewers and pins fashioned out of tusks'. Her 'undulating body kept time to the beat of the girls' hands and the low, crooning chant. Presently, she affected to find the clew she sought, and sprang aloft with a series of wild pirouettes, shaking her spears and brandishing her little shield in a frenzied fashion.'[11] The other women 'joined in hunting out a phantom foe, and triumphed over his discovery in turn, but being older than Nozilwane, were soon breathless and exhausted, and glad to be led away by some of the attendant women to be anointed and to drink water'.[12]

With the sun setting and the guests thirsting for a second cup of tea, something was needed to bring the display to a close. "'Let us test their powers of finding things," said one of the party. "I have lost a silver pipe stem, which I value much."' Though not identified in the article, it is possible this was Haggard. 'So the five wise women were bidden to discover what was lost, and where it was to be found.'[13] Nomaruso stepped forth sporting 'a magnificent snake skin, studded besides in a regular pattern with brass-headed nails, which floated like a streamer down her back' and a 'magnificent jupon of leopard skins decorated with red rosette ... "Is it lost by the great white chief?" (meaning their own King of Hearts, their native minister [Shepstone]). "No, it is lost by an ordinary white man. Let me see what it is that is lost. Is it money? No. Is it a weighty thing? No, it can be always carried about." When Nomaruso ran out of ideas, Nozilwane stepped into the breach: "His pipe ... A thing which has come off his pipe;" and so it is.'[14]

Did the pipe stem belong to Haggard? And what did he make of these 'witches'? In his autobiography, he remarks: 'Often I have wondered whether they are merely frauds or whether they do possess, at any rate in certain instances, some share of occult power. Certainly I have known them do the strangest things, especially in the way of discovering lost cattle or other property.' At Lady Barker's tea party, Haggard remembered, 'the doctoress soon discovered an article I thought was gone forever'.[15]

Though the 'witch dance' defied Haggard's descriptive powers, an experience less than two months later would spark his nascent talent into dramatic life. On Easter Sunday when Haggard wrote to his mother, he had heard Colenso preach at St Peter's, the Anglican cathedral of Pietermaritzburg.[16] The description 'cathedral' reflected the structure's status as the seat of a bishopric rather than its diminutive size and appearance: a restrained example of Gothic revival constructed from local sandstone in the manner of an English parish church, a reassuring edifice for those who thought of England as home. The cathedral was packed not, as one might expect, in observance of the most important day in the Christian calendar but in 'expectation of hearing something from the Bishop of Natal on the subject of Mr. Brooks's death'.[17] Thomas Marwick Brooks, one of Colenso's best friends, 'who had stood by him when all deserted him',[18] had shot himself during the preceding week. A lawyer by profession, Brooks had worked on an acting basis as the Natal Secretary for Education for several years and shortly before his death had completed a mammoth report on the state of education in the colony. The *Natal Witness* speculated that pressure of work and shabby treatment by the colonial authorities had driven Brooks to take his own life. Haggard claimed Brooks's suicide could be attributed to one of Colenso's daughters having refused to marry him despite several proposals.

Expectations of Colenso's sermon were more than fulfilled; in Haggard's estimation it was 'by far the finest I ever heard him preach'.[19] Colenso took as his theme the final words of Jesus on the Cross: 'It is finished.' The sermon nearly finished Colenso, who 'quite broke down ... all the last part of his sermon he was literally sobbing. It was touching to see stern-faced Colenso, whom nothing can move, so broken. He is a very strange man, but one you cannot but admire, with his intellect written on his face.'[20]

In the same letter Haggard informed his mother he was about to go 'up-country ... to explore Weenen or the Land of Weeping, so called from the weeping of women and children after the great massacre of the Dutch'.[21] *Witness* readers were informed that Bulwer was visiting the area 'to acquire a more intimate personal knowledge of the county, and to examine the conditions of the Natives of the district'.[22] The trip was to be under the guiding hand of Theophilus Shepstone and would also serve as practical demonstration of the Secretary for Native Affair's power and influence over the African population; a not too subtle reminder that while Bulwer might be Westminster's appointee, it was Shepstone, the colonial, who had his finger on the pulse of the colony. Bulwer would be 'accompanied by his aide-de-camp, Captain Cox and his private secretary,'[23] the 19-year-old Haggard, private secretary by default though still without a confirmed post or any remuneration.

The tour would be Haggard's first venture into the African interior beyond the domesticating reach of white settlement. Until now his experience of rural Natal had been confined to trips between Pietermaritzburg and Durban and the environs of the colony's capital; terrain markedly different from the wind-sculpted fields and hedgerows of his native East Anglia but nonetheless a cultivated landscape. This journey into the hinterland with Bulwer and Shepstone opened Haggard's eyes to the dramatic qualities of African scenery and the culture and customs of its indigenous peoples.

Bulwer's tour took a similar route to Colenso's diocesan reconnaissance with Shepstone in 1854, including visits to some of the same chiefs encountered by the bishop, including Phakade kaMacingwane, paramount chief of the Chunu.[24] Phakade was one of Shepstone's favoured *amakosi* and visits to his homestead a fixture of the familiarisation tours laid on by the Secretary for Native Affairs for newly appointed dignitaries such as Bulwer. For Haggard the visit to Phakade's homestead would be the high point of the tour, which also took in the small settler towns of Estcourt, Colenso and Ladysmith. An earlier traveller, John Sanderson, describes the route from Pietermaritzburg to Ladysmith, 'nearly parallel with the Drakensberg, whose sharp jagged outline, of tolerably uniform level on the whole, rises like a wall against the western sky'.[25] In 1876 Haggard saw the Drakensberg – *uKhahlamba*, 'the Barrier of Spears' – for the first time. In the cold, clear air of early autumn the mountains loom strikingly close, a magnificent and imposing wall, instantly recognisable as 'Haggard mountains' from his African romances: flat veld in the foreground, ahead the mountain range; grey, abrupt, impenetrable, through which, on closer examination, Allan Quatermain and co. will discover a secret way known to few leading to a lost kingdom.

From Ladysmith they would have ridden south-east towards Weenen, Haggard on a Basuto pony, 'carrying a gun, as was our custom when on trek'.[26] From the fertile hills of the mist belt they entered 'the mountainous bush-land' of 'The Thorns', which, 'though the roads are terrible, is much pleasanter to travel through as it is more varied. Also you can make little dives into the bush in search of a little shooting, though it is very necessary to take your bearings first.'[27] Haggard neglected to do so and got completely lost. Nightfall found him wandering in the dark and soaked to the skin thanks to an afternoon thunderstorm, when he 'suddenly stumbled on a Kaffir coming through the bush. An angel could not have been more welcome.'[28]

A new problem presented itself: 'I knew no Kaffir, he knew no English. Luckily I did know the Kaffir name of Mr. Shepstone [Somsewu] which is known by every black in South Africa.'[29] The African knew Shepstone and his party were in the area and brought Haggard safely back to the waggons, where Haggard 'found the Governor in a dreadful state of alarm'.[30] Understandably, Bulwer was *in loco parentis* and took a genuinely protective interest in his young charge, but it was the 58-year-old Shepstone who won Haggard's love and loyalty, and it was on this trip that the older man cemented his place in Haggard's affections. By the end of the year Bulwer and Shepstone would be at loggerheads over Haggard's future, but on that night in 'The Thorns' there was a collective sigh of relief at Haggard's safe return. The following day the party set their faces towards that great mountain, 'towering high above its fellows, called Pagadi's Kop'.[31]

It was a slow uphill progress to Phakade's homestead, and after 'a hard and stiff climb' they reached 'a perfectly level space ten or twelve acres in extent, exactly in the centre of which was placed the chief's kraal'. Riding to the western edge of this plateau, they enjoyed 'one of the most perfectly lovely views it is possible to imagine'. The sight would forever be imprinted on Haggard's imagination, drawn upon time and again in the writing of his African romances:

> It was like coming face to face with primeval Nature, not Nature as we civilised people know her, smiling in cornfields, waving in well-ordered woods, but Nature as she was on the morrow of the Creation. There to our left, cold and grey and grand, rose the great peak [Pagadi's Kop, now Ntanyana], flinging its dark shadow far beyond its base. Two thousand feet and more beneath us lay the valley of the Mooi, with the broad tranquil stream flashing silver through its midst. Over against us rose another range of towering hills, with sudden openings in their blue depths through which could be seen the splendid distances of a champaign country. Immediately at our feet, and seeming to girdle the great gaunt peak, lay a deep valley, through which the Little Bushman's River forced its shining way. All around rose the great bush-clad hills, so green, so bright in the glorious streaming sunlight, and yet so awfully devoid of life, so solemnly silent. It was indeed a sight never to be forgotten, this wide panoramic outlook, with its towering hills, its smiling valleys, its flashing streams, its all-pervading sunlight and its deep sad silence.[32]

A silence due to an absence. 'Some few years ago those hills, those plains, those rivers were teaming each with their various creatures', explained Haggard, and from the same vantage point a traveller would have seen 'herds of elephants cooling themselves', hippopotami at play in the river pools, and on the hills and plains 'droves of buffalo and elands', zebra and 'swarms of springbok' and other antelope. Haggard was in no doubt as to the cause of their disappearance: 'All alien life must cease before the white man, and so these wild denizens of forest, stream, and plain have passed away never to return.'[33]

At the royal homestead they were hosted by Phakade's eldest son and heir, Gabangaye, who ushered them through to the 'dwelling-places of the chief's family, fenced off from the rest by a hedge of Tambouki grass'. After being greeted by Phakade's wives, a daughter, 'tall, and splendidly formed, with a finely cut face',[34] bade them enter the hut, which they did on their hands and knees. Haggard noted the flooring, a mixture of clay and cow dung, looking 'exactly like black marble, so smooth and polished had it been made, and on its shining level surfaces couches of buckskin and gay blankets were spread in an orderly fashion'.[35] In the company of Gabangaye and Phakade's wives 'we partook of the beer and exchanged compliments, almost Oriental in their dignified courtesy, in the soft and liquid Zulu language'.[36] The party then rode on to their camping place, by when the 'stars were shining in southern glory' and 'supper and bed were more than usually welcome. There is a pleasure in the canvas-sheltered meal, in the after-pipe and evening talk of the things of the day that has been and those of the day to come, here, amid these wild surroundings, which is unfelt and unknown in scenes of greater comfort and civilisation.'[37]

The dance performed the next day was held in front of their camp. Haggard wrote a description of the dance for his father and most likely made notes which he worked up into an article, 'A Zulu War Dance'. Haggard's sense of the romantic and spectacular, later employed to best-selling effect in his adventure stories, is already well in evidence here, as is his rendition of Zulu speech patterns.

> During the morning we could hear snatches of distant chants and caught glimpses of wild figures threading the thorns, warriors hastening to the meeting place … Suddenly there stood before us a creature, a woman, who, save for the colour of her skin, might have been the original of any one of Macbeth's 'weird sisters'. Little, withered, and bent nearly double by age, her activity was yet past comprehension. Clad in a strange jumble of snake skins, feathers, furs and bones; a forked wand in her outstretched hand, she rushed to and fro before the little group of white men crying. Her eyes gleamed like those of a hawk through her matted hair, and the genuineness of her frantic excitement was evident by the quivering flesh and working face, and the wild, spasmodic words she spoke. The spirit at least of her rapid utterances may thus be rendered:
>
> 'Ou, ou, ou, ai, ai, ai. Oh! Ye warriors that shall dance before the great ones of the earth, come! Oh! Ye dyers of spears, ye plumed suckers of blood, come! I, the isanusi, I, the witch finder, I the wise woman, I the seer of strange sights, I the reader of dark thoughts; call ye! Come, ye fierce ones; come, ye brave ones, come and do honour to the white lords. Ah, I hear ye! Ah, I smell ye! Ah, I see ye; ye come, ye come!'[38]

This startling figure, the prototype for 'Gagool the witch-finder' in *King Solomon's Mines*,[39] was replaced by another, Phakade's *imbongi* or praise-singer, standing 'before us with lifted weapon and outstretched shield, his plume bending to the breeze, and his savage aspect made more savage still by the graceful, statuesque pose, the dilated eye and warlike mould of the set features'.[40] Striking his shield, the *imbongi* gave the royal salute to Bulwer: 'Bayete, Bayete, O chief from the olden times, O lord and chief of chiefs!'[41] then sprang forward and flew hither and thither chanting the praises of Phakade: 'Pagad', the brave in battle, the wise in council, the slayer of warriors ... Pagad' and his soldiers are coming; tremble all ye, ou, ou, ou!'

The praises ended, their echo seguing into 'a deep murmuring sound like distant thunder; it swells and rolls, and finally passes away, to give place to the sound of the rushing of many feet', and over the brow of a nearby ridge dashed 'a compact body of warriors, running swiftly in lines of four, their captain at their head, all clad in the same wild garb as the herald. Each bears a snow-white shield carried on the slant, and above each warrior's head rises a grey heron's plume.' These were the advance guard of the 'Greys' – veteran troops – and as they came into full view 'from every throat out burst the war-song of the Zulus'.

The 'Greys' took up position on the plain, to be followed by another *ibutho* (regiment) bearing 'coal-black shields' and 'drooping plumes ... black as night; they fall into position next the first comers, and take up the chant. Now they come, faster and faster ... red shields, the dun shields, the mottled shields, the yellow shields ... till at length there stands before us some five hundred men, presenting, in their savage dress, their various shields and flashing spears, as wild a spectacle as it is possible to conceive.'

The war song continued 'louder and louder, a song of victory and triumph. It rolls against the mountains, it beats against the ground: "He is coming, he is here, attended by his chosen. Now shall we go forth to slay; now we shall taste of the battle."' Enter Phakade kaMacingwane, 'swathed in war-garments of splendid furs' and accompanied by hand-picked warriors. 'He is old and tottering, and of an unwieldy bulk', supported by two attendants, while a third bears his shield, and a fourth 'a cane-bottomed chair'.

> With a shout, the old man shakes off his supporters and grasps his shield, and then, forgetting his years and his weakness, he rushes to the chieftain's place in the midst of his men. And as he comes the chant grows yet louder, the time yet faster, till it rises, and rings, and rolls, no longer a chant, but a war-cry, a paean of power. Pagadi stops and raises his hand, and the place is filled with a silence that may be felt. But not for long. The next moment five hundred shields are tossed aloft, five hundred spears flash in the sunshine, and with a sudden roar, forth springs the royal salute, 'Bayete!'

Now the warriors dance, first manoeuvring in silence, 'but as their blood warms there comes a sound as of the hissing of ten thousand snakes, and they charge again and charge again ... writhing, twisting and turning, and to all appearances, killing and being killed, whilst the whole air is pervaded with a shrill, savage sibillation'. Solo dancers emerge from the mass and dart 'hither and thither with wild activity, he bounds five feet into the air like a panther, he twists through the grass like a snake, and, finally, making a tremendous effort, he seems to slay his airy opponent, and sinks exhausted to the ground'.

More songs, chants, dances, and once again the warriors 'engage in mimic combat, once more they charge, retreat, conquer, and are defeated, all in turns'. To their front 'exciting them to new exertions, with word and gesture, undulate in a graceful dance of their own the "intombas", the young beauties of the tribe, with green branches in their hands, and all their store of savage finery glittering on their shapely limbs ... and round them again dance the children, armed with mimic spears and shields'. The dance ends and, following a final salute, the warriors 'departed over the ridge from whence they came', the last figure standing out 'for an instant against the flaming background of the westering sun, and then dropped, as it were, back into its native darkness beyond those gates of fire'.

Divesting himself of his 'heavy war-dress', Phakade 'sat down amicably amongst us' taking Shepstone by the hand.

> 'Ah! t'Sompseu, t'Sompseu, the seasons are many since I first held this your hand. Then we two were young, and life lay bright before us, and now you have grown great and are growing grey, and I have grown very old. I have eaten the corn of my time, till only the cob is left for me to suck, and, *ow*, it is bitter. But it is well that I should clasp this your hand once more, oh, holder of the Spirit of Chaka, before I sit down and sleep with my fathers. *Ow*, I am glad.' [42]

At this point Haggard's article comes to an end, but in *The Cloak That I Left* Lilias continues the scene, the young man who would become her father sitting in the shadows listening to Shepstone and Phakade's conversation 'until a full moon topped the edges of the further side of the valley and flooded all that wild and lovely place with a silver radiance'. When Phakade rose to take his leave, his 'parting words came clearly to Rider's ears and were written down in the little notebook he carried'.[43]

> 'Your council is good, t'Sompseu, and perhaps while your arm is still strong, and you hold it out to shield the white peoples they may dwell in safety beneath it. But I tell you t'Sompseu, that Cetywayo's regiments grow thirsty for blood ... Cetywayo's heart is soft towards you, he does not want war with the English, but he is but one mind against many who would tread the red road of the assegai – the road that was trodden by the great Elephants Chaka and Dingaan.'
>
> 'Is it so, Pagate?' Shepstone replied quietly. 'Then I tell you as I told the King, that the Queen of England is the most mighty one in the whole earth, and though her foot, of which you see but the little toe here in Africa, seems small to you, yet if she is angered it will stamp the Zulu flat, so that they cease to be.'
>
> 'Ow! Sompseu, truth and wisdom dwells in your heart, and it may be so, but first there will be a very great killing.'[44]

Phakade's parting words would prove prophetic. That they are recorded by Haggard raises a number of questions. Contrary to claims by Lilias, her father did not speak isiZulu; he admits as much above in his chance meeting with the lone Zulu when lost. So how was he able to record this conversation? Was a translator present? Did Shepstone translate? Another question concerns Haggard's 'little notebook'. Lilias makes several references to a diary kept by Haggard during his years in southern Africa. This is consistent with a reference to Haggard's African diaries in an article by the Haggard bibliographer J.E. Scott, in which he states that Haggard 'always carried in his pocket a little notebook in which he used to jot down such details as appointments, addresses, and ideas and plots for stories. Some thirty-five of these notebooks – the first dated 1874, when he was eighteen, the last 1925 (he died on May fourteenth of that year) – are still in existence.'[45] They no longer appear to be. The Norfolk Record Office, main repository of Haggard material, holds '29 rough diaries, c.1882–1925'. The Cheyne Collection holds Haggard's notebook diary from 1878 (a small A6 pocket-sized diary in which Haggard made occasional and brief notes, hardly a diary), but no other notebook diary appears to have survived from the African period of Haggard's life. Certainly no biographer has seen them. Morton Cohen, who worked closely with Lilias when researching his biography, didn't see these diaries.[46] Their disappearance could be explained by their having been destroyed because of what they contained, a view endorsed by Cohen.[47] Lilias is remarkably frank in *The Cloak That I Left*, but there are some matters she does not disclose, matters relating to Haggard's life in South Africa known only to close family members. As will be seen, their nature and the possibility of future revelation could well explain the destruction of Haggard's African diaries.

When Bulwer and his retinue returned to Pietermaritzburg, the *Natal Witness* reported that the Lieutenant Governor, 'who has the reputation of working too hard, came back ... all the better for his trip'. The same report also mentioned 'Mr Haggart, private secretary'.[48] Perhaps Haggard found consolation for the continued misspelling of his surname in the Zulu name which was likely given him during the trip: *Lundanda uNdandokalweni*, which, according to Lilias, 'means "One who walks upon the hills" or "the tall one who travels on the heights"'.[49] Haggard himself wrote that 'the Zulus gave me the name of Indanda which meant, I believe, one who is tall and pleasant natured'.[50] In later life he was told it meant 'the tall man who walks along the ridges or on the mountains'. Never having been 'addicted to this form of exercise I presume that the interpretation is metaphorical and spiritual, i.e. one who keeps on high ground or it may mean one who appears to be thinking of far away things'.[51] The name may also have an ironic application, such as 'the man with his head in the clouds' – an interpretation Haggard acknowledged.[52]

New name or not, Haggard's trip to 'The Thorns' and the 'great war dance' he witnessed inspired him to produce 'the first thing I ever wrote for publication'.[53] 'A Zulu War Dance' was run in the *Gentleman's Magazine* of July 1877. Though the first article to be written, it was preceded in print by another, titled 'The Transvaal', published in the May 1877 issue of *Macmillan's Magazine*. That these articles came to be published was, as we shall see, thanks to the good offices of Lady Barker and her husband Frederick Broome.

Safely back in Pietermaritzburg, Haggard continued as acting secretary to Bulwer, copying dispatches, receiving guests, and doing 'my other duties, probably not as well as I might have done'.[54] There was the Agricultural Show, an annual jamboree held over several days, including the judging of prize animals, various entertainments and displays, attracting settlers from all over the colony. At the bazaar Haggard bought 'the skin of a boa constrictor [rock python] and the egg of an ostrich'.[55]

On 24 May Haggard was in attendance alongside Bulwer and the blimpish Sir Arthur Cunynghame, Commander-in-Chief of the Army in South Africa, in Maritzburg for a review of the troops: the 13th Regiment from Fort Napier together with the volunteer regiments, the Maritzburg Rifles, the Natal Carbineers, and the cadets from Hilton School.[56] The review was held in honour of Queen Victoria's birthday, celebrated that evening with a ball at Government House – 'an awful nuisance but a great success', according to Haggard,[57] but approved of by the *Witness*: 'an excellent innovation was introduced by the laying out of a capital supper in a capacious marquee which enabled everyone to enjoy the most important event of the day without crowding'.[58] Haggard made a friend in Cunynghame's aide-de-camp, Lieutenant Nevill Coghill, 'a particularly light-hearted young man full of good stories'.[59]

At another dance held at Government House on 6 June, Haggard witnessed 'a very curious sight'. Conversation after supper turned to the subject of running, and an officer laid a wager of five pounds to anyone game enough to run a hundred yards. Frederick Broome 'who used to be a great hundreds runner promptly took him up'.[60] A match was instantly arranged to take place on the road in front of Government House 'lit up by a brilliant South African moon'. Dancing stopped and everyone went outside. 'The distance was marked out and off they went. Broome won, coming in at a tremendous pace, but just as he breasted the tape he tripped, fell and went rolling over and over down the hill amidst clouds of dust and derisive cheers. It was certainly a ludicrous sight to see a weighty and respectable Colonial Secretary enacting the part of a shot rabbit, at two o'clock in the morning in front of a ballroom full of people.'[61] Haggard enclosed some photographs of Government House in a letter to his mother, pointing out his room. Other photographs included one 'of Kafir Witches, which is more curious than beautiful', and another of 'a Kafir Christianised or scoundrelised'.[62] This white settler trope was expanded on by Haggard in response to a letter from his mother in which she expressed approval of missionaries:

> A Christian Kafir is a gentleman to be avoided, he grafts the views of the white man onto his own, with no pleasing result. Most of the German missionaries give up their attempt in all but in word and take to farming their Government grants. The Wesleyans and the Catholics are the only ones that do any good, and their success

is very partial. It is a sad fact but not the less a fact. I daresay all this will right itself in time.[63]

Haggard is silent regarding the Christian Africans of Edendale, of whom Lady Barker wrote sympathetically in one of her 'Letters from Africa'.[64] The township of Edendale had been established on the eastern fringe of Pietermaritzburg in 1851 by the Methodist missionary James Allison 'after leading his following of African Christians from Swaziland'.[65] Such Christian converts were known as *amakholwa* (believers), 'educated Africans who sought exemption from "tribal authorities" and "tribal law"'.[66] White settlers saw them as a threat, fearing they would have 'a more powerful claim to equal rights than an uneducated population devoted to their ancient belief'.[67] The *amakholwa* were also formidable farmers and 'pioneers in many branches of commercial agriculture, experimenting in the 1850s with coffee, cotton, arrowroot, and sesame, and in the 1860s with sugar'.[68] The *amakholwa* of Edendale were loyal subjects of the Crown and would fight on the side of the British in the Anglo-Zulu War of 1879.

Haggard's secretarial duties included writing letters to next of kin concerning deceased relatives, for example, to a Mrs Cowley in England enquiring after her son Richard 'and enclosing a letter for him, which I was required to return as poor Cowley died eight or nine months ago of the Zambezi fever'.[69] Haggard knew Cowley's companion Norman Macleod of Macleod. Macleod and his fellow Scot, William Frederic Fairlie, both officers of the 75th Regiment, 1st Gordon Highlanders, stationed at Fort Napier from 1871 to 1875, had 'travelled north from Natal to see Victoria Falls and shoot big game' with Cowley, 'a young fellow out here by way of learning farming',[70] who was 'anxious to make a name as a lion hunter'.[71] Cowley achieved his objective, killing a lion 'that charged him determinedly'.[72] Macleod and Fairlie set off for the Victoria Falls and got within eight miles when their party was brought down by fever. On returning to the base camp, they found everyone 'also had fever and poor Cowley was dead'.[73]

Pietermaritzburg was the starting point for many an expedition north of the Limpopo. Charles Montague Duncan Stewart, a good friend of Haggard's in Maritzburg, planned a two-year trip 'in that same country only he wants to reach Lake Nyanza [Lake Victoria in Kenya]. Taking the utter foolhardiness into consideration I should say the odds are against him ever coming back.'[74] Stewart was an experienced hunter. 'Old hunters who have hunted with him tell me they have never seen his equal for utter disregard of danger ... But he will be in more danger from fever than anything else. I am sorry he is going but it is no good trying to deter him.'[75]

In a postscript to his mother, Haggard said he would be 'riding down to Durban' the following week 'to be groomsman to my friend Beaumont who is about to plunge into matrimony. I would rather not have gone but Beaumont wished me to come and the Governor seemed to think I had better, so I must go, frock coat, tall hat and all'.[76] It was fortunate he did as Beaumont's 'garment sent out from England was more suitable to a funeral than a wedding', whereas Haggard's frock coat 'which I had only worn three or four times was the exact thing and fitted him like a glove'.[77] It had been agreed beforehand there would be no speeches at the marriage breakfast, so Haggard 'found it rather trying to be suddenly requested to return thanks for the bridesmaids which is not an easy speech to make. However I managed to rise to the emergency and got through with flying colours.'[78]

Haggard remained in Durban for a three-day holiday after the wedding and enjoyed the change 'as it was the first holiday I have had with the exception of the week when I was sick'.[79] He also reported 'stirring news from the Transvaal, telling of the first skirmish between the Boers and Secocoeni, a native chief of very considerable power'.[80] This was the first move in what became known as the Boer–Pedi War or the First Sekhukhune War.

5

'A STRANGER IN STRANGE LANDS'

The Boer–Pedi war in the Transvaal, coming so soon after the Langalibalele 'rebellion', presented another opportunity for the British Colonial Secretary, Lord Carnarvon, to advance his confederation policy. The Cape Colony and Natal were logical components of a British southern African confederation, but what of the Boer republics, the Orange Free State and Transvaal? Carnarvon pinned his hopes on negotiation, but what had worked in Canada was not going to be so easy in South Africa. 'Confederation was intended to be South Africa's great leap forward',[1] but attempts to mount a conference devoted to the subject in Cape Town in 1875 generated so little enthusiasm among prospective participants that it failed to materialise. Undaunted, Carnarvon organised another, this time under his personal supervision in London in 1876.

Thanks to its mineral wealth the Transvaal was the most coveted piece in Carnarvon's confederation jigsaw and ripe for the plucking. Lack of internal governance and poor financial management saw the republic perpetually on the edge of bankruptcy while the white inhabitants engaged in near-constant warfare with the Pedi, who were equally determined to maintain their independence and retain their land in the north-eastern Transvaal. The Boers were well aware of their republic's mineral wealth but lacked the will and the methods to exploit it, something, especially under President Thomas François Burgers, they were actively trying to remedy. Burgers, a liberal clergyman educated in Holland, had been elected in 1872 as the man to haul the Transvaal into the nineteenth century. Overtures were made to foreign powers for aid and investment; there was talk of an alliance with the Portuguese and of building a railway from the highveld to Delagoa Bay on the coast of the Portuguese province of Mozambique, thus ending the Transvaal's and Free State's dependence on Natal for access to the high seas and international trade via Durban. If this was achieved, what would they have to gain from confederation? The British feared the Transvaal would be developed, but not by them.

War with the Pedi under their king Sekhukhune was the perfect excuse for British intervention in Transvaal. Since the first trekkers entered the region in the 1830s there had been conflict over land, cattle and forced labour, between the Boers and the Pedi. A treaty demarcated the Steelpoort River as the boundary between the two opponents. North of the river the Pedi consolidated around their stronghold at Tsate within the defensive shelter of the Leolu Mountains, a tough nut for either of their traditional enemies, the Boers and the Swazi, to crack. In 1876 the removal of beacons along the boundary with the north-eastern Transvaal by the Pedi precipitated war. The early stages of the campaign went well for the Boers and their Swazi allies, but the latter retired disgusted at being deployed by the Boers to do most of the fighting. The Boers were left to assault Tsate alone. This ended in a humiliating and bloody failure, leaving them with no stomach for further hostilities.

In a bid to contain the Pedi, a fort – named Fort Burgers after the president – was constructed close to the border, but when no burghers could be persuaded to man it, the Pretoria authorities – promising land in return – raised a mercenary outfit, the Lydenburg Volunteer Corps. Adventurers and freebooters from the Kimberley diamond fields signed up, many of whom had already been drawn to the Transvaal by the discovery of gold in the Lydenburg district and Pilgrim's Rest. The volunteer corps was commanded by the Prussian ex-officer Captain Conrad von Schlickman, one of the leaders of the Black Flag Revolt against Cape colonial authority on the diamond fields. A second fort, Fort Weeber, named after the landdrost at Middelburg,[2] was garrisoned by the local Middelburg Burgher Volunteers under Captain Ignatius Ferreira, another veteran of the diamond fields.

Low-level warfare continued, raid followed counter-raid, effective enough on the part of the Pedi to force Schlickman to appeal for more volunteers. Enter the 'amazing rapscallion' and leader of the Black Flag Revolt, the self-promoting Irish Fenian Alfred Aylward. [3] When Schlickman was killed in an ambush, Aylward assumed command and the war 'degenerated into a series of petty marauding expeditions conducted with daily increasing animosity and barbarity on both sides, and tending to lead to no conclusion.'[4]

The Boer–Pedi War swung the gaze of the British government irrevocably towards the Transvaal. While Haggard was holidaying in Durban at the end of July, Shepstone arrived in London to attend Carnarvon's confederation conference. President Brand of the Orange Free State was also present; the Transvaal's President Burgers claimed not to have been invited. The conference began on 3 August, but little of import was discussed and on 15 August the conference was adjourned, never to resume. Shepstone was still in London on 14 September when a 'wildly misleading' telegram arrived saying the Boers had been routed by the Pedi and the citizens of Lydenburg were calling for the British to take over the Transvaal.[5]

A war between the Pedi and the Boers in the Transvaal had worrying ramifications for the rest of southern Africa. Sekhukhune was an ally and tributary of the Zulu king Cetshwayo, himself mired in a long-running border dispute with the Transvaal.[6] As a consequence Cetshwayo was 'on the worst of terms with the Boers' and there were fears 'he and his 30 000 armed men supposed to be hovering like a thunder cloud on the borders of Natal will take the opportunity to have a shot at them too'.[7]

The Swazi were also part of the equation. Their increasingly fragile alliance with the Boers meant there was a danger that if they patched up their differences with the Zulu, all three African polities could make a concerted attack on the Boers and the British would inevitably be drawn in. 'War here between white and black is a terrible thing', Haggard told his mother. 'No quarter is given and none asked, though perhaps on the whole the white man (if Dutch) is more cruel than the savage.'[8] The British feared a Pedi victory over the Boers would be followed by a Zulu invasion of the Transvaal, leading to a 'general native war'.[9]

The failure of the Boers to conclusively defeat the Pedi, in addition to their administrative and financial woes, threatened the stability of the whole region: the perfect excuse for British intervention. Carnarvon seized the moment. Shepstone was ordered to return to South Africa immediately as a Special Commissioner (his authority was reinforced with a knighthood) and to proceed to the Transvaal and assess the situation; secretly he was instructed to bring the Transvaal under British rule, ideally with its government's consent; if not, without.

Haggard had been in Natal for over a year acting as Bulwer's secretary and general dogsbody but without an official paid post or any clear career prospect. Haggard's father applied pressure on his son, who replied saying he was still trying to ascertain if an appointment in South Africa might be a 'stepping stone' to something better. He would either accept a post or return to England 'and read for some profession, such as the Bar' as there was nothing to be gained 'by my staying on here in my present capacity'. Haggard thought he might be better off on Shepstone's staff, but Bulwer was 'too constitutionally cautious and timid even to give one the chance of doing anything'. Whatever the outcome, Haggard would 'never regret the year I have spent here, both on the experience of life and men that it has given me and of the one or two good and powerful friends it has made me'.[10] He undoubtedly counted Shepstone among them.

Shepstone was awaiting his commission signed by the Queen for the annexation of the Transvaal. He didn't want to depart before having the commission in his hand and was also playing a waiting game to see how belligerent the Zulu might become and thus strengthen his hand with the Boers. The precise nature of Shepstone's mission was not known, but Haggard thought it probable Shepstone was 'to proceed to the seat of the War, in the capacity of Special Commissioner' and, if that was the case, Haggard hoped to accompany him, 'provided I can obtain the Chief's permission'.[11] Thus began a tug of war between Bulwer and Shepstone as to Haggard's future. When Shepstone requested he be allowed to take Haggard 'on his staff to the Transvaal', Bulwer 'cut up very rough about it'.[12] Haggard attributed Bulwer's opposition to jealousy: Shepstone had 'higher powers than himself and [he] cannot bear the idea of anybody connected with him having a finger in the fire. However I hope to manage it yet.'[13] According to Sir Garnet Wolseley, Bulwer disliked Shepstone 'very much' and, prior to Bulwer's arrival in 1875, 'the natives had always been kept in ignorance by Shepstone of the fact there was a Governor of the Colony always giving them to understand that he himself was their supreme ruler.'[14]

Haggard was determined to leave Pietermaritzburg and travel north, either with Shepstone to Pretoria or with his friend Stewart on the first stage of his hunting expedition, thereafter returning to England and reading for the Bar. His preference was to go with Shepstone either as a guest or on his staff. 'I can hardly see why Sir Henry should go out of his way to prevent my having this chance, for it would be an undoubted chance ... I am going upcountry anyhow so why should he object to my availing myself of Sir Theophilus's kind offer goodness only knows.'[15] The days of 'friendly jaws' were long gone: the 'Governor is not an easy man to get on with under any circumstances.'[16]

Apart from Bulwer's dislike of Shepstone, there may have been another reason why Bulwer was so opposed to Haggard's transfer: concern for his health. Haggard admitted to his father he had 'not been very well lately' and had been advised not to go down to the coast again 'as the heat there would probably give me an attack of the liver'. This was possibly jaundice, though subsequent descriptions of recurrent symptoms are suggestive of hepatitis. According to Haggard, the 1876 winter season in Pietermaritzburg had been 'a very peculiar one, and very fatal to children'. Three children had died in a 'refuge for the destitute', one of them 'poor little "Goldie" ... a great friend of mine. I was playing with her a day or two before. This place is certainly unhealthy for women and children, all the English ladies who come here are more or less ailing.'[17] Bad health had sent Lady Barker back to London with her two children – 'repeated attacks of dysentery have nearly killed me.'[18]

Haggard acknowledged Lady Barker had been 'very kind to me' and told his father she would be glad to meet him and 'tell you all about me.'[19] Barker and her husband Frederick Broome had encouraged Haggard's literary aspirations and, in a letter to his father dated 6 October 1876, Haggard spoke for the first time of writing articles for publication, adding a cautionary postscript: 'Don't say anything about my having written things in magazines.'[20] A colonial official, even a lowly unpaid one, could be seriously disadvantaged by publishing articles interpreted as critical of settler society.

Whatever the reason for Bulwer's obstructive behaviour, the atmosphere at Government House became increasingly tense. Shepstone wanted Haggard in the Transvaal for two reasons: 'First, we are very good friends and he was kind enough to say he wished to have me as a companion. Second, I imagine there will be a good deal of what is called the champagne and sherry policy up at Pretoria and he wants somebody to look after the entertaining. It will be a most interesting business, and if [Bulwer] prevents me from going I cannot help thinking he will be inflicting a somewhat wanton injury on me.'[21] Bulwer suddenly capitulated, and in a short letter on 13 December 1876 Haggard told his mother he expected to start for the Transvaal soon, Bulwer having 'consented to allow me to go for a couple of months in a private capacity on the condition I should hold no official position'. This was a pity as he could have been well paid and 'been favourably mentioned [at] home, and all the rest of it. I look on it as a chance lost ... It will take us about a month to trek to Pretoria. Our party will consist of eight or nine – and about eight wagons and two or three mule wagons.'[22]

Haggard was still 'very seedy' but anticipated the trip would set him up again. 'I have got so horribly thin, and the slightest thing seems to upset me ... I think I had better come back and read for the Bar, for putting other reasons aside, I believe the first hot climate I went to if I got in the Col. Service would do for me, and the Doctor hinted as much to me.'[23] The doctor was Vacy Lyle, who was going to the Transvaal as Shepstone's personal physician. He had accompanied Shepstone to Zululand in 1873 and given Cetshwayo a medical examination at the time of the bogus 'coronation'.

Melmoth Osborn, witness to the battle of Ndondakusuka in 1856, was another of Shepstone's handpicked band of brothers, summoned from his current post as magistrate at Newcastle in northern Natal to take up the position of Shepstone's secretary. Known among the Zulus as Malimat or Malemate, a corruption of his first name, Osborn was to become another of Haggard's mentors, 'shrewd, kindly, honourable, the truest of friends, the bravest of men' and belonging 'to that class which Pope defined as the noblest work of God'.[24]

Sporting a 'rich Irish accent'[25] and a monocle was Major Marshall Clarke, Shepstone's aide-de-camp, truly a long way from Tipperary where he was born in 1841. Educated at Trinity College Dublin and the Royal Military Academy in Woolwich, Clarke had lost his left arm during service in India when 'armed only with a carving knife he fought a tiger single-handed'.[26] He had also been at Shepstone's 'coronation' of Cetshwayo and taken part in the Langalibalele campaign.

William Morcom, a 'quiet, sarcastic little man',[27] was the mission's legal adviser. Frederick Fynney was coming along as interpreter and a sounding board for Shepstone on 'native matters', while the military were represented by Colonel Edward Brooke of the Royal Engineers and Captain James Fencott 'Jumbo' James of the 13th Light Infantry. Sub-Inspector Frederick L. Phillips was in charge of the mission's escort of twenty-five troopers from the Natal Mounted Police.

These appointees were joined by Shepstone's son Henrique, who would later be appointed the Transvaal's Secretary of Native affairs, and Haggard as a guest. Joseph Henderson, a prominent Pietermaritzburg businessman and banker – his daughter Kate was married to Shepstone's son George – preceded the mission in order to keep Shepstone 'informed of conditions and to smooth his way with the Boers'.[28]

Henderson travelled with Percy Whitehead, a fellow businessman with mining interests in the Transvaal.

Shepstone's mission was undertaken without any clear statement of intent. 'All we can say', wrote the frustrated editor of the *Natal Witness*, 'is that [Shepstone's] present plans are understood to be to start for the Transvaal before these lines appear in print ... Whether it is true that 40 mounted police are going as guard of honour we cannot say. All we can say is that if they do go and cross into the territory of the Transvaal, or if a single man of them does, it will be an invasion of that country.'[29] The editor was incorrect as to the number of mounted policemen but right in one regard: this was an invasion – the invasion of an independent state justified as being in the best interests of its inhabitants, a familiar justification for colonial creep employed in other parts of the British Empire.

Haggard left Pietermaritzburg on the afternoon of Friday, 15 December: 'four of our party, two on horseback, and two on the box of an ox-waggonette, proceeded down the streets of Maritzburg in the rain' looking, in their 'flannel shirts and mackintoshes, "like gentlemen about to extend British influence" as a local newspaper sarcastically remarked'.[30] Secreted in Haggard's waggon was a Union Jack. Members of the mission – Shepstone would join them in Newcastle – left Pietermaritzburg in small parties, making the formidable ascent up Town Hill, 'which in bad weather has often delayed a heavily laden wagon for a fortnight before it reached the summit'.[31]

Haggard's group arrived in Howick, a village 18 miles north of Pietermaritzburg, late on Friday night to find 'eight wagons, each with its span of sixteen oxen, drawn up and tents pitched for our reception'.[32] Saturday dawned fine and clear, but an early departure was prevented as some of the waggons had to be repacked and two oxen shot after coming down with redwater fever. When the party finally got going, a 'hot wind had set in, a violent north wind which comes straight from the burning plains of the interior, withering and scorching everything in its course'. After a short trek they outspanned 'just before a thunderstorm struck ... It set in wet for the night, and a wet night in camp is very wretched.'[33]

On Sunday night camp was pitched on 'one of the coldest spots in the colony, a high plateau at the foot of the Karkloof heights'.[34] The next day they descended from this forested area onto rolling grasslands ghosted to the west by the Drakensberg. A further day's trek brought them to the ford across the Mooi River and the following day they arrived at Estcourt, 'a pretty little place with about a hundred inhabitants, on the Bushman's River', where 'we all got our papers and letters, which were more than welcome'.[35] The sandstone Fort Durnford stood guard over the ford on the river and there was a well-established hotel.[36] Next stop was the 'very small village' of Colenso, congregated around a ford on the formidable Thukela. Named after the bishop, it was referred to by the Zulu as eSkipeni, 'the place of the boat', and it consisted of 'two inns, a store, a blacksmith's shop, and three or four other small houses'.[37] Fording the Thukela, one of the waggons was stranded on a rock.

The wide river, with its roaring rapids and wooded banks over which the evening light was fast darkening into night, made a strange frame for the picture of the wagon, stuck fast in its centre, the confused and bellowing oxen, the naked drivers up to their middles in water, shouting and clapping their tremendous 'voorslag' whips cut from the hide of a seacow [hippopotamus]. At length, the eight drivers with their attendant voorloopers managed to get the oxen's heads straight, and seizing the moment to let into all the unfortunate beasts with their great whips, accompanied with a volley of wild cries, got them to pull the wagon out.[38]

On the afternoon of Christmas Day the party forded the Klip River, and in Ladysmith that evening Haggard wrote to his mother wishing her and all at Bradenham Hall 'a merry Xmas, and a happy new year', knowing the letter would not get there until Christmas was all but forgotten, but when it did

it will show you that I did not forget you in this distant place today. It is indeed strange to me who have been riding along all day through these boundless and desolate African plains, under a tropical sun with a flannel shirt and cartridge belt, and a pair of riding trousers for clothing to think of you at home with your warm fires, your holly, and your church bells ... To be as a stranger in strange lands, living as it were, by oneself, makes one think very tenderly at times, and especially at such times as these of the old house, the old days, and the old familiar faces. I hope you won't think I am getting sentimental, but one must be made of hard stuff not to feel a little bit home sick at times when one is lonesome – However if all goes well, and my father approves, I hope another Xmas will see me with you, and tonight I shall drink all your healths according to the good old custom in some champagne I have worked out of the inner recesses of the wagon.[39]

Haggard was enjoying the camaraderie of travel. 'We all get on very well together, but doing 15 miles a day is slow work, especially here. When we get among the game it will be better fun. However it does one good, I have got a healthier look about me already, and with the exception of a few hours now and again, I feel fairly well.' Haggard wanted to get his health back before they reached Pretoria, where there was the possibility of fever. 'The Transvaal is very healthy in the winter but in the low veldt in the summer there is always some miasma knocking about.'[40]

By now there was no doubt as to the purpose of the mission: 'If things succeed it will be a good business for all concerned.' Haggard expected success as the 'Zulus are looking very nasty and altogether I should not be much surprised if another three months find the great Union Jack in my own waggon floating over Pretoria.'[41]

From Ladysmith they headed north 'day after day, until we were ascending the high and healthy slopes of the Biggarsberg, where the weather, which has been terrifically hot, broke with a great storm'.[42] As they drew near the Ingagane River, the country 'grew less desolate and more fertile than among the rock strewn hills we had been passing through'. Newcastle wasn't far distant, so they decided on a night trek.

I shall never forget that night. Behind us the moon, all the brighter for its background of inky clouds, was flooding the mountain plain and valley with wonderful light ... It fell upon the great distances of rolling plain and made them more limitless still. It lit the hill behind us, and turned the upright slabs of rock into enormous and fantastic gravestones. Its rays even reached the base of the Drakensberg towering on a dim horizon, their heads now and again crowned with fire by the flickering summer lightning.[43]

Newcastle was the centre of a coal mining and farming area as well as an official post halt, the halfway stop between Durban and Pretoria. In 1876, with the annexation of the Transvaal in mind (and possible hostilities with the Zulu), a small fort was built on a hill north of the town as a base for British troops.

At Newcastle Haggard spent £8 on a 'three-legged sporting pony – I say three legged because his fourth prop could hardly be called a leg'. Haggard was confident his new mount, named Dot-and-go-one, would soon build up its game leg after 'forty miles a day for three or four consecutive days, and nothing but grass to eat'.[44] Haggard's other horse, Metal, 'so called because of the metallic nature of his mouth', was a 'handsome pony, just like a little wooden horse, possessing great speed and endurance. His weak point is he abominates the report of a gun ... so that he is altogether useless as a shooting pony, except to ride into the game on – and then you can't hold him.'[45]

From Newcastle Shepstone wrote to President Burgers 'about his wish to visit the Transvaal and received the desired invitation'.[46] Now it was invasion by invitation, as well as an 'open secret that [Shepstone] was empowered to take over the country'.[47]

The rain sluiced down as the mission trekked out of Newcastle on the afternoon of 2 January 1877 for Laing's Nek, one of the main passes of the northern Drakensberg; and at the foot of the treacherous Sliding Hill, 'almost impassable in wet weather',[48] the waggons 'had to come up with double spans – a very good bit of driving'.[49] At the head of the pass the road levelled out and they travelled on past the crouching moss-green mountain of Majuba, the Hill of Doves, to Wesselstroom (later Wakkerstroom) before turning north-west towards the Vaal River.

While Haggard was setting his face to Sliding Hill, Sir Henry Bulwer was at his desk at Government House in Pietermaritzburg penning a letter to Haggard's father regarding his son's prospects after a 'year and five months' in South Africa. Haggard, said Bulwer, was 'undecided and unsettled' on the question of entering the Colonial Service and 'had turned his thoughts to the English Bar and to some extent (I ought to mention it) to literary work'. Bulwer thought the Bar offered 'a larger and broader field than the Colonial Service', though Haggard must be

fully prepared to work at the Bar since it is a bona fide profession and not as many men do as a covering cloak for literary success or other pursuits ... I do not think that he takes kindly at present to the formal routine work of Offices or to work that is not congenial to his tastes that are literary; but I doubt not that they will come right in course of time. He is a very fine young fellow full of spirit and pluck with many most excellent and admirable qualities of head and heart and with a very amicable disposition.[50]

Two weeks prior to Bulwer writing his letter, Haggard's future had been the subject of a 'family conclave' at Bradenham Hall held by his father, mother, sister Mary and brother Jack. In a letter written the next day, Haggard's father informed his son that the 'result of our joint cogitations is, *that you must yourself be the best judge of what is best, and that you had better come home as soon as you like ...* what you do when you get here, is time enough to settle when you arrive.' William Haggard's advice was similar to Bulwer's: 'If you got to the Bar, it will be for one or two reasons, either to practise at it regularly or to make it (and it is a very good one) a stepping stone in Colonial Life.'[51]

William Haggard also pointed out that his son had the option of taking up 'your original intention of going to St John's College, Cambridge'. The classical scholar Sir John Edwin Sandys, a friend of William Haggard's, 'would give you every help and assistance.'[52] Haggard's father thought it a 'great advantage to have a University Education'. He had been opposed to it 'at the time that you left school too early and went into this humbugging cramming system' – as if his son had had any choice in the matter. Haggard could study law at Cambridge while 'keeping your terms at Inn of Court', at the same time maintaining colonial connections via correspondence 'with Sir Theophilus and other colonial friends'. It didn't matter whether Haggard entered an Inn either 'at Easter or October' in 1877, 'but I think it does signify that you return as well acquainted with S. Africa as you can be, and I hope take notes in your travels there.'[53] A few days later William Haggard sent another letter, telling his son that on returning to England he should 'go to work for the Bar at once ... or give up the idea of Cambridge, but really I do not know which is best.'[54] Given the bewildering vacillations of Bulwer and his father, no wonder Haggard was drawn to Shepstone and his rock-like certainty.

On Wednesday, 3 January 1877, Shepstone's mission splashed across the border, 'a little spruit [the Coldstream], and entered the Transvaal.'[55] The 'disturbed condition of things' was soon evident. They met a Boer family, 'one of sixty others flying from the Wakkerstroom district, where the Zulus had come over and massacred fifty refugees living on Transvaal territory, and showed signs of doing the same to their masters.'[56]

So began their journey over 'the great Transvaal wastes. Day after day we passed over vast spaces, stretching away, north, south, east and west, without a tree, a house or any signs of men, save here and there a half-beaten wagon track.' Game was abundant: 'we saw about a thousand head of springbok, bounding along with a succession of springs of about eight feet into the air, coming down lightly as cotton-wool. We chased this troop and fired at them but they would not let us get within six hundred yards.'[57]

Two days later they came in sight of Stander's Drift, on the Vaal River, 'a mere hamlet of barely half a dozen houses',[58] where a burgher commando led by Field Cornet Adriaan Stander, after whom the drift was named, awaited them on the south bank of the river.[59] Shepstone's approach was heralded at midday by 'an officer of the Natal Mounted Police with a mounted escort of Police'[60] emerging from a cloud of dust followed by the waggons with another troop of mounted police at the rear. The commando fired 'a volley of welcome, and then turning, galloped in the lead and crossed the river. Here they again lined the road, and on the river being crossed by Sir Theophilus, fired another salute.'[61]

Once dismounted, the first person Shepstone greeted was the former Hanoverian nobleman Baron Bernhard Ludwig Schwikkard, who had renounced his title at the accession of Queen Victoria to the British throne in 1837 'to become a British subject, and to try a life of adventure under the British flag'.[62] Schwikkard had come to Natal and joined the small group of British settlers at Port Natal. In the conflict with the Boers in 1842 he was captured, clamped in the stocks and jailed for nine months for having fought on the British side. After the British annexation Schwikkard farmed on the Natal south coast, returning briefly to Germany to marry his fiancée Louise Marie Amelia Schronn. When the farming venture in Natal failed, the couple went to the Australian goldfields at Ballarat where 'the fever of the quest for gold entered [Schwikkard's] veins and remained there till he died'.[63] Louise's bakery and butcher business made more money than her husband's gold prospecting and they came back to Natal. The Schwikkard family and one of their sons, Otto, would become an integral part of Haggard's life in southern Africa.

At 14, Otto left school and went gold prospecting with his father. They struck a promising seam in an area close to the location of the future city of Johannesburg and were about to explore further when they got word Mrs Schwikkard was seriously ill. They returned home immediately; she subsequently recovered. At Stander's Drift Schwikkard told Shepstone that the richest goldfields in the Transvaal 'would be between Pretoria, Heidelberg and Potchefstroom'.[64] Schwikkard was right: he and Otto had narrowly missed discovering the gold-bearing reefs of the Witwatersrand.

Since then Otto had been on commando in the Boer–Pedi War, returning early in January 1877 to find his parents excited at the prospect of the imminent arrival of Shepstone, whom his father had known since the 1840s. Otto was a member of Stander's commando and later recalled Shepstone chatting with members of the commando 'with the utmost friendliness and an entire absence of airs'.[65] He was greatly impressed by Shepstone 'whose manner to his father and all their friends was so genuine and friendly'.[66] Otto recalled Haggard as 'a slight young fellow, about twenty years old with the beginnings of a moustache ... who had a quick smile and ever-ready pleasant word'.[67]

John Eustace Fannin, a Natal government land surveyor working in the area at the time, also came to meet Shepstone and enjoyed 'a little talk with Sir T. and lunch with him and others', after which Shepstone 'explained the objects of his mission ... I think good will come out of the affair – the feeling of the assembly was unmistakably in favour of English intervention in Transvaal affairs'.[68]

Then it was on to afternoon tea at the Schwikkards' where a cake was provided in early 'celebration of Theophilus's sixtieth birthday'.[69] The evening was given over to a 'grand dinner ... at which it was discovered that Mr Stander and Sir Theophilus had been comrades in the same camp in a Kaffir war forty years before!'[70]

The following morning Shepstone asked Schwikkard if he could take his son Otto to Pretoria as he 'knew the Boer people and their ways' and 'wanted someone besides himself who could speak the Taal [the language, i.e. Afrikaans], and he thought Otto would be useful'.[71] Schwikkard agreed, a Gladstone bag was packed and Otto went to Pretoria, 'leaving his father and mother waving to him among the people of the settlement who had gathered to say goodbye'.[72]

In his autobiography Haggard recalled with nostalgia these days of travel to Pretoria: 'Those camps were very pleasant, and in them, as we smoked and drank our "square-face" after the day's trek, I heard many a story from Sir Theophilus himself, from Osborn and from Fynney, who next to him, perhaps, knew as much of the Zulus and their history as any living in Natal.'[73] Shepstone and Osborn told their stories of the battle of Ndondakusuka and Haggard heard tales from Mhlopekazi, 'head native attendant to Sir Theophilus'. Reputed to be a Swazi of high birth, Mhlopekazi was 'a tall, thin, fierce-faced fellow with a great hole above the left temple over which the skin pulsated, that he had come by in some battle. He said that he had killed ten men in single combat ... always making use of a battleaxe. However this may be, he was an interesting old fellow from whom I heard many stories that Fynney used to interpret.'[74] Renamed Umslopogaas, a corruption of his real name, and with his axe the Woodpecker, Mhlopekazi was a major character in three of Haggard's books: *Allan Quatermain*, *Nada the Lily* and *She and Allan*.[75]

6

'ONE OF THE HARDEST JOURNEYS IMAGINABLE'

Cotton-wool clouds, laundry-white on blue, sailing from horizon to horizon, below a string of waggons creaking and lurching over the undulating grasslands of the highveld populated by abundant herds of game and wild ostriches: 'magnificent birds travelling along with the speed of a racehorse, three or four abreast, with their wings half-open and their long plumes fluttering behind them'.[1]

Shepstone and his party 'were welcomed at every dorp and hamlet', and at the town of Heidelberg an address read aloud to the assembled crowd in the main square assured the Special Commissioner 'that we shall agree to anything you may do in conjunction with our Government for the progress of our state, the strengthening against our native enemies and for the general welfare of all the inhabitants of the whole of South Africa'.[2]

Fifty-three miles and three days later, on Saturday morning, 20 January 1877, Pretoria lay six miles away as Shepstone's mission outspanned on the banks of Sesmyl Spruit (Six Mile Stream). On Sunday 'hundreds of people' from Pretoria came out to their camp 'for there was a vast amount of enthusiasm at the prospect of some development which would bring safety and prosperity to the State'.[3] Taking advantage of the halt, Haggard wrote a letter to his mother. His return to Pietermaritzburg had been postponed and Dr Lyle, Shepstone's physician, vetoed his 'undertaking five days and nights in the Post Cart' in his present state: 'I have been and am very seedy. The root of the evil appears to be the stomach which has affected the liver, which in its turn has touched the heart. I was rather bad yesterday but got the worst attack I have yet had this morning. It only lasted about an hour, beginning with faintness and nausea, and going on with pain about the heart and choking. It left me very weak, but I am getting all right now.'[4]

Lyle assured Haggard there was 'nothing to be frightened of ... he is sure it is not organic, but simple acute stomatic derangement ... but I only hope I will get better soon for this sort of thing makes one a burden to oneself and everybody else'.[5] Haggard thought Bulwer unlikely to insist on his immediate return to Pietermaritzburg because of his poor health, but 'he will be pretty sure to think that I am trying to do him. I really don't care what he thinks, as I value my health, or what is left of it, more than I do his fads.'[6] Healthier political and social prospects lay ahead: 'The Zulu demonstration [the raids in the Wakkerstroom district] has had a wonderful effect on Burgers who I think is throwing up his hand. There are going to be some gaieties at Pretoria in honour of our arrival, dinners and balls. I hope I shall be well enough to go.'[7]

The camp at Sesmyl Spruit was struck on the morning of Monday, 22 January, 'and every man, animal and waggon made to look as spick and span as possible' for the final leg of the journey.[8] The traveller after 'a weary and monotonous journey across treeless plains cannot but be struck with the beauty of [Pretoria's] situation', wrote Lyle. Once through a pass 'between low rocky mountains', the view opens up for the traveller to see 'an upland valley, and there nestles Pretoria, the houses gleaming in the sunshine and overshadowed by weeping willows, clothed in a foliage of tenderest green, or by the exotic eucalyptus with its mast-like stem and smoke-tinted leaves'.[9]

Pretoria, like Pietermaritzburg, lay in a valley surrounded by hills and was similarly laid out in a trekker grid pattern of parallel lines, 'ten streets east and west, eight streets north and south; in each case losing their outlines in the open veldt or in the Aapies River, which wanders along the northern boundary with a gurgling trickle, but which can become a raging, foaming torrent in the wet season'.[10] In 1877 Pretoria was 'no more than a village (*dorp*), consisting of only about eighty houses, most of them under thatched roofs, and of the essential native location'.[11]

Shepstone was escorted into town in President Burgers's state carriage. According to Haggard, 'the whole town was decorated, and a band of Good Templars took the horses out and dragged the wagon in fine style. We had done the 370 miles in thirty-eight days – not bad travelling.'[12] Cheering crowds greeted their arrival at Church Square, around which 'congregated the public offices, the banks, hotels, and some of the chief stores, or shops of the place' and, at its centre, a Dutch Reformed church.[13] After a welcoming address and the singing of 'God Save the Queen', Shepstone outlined the object of his mission:

> Recent events in this country have shown all thinking men the absolute necessity for closer union and more oneness of purpose among the Christian Governments of the southern portion of this continent: the best interests of the native races, no less than the peace and prosperity of the white, imperatively demand it, and I rely upon you and your Government to cooperate with me in endeavouring to achieve the great and glorious end of inscribing on a general South African banner the appropriate motto – '*Eendragt maakt magt*' (Unity makes strength).[14]

Shepstone was assigned a house on Church Square while the rest of the party pitched camp in an adjacent square. Shepstone and his staff lunched informally with President Burgers, but come evening there was 'a tremendous public dinner of welcome, with speeches, many and long after it'. The dinner was given in the Volksraad

Zaal (legislative chamber) and 'those walls accustomed to furious denunciations of everything English rang to the tune of *Rule Britannia* ... and *God Save the Queen*'.[15] Rumours that Shepstone planned to hoist the Union Jack after dinner saw 'seventeen valiant burghers' waiting for the moment 'when they should make for themselves an immortal name by shooting the lot of us'. But 'no flag was hoisted, and therefore no one was shot'.[16]

Shepstone immediately launched his champagne-and-sherry policy 'precisely as Wolseley had done in Natal, where his brilliant lieutenants had dazzled the eyes of Pietermaritzburg maidens', William Morcom, the mission's legal adviser, told his family in his weekly letter.[17] Haggard acknowledged the fairer sex 'were of great service to the cause of the mission, since they were nearly all in favour of a change of government, and, that being the case, they naturally soon brought their husbands, brothers, and lovers to look at things from the same point of view'.[18]

Luncheons and dinners, banquets and balls flew by in furious succession and, much to his chagrin, Haggard was frequently called on at short notice to toast 'the ladies'. The popping of corks didn't suppress opposition to the British presence, however, and 'within a few days of our arrival', Haggard recorded, 'the Boers were massing on the road from Potchefstroom, with the intention of coming to Pretoria and taking the Special Commissioner, his staff and escort, back to whence they came'.[19] They rode into town on 6 February. 'The best part of the cavalcade was the horses, the Boers have very good horses, but the riders, the flower of Boer chivalry, they were about as sulky, greasy, unwashed looking individuals as it is easy to imagine.'[20]

The mission's Zulu staff stood impassive and silent before going 'we thought to their work', but shortly afterwards were heard 'the savage notes of a Zulu War song' and on investigation they were found to be sharpening their assegais – 'they fully expected to fight their hereditary enemies the Boers and were totally disappointed at its non-occurrence'. Masuku, Haggard's personal servant, cleaned Haggard's rifle and pistols, plus a 'double barrel smooth bore'.[21]

The burghers demanded an explanation from their president as to Shepstone's presence in their country's capital. Burgers told them the Special Commissioner was there to 'discuss certain complaints' and to 'bring about confederation, which however, would not be approved by the Government without the consent of the majority of the people'.[22] Satisfied with the response, they rode off. However, two burghers struck a blow 'at British influence' by attempting to steal Haggard's horses, Metal and Dot-and-go-one, a theft thwarted by some Africans on the scene. Masuku was aghast when told of the incident and mimicked stabbing them with an assegai, making 'the terrible "sgwe, sgee" (the sound a Zulu makes as he passes and repasses his spear through the body of a fallen enemy) which plainly showed what he would do if he had the chance to seize the rascals who tried to steal his master's horses'.[23]

Bad weather, not Boers, caused greater discomfort. After five days of heavy summer rains it became apparent 'we had encamped in a swamp where one might have shot snipe. Our tents became mushroom grounds that would have filled the breast of a British gardener with envy.' When fever broke out, refuge was taken in the waggons, but eventually 'our ground got so bad that we could stop no longer' and they moved to accommodation with firmer foundations.[24] According to Morcom, Pretoria lay 'so low that every possible artificial means should be taken to promote the efficient drainage of every part of it', and he attributed the 'feverish attacks, the sore throats and the mortality among children' to the unhealthy atmosphere.[25]

Haggard and Morcom were among a small group who rode out one afternoon to see the famous Wonderboom (the amazing tree), one of 'the most wonderful vegetable products in the neighbourhood of Pretoria'.[26] Canter turned full gallop when 'a rain storm of the sort peculiar to South Africa'[27] brewed up behind them, and they took shelter in an African homestead on the side of a hill, where they were received 'very hospitably especially when they found we were not Boers come to levy taxes' and Haggard handed around his tobacco pouch.[28] Storm over, the riders set off again, heading through a narrow pass, once 'the site of a large Native town probably of 8 or 10 thousand inhabitants to judge from the number of kraals, walls and the fortifications'.[29] The abandoned ruins, prefiguring many such in Haggard's romances, were once Kungwini, a royal homestead of the Ndebele leader Mzilikazi, overrun by the Zulu in 1832.

A quarter of a mile from these ruins grew the Wonderboom, a fig tree of the species *Ficus salicifolia*.

> The main stem or trunk is comprised of several shoots from the root these shoots having become joined together near the root branching out on all sides at no great height from the ground. Some of these branches have bent over and entered the ground and taken root there and there a large extent of ground is covered by the tree and its off shoots. The foliage is very thick and the shade which it affords to the traveller very refreshing.[30]

Haggard noticed that even in this 'remote place' some 'English snob' couldn't resist the temptation to 'cut in nice big capitals a monument that should speak of him to future generations.'[31]

Haggard set down many of his impressions of those first weeks in Pretoria in an article titled 'Camp Life in Pretoria'. It was never published, but another written by Haggard while in Pretoria did make it into print. Haggard sent this article minus a title to Frederick Broome in Natal, who forwarded it to Lady Barker in London, requesting she pass it on to Alexander Macmillan with a view to publication. Macmillan expressed interest and, when he asked for a title, she suggested 'The Transvaal', adding that perhaps Haggard's name be omitted as he was on Shepstone's staff, 'and it might make a difficulty, but you know best'.[32] The article ran above

Haggard's name in the May 1877 issue of *Macmillan's Magazine* and, appearing prior to 'A Zulu War Dance', marks the beginning of Haggard's literary career.

'The Transvaal' is an apologetic for the annexation. The Transvaal Boers are depicted as a stubborn people with a 'strong aversion to control', especially by the British, a people possessed of a 'wandering and nomadic spirit' and a taste for vast tracts of land which made them head off into the wilderness 'on the slightest pretext, such as a season's drought or the increase of population in their neighbourhood'. Haggard concedes that 'these strange men possessed in many cases minds and qualities far superior to what their shrinking hatred of civilisation would have the observer to suppose'. He conjured up a portrait of 'the average Dutch Boer' with his wife and 'numerous children' as an 'awkward-looking man, of large stature, and somewhat heavy, obstinate face, which is lit with a broad and kindly smile of greeting. His home, it is true, is not over clean, nor are his habits over nice, but his hospitality is most hearty, and the best he has is at your disposal. You will find him intensely religious, believing his Bible down to the very pictures ... and you will also find him intensely prejudiced against everything modern and civilized.'[33]

Pretoria was home to a small but cosmopolitan white community, and Haggard thought the capital a 'wonderfully gay place considering the difficulties under which it labours'. He attributed the gaiety

> to the large Hollander element in Pretoria society, which is made of up of Dutch, English and Hollanders. The Dutch or Boer element hates the English and Hollanders, the English dislike half the Dutch, abominate the Boers and call them '*les barbare*[*s*]'. In fact everyone hates everyone in a manner wholly Christian. The Boers vituperate the Hollanders, because they are better educated than they, and hold all the highest Government posts; and the Hollanders hold out the red rag to the Boers by playing croquet all Sunday afternoon, and dancing all Sunday night, crimes worthy of death in the eyes of the fanatical doppers (a religious sect whose puritanical tenets are much believed in by the Boers).[34]

Croquet was played in an atmosphere of high seriousness. Cheating was frowned on, 'and if you do it too often you won't be asked again'.[35] Flirtation during play was equally taboo. Pleasure was reserved for dancing – 'everybody here dances, and dances well'. Haggard was much involved with arrangements for balls hosted by Shepstone; a ball for '150 people one night' was followed the 'next evening by a children's party'. The latter was for 'little girls' of whom there were a large number of 'all nations in the town ... and all of them dance beautifully. It was a fearful exertion, as one had to manage two little girls every dance, taking another as soon as one was tired, and careering round the room with your head in a line with your knees.'[36]

The Zulu staff concluded that the constant round of dances was of military significance. One morning Masuku told Haggard he was glad he knew 'now that we are going to fight, since last night I saw Somptseu and all the Inkoosis in their fighting dress dancing the war dance with the white intombas (marriageable girls)'.[37]

Negotiations with the Transvaal authorities were ongoing, Shepstone telling the burghers he had come to address concerns over hostilities with the Pedi as well as the financial situation of the current administration and the need for reform. Confederation was presented as the remedy for all ills. Only as time passed did the 'master of the art of vagueness'[38] reveal the iron hand within the silk glove: his authorisation to summarily annex the Transvaal if negotiations didn't lead to the satisfaction of British desires.

The burghers were not entirely passive. According to Haggard, many threats 'were uttered against us ... Indeed there is no doubt that at times during these months we went in considerable risk.' Haggard and Morcom were working late one night copying dispatches and had not drawn the curtains. 'Sir Theophilus came in and scolded us, saying that we ought to remember that we made a very easy target against that lighted background. Then he drew the curtains with his own hand.'[39]

Haggard attended several sittings in the Raadsaal (council chamber), a 'long low room with a deal table running down the middle, round which sit thirty Boers, many of them heavy faced and unintelligent'.[40] One burgher stood out, Paul Kruger, 'then a middle-aged man with a stern, thick face and a squat figure'.[41] The famous Boer patriarch, born in the Cape in 1825, had trekked north with his parents in 1835. At the age of 11 he took part in the battle of Vegkop which saw off Mzilikazi and the Ndebele. In Natal the young Kruger witnessed the Zulu descend on the Boer encampments at Weenen after the killing of Piet Retief and his men. Thereafter his family trekked to the highveld and settled in the Magaliesberg. Kruger was accepted as a burgher, a fully fledged citizen, at 15; at 16 he owned two farms and at 17 he married his first wife, Maria du Plessis, who died four years later. His second marriage to Gezina du Plessis would last 54 years and produce 16 children and 120 grandchildren. Kruger's hunting exploits and his bravery in combat were part of Boer folklore and he became Commandant General of the ZAR in 1863, resigning a decade later on the election of Thomas Burgers as president. Dour in manner and uncouth in behaviour, Kruger was a devout member and lay preacher in the ultra-conservative Dopper Church. He believed the world was flat because the Bible told him so, but he was not to be underestimated; he was a wily and canny opponent. Kruger impressed Haggard 'more than did any of the other Boers'.[42]

Negotiations continued, Shepstone moving inexorably towards his objective while the burghers quarrelled among themselves. On 1 March Shepstone told the Executive Council that there was 'but one remedy to be adopted, and that was that the Transvaal should be united with English Colonies of South Africa under one head, namely the Queen, saying at the same time that the only thing now left to the Republic was to make the best arrangements it could for the future benefit of its inhabitants, and to submit to that which he saw to be, and every thinking man saw to be, inevitable'.[43] In the ensuing furore and in a final bid to assert its independence, the Volksraad approved a reform plan proposed by President Burgers and rejected Carnarvon's confederation bill. Shepstone's 'hopes of annexing the Transvaal with the consent of its government dwindled to virtually nothing'.[44] They were even more tenuous on the discovery that the Pedi had been 'so thoughtless as to conclude peace with the republican government while Shepstone was actually in Pretoria negotiating its downfall'.[45]

According to a treaty negotiated by Commandant Ignatius Ferreira with Sekhukhune, signed on 5 February, the Pedi king consented to become a subject of the state and agreed on a boundary to his territory as well as handed over 2,000 head of cattle in compensation for those stolen by the Pedi. The treaty left Shepstone with few cards to play, and he had his work cut out to exaggerate the Zulu danger in order 'to terrify the Boers ... into accepting British rule'.[46] Haggard acknowledged that 'if the Transvaal Government had really induced Secocoeni to become its subject, one of the causes of the proposed British intervention ceased to exist'[47] and the Boers would have been entitled to expel the British from their country.

Just when it looked as though Shepstone's bluff had been called, he was thrown a lifeline: a brief message written by Sekhukhune was passed on to him by Alexander Merensky, a German missionary at the Botshabelo mission station north of Middelburg. It read in part: 'the Boers are killing me, and I don't know the reasons why they should be angry with me; Chief, I beg you come with Myn Heer Merensky'.[48] The plea was accompanied by a letter from Merensky stating that Sekhukhune 'had distinctly refused to agree to that article of the treaty by which he became a subject of the State'.[49]

Shepstone suggested that Ferreira, who negotiated the treaty, might have been in error, and that a joint commission be sent to Sekhukhune to ascertain the truth. This was agreed and a commission was set up consisting of two representatives of the Transvaal government, W.J. van Gorkom and J.C. Holtshausen, and two British representatives, Marshall Clarke and Melmoth Osborn, with Haggard as secretary.

The British trio left Pretoria on 17 March, making for Fort Weeber to join the two burghers already on their way and continue together to the Pedi capital, Tsate, to investigate the treaty and, if necessary, ratify a new one to the satisfaction of both British and Transvaal authorities. The mission was expected to take two weeks and the proclamation of annexation was postponed until its return. Haggard was eager to take advantage of 'a great chance' to see 'what I expect will be a very curious business – and of what one is certain never to see again, besides the information I should get will be wonderful'.[50] This would be sufficient indeed for another article, 'A Visit to the Chief Secocoeni', published in the *Gentleman's Magazine* in September 1877.[51]

There were still concerns over Haggard's health. Shepstone told Bulwer he 'was loath to let him [go], but he pressed me until I consented', only on condition that at any 'sign of unnatural fatigue' Haggard stopped 'somewhere he could be taken care of'. Shepstone judged Haggard 'strong enough when he left', and how he stood the journey would 'be good criterion to judge by whether he could take the longer one in the post cart he proposes'.[52] This proposed journey was not the original planned return to Pietermaritzburg. Haggard had volunteered, following the annexation, to take the official dispatches by post cart from Pretoria to Cape Town – an 1,800-mile journey – and from there to England.

Disquiet over Haggard's health was not unwarranted, as where they were headed was fever season. 'However fever or no fever we had to go.' Speed was of the essence as the precise terms of the treaty with Sekhukhune had to be clarified before Shepstone could promulgate the annexation. With the clock ticking, the small party took only 'four riding horses, three for ourselves and the fourth' for Clarke's Zulu servant named 'Lankiboy', who also led a packhorse, and carried an enormous knobkerrie 'stuck in his button hole, as though it were a wedding bouquet'. Their saddlebags contained 'a change of clothing, and in front we strapped a rug and a mackintosh. Our commissariat consisted of four tins of potted ham, and our medicine chest of six dozen bottles of quinine, some Cockle's pills, and a roll of sticking plaster, which, with a revolver and a hunting knife or two, completed our equipment.'[53]

Riding due east from Pretoria, they arrived at 'a Boer's house' and 'off-saddled to feed our horses'. In 'A Visit to the Chief Secocoeni', Haggard gives full rein to his anti-Boer prejudice: 'at no time are they a pleasant people to deal with, and just now they are remarkably unpleasant towards Englishmen'. The party obtained forage for the horses, but when their host realised who they were, he refused them bread or eggs. 'Finally, we succeeded in buying three cups of milk for a shilling, "as a favour", and that is all we got from sunrise to sunset.'

Sixty miles further on they came 'to a Boer's house where we had to sleep'. Haggard was dismissive of his hosts and their dwelling – 'the grime and filth of it baffles description'. After supper – a cue for a critique of eating habits and etiquette – Haggard and his companions fled outside 'to escape the feet-washing ceremony (all in the same water) which this "simple pastoral people" indulge in, and which they expect the barbarous "uitlander" (stranger) to enter into with enthusiasm'.

For sleep 'a luxurious couch' was made up for them on the floor, 'consisting of a filthy feather-bed and an equally filthy blanket'. Haggard blew out the candles. Enter fleas: 'Sleep was impossible; one could only lie awake and calculate the bites per minute, and the quantity of blood one would lose by daybreak.' Come morning, 'very glad we were when we had paid our bill and were in the saddle once more, riding through the cold morning mist that lay in masses on all the ridges of the hills like snow on mountains'.

From where did Haggard's crude prejudice towards the Boers arise? Such prejudice was evidently widely enough shared in British settler society for Haggard to think nothing of publicly expressing it in print. Some sources suggest he may have been influenced by Shepstone. Sir Bartle Frere, a future Cape Governor, thought

Shepstone had 'no sort of sympathy with the Boers'.[54] John Kotzé, the Transvaal judge with whom Haggard would work closely, shared Frere's opinion, stating that Carnarvon found in Shepstone 'a willing and shrewd lieutenant ... who had but a scant sympathy, if any, with the South African Boers'.[55] Sympathy, scant or otherwise, is not an automatic identifier of racism; it could equally be read as an indicator of Shepstone's political stance. This view was supported by Haggard, who refuted Frere's assertion: '[Shepstone] was full of sympathy for the Boers, and understood them as few men did. Moreover he appreciated all their good points, and most of them admired and were attached to him personally. Had this not been so he could never have annexed the Transvaal with such comparative ease.'[56]

Even if Shepstone is absolved, that is not to say political antipathy didn't shade into prejudice among Haggard's other friends and colleagues. This was certainly Kotzé's view. In his court circuits with Haggard, the judge made a point of visiting local farmers and was 'invariably met with kindly greeting and hospitality. Haggard could not, however, be persuaded into visiting the homes of the Boers. He was strongly prejudiced against them, and so avoided them, although they had never offended him in any way.'[57] Accounting for Haggard's attitude, Kotzé pointed his finger squarely at the 'environment at headquarters in Maritzburg' and 'the general feeling of the circle in which he moved in Natal towards the Boers'.[58] A pity, thought Kotzé, for had Haggard 'understood the Boers, he would have written of them with better knowledge and spirit'.[59] That Haggard didn't would not be without consequence.

Putting prejudice behind him and with more than sixty miles to cover, Haggard thrilled at galloping Metal across the 'wild beauty' of the highveld. Ahead lay Botshabelo (Place of Refuge) – 'the most important mission station, and one of the very few successful ones, in South-eastern Africa' founded by Alexander Merensky in 1865. Botshabelo stood on 'the brow of a hill surrounded by garden and orchards', below which were 'dotted numbers of kraals, to say nothing of three or four substantial houses occupied by the assistant missionary and German artisans'. Merensky's house stood next to the thatched red-brick mission church. Overshadowing the station was a fort 'consisting of thick walls running in a circle with upstanding towers, in which stand one or two cannon'. The medieval-style fort still stands today, 'a unique blend of Western and Sotho architecture'.[60]

Merensky had been 'forced by the pressure of circumstances to teach his men to use the rifle, as well as the truths of Christianity; to trust in God, but also to keep "their powder dry". At a few minutes' notice he can turn out 200 well-armed natives.' Botshabelo and its martial missionary would be relocated to East Africa in *Allan Quatermain* and Merensky renamed Mackenzie.[61]

Haggard, Clarke, Osborn and Lankiboy spent the night at Botshabelo and in the morning rode to Middelburg, midway between Pretoria and Lydenburg, where they were warmly received by 'the handful of English residents' and where they interviewed Gideon, the African who had acted as interpreter between Ferreira and Sekhukhune as well as 'two natives, Petros and Jeremiah, who were with him'.[62] The two insisted Sekhukhune 'had positively refused to become a subject of the Republic, and only consented to sign the treaty on the representations of Commandant Ferreira that it would only be binding as regards the two articles about the cattle and the boundary line'.[63]

At Middelburg the party exchanged their horses for a waggon as it was impossible to proceed to Fort Weeber otherwise, 'because of the deadly nature of the country for horses'. Horses in southern Africa were subject to a 'mysterious disease' for which there was no cure 'and very few horses pull through – perhaps, five per cent'. These animals were known as 'salted horses', less liable to contract the disease a second time.[64] An ox-drawn waggon was hired and provisioned, and they took three horses, the 'oldest and least valuable', as the final stretch of mountainous country between Fort Weeber and Tsate could not be traversed by waggon. The waggon was driven by two young Boers, 'terrible louts, with gaping mouths just like cod-fishes. However they understood how to drive a waggon.'

They headed north-east from Middelburg on 20 March, camping 'after a twenty miles trek, just on the edge of the bush-veldt'. The following day they dropped down from the highveld plains into 'a beautiful bush-clad valley with mountains on either side. It was like making a sudden descent into the tropics. Not a breath of wind stirred the trees, and the sun shone with a steady, burning heat. Scarcely a sound broke the silence, save the murmur of the river we crossed and recrossed, the occasional pipe of a bird, and the melancholy cry, half-sigh, half bark, of an old baboon, who was swinging himself along, indignant at our presence.'[65]

The sun hot 'and the road fearful', they were glad to reach Whitehead's Cobalt Mine, one of Percy Whitehead's ventures.[66] Before departing, Haggard, Clarke and Osborn explored the hillside mine, then leaving 'this awful hole', they rode on past old copper workings, circular pits abandoned by Africans a century before, until they came to the banks of the Olifants (Elephants) River:

> You cannot see the river till you are right upon it, owing to the great trees with which its steep banks are fringed and in the early morning it is quite hidden from bank to bank by a dense mass of billows of white mist, indescribably strange to look upon. The close odour, the long creeping lines of mist, the rich rank vegetation, the steady heat of day and night, all say one word, 'fever', and fever of the most virulent type.

As with horse sickness, the cause of malaria was not known, and at the time it was thought to emanate from such sinister mists. Haggard confessed to a 'latent fear' he would 'someday begin to feel hot when he ought to be cold, and cold when he ought to be hot, and so be stricken down, to rise prematurely old, or perhaps to die, and be buried in a lonely grave covered with stones to keep off jackals'. This fear was not without foundation, as they were 'travelling in the very worst fever-month, March, when the summer vegetation is commencing to rot, and throw off its poisonous steam. What saved us ... was our temperate living, hard exercise, and plenty of quinine, and tobacco, smoked.'

As the name of the river suggested, this was game country, yet they 'saw very little and killed nothing', partly because they didn't 'dare go out of hearing of the waggon-wheels, for fear of getting lost in the bush', but also because the big game had been shot out – 'a few years back this veldt swarmed with big game, with elephants and giraffes, and they are even now occasionally seen' – though not by Haggard. They rode north along the bank of the Olifants 'through the sunrise, through the burning midday and glowing sunsets, steering by the sun and making our own road until the river's confluence with the Elands [River]', where they struck east onto higher ground, away from the 'low, hot valleys' covered with mimosa trees 'into the region of the sugar bush, which thrives upon the hillsides'.

On 25 March they entered the valley where Fort Weeber stood to the west of the Leolu Mountains. The fort was garrisoned by the Middelburg Burgher Volunteers and commanded by Ferreira, who had negotiated the treaty with Sekhukhune. The garrison was reduced to 'abject poverty', not having 'received any pay except Government "good-fors" (promissory notes, generally known as "good for nothings")'. Nor were the volunteers able to mount offensive operations as eighty-two of their ninety horses had died of horse sickness. Notwithstanding this down-at-heel state of affairs, the garrison 'gave us a very grand reception. As we rode up, they fired a salute of twelve guns.' After a formal address read by Ferreira, 'a more practical welcome followed in the shape of a good dinner'.

Van Gorkom and Holtshausen, the two Transvaal representatives, were already at the fort, and on the morning of 27 March the full commission, now including Ferreira, Captain Gerrit van Deventer ('an excellent man who could sit a bucking horse better than anyone I knew')[67] and an unnamed interpreter, began their 36-mile ride to Tsate. 'Poor unfortunates, we little knew what was before us when we rode gaily away!'

Riding through hilly country 'entirely composed of boulders of granite, weighing from five to 1000 tons', they passed the ruins of Phiring, the Pedi capital abandoned in 1853 after conflict with the Boers and the Zulu, before coming to 'a great alluvial valley nine miles wide'. Human skeletons were scattered across the plain, witness to 'the only real fight between the volunteers and Secocoeni's men' in August 1876. At the foot of the Leolu Mountains there were abandoned homesteads, many razed to the ground by the Middelburg volunteers; their inhabitants fled into the mountains and built new homesteads in 'inaccessible places', their 'white huts peeping out all over the black rocks'.

The scenery visible from the top of the pass over the Leolu Mountains to Tsate was 'inexpressibly wild and grand ... forty miles in front of us towered up another magnificent range of blue-tinged mountains known as the Blue Berg [Blouberg mountains], whilst all around us rose bush-clad hills, opening away in every direction towards gorgeous-coloured valleys'. From this viewpoint they descended 'a most fearful precipitous path consisting of boulders piled together in the wildest confusion, from one to another of which we had to jump, driving the horses before us'. Halting for a rest halfway down, they noticed 'that the gall was running from one of the horses' noses'. Despite being 'salted', the animal had succumbed to horse sickness and was left to die.

A gully at the foot of the pass brought them to the valley floor, and in the distance stood Tsate, Sekhukhune's 'beautiful, fever-stricken home', in the shadow of a prominent koppie (hill), lone outlier of the surrounding mountain ranges. They rode on through 'the still hot eventide' until they came to the town below the koppie they had seen from a distance, a 'fortified kopje perforated by secret caves where the ammunition of the tribe is hidden' – Ntswaneng, the 'Fighting Koppie', the Pedi citadel of last resort in the event of attack.

They were taken to a thatched sleeping hut with a verandah standing in a courtyard 'beautifully paved with a sort of concrete of limestone which looked very clean and white, and surrounded by a hedge of reeds and sticks tightly tied together, inside which ran a slightly raised bench, also made of limestone'. The interior of the hut was 'ornamented in the Egyptian style with straight and spiral lines, painted on with some kind of red ochre, and floored with a polished substance'. There, after dining on a sheep slaughtered for their benefit, they spent the night. Breakfast was served on an assegai blade, one in each hand of a Pedi, 'on which were respectively speared a leg and a side of mutton'. They cut slices with their hunting knives and ate with their fingers.

Later that morning came a message from Sekhukhune 'that it was now time to talk'. It was a short walk to 'the chief's private enclosure, where stood his huts.' Sekhukhune 'rose from the ox-hide on which he was seated under a tree, and came to the gate to meet us'. Haggard described Sekhukhune as being of 'middle size, about forty-five years of age [he was 62], rather fat, with a flat nose and small, twinkling, black eyes, he presented an entirely hideous and semi-repulsive appearance. His dress consisted of a cotton blanket over which was thrown a tiger-skin kaross, and on his head was stuck an enormous white felt hat, such as the Boers wear.' Introductions over, Sekhukhune returned to his ox-hide and, apart from occasionally shouting 'out some instructions', left 'Makurupiji', the name given to Sekhukhune's 'mouth' or prime minister, to speak on his behalf. He gave an account of the meeting with Ferreira when the treaty was drawn up 'in almost the same words as had been used by the interpreters at Middelburg' and 'denied having consented to become a subject of the Republic or to stand under the law, and added that he feared he "had touched the feather to" (signed) things that he did not know of in the treaty'.

During the four-hour meeting Sekhukhune chewed 'an intoxicating green leaf very much resembling that of the pomegranate, of which he occasionally sent us some'.

Perched on a log in the blazing sun, Haggard took notes 'to the best of my ability ... as the interpreters rendered the conversation from Sesutu [Southern Sotho] into Dutch and English'.[68] Ferreira cross-examined Sekhukhune 'but entirely failed to shake the evidence': the king had signed the treaty 'on the distinct understanding that he was not to become a subject of the State'.[69] Ferreira was furious. In his autobiography Haggard says Ferreira, whom he refers to as Mr A, 'rose in a rage, real or simulated, and withdrew, taking with him the Dutch Commissioners'. Van Deventer also left.

Clarke, Osborn and Haggard remained with Sekhukhune, who spoke to them directly as Osborn refused to communicate via a third party. 'It was very curious to see this wily old savage shoving a handful of leaves into his mouth, and giving his head a shake, and then making some shrewd remark which went straight to the bottom of whatever question was in hand.' Sekhukhune said he wanted the British to save him from the Boers, 'who hunt me to and fro, and shoot my people down like wild game'. He said that 'many thousands of the black peoples' under English rule were 'happy and at peace. I know that if I do likewise I shall be as a wife to the British Government, and knowing a wife's duty to her husband I will not fail to render it due obedience' – but queried whether he had to 'repay the two thousand head of cattle ... seeing the war was not of my making?'[70] Osborn told Sekhukhune that as he had given his word regarding the cattle, he should hand them over. Sekhukhune agreed to this and 'some other rulings about territory', and the delegation's impression was that 'he indeed wanted to come under the sovereignty of Britain'.[71]

Rather than 'risk the fever for another night', Clarke, Osborn and Haggard left for Fort Weeber immediately. Their return journey very nearly took them into a well-planned ambush, unmentioned by Haggard in his article owing to political sensitivities; only in 1906 did he record in a memorandum what happened.[72] When leaving Tsate, there was a problem 'in getting guides to lead us over the forty miles of plains and mountains that lay between us and Fort Weeber'. At last they procured two teenagers, Sekouili and Nojoiani, 'whom we named "Scowl" and "No-Joke", as those words somewhat resembled their native appellations'.[73]

On the pass over the Leolu Mountains they encountered the carcass of the horse left to die the day before, already half skinned 'by some passing Basuto', and another dying of horse sickness, abandoned by the Boer commissioners who had preceded them. By the time they reached the crest of the pass, the sun had set and the moon had risen. 'A discussion rose between us as to which of the two paths we should follow, I urged that we should take the lower path because the view of the moonlit valley would be so much better from it, and this ultimately we did though our two guides remonstrated violently at our doing so.' Haggard's romantic whim saved their lives.[74] During the descent they became aware 'of a great commotion going on amongst the rocks a mile or so to our left, where ran the road we should have followed. War-horns were blown, and a Basuto warrior armed with gun and spear rushed down to look at us, then vanished ... So we crossed the mountains in safety.'[75]

Only after the annexation in April, when Van Deventer was 'taken into the service of the English government',[76] did they learn of the 'cruel and appalling plot'[77] to murder them. Van Deventer told Osborn and Haggard that Makurupiji had visited Fort Weeber prior to the arrival of the commission and spoken with Ferreira, who convinced him the English would 'take all their women and cattle and make slaves and soldiers of all their men' and that the only way to prevent this would be to ambush and kill Clarke, Osborn and Haggard on their return journey from Tsate.[78] Van Deventer said this was why Ferreira 'pretended to get into a rage and ridden off with the two Boer envoys ... lest they by some accident should be involved in the massacre'.[79]

In his memorandum Haggard says Ferreira planned the murders to prevent them revealing that the treaty had been forged, 'in which event [Ferreira's] credit would be saved and the S. African Republic he served would be freed from a great embarrassment'.[80] The ambush 'was set upon the upper path by which we had come and by which our two guides, Scowl and No-Joke, were directed to take us back. The accident of our taking the lower road, according to Van Deventer, alone preserved us from a particularly unpleasant death'.[81]

Ahead of the British party on that fateful night, Ferreira, Van Deventer, Van Gorkom and Holtshausen were met 'by some of the Boer troopers' and told 'we had escaped the ambush and were riding towards him'.[82] Ferreira, according to Van Deventer, 'lost all control of himself and called for volunteers to shoot us down'. Holtshausen, hearing of the plot for the first time, as had Van Gorkom, 'intervened with great effect, shouting out that if this wicked deed was done he "would publish it in every court in Europe"'.[83] No volunteers came forward and Haggard, Osborn and Clarke, blissfully unaware of the plot to kill them, arrived at Fort Weeber about daybreak to be 'enthusiastically received by Captain Ferreira'.[84]

The following morning when Haggard and Osborn left for Pretoria, Clarke headed north with Lankiboy on a prearranged mission to the restive Lydenburg goldfields 'to keep them quiet for the present at least'.[85] After taking a different route to avoid fever country, Haggard and Osborn arrived back in Pretoria at 'about eight o'clock at night, on the sixteenth day of our journey' – Monday, 2 April – to be 'greeted as those who had come out of the jaws of death'.

Masuku, on hearing Haggard calling him, exclaimed in isiZulu: 'He has come back! By Chaka's head I swear it! It is his voice, his own voice that calls me; my father's, my chief's!' Once the horses had been attended to, Masuku showed Haggard 'how he had kept everything secure in my tent, and said solemnly in his broken English: "I very glad you came back, sir; I no like to live without you, Inkose." Poor Masuku! He had been dreadfully disappointed at not being allowed to come with me. "Surely," he said, "where my chief goes, there I should go too."' Shepstone was most likely even more relieved than Masuku at Haggard's safe return, writing immediately to Bulwer:

'Osborn and Haggard returned ... Haggard wonderfully set up instead of knocked up as I feared by the hard work the journey gave him.'[86]

For Haggard the mission to Sekhukhune had been a resounding success, his health was restored and he had enjoyed another thrilling experience in Africa. He recommended his mother read his article 'A Visit to the Chief Secocoeni' when it was published in the *Gentleman's Magazine* as it 'will give you some idea of what travelling is like here'.[87]

There was a sequel to Ferreira's plot to kill Clarke, Osborn and Haggard. After the annexation, Ferreira applied several times for employment 'under the new regime'.[88] These requests were refused. Finally the frustrated Ferreira went to see Osborn, now Government Secretary, and in an adjoining room Haggard heard their raised voices. 'Ferreira was blustering and demanding to be employed as a right. At last he asked why he should be left out when so many of the other Boer officials had received appointments. Thereupon Mr Osborn answered – "Damn it, Captain Ferreira, you know why!"' Ferreira did not respond, but Haggard saw him 'walk out of the room and the house with a very crestfallen air'.[89]

Ferreira's guilt was common knowledge in Pretoria's administrative circles.[90] This raises the question: did Sekhukhune know of the plot to kill Clarke, Osborn and Haggard? Haggard thought it 'very possible' but that his involvement could never be proved conclusively.[91]

Elsewhere in southern Africa another of the players in Carnarvon's confederation game was taking up his position. On 31 March 1877 Sir Bartle Frere arrived in Cape Town to take over from Sir Henry Barkly as Governor of the Cape. An 'imperial pro-consul of the first order',[92] the 62-year-old had been handpicked by Lord Carnarvon. Frere's career had begun in the Bombay Presidency of the 1830s. He steered the province of Sind through the Indian Mutiny with a minimum of disturbance and, as Governor of Bombay, overhauled the city's sanitation. When he left India in 1874 Frere's reputation 'as an administrator and as a humanitarian was impeccable'.[93] Posted to the court of Sultan Barghash bin Said of Zanzibar, he pressured the potentate into ending his involvement in the slave trade. Now Frere was in South Africa, ready and willing to corral the region's reluctant republics into a confederation, the last hurrah of an illustrious career.

In Transvaal the British annexation was imminent, the joint commission having proven Sekhukhune had not agreed to become a subject of the Boer republic, though even this desired outcome had its drawbacks: the Pedi threat having evaporated, Shepstone's main prop for annexation 'was to promote the image of the Zulu as a fierce and aggressive menace to white people'.[94] At the beginning of April tensions on the Zulu border were represented 'to be extremely threatening' by Shepstone, 'who *seems* to have feared an almost immediate invasion of the Transvaal by Cetewayo's impis'.[95] The Zulu army had obligingly mustered on the Transvaal border in response to a reported Boer invasion of Zululand in the offing. When this report proved false, the Zulu army stood down. On the eve of the annexation, Shepstone sent a message to Cetshwayo 'warning him to abstain from all hostile intentions against the people of the Transvaal',[96] and the Zulu king withdrew his regiments.

On 9 April Shepstone told the Raadsaal he was 'about to declare the Transvaal British territory', having come to the conclusion he could 'see no possible means within the State by which it could free itself from the burdens that were sinking it to destruction'.[97] There was little resistance. While it might not be true, as Shepstone claimed, that a majority of the Boers accepted the British presence, the country was undoubtedly deeply divided and many Boers, as well as British settlers, welcomed British rule 'as the only way to safeguard life and property'.[98] Burgers issued a formal protest against annexation and the Executive Council appointed two of its members – Kruger and Eduard Johan Jorissen, the State Attorney – to travel to London and seek its reversal. Burgers's last act as president was to order his burghers to refrain from any violent act that might jeopardise the success of their mission.

On the morning of Monday, 12 April 1877, 'the momentous and fatal step … so disastrous in its ultimate results' was taken.[99] On that early autumn day the Transvaal was declared British territory, 'an anxious moment for all concerned'.[100] At eleven o'clock Shepstone's staff proceeded from what became Government House to Church Square, where a crowd awaited them. Shepstone remained behind with the police escort. 'That there was a possibility of trouble we all knew, for many threats had been made, but in that event twenty-five policemen would not have helped us much.'[101]

In the square Osborn read aloud the proclamation of annexation to the crowd, 'largely composed of English folk or of those who were not unsympathetic'.[102] The Transvaal republic was held to have irretrievably broken down owing to its inability to maintain authority over the land in the north, now effectively under control of 'aboriginal tribes', to the point that 'all confidence in its stability once felt by surrounding and distant European communities had been withdrawn'. In addition, commerce was 'well-nigh destroyed' and the country 'in a state of bankruptcy'. The white inhabitants, 'discontented with their condition, are divided into factions', all indications pointing toward 'civil war, with its attendant anarchy and bloodshed'.[103]

The Pedi defeat of the Boers in 1876 had dealt a mortal blow to the 'reputation of the Republic' and represented a 'culminating point in the history of South Africa', disclosing 'for the first time to the native powers outside [the Transvaal], from the Zambesi to the Cape, the great change that had taken place in the relative strength of the white and black races' – a disclosure that 'at once shook the *prestige* of the white man in South Africa, and placed every European community in peril'. Matters had 'become so grave, that neither this country nor the British Colonies in South Africa can be saved from the most calamitous circumstances except by the extension over this state of Her Majesty's authority and protection'. Consequently 'the South

African Republic ... shall be taken to be British territory' and all 'orderly, right-thinking, and peace-loving people of the Transvaal' were expected to support 'her Majesty's authority'.[104]

The Transvaal would retain its 'separate Government, with its own laws and Legislature', and arrangements would be 'made by which the Dutch language will practically be as much the official language as the English'. 'Equal justice' was guaranteed 'to the persons and property of both white and coloured'. But there were limits to British magnanimity: 'the adoption of this principle does not and should not involve the granting of equal civil rights, such as the exercise of the right of voting by savages, or their becoming members of a legislative body, or their being entitled to other civil privileges which are incompatible with their uncivilised condition'. Nor would their lives be without regulation: 'native tribes living within the jurisdiction and under the protection of the Government must be taught due obedience to the paramount authority, and be made to contribute their fair share towards the support of the State that protects them'.[105]

Osborn, no less than the waiting Shepstone, must have visibly relaxed when 'the proclamation was received with hearty cheers'.[106] Burgers was not present and his formal protest – the draft of which had been approved by Shepstone – was read on his behalf and 'received in respectful silence'.[107]

In *Finished*, the final volume of Haggard's Zulu trilogy, Allan Quatermain is a witness to the proclamation of annexation and to his creator's role in it. A 'tall young fellow, yourself, my friend', writes Quatermain, handed the proclamation to Osborn, who 'began to read in a low voice which few could hear, and I noticed that his hand trembled. Presently he grew confused, lost his place, found it, lost it again and came to a full stop.' After an awkward pause 'you, my friend, grabbed the paper from his hand and went on reading it in a loud clear voice'.[108] That Haggard took up the reading of the proclamation from Osborn went unrecorded elsewhere and could be dismissed as fiction, but during Haggard's visit to Pretoria in 1914 the Administrator of the Transvaal, Johan Rissik, confirmed the incident. "'At that moment," said Rissik, who of course was an ardent Dutchman, or rather Hollander, "I would gladly have shot you."'[109]

Immediately after the proclamation, a photographic session was held at Government House. Behind the camera on its tripod was the Swiss photographer Henri Ferdinand Gros, owner of a 'Photographic Gallery' in Pretoria offering a variety of services, including photographs 'taken in the Newest Style at Shortest Notice'.[110] The group photographs taken by Gros on this occasion are, as far as is known, the only images of Haggard during the years he lived in South Africa.

News of the annexation 'was received all over the country with a sigh of relief, and in many parts of it with great rejoicings', according to Haggard, and nowhere 'was there the slightest disturbance, but, on the contrary, addresses of congratulation and thanks literally poured in by every mail'.[111] Shepstone hosted his first official dinner on 26 April, and 'as in duty bound the toast of the Queen was given for the first time in the Transvaal by the first Administrator thereof'.[112]

Soldiers of the Queen from the Maritzburg garrison at Fort Napier, already standing to on the Natal border prior to the annexation, were now approaching Pretoria, and many residents rode out to see them on the route of march, the regimental band being a particular drawcard. With them was Otto Schwikkard, now assigned to the army's Commissariat Department and returning to Pretoria after attending the deathbed of his father in Standerton. On the outskirts of the town, Schwikkard was injured when the cart being driven by an officer overturned. The officer broke a leg while Otto 'sustained a slight scalp wound'.[113] Haggard and Dr Lyle went to fetch the two casualties in a mule waggon.

A battalion of the 13th Regiment arrived in Pretoria on Friday afternoon, 4 May, 'and the townspeople were to be seen proceeding to the Poort road in carriages of every description, in wagons, on horseback, and on foot'. The troops marched through the pass at 3.30 pm, the band playing 'Rule, Britannia'. The 'feeling of rejoicing and relief' at the sight of the troops 'was so profound that when the band began to play "God save the Queen" some of the women burst into tears'.[114]

With British redcoats in place, all was ready for Shepstone's next piece of imperial theatre, the raising of the Union Jack over the Transvaal. Haggard was present. On 24 May, Queen Victoria's birthday, the British flag was formally hoisted at Pretoria in the presence of 'a large gathering of English, Boers and natives.[115] The band played "God save the Queen", the artillery boomed a salute, and at midday precisely, amidst the cheers of the crowd, Colonel Brooke, R.E., and I ran up the flag to the head of the lofty staff.[116] For Haggard 'it was one of the proudest moments of my life',[117] and he was in no doubt as to the significance of the event: 'It will be some years before people at home realise how great an act it has been, an act without parallel. I am very proud of having been connected with it. Twenty years hence it will be a great thing to have hoisted the Union Jack over the Transvaal for the first time.'[118]

As we have seen, Haggard planned to go home to England via the Cape carrying the official dispatches after the annexation. This arrangement had changed inasmuch as Shepstone preferred to use the established mail channels, as a bearer 'might be delayed on the road by sickness or accidents, and that in performing a long journey of the sort, a mail bag had a better chance of getting safely and swiftly to its destination than increasing it'.[119] But Haggard was still going to England, for Shepstone was sending him at the same time as the dispatches with 'credentials to the Colonial authorities, empowering you to give such information as my dispatches do not and cannot contain, which is a great deal (Sir T is not a voluminous writer like Sir HB) and in this way you will be a living dispatch'.[120] Haggard thought this would undoubtedly redound to his credit and was 'indirectly a great compliment to myself'. Bulwer gave his blessing.[121]

There was another motive for Haggard's return, not mentioned in his letter: 'I was very anxious to come home after several years' absence from England, on "urgent private affairs". To be frank, I desired to bring a certain love affair to a head by a formal engagement, which there was no doubt I could have done at that time.'[122] Haggard intended formalising his engagement with Lilly Jackson. However, 'it was impossible for me to get leave at the moment' – he had been given a position in Shepstone's new administration though it is not known what it was. 'Yet the matter was one that would admit of no delay', and so Haggard told Shepstone what he hadn't told his father, obtaining a promise 'that if I resigned my appointment in order to visit England, as it was necessary I should do, he would make arrangements to ensure my reappointment either to that or to some other billet on my return.'[123] On that basis Haggard sent his luggage forward to Cape Town, but on the day before his departure he 'received a most painful letter' from his father. 'Evidently he thought or feared that I was abandoning a good career in Africa and about to come back upon his hands. Although it was far from the fact, this view may or may not have been justified. What I hold even now was not justified was the harsh way in which it was expressed.'[124]

In his letters home Haggard had made abundantly clear his future plans, including coming back to England; his father had even given advice about what to do when he came. True, his father would not have received his son's letter written in March about accompanying the official dispatches and the attached kudos; nevertheless this thunderbolt of a letter must have seemed totally inexplicable to Haggard, and its impact was immense: 'The words I have forgotten, for I destroyed the letter many years ago, immediately upon its receipt, I think, but the sting of them after so long an absence I remember well enough, though some four-and-thirty years have passed since they were written, a generation ago.'[125] The sting was such that immediately after reading the letter, Haggard withdrew his resignation and 'cancelled the passage I had taken in the post-cart to Kimberley *en route* for the Cape and England. As a result the course of two lives was changed. The lady married someone else, with results that were far from fortunate, and the effect upon myself was not good.'[126]

In a curt response to his father's letter, Haggard said he had abandoned 'my idea of coming home.'[127] In his autobiography, filial loyalty sees Haggard partially defending his father's action, but the pain is evident. 'I should have remembered that when he wrote his letter my father could not have known that I was coming home ... to give *viva-voce* information to Lord Carnarvon as to all the circumstances connected with the Annexation.'[128] Haggard says he acted out of 'hurt pride and anger', excusing his lack of judgement with the fact 'I was very young, only twenty, and that I had to make up my mind on the spot while, as the Zulus say, "my heart was cut in two".'[129]

There is a strong possibility Haggard's mother and his sister Mary 'were privy to the secret and private reasons for my journey' through the Jacksons, and had alerted his father, prompting the intemperate letter.[130] Lilias acknowledges William

Haggard may well have 'suspected there was a love affair' behind his son's 'sudden desire to come home, and he had already suffered more than a little from the tumultuous and varied excursions with diverse ladies indulged in by his elder sons',[131] and adds that 'no member of the Haggard family' was 'to be trusted within sight of pen and paper when they are what is politely called "a bit worked up"'.[132] Subsequent correspondence indicates William Haggard's anger was most likely provoked by his son breaking ties with family friend Sir Henry Bulwer.

Lilly Jackson's feelings on the matter are not known. Her family liked Haggard 'but did not trouble themselves very seriously about an entirely penniless lad, son of an obscure Norfolk squire, without any sort of prospects, who had fallen so desperately in love with the beauty of the family'. No doubt he would soon get over it. 'As to the girl herself, probably she had no idea of the strength and persistence of Rider's affection.'[133] Haggard possibly delivered his own judgement when describing Eva Ceswick, Lily's fictional incarnation in *The Witch's Head*, as 'very loving, very sweet and very good, but she did not possess a determined mind'.[134]

Haggard didn't write to his father again until 1 June. Bruised feelings were one reason, but he was also waiting for confirmation of his appointment to a paid government post in order to deliver an assertive riposte to his father as evidence that he was quite capable of managing his own affairs. At the beginning of the letter Haggard states he doesn't

> think that it will be of any good to dwell any more on what is to me, in some ways at least, a rather painful subject ... in so far as regards what you say about myself, and my relations with, and conduct to Sir Henry Bulwer. Still as I may not hereafter allude to the matter again, and as it may be some years before I have any chance of explaining to you personally the circumstances of the case, I wish to say there are two sides to every question, it is probable that my conduct has not been so entirely bad and wrong as you seem inclined to believe. Also I repeat that my leaving Sir Henry was his doing, not mine. He told me plainly that I must make up my mind, either to take a small appointment or to go home and enter some profession. I did not see my way about the appointment, so I decided to come home. Since then he changed his mind.[135]

Then comes the *coup de grâce*: 'I received to-day my letter of appointment as English Clerk to the Colonial Secretary's Office with a salary of £250 per annum.' Haggard also hoped to be appointed Clerk to the Executive Council, 'as soon as there is an Executive to be Clerk to', which was worth another £100, though this had been cut to £50 as 'it is not desirable to give offence by making my pay higher than that of any other clerk in the service, and though virtually I shall stand first on the list, it is thought better that I should not be nominally either under or over the one or two drawing equal pay'.[136] Bulwer 'could never give me anything better if so good' even if he were to stay ten years in Natal. 'Transvaal is more than six times [Natal's] size ... it will before long, with its natural wealth and splendid climate, be one of the most splendid foreign possessions of the British Crown, and if as is probable gold is discovered in large quantities, it may take a sudden rush forward, and then one will be borne up with it. So that whatever happens I think that I shall always do pretty well here.'[137] In the long term Haggard's plan was to 'rise to the position of a Colonial Governor, and to do that I must trust to good fortune and my interest ... At any rate I have now got my foot on the first rung of the Colonial ladder, and D.V. [*Deo volente*, God willing*] I intend to climb it.'[138]

For Haggard the 'great thing' was that he was now 'independent and shall, I hope, put you to no more expense or trouble, both of which I am afraid I have given you too much already'.[139] Operating from a position of strength, Haggard broached the vexed question of finance. 'I fear I shall have to draw on you once more for 20 pounds in order to meet some debts which I must pay before the month is up in connection with the transhipping of my baggage to Cape Town and back, etc. I shall be very sorry to put you to that expense, my dear Father, but I trust that it will be the last time I shall ever have to do so.'[140]

Haggard's more immediate concern was permanent accommodation. Property was in short supply in Pretoria; the annexation had created a property boom and a 'building site that would have sold for 40 pounds before is now valued at 130 pounds'. On the probability 'I shall stay in this country for many years', Haggard said his best option was 'to build something sooner or later'.[141]

7

'PLEASANT RECOLLECTIONS'

At five o'clock on the afternoon of Wednesday, 25 April 1877, John Kotzé and Lewis Ford, previously unknown to each other, stepped up from the dust of a Kimberley street into Cobb's coach to Pretoria. Neither was sure of what lay ahead, but each pinned his future on the outcome, and both would play significant roles in Haggard's life.

The 31-year-old Lewis Peter Ford was born in London in 1846 and came to South Africa with his parents in 1851. Having read law at the South African College (now the University of Cape Town), Ford enrolled as an attorney in 1866 and was appointed deputy sheriff of Richmond and Murraysburg in the Cape Colony. In 1871 he and a friend, a Dr Fockers, visited the Kimberley diamond fields and both 'made up our minds to move there'.[1] Ford brought with him his wife Ellen and their four children. The diamond fields were 'an Eldorado for lawyers',[2] and Ford quickly built up a successful practice as well as being actively involved in the diggings.

Ellen was not enamoured of life in Kimberley and returned to Cape Town with their children. The couple divorced and Ford married one of Fockers's patients, Johanna Lehmkuhl, daughter of Frederick Lehmkuhl, a 'domineering, but impecunious German immigrant'.[3] The 22-year-old Johanna was, according to Ford, 'a complete invalid', rendered near immobile by paralysis in her lower body. Under Fockers's care Johanna began to recover and Ford took her on outings in his 'one horse, four-wheeled carriage for two'. Johanna was 'such a bright, happy creature, and so pretty' that Ford decided he could give her 'all the care she needed if I married her. And so I did.'[4]

At this stage Johanna was on crutches and without 'hope of her ever being able to do without them'. Or so Ford believed. Not long after the birth of their first child, Johanna 'gave a scream … she felt her ankle move.' Ford 'caught hold of the foot and slowly bent it into position'. Fockers put 'on a splint and bound the foot so it could not go back again' prior to obtaining 'a boot and steel brace'. A few weeks later Johanna was able to do 'without her crutches', but her legs having lost their muscle, she 'had to learn to walk' and in a few months she was 'as well as any woman'.[5] The couple would go on to have five more children, though Ford, as will be seen, was not the biological father of one of them.

When the Black Flag Revolt in Kimberley broke out, the British government lost patience with the instability in South Africa's diamond fields and imposed stricter controls to resolve the continual claim disputes. When a royal commission recommended the lifting of limits on the number of claims individuals could own, the magnates moved in. Minor players like Ford were squeezed out, Kimberley 'collapsed financially, and everyone who could left'. Ford went to Pretoria 'with £5 in my pocket'[6] in the hope that 'following the Annexation there might be an opening for an English lawyer'.[7]

Ford's fellow passenger, 27-year-old John Kotzé, the son of a Cape parliamentarian, was born in Cape Town in 1849 and, like Ford, attended the South African College. To qualify for the Bar, in 1869 Kotzé went to read at the Inner Temple in London, where he met and married Mary Aurelia Bell. The couple returned to the Cape with their infant daughter in 1874. Kotzé practised law in Cape Town before moving to Grahamstown, the second largest town in the Cape Colony. In February 1877 he received a telegram from President Burgers offering him the post of Chief Justice of the Transvaal: 'If you accept, prepare to start without family.'[8] Kotzé accepted and set off by coach for Pretoria via Kimberley. His arrival there coincided with that of the Transvaal mail coach bringing news of the British annexation. Kotzé was uncertain as to where this placed him *vis-à-vis* the position offered by Burgers but decided to continue his journey as planned, which is how Ford and Kotzé found themselves travelling together on the three-day journey to Pretoria.

On arrival in Pretoria shortly after noon on Saturday, 28 April, Kotzé booked into the Edinburgh Hotel in Church Square and, after lunch and a short rest, he walked over to nearby Government House to consult the new Administrator about his future. Kotzé was impressed by Shepstone: 'His face indicated strength and kindness, with quick observant eye, well-shaped head, easy manner and pleasant address.'[9] Kotzé was so moved by Shepstone's 'seeming genuineness' that he requested the older man 'speak to me as a father to a son'. Shepstone responded by saying he considered the establishment of a High Court 'a matter of pressing necessity' and would get back to Kotzé in a week's time, in the meantime requesting details of President Burgers's job offer. Kotzé then spent a 'pleasant hour' with Burgers and his wife Mary, whom he knew well.[10]

Two days after the Burgers left Pretoria on 7 May, Kotzé was called to Government House, where he bumped into State Attorney Jorissen and Paul Kruger, who had just paid their respects to Shepstone 'preparatory to leaving for London to lay the protest of President Burgers on behalf of the Republic before Her Majesty's Government'.[11] After a brief conversation with the two men, Kotzé had a long meeting with Shepstone, who wanted to 'create a high court for the Transvaal consisting of a single judge'.[12] Kotzé was the judge. At 27 he 'established a record by being the youngest member of the bar ever appointed to the judicial bench under the Crown'.[13] Despite his age Kotzé was better qualified for the job than any other judge in the Transvaal.[14] An acting Attorney General was temporarily required to replace Jorissen and Shepstone asked Kotzé for a recommendation. Not having had time to gauge the capacity of any local candidates, he suggested his recent travelling companion. Thus Ford became acting Attorney General and immediately sent for his wife and children to join him in Pretoria. The opening of the new High Court took place on 22 May. Kotzé missed the raising of the British flag two days later, as he was en route to Grahamstown 'for the purpose of bringing my family to Pretoria'.[15]

The appointment of the 'boy judge', as Kotzé was inevitably dubbed, raised a few eyebrows. Morcom for one was sceptical,[16] though he was silent when the 20-year-old Haggard was tapped to be acting Master and Registrar of the High Court owing to the illness of the current incumbent, 29-year-old Hendrik van Breda, formerly the Treasurer General in Burgers's administration. Haggard's job as English Clerk was not exactly onerous, which is probably why Shepstone found something more useful for him to do. However, Breda 'recovered sufficiently to scrape through his business while lying in bed. It is my opinion that he will have to take six months' leave if he wishes to save his life, and in that case I shall get the acting appointment.'[17] Haggard was keen to have Breda's position as it was 'an important post and gives one legal experience'; he would also 'draw half the Registrar's pay which would be £250 per annum and half my own which would be £125 per annum. However nothing is settled about it yet, and perhaps the unfortunate fellow's liver will get better.'[18]

As the new administration set up shop, further moral support for the British presence in the Transvaal came in the shape of Lieutenant General Sir Arthur Cunynghame, who reviewed the 13th Regiment's manoeuvres on his way to the north-eastern Transvaal for a hunting trip; Haggard renewed his friendship with the general's aide-de-camp, Nevill Coghill.

Shepstone was also on the move. On 16 August 1877 he embarked on a tour of the eastern and southern districts of Transvaal, travelling via Middelburg to Lydenburg, then south via New Scotland to Wakkerstroom, reaching Utrecht, close to the border with Zululand, on 21 September. Shepstone had inherited the border dispute between the Transvaal and the Zulu. As Secretary for Native Affairs in Natal, he had supported the Zulu claims, intent on preventing Boer access to the Indian Ocean, but now that the Transvaal was under British control Shepstone, 'chameleon-like, took on all the policies and attitudes of his predecessors'.[19] Zululand must be subjugated, as 'there was no longer any reason why the Zulu should delay the fulfilment of their destiny as workers in Natal and elsewhere'.[20]

The Zulu expected Shepstone to settle the dispute in their favour, but in a cynical and expedient volte-face Shepstone backed the Boer claims to the hilt. The Zulu understandably felt betrayed and displayed outright hostility towards him. Shepstone was angered at their response: the Zulu were supposed to be meekly submissive to their White Father – 'the sooner the root of all evil, which I consider to be the Zulu power and military organisation is dealt with the easier our task will be,' he reported to Lord Carnarvon.[21] '[I] have been thrown over by my father' was Cetshwayo's response.[22]

The rift between Cetshwayo and Shepstone widened; intemperate words on both sides exacerbated the situation. Bulwer in Natal viewed 'the developing crisis with mounting disquiet'; he thought Shepstone's tactics 'potentially disastrous'[23] and initiated an arbitration process but gained 'very little support for his peace initiative in the Transvaal or Natal',[24] which was derided by white settlers on the one hand and sniped at by members of the Shepstone bureau. Undaunted, he appointed a three-man Border Commission to investigate the boundary claims.

Haggard's appointment as acting Master and Registrar was confirmed on 3 August 1877 after Breda went on extended sick leave. A few days later Haggard accompanied Kotzé on the judge's first tour of the Transvaal court circuit, an 800-mile journey that would see them visit the magistracies of Middelburg, Lydenburg, Wakkerstroom, Standerton, Heidelberg, Potchefstroom and Rustenburg, before returning to Pretoria. Haggard's 'most pleasant recollections' of his life in the Transvaal were those 'connected with my journeys on circuit in company with Judge Kotzé'.[25]

Haggard and Kotzé travelled in a 'comfortable spring wagon', and 'a similar vehicle was allotted' to the High Sheriff, C.J. Juta, and the acting Attorney General, Ford, who accompanied them. Juta was to select 'suitable deputies in the various districts' while Ford would 'conduct prosecutions on behalf of the Crown'. The waggons were 'each drawn by eight oxen, of which a driver and leader (*voorloper*), the latter generally a young native, had charge'. They were 'comfortably fitted up, and each of them was provided with four lockers, so that we were able to take in an ample stock of provisions, etc., for the journey', including a 'folding table and canvas chairs, as well as necessary cooking utensils'.[26] Personal servants – in Haggard's case, Masuku – were also in attendance.

Trekking east towards Middelburg, they saw 'quantities of springbok and blesbok', but of the four officials only Kotzé and Haggard had rifles. They had 'very good sport' and were also able 'to keep ourselves and the boys well supplied with fresh meat'. Haggard was riding his favourite horse, Moresco, 'the most remarkable which I ever knew'.[27] Being a 'salted horse', he was 'very valuable in consequence'.[28]

On the morning of the third day of their trek Haggard and Moresco went in pursuit of a small herd of wildebeest. Failing to make a clean kill, Haggard rode after the wounded animal and before long he found himself lost on the veld. Meanwhile the waggons lumbered on for three or four miles before outspanning for the night. When Haggard hadn't appeared at camp by the time 'we had finished our supper, we got rather anxious'. Taking his knobkerrie, Masuku 'walked back along the road we had come, in order to search for his master'.[29] To everyone's 'great relief' Haggard and Masuku 'turned up about three a.m.'[30]

This was the second time Haggard had got lost in the wilds and on this occasion he became totally disoriented, wandering 'aimlessly, without plan, till an accident happened'. His horse fell, and he was thrown and knocked unconscious. He came to, finding himself 'lying in swampy ooze, still holding the rifle, with the horse, that was too weary to run away, standing within a few paces'.[31] Seeing the setting sun, Haggard realised he had 'been heading west when he should have been heading east'.[32] Haggard remounted and rode on as night fell and the moon rose. When his horse refused to travel further, he dismounted and wrapped himself with the horse's saddlecloth to keep warm. Exhausted and frightened, Haggard was faced with the possibility 'that I should not live to see another dawn. The loneliness was awful, and the silence broken only by the howling of hyenas or other night beasts'.[33] He hazarded some shots at passing antelope but 'they galloped off untouched'. He lay down again; 'all fear had left me and I seemed to desire nothing except sleep'. Thinking he heard a voice, he 'sat up and fired my last cartridge'.[34] Mazooku didn't hear the rifle shot but 'his quick eyes saw the flash from the mouth of the rifle' and, walking towards where it had come from, 'at length caught sight of the outline of a horse standing against the sky, and so found me sinking into coma'.[35] Haggard made use of this incident in *Queen Sheba's Ring*, where three lost adventurers are rescued thanks to the sound of a rifle shot and the muzzle flash.[36]

At Middelburg, Kotzé 'administered the oaths of office and allegiance to all officials and servants of the Government',[37] as he would at all the magistracies on this first court circuit since the annexation. While at Middelburg, the four officials took the opportunity to visit the Botshabelo mission station where Haggard had overnighted earlier in the year with Clarke and Osborn. Merensky, 'full of life, energy and information', struck Kotzé 'as of a type superior to the ordinary African missionary'.[38] Impressed by the mission station's self-sufficiency and its 'thriving trading business', Kotzé bought his wife 'a pair of pretty square German porcelain vases'.[39]

Legal duties done, the party left for Lydenburg, travelling north-east over the highveld plains, swarming with 'springbok and blesbok in their tens of thousands' and 'black wildebeest in troops of about forty to three hundred'.[40] Early one morning Kotzé shot his first blesbok, 'and I made my first acquaintance with what is undoubtedly the finest breakfast dish of the veld – freshly-fried blesbok liver'.[41] The 'excellent bird shooting along our route' also made for good eating. Haggard's shooting skills were widely acknowledged, but on this trip he revealed an unexpected talent:

> this genial, high-spirited and romantic young man, bred and educated as befits a gentleman's son, proved himself to be an excellent cook! He prepared for our evening

meal dishes which would have done credit to a first-class chef. In a baking pot he baked venison, as well as korhaan and red-wing partridge, in a manner that could not be excelled, and he steamed the potatoes to perfection. He would also, on occasion, prepare more dainty dishes, such as roast snipe on toast, which were simply delicious.[42]

Fording the Elands River, they made for the high ground overlooking the Crocodile River valley. They managed the steep descent without mishap and came to a trading store 'kept by a jovial German named Heimann, who spoke English and Dutch quite well', where they outspanned for the night and 'obtained fresh milk, eggs and home-made bread'.[43]

Early next morning, by the time 'the rising sun tipped the mountains with gold we were well on our journey'.[44] Crossing a drift over the Crocodile, they headed up the valley to Lydenburg, halting briefly at Koppie Alleen (Lone Koppie) 'under the shelter of which stood the hospitable homestead of Commandant Coetzee and his wife'.[45] This was probably D.R.G. Coetzee, who 'played a prominent role in supplying his fellow burgers with [African] children' – just one of a 'variety of other political and trading relationships with the Pedi and Swazi'.[46]

Lydenburg was a lively regional trading centre with banks, a post office and 'three large stores where every description of goods is sold, from a plough to a bottle of Florida Water, or a fiddle and a pair of babies' boots'.[47] The party had hoped to meet Shepstone in Lydenburg but he had gone on to Pilgrim's Rest with Clarke, now Special Commissioner of the district, who had placed his house at their disposal. 'Clarke's servants were well-trained Zulus, and they attended us remarkably well.'[48]

A brief court session at Lydenburg allowed time for Kotzé, Ford and Haggard to visit Pilgrim's Rest, the heart of the goldfields, 38 miles away. The small town was in festive mood thanks to a dinner and a ball being given 'by the diggers in honour of Sir Theophilus', to which 'we were also invited'.[49] A fellow guest was the Portuguese Vice Consul, Alois Nellmapius, who invited them to stay the following night at his camp at New Caledonia, a few miles to the north. Born in Budapest in 1847, Nellmapius came to southern Africa in 1873. In 1875 he submitted a proposal to the Transvaal government to build a road from the goldfields to Lourenço Marques on the coast of Mozambique. Given the go-ahead, Nellmapius formed the Lorenzo Marques and South African Republic Transport Company to construct the road and was rewarded with four farms. Kotzé, Ford and Haggard rode the next day to Nellmapius's camp where he lived in three tents, one as a living room, the other two 'fitted up as bedrooms'. They had a 'pleasant evening, for Nellmapius was an educated man ... and also very optimistic in the mental pictures he drew of the country's future prosperity'.[50] He also served an 'excellent dinner, prepared by a competent Indian cook'.[51]

After returning to Lydenburg and making their farewells, Kotzé and party began 'our long trek to Wakkerstroom'.[52] The route 'lay almost due south, and we had once more to traverse the Crocodile Valley and ascend its southern rim in order to reach the high veld beyond the top of the mountains'.[53] One night while they were outspanned in the New Scotland area, 'the great horse-breeding district of the Transvaal', Moresco broke the rein securing him to the waggon and 'made off after a troop of mares'. The court circuit's tight timetable only allowed for a brief search which proved fruitless, but three mornings later when Haggard alighted from the waggon he shared with Kotzé, he found Moresco 'standing untied among our other horses'. Having 'tired of the company of the mares, [he] had deliberately taken up our spoor and followed it until he found us forty or fifty miles away'.[54]

En route to Wakkerstroom they called in at Emigratie, a farm owned by Hendrik Theodorus Bührmann. An official in the Lydenburg district with an inside track on land deals, Bührmann had accumulated a healthy portfolio of over twenty farms and, like Coetzee, was also involved in the trade of African children. On Bührmann's advice they took the shorter route to Wakkerstroom from his farm, as it was in a better state of repair than the main road. Not so the waggon. A couple of days later 'the hind axle of our wagon broke just inside the box, which prevented us from proceeding any further'.[55]

Ford and Juta continued on to Wakkerstroom in their waggon to organise a relief party while Kotzé and Haggard were left 'befogged on what was really the top of a spur of the Drakensberg. The mist was so thick we could scarcely see more than a yard ahead.'[56] With a well-filled water cask 'to keep the kettle going' and plenty of provisions, the two settled in for the night attended by Masuku and 'our Hottentot wagon-driver'.[57] They retired to the waggon, 'lit our lanterns, and whiled away the long moments by reading a play or two of Shakespeare, each taking an act in turn'.[58]

The mist cleared the next morning, and a rescue and repair party arrived. Once the broken waggon had been relieved of its wheels and secured on an ox-waggon, they all set off for Wakkerstroom, where a new axle was sent for from Newcastle, 50 miles away. Wakkerstroom was 'a straggling-looking town' with a large vlei (pool of water) half a mile to the south, home to 'a large species of bull frog ... its blowing or bellowing could be distinctly heard at night-time in the town'.[59] Haggard and Kotzé stayed at the home of Anna O'Reilly, the widow of a former landdrost. Coincidentally, Kotzé knew her brother Edward Gilfillan, who lived at Cradock in the Cape Colony.

Boundary disputes constituted the main court business at Wakkerstroom and the sessions concluded with a dinner at the Traveller's Inn, owned by the former Royal Navy officer Edward Hazelhurst, an English immigrant who had worked as a lumberjack in the forests around Pietermaritzburg and opened the hotel in 1876 after a failed attempt to make his fortune on the Kimberley diamond fields.

Leaving Wakkerstroom they trekked north to Heidelberg, passing Meek's farm and store, which was later described by Haggard in *Jess* where it is renamed Luck's:

a curious establishment on the Pretoria road [that combined] the characteristics of an inn, a shop, and a farm-house ... If the traveller is anxious to obtain accommodation for man and beast at a place of this stamp he has to proceed warily, so to say, lest he should be requested to move on. He must advance, hat in hand, and ask to be taken in as a favour, as many a stiff-necked wanderer, accustomed to the obsequious attentions of 'mine host', has learnt to his cost.[60]

It may have been at Meek's that Haggard met Anthony Trollope, then visiting South Africa to gather material for a book along similar lines to those he had written on Australia and New Zealand. Trollope took the same route from Pietermaritzburg to Pretoria which Haggard travelled in 1876.[61] Haggard first met him 'in a towering rage at a roadside inn because he could not get any breakfast' and later in Pretoria. Trollope 'stopped in the country about twelve days and now is going home to write a book about it – in which no doubt he will express his opinion with a certainty that an old Resident would hesitate to adopt. I talked with him a good deal, he has the most peculiar ideas about things and is as obstinate as a pig – I call such a proceeding downright dishonesty making use of a great name to misrepresent a country.'[62] Haggard was more circumspect in his autobiography than when writing to his mother in 1877, providing an 'alternative' meeting with the famous author in Pretoria:

I had been sent away on some mission ... and returned to Government House late one night. On going into the room where I was then sleeping I began to search for matches, and was surprised to hear a gruff voice, proceeding from my bed, asking who the deuce I was. I gave my name and asked who the deuce the speaker might be. 'Anthony Trollope,' replied the gruff voice, 'Anthony Trollope.'

Mr. Trollope was a man who concealed a kind heart under a somewhat rough manner, such as does not add to the comfort of colonial travelling.[63]

At Heidelberg there occurred the only refusal to take the oath to the new administration, as the landdrost Frederik Maré objected to serving the British government.[64] While the court was sitting at Heidelberg, Haggard rode to Pretoria, sixty miles to the north, for a brief visit. Here a stressed Osborn said he might have to request Shepstone 'for my return, as he could not get on in his office alone, the work was too heavy'.

Writing to his mother, Haggard said he would 'personally rather be back in his office' as he wasn't certain of being confirmed as Master and Registrar if Breda died or resigned. The salary of '£400 per annum with pickings' was definitely attractive but had to be offset against the nature of the post, which involved 'a constant battle with three rascally attorneys who want to carry on the same knavery as they did under the last Government'.[65] The three 'rascally attorneys' were the 'legal fraternity' of Potchefstroom, who hailed 'from the Netherlands: Mr G. Buskes, Mr Van Eck and Fred Kleyn'.[66] History would confirm Gerhardus Hendricus Buskes's classification as a rascal.[67]

Haggard rejoined Kotzé, Ford and Juta on the road between Heidelberg and Potchefstroom. Their arrival at the latter town coincided with the October *nachtmaal*, 'a church feast … generally observed three times in the year – in April and October and at Christmastide' when surrounding farmers and their families came to town to take Holy Communion, baptisms and marriages were celebrated, and young people examined and confirmed in membership of the Dutch Reformed Church.[68]

From Potchefstroom the party travelled north to Rustenburg past a range of hills called the Gatsrand (ridge of holes or caves), and visited 'one of the caves of Wonderfontein' with a young farmer as their guide.

> We had each provided ourselves with packets of candles, and by the light of these the moist and glistening stalactite formations presented an unusual and pretty sight. The dripping water from above, charged with lime, had formed numerous pillars of varying thickness … In the centre, about eight feet from the floor, there was an opening in a very thick pillar resembling a pulpit. This evidently made an impression on Haggard, who took a good note of what he saw, for a decade later he well described and immortalized this cave, including the pulpit, in his *King Solomon's Mines*.[69]

North of the Magaliesberg the country 'was far more tropical in appearance than that through which we had previously passed' and they found Rustenburg 'a pretty little town, with its orange and citrus trees in bloom'.[70] There Haggard responded to a letter he had received from his mother. 'We have been leading a curious sort of life for the last two months in the veldt for eight or ten days and then a stint of work then more veldt … It is a savage sort of existence, but it certainly has attractions, shooting your own dinner and cooking it. I can hardly sleep in a house now, it seems to stifle one.'[71] In the letter Haggard also mentioned the murder of Robert Bell – 'I knew him well' – a justice of the peace and border agent in the New Scotland area on the Transvaal border with Swaziland. Bell and eight policemen had been murdered by Swazis on 22 September, shortly after Haggard had passed through the area. 'I do not think that the crime had any political significance, but it will have a bad effect.'[72]

Haggard was 'very much astounded' to hear of his brother Jack's engagement to Etta White, one of two sisters he had taken up with in Tours when the Haggard family were staying there in 1875. It was to be a long engagement – Jack was now on half-pay and without prospects.

He also sent news of war in the Eastern Cape with Sarhili kaHintsa, king of the Gcaleka branch of the Xhosa. 'It is quite possible that we are on the eve of a vast native war. If the natives gain any considerable success there will be a general rising. Cetewayo has for some time been in communication with [Sarhili], which … looks ominous.'[73] This claim was probably an invention of Shepstone's, who saw Cetshwayo as eternally 'encouraging disaffection and disturbance' and 'the root and strength of all native difficulties in South Africa'.[74] Similar sentiments expressed in private communications and public dispatches inexorably moved the authorities to consider invading Zululand. Haggard echoed his master's voice: '[Cetshwayo] has also been trying to enter into an alliance with his old enemies the Swazies, and the Zulus are panting for war.'[75]

The initial stages of the war in the Eastern Cape were fought by colonial troops alongside African levies, but when the fighting flared up into a fully fledged war – the Ninth Cape Frontier War – Frere summoned the imperial troops scattered around the Cape Colony, including the 1/24th Regiment. The war, prosecuted with vigour by Frere, ended in the middle of 1878. During its cruel and bloody course Arthur Cunynghame, Commander-in-Chief of the Army in South Africa, fell victim to colonial politics and was replaced by Frere's friend Lieutenant General Sir Frederic Thesiger.

8

'A CRUSHING BLOW'

Pretoria, October 1877. Hendrik van Breda was still on sick leave in the Cape and Haggard, living in Breda's house, was making do with 'a box for a washstand and a deal table and an iron bedstead whose bottom has irredeemably gone to the bad'.[1] Linen and crockery had arrived from Bradenham and Haggard was glad to hear from his mother that some respectable furniture was on its way.

The Transvaal High Court began sessions in November and Haggard continued as acting Master and Registrar. The job gave Haggard a window into the seamier side of the legal profession, some aspects of which he found profoundly shocking: 'This place has for years been the receptacle for all those gentlemen who were too great blackguards for even the Cape Colony and Natal to put up with and that is saying a great deal. Here they have thriven and grown fat, and they don't at all like the new state of things which throws a little light on their proceedings.' Haggard was unable to find 'a single man' he could trust to do a land valuation in Wakkerstroom. A dose of dysentery added to Haggard's dissatisfactions; he had been 'pulled down a little but am nearly all right now'.[2]

Shepstone was still on the Zulu border. Haggard thought matters wouldn't be settled without an appeal to arms, and 'one last struggle between the black and white races'.

> That it will be a terrible fight there is no doubt for Zulus are brave men ... They are panting for war as they have not 'washed their spears' since the battle of the Tugela [Ndondakusuka] in 1856, when the two brothers fought for the throne ... It will be a magnificent sight to see about 20 000 of these fellows coming sweeping down, but more perhaps picturesque than pleasant. However I have but little doubt that we shall beat them. Besides the thing may blow over. I am going to volunteer this afternoon.[3]

Haggard wasn't volunteering to fight the Zulu, though; volunteer units were being raised to counter threats from the Boers and Sekhukhune's Pedi.

On Friday, 4 January 1878, 'large numbers of Boers' converged on Pretoria to hear Kruger and Jorissen's report-back on their mission to England, and it was rumoured if the report proved 'unsatisfactory they intended to resort to violence'.[4] Early on Saturday afternoon the Boers, 'variously estimated at from 1,100 to 1,500 men, most mounted, and many of them carrying rifles', entered the city. Apart from one of them threatening to shoot the Treasurer, Nicolaas Swart, and another forcing his way into Government House to find Kruger, the crowd behaved 'in a fairly orderly manner and refused to be excited by acts of violence by the agitators who were moving in its midst'.[5] Kruger apologised for Jorissen's absence – he was temporarily out of town – and postponed the meeting until Monday, saying 'he had been received with every kindness by the English Government and that although it was true he had failed to get the country back he had succeeded in every other particular'. Kruger told the assembly they shouldn't be angry with the British government about the annexation, 'but with those "traitors in their midst" who had brought it about'.[6]

It was a tense weekend. Firearms were banned from the Monday gathering, a guard was placed on the Artillery Yard in the military camp, and on Sunday night two seven-pounder guns were positioned on a 'new redoubt which effectively commanded the Boer Camp, round the Dopper Church at the lower end of the Town'.[7]

On Monday morning at ten o'clock the deputation's report was read out to the reassembled burghers. Kruger and Jorissen proposed drawing up a petition 'for signature by burghers throughout the country in order to show that the people were opposed to the annexation'.[8] The mood of the crowd was subdued and they gradually drifted away until 'by four p.m. the Town was empty, and a very serious crisis successfully passed through'.[9]

In Jorissen's absence Lewis Ford had fulfilled 'his duty satisfactorily' as acting Attorney General but 'cherished the misplaced ambition of being raised to the Bench'. Kotzé pointed out that on Jorissen's resumption of duty Ford's appointment ceased and that he had 'no claim whatever to a seat on the Bench'.[10] The friendship forged on the mail coach from Kimberley ended abruptly and the Kotzé family cut the Ford family in public. In court Kotzé expressed unhappiness at 'the grave breaches of professional etiquette by Ford's office' and granted 'a *rule nisi*, ordering Ford to "show cause why he should not be suspended or struck off" the roll'.[11]

February 1878. Shepstone remained on the Zulu border. The 'Zulu business' continued to hang fire. Haggard was in no doubt the 'most pressing danger' was from the Boers: when he came back, Kruger 'was entirely with us, but since his return has become intimidated by the blood and thunder party, and now declares that he considers himself to be still vice president of the country'.[12] The Boers were on the brink of demanding their own government be brought back. When Shepstone finally returned from the Zululand border towards the end of March, he issued what became known as the 'Hold-your-jaw' proclamation declaring the agitators' gatherings illegal. To little effect, for a meeting went ahead on 4 April 1878 at which

Kruger and Piet Joubert were chosen to go to London to make a further appeal 'to Her Majesty's Government by laying indisputable proof before the Secretary of State that the great majority of the people were against the annexation.'[13]

With Boer agitation temporarily tamped down, attention turned to the Pedi. Sekhukhune had taken advantage of British preoccupations with the Zulu and the Boers to deal with some rebellious tributary chiefdoms, including that of the Maserumule, sending an impi to back his sister Lekoglane's claim to the paramountcy. Such aggression could not go unpunished, and Clarke raised a force of volunteers of white and African levies in Lydenburg and reoccupied Fort Weeber. Sekhukhune said he had no quarrel with Clarke and told him to keep his distance. Clarke refused to back off and the Pedi retaliated by raiding farms. The First Anglo-Pedi War had officially begun, but, unable to respond effectively with a largely untrained force, Clarke abandoned Fort Weeber, which the Pedi promptly burnt down.

The uprising played to Shepstone's fears of a native conspiracy between Sekhukhune and Cetshwayo to drive the whites out of southern Africa. When another three companies of the 13th arrived in Pretoria in March, there were sufficient imperial troops for some to be dispatched to the north-eastern Transvaal. Auxiliaries were raised, including a mounted police force under Alfred Aylward, as well as fifty mounted volunteers in Pretoria under Captain Gerrit van Deventer (the Ferreira murder plot whistleblower). Haggard's friend Charles Stewart had returned to the Transvaal after his hunting trip north of the Limpopo, and Haggard was instrumental in getting him a post with a volunteer unit.

A force led by Clarke made up of several volunteer units, including Van Deventer's, the Zulu Police and African levies, attacked the Maserumule stronghold on 5 April. Their mountain fortress proved impervious to assault, at least with the troops at Clarke's disposal, and a further attempt on 6 April met with the same result. One of the casualties was Van Deventer, who died of his wounds. With no choice but to withdraw, Clarke initiated a raiding campaign to destroy crops and starve the Pedi into submission. Stewart took part in an offensive action at Magnet Heights several miles east of Fort Weeber and took over the leadership of the Zulu Police unit when its white officers were wounded.[14] 'It must have been an uncommonly smart action, and not a pleasant thing for a few men to have to hold back … many hundreds of men, as Stewart did for some time.'[15] In June Lekoglane gave up her claim on the Maserumule chieftaincy and sought refuge with her brother Sekhukhune. Imperial troops set up garrisons at Middelburg and Lydenburg.

In the same month the war against the Xhosa in the eastern Cape was winding down and Lieutenant General Thesiger could apply his mind to the Zulu and the Pedi. He ordered the 80th Regiment up to Transvaal and placed Colonel Hugh Rowlands, VC, in charge of all imperial and colonial forces there, including 200 men of the Frontier Light Horse under Major Redvers Buller as well as 500 Swazi auxiliaries which Stewart had been sent to Swaziland to recruit.[16] Haggard and

Osborn also raised 'over 500 natives from Rustenburg to join the Forces'.[17] Confident he now had the troops for the job, Rowlands headed into the Pedi heartland to attack Tsate. Haggard predicted a 'heavy casualty list for the fortifications are very strong', as he well knew from his visit the previous year. 'Stewart and his Swazis will be a great assistance ... for they go over the walls with a rush and care very little for the butcher's bill.'[18]

Haggard hoped to be present for the attack but was unable to obtain leave. However, the attack never took place: the Pedi harassed Rowlands's advancing force, which was further disadvantaged by lack of forage and water due to drought. Then the fever season arrived. 'Operations will now have to stand over until next winter and probably the Zulus, seeing what powerful allies they have in fever and horse sickness will begin.'[19] A successful attack on a Pedi stronghold near Fort Burgers on 27 October salvaged British pride, but the war was over and Rowlands was ordered to redistribute his men along the Zululand border.

'I am one of the marked men who are to be instantly hung on account of that Secocoeni article I wrote.' Haggard's sentiments on the Boers expressed in 'A Visit to Secocoeni' had come back to bite him. 'Some spiteful brute translated it into Dutch with comments and published it in the local papers. The Boers are furious; there are two things they cannot bear – the truth and ridicule.'[20] Not a reassuring announcement for a mother to receive from a son so far away; neither was the postscript: 'I have a pleasing duty to perform early tomorrow – go and see a man executed.'[21]

The man was Mbekane Malaza,[22] a Swazi *indvuna* (Siswati equivalent of *induna*, or councillor) living in the Transvaal in the New Scotland area close to the border with Swaziland. Malaza and some of his retainers were found guilty of the murder of Robert Bell and eight native policemen, which occurred while Haggard was on circuit with Kotzé. The case was tried by Kotzé in December 1877, the jury found all the men guilty of murder, and they were sentenced to death by hanging. Shepstone confirmed Malaza's sentence but commuted those of his men to life imprisonment.

Haggard gives an account of Malaza's execution in his autobiography, describing him as 'a Kaffir chief of high blood ... a most dignified and gentlemanlike person'.[23] Not so the hangman, who was 'hopelessly drunk'. As for the High Sheriff, C.J. Juta, it was all too much and he 'retired into a corner of the yard, where he was violently ill'. The duty to direct proceedings devolved to Haggard. 'So I stood over that executioner and forced him to perform his office. Thus died this brave Swazi gentleman.'[24]

That Malaza was hanged is certain, but the conduct of those involved in his execution is less so. Kotzé claims Haggard's account was 'pure romance, and not in keeping with fact'.[25] The sheriff wasn't 'overcome that morning' to retire 'sick into the corner of the gaol yard, but [Haggard] himself; nor was the hangman intoxicated'.

That Haggard was 'left alone to force the unfortunate hangman to do his duty is wholly imaginary'.[26]

Kotzé softened this judgement, written after Haggard's death, saying he had no desire to suggest that 'my old friend wrote with any intent to misrepresent the truth': Haggard possessed 'an extraordinary mind' but was 'emotional and much given to romancing'.[27] According to Kotzé, Haggard asked if he could be present at the execution. Surprised 'at the strangeness' of the request, Kotzé told him 'it was usual for only those whose duty required it, to be present on such an occasion', but if he had the sheriff's consent, which Haggard did, he could attend. When Malaza was about to be hanged, Haggard 'was overcome and moved away towards the corner of the yard' and the sentence was carried out 'without any hitch'. Later the same day Haggard told Kotzé 'he felt queer and upset and could not look to see the end'. Juta also 'told me [Kotzé] that Haggard's nerves failed him'.[28]

In 1914, when Haggard met Kotzé in Cape Town, he conceded the judge's memory was 'certainly better' than his own. 'Several times he corrected my recollection of particular events, even to the words used in connection with them.'[29]

Hendrik van Breda had returned from Cape Town 'looking worse than ever' and Haggard continued acting as Master and Registrar. When Breda died on 20 March, Haggard was sure he would take over his post 'unless something unexpected occurs'. This was a distinct possibility as there was active opposition to Haggard's appointment, especially as he had been the driver of the rule of court 'making the taxation of every bill of Costs, between Attorney and Client as well as between Party and Party compulsory'.[30] This was something he deemed necessary as some advocates and attorneys took to agreeing to each other's bills of costs and not forwarding them for taxation.

Haggard had won the day and in the first week of April 1878 he saw the official minute appointing him Master and Registrar. 'I believe I am by far the youngest head of Department in South Africa.'[31] Haggard was especially gratified to have 'got the better of those lawyers who petitioned against me'.[32] Despite this, one can't help thinking the lawyers had a case given Kotzé's insistence on legal qualifications. When Haggard began his acting appointment in August 1877, he hadn't 'the slightest knowledge of my work ... nor had I anyone to teach me'. Haggard was confident he had 'to a great extent overcome' these obstacles and 'now I am going to see if I can instil a little honesty within the legal practitioners of the Transvaal'.[33] In a letter to his mother Haggard said Shepstone 'was very civil' when he thanked him for the appointment, 'telling me that it suited me and I suited it, so it was satisfactory for everybody'.

At dinner that evening 'Mr Sargeaunt proposed my health in very flattering terms indeed so it all went off very nicely'.[34] William Sargeaunt, who had worked alongside Shepstone as Colonial Secretary in the 1850s, had left Natal and later became a Crown Agent. It was in this guise, as an auditor of empire, that Sargeaunt came to Pretoria in September 1877. Lord Carnarvon, increasingly perturbed by the Transvaal's empty treasury, dispatched Sargeaunt to investigate the new colony's finances and lend his expertise to Shepstone and compile reports for the Colonial Office.

Meeting Sargeaunt for the first time, Haggard thought him 'a very nice pleasant man, one with a vast deal of experience'.[35] On Sargeaunt's clerical staff was Arthur Cochrane; two months younger than Haggard, he would become a close friend. Sargeaunt was also accompanied by his 20-year-old son John and Captain Robert Patterson, 'a man in early middle life, florid in appearance, and rather stout in person, of an open manner and a genial disposition'. Patterson possessed considerable private means, and in 'an ill-omened moment a desire entered into him to visit what were then the less explored districts of Africa'.[36] He had attached himself in an unofficial capacity to Sargeaunt's mission and spent most of his time with John Sargeaunt, taking 'journeys into the neighbourhood of Secocoeni's country and elsewhere for the purpose of shooting game'.[37] His appetite 'whetted by these pleasant and successful excursions', Patterson determined, before returning to England, to visit the Victoria Falls.[38]

Under the British administration, Pretoria was 'a fairly gay community' and the 'presence of the military with the regimental band helped to make things pleasant. Frequent picnics, riding parties, croquet, and, of an evening, whist and musical "At Homes" … were the usual diversions; while dancing and an occasional ball, given in turn by the townsfolk and the officers of the garrison, made up the amusements of our little capital.'[39] Twice a week the band of the 13th Regiment played 'a selection of music, either in the Market Square or at the flagstaff in camp, and thither the citizens would flock like a Hyde Park crowd'. The male display habits of the young subalterns were particularly noticeable: 'They would appear dressed in mufti of the most extreme fashionable cut, and strut up and down like peacocks, objects of special admiration.'[40] Amateur theatricals 'sought to make up to Pretorians for anything they might be missing on the professional stage' and Haggard 'filled his part well' in *Betsy Baker, or, Too Attentive by Half*, a one-act farce by a master of the genre, John Maddison Morton.[41]

Life at Government House 'was conducted in a simple and homely way'. Both Shepstone and Brooke, his chief of staff, 'understood the art of entertaining and welcoming their guests. Sir Theophilus was very popular, especially with the younger generation, on account of his kindly disposition and fatherly manner, and he was much respected.'[42] He regaled guests with 'after-dinner anecdotes of frontier life on the Cape Border and of his numerous other native experiences', told 'with a clearness and impressiveness that made it a real pleasure to listen to him'.[43]

On the Queen's birthday in 1878, a year after the British flag was flown for the first time over the Transvaal, the soldier, traveller and writer Edward Sandeman was in Pretoria: 'a whole holiday was declared, and every flag in the town was displayed'.[44] Early on the morning of 24 May, after a royal salute, Shepstone reviewed the troops and 'the whole town turned out to look on'. The playing of the national anthem provoked three 'very hearty cheers' for Her Majesty from 'all the Englishmen, with their heads uncovered, although the sun was at 90° in the shade. The Dutch neither cheered nor took off their hats, and looked sullenly on; but did not attempt any anti-demonstration, much as they would have liked to.'[45]

There was a ball and supper at Government House that evening. Shepstone received guests in a 'huge reception room' specially created in front of the house 'by extending canvas from the top of the house verandah to the other side and putting cloth on the ground'. This covered the orange trees and flowering shrubs in the garden as well as full-grown trees from the branches of which 'were suspended rows of Chinese lanterns and other illuminations'. A canvas-covered supper room also opened out of the reception area, which left three ground-floor rooms of Government House free for dancing to the music of the 13th band, 'placed in the verandah'.[46]

Sandeman was struck by the settings and the decor and even more by the feminine fashions: prepared for 'the most extraordinary attempts at ball-dresses' in this colonial backwater, he found instead 'the dresses were as good as at any ordinary English county ball'. Sadly the gentlemen 'were not equally happy in their costumes' but the 'various military uniforms gave a bright colouring to the scene; and on the way home at two o'clock in the morning, we all agreed that there had never been seen a prettier ball or been more thoroughly enjoyed than that on her Majesty's birthday, 1878, at Pretoria.'[47]

Birthday celebrations over, it was back to work. Haggard was drafting a new costing model 'for the benefits of my friends the lawyers ... under the old tariff do what I will I cannot keep the law costs down, they are something enormous, the most trifling case will cost two or three hundred.'[48]

On the domestic front Haggard was resigned to the fact he would have to purchase land and build his own house in order to secure decent accommodation: 'It will be the cheapest way, and by far the most comfortable.'[49] In May Haggard decided 'to build a nice house' with Arthur Cochrane; 'it will be a very sound investment'. Haggard bought 'two acres of land at the top end of the Town where land will soon become very valuable'.[50] Haggard and Cochrane – they referred to themselves as The Firm – moved onto the property towards the end of July, living in hastily constructed stables 'until we up the house'. Haggard asked his mother to send some seeds for the garden and some acorns, hazelnuts 'and a horse chestnut or two ... I want to raise some of the English trees here.'[51]

In early September 1878, when Haggard was on his second court circuit with Kotzé, the building of the house had not yet commenced, but Cochrane had 'moved to the future stable which is acceptable. It will be a precious squeeze there till the house is built, but we have built a lean-to for a kitchen.'[52] The stable grew 'into a sort of cottage' with a 'temporary stable at the back'.[53] In November the two were 'very busy gardening, planting out vines &c.' and, at last, about to begin building, 'but not on our original plan which proved too expensive'.[54] The eventual result was a small two-room cottage with an outside kitchen, ironically christened 'The Palatial'.

A salaried official in a brand spanking new British colony and the prospect of a splendid career ahead, Haggard basked in the 'first years of manhood, when I was connected with great men, and great events'.[55] His heart was buoyed by the thought of Lilly Jackson waiting faithfully for him back in England.

Haggard's entries in his pocket-sized De La Rue 'Indelible Diary and Memorandum Book' for the year 1878 are infrequent and brief: on 9 March, 'Letter from Mary re Lilly', followed the next day by the equally terse: 'Wrote proposal.'[56] Haggard's sister Mary was party to both sides of the romance between Lilly Jackson and her brother, and in her letter she most likely told him Lilly was being courted by a suitor with serious intentions. Haggard countered with a formal proposal to Lilly.

Subsequent diary entries, for 17 and 24 March, record simply: 'Wrote Lilly.'[57] There are no further mentions of her name and no diary entries at all from mid-April until 20 June. Writing of the early part of 1878 in his autobiography, Haggard says his 'love affair ... unexpectedly developed ... with the result that for some little space of time I imagined myself to be engaged and was proportionately happy. Then one day the mail cart arrived and all was over.'[58] Lilly announced she was going to marry the other man.

'It was an ordinary enough tale', comments Lilias. 'Africa was a long way from England and the impecunious man was a long time coming home. The rich and desirable match meanwhile dwelt persistently on the doorstep', an opportunity of which a 'strong-minded elder sister' continually reminded her. 'Perhaps it was not in [Lilly's] gentle and rather stupid character to withstand any particular pressure – perhaps she was not very much in love with Rider, almost certainly she had no idea of the depth and strength of his affection for her.'[59]

The Haggards at Bradenham 'did their best'.[60] When Mary informed her parents of looming disaster, William Haggard, 'warm-hearted and sympathetic as he always was with his children when his temper did not get the better of him', wrote to Lilly and 'offered a home at Bradenham until Rider could get back from Africa'.[61] In *The Witch's Head*, Eva, engaged to the absent hero Ernest Kershaw, is offered 'a home and protection' by Ernest's guardian while being courted by another man. Eva thanks Ernest's guardian 'for his kindness', regretting 'that circumstances and "her sense of duty" prevented her from accepting the offer'.[62] Similarly Lilly: she declined the invitation from Haggard's father and wrote a 'sad little letter' to Rider in Pretoria and 'married the other man'.[63]

Lilly's letter was 'a crushing blow' to Haggard, 'so crushing that at the time I should not have been sorry if I could have departed from the world. Its effects upon me also were very bad indeed, for it left me utterly reckless and unsettled. I cared not what I did or what became of me.'[64] A measure of Haggard's recklessness can be found in *The Witch's Head* when Ernest, in similar circumstances, tells his mentor Alston (an amalgam of Shepstone and Osborn) that Eva 'has thrown me over'. Alston points out

> a shapely Kafir girl passing with a pot of native beer on her head, 'you had better take that Intombi [young woman] to wife than such a woman as this Eva. She at any rate would stand by you in trouble, and if you fell would stop to be killed over your dead body. Come, be a man, and have done with her.'
> 'Ay, by Heaven I will!' answered Ernest.[65]

Citing the above, the Haggard biographer D.S. Higgins speculates that Haggard had a sexual relationship with a black woman. This is a credible enough claim given the place and time. Shepstone, Haggard's chief and mentor, had had such a relationship as a young man and may even have fathered a child.[66] While there is no documentary evidence to support Higgins's conjecture, there is with regard to Haggard having an affair with a married woman, Johanna Ford, the wife of his friend and colleague Lewis Ford.[67] In addition to Haggard's liaison with Johanna Ford, Cochrane was in a relationship with Johanna's sister, 17-year-old Josephine Lehmkuhl.[68]

The beginning of Haggard's affair with Johanna Ford cannot be dated precisely. If, after receiving Lilly's letter, he wrote pleading his cause, the correspondence ceased for certain on Friday, 19 July 1878. On that day Haggard wrote in his diary: 'Heard of Lilly's *Marriage*.'[69] On 4 June 1878 Lilly Jackson married stockbroker Francis Bradley Archer in St James's Piccadilly. A few days after making that diary entry, Haggard left Pretoria on his second court circuit of the Transvaal, returning at the end of September. Haggard must have embarked on his affair sometime between September and the end of the year, as by January 1879 Johanna Ford was pregnant with his child.

On his second court circuit Kotzé was accompanied solely by his Master and Registrar, Haggard, but otherwise the tour was much as the first, a blend of work and pleasure. One morning on their way to Lydenburg from Middelburg while they were hunting in the mountains above the Crocodile River valley, snow began falling. Haggard and Kotzé hastened back to their waggon. By noon they were snowed in and they stayed put for three days, 'making ourselves as comfortable as possible under the circumstances'.[70]

Two days of court business in Lydenburg saw them two days ahead of schedule, so they ascended 'to the high-veld plains by the main road running south to Natal' where the sport began; the veld 'literally swarming with springbok, blesbok and gnu ... Haggard, as usual, provided a first rate dish for supper'.[71]

In Wakkerstroom – staying once again at Anna O'Reilly's 'hospitable and comfortable bungalow' – the court sitting involved 'disputes of boundaries and beacons', some so complex the court had to sit for 'some days at night as well, in order to get through the work in time'.[72] Haggard considered these cases 'the most productive of false swearing and the most lucrative of all cases in this country. Boers are so pig-headed, that egged on thereto by some high principled member of the Bar, they will frequently spend £1000 over a strip of land not worth £350 and only stop when they are ruined'.[73] Such clients were easy pickings for unscrupulous members of the Bar. 'At the present moment two learned counsel are sitting opposite me. One of them fled from justice in the late Colony' while the other, William Emil Hollard, 'began life as a deserter from the German legion, has been imprisoned for theft, has been a gun runner, is accused of every crime in the calendar, murder not excepted, and has been hunted by nearly every Govt.'[74]

At Heidelberg the schedule was a light one and, while Kotzé visited friends, Haggard rode up to Pretoria planning to rejoin Kotzé in Potchefstroom (however, shortly after his arrival he and Osborn, as we have seen, were sent to Rustenburg to raise a native levy to fight the Pedi). Haggard arrived in Pretoria just before Captain Patterson and John Sargeaunt left for the Victoria Falls on their hunting expedition, an adventure now become a diplomatic mission to the Ndebele king, Lobengula kaMzilikazi. A letter, signed by hunters and traders in the Tati goldfields, complaining of their treatment by Lobengula and requesting punitive action, had been passed up the line to Frere and back down again to Shepstone, who appointed Patterson as an official envoy to take a letter to the king informing him that Patterson had been appointed to investigate the verity, or otherwise, of the complaints.

Haggard and Cochrane would have liked to accompany their friends and see the famous falls but were unable to obtain leave and had to content themselves with riding out from Pretoria to the place 'of the first outspan, where we bade our friends goodbye'.[75] Patterson and Sargeaunt were accompanied by Gray Palmer, an 'interpreter, a hunter and guide of experience', and two of Haggard and Cochrane's servants, 'Khiva, a Zulu boy who spoke English perfectly, and Vent-vogel or Wind Bird, a clever Hottentot driver, together with a few other natives'.[76]

As Haggard settled back into life in Pretoria, the full impact of the 'crushing blow' dealt him by Lilly's rejection and her subsequent marriage began to play itself out. An indication of his state of mind can be inferred from a letter to his mother written on 18 November 1878, which was markedly different in tone and style from his usual chatty correspondence:

> The circumstances of my life are so different in all their details that they can hardly interest you, and there are no mutual friends to give you news of. I mention this in

excuse of what must seem to you very stupid and bare-boned letters ... My father will have told you that I proposed coming home if I can manage to get leave. Several reasons have led me to this determination which I will not enter into now, but in addition to these I think I have been away long enough and am I confess getting terribly homesick. People at home don't realise what it is living for years in a far off foreign country among people whose ways are not your ways, and whom you would set down in England as a set of barbarians, never seeing a face that you had known or cared for: living in fact as though you had never had any past. I know that people pooh pooh that sort of thing and rightly, but the fact remains that it tells on a fellow after a year or two, and gives him what is vulgarly known as the 'Blue Devils', a complaint I am suffering from now.[77]

Depression and the complications of his affair with Johanna Ford reinforced Haggard's desire to come home on leave. There is an oblique reference to his affair in the less than enthusiastic response to his father's plan for his ward George Mayes (also known as George Blomefield) to come out to the Transvaal: 'there are many temptations for a young fellow to go to the bad, and few of the restraining home influences to keep him straight'.[78] He feared for Mayes: 'A colony is an awful place to send a young fellow to unless he has something to keep him straight, such as being engaged to some nice girl at home or something of that sort.'[79]

Writing his autobiography over thirty years later, Haggard was still unable to fully confront this period of personal turmoil: 'Here I will leave this subject of which even now I find it painful to write, especially after a morning spent in the perusal of old letters, some of them indited by the dead.'[80] The closest Haggard got to writing about his 'utterly reckless' behaviour in Pretoria was in *The Witch's Head*:

Eva's desertion struck [Ernest's] belief in womanhood to the ground ... He took to evil ways, he forgot his better self. He raced horses, he devoted himself with great success to love-affairs that he would have done better to leave alone. Sometimes, to his shame be it said, he drank – for the excitement of drinking, not for the love of it ... He had no object in life. But at times a great depression and weariness of existence would take possession of him ... he hated life, and in his calmer and more reflective moments he loathed the pleasures and excitements by means of which he strove to make it palatable.[81]

Lilias says her father's response to Lilly's marriage 'increased the mysticism of Rider's nature, convincing him that in this world the perfection of human love and companionship cannot, for more than a very brief period, reach its fruition'.[82] This view Haggard expressed in his first novel *Dawn*:

And surely this holds also good of those who have loved and lost, of those who have been scorned or betrayed; of the suffering army that cry aloud of the empty bitterness of life and dare not hope beyond. They do not understand that having once loved truly it is not possible that they should altogether lose: that there is to their pain and the dry-rot of their hopes, as to everything else in Nature, an end object ... for there are many who have the memory of a lost Angela [read Lilly] hidden away somewhere in the records of their past, and who are fain, in the breathing spaces of their lives, to dream that they will find her wandering in that wide Eternity where 'all human barriers fall, all human relations end, and love ceases to be a crime'.[83]

Lilias is reticent as to detail but acknowledges the life-changing shock of Lilly's rejection upon her father: 'Boy as he was, he learnt what it is to walk through that pitiless country which is entered through the gate of such sorrows. He understood why men took to drink or drugs or any bodily madness – to seek forgetfulness, to stifle that persistent ache which he thought at times had lifted, but oh! bitter deception, awoke and twisted his heart at the broken notes of a bird, a scent, the fragment of a tune.'[84]

Haggard expressed his feelings in *Dawn*: 'although it is, fortunately, not often in the power of any single passion to render life altogether worthless; it is certain that, when it strikes in youth, there is no sickness so sore as that of the heart; no sorrow more keen, and no evil more lasting than those connected with its disappointments and its griefs'.[85] Even if not told by her father, Lilias knew what had occurred in Pretoria: his correspondence and that of others were to hand when writing her memoir: 'there is no doubt "the accursed Amyand blood" was having its fling, the inevitable feminine complications ensued'.[86]

Haggard was not the only person in Pretoria with a complicated personal life; the town's citizens were pruriently anticipating the pending Weatherley vs Weatherley divorce case set down to be heard on 2 November. Colonel Frederick Augustus Weatherley had sued his wife Maria Louisa Weatherley on the grounds of her adultery 'with one Gunn of Gunn, otherwise known as Captain Gunn'.[87]

The origins of the divorce case lay in the equally sensational 'Gunn of Gunn conspiracy case'.[88] The Gunn of Gunn, a Scotsman, more formally Charles Grant Murray Somerset Seymour Stuart Gunn, had come to South Africa 'in order to escape the consequences of having killed a man in a duel'[89] and ended up on the Kimberley diamond fields claiming to be a member of the 13th Hussars and with the 'unblushing impudence to sport, not only the Iron Cross of Prussia, but the Victoria Cross, won, as he asserted, in some hairbreadth Indian adventure'.[90]

In 1876 Gunn responded to Captain von Schlickman's call for volunteers to serve in the Zuid-Afrikaansche Republiek against the Pedi by recruiting 'five decent men and twenty ruffians – the sweepings of Kimberley jail'.[91] In Pretoria Gunn put up at the Edinburgh Hotel, run by a fellow Scot, and set up a recruiting office on the premises, kitting out the 'Gunn Highlanders' in a multi-coloured uniform of his own design.[92] His 'most magnificent idea was when he established two gallowglasses and a piper ... to attend on him as he were indeed a "Lord of the Isles"'.[93]

A nonplussed and eventually exasperated President Burgers sent Gunn and his men on to Fort Burgers near Lydenburg. He carried on much as he had in Pretoria and was arrested. Behind bars Gunn began agitating, making himself out to be 'a much ill-used person'.[94] Transferred to Pretoria, he remained in gaol until the British annexation when, according to one account, he was released under a general amnesty. Gunn immediately set about re-establishing himself as a force to be reckoned with, writing for *De Volkstem* and even standing in for its editor, Jan Celliers, on occasion.[95] When an appointment in Shepstone's administration – something Gunn believed his rightful due – didn't materialise, he turned to intrigue, which brought him into alliance with the similarly aggrieved Frederick Augustus Weatherley.

Colonel Weatherley had served in the Crimean War and the Indian Mutiny. In 1868 he and his wife Maria returned to England, where he was given a command in the Sussex Artillery Volunteers as a lieutenant colonel. In 1872 he invested in the Eersteling Gold Mining Company, formed 'for the purposes of carrying on operations in the district of the Zoutpansberg, in the Transvaal'.[96] In 1875, his investment showing 'decidedly uneven prospects of a return', Weatherley, with his wife and their sons Cecil and Rupert, set out for the Transvaal 'to assess the situation for himself'.[97]

They arrived early in 1876, and it wasn't long before Weatherley joined the Boer republic's forces in their war with the Pedi. When the conflict drew to its inconclusive end, Weatherley settled in Pretoria and became 'a vocal supporter for annexation'.[98] After the annexation Weatherley advised the new administration on 'raising auxiliary forces for local defence' and expected 'to be given a prominent military post' for services rendered. When no post was forthcoming, he took it as a personal slight and became 'a bitter opponent of Shepstone's administration'.[99] Weatherley and Gunn were natural allies and thus began 'a private agitation ... by a few disaffected persons' with the object of having Shepstone removed from office and replaced by Weatherley.[100]

Haggard considered Weatherley 'the dupe of the other conspirators', of which there were four, including the 'good-looking desperado', the Gunn of Gunn.[101] Haggard says Gunn was released from gaol without trial not as a result of any amnesty but because of Weatherley 'interesting himself strongly on his behalf'.[102] On his release Gunn requested that Shepstone 'publish a Government notice declaring him innocent of the charges brought against him'.[103] Shepstone declined to do so. The other two conspirators were an unidentified lawyer 'who felt himself injured because the rules of the High Court did not allow him to practise as an advocate',[104] and *De Volkstem* editor Jan Celliers, who had 'lost the Government printing contract ... Of course, there was a lady in it; what plot would be complete without? She was Mrs. Weatherley.'[105]

The four men petitioned Sir Bartle Frere to remove Shepstone, 'setting forth a string of supposed grievances',[106] and Weatherley went to Cape Town in May 1878 to see Frere in person. With Weatherley safely out of the way, his co-conspirators drew up a second petition. Once this had been signed by the handful of people close to the conspiracy, nobody else was forthcoming, so the conspirators forged 'no less than 3883 signatures, of which sixteen were proved to be genuine, five were doubtful, and all the rest fictitious'.[107] As soon as Weatherley became aware of this outrageous deception, he apologised 'for his share in the agitation'.[108] The lawyer vanished and Celliers continued to edit *De Volkstem*. Gunn was briefly placed under arrest, but there seems to have been no further action taken against him. By then his affair with Mrs Weatherley was public knowledge.

On his return from the Cape, Weatherley's sons – 18-year-old Cecil Paulet and 14-year-old Rupert – told their father 'of their mother's conduct' with Gunn. Weatherley's first response was disbelief, but when his suspicions were aroused 'he determined to obtain proof of her guilt'.[109] Having done so, Weatherley sued for divorce on the grounds of his wife's adultery with Gunn 'at diverse times between the 1st day of June and the 20th day of October, 1878'.[110]

Maria Weatherley was represented in court by none other than Lewis Ford, while her aggrieved husband was represented by Haggard's bête noire, William Emil Hollard, and Advocate Henry Cooper.[111] The case was heard by Kotzé during November and December, with Haggard as court registrar.

The case threw further lurid light on Gunn's conduct. When Weatherley left for Cape Town, Gunn had also 'carried on an improper intercourse with the coloured servant girl Malattie'.[112] The case further exposed Gunn's spurious claims to an illustrious military career. On the stand Gunn said he 'had seen active service and had been on the staff of Lord Napier of Magdala'. A 'skilful cross-examination' by Hollard forced Gunn to admit that his position on Lord Napier's staff 'was that of a common orderly!' This led to Gunn 'challenging the advocate to a duel with pistols. The challenge was promptly accepted by Hollard, who had been a member of the German legion and accustomed to the smell of powder.' The parties turned up at the appointed time and place with their seconds, 'but, as might have been expected, the valiant Gunn of Gunn offered Hollard an apology, and thus ended the fiasco'.[113]

Kotzé delivered his judgment on 20 January 1879.[114] By then Ford's wife Johanna was pregnant with Haggard's child.

On a blank page of his 1878 pocket diary, Haggard wrote the date 20 January 1879 and noted 'Weatherley judgement delivered',[115] adding that Frederick Broome had invited him to Mauritius where Broome was now Colonial Secretary. 'I have half a mind to go there and fly from the devil.'[116] There was much for Haggard to fly from. Quite apart from his chaotic personal life, the British had invaded Zululand in mid-January. Weatherley was directly involved in the preparations for the war. Indeed, shortly after he sued for divorce, he had been commissioned by Lieutenant General Thesiger, now Lord Chelmsford following the death of his father in October, to raise a body of volunteers 'for service against the Kafirs'[117] and 'formed a unit of 150 men initially known as "Weatherley's Border Lances" (not Lancers, as is often given), commonly called the Border Horse'.[118]

The Weatherley divorce case was well under way in early December when Gray Palmer, guide and interpreter for Patterson and Sargeaunt's trip to Matabeleland, arrived back in Pretoria, bearing tragic news which Haggard recorded in his diary: 'Heard of Patterson's and Jack's death, a truly awful calamity. I was the last of us that saw them alive.'[119]

Patterson and his party were received by King Lobengula at Bulawayo on 10 September. When the monarch proved unreceptive to Shepstone's letter, Patterson made the mistake – either as a threat or a none too subtle warning – of mentioning the name of a rival heir to the Ndebele throne: Kuruman, the gardener employed by Shepstone in Pietermaritzburg.[120] With his diplomatic duty done, Patterson continued with his original intention of seeing the Victoria Falls, and so Patterson, Sargeaunt and Evan Morgan Thomas, son of the missionary Thomas Morgan Thomas, who had joined them at Lobengula's homestead, plus Khiva and Ventvögel with twenty guides and bearers provided by Lobengula, headed off on the twelve-day journey to the famous falls. They did not return.

The first reports to reach Pretoria said the party had died from drinking from a waterhole poisoned to trap game. According to another account, a group of local people terrorised by Patterson's Ndebele escort had gone ahead of the party and poisoned the waterhole. Then news reached Shepstone that Patterson's party had died as the result of an accident. The truth finally emerged when Palmer, who had remained behind at Lobengula's homestead, returned to Pretoria. Patterson, Sargeaunt, Thomas, Khiva and Ventvögel had been assegaied by their Ndebele escort on the orders of Lobengula. The story of the Patterson expedition would become a key ingredient of *King Solomon's Mines*.

9

'DISASTER IN ZULULAND'

The year 1879 was one of war in southern Africa. It began peacefully enough in Pretoria with the advent of the inaugural Anglican bishop of the Transvaal. The imposing six-foot, two-inch Henry Brougham Bousfield had been consecrated the first Bishop of Pretoria at St Paul's in London on 2 February 1878. Haggard was amused by reports of Bousfield's farewell speeches in England, judging from which the bishop 'seems to think he is going to a place "where cannibals with eager feet welcome the man they mean to eat" ... The idea English people have of their colonies and the inhabitants thereof is certainly a curious one.'[1]

Bousfield was delayed in Natal as there was a lack of forage for trek-oxen after a dry winter was succeeded by summer drought. They began their journey to the Transvaal on 3 December, arriving on 7 January 1879, when they outspanned on the rise above the Aapies River and saw a 'party with a carriage and horsemen ... drawing towards them in a cloud of dust'.[2] Among them were Haggard and Godfrey Lagden. The 26-year-old Lagden, son of an Anglican parish priest, who, lacking 'influential family connections or academic talent ... seemed destined for a humble career'[3] and, after schooling at Sherborne, had become a post office clerk before throwing it up to come to the Transvaal, where he obtained a clerical post in the new administration. He became part of Haggard and Cochrane's circle and was a frequent hunting partner. He subsequently married one of Bishop Bousfield's daughters, Rebekah Francis.[4]

The carriage was a four-seater spider driven by its owner, Henry Cooper, accompanied by John Kotzé and the Reverend Arthur Law, the senior Anglican priest in Pretoria, who was clutching an address of welcome for the bishop. The bishop and his wife Charlotte transferred to the spider for the drive into Pretoria. As they splashed across the Aapies River, Kotzé remarked: "'Bishop, you are now within the town." The Bishop exclaimed: "Pretoria, henceforth thou art a city, for I am in thee!" Cooper nudged my knee and flicked the horses, while I was highly amused.'[5] Unfortunately Haggard left no record of what he thought of the bishop on meeting him. He was very likely preoccupied with his personal predicaments while his letters from this period are dominated by war with the Zulu, whose opening moves were playing out while the bishop and his cavalcade trekked to Pretoria.

War with the Zulu had long been a subject of Haggard's correspondence. Writing to his father on 13 April 1878, Haggard declared 'this country will never really go ahead till we have finally settled the Zulu question'.[6] Delaying matters were a number of factors, including Boer agitation over the British annexation and the Pedi threat in the northern Transvaal. And where did the Swazi stand? With their friendship towards the Boers wavering, if they patched up their differences with the Zulu, all three indigenous peoples could make a concerted attack on the Boers – the native conspiracy of Shepstone's and Frere's imaginings. 'War here between white and black is a terrible thing,' commented Haggard.[7] The only time Haggard recalled Shepstone being angry with him – 'for he was very tender to my faults' – was when Haggard suggested that the Transvaal would be better left unannexed. '"Then," I said, "the Zulus and the Boers will destroy each other, and the Transvaal will fall like a ripe apple into the lap of Great Britain."' Shepstone was furious and angrily demanded of Haggard whether he understood what he was saying as 'such a policy would mean the destruction of thousands of white men, women and children by the Zulu assegais, to be followed probably by a great war between white and black'.[8]

With the benefit of hindsight, Haggard thought his opinion, 'tainted though it may have been with the callousness of youth', was 'absolutely sound'.

> For what happened? First we had to fight the Zulus and slaughter them by thousands, paying no small toll ourselves, and then we had to fight the Boers, not once, but twice. If we had allowed them to exhaust themselves upon each other the total loss of life would have been no greater, if so great, and the settlement of South Africa would have been effected without the shedding of British blood; moreover, in the end the Boers would have implored our assistance and gladly have accepted our rule.[9]

The Ninth Cape Frontier War had ended in August; it had taken over a century and a quarter before the Cape's eastern frontier was finally pacified. Sir Bartle Frere, the British High Commissioner, could now concentrate on the confederation of southern Africa; the Zulu were the final obstacle in his view, but he was blind to the fact that the disaffected Boers of the Transvaal and those of the still independent Free State constituted an even greater obstruction. Perhaps confederation had always been a dream too far, no more so than the present when Lord Carnarvon, its main proponent, was no longer Colonial Secretary, having resigned in January 1878. With Carnarvon gone, the British government's desire for confederation evaporated. His successor, Sir Michael Hicks Beach, considered its achievement highly unlikely and preferred peace with the Zulu.

When, to Frere's horror, Bulwer's Boundary Commission decided in favour of the Zulu, a hoped-for *casus belli* disappeared. Frere suppressed the commission's findings and sent up a smokescreen of prevarication while continuing preparations for war.

More British troops were sent to Natal, ostensibly for defence, Frere overruling the objections of Henry Bulwer, the Natal Governor, who rightly suspected they would be deployed to invade Zululand. Lord Chelmsford set up his headquarters in Pietermaritzburg in August 1878 and Frere banked on the swift subjugation of Zululand, swift enough to take advantage of the time-lagged telegraphic communications between Cape Town and London so as to present the Colonial Office with a fait accompli.

Shepstone obligingly exaggerated the Zulu danger: 'At this moment the Zulu power is a perpetual menace to the peace of South Africa.'[10] Cetshwayo was well aware of these aggressive developments thanks to his own spies and his channel of communication with Bishop Colenso, through whom he made his desire for peace known, appealing to Bulwer: 'the English are my fathers, I do not wish to quarrel with them, but to live as I have always done, at peace with them'.[11]

The findings of the Boundary Commission remained under wraps, while Frere claimed he was awaiting Shepstone's comments: a spurious excuse to buy time and cook up an ultimatum which would force the Zulu onto the battlefield. Alleged transgressions of promises made by Cetshwayo at his 'coronation' by Shepstone in 1873 formed the basis of a document to be handed to the Zulu simultaneously with the findings of the Boundary Commission. Bulwer was bullied into acquiescence.

On 11 December 1878 a delegation, headed by Shepstone's brother John, Natal's acting Secretary for Native Affairs, with Frederick Fynney as interpreter, met with their Zulu counterparts on the Natal bank of the Lower Drift on the Thukela. After first announcing the good news – the finding of the Boundary Commission – they presented the Zulu delegation with an ultimatum: a list of demands, including the abolition of the Zulu regimental system and others undermining the authority of the king; demands impossible to meet, as compliance would destroy the very fabric of Zulu society. War was inevitable.

On 11 January 1879 the British invaded Zululand in a pincer movement, attacking with columns from the north-west, the west and the south. Cetshwayo ordered his commanders to drive the British back into Natal but not to pursue them across the Natal border. 'It is the whites who have come to fight me in my own country', he said, 'and not I that go to fight with them. My intention is only to defend myself in my own country'.[12]

On the morning of 22 January, Lord Chelmsford, accompanying the central column, moved out of a temporary camp below the mountain of Isandlwana with a strong force. Natal African troops under Colonel Durnford were ordered up from Rorke's Drift to reinforce the camp; they constituted nearly half of the forces at Isandlwana, while the rest were imperial troops and colonial volunteer units. A Zulu attack on the camp was thought unlikely, but the unlikely happened and the defenders of the camp were all but annihilated. Encouraged by the victory, a Zulu impi disobeyed the king's orders and crossed the Mzinyathi (Buffalo) River into

Natal to attack the British post at Rorke's Drift, but was repulsed. Another British column was cut off and besieged in Eshowe. A fourth column commanded by Colonel Evelyn Wood halted at Kambula. A fifth was held in reserve near Lüneburg on the north-west border of Zululand. The invasion stalled. Frere was denied his swift victory; he had gambled and lost, 'and proved to be an extraordinarily bad loser, spending the rest of his life insisting upon the rectitude of his actions'.[13]

Two days after the Zulu victory at Isandlwana, on the morning of 24 January, Haggard, enjoying an 'after-breakfast pipe' in the garden of 'The Palatial' heard 'the shrill voice of an old Hottentot washerwoman vehemently explaining something' to the cook prior to emerging from the tin-roofed kitchen with a bundle of laundry.[14] Haggard asked what news she brought. '"Ah, Baas," she answered, "bad news, very bad. Cetywayo the King has attacked the *rooibaatjes* (red-jackets – *i.e.*, English soldiers) down yonder in Zululand and killed them by hundreds. Yes, yes, they lay like leaves upon the plain, red winter leaves – steeped in blood."' The startled Haggard showed no sign of surprise 'as it is not wise to betray emotion when talking to black people'. British upper lips must remain stiff at all times. How could she know this as 'the Government have no news of such a thing?'[15]

> 'It was told me, Baas,' she answered, and no more would she say.
> 'Then a lie was told you, old vrouw, for where is the man who can run, or the horse that can gallop, over more than three hundred miles of veldt in thirty hours even to bring bad news?'
> 'As you will, Baas,' she answered good-naturedly; 'a lie was told me – oh, yes, a lie was told; but all the same the *rooibaatjes* lie dead.'[16]

Masuku saddled up Black Billy, another favourite horse, and Haggard rode off to the government offices to see Osborn and find out if 'the Government had any such intelligence, to which he replied "None"'. Greatly relieved, Haggard responded by saying it 'must be nonsense for the news could never have reached here in the time', there being no telegraph in 1879.

> 'Don't you be so sure of that, young man,' [Osborn] replied. 'The Kaffirs have ways of sending messages of which we know nothing.'
> 'Yes, we do,' I answered, 'they call them from hill to hill: but there are no hills on the high veldt, so it must be nonsense, unless it is magic.'
> 'Never be cocksure about anything in this wide world, my boy,' said my mentor, oracularly, and we parted.[17]

In his autobiography Haggard claimed to have expected the 'disaster' of Isandlwana and wrote to friends in England 'prophesying that it would occur'. To 'their great astonishment' the reception of his letter coincided with the telegraphic message bringing 'news of the great destruction'. He credited his foresight 'to the training that I had received under those who knew the Zulus better than any other men in the world'.[18] Haggard prophesied, others dreamt: 'a lady I knew in Pretoria' dreamt 'she saw a great plain in Zululand on which the British troops were camped. Snow began to fall on the plain, snow that was blood-red, till it buried it and the troops. Then the snow melted into rivers of blood.'[19] Was the dreamer Johanna Ford? Haggard's affair with her was well under way by this time.

One wonders if Haggard recalled the conversation between Shepstone and Phakade back in 1876 when the chief acknowledged that though the British might defeat the Zulu, there would first be 'a very great killing'.[20] Phakade's warriors fought on the side of the British as part of the Natal Native Contingent, playing a critical role in the battle at the centre of the line where the two companies of the Chunu were exposed to the full fury of the Zulu attack. In all, 243 Chunu were either killed or missing in action, 80 per cent of their strength. Phakade lost his son and heir Gabangaye, whom Haggard had met, and his grandson Mbonjana. Phakade was shocked at this huge blow and, stricken with grief at the loss of his son, he sought the refuge of a remote homestead while his people turned to mourning. He died a year later in 1880.

The official report of the Zulu victory at Isandlwana reached Pretoria on 26 January. Haggard wrote a terse letter to his father telling him of 'the terrible disaster that has befallen our troops in Zululand ... I suppose most white men will have to turn out especially if the Boers join the Kafirs. Don't be alarmed however and don't publish this.'[21] How not to be alarmed? Shepstone had lost a son, George, a captain in the Natal Carbineers. Others who died were Osborn's son-in-law, Edward Hitchcock, quartermaster of the Newcastle Mounted Rifles (he ran the popular Newcastle Hotel in civilian life), and another well-known Newcastle figure, Captain Robert Bradstreet.[22]

In a more composed letter written on 31 January, Haggard said 'it was the old story of underestimating your enemy'[23] and described how Lord Chelmsford on the morning of 22 January had split his force and left the camp 'under the command of Colonel Durnford', a friend and supporter of Bishop Colenso and now, conveniently dead, the scapegoat for the defeat, who

> though a nice fellow personally was a headstrong rash man, and irony of fate, a violent Zulu partisan, instead of at once drawing the wagons into a park, marched out with his whole force, in open order, and gave battle about a mile from the Camp ... the Zulus came on with that terrible dash of theirs. In vain the troops mowed them down by hundreds, others filled their places. They assegaaied the gunners at the guns, they cut up the native contingent which appears to have fought well, killing Colonel Durnford and George Shepstone and many others, and finally drove them back, fighting in little knots, first to the Camp, then through it, then down to the banks of the [Mzinyathi River] where a last stand was made, then into it, where they were drowned.[24]

In Utrecht, 50 miles north-west of the battlefield, Shepstone received news of the Zulu victory and the death of his son within a day. He wrote to Osborn: 'the blows which Providence inflicts must be borne. I cannot help thinking, however, that had they taken the simple precaution of turning their wagons into a defensive laager, the catastrophe would not have happened'.[25]

Haggard told his parents he would 'very likely go down to the border with a Volunteers' Troop shortly. The emergency is too grave, and mounted men are too urgently needed, for us to hang back now, especially when one's example may bring others.' Haggard and Lagden had set about raising a mounted corps; so far they had twenty-two volunteers, twelve of whom were English officials – so many that Haggard doubted Shepstone would allow them to go. 'However I intend to go if I can, for I think it is the duty of us Englishmen to set an example ... and if anything should happen to me, it must and I am sure will be your consolation that it will be doing my duty.'[26]

The citizens of Pretoria were stunned by the Zulu victory at Isandlwana. Business was suspended, 'and the streets were filled with knots of men talking, with scared faces, as well they might: for there was scarcely anybody but had lost a friend, and many thought that their sons or brothers were among the dead on that bloody field'.[27] Haggard knew 'many of the officers of the 24th who fell', particularly mourning his friend 'the gallant Coghill',[28] who died with Lieutenant Teignmouth Melvill on the banks of the Mzinyathi while attempting to save the 24th Regiment's Queen's Colour.[29] Haggard also knew one of the handful of British officers to survive the battle of Isandlwana, Captain Edward Essex of the 75th (Stirlingshire) Regiment, a special service officer appointed director of transport, who described his flight from the battlefield to Haggard: 'All he could recall was a kind of refrain which came into his mind. It ran "Essex, you ------ fool, you had a chance of a good billet at home, and now, Essex, you are going to be killed!"'[30] His escape earned him the nickname 'Lucky' Essex.

In Pretoria the immediate response to the British reversal was, as Haggard indicated in his letter, to raise a volunteer corps. Haggard, Lagden and a colleague, Richard Kelsey Loveday, a clerk in the Deeds Office, 'took a very active part in the raising of this corps'.[31] Haggard was elected adjutant of what became the Pretoria Horse, and 'one of the two lieutenants, the captain being a Mr R. Jackson, a colonial gentleman of great experience'.[32]

A call went out for reinforcements from Britain as well as British colonies closer to hand, including Mauritius, where Frederick Broome, now acting Governor as well as Colonial Secretary, judged the situation 'sufficiently desperate to justify sending almost the entire Mauritian Army to the aid of the colonists'.[33] Lady Barker organised a fund to buy medical supplies for the relief of the sick and wounded. She would later describe the Anglo-Zulu War as one 'which many people think was both cruel and unnecessary and which never need have happened at all'.[34]

The Pretoria Horse were initially ordered to proceed to Zululand as part of Weatherley's Border Horse,[35] but when Weatherley and his men left Pretoria for the Zululand border on 30 January, Haggard and his fellow volunteers were not among them. Their orders had been countermanded as the Boers, seeing their chance while the British were occupied in Zululand, were threatening rebellion 'so vigorously that it was deemed necessary to retain us for the defence of Pretoria'.[36]

Haggard stood among the cheering crowds when the Border Horse rode out of the city, Weatherley at their head riding alongside his 14-year-old son Rupert.[37] That the Pretoria Horse's original orders were revoked 'was fortunate' for Haggard and his fellow volunteers 'since otherwise in all human probability our bones would now be rotting beneath the soil of Zululand'.[38] After taking part in raiding operations, the Border Horse were ordered to Colonel Evelyn Wood's camp at Khambula from where on 28 March they rode out to take part in the action at Hlobane, at which forty out of the fifty-five members of the Border Horse were killed, including Weatherley and his son Rupert.[39]

An indirect casualty of the war was Theophilus Shepstone. Sargeaunt's report on the Transvaal's finances suggested 'matters were so shaky that crown colony rule should perhaps be set up'.[40] Shepstone had been unable to collect taxes, failed to conciliate the Boers, and proved unable to remove the Pedi threat. Frere was 'at his wit's end with Shepstone's inability to get to grips with governance in the Transvaal' and in August 1878 agreed with Hicks Beach that Shepstone be replaced.[41] Frere was damning in his comments on Shepstone in correspondence with the Colonial Office. This was a singular betrayal considering Shepstone had been a willing ally in furthering the Governor's agenda. Shepstone was recalled, Hicks Beach requesting he 'come home on leave and consult with me', and was replaced temporarily with Major Owen Lanyon, 'who has administered Griqualand with energy and ability'.[42] A dour, humourless Irishman and ardent dispenser of discipline, Lanyon could be relied on to give short shrift to troublemakers; he had put down rebellion by the Griqua, Batlhaping and other dispossessed peoples with brutal efficiency.

Shepstone continued to play an active role in the run-up to the Anglo-Zulu War and, though he knew his 'recall' would be permanent, he was reluctant to let go the reins of power and influence, writing to Lanyon that he was 'in no great hurry'[43] and wouldn't dream of departing before briefing him in Pretoria.[44] When Lanyon took up his post on 11 February 1879, Shepstone 'finally made a low-key rather pathetic exit from the Transvaal'.[45] He left in May 1879 for England, where, as with the Langalibalele affair, 'he miraculously escaped responsibility for the conflict in Natal'.[46] This time Frere was the preferred sacrificial victim. He refused to take any responsibility and consequently died 'a slow and agonising political death in public'.[47]

In February 1879 some Boer farmers living about twenty-five miles north of Pretoria encountered an impressive Zulu who claimed he was a chief induna (councillor) of King Cetshwayo sent by his king at the head of an impi 'between twenty and thirty thousand men, to fall upon Pretoria and destroy it utterly'.[48] After delivering his message, the man departed. The story was credible, for a Zulu army could well have moved north-east without being detected. Haggard was ordered to mount and parade his men. The men were inexperienced, the horses half-broken, and the result was chaos: a sergeant major was taken to hospital and the injured treated on the spot by the corps's doctor.

Later that night a guard on the outskirts of town fired his rifle, the agreed signal in the event of a Zulu onslaught. 'But no Zulus came, and when at dawn we sallied forth to search the surrounding country, the red rays of the rising sun fell only on the green veldt and the rocky hills, instead, as we half feared, of being reflected from the broad blades of twenty thousand stabbing assegaais'.[49] There was no Zulu army. The whole thing had been a hoax. Given that 'tidings of slaughter reached us nearly every day – also that news of the Zulu advance into the white man's country was hourly expected – it is not wonderful that even those best qualified to judge were deceived by this tale of Cetywayo's impi'.[50]

Zulu warriors might be illusory, but disgruntled Boers were not. Kruger and Joubert had returned from London on 11 January 1879, their mission a failure. News of 'our disaster' at Isandlwana was received by the Boers 'with great and unconcealed rejoicing, or at least by the irreconcilable portion of that people', according to Haggard. 'England's necessity was their opportunity, and one of which they certainly meant to avail themselves.'[51] Notices were issued summoning the burghers of the Transvaal to attend a mass meeting on 18 March. About 3,000 Boers assembled 30 miles north of Pretoria and 'formed a semi-permanent armed camp' at Salt Pan.

Haggard and 'six or eight picked men' were sent to Ferguson's Hotel five miles south of the camp, from where British spies 'crept out and reported to me what had taken place during the day'.[52] This information was sent by messenger to Pretoria, a relay of fresh horses and riders ensuring the news reached the capital across rough country in about an hour. The Boers got wind of what was going on and a group 'from thirty to fifty men ... rode to the inn fully armed, with the avowed intention of shooting us'.[53] The Boers entered Ferguson's and 'stormed and threatened'. Haggard had ordered his men to do nothing 'unless we were actually attacked, when all had liberty to sell their lives as dearly as they could'. Haggard 'sat in my little room surveying them through the open door', pretending to be engaged in 'some ordinary occupation, such as reading or writing'.[54] The tense stand-off was on the verge of a deadly climax when a Sergeant Glynn saved the situation. A Boer in mid-harangue paused to light his pipe and threw the lit match on the wooden plank floor. Glynn quickly seized the match, 'blew it out, and exclaimed in tones of heartfelt gratitude and relief, "Dank Gott!" (Thank God!) "For what do you thank God, Englishman?"' Glynn said if he hadn't blown out the match they would all be 'in small pieces' as the British government had 'stored two tons of dynamite under that floor'. '"Allemagte!"(God Almighty) said one of them. "Allemagte!" echoed the others ... In a few minutes not one of them was to be seen.'[55]

Shortly after this incident Haggard was relieved by Lieutenant Fry and returned to Pretoria. Fry had been at Ferguson's Hotel no 'more than a day or two before he and all his troopers were hunted back into Pretoria by a large mob of armed Boers whom they only escaped by very hard riding'.[56]

By degrees the Boers were edging closer to Pretoria 'till at last they pitched their laagers within six miles, and practically besieged it'. Commerce came to a halt, 'houses were loopholed and fortified, and advantageous positions were occupied by the military and the various volunteer corps'. The Pretoria Horse occupied a building normally used for stabling government mules but transformed it into a fort, sinking a well and building bastions 'for sharp-shooters'.[57] Word came that several thousand Boers were marching on Pretoria. Jackson and Fry were on duty elsewhere and Haggard was in charge of the corps. He posted the best shots, Cochrane among them, 'upon the upper platform, and the rest at the loopholes we had prepared upon the ground floor and upon the little external bastions'.[58] They stood to until dawn, when the news came that 'the Boers had drawn off, leaving Pretoria unmolested, after which we went to bed feeling as flat as ditch water'.[59]

In mid-April 1879 Frere visited the Transvaal to meet Boer leaders and assist Lanyon in overhauling the administration. Haggard commanded the guard of honour escorting the Governor into Pretoria. New to soldiering and totally untrained, Haggard was 'not well acquainted with the ceremonial words of command'. When Frere came in sight, he correctly 'ordered the corps to present arms' but had forgotten the order that followed. Eventually he shouted '"Put 'em back again!" Well, it served. The Pretoria Horse grinned and the arms went back.'[60]

Frere spent a fortnight in Pretoria and met the Boer leaders, including Kruger, several times; they demanded independence and submitted a petition to that effect. Frere handled the situation well and, though he conceded nothing, was conciliatory enough to earn the respect of the Boers. Haggard suggested the reason for the eventual Boer acceptance of the existing status quo was that the end of the Anglo-Zulu War was in sight, which meant there would soon be 'plenty of troops available to suppress any attempt at revolt, but they also saw to what lengths they could go with impunity ... The lesson was not lost on them; but they postponed action till a more favourable opportunity offered.'[61]

The advent of so many imperial troops into southern Africa rendered the Pretoria Horse redundant. Haggard's brief military career came 'to a sudden end, for which I was sorry, for I had found the occupation congenial'.[62]

Haggard met Frere on several occasions, both on an official basis and socially. Frere and his mother 'had been friends when they were young together in India'[63] and he was also a schoolfellow of his father. Frere 'was very civil to me and asked me to remember him most kindly to my Father and yourself', Haggard told his mother. 'They say however that he intends to get rid of all the annexationists to please the Boers.'[64] Pleasing the Boers was something Haggard had signally failed to do in his published articles. Frere had read them and 'rightly reproached me for my indiscretion'. In his defence Haggard said he had written nothing but the truth. '"Haggard," [Frere] said in his suave voice, "do you not know that there are occasions on which the truth is the last thing that should be uttered? I beg you in future to keep it to yourself."' Haggard conceded Frere's censure 'was well deserved'.[65]

Before departing for Cape Town, Frere confirmed Lanyon's appointment. Shepstone, now in England, realised Frere had avoided visiting the Transvaal until he was out of the picture. This deliberate slight was the final straw and the 62-year-old Shepstone decided on retirement. Despite this, he would continue to exert influence over political affairs in Natal behind the scenes, through his brothers Offy and John and his friend Melmoth Osborn.

With Lanyon as Administrator, a new order came to power in the Transvaal. Godfrey Lagden was appointed Lanyon's private secretary, and it was probably through him that Haggard and Cochrane learnt which way the wind was blowing and that the time had come for them to make their exit. Quite apart from a new regime, it had become 'obvious that they would be better out of Pretoria'.[66] Ford's wife Johanna was pregnant by Haggard, and Cochrane was in a complicated relationship with Johanna's sister Josephine.

Following the defeat at Isandlwana, the Anglo-Zulu War went into a holding pattern, the British regrouping and skirmishing while awaiting reinforcements from Britain. In mid-March the British and the Zulu returned to the offensive. Zulu irregulars – estimated between 800 and 4,000 – overran 'a convoy and its escort of men from No. 5 column' at the Ntombe River drift on 12 March, killing 61 British soldiers, a civil surgeon, 2 white waggon conductors and 15 black drivers.[67] On 28 March there was a running battle on the mountain of Hlobane when the Zulu army, advancing towards Wood's camp at Khambula, 'cut off and routed the British raiding the mountain for cattle'.[68] As we have seen, Weatherley's Border Horse was annihilated, and the British lost over 200 men. The following day a Zulu force attacked Wood's entrenched position at nearby Khambula and sustained heavy losses. The tide had turned in favour of the British. Haggard was not impressed. 'I suppose there must be great glorification at home over the Kambula affair, though in reality there is little cause for satisfaction. The blunder of the day before [at Hlobane] is far worse than that of [Isandlwana] ... It is blunder, blunder, blunder, all through the piece.'[69]

Haggard and Cochrane resigned at the end of May 1879. In his letter of resignation Haggard stated he was resigning 'for private reasons only' since the post was one, had 'circumstances permitted, I should have been proud to continue to fill'.[70] His mother's poor health was one reason, as he had received a letter from his father telling him if he 'did not come and see her quickly I might never see her again at all'.[71] The official response to Haggard's resignation came from Osborn: 'his Excellency ... regrets that the Government should lose the services of an officer who has performed difficult duties so satisfactorily'.[72] Formality was strictly for the record, for informally Osborn, Haggard and Cochrane had come to a mutually beneficial arrangement. Haggard and Cochrane bought Osborn's farm in Natal, a small estate called Rooi Point just outside Newcastle, which Osborn had acquired in the 1860s when magistrate at Newcastle and where he built a farmhouse named Hilldrop.[73] The sale price for the farm was initially £1,500 but Osborn reduced it to £1,400. Haggard and Cochrane paid '£1000 down and 400 at eight months'.[74] They postponed selling 'The Palatial' in the hope it would rise in value, and opted to rent it out. Their first tenants were members of the Schwikkard family.

Haggard and Cochrane intended leaving Pretoria in the first week of June; thereafter Haggard would stay 'about a month on the farm, and then come on home' for a holiday, leaving Cochrane to manage the farm. He would be returning to England with Osborn's 16-year-old son Jack in tow – 'I have got to put him to school in England' – and was considering sending him to the Reverend Henry Graham at Garsington.[75] Haggard's plans, his resignation and the purchase of the farm, were well in motion when he wrote to his father on 19 May. Not wanting a repeat of the events of 1878, he made sure everything was accomplished well before his father received his letter. 'Believe me father I am acting wisely in taking this step. Several more of the officials have followed our example and resigned. Unless they do something they will soon have nobody left.'[76]

Haggard assured his father that Shepstone approved of his resignation and 'never supposed I should always stop in the service as it was simply "starvation"' but thought 'I should go in for being a lawyer and that is why he appointed me Registrar'.[77] Haggard would have done so but for reservations about obtaining local qualifications. The farm was 'a charming place, and I think if we can settle anywhere we should there, for it has many advantages – Mr Osborn advises us to go in chiefly for ostriches'.[78] The property's development potential was bright: 'In a few years' time when the railway reaches Newcastle a great deal of that land can be cut up for villa residences.' He also mentioned that Shepstone, who would be 'in England very shortly', was 'well acquainted with Roy [Rooi] Point, and there is not a better judge of land in the country'.[79]

As might be expected, Haggard's resignation was 'not popular at home when they heard of it, he had done extremely well, and his future seemed assured. By the time they did hear, everything was settled.'[80] In Pretoria Chief Justice Kotzé expressed his regret at losing Haggard's services and also gave Haggard some extra ammunition for use when he arrived at Bradenham: 'The Civil Service in the Transvaal offers no inducement for young men of ambition or ability, and hence farming if properly conducted affords a far better prospect to those willing and able to work.'[81]

Richard Loveday, Haggard's comrade in the Pretoria Horse, succeeded him as Master and Registrar, and prior to Haggard's departure the solicitors of Pretoria gave a public dinner in recognition of Haggard's work. Meanwhile Kotzé was preparing for the year's court circuit; he was to be accompanied by Bishop Bousfield, 'desirous of visiting his clergy and people in the outlying parishes', and Henry Cloete, who 'was to act as Crown Prosecutor'.[82] On the day of his departure Kotzé sent the waggons on ahead before riding out with the bishop, Cloete and Haggard. 'It was his last ride with me ... I was sorry to part with him, for Haggard was an efficient Master and Registrar, as well as a pleasant and genial companion.'[83]

An entry in Lagden's pocket diary on 7 June 1879 records: 'Cochrane and Haggard left'.[84] The two rode south to 'a Boer stead somewhere in the neighbourhood of where Johannesburg now stands'[85] and bought eight ostriches, 'fine two-year-old birds, about 7ft high'.[86] These were to be herded 200 miles across country to Hilldrop by 'our factotum Baker',[87] specially hired for the job. On their way to Newcastle, Haggard and Cochrane stayed with the Schwikkards in Standerton, where it was arranged that if trouble broke out in the Transvaal, as Haggard 'confidently expected', they were to come and stay at Hilldrop.[88]

By the middle of June, Haggard and Cochrane were at the farm awaiting the arrival of their ostriches and settling into their new home. The farmhouse was

an extremely good one, well-built, and finished, with kitchen, stable and waggon house outside ... charmingly situated about two miles from the mining town of Newcastle, under the lee of a big hill that shelters it from all the high winds that are so unpleasant in Natal. From the windows I can as I write, see thirty miles, right to the Utrecht mountains that bound the horizon ... All the grounds are planted with syringa groves and orange trees, that will grow nowhere else in the district and choice grafted fruit trees. In fact we reap the results of Mr Osborn's fifteen years' labour, who raised this place out of the bare veldt.[89]

The closer Haggard was to getting home the more he tried to pre-empt a hostile reception:

I expect to find my reasons for this change in life treated with something like contempt and to be told pretty plainly that I am a fool for my pains ... there are two things that everybody ought to remember in so doing, first that I am thoroughly acquainted with the country, its circumstances, prospects, and everything connected with it, which they certainly cannot claim to be, and, secondly, that as a general rule, a man is the best judge of his own actions ... I only hope that what I have to say will not be received in an angry spirit, or that my short stay, the last for some years, will not be made unpleasant through it.[90]

The Anglo-Zulu War was drawing to its close, and Haggard concluded his letter with mention of 'another blunder made worse by arrant cowardice': the killing of Louis Napoleon, the French Prince Imperial, on 1 June 1879. 'It is sad to think that the last of the Napoleons should have met his end at the hands of three or four Kafir cowherd boys, for I don't believe there were more. I hope those cowardly fellows with him will be shot to a man.'[91] Other reminders of the war were closer to hand. 'Mrs Hitchcock, Mr Osborn's daughter, is here now, she lost her husband at [Isandlwana] when her baby was three days old. I don't think she is nineteen yet.'[92]

By early July Haggard was in Pietermaritzburg, 'I thought I should have been utterly forgotten by now but even the kafirs in the street remember me and salute.'[93] Staying in his old quarters at Government House, he was once again in the company of Sir Henry Bulwer, who 'seems rather to agree with me than otherwise in what I have done'.[94] Writing to his mother, Haggard told her he was 'a step nearer home' and would be sailing shortly. 'Dearest Mother, you can't know how happy I feel at the prospect of seeing you again ... it seems more like ten years than four since I left home.'[95]

On 4 July, the day after Haggard wrote to his mother, the Zulu were brought to bay at the battle of Ulundi. In the Zulu heartland near Cetshwayo's royal homestead Ondini, the Zulus attacked a British square. They were decimated by the gunfire. Cetshwayo fled and the British burned down Ondini. Chelmsford had his victory, but it was his last. His replacement had been decided at the end of May when the cabinet in Westminster under Lord Beaconsfield, frustrated at wars and rumours of wars plus defeated and indecisive generals, decided on the immediate appointment of General Sir Garnet Wolseley as Commander-in-Chief, Governor of Natal and the Transvaal, and High Commissioner for South-East Africa, thereby anointing him the chief civil and military authority in south-eastern Africa, outranking Lord Chelmsford and Bulwer, and confining Frere's influence to the Cape Colony.

Wolseley arrived too late to deliver the *coup de grâce* to the Zulu, but there remained the Pedi in the Transvaal. By August Wolseley was in Pretoria planning his campaign to bring Sekhukhune to heel. Among those he consulted was Haggard's would-be nemesis, Ignatius Ferreira, now captain of an irregular mounted corps that he had raised, Ferreira's Horse. Wolseley heartily disliked Ferreira but was happy to make use of his local knowledge and his ruthlessness. Ferreira briefed Wolseley on the Boer attack on Tsate in 1876, recounting 'deeds that showed he did not regard killing a native as killing a human being'. Concerning Wolseley's planned assault, Ferreira was 'most anxious' Tsate should 'not be burnt until it is well looted as he says it is full of money and valuables and he knows where to find them'.[96]

In November 1879 Wolseley marched on Tsate with a combined force of imperial troops, volunteer units, and 8,000 Swazi warriors. The rains had been good and there was no problem obtaining forage. Wolseley's forces advanced on the Pedi capital, and on 28 November a particularly savage six-day battle began in which the Swazi gave no quarter. Sekhukhune lost fifteen members of his immediate family, including his son and heir, Morwamotse. The final defenders died of thirst and starvation in the caves of Ntswaneng, the Fighting Koppie.[97] Sekhukhune surrendered to Marshall Clarke and Captain Ferreira (who didn't find any treasure) and was taken by Wolseley to Pretoria and paraded through the streets.[98]

And King Cetshwayo? When he refused to give himself up, the British began a brutal game of hide-and-seek in the kloofs and hills of Zululand. Homesteads were destroyed and cattle confiscated wherever it was thought Cetshwayo had taken refuge, and torture was used to elicit information as to his whereabouts. He was captured on 28 August and taken to the British headquarters at Ulundi before being escorted to Port Durnford on the coast, from whence the Zulu king sailed to Cape Town and captivity.

10

'MY OWN SWEET LOVE'

The island of Ascension was the first port of call on the voyage to England for Haggard and young Jack Osborn. In 1879 Haggard's brother Jack was serving there aboard HMS *Flora* on harbour service, allegedly posted to Ascension because 'he had quarrelled with every commanding officer under whom he had served'.[1] Still engaged to Etta White, Jack was unhappy and lonely, corruption was rife in the navy stores department, and his only company off duty were his two dogs, Spice and Black. For Jack, his brother's visit was all too short – 'three hours only'[2] – most of it spent organising the collection of a 'gigantic turtle' as a present for their father.[3] The reptile inspired a quatrain from a 'sportive passenger on the ship'.[4]

> 'Tis true, O my Father, from distant lands
> I've come, a bad penny, back on your hands;
> But when once you have tasted this nice green fat,
> You won't care, O my parent, one kipper for that.[5]

The writer was Frederick Broome. He and Lady Barker were heading to their London home for a spell of leave from Mauritius.[6] Haggard discussed 'subjects which would make first rate articles'[7] with them, and Barker wrote to her publisher, Alexander Macmillan, boosting Haggard's prospects: 'He is at this moment hard at work writing an article on "volunteering in the Transvaal" from his own practical experience which ought to be excellent and he has the materials for another at hand on "The Justification of the Annexation of the Transvaal" ... What I want to know is if you have room for either and if so when?'[8]

Haggard disembarked at Plymouth in early August, while Osborn and the turtle sailed on to London Docks. Haggard was met by his brother Andrew, stationed at Plymouth with the 25th Regiment, the King's Own Borderers. 'I have arrived safely in England,' Haggard informed his father, mentioning seeing Jack on Ascension and that he was bringing 'a live turtle from there for you, if you care to have it'.[9] The turtle, as Broome's quatrain indicated, was a peace offering. Haggard planned on staying a few days with Andrew (then cohabiting with his fiancée, Mary Dixon) before going up to London to collect the turtle and Osborn, intending to bring the latter to Bradenham and consult his father about 'making arrangements for him'.[10] Haggard ducked any discussion of his own plans: 'it will be much easier to explain things to you than to write them. I shall go and see Sir Theophilus in London.'[11]

Shepstone had been in England since 24 June. On 7 July he went with William Sargeaunt and Haggard's parents to the Royal Agricultural Show at Kilburn, where in conversation with William Haggard he expressed himself not as favourably disposed to Haggard's resignation and his farming venture as he had been in the letter quoted by Haggard in correspondence with his father. Andrew, told of this conversation by his father, passed on the bad news to his younger brother. The two immediately launched a campaign in Rider's defence, Andrew writing the opening salvo stating that after much discussion with his brother he was 'of the opinion his step has been a very wise one'. Andrew had sight of letters from Shepstone and others 'in responsible positions' approving of his move, 'so I think Shepstone can only have been agreeing with you out of utility'; once their father had 'heard what he has got to say you will agree with him that he has done well, and not thrown up the service out of mere caprice'.[12]

Anticipating an angry reception for the prodigal son at Bradenham, Andrew poured liberal amounts of oil upon troubled waters: 'it strikes me his four or five years' foreign service have developed his ideas so as to make him a sharp fellow who is by no means likely to take an important step like this without good weighty reasons and good advice'.[13] Something of a prodigal himself, Andrew was not the best of advocates for his brother, and William Haggard was horrified at Andrew's revelation that Rider would 'like me to join him in his enterprise. If I could get the cash together, about a thousand – I should not be at all averse to doing so.'[14]

In London Haggard met up with Jack Osborn at Lane's Hotel in St Alban's Place in lower Islington, an establishment popular with 'the rowdier class of youngsters',[15] using his club Windham's in St James's Square as a poste restante.[16] Haggard saw Shepstone on 14 August and subsequently invited him to Bradenham. The homecoming could not be postponed any longer and Haggard finally took the train to Bradenham, regrettably minus the turtle, which in 'some mysterious way' had 'got lost in the London Docks. Personally I thought the occurrence fortunate, for what would have been done with the creature if I had succeeded in conveying it safely to Bradenham Hall still alive and flapping, I cannot conceive'.[17] His father was less sanguine, and the absence of the promised turtle precipitated a temper tantrum – 'he wanted his turtle and said so'.[18] Everyone else was glad to see Haggard home, especially his mother, 'but my father did not welcome my reappearance with whole-hearted enthusiasm. He remarked with great candour that I should probably become "a waif and a stray", or possibly – my taste for writing being already known – "a miserable penny-a-liner".[19]

Bowing to paternal pressure, Haggard wrote to Osborn in Pretoria saying he was considering a return to the Colonial Service. Attempting to please his father and at the same time assert his independence, Haggard decided to combine a career in the Colonial Service with farming in Natal and ordered a corn-grinding mill, an engine, boiler and pump for export to Hilldrop from Western & Co. Engineers in Lambeth, a company run by the Western brothers, one of whom, Maximilian, was married to Haggard's older sister Cecilia, known as Cissie.

Andrew wrote from Plymouth enquiring after Rider, a letter indicative of how the Haggard family perceived Rider: 'I hope you will agree with me that he is not such a fool as we thought him.'[20] Andrew repeated his interest in investing in the Natal enterprise, but his father quashed any such move that might lead to Andrew, who promised to be 'a brilliant soldier, departing from his regiment to join Rider in a wild-cat scheme, apparently financed with the family's funds'.[21]

Despite the painful encounters with his father, Haggard was determined to enjoy the summer holidays at Bradenham Hall, where his younger sister, Mary, had invited some of her friends to stay. Haggard joined in the fun, sallying out on picnics, painting watercolours and composing serio-comic character sketches. Haggard was particularly struck by 19-year-old Agnes Barber, the daughter of Fairless Barber, a solicitor who lived in Rastrick, Yorkshire. His wife Maria had 'received an unusually liberal education' in Koblenz, Germany, studying French, German and Italian. She boasted a 'fine taste in literature' and was said to have 'possessed powers of telepathy and Mesmerism, which ... were passed on to her children'.[22] The couple had three daughters, Agnes, Mabel and Margaret, the last of whom went on to write and publish under the pseudonym Michael Fairless.[23] Aggie, as she was known, was 'one of the most peculiar individuals that I ever came across in my long and varied experience', according to Haggard's sketch of her. 'All her passions are strong, especially her love and hate ... She has a most insane desire to take care of all she loves whatever the consequence may be to herself. She will never marry till she finds a master and then will make a devoted but not jealous wife.'[24]

Aggie inherited her mother's interest in literature and was an ideal mate for Haggard. In many ways they were kindred spirits: with Aggie he could discuss his literary aspirations and dreams. However, he well knew, given his father's precarious financial circumstances brought about by the agricultural depression of the 1870s, that if he were to marry it would be advisable to marry into money. According to Aggie's grand-niece Judith Hickey, 'Rider and Aggie became close friends but he could not consider her as a possible wife as Aggie had no fortune, which he knew his father expected of him.'[25]

Shepstone arrived at Bradenham on the last day of September to stay for a week. He was immediately plunged into Norfolk rural life, attending agricultural meetings and being introduced to local landowners. On Saturday, 4 October, Shepstone visited Norwich with Rider and Mary and their sister-in-law Julia, wife of brother Bazett. On the Monday Shepstone went to East Dereham and lunched with Colonel William Bulwer, a relative of Sir Henry Bulwer. 'Mr and Mrs Haggard and Miss Haggard went also.'[26] Shepstone took a shine to Mary, whom he nicknamed Lulamile,[27] and they struck up a correspondence. On his departure for London Shepstone left a note for his host to the effect that given his knowledge of the location of Haggard and Cochrane's farm, it would, over time, 'increase in value'.[28]

Haggard's father had come to some form of accommodation with his son and devised a plan to purchase a partnership in the Natal farm for his ward George Blomefield, the aforementioned 'illegitimate child of old Colonel Blomefield of Necton Hall, Norfolk'.[29] After the colonel's death Haggard's father persuaded his sister, who inherited Necton, 'to make a settlement on [George] and have him educated'. With £1,000 from Blomefield's inheritance, Haggard's father, 'anxious' that his ward make a career 'in some country where his birth history was not known, arranged that he should enter into partnership with us'.[30] William Haggard may also have intended Blomefield as a substitute for his son, allowing Rider to extricate himself from the farm and concentrate on finding a more secure career.

As summer gave way to autumn, Haggard found comfort in finding 'all belonging to me alive and for the most part well'. However, with his 'two greatest friends' from Scoones, 'Arthur L. and Justin Sheil, it was otherwise.' The former, of whom nothing is known, had died. 'My recollection is that Arthur L.'s illness began in a form of religious mania. If so, my other great friend, Justin Sheil, also passed into the shadow, or the glory, of religion.'[31] Sheil had entered the novitiate of a Roman Catholic order, the Cistercians of the Strict Observance, better known as the Trappists, at Mount St Bernard Abbey in Leicestershire.[32]

In a letter invoking the thoughts of Auguste Comte and Georg Wilhelm Friedrich Hegel and the theories of Charles Darwin, Haggard attempted to dissuade his friend 'from the career which he had chosen in language that must have seemed to him almost impertinent'.[33] Sheil's assertive response accused Haggard of deriving his knowledge of Catholicism from 'some vulgar Protestant pamphlet, and all your ideas of its institutions and ways from what I suppose you were told in the nursery'. Having got that off his chest, Sheil assured Haggard he was not offended; 'many who call themselves my friends think the same, but you are the only one who has taken sufficient interest in the matter to tell me so, and therefore I thank you'.[34]

Haggard devoted several pages of his autobiography to Sheil's correspondence, a reflection of his own fascination with religious belief: 'I am not prepared to quarrel with any religion worthy of the name, unless it be that of Mahomet in certain of its aspects. I have learned that they all spring from the same light, though the world being, as it were, cut crystal, that light flows from its facets in different-coloured rays.'[35] Whatever his views on his friend's chosen path, Haggard must have envied Sheil being master of his own destiny at a time when he was struggling to take control of his.

In a letter from Melmoth Osborn thanking William Haggard and his family for their kindness to his son Jack, Osborn said he was glad to hear from Rider that there was 'a chance of his re-entering the Colonial Service' and had written 'strongly advising him to do so provided he could secure a fair position on entering'.[36] In this letter Osborn told Haggard such a course 'would simply be following a pursuit for which you are eminently suited and abandoning one [farming] for which you are not'.[37]

Haggard went to London and visited the Colonial Office in Whitehall, where he obtained an interview with Robert Herbert, Permanent Undersecretary of State for the Colonial Office and a brother of Lord Carnarvon. Haggard then wrote to the Colonial Secretary, Hicks Beach, requesting he be allowed to withdraw his resignation as Master and Registrar of the High Court of the Transvaal – 'a variety of circumstances have caused me to regret having left the service' – and he asked to 'be allowed five months' leave of absence from date hereof on urgent private affairs'. Haggard gave Shepstone as a reference.[38] Haggard wrote to Herbert informing him of his 'official letter' to Hicks Beach, pointing out 'that the gravity of my request can work no injustice to the gentleman who is at present acting in the office in question ... since I have no wish to return to Pretoria, indeed there are reasons that would prevent my doing so'.[39] Haggard would not be welcome in Lanyon's administration and there was also the matter of his relationship with Johanna Ford. 'I only ask to withdraw my resignation, because I am aware that it will be easier and more regular for me and as a member of the Colonial Service to be transferred or promoted to some post in Natal if possible or failing Natal to some other Colony, than to be appointed straight away.'[40]

Haggard's letters to Arthur Cochrane in Natal are no longer extant, but most of Cochrane's to Haggard have survived, filled with gossip and laddish badinage. Cochrane comes across as erratic in mood and behaviour as well as exhibiting a quick temper: exasperation with African farm workers escalated into physical assaults. But also evident are Cochrane's affection, loyalty and subservience to Haggard. A long letter written in mid-August 1879 concerning Cochrane's 'troubles ... various and numerous'[41] ranges across running the farm, problems with African staff, 'The Firm's' financial health, and his on-off love affair with Johanna Ford's sister Josephine Lehmkuhl (known as Phinny). Cochrane was anxious to know how 'our move' had been viewed in England. 'I hope your father took it well.'[42]

The news in Cochrane's letter dated 22 September, which Haggard received in late October, was hardly unexpected but must still have come as a shock: Haggard was now a father, his daughter by the 'Gay Missus' (as Haggard and Cochrane referred to Johanna Ford), named Ethel Rider, was born on 16 September 1879: 'we are to be Godfathers – at least I am – Mr Ford said he felt highly honoured at the compliment? we paid him and his family – what a rum world this is'.[43]

Ford, unless he was a complaisant husband, didn't know Haggard was the father of Ethel. Cochrane had been told of the baby's birth in a letter from Josephine that was otherwise devoted to their relationship. Cochrane longed for Haggard's advice 'and shall be right glad for many reasons to see your old face again – I find it very lonely here'.[44] This condition was contradicted by the news that Cochrane had 'such a number of visitors lately all women folk, & say they all come to see the ostriches ... however they are very nice and occasionally we've had a waltz in the big room and amused ourselves singing etc. ... one was a snorting fine girl, she told me that it was *not* to see the ostriches that she came.'[45] Cochrane was alarmed to learn Haggard was looking to return to the Colonial Service: 'I should feel terribly if you did make up your mind to return to the service.'[46] A postscript updated Haggard on personal matters with what appears to be a sexual code phrase: 'No news from Pretoria nothing since the birth of the youthful young one. Ivory brushes and the consequences beware!!!'[47]

Cochrane welcomed news of a partner in 'The Firm': 'Blomefield's £550 will of course be very handy and will indeed be a godsend'.[48] To shore up finances, Cochrane also intended writing to Lewis Ford, who was handling their legal affairs in Pretoria, about mortgaging 'The Palatial'. 'Bye the bye mentioning that name reminds me of a sentence [in a letter from Josephine] 'viz. "Mrs F's baby is a dear little thing, a big child not one of those puny little things". I studiously avoid alluding to the child in any of my letters.'[49]

Cochrane's relationship with Josephine remained unresolved. Following sexual intercourse with Cochrane, she had threatened to kill herself unless he married her. Johanna Ford encouraged Cochrane to agree to an engagement to her sister on the basis 'it was not to be binding' but it would stop Josephine committing suicide. 'So far it has gone *no further*. I am afraid there will be a heavy reckoning day for us two when we go to Pretoria ... and you more than I may think yourself devilish lucky if you get out of the business all clear. As for me if the worst came to the worst I could marry the girl – but you have not even that resource.'[50]

There was further unsettling news for Haggard: Moresco, his favourite horse, had 'bolted one night late with a lot of mares – and I can hear nothing of him'. Cochrane had offered a reward but without success. 'I hope to goodness he will turn up again. I am fearfully anxious and put out about it.'[51]

In early November Haggard received a response from the Colonial Office, saying his letter had been 'referred to the Governor of the Transvaal for his consideration'[52] – Sir Garnet Wolseley. Haggard's request to withdraw his resignation was refused. Nor was he enjoying success as a 'penny-a-liner'. Lady Barker had failed to work her magic with Macmillan and on 3 November Haggard wrote to Chatto and Windus, publishers of the *Gentleman's Magazine*, reminding them they had published 'A Zulu War Dance' and 'A Visit to Secocoeni' two years previously and asking if they would 'care to take "Volunteering in the Transvaal", giving my experience as officer of a corps raised in Pretoria on receipt of the news of the Isandlwana disaster and afterwards employed by the Boers'.[53] They didn't.[54]

On 8 November Cochrane wrote a letter to Haggard containing a bombshell:

> I enclose a telegram telling of the sudden death of my young God child and your –? yes, the poor little thing is dead and perhaps a good thing for all concerned. I suppose the Gay Missus will take on fearfully ... I hope to goodness there will be no ravings etc. or any unhappy sentences which may be spoken while under the influence of the great grief. She will look upon it as a punishment and I think that is for the best.[55]

In a subsequent letter Cochrane told Haggard: 'Mrs F seemed fearful cut up at the loss of *the* baby ... Phinny seems to have had a great affection for it, and mentions casually that it was not like any of *Mr Ford's* children.'[56]

When was the letter of 8 November received and read by Haggard at Bradenham Hall? The mail ships would have taken around thirty days on the voyage from Durban via Cape Town to England. Add a few extra days for the letter to travel by post cart from Newcastle to Durban and a shorter delay at the English end, and the likelihood is he received it in the latter half of December just before Christmas. The timing is pertinent: by that date Haggard was engaged to be married.

Judging from Haggard's correspondence with the Colonial Office, he intended to stay five months in England, returning to Natal early in the New Year. He must have wondered if his return to southern Africa wasn't a case of out of the frying pan into the fire: in England his father was an ever-nagging presence, but uncertain career prospects and unknown complications of a personal nature awaited in South Africa. As his hopes of continuing a career in the Colonial Service had been dashed, his sole employment would be the Natal farm. None of this is mentioned in his autobiography, other than the strain and tension caused by his father, and even in that department 'things righted themselves by degrees, as somehow they generally do when one is young and not afraid to take chances. To begin with ... I did the wisest and best deed of my life and engaged myself to be married.'[57]

Haggard's sister Mary had invited more of her friends to stay at Bradenham. One of them was Louisa Margitson, who came for three or four days towards the end of November. During her visit Haggard proposed and Louisa accepted. The 20-year-old Louisa Margitson was an orphan in the guardianship of her three uncles: William Hartcup, her late father's brother-in-law and a solicitor in Bungay; and her mother's brothers, her favourite uncle Frank Hamilton and his younger brother William.

Louisa or Louie, as she was known to family and friends, was the first child of John Margitson and Elizabeth Mary Anna Margitson (née Hamilton), born on 6 October 1859. Three subsequent children, all boys, died within days of their birth and were buried in the Margitson vault at St Mary's in Ditchingham, where the Margitsons lived at nearby Ditchingham House on the Norfolk estate purchased by her great-grandfather in 1817. The 'House', as it was known locally, was a three-storeyed

'Georgian red brick box with a block of chimneys in the centre of the roof',[58] visible from the Bungay to Norwich road across a stretch of lawn with an ornamental pond. The estate extended to the banks of the Waveney River and the town of Bungay lay a mile to the south on the Suffolk side of the river. Here in Bungay, in 1860, John Margitson founded the fourth battalion of the Suffolk Rifle Volunteers.

Illness and the death of family members were a feature of Louie's early life; at various times she suffered from diphtheria and influenza as well as the usual childhood complaints. When her father contracted tuberculosis in 1867, its symptoms were 'only too familiar',[59] having caused the death of three of John Margitson's sisters. On medical advice the small family of three and Elizabeth's unmarried sister Hannah travelled to Switzerland in search of a cure, moving from Geneva to Berne and finally the small city of Thun, where John Margitson died on 7 July 1868. Mother, daughter and aunt returned to England in September 1868: Louie, 'thin and with a very bad cold', was 'very nervous all the way home ... she did not feel safe without her father'.[60]

At Ditchingham House, Louie enjoyed a 'happy girlhood ... with her horses and her dogs and her schoolfriends' and, following tuition by a governess, was sent to school at Lowlands just outside Bungay, 'where the daughters of many local gentry went'[61] and where Louie made friends with Mary Haggard.[62]

After the death of her father, Louie's uncle Frank Hamilton, a London doctor, 'watched over her with the greatest care, as she was always considered to be delicate'. Nonetheless Louie 'grew up to be an extraordinarily robust woman but the tragic losses that the Margitson family had suffered with her young aunts made everyone nervous about this only fatherless child'.[63]

In the mid-1870s Louie's mother was diagnosed with pernicious anaemia, 'for which there was no known cure'.[64] Specialists in London were consulted and from 'then on the tragic history of John's illness was to repeat itself'.[65] Elizabeth Margitson died on 28 September 1878 in the spa town of Bad Schwalbach, Germany. Louie returned to Ditchingham House to live with a relative, her cousin Rose Hildyard. Louie was left 'in sole possession of a modest but worthwhile estate that until her twenty-first birthday on 6 October 1880 was managed by her uncle and trustee, William Hartcup'.[66]

Haggard and Louie had known each other for three days when he proposed to her in the Philosopher's Walk at Bradenham.[67] Even allowing for 'the impulsive Haggard temperament, this was quick work'.[68] Haggard married for love but had the good fortune, or the good sense, to fall in love with someone possessed of money and land. That a jobless younger son was marrying an heiress was certainly the uncharitable interpretation of some at the time and it remained a sensitive issue for Haggard, who addressed the matter in his autobiography: '[Louie's] parents died in her youth, leaving her the heiress to certain landed property which would have been valuable had real estate in Norfolk retained the worth which it had at the time of their death ... Now its net rentals, although it is totally unencumbered, about pay for the upkeep of the house and gardens. I mention these facts because I see it recorded in works of reference that I married an "heiress", which is an elastic term.'[69] Elastic but inescapable. It could also be applied to what would turn out to be an increasingly protracted engagement, a saga worthy of a three-decker Victorian novel packed with thwarted love, anonymous letters, evil uncles, zealous guardians, courtroom confrontations, a dash of madness, and servants caught *in flagrante* in the pantry.

And what of Johanna Ford and the infant Ethel Rider? Did Haggard confess all to his prospective bride? Yes, he did. Haggard was totally transparent regarding his romantic life with regard to both Lilly and the 'Gay Missus'. At the time of his proposal to Louie he had yet to hear of the death of Ethel Rider, news of which arrived just before Christmas, when he probably agreed with Cochrane the death of the 'poor little thing' was 'perhaps a good thing for all concerned'.[70]

The brief acquaintance, long enough for Haggard to fall in love with Louie, was also sufficient for his brother Andrew, on leave at Bradenham, to do the same. On finding his younger brother had proposed to Louie and been accepted, Andrew was distraught and poured out his heart to Louie, swearing her to secrecy. Meanwhile Haggard and Louie waited in suspense to hear if her guardians would consent to their marriage. Haggard went down to London to stay at his club Windham's, where on Friday, 29 November 1879, he received a telegram from Andrew: William Hartcup had given his verbal approval – 'it has taken a great weight off my mind', Haggard wrote to Louie. 'My darling, I did not know how much I had got to love you till I left you yesterday ... I can only hope that your Uncle [Frank Hamilton] will follow Mr Hartcup's lead, and there will be no difficulties thrown in our way.'[71] The next step was for Haggard to be invited to visit Louie and her relatives at Ditchingham and Bungay.

Haggard's parents contacted William Hartcup to enquire about Louie's income. The answer was satisfactory and Haggard's mother told her husband she considered their son a 'fortunate young man ... it is a great satisfaction to us to know Rider is likely to be so well settled, and no further anxiety there – and it is a happy consequence of his coming home, which appeared to you at first a doubtful move.'[72] Their son may have been 'well settled' but there can be no doubt he and Louie were very much in love, as their daily correspondence abundantly demonstrates: 'My past life has been so very lonesome and unhappy, that the prospect of your sweet companionship, of your true love, seems almost too good to be true. It is light coming out of darkness into light ... if it is in the power of man to make you happy, you shall be happy – My past may have been reckless enough, but my future shall atone for it.'[73]

On Monday evening, 2 December, Louie wrote to Haggard's mother from Ditchingham, apologising for not having written earlier to thank her 'for all your kindness to me, but I thought I had better wait until I had spoken to my Uncle & heard what he thought from his own lips. He seemed *quite* satisfied, & does nothing but laugh at me!! So I trust all will go smooth now.' Louie thanked her future mother-in-law for welcoming her 'so heartily to your family on such a short acquaintance, & God helping me I will be a true and loving wife to Rider so that you may never regret my visit to Bradenham Hall'.[74]

The same evening Louie wrote to Haggard to report seeing Uncle William and that all was 'smooth in that quarter', but as to Haggard visiting Ditchingham House, 'they don't seem to think it would be correct' as 'the neighbourhood knows nothing at present. I hope something will be settled soon.'[75] Louie asked Haggard if he had told 'Sir Theophilus yet of your folly in engaging yourself to a girl after 5 days' acquaintance!' Haggard had indeed told Shepstone – he was in London until the New Year – who wrote to William Haggard to say he was 'exceedingly glad [Rider] has now the heart of a lady who from all accounts is quite worthy of him ... Yes, your son is emulating me in so far that he is carrying out a process of annexation; his territory is smaller and its inhabitants fewer than mine were; but I suspect he has the best of it, because his Republic and its President are more loyal and loving to him, than mine were to me.'[76]

Melmoth Osborn wrote to Haggard offering his 'sincere and hearty congratulations on the prospect of happiness before you'. Osborn penned his letter from 'the heart of Zululand, where I hold the office of British Resident'.[77] After Cetshwayo's capture in August 1879 and his removal to Cape Town, Wolseley set about a post-war partition of Zululand; a ham-fisted attempt at recreating a pre-Shakan Zulu society, dividing Zululand into thirteen separate chiefdoms and imposing new chiefs on areas and communities with which they had no previous connection, often in reward for siding with the British during the Anglo-Zulu War. The primary aim of the settlement was to prevent the resurrection of the Zulu monarchy and protect the security of Natal while at the same time avoiding the expense and responsibilities that came with annexation. Among the newly appointed thirteen chiefs were the main beneficiaries of the settlement, John Dunn (last encountered at the battle of Thukela in 1856), Zibhebhu kaMaphitha, chief of the Mandlakazi, and Prince Hamu kaNzibe of the Ngenetsheni, the latter two vocal and aggressive opponents of the Zulu royal family and their supporters, the uSuthu. Wolseley's settlement cynically exploited existing conflicts within the Zulu nation in a bid to divide and rule. 'Political expediency, cultural arrogance and ignorance played a far more important part in the planning of the settlement than did conscious manipulation.'[78] Whether by accident or design, the settlement was a recipe for civil war.[79]

Love letters continued to fly between Louie from Ditchingham and Haggard from London and Bradenham. They swapped news of the snowy weather in their part of the world, ice skating on local ponds, Louie's beloved horses – 'you will be *quite* jealous of them I forewarn you!! You should have seen me fondling and kissing them this morning!!!!!'[80]

Louie hunted out lodgings for Haggard close to Ditchingham, where their engagement was now public knowledge, but worryingly the 'gentleman in London', presumably Frank Hamilton, had given neither an opinion nor consent. Haggard's father suggested his prospective daughter-in-law be made a ward of Chancery if her guardians withheld consent. As a ward of the court Louie would come under its protection and, as she stood to inherit, the Court of Chancery would assume responsibility for her until she came of age. When William Hartcup refused his written consent, William Haggard wrote to his solicitor, Fred John Blake, asking him to represent his son and Louie. 'There are evidently rocks ahead for us', Haggard wrote to Louie, but two things were certain. '1. That I don't see my way to stopping in England till next October [when Louie came of age]. 2. That I won't leave England without you ... If it comes to the worst we must go to the Court that is all, though I should be sorry if we are driven to it.'[81]

Haggard told his brother Will – now serving in Teheran – that Louie was

> willing to come to Africa, so we propose returning there shortly, i.e. as soon as we can get satisfactorily married. There is property concerned, and trustees, who, as I dare say you know, are gentry difficult to deal with. They want us to postpone the marriage till she comes of age next October, but we don't see the force of it in any way. I *want* to get married next April – whether I shall manage or not is another matter.[82]

William Hartcup having had a change of mind, Frank Hamilton was reluctant to give his consent, aware that Haggard's career prospects were less than brilliant. In spite of Louie's guardians' lack of consent to their marriage, Haggard and Louie met in Norwich on Saturday, 13 December. He accompanied her back to Bungay and installed himself in lodgings which she had found from where he could visit her at Ditchingham House. Thereafter Louie spent Christmas and New Year with the Haggards at Bradenham Hall, taking part in the traditional festivities, which included amateur theatricals complete with a handsomely printed programme for the double bill of the comedietta *Two Heads Are Better Than One* and the farce *Ici on parle français*.[83] Of the five performers appearing in the first, four were Haggards: 'Mr. Rider Haggard, his brothers Mr. Bazett Haggard and Mr. Arthur Haggard', and their sister Mary.[84] In the second there were seven actors, which included the same four Haggards and 'Miss Margitson'.[85]

These activities outraged William Hartcup and reinforced his opposition to the marriage. He was particularly provoked by Haggard's visit to Ditchingham before Christmas. Haggard was there again in January, when Louie received an angry letter from her uncle: 'I exceedingly object to your reception of Gentlemen visitors for in your unprotected position it is neither maidenly [n]or Dignified and if the gentleman who offers you his hand has any true regard for your position he would not be required to be told that your House cannot at present be used as if it were his own home.'[86] Hartcup said Louie's aunt Hannah (living at Ditchingham House *in loco parentis*) was completely under Louie's thumb and 'bends to your requirements – had it not been so she would never have occupied a room Downstairs with her children whilst you and Mr Haggard were privately occupying a separate room upstairs, a proceeding which I am sorry to say has been made the subject of comment by others'.

Hartcup insisted that in future Louie didn't invite 'staying Visitors to your House without first consulting me nor can you accept Invitations for staying out yourself without my consent'. He also instituted financial restraints, forbidding Louie to draw any cheques until he had inspected her past bank accounts. Hartcup said he wrote with 'no feelings of unkindness' and advised Louie to 'defer your reply until your Visitors have left you and you are able to write in peace and quietness for letters written under excitement are valueless to the receiver and often times ... very much to be regretted'.[87]

Angry and unabashed, Louie took to verse:

> Oh where oh where is your daring Rider gone?
>   He's gone to fight old Hartcup for the settlements aren't done.
> And it's oh in my heart that I wish him safe at home.

> Oh and when and oh when will your Norfolk lad come home,
> When lawyers are defeated then straight back he will come,
> And I'll crown him with laurels my bonnie Norfolk man.[88]

William Hartcup beat the Haggards to the draw by making Louie a ward in Chancery, thus ensuring the marriage could not take place until 'the case was through the Courts'.[89] Louie stood her ground, spending most of her time with the Haggards at Bradenham or in London, where, in February, she stayed in lodgings in Belgravia, accompanied by her mother's sister Mrs Louisa Hildyard, while Rider resided nearby with Bazett and his family. Louie and Rider visited her maternal relatives in Clapton, including uncles Frank and William. Later in the same month an appeal on behalf of Haggard and Louie came before Sir Richard Malins, Vice Chancellor in the Court of Chancery. Shortly before the hearing, Louie came down with measles and Rider nursed her back to health.

Malins's verdict was in the young couple's favour. Louie was triumphant. Malins was 'favourably impressed' from the outset, but a testimonial from Shepstone 'settled the question, and old Malins said he thought it was a very "suitable match"'.[90] When Hartcup's lawyer 'tried to bring in something about only four days' acquaintance ... Malins shut him up with – "Have you never heard of love at first sight before?"'[91] On the question of impropriety, brought up with regard to Haggard having nursed Louie through measles, Haggard's response, 'Of course I did – and I should like to know who else had so much right', amused 'Malins greatly'.[92] Malins approved of the match but told the couple that until the appointment of a guardian, 'we had better not see too much of each other and limited us to two days a week'.

Louie opposed the court's proposal that William Hartcup and his wife (another Louisa) be appointed her guardians; if they were, she insisted on having her aunt Hannah as her female guardian. This was granted 'but not unnaturally produced another royal row with the Hartcup family, with every sort of accusation of base ingratitude and unbecoming and undutiful behaviour'.[93] Haggard counselled her not to worry: 'Naught but death shall come between you and me, and even that shall not divide us.'[94] Louie and her aunt moved to Eastbourne to wait out events, and to relieve the stress Haggard advised her to 'take just as much quinine as will go on a three-penny bit, and you'll be right as ninepence'.[95]

In early March a furious Hartcup turned up at Ditchingham House without consulting Louie or her aunt, and fired Hood the groom, allegedly because he had been 'found in company with the parlourmaid in the pantry and harness house'.[96] Hood was a favourite of Louie's, as he was good with her beloved horses. She informed her uncle William Hamilton, who took her side and sent a long letter of complaint suggesting that the dismissal 'of the parlourmaid instead of Hood, and her replacement by an older woman' would be 'much more palatable to Louisa and my sister, and equally put an end to the courting at the house which you disapprove'.[97]

Louie had kept her promise to Andrew not to tell her future husband about his avowal of love, but Andrew was becoming a nuisance. 'I had a letter from Andrew today which has not improved my spirits,' she informed Rider; 'there is such an undertone of bitterness running through all he says. He has also I fear been getting into fresh scrapes, making love to four young women at once! Remember this is *strictly private*, don't lead him to suppose I have made these remarks if you write to him.'[98]

At the time Haggard was in Herefordshire visiting the Maddison Greens at Lyonshall and his aunt Fanny, his father's sister married to William Fowle, vicar of St George's Church at Brinsop, bringing them up to date on his marriage plans, prior to seeing his brother Arthur at Pembroke College, Cambridge, where he probably also met Frederick Jackson and had news of Lilly.

Meanwhile Andrew went to see Louie and she endured 'a very painful interview ... which she attributed to his "'unnatural excitement'".[99] He refused to release Louie from her promise, but the bizarre content of a subsequent letter decided Louie the time had come to speak to Rider. Andrew accused Louie and Rider of writing anonymous letters to his fiancée, Mary Dixon, in Plymouth and turning her against him; apparently the discovery on his part was the result of a divine revelation. The deity aside, someone had told Mary Dixon that Andrew 'was looking for a wife elsewhere'.[100]

Supernatural references and the substance of the letter suggest a degree of mental unbalance. Louie forwarded Andrew's letter to Rider as well as replied to it herself: 'I thought you knew me better than to imagine I could lend myself to anything so unladylike as clandestine correspondence. You are under some extraordinary delusion.'[101] Rider forbade his brother to have any further communication with Louie and told her he thought Andrew 'must have been off his head when he wrote to you that wonderful epistle'.[102]

Who did write the anonymous letters to Mary Dixon? A possible candidate is Haggard's sister Cissie, who was suffering from severe mental illness and prophesying 'the most awful evil to all and every member of her family'[103] as punishment for their sins. Haggard dubbed her a 'modern Cassandra',[104] and remarked that Cissie and Andrew 'had better set up a private Bedlam'.[105]

The arrival of Jack Haggard at Bradenham Hall must have come as a welcome relief amidst all these dramas. He had been invalided home from Ascension owing to bad health, his teeth having 'rotted from years of poor diet, with the consequence of chronic indigestion.'[106] The brothers enjoyed themselves shooting and planning 'imaginary voyages around the world ending up in Jack's idea of paradise, Vancouver Island'.[107]

In Natal, Cochrane was enjoying his own share of emotional turbulence. Haggard had written expressing his view that, owing to 'certain past incidents' involving both of them, Cochrane marrying Josephine Lehmkuhl and bringing her to Hilldrop 'might lead to hopeless complications with her not too desirable family', and if he was bringing 'out a bride the situation would not, frankly, be possible'.[108] Cochrane assured Haggard he felt safe from the bonds of matrimony as long as he didn't set foot outside Natal, though he admitted, 'I *do* like the girl, and can't help it, but as long as I am A.C. [Arthur Cochrane] and not a fool, I shall not be induced to try the double bed business. Unless, as I say, I am again collared when I should fear myself greatly.'[109]

Cochrane was well and truly collared when Lewis Ford and Josephine visited him at Hilldrop. 'I wanted to tackle Ford but Phinny would not allow me and I went and did as she asked me – viz. told Ford that I was engaged to her – a lie – but one that was meant well – what with threats of poison etc. and tears – I was simply worn out and did anything for peace sake.' He intended to break off his engagement with Josephine gradually, and 'if she has any spirit she will take in the situation and break it off herself'.[110] When Josephine realised Cochrane was backing down, she 'tried to commit suicide using laudanum'.[111] Then Cochrane received a letter from Haggard announcing he was not returning to Natal until much later in the year. Cochrane was shattered and, on learning Josephine was coming through Newcastle by post cart en route to Grahamstown, where she planned to enter a convent, he 'galloped to the top of a mountain, intercepted the coach and clasped the distracted maiden in his arms. He extracted a promise that she would not take the veil' and 'swore he would marry her as soon as he was in a position to do so'.[112]

Haggard accepted the situation and sent a letter of congratulations to Cochrane, who, in reply, told his friend he need not fear that the 'Fords or any of Miss L's people' would be allowed to take advantage of my having married Joe to thrust themselves upon the Firm ... from what I can gather from [Mrs Ford's] letters and from Joe's I fancy the once gay Missus has gone or is going gradually to decay, such as loss of hair. Ford says she is getting idiotic. I suppose it will be a case of the 'prussic' [acid] when the morning arrives for the celebration of your nuptials but joking apart – she really seems to be entirely *crushed*. She is very anxious to know the day of your marriage and begs me to let her know when it will be.[113]

Regarding Haggard's eventual return, Cochrane urged that he bring a cook, 'that is more important than anything else ... God knows how glad I shall be to see you again old boy it seems a long, long time since you left – and I want help badly.'[114] The mill and its component parts which Haggard purchased in London had arrived, but when the engine for the mill was unpacked, it was found to be 'severely damaged' owing to 'being sent upside down'.[115] The need to generate income was imperative, so Cochrane began manufacturing bricks and was also thinking of selling 'The Palatial', where a new tenant had been installed after the Schwikkards left at the end of their lease and relocated to Newcastle.

Haggard was still of a mind to apply for a Colonial Service position and Cochrane was happy to adjust the deed for the farm to 'arrange what is best according to what you will do'.[116] He was also '*very anxious*' to know when George Blomefield was coming, as work on the farm was 'exceedingly hard for me alone' and he feared the consequences if his health failed: 'what would become of the place and the Kaffirs – it is only by constant attention and the severest discipline that I am able to get them to do their duty ... if it had not been for Keane Osborn's [a relative of Melmoth Osborn] help I should have *bust* some time ago'.[117] Fortunately the brick-making project had taken off, and Cochrane and Osborn had manufactured 70,000 bricks at £3 per thousand for one client and 30,000 for the mill house. He had also begun a speculative joint venture, to mine a nearby coal seam.

Haggard's intention was to take over the farmhouse when he arrived with Louie; Cochrane would set up bachelor quarters in the mill house. Cochrane was only 'too delighted to do anything which will serve to bring us near together again. Our friendship is of no ordinary sort – I feel to you as a brother, almost can I say that you are placed above them – so you may guess what good news it was to me – when I heard that in all probability you will live here for a time.'[118]

The Newcastle races and a week of revels at the end of May promised a welcome respite from Cochrane's labours, and he was training several horses with an eye on the Newcastle Plate. One of the mounts was 'an Arab of Sir Garnet's which he sold to Osborn'. He was also training the horse of a friend called Tucker. 'Mrs Tucker is very nice and ladylike and with Mrs Beaumont [wife of William Beaumont, now resident magistrate at Newcastle] could be very charming friends for Mrs Haggard – the people (aristocracy) of Newcastle look forward to your arrival with no ordinary amount of impatience and curiosity, they are quite prepared to be friendly and nice.'[119]

Cochrane's catalogue of colonial high jinks during the Newcastle races very likely mirrors the bachelor life that Haggard and Cochrane led in Pretoria: 'I regret to say that I have been utterly and totally "on the spree" – you must not think that I have been drunk for a week – but our Races came off – 2 dances – a football and cricket match, a dinner and 2 luncheons – at the end of which programme your humble servant was a decided wreck.'[120] As well as officiating at the races as starter, Cochrane and the district surgeon, Dr Charles O'Grady Gubbins, 'a very jolly Irishman ... gave a dance at Hill Drop', where 'oceans of champagne' were on hand as well as the regimental band of the 58th from Fort Amiel in Newcastle. Cochrane embarked on a serious flirtation with an officer's wife and the next morning was so 'wrecked' he was unable to play in the cricket match, but had recovered sufficiently by the evening to claim more dances with the officer's wife and 'after that I slept at Camp had breakfast and lunch and dinner and returned to Hill Drop a Spectre'. The following evening Cochrane 'dined with the husband of the lady and played Loo – slept at Camp and in the afternoon held a levee here, Champagne and tea, that ended my week, such a week all we used to do at Pretoria melts into insignificance before the orgee [sic]'.[121]

Cochrane's letter contained an unexpected item of good news: he had found Moresco in the local pound for stray livestock. At first he didn't believe it could be Moresco but 'sure enough it was the old boy – with big legs – and sore back – and as thin as a rake – my delight you can imagine'. Cochrane was shocked at Moresco's condition: 'I took him home and have been nursing him ever since.'[122] Subsequent enquiries found that Moresco had been stolen and ridden to the Cape Colony, 'nearly a thousand miles away, and that the horse had escaped thence and found a path back to his home'.[123]

Cochrane planned a trip to Pretoria in July to sell 'The Palatial'. 'I thought perhaps Lagden or some of the young blades of Pretoria might like to have it ... but I hear there has been quite a panic up there, everybody has been coming to smash, and I imagine property must be rather low just at present.'[124]

Sir Garnet Wolseley had departed from Pretoria early in April 1880, leaving Lanyon to take up the reins. Lanyon had never been popular with the Boers and, when news of Gladstone's landslide Liberal victory on an anti-imperial ticket reached Pretoria in mid-April, hopes were raised that British rule might be revoked and independence regained. This view was shared by Chief Justice Kotzé, who informed Haggard that Pretoria was 'no longer what it was' and advised him to 'abandon the idea' of looking for a job in the Colonial Service and read for the Bar instead, which wouldn't take more than three years and leave him with the 'certain prospect of a judgeship' and enable him 'without much difficulty to get into the Cape Parliament. Mrs. Haggard will be pleased with Grahamstown (which I would recommend in preference to Cape Town), and you will have a *fine* and *thoroughly independent* career before you.'[125] Haggard acknowledged Kotzé's advice 'was sound' and in the future he would occasionally wish he had acted on it, but what 'chiefly stood in my way ... was my agreement with Cochrane, whom I did not like to desert, although he generously offered to release me. Also I wished to be up and doing, and did not like the idea of those three years of comparative inaction which would have prevented me from earning anything more till I was twenty-seven.'[126]

Cochrane succeeded in selling 'The Palatial' for '£540 *cash* ... we have done very well indeed ... I shall write to Osborn and tell him that the money is ready for him – £420 – then the farm is paid for – thank God.'[127] While Cochrane was away, Blomefield had arrived at Hilldrop. 'I like him you will be glad to hear, and fancy that he will make a provident and hard worker ... he will be a great addition to the Firm.'[128]

In early July Haggard made another attempt to secure a post in Natal, taking advantage of the appointment of Sir George Pomeroy Colley to replace Wolseley as Governor of Natal and High Commissioner for South-East Africa in April. Haggard had met Colley at Government House in 1875 when, after Wolseley's departure, Colley remained behind before travelling through the Transvaal and Swaziland to Delagoa Bay.[129] Haggard asked to be considered as a candidate for the post of Assistant Colonial Secretary in Natal. A brief acknowledgment from Colley's private secretary informed Haggard that Colley had 'already made a recommendation for the post of assistant Colonial Secretary'. His surname being misspelt as 'Haggart' can only have added salt to the wound.[130]

Henry Rider Haggard and Mariana Louisa Margitson were married at St Mary's, Ditchingham, on Wednesday, 11 August 1880. They had hoped to tie the knot a month earlier on 13 July 'but this had to be abandoned as the lawyers were not ready'.[131] William Hartcup fought to the bitter end to prevent the marriage: objecting to the cost of Louie's wedding dress and telling the vicar of St Mary's not to put up the marriage banns as Louie was under age. The impasse was finally resolved by a meeting between William Haggard and the Bishop of Norwich, John Pelham, while Rider wrote to the vicar, William Scudamore, a friend of Louie's deceased father, 'telling him if further obstructions were thrown in the way of the wedding taking place he must be prepared to take the legal consequences'.[132]

Scudamore wrote to Louie imploring her 'to heal the breach' and get the Hartcups to the wedding at all costs: 'Their absence from it will never be forgotten in the neighbourhood, in which your family have been respected and where all desire to see you in your right position ... Ask yourself what would my father wish me to do in this matter, if he were alive?'[133]

Scudamore's offer to visit Louie in order 'to assist her to a better decision'[134] was given short shrift: 'as I am quite sure that nothing you can say will alter my opinion, I think we had better avoid an interview which might be painful to both of us. I shall be much obliged if you will not refer to the subject again.'[135] The Hartcups did not attend the wedding.

The wedding was an occasion for general celebration. The 'assembled crowd of villagers and neighbours from Ditchingham and surrounding parishes', together with the 'combined choirs of Ditchingham and Pirnough' plus the 'officiating clergymen and the Bride and Bridegroom', made 'the whole scene very imposing and will doubtless remind the wedding pair in their South African sojourn of the associations of Old England and Home'. As the 'noble peal of bells' in the tower of St Mary's 'gave out its joyous chimes', the newly married couple returned to Ditchingham House 'under triumphal arches of laurel decked with flowers, corn and appropriate emblems and mottoes' including 'Happy may they be'.[136]

Louie made sure her imprint was on the day and the couple 'departed on their honeymoon in style behind four grey horses ridden by postilions' to make 'a royal progress through the streets of Norwich'. Haggard had reservations as to the wisdom of what might be read as a defiant gesture, but Louie was determined 'everyone would know they were bride and bridegroom ... All her little world knew of the opposition to her marriage – she would show them she was proud of her husband and not ashamed – hence the triumphal progress.'[137]

Triumph came at a price. Haggard recorded the 'net result of the whole business was that, including the cost of the settlements, a very moderate estate was mulcted in law expenses of a sum of nearly 3000 pounds!'[138]

The couple's honeymoon was spent in the Lake District, and on their way home Haggard and Louie made 'a pilgrimage' to Mount St Bernard's Abbey to see his friend Justin Sheil, now Brother Basil, 'because in my vanity I thought that if we could come face to face I might be able by my personal influence to induce him to return to the world'.[139] Haggard was permitted to see Sheil alone and again he tried to dissuade Sheil from his chosen path – 'my beseeching he put aside with the most sweet and tender gratitude. "Many have scolded and lectured me," he said; "you are the first who ever came here to try to snatch me from what you believe to be an intolerable fate."'[140] Haggard conceded defeat, and he and Louie were shown around the monastery and its school and farm by Brother Basil. 'Then came the farewell. I shook Sheil's hand and looked into his patient eyes. The door clanged to behind us. It was our last meeting in the world.'[141]

Haggard's wedding was celebrated at Hilldrop by Cochrane, Osborn and Blomefield: 'we drank to you and your wife and gave you each three times three ... and now that you are married I can only hope that I shall have in your wife as true and staunch a friend as I have found you to be.'[142]

Moresco remained 'in a fearful state, he does not seem to be able to pull himself together again, and his back won't heal. I have done all I can for him with the limited means at my disposal – and we are now trying to burn the flesh away in order to start afresh.'[143]

In London Haggard and Louie booked their passage to South Africa and purchased 'a vast amount of household equipment and furniture' and arranged 'the final details of Wills and Settlements which could not be done until after Louie's twenty-first birthday on October 6th'.[144] At Whiteleys in Westbourne Grove they bought the entire household contents for Hilldrop, from a humble rolling pin to an expensive 'Ash Bedroom Suite complete'.[145] From Jolly & Son of Norwich, 'inventors of the celebrated Landaulet Broughams, Anglo-American Phaetons and Fulcrum Dog Carts', Haggard ordered one of the phaetons, 'a high and lightly constructed carriage with a covered seat in front and a footman's seat behind', which, with packing, came to £81.17s, the price offset by trading in an 'old waggonette' and thus reduced to £65.1s.[146] He also purchased a second-hand grand piano.

While Rider and Louie were preparing for their departure for South Africa, Andrew Haggard and Mary Dixon married secretly on 18 October 1880. Mary was already suffering from tuberculosis. She would die on 22 January 1881, 'leaving behind a child, probably a daughter, of whom there is now no trace'.[147]

Before dawn on 8 November 1880, Haggard and Louie – now three months pregnant – together with Lucy Gibbs, Louie's maid, Stephen Lanham, a groom from Bradenham, three dogs, two retrievers, Jet and Stray, plus Bob, a terrier and last-minute present from Jack, and two parrots, sailed from London via Dartmouth for South Africa. 'Weather cold but fine and a little swell,' wrote Louie in her diary, adding that 'many people were seasick, including Gibbs'.[148] Louie caught up with her correspondence, while her husband was 'in a great stew about himself as feeling rather seedy. He imagined he had scarlet fever.'[149]

Well out into the English Channel, the rough seas proved too much for Louie and she too 'succumbed to the horrors of seasickness', only recovering when close to Madeira, which they reached in the early hours of 17 November. They went immediately ashore at 1 a.m. in the 'bright moonlight' to 'buy some of the well-known Madeira chairs ... and then to the fruit shop where we all indulged largely in oranges, bananas, mangoes etc.' Returning aboard just before four in the morning 'and indulging in some champagne and sandwiches which were procured surreptitiously from the head steward we went to bed once more and slept peacefully till 7.30.'[150]

On the long voyage to Cape Town a committee was formed to arrange amusements. Louie suggested 'we should try and get up "Pinafore"'.[151] At which point she lost interest in her diary and didn't return to it until December, by when she was in Pietermaritzburg.

11

'LAND OF MURDER AND SUDDEN DEATH'

'Fight against it as I will indolence overtakes me,' Louie confessed to her diary on 28 December 1880 and, making 'one of those good resolutions by which the lower regions are paved', she recommenced the neglected diary, first bringing it up to date. The Haggards had disembarked at Durban on Sunday, 12 December, and after a short stay in the city organising three waggons 'to take up our things [to Hilldrop] ... came on by the new railway to Maritzburg'.[1] Four years after the first sod was turned in 1876, the Durban to Pietermaritzburg line had been officially opened at its inland terminus on 1 December 1880.

The Haggards booked into Moseley's Hotel for a couple of days before moving to the Shepstones' home in Loop Street on Sunday, 19 December. Cochrane had sent two horses down from Hilldrop, whither they intended starting on Thursday, 23 December, but heavy summer rains delayed their trek and they spent Christmas Day with the Shepstones. 'Rather different from England', noted Louie. 'Very hot here.' In the midst of the seasonal festivities came news of 'the Boer outbreak and the murderous attack on the 94th. Things looking very queer.'[2] The Transvaal Rebellion had begun.[3]

The British annexation of the Transvaal was not to be reversed – Wolseley had issued a proclamation to that effect in March 1880 – but Boer expectations had been raised by the incoming British prime minister, William Gladstone, who had 'virulently attacked Tory confederation policy in South Africa' during his 1880 election campaign.[4] The imperatives of power inevitably bred compromise, and from the outset Gladstone's government, 'elected on a largely anti-imperialist platform found itself uncomfortably squelching in too many imperial quagmires',[5] including Ireland, Afghanistan, the Sudan and South Africa.

In the case of the Transvaal it was thought the best course was to allow the status quo to continue, and Lord Kimberley, back as Colonial Secretary, reiterated the British government's determination not to reverse the annexation. Further Boer appeals to the British government fell on deaf ears; in some quarters it was hoped the recall of Sir Bartle Frere might ameliorate matters, but these hopes were scotched by growing unrest in the Transvaal encouraged by Lanyon's 'rigorous efforts to collect taxes'[6] and his total underestimation of the Boers' strength of purpose. Wolseley's replacement, Major General George Colley, withdrew imperial troops from the Transvaal, with the result that the British were caught completely off guard by the Boer declaration of a republic on 16 December 1880: the Day of the Covenant, commemorating the trekkers' vow to God prior to their victory over the Zulu at the battle of Ncome (Blood) River in 1838. The isolated garrisons at Pretoria, Marabastad, Potchefstroom, Lydenburg, Wakkerstroom, Standerton and Rustenburg suddenly found themselves under siege, and the British in the Transvaal looked to Natal for relief as Boer forces occupied 'the only viable entrance to the Transvaal from Natal at Laing's Nek',[7] just north of Newcastle.

The 'murderous attack' on the 94th Regiment referred to by Louie occurred on 20 December 38 miles east of Pretoria at Bronkhorstspruit. Here a British force of around 300 men retiring from Lydenburg to Pretoria found their progress halted by a Boer commando who, under a flag of truce, informed the British commander that any further advance would be judged a declaration of war. The parley was fruitless; the British advanced, the Boers closed in and opened fire – 56 soldiers were killed and 92 wounded, several dying later of their wounds. The Boers lost one man and four wounded. British settlers considered the attack an act of treachery; for the Boers it was their first victory.

The Haggards resolved 'against going up country at present', because if the 'Free State and Cape Boers join [the Transvaal Boers] they would have no great difficulty in accomplishing their object for a time so our present position is that of being stranded here while our things have all gone on'.[8] Her husband was in a quandary. Newcastle was close to the Transvaal border. 'Did I dare take my wife thither? ... To advance seemed too risky; to remain where we were was both wearisome and, with our servants, ruinously expensive.'[9]

The Haggards returned to Moseley's Hotel to sit out events, passing the time with carriage drives to scenic spots around Pietermaritzburg, strolling in the Botanical Gardens and calling upon old friends, such as John Shepstone and the Hendersons, as well as paying frequent visits to the Shepstones. To fend off boredom Haggard obtained some work in the government offices, where Louie joined him to 'do copying, so we are not quite so dull as before', though both were 'getting very sick of Maritzburg'.[10]

On New Year's Day 1881, Colley began moving the garrison troops at Fort Napier up to the Natal border. In the afternoon the Haggards went for a drive to see them on the march 'but only fell in with the wagons, a good many of which had stuck in the mud, the road being very bad'.[11]

On Monday, 3 January, Haggard heard that Newcastle was 'in a state of panic ... and the townspeople had gone into laager'. Two days later came news of the shooting of Captain J.M. Elliott and Captain R.H. Lambart, prisoners of the Boers. Both were granted parole conditional on not bearing arms for the duration of the war and escorted to the border. The two men were forced to cross the Vaal, then in flood, and when their cart overturned, the escort on the bank opened fire. Elliott was killed but Lambart managed to escape.[12]

In Maritzburg midsummer days were crossed off the calendar. On 9 January the couple dined at Government House on the evening before Colley left 'to take personal command of the troops at Newcastle'.[13] On that hot and humid January evening 'there were thirteen of us', recalled Haggard, 'of whom three were ladies – Lady Colley, another lady whose name I forget, and my wife'. The other guests were officers and members of Colley's staff. Haggard was sitting next to young Lieutenant Robert Elwes, recently out from England, who told him that shortly before his departure he had seen Haggard's father at King's Lynn station 'talking to the barmaid'.[14] Elwes had written out the dinner menus in French, a duty once Haggard's, and had rendered one of the dishes as *patés de mince*. Lady Colley had never heard of the dish and cast an enquiring glance at Elwes.

> '*Patés de mince*, Lady Colley,' he stammered presently, his youthful face covered with blushes, 'is the French for mince pies.'
> Poor Elwes! He did not hear the last of his *patés de mince* during that meal.[15]

Colley left for Newcastle the next day to join the Natal Field Force based at Fort Amiel in Newcastle and lead it into the Transvaal to relieve the besieged garrisons.[16] It was 45-year-old Colley's first independent field command, and his departure for the front prompted Shepstone to write in his diary: 'I hope he will not act rashly.'[17] 'Hurrah!' wrote Louie in hers the same day. 'The Boers have retreated across the border so we think of starting up country this week.'[18] This must have been a rumour, as the Boers remained encamped just south of the Natal border at Coldstream.

Rumour or no, knowing British troop reinforcements were on their way from India and unable to find any temporary accommodation in Maritzburg, the Haggards made their farewell calls, bought two more horses for the spider to add to the pair sent by Cochrane, and, with the garden at Hilldrop in mind, visited the Botanical Gardens to order some tree seeds and, as per Cochrane's recommendation, employed a cook, a Mrs Hyndeman, who would come to Hilldrop later with her husband. The Haggards dined with the Shepstones on the evening before their departure. 'Sir T.' was 'very averse to our starting so soon',[19] but the pregnant Louie was bent on leaving a 'fearfully hot'[20] Pietermaritzburg.

On Thursday, 13 January, the Haggards began the 175-mile trek to Newcastle. The rainy season was well under way and the roads were in a terrible state, 'being cut up by the passage of guns and troops. Indeed, there were no roads – simply, in that wet season, breadths of mud-holes sometimes a hundred yards wide, of which hole you might take your choice.'[21] The light-weight well-sprung Spider Phaeton was not the ideal conveyance for 'an extremely arduous journey',[22] and Louie's maid, Lucy

Gibbs, was thrown out of it several times, on one occasion falling 'right between the wheels'; fortunately she 'only bruised her arm a little and got a good shaking'.[23] The pregnant Louie was 'in a state in which great exertion was undesirable' but, thanks to the condition of the roads, ended up walking 'a good part of the way, in fact we all did, as it was quite as hard work hanging on driving as walking'.[24]

Rain forced them to stay over at the Castle Hotel with its 'funny little imitation of a castle at one side of it' on the banks of the Mngeni River in Howick.[25] The next morning, a sunny one, Haggard enjoyed a swim in the river and both were impressed by the Howick Falls, 'the finest I have ever seen' and, courtesy of the rain, 'more than usually beautiful'.[26] Back on the road, they reached Colenso, galloping ahead of a thunderstorm, the lightning 'striking behind us' and reducing Gibbs 'to a perfect jelly of terror'. Louie told her to stop making an exhibition of herself. '"Look at me, I'm not frightened." "No, ma'am, I see you ain't," answered the gasping Gibbs, "and I tell you straight I don't call it ladylike!"'[27]

In between storms, the sun beat down and temperatures hovered in the mid-thirties. Louie's face had become 'the colour of a boiled lobster and is in consequence very uncomfortable. Wear what hat you will nothing seems to keep out the sun & of course over rough roads you want your hands to hang on with & cannot always hold up an umbrella.'[28]

The effects of the Transvaal Rebellion were evident for all to see: 'At almost every stage we meet fugitives from the Transvaal, but they all seem to look upon Newcastle as safe.'[29]

On the final stage of their journey, with Newcastle 31 miles to the north-east, they encountered 'a swollen spruit which a man with some wagons declared was too deep for us. However we were not going to turn back over the fearful road we had come so we dashed bravely and got through all right'.[30] Haggard provided a more dramatic account in his autobiography, complete with 'two brawny Zulus' hanging on the side of the spider in order to prevent it overturning. The horses lost their footing in the deep water and 'struck out for the further shore of the drift'. The carriage, taking on water, began to float, 'but the brave Kaffirs hung on'. Gibbs 'wailed softly', clasping the dog Bob 'to her breast'. It was touch and go until 'the horses got their feet again, and we dragged through, damp but safe'.[31]

They reached Newcastle on 24 January, Louie 'feeling tired and seedy'.[32] Cochrane met them on the road and they all went into town for lunch before driving out to Hilldrop, 'which we found in a fearful state of confusion' as they were not expected so soon.[33] The farmhouse was 'full of fugitives from the Transvaal, friends of Mr Cochrane's' – the Schwikkard family.[34]

Otto Schwikkard, on his discharge after the Anglo-Zulu War, had bought two ox-waggons and set up as a transport rider, bringing goods up to the Transvaal from Durban harbour or the railway head, by then at Botha's Hill. The Transvaal Rebellion placed him in a dilemma; he had ridden with the Boer commandos against

Sekhukhune but had fought on the British side in the Anglo-Zulu War. In the event of war 'he would be a marked man if he remained in the Transvaal' and was advised to 'move his family, stock, waggons and household belongings to Natal'.[35] The family headed for Newcastle where Otto enlisted as a scout attached to the British Headquarters Staff, while his mother Louise and several of her younger children came to stay at Hilldrop.

Haggard was reunited with other old friends in Newcastle, including William Beaumont, the resident magistrate, with whom he had sailed to Natal in 1875. Another friend and fellow member of Shepstone's band of brothers was Inspector Frederick Phillips of the Natal Mounted Police, while the Anglo-Zulu War veteran Edward 'Lucky' Essex, now a brevet major, was on Colley's staff. There was an especially warm welcome for Haggard from Masuku, who had returned to his home in Natal when Haggard left for England and was now back to take up his place as Haggard's personal servant.

Cochrane and Blomefield were in good health, but there was no denying 'we have come up in very troublous times', Haggard told his father. 'When for various reasons we made up our mind to come up, Newcastle was looked on as one of the safest places in the Colony owing to the large body of troops there ... Then, to our dismay, we learned that on the very day of our arrival Colley had moved out to attack [Laing's] Nek.'[36] On 24 January a British force left Newcastle heading north and on 26 January made camp on the diminutive Mount Prospect. In response the Boer Commandant General, Piet Joubert, advanced south to Laing's Nek, the gateway to the Transvaal, taking up entrenched positions on the heights on either side of the road. On the morning of 28 January 'the sound of firing' was heard at Hilldrop, and in the afternoon Haggard received a note from Beaumont saying the attack on Laing's Nek had been a failure and the British troops forced 'to retire to their waggon laager, after heavy loss'. Beaumont didn't think that Newcastle was in any danger, but if there was cause for alarm 'I will send out a runner to warn you'.[37]

British cavalry and infantry had advanced up the slopes towards the Boers who were holding Laing's Nek after a reconnaissance by Major Essex and a group of scouts, including Otto Schwikkard, to establish the Boer positions. The British cavalry charge was beaten off and the infantry advance climaxed with a charge on the Boer position in which four out of five of Colley's staff officers who joined in the attack – all mounted – were killed, including the Haggards' dining companion in Pietermaritzburg, Lieutenant Elwes.[38] The surviving staff officer was 'Lucky' Essex – 'his usual good fortune attended him, for though his horse was killed and his helmet knocked off, he was not touched'.[39] The British losses were heavy: 84 men killed and 113 wounded; the Boers losing 14 killed and 27 wounded. It was a major reverse, and the recently arrived reinforcements from India were urgently moved up to Newcastle under General Sir Evelyn Wood, Colley's second-in-command.

As Shepstone feared, Colley had been rash. 'Nobody dreamed that Sir George Colley could be mad enough to try and force the passes with such a handful of men, and I believe he was again and again warned of its impossibility,' Haggard told his father. 'Every time one sees a Kafir runner coming to the house one feels anxious lest he should be the announcer of some fresh evil.' [40] At the end of January the Schwikkards moved into Newcastle; Louise Schwikkard promising to return for Louie's confinement, which was expected in June.

Around midday on 8 February, guns could be heard at 'work in the neighbourhood of the hill Schuins Hoogte [Sloping Heights], about eleven miles from our farm'.[41] Haggard read a letter from his mother while 'the air was alive with the roar of cannon and the crash of gatlings and musketry ... with what result we are entirely ignorant, but the fighting lasted more than two hours'.[42]

Following their victory at Laing's Nek, mounted parties of Boers harassed the British communication and supply route between the camp at Mount Prospect and Newcastle as well as raided farms south of the town. Colley decided on a show of strength, and on 8 February he led a force south from Mount Prospect across the Ingogo River along the road towards Newcastle. In response to a Boer attack, they moved off the road and took up a defensive position on the low plateau of Schuinshoogte. Lack of cover left the defenders exposed and the Boer marksmanship was deadly.

Otto Schwikkard was keeping his head down – he had scouted behind enemy lines prior to what became known as the Battle of Ingogo – and now he was dispatched back to Mount Prospect to call up reinforcements. The British managed to hold out until sunset when the Boers retired and rain set in. Colley retreated back across the Ingogo in a night march to Mount Prospect, and when the Boers returned at first light, they found the plateau deserted apart from a group of wounded men. British casualties were high – 53 killed and 63 wounded. The Boers are estimated to have had 8 killed and 10 wounded, 2 of whom subsequently died. 'Lucky' Essex again survived to tell the tale.

At Hilldrop the Haggards were sleeping in their clothes 'ready to make a bolt of it'[43] and were 'kept advised of all that happened through the Zulu natives dwelling on our farm'. Masuku and 'his friends night and day guarded us as a mother might her child'.[44] Boer incursions into Natal continued. 'Every night we were obliged to place out Kafirs as scouts to give us timely warning of the approach of marauding parties, and to sleep with loaded rifles close to our hands, and sometimes, when things looked very black, in our clothes, with horses ready saddled in the stable.'[45] One night 'in the stillness' Haggard heard 'the galloping of a vast number of horses. Some five hundred of the enemy had taken possession of the farm next to our own, which they looted.'

There were numerous false alarms. Haggard was sitting up late reading in the drawing room, the door on to the verandah ajar, when a voice outside demanded 'if the place was in the possession of the Boers'. The voice was followed by 'a full-cocked revolver' coming around the door and 'a line of armed figures in a crouching attitude stretching along the verandah into the garden beyond. It turned out to be a patrol of the mounted police.' They had been told the Boers had seized Hilldrop and 'had come to ascertain the truth of the report'.[46]

When rumours spread that the Boers planned to mount an attack on British reinforcements marching up from Pietermaritzburg, 'we colonists saw a chance' of cutting them off and the creation of a volunteer corps was mooted.[47] Haggard was undecided whether to join because of family responsibilities: 'I remember my young wife coming out of the house into the garden, where some of us were talking over the matter, and saying, "Don't consider me. Do what you think your duty."'[48] The authorities, anxious to prevent the war spreading to the civilian population, forbade the formation of a volunteer unit and Beaumont personally delivered the order to Haggard. 'It was a peculiar errand that he had to perform, but the British lion was a humble animal in those days; its tail was tucked very tightly between its legs.'[49]

As stories circulated that a major battle between the Boers and the British reinforcements now approaching Newcastle was to be fought on the southern boundary of Haggard's property and that the Boers intended occupying Hilldrop and the hill above, 'we retreated into laager in Newcastle' and spent a few 'very uncomfortable days'[50] with friends of Cochrane, the Tuckers. Mrs Tucker 'kindly put up a bed for [Louie] in her sitting room and Rider slept on the floor'.[51]

The British troops marched unscathed into Newcastle on 17 February and the Haggards returned to Hilldrop, where they got 'the house straight again' and cut hay in-between the heavy afternoon rains. They also 'discovered that someone had been stealing the feathers off two of the ostriches'. The two culprits were taken into Newcastle 'to receive the just rewards of their deeds, namely 20 lashes and two months' hard labour'.[52]

The weather was 'oppressively hot' on Sunday afternoon, 27 February, and, sitting on the verandah after lunch, Haggard 'thought he heard guns', but everyone else thought it was thunder. Nonetheless Haggard and Cochrane rode into town 'and came back with the startling news that an engagement had taken place near the "Nek", our loss was great and Sir G. Colley missing'.[53]

Peace negotiations with the Boers had been under way for some time behind the scenes, and Colley was ordered by the British government (now in direct telegraphic communication with South Africa) not to undertake offensive operations until a Boer response to a peace proposal had been received. Anticipating a negative response, Colley decided to occupy the mountain of Majuba commanding the western flank of the entrenched Boer positions at Laing's Nek. This was achieved with a night ascent up Majuba's southern face. By sunrise on Sunday, 27 February, Colley occupied the summit. Colley didn't intend this as an offensive operation, but the Boers interpreted the troop movements differently and advanced up Majuba's northern face, skilfully using dead ground and maintaining a heavy fire on the British, who were exposed on the skyline. When other Boer commandos advanced up the eastern and western sides of the mountain, the British position collapsed, Colley was killed and the survivors fled back down the mountain. Haggard reflected that less than two months after that farewell dinner on a hot night in Pietermaritzburg, 'Lady Colley, the other lady, my wife and I were the sole survivors of that dinner-party'.[54]

The Boer victory at Majuba was a humiliation: the 'might of the British Empire had been defeated by a small infant republic with no standing army'.[55] Of the British combatants, 92 officers and men were killed, 131 wounded and 57 taken prisoner. One Boer was killed and six wounded, one of whom subsequently died. Otto Schwikkard had been involved in a preliminary reconnaissance of Majuba on 25 February and, in a brief skirmish with a party of Boers, fell from his horse and injured his ankle. He returned safely to camp but required hospitalisation in Newcastle. Essex had yet another escape, by default; he had been ordered to remain at Mount Prospect.

Alexander Merensky, the German missionary from Botshabelo, was on the Boer side at Majuba, conscripted as a military medic.[56] Another familiar face among the Boers was Alfred Aylward, veteran of the Black Flag Revolt turned mercenary in the Transvaal and now reinvented as a war correspondent. His claims of British atrocities against the Pedi had embarrassed Shepstone's administration and he was given a year's pay and free passage back to England, where he supervised the publication of his book *The Transvaal Today*, a surprisingly objective piece of reportage. He returned to South Africa during the Anglo-Zulu War to become an erratic but innovative editor of the *Natal Witness*.[57] His open support for the Boer cause offended the patriotic sensibilities of his readers and, in danger of being lynched, he left Pietermaritzburg in disguise and was next spotted 'on the summit of Majuba as an adviser of sorts to the Boer forces'[58] and correspondent for the *Daily Telegraph*, which ran his account of the battle.

With Colley dead, Evelyn Wood was appointed acting Governor of Natal and High Commissioner of the Transvaal, and on 4 March he met General Piet Joubert and agreed to a truce.

'We are not altogether in an enviable position,' Louie told her mother-in-law, describing the British troops as 'panic-stricken' by their string of defeats, though she gave due credit to the tenacity of the Boers: 'Their coolness and pluck are wonderful, and they have not made *one* false move yet. Add to this the fact that they are all splendid shots, and you will agree that it is no mean foe with whom we have to deal, though this is what our officers and men would not first believe hence these sad disasters.'[59]

Unlike the war, indeed thanks to it, Rooi Point farm was flourishing. Haymaking was 'a new departure in that district in our time', Haggard recalled with pride, and the presence of so many horses thanks to the military meant that good forage was in demand, so prices were high. 'I remember selling the result of about a month of my own work for £250, and never in all my life have I been prouder of anything than I was of earning that money, literally with my hands and by the sweat of my brow.'[60]

The ostriches were also 'doing nicely' and some had 'splendid feathers', Louie told her mother-in-law, but to Louie's great frustration Mr Hyndeman had arrived minus his wife, the cook; 'so afraid of the Boers', she had stayed behind in Ladysmith. Louie insisted she put in 'an appearance as soon as possible ... Our hearts misgive us though at the thought of the life she will lead us with her fancies and I daresay we shall wish her back at Ladysmith.'[61] Mrs Hyndeman evidently lived up to expectations and is noticeable by her absence from Louie's diary until 14 July: 'Mrs Hyndeman departed early this morning hip, hip, hurrah!! All faces beam with delight. I have taken charge of the cooking for the present.'[62]

Moments of delight were to be savoured in this time of uneasy truce. The tense atmosphere was exacerbated by an outbreak of horse sickness 'raging at Newcastle ... so badly indeed that we lost £200 worth of animals in a month'. Haggard had no fears for Moresco 'since he was "salted" ... we believed that he could not take it again'.[63] He was mistaken. Moresco had contracted the sickness 'in its worse form, but we knew nothing of it until he was dying'.

> In the middle of the night we were awakened by a sound of somebody banging on the back door of the house. It was Moresco. He had come down from the hill side, contrived to jump or clamber over the wall, dying though he was, and now with his head he was knocking on the door to call us to his assistance. We could do nothing for him; we drove him through the gateway, and there by the wall we found him still and dead in the morning.[64]

One of Louise Schwikkard's horses stabled at Hilldrop also succumbed, and the retriever Jet died of distemper.

The guns remained silent and the daily round of the farm continued undisturbed, apart from the dispatch of poisonous snakes close to the house and the seasonal afternoon thunderstorms. The truce held and social life resumed. The district surgeon Dr Charles Gubbins and his wife Maud[65] dropped by, and 'Lucky' Essex called one afternoon, staying on to dinner. 'We were very glad to see him. He is going down country for the present having got some appointment in Durban.'[66]

News filtered down that peace with the Boers was on the cards, 'much to our disgust',[67] and an armistice was agreed on 23 March. Two days later Louie learned 'that we are going to give back a great part of the Transvaal to the Boers and that there is to be a two months' cessation of hostilities and a commission formed to finally settle the terms of peace. Colonists and soldiers are alike very indignant.'[68] The appointment of a royal commission to negotiate peace terms meant the retrocession of Transvaal was certain. British colonials felt abandoned by Gladstone's government. Haggard experienced the retrocession as a 'great betrayal, the bitterness of which no lapse of time ever can solace or even alleviate'.[69]

Haggard was in Newcastle when the news arrived:

> Some thousands of people were gathered [on the market square], many of them refugees, among whom were a number of loyal Boers, and with these soldiers, townsfolk and natives. I saw strong men weeping like children, and heard English-born people crying aloud that they were 'b----y Englishmen' no more ... An idea suddenly ran through the crowd; 'they made a rude effigy of Mr. Gladstone and, as was done in most other loyal parts of South Africa, burnt it with contempt and curses.[70]

As for the 'unfortunate loyal inhabitants' in the Transvaal, they simply packed up and left; 'they came pouring down through Newcastle by hundreds; it was the most melancholy exodus that can be imagined. There were people of all classes, officials, gentlefolk, work-people, and loyal Boers, but they had a connecting link; they had all been loyal, and they were all ruined.'[71]

On the evening of 29 March, Wood and Colonel Redvers Buller visited Hilldrop 'on business for a few minutes'. Louie was 'not much taken with either of them'.[72] The next day a message from Wood enquired 'if we should feel inclined to let Sir Hercules Robinson have this house to hold the [peace] conference in ... at £200 for the month'.[73] An imperial professional, 56-year-old Robinson had arrived at the Cape in January after being appointed to replace Frere as Governor and High Commissioner for the Cape Colony. Born in Rosmead, Westmeath, Ireland, Robinson enjoyed a brief military career after training at Sandhurst; a career he quickly finessed through marriage and an influential father-in-law into a highly successful one in the Colonial Service. He had hardly settled into the governorship of New Zealand when he was dispatched to the Cape.

Haggard and Cochrane signed an agreement to let Hilldrop at the end of April as a residence for Robinson and his staff, all except for one room – the Haggards' bedroom which was for use by Louie.[74] 'We shall have to live in a kind of picnic fashion,' Louie informed her mother-in-law, 'our house-room will consist of a bedroom and two tents!' – one for a kitchen and the other for Jack Haggard, who was expected in early May. Cochrane and Blomefield would bed down in the mill. 'Happily the rains seem to have come to an end for this season and we are now having bright sunny weather, just the right sort for camping out.'[75]

The social round went on uninterrupted – visits to the Beaumonts, the Tuckers and Louise Schwikkard. In due course the withdrawal of British troops from the Transvaal brought with them Owen Lanyon and Marshall Clarke, both of whom visited Hilldrop several times.[76] Another visitor from Pretoria, who stayed several days at Hilldrop, was Lewis Ford. With Ford, Haggard and Cochrane all under one roof, there are no letters to offer a glimpse of their interactions during this time.

During April the steam-driven grinding mill (now repaired) was erected at the foot of the 'boulder-strewn hill' behind the farmhouse and started for the first time. Standing on a ladder, Blomefield adjusted the safety valves when 'a tremendous noise was heard and rush of steam and water came out'. Everyone 'fled for their lives thinking something fearful had happened', while Blomefield 'came down with a crash upon his head, happily without hurting himself at all. I am sure one of them will get blown up in the end, and am only glad Rider's talents do not lie in the machinery line.'[77]

A qualified engineer, Mr North, was hired to run the mill in the hope 'we should make our fortunes or at any rate do very well as millers'.[78] Brick-making was the better option – 'for which there was a good market in Newcastle', thanks to the sudden concentration of troops and refugees.[79] It was hard work, so much so that 'Natal Boers used to ride from quite a distance to see two white farmers actually working with their own hands. One of the curses of South Africa is ... the universal habit of relegating all manual toil, or as much of it as possible, to Kaffirs, with the result that it came to be looked upon as a more or less degrading occupation only fit for black men.'[80]

Farming ostriches was also a first in that part of Natal, perhaps with good reason. One gave Cochrane a 'frightful drubbing', and through a pair of opera glasses Haggard saw 'an unfortunate Kaffir barely escape with his life ... by going to earth in an ant-bear hole'.[81] The birds also exhibited a magpie-like tendency to 'pick up pocket knives or anything that attracts them'. One bird swallowed a bone that caught in its gullet. Haggard and Cochrane operated using a cutthroat razor, and not surprisingly the ostrich 'resented our surgical aid'. They removed the bone, but when the bird turned up a few weeks later 'with another bone immovably planted in exactly the same place', it was left to its fate.[82]

Haggard and Cochrane tapped another source of income, buying and hiring out draught oxen and waggons to the authorities for transport, 'though from these trips they returned dreadfully footsore and poor'.[83] Some were sent down to the bushveld to recover. A message came back informing them that the animals had died from eating a poisonous herb called tulip. 'We often wondered whether "tulip" really accounted for their disappearance from our ken.'[84]

On 28 April there came a telegram: Jack Haggard was in Cape Town. He had come to southern Africa seeking to combine a visit to Hilldrop with finding an appointment in the Colonial Service. Haggard feared his brother had 'arrived at a bad time for Govt employ as the country is flooded with kicked out Transvaal officials who of course have some claim'.[85] Jack planned to arrive in Durban on 2 May and then travel upcountry to Newcastle. With the Cape Governor, Sir Hercules Robinson, also heading that way, Jack decided to delay presenting his letters of introduction until they met in Newcastle. There was no delay when it came to romance: in Durban Jack wooed a Miss Noffman.

Haggard was right, it was not great timing on his Jack's part: employment prospects were negligible and, in addition, Haggard and Louie were 'seriously debating clearing out of this part of the world'. The war and its outcome had strengthened Haggard's 'conviction that henceforth we can look for no peace or security in S. Africa' and that it was 'no place for an Englishman to make a home in'.[86] Haggard was not without regret at this conclusion: 'we were just beginning to do well, and had there been no war I think this would have developed into a very thriving concern'.[87] The Haggards weren't planning to return to England but had 'fixed on Vancouver Island for our next Colonial venture', a choice likely inspired by Jack's praises of the island paradise.

> I daresay you will wonder at our wishing to go elsewhere, but there are several reasons that impel us to do so. First we both like Colonial life, next, it is satisfactory to be earning one's own living, and thirdly and chiefly I am very anxious to form connections with some country in which it is possible for a man of moderate means to start his children in some respectable career in which they can earn their livelihood and have a fair chance of getting on in the world. This I had hoped to do in Natal but events have been against us.[88]

On Friday, 6 May, Robinson's servant came to take over the house, 'so we cleared most of the things and got the rooms ready'. Robinson would be joined by two other royal commissioners, President Johannes Brand of the Free State and Sir Henry de Villiers, the Chief Justice of the Cape. Robinson moved in on the Sunday. Haggard and Cochrane dined with him on Monday evening and thought him 'a very pleasant old gentleman'.[89] The commission occupied the farmhouse for five weeks. The irony of the situation did not escape Haggard: 'It was a strange fate which decreed that the Retrocession of the Transvaal, over which I had myself hoisted the British flag, should be practically accomplished beneath my roof'.[90]

The first official sitting of the commission took place on 10 May in Newcastle. Three days later Jack arrived at Hilldrop bringing 'good news of all at home',[91] along with his terrier Spice, 'who signalised her arrival by fighting the household cat at the top of a tree'.[92] In Pietermaritzburg Jack had spoken to Shepstone about the possibility of employment, but there was none to be had and, when he presented his letters of introduction to Evelyn Wood, he was told that 'all vacant appointments in this Colony will be offered to men who have lost their own in the Transvaal'.[93] Strangely, given his past eulogies, Jack wasn't in favour of relocating to Vancouver. 'His account of Vancouver Island is such as to make us abandon our idea of forming a company and going there, so I suppose we must stay on here and then come home.'[94]

While the commission occupied Hilldrop, Louie gave birth on the morning of Monday, 23 May: 'Baby was born at ¼ to 6am.'[95] Haggard telegraphed the news to Bradenham Hall, writing to his father the following day. Owing to a miscalculation, the baby was not expected for another three weeks, so when Louie's labour pains began on Sunday evening they were judged to be false. 'Towards five o'clock on the following morning the pains increased in severity and it became clear this was the real thing.' Haggard sent at once for Dr Gubbins and Mrs Schwikkard, 'but within half an hour of that the child was born'. Prior to the doctor's and Mrs Schwikkard's expected arrival, there was 'considerable anxiety' as the maid Gibbs 'did not know what to do. Indeed Jack and myself were by no means certain we would not be obliged to do what was necessary ourselves.' Mrs Schwikkard arrived, 'bringing the cheerful news Gubbins was away on holiday'. Fortunately Mrs Schwikkard 'had considerable experience in this sort of thing [she had nine children] and so she soon got things pretty straight'. In the absence of Gubbins, Haggard sent for Surgeon Major William Johnstone, 'a friend of mine who is one of the head military doctors ... and before three hours were over he was here and did what remained to be done very satisfactorily'.

Haggard was pleased to report mother and child were doing 'as well as possible ... The child is a very perfect and fine boy, he weighed nine pounds just after birth ... He has dark blue eyes and is a fair child – with a good forehead, and I think that is all I have to tell you about him.'[96] Shepstone sent his congratulations. 'Fortunately everything that is born in a stable is not a horse, or your boy would be a Boer or a Royal Commissioner; the latter he may become, the former never.'[97]

A notable visitor to Hilldrop during this time was the 'popular young authoress', 26-year-old Lady Florence Dixie.[98] An enthusiastic sportswoman and proto-feminist – she refused to ride side-saddle and designed her own clothes – Dixie acquired her title courtesy of her marriage to the somnolent but pliable Sir Alexander Beaumont Churchill Dixie. In 1878 Dixie travelled to Patagonia with her husband and brothers, chronicling their journey in her book *Across Patagonia*. Seeking further adventure, she looked to the war in South Africa and was appointed as a war correspondent (reputedly the first female one) to the *Morning Post*. The war was over by the time she arrived, but nevertheless she set out for the front, galloping across the veld and camping under the stars. At Newcastle she met up with a cousin, Captain Douglas of the 15th Hussars, and toured the battlefields with him, making a special visit to the military cemetery at Mount Prospect to pay her respects at the grave of Robert Elwes. 'We had been playmates in childhood, and friends in later years. Standing by the grave of the gallant boy, I found old scenes recurring with great force and vividness.'[99]

Dixie and her husband were invited by Robinson to dine at Hilldrop but got lost on the way, a matter 'of slight moment, for were not the reward of a good dinner and the luxury of a real house and its comforts awaiting us? Poor Sir Hercules Robinson! he did not call them comforts – what to us was luxury was to him the reverse.'[100] Haggard was unaware of Robinson's unhappiness with the accommodation and only briefly met Dixie at the time of her visit. A year later Haggard and Dixie would be adversaries in print.

The commission left Hilldrop on 2 June 1881 to continue their negotiations in the Transvaal, where the Pretoria Convention between the Boers and the British was signed on 3 August. Before the commissioners' departure Haggard and Jack were invited to dine, the latter using the opportunity to enquire about employment, again without success. Haggard wrote to Shepstone the following day, expressing his liking for Robinson and suggesting Shepstone write 'some vindication' of his policies in the Transvaal. 'It would carry great weight ... since it must be remembered that after all the respectable part of the nation at home is deeply disgusted with this business. I don't see why these asses should go on braying eternally without some contradiction.'[101] Shepstone demurred: there was nothing 'to be said about the Transvaal that would have the slightest effect just now; the humiliation is determined upon and must be endured: natural causes and natural processes are all that can now be looked for to bring about amelioration.'[102]

Shepstone's omission would be remedied by Haggard with his first book, *Cetywayo and His White Neighbours*, published in June 1882. Meanwhile Haggard vented his frustration in a detailed letter to Frere, who pronounced the missive 'one of the best accounts I have read of the present miserable state of affairs in the Transvaal' but took a similar line to Shepstone: 'I have done my best to make the truth known publicly and privately and have not yet given up hopes that the terrible evils of England forsaking her children may be averted. But *how* I hardly see. At present Mr. Gladstone is practically supreme in such matters, and his one idea seems to be to reverse all that has been done hitherto by his predecessors.'[103]

On 11 June 1881 'baby was christened by the name of Arthur John Rider'. Cochrane and Jack were godfathers and Louise Schwikkard godmother, standing in as proxy for Louie's aunt Louisa. 'Had a nice lunch afterwards and drank the youngster's health. Also Jack's, it being his birthday.'[104] The infant's first two names reflected those of his godfathers', but in his early years the child was referred to as Rider and later, 'by his own wish', he was called Jock to avoid confusion with his father.[105] Haggard forwarded Jock's birth registration and baptismal certificates to Fred Blake in London, telling his solicitor the outlook for South Africa was 'very black and I am beginning to be doubtful if it will be a safe place for respectable people to live in. More mischief has been done in the last six months and the seeds of more trouble and bloodshed sown than it is possible for anybody who does not live in the country to understand.'[106]

At Hilldrop on 14 June, Lieutenant Ian Hamilton and Captain Augustus Morris, each with an arm in a sling, 'called to see the ostriches'. Both had been wounded at Majuba and mentioned in dispatches.[107] Hamilton played a significant role in the battle, holding a section of the perimeter, and was shot in the wrist during the British collapse. He would go on to be the future hero of the march on Pretoria in the Anglo-Boer War, commander-in-chief at Gallipoli in 1915 and a close friend of Winston Churchill. His acquaintance with Haggard dated from this visit to Hilldrop.[108]

Two days later Melmoth Osborn dropped by on his way from Zululand to Pretoria, where his presence was required by the royal commission. While Osborn and the others were inspecting the mill, a Zulu servant named Foulata came to Louie at the farmhouse, 'saying something about a fire and on going to look what was our horror to see a big grass fire coming up at the back of the house like a race horse'. The groom Stephen Lanham 'rushed off to help beat it out and Jack who came home just then also lent a hand and after great exertions they managed to turn it up the hill and saved the stables etc. which otherwise would have been burnt'.[109] Foulata would give her name to a key character in *King Solomon's Mines*, one half of an interracial romance with the naval captain John Good, a character partially based on Jack.

Osborn, on his way back from Pretoria, came for breakfast on 1 July, after which 'Jack started with him for Zululand' for a dash of experience at the cutting edge of colonial service. According to Haggard, his brother accompanied Osborn 'to try and put a stop to a big row ... One of the old tribal chiefs has asserted himself and ousted a puppet Govt Chief set over his tribe by Sir G. Wolseley ... Thus civil war is pending in Zululand and Osborn has gone to try and stop it Jack accompanying him.'[110] Osborn was in central Zululand, where his Zulu-style homestead consisted of a number of huts and rondavels located at the foot of Nhlazatshe, a sugar-loaf mountain. The Wolseley settlement was fast unravelling, and the relationship between rulers and ruled became increasingly tenuous, especially as the appointed chiefs abused their positions to settle old scores. An uSuthu deputation, supporters of the Zulu royal house, had gone to Pietermaritzburg in May 1880 to protest against their 'treatment at the hands of Hamu and Zibhebhu and to ask if Cetshwayo might be allowed to return to Zululand'.[111] They were redirected to the British Resident, so they came to Nhlazatshe and laid their grievances before Osborn. In January 1881, after six months of dithering, Osborn held an inquiry into the treatment of the uSuthu chiefs.

When Jack Haggard left Nhlazatshe in early August, Osborn was preparing for Wood's visit to Zululand to deliver judgment on the complaints from the uSuthu on 31 August 1881. On the appointed day Wood and his staff with a large military escort including a military band, together with Osborn and the *Morning Post* correspondent Lady Florence Dixie, sat down to meet the uSuthu. Five of Cetshwayo's brothers were present as well as his son Dinuzulu. They assumed their grievances would be addressed, but they had misread the situation. Osborn was Shepstone's man and shared his master's views regarding Cetshwayo; Zibhebhu's rule must be respected and the complaining *amakosi* (chiefs) expelled from their districts and sent elsewhere. It now became clear to the uSuthu that 'the authorities intended to co-operate with the appointed chiefs in their destruction ... They had come to Osborn for redress and been viciously punished for it.'[112]

Instructed not to ask the Zulu any questions at the Nhlazatshe meeting as to their feelings about Cetshwayo, Dixie smelt a rat and undertook her own 'pilgrimage of inquiry'.[113] This brought her into contact with the Colensos, who helped facilitate an interview with Cetshwayo in Cape Town. She wrote a sympathetic account published in the *Morning Post*, which included 'an impassioned plea for his restoration'.[114] On her return to England she vigorously campaigned for the king's release and reinstatement, writing letters to the Queen and the Prince of Wales, and articles for the *Morning Post* and *Vanity Fair*, as well as a book on her experiences in southern Africa, *In the Land of Misfortune*.

At Hilldrop on 11 July, Haggard and Louie sat down and made 'a rough calculation of what the past six months has cost us and found to our horror that including our debts and expenditure it was about £450'. In the afternoon, hoping for some light relief, they 'rode over to a Kaffir dance but found on our arrival that there was a fight going on which Mr Cochrane stopped with some difficulty after one or two men had been severely hurt'.[115]

On 24 July Haggard received a letter from his father 'urging our return home'.[116] Why exactly is not known, but it may have had something to do with William Haggard's finances as Blake, the family solicitor, had also written to Hilldrop recommending they return. Haggard made up his mind to leave as soon as possible. Though he had given due consideration to what his father and Mr Blake had written, the real reason for coming back 'in such a hurry' was the state of the country, 'so unsatisfactory and so dangerous that I do not, having the safety of others at stake, feel justified in remaining'. Cochrane, 'suffering from a prolonged attack of dysentery', would come with them; 'a rest and a change of air is the only thing that will pull him together again'. Once recovered, Cochrane would return to Hilldrop. In the meantime the farm was to be left in the charge of George Blomefield and Mr North. Haggard hoped to 'get away about 30 August'.[117] Haggard gave similar reasons for leaving to Shepstone: 'I don't see how respectable people can be expected to stop up here in this land of murder and sudden death.'[118]

On 1 August Louie began packing and 'Rider went to town to arrange with an auctioneer about selling our furniture'.[119] Jack was yet to return from Zululand and everyone was apprehensive about his reaction to the news of their departure. They needn't have been, for when Jack returned on 5 August, he was all for returning to England as well.

Rider and Louie celebrated their first wedding anniversary on 11 August and, accompanied by friends, 'went for a very jolly picnic to Tiger's Kloof', a local beauty spot close to Hilldrop.[120] The same day the last of their luggage 'left for Maritzburg'.[121]

Southern Africa was not quite finished with them yet: on 17 August a Zulu named Indabezimbi arrived at Hilldrop and 'asked permission to settle on the farm. He had been robbed and nearly murdered by the Boers.' Haggard and Cochrane spent most of the day taking Indabezimbi's statement and 'that of his wives',[122] statements later appended to *Cetywayo and His White Neighbours* to illustrate the 'treatment the Kafir must expect at the hands of the Boer, now that he is no longer protected by us'.[123] The name of one of Indabezimbi's wives, Gagaoola, would be bestowed on a major character in *King Solomon's Mines*, the ancient sangoma, referred to as Gagool or Gagaoola.[124]

Everyone at Hilldrop rose 'very early' on 23 August, the day of the auction. There were 198 lots, including the phaeton, the contents of the dining room, two bedrooms, pantry, wine cellar, kitchen and verandah, along with sporting items, such as a 'double-barrelled gun, central fire, No. 12, hammerless, highly finished, right barrel modified choke-bore, left barrel full bore; an excellent killing gun'.[125] The imported items were the main attraction, as 'such articles were then rare at Newcastle'. The grand piano, bought 'second-hand for £40 in England, fetched £200, and the other things went at proportionately good prices. During the auction bidders 'got hold of a stock of wine which was exposed upon the verandah and therein drank our healths, whereon the watchful auctioneer knocked it down to the drinkers at a high price per dozen'.[126] The auction 'continued until dark', recorded Louie, and after 'it was all over we drove into town and I believe we were none of us sorry to think that the worry and confusion of the last few days was over and that we were really starting on our journey though both Rider and I were very sorry to leave dear old Hilldrop.'[127]

Haggard recalled in his autobiography feeling sad 'as we drove down the dusty track to Newcastle, and the familiar house, surrounded by its orange trees, grew dim and vanished from our sight. There my son had been born; there I had undergone many emotions of a kind that help to make a man; there I had suffered the highest sort of shame, shame for my country; there, as I felt, one chapter in my eventful life had opened and had closed.'[128] The saddest farewell was to Masuku:

> The poor fellow was moved at this parting, and gave me what probably he valued more than anything he possessed, the kerry [stick] that he carried ever since he was a man – that same heavy, redwood instrument with which more than once I have seen him battering the head of some foe ... were I to revisit Africa today, I have not the faintest doubt but that he would reappear. I should go out of my hotel and see a grey-headed man squatted on the roadside, who would arise, lift up his arm, salute me and say 'Inkoos Indanda, you are here; I am here, come back to serve you.' ... I do not know that I felt anything more in leaving Africa than the saying of good-bye to this loving, half-wild man.[129]

The journey to Durban was a repeat of their trek upcountry: unplanned overnight stays due to rain-soaked roads and, this time, heavy snow falls, the drifts forcing them to 'drive along the side of the road where the snow was not so thick'.[130] On the road to Mooi River they encountered a man with two waggons. Thirty-one of his oxen had died 'of the cold the previous night'.[131] The 'last survivor stood over them, his great horns swinging to and fro'. By the nearest waggon 'sat a man and woman, rude, unwashed Boers. We asked them if the snow had killed the oxen, and the man answered "Ja." "They were all we had," added the woman, in an unemotional voice.

"Now we are beggars.'"[132] Unknown to the Haggards, Otto Schwikkard was also a victim of the storm. The oxen for his transport business were wiped out by the same August snows of 1881; he lost 256 animals.[133]

The Haggards arrived in Pietermaritzburg on Monday, 29 August. Shepstone had left for Durban 'having heard of the snow up country and thinking we could not possibly get through'.[134] Though they managed the trek, their luggage was delayed by the weather on the top of Maritzburg's Town Hill. They wouldn't see it again until in England. That afternoon they caught the three o'clock train to Durban and on Tuesday met up with Shepstone and their friend Major Essex while Jack 'went to call upon Miss Noffman (otherwise his "limp lank long Lily love")' who 'came to call upon us in the afternoon'.[135]

At eight o'clock the next morning they boarded the tug that would take them out to the *Dunkeld* beyond the bar. Their departure was blighted by the death of their terrier Bob, 'apparently from poison. He was not well last night but we did not think it anything serious.'[136] Major Essex waved them goodbye and on 'Wednesday, the 31st August, from the deck of the *Dunkeld*, we saw the shores of Natal recede from our sight forever'.[137] Or so Haggard believed when writing his autobiography thirty years later.

Sailing south to Cape Town, Louie and Gibbs both succumbed to the seasickness that had afflicted them on the outward journey from England. On 2 September the *Dunkeld* arrived at Port Elizabeth and they transferred to the *Dublin Castle* for the voyage to England, but not before hearing of the 'terrible *Teuton* wreck'.[138] The RMS *Teuton*, bound for Port Elizabeth from Cape Town, had struck a rock on the night of 30 August. Only 11 passengers and 25 crew members survived out of the 272 people on board.

This tragedy, so close in time and geography, can only have reinforced Haggard's philosophic fatalism and his depressive morbidity in the face of implacable fate, his sense that 'this world is one of the hells'.[139] Haggard had been no stranger to sudden and violent death in southern Africa, often the consequence of a frontier settler society bent on dispossessing and subjugating the indigenous inhabitants. He could compile a long list of friends and acquaintances who had died in the wars against the Pedi, the Zulu and the Boers; there were deaths due to murder, disease and fever, and there were his own brushes with mortality – lost in the veld; unwitting object of a frustrated assassination plot – and the death of his illegitimate child, Ethel Rider. In his fiction Haggard's alter ego, Allan Quatermain, would voice his creator's views on the fragility and uncertainty of human existence, and in many of his novels Haggard explored notions of life – and love – after death; the brevity and the suffering of human existence fuelling his own search for eternal verities. Meanwhile the mundane held sway: in Cape Town, Louie bought a new dress and hat, 'all my luggage having been left behind'.[140]

They sailed on 6 September, breaking their journey at Madeira, where they spent a fortnight awaiting their luggage while enjoying the sights, relaxing and writing letters. When the *Kinfauns Castle* arrived on 5 October, nothing 'was to be heard [of our luggage] so we are no better off than if we had gone straight home'.[141]

12

'WRITE A BIT, DON'T YOU?'

On arrival in England, the Haggards spent time in London visiting Louie's relatives and showing off Jock while Haggard put out feelers for employment. As Ditchingham House was occupied by a tenant, they decided to base themselves at Bradenham Hall in order to have a rest 'after our African adventures'.[1] Haggard spent the first few days shooting with his brothers Will and Jack. Stephen Lanham, the groom, returned to his duties in the Hall's stables while Lucy Gibbs 'remained in our service for a year or two, then left and vanished away as modern domestics do'.[2] Louie's diary entries gradually petered out, ending with the short statement: 'Baby cut his first tooth.'[3]

Lilly Jackson's brother Frederick was a guest at Bradenham at this time. He was planning a hunting expedition to Kashmir, and Haggard was enthusiastic with advice; hunting was a subject of mutual interest and so 'flowered the deep affection that existed between the two men throughout their lives'.[4]

The weeks at Bradenham were 'happy days' for Haggard, filled with 'the well-remembered round of partridge shooting, dinner-parties with old friends who had known him since his birth, and Sunday by Sunday the walk across the park to the little church'.[5] One Sunday afternoon, leaving Louie to wheel Jock in his pram up and down the Philosopher's Walk, Haggard went indoors and upstairs to the library to see his mother. She was in the company of his brother Andrew and Bessie Ravenshaw, a family friend. Andrew was paging through a manuscript of his recently completed first novel.[6] Haggard had read the manuscript and thought it 'rather a bad novel, but nothing would have induced him to say so – Andrew disliked criticisms'.[7]

Bessie and his mother went to find Louie and the baby while Haggard stood at the window enjoying his favourite view: 'the drive leading to the road on the left backed by the Long Plantation, the group of great oaks and beeches, the green sweep of pasture and the footpath running down to the church and village'.[8] Lilias says her father, who must have been her source, was musing on ideas of 'England and home', wondering if 'any man could know the full meaning of those two words who had not lived abroad? – yet already he found himself regretting the hard and dangerous life'.[9] Now rested after his 'African adventures', what was he to do next? As if privy to these thoughts, Andrew 'looked up from his manuscript and said idly: "Well, old chap, what are your plans for the future?"' His brother had no idea. His father wanted him to take up law, but Haggard couldn't see himself 'sitting on my tail for ever in musty courts in London – I wouldn't mind if I could get out to Africa again.' Andrew suggested he should 'read for the Bar and fill up your time writing – you do write a bit, don't you?'

'Only a few articles on African affairs. I should like to write a book though about all this business of Cetywayo – after all, I was there and saw it from the inside.'

'No one wants to hear about that, old chap, the whole thing has raised enough stink as it is; write a novel.' ...

'Do you think I could?'

Andrew rose, and with a magnificent gesture waved his voluminous manuscript under Rider's nose.

'Do I think you could? Certainly I do! Our mother can and has written various things, I have already written one, as you see. It is evidently in the blood! Take my advice, old fellow, and try your hand at it. There are precious few things we cannot do if we try.'[10]

The brothers long remembered this conversation, Andrew always maintaining that 'Rider owed his literary success to the advice given'. Andrew left the library and Haggard sat down until the sound of slamming doors downstairs, his father's voice 'roaring to the patient Hocking to find his slippers, the barking of dogs, and the clatter of cups heralded the family coming to tea.[11] When Haggard went down to join them, his mind was made up to read for the Bar.'[12]

By Christmas Haggard, Louie and Jock were living at Weston Lodge, a small rented furnished house in the South London suburb of Upper Norwood, from where Haggard presented himself at Lincoln's Inn on the presumption his admission would be immediate. To his dismay he was expected to take an entrance examination. He appealed to the Benchers, the governing body of the Inn, that an examination was 'perhaps superfluous' given his experience as Master of the High Court of the Transvaal. His appeal was refused. 'So I set to work and, with the assistance of a crammer, in a month learned more Latin than I had done all the time I was at school',[13] and well enough to pass 'the examination at the head of the batch who went up with me'.[14]

He began reading for the Bar examinations and, when time allowed, faithful to his original idea of writing an insider's view of the annexation of the Transvaal and the Anglo-Zulu War, started work on what would become his first book. To ensure its accuracy he 'purchased all the Blue-books dealing with the period of which I was treating, and made précis of them.'[15] The result was *Cetywayo and His White Neighbours.*

The timing for such a title looked exactly right. Lady Florence Dixie's campaign on behalf of the Zulu king, aided and abetted by the Colensos, had paid off: Cetshwayo was due to visit England in the summer of 1882 to plead his cause and request he be restored to his throne, but when Haggard finished his book at the end of April 1882, he was confronted by a difficulty he hadn't anticipated, 'finding somebody willing to publish it'.[16] He fired off letters to potential publishers describing the book as the product of six years' experience in South Africa 'in official and private capacities' and recommending sections of the book most likely to ensure its sale 'both here and in the Colonies ... As you are no doubt aware, the ex-king will visit England very shortly, when I think an opportunely published work on the subject would find a ready sale.'[17]

The reaction was overwhelmingly negative: 'nobody wanted anything to do with either Cetewayo or his white neighbours. At length I was faced with the alternative of putting the results of my labours into the fire or of paying for their production in book form.'[18] Trübner and Co., run by the scholar and publisher Nicholas Trübner, expressed interest in such an arrangement and Haggard sent them the manuscript on 14 May 1882. On 18 May Trübner and Co. informed Haggard they would take his manuscript and turn it into a book of 320 pages with a print run of 750 copies on receipt of 'a cheque for the sum of £50 sterling'.[19] Haggard sent the cheque by return of post.

Cetywayo and His White Neighbours, or, Remarks on Recent Events in Zululand, Natal, and the Transvaal was published on 22 June 1882, Haggard's twenty-sixth birthday. The book is, to quote the historian Jeff Guy, 'an extremely lucid, cleverly presented statement of Shepstone's views on South African affairs'.[20] Haggard's bias and his loyalty to Shepstone undoubtedly stamp the book, but it remains an invaluable primary source and by any yardstick an impressive first book: an assertive, combative, confident polemic in which Haggard expresses his views on affairs in South Africa, including the annexation of the Transvaal, the Anglo-Zulu War, the Transvaal Rebellion and the retrocession of the Transvaal.

In the book's first section, 'Cetywayo and the Zulu Settlement', written in expectation of Cetshwayo's visit to England, Haggard attacks Dixie and her recent pamphlet, 'A Defence of Zululand and Its Kings', an attack which segues into a broadside against supporters of Cetshwayo's restoration, including Bishop Colenso ('as usual working his own wires, and creating agitations to forward his ends'),[21] and proceeds to demolish *History of the Zulu War and Its Origin* by Colenso's daughter Frances. However, Haggard does concede the Natal government 'had no right to dictate the terms to a Zulu king on which he was to hold his throne' and that Zululand 'was an independent nation'.[22]

Haggard stresses Cetshwayo's 'bloodthirstiness, so strenuously denied by his apologists',[23] and lambasts the king's 'lady advocates'.[24] Acknowledging the 1878 ultimatum was a thin pretext on which to wage war, he justifies it on the basis that Sir

Bartle Frere 'was afraid, and had good reason to be afraid that, if he did not, Cetywayo would before long sweep either the Transvaal or Natal'.[25] As to whether Cetshwayo should be restored to the Zulu throne, Haggard was indecisive: 'the Government that replaces Cetywayo on the throne of his fathers will undertake a very grave responsibility, and must be prepared to deal with many resulting complications, not the least of which will be the utter exasperation of the white inhabitants of Natal'.[26]

Unexpectedly, given what we know of his private feelings, Haggard fulsomely saluted the reappointment of Sir Henry Bulwer as Governor of Natal: being of 'a temperate and a cautious mind, he may be more safely trusted to pilot a country so surrounded with difficulties and dangers as Natal is, than most men'.[27]

The greater part of *Cetywayo and His White Neighbours* is devoted to the Transvaal: its history, the annexation, the Transvaal Rebellion and the retrocession. Shepstone is the undisputed hero of the annexation: 'without shedding a single drop of blood, or even confiscating an acre of land, and at no cost, annexed a great country, and averted a very serious war'.[28] Haggard's prejudice against the Boers comes into play, restating much of what he had got into trouble for in his earlier articles. Like 'the Israelites of old', the Boers 'think they are entrusted by the Almighty with the task of exterminating the heathen native tribes around them, and are always ready with a scriptural precedent for slaughter and robbery'.[29] Not so the Englishman, who though 'he may not be very fond of him, at any rate regards the Kafir as a fellow human being with feelings like his own. The average Boer does not. He looks upon the "black creature" as having been delivered into his hand by the "Lord" for his own purposes, that is, to shoot and enslave.'[30]

Haggard believed the African inhabitants of the Transvaal were most negatively affected by the retrocession and their return to Boer domination was 'a cruel injustice', especially as they had no say in the matter.

> It is generally considered that the white man has a right to the black man's possessions and land, and that it is his high and holy mission to exterminate the wretched native and take his place. But with this conclusion I venture to differ ... I cannot believe that the Almighty, who made both white and black, gave to the one race the right or mission of exterminating, or even of robbing or maltreating the other, and calling the process the advance of civilisation. It seems to me, that on only one condition, if at all, have we the right to take the black man's land; and that is, that we provide them with an equal and a just Government, and allow no maltreatment of them, either as individuals or tribes: but, on the contrary, do our best to elevate them, and wean them from savage customs. Otherwise, the practice is surely undefensible.[31]

Such views, liberal for their time, are repeated in Haggard's subsequent novels and would be re-articulated with prophetic force in *Diary of an African Journey*, the record of his 1914 visit to South Africa. Haggard would never become a Dixie or a Colenso, capable of pinpointing the injustices of the time and identifying their origins in colonial systems of administration and government; that final leap into enlightenment was prevented by the constraints of his class and a patriotism founded upon the unquestioning faith that whatever was British must inherently be best. But Haggard's faith was not entirely blind and didn't prevent him protesting against British policies when he felt they failed to live up to the high ideal of Britain's civilising (and Christianising) imperial mission. Haggard's innate sense of fair play took him in the right direction but left him without a map or mode of thought to progress further.

Cetywayo and His White Neighbours was widely reviewed on publication. *Vanity Fair* recommended it to those wishing to become more informed on South African affairs,[32] though a caustic review in the *Daily News* accused Haggard of belabouring commonly stated views on Cetshwayo and the consequences of the retrocession of the Transvaal – 'the most amusing thing in Mr. Haggard's book is his solemn warning that our policy, which he is pleased to stigmatise as "sentimental", may end in alienating the affections of "the Colonists", etc.'[33] An otherwise favourable review in the *Spectator* criticised Haggard's caricatures of the Boers.

The *Saturday Review* welcomed an eyewitness account of the 'melancholy story of English irresolution and disgrace', and said that while Haggard's book might be less popular than Captain Walter Ludlow's *Zululand and Cetewayo*, published at the same time, his was the more important volume.[34] Ludlow's *Zululand and Cetewayo: Containing an Account of Zulu Customs, Manners, and Habits, after a Short Residence in Their Kraals* was a first-person narrative based on Ludlow's 1880 tour of Zululand, a non-taxing read, patronising and racist; brimful of hunting stories and humorous anecdotes, it undeniably had greater popular appeal, something Haggard acknowledged in a letter to Aggie Barber: 'I cannot conceal from myself the fact that [*Cetywayo and His White Neighbours*] is rather heavy reading ... it seems to have been generally accepted as more or less of a standard work, so I ought to be satisfied I suppose. Of course one can hardly expect to make much of a financial success of such a work. Ludlow's book is so much more likely to do that (if you like I will send it to you to read).'[35]

The status of 'a standard work' did not translate into sales; the book might be an 'able and statesmanlike discussion of our leading difficulties in South Africa' but, as the *British Quarterly Review* pointed out, recent events in Zululand rendered it out of date.[36] By June 1882 Wolseley's settlement had collapsed and Zululand was descending into civil war.[37] Zibhebhu and Hamu continued their persecution of the uSuthu, and Cetshwayo begged to be allowed to return to Zululand in order to prevent the slide into total chaos.

At the end of May, Haggard and his family moved to Ditchingham House, where they were joined by Aggie Barber to help Louie, now pregnant with her second child. Aggie didn't stay long, leaving to return to her mother in Bungay in July when the Haggards decamped to Bradenham Hall.[38] While Louie packed, Haggard posted off copies of *Cetywayo and His White Neighbours* to persons of influence, including Lord Randolph Churchill, a virulent opponent of Gladstone, and Lord Carnarvon, architect of the confederation policy, who was pleased to find his views 'endorsed by one who had such good opportunities of judging as yourself', adding that the 'English public was so deceived by misrepresentations of the annexation of the Transvaal that the real history was never understood ... A true statement of it is therefore very valuable, and I am grateful to anyone who has the courage to say what really did occur.'[39]

Determined to cement a reputation as an expert on South African affairs following the publication of *Cetywayo and His White Neighbours*, Haggard began writing letters to the press. He was subsequently approached by the *South African* to write six articles, which appeared weekly from 28 September to 9 November; titles included 'Some Aspects of the Native Question in the Transvaal' and 'The Restoration of Cetywayo'.

King Cetshwayo kaMpande came to London in August 1882 and was accommodated at 18 Melbury Road, Holland Park, attended by three indunas. The king took in the sights: visiting the Zoological Gardens in Regent's Park, touring the Houses of Parliament and looking in at the Woolwich Arsenal. He also had three unsatisfactory meetings with the Colonial Secretary, Lord Kimberley, concerning his restoration and the reconstruction of Zululand. The conditions laid down for his return made it clear that Cetshwayo would not be ruling over a kingdom as it had been prior to the war of 1879.

On 14 August, Cetshwayo and his party visited Queen Victoria at Osborne House, her summer retreat on the Isle of Wight. The Queen said she respected him as a brave enemy and hoped he would now become a firm friend, presenting him with a silver cup as a memento of the occasion and commissioning a portrait by Carl Rudolph Sohn.[40] Cetshwayo told *The Times* that Queen Victoria 'received me kindly, and I respect her very much. She, like myself, was born to rule men. We are alike.' The Queen also invited Cetshwayo to visit her residence at Windsor, where he encountered the memorial to the Prince Imperial in his tour of the castle and was 'filled with regret, although he said he was in no way to blame, as he did not order him to be killed'.[41]

Cetshwayo's expectation of returning to Zululand immediately on his return to South Africa was dashed by Natal officials fearing a reunified Zululand. In December 1882 he finally learned his fate. Zululand was to be partitioned into three areas: a northern territory under Zibhebhu; a Reserve Territory to the south administered by Natal; and a central portion that he would be occupying. Cetshwayo reluctantly agreed to this new dispensation and set sail from Cape Town, arriving on 10 January 1883 at Port Durnford on the coast of the Reserve Territory, where he was met by Theophilus Shepstone, ushered out of retirement to supervise the king's restoration. Cetshwayo was formally installed on 29 January before a crowd of around 6,000 people. To Shepstone's annoyance over forty uSuthu leaders protested against the terms of Cetshwayo's restoration. Once Shepstone had departed, the king and his attendants moved on to the Mahlabatini plain, where his followers began building a royal homestead east of that destroyed in 1879. Cetshwayo had returned to Zululand but not in triumph. Sandwiched between his arch-enemy Zibhebhu to the north and unsympathetic Natal officials to the south, he faced an uncertain future.

Earlier in 1882 Arthur Cochrane and Jack Haggard returned to Natal under separate arrangements, planning to meet up at Hilldrop. Jack was accompanied by Charles Torkington, who was mentally ill and in Jack's care. Torkington's doctor had recommended a long journey to foreign climes. Cochrane's intention was to join George Blomefield in making the farm a going concern, with Jack lending a hand while keeping an eye out for a colonial posting. They found the farm teetering on the brink of disaster. Blomefield had neglected the farm to concentrate on mining coal. 'He has simply ruined the farm by this,' Jack wrote to his father, 'and had Cochrane and Rider not a penny to fall back on it would be a bad look out for them indeed'.[42] Blomefield had also 'managed to get at very bad loggerheads with all the Kaffirs on the farm ... hardly a man would work for George. Now they are all at work again', and more work was 'done during the last month or six weeks than during the whole preceding year'.[43]

Blomefield continued to be a liability, verbally abusing and physically assaulting African workers – 'although the Colony is undoubtedly the best place for him, it remains to be seen if he won't ruin himself by his violence and want of intelligence'.[44] Meanwhile Torkington, 'as mad as he can be', was threatening suicide. These dramas were offset by the farm looking its best in the African spring, 'and the more I see and know of the farm the more I should advise Rider to hang on to it ... its position, wealth in coal and iron, beautiful springs and many other advantages, make it far more valuable than any farm near here'.[45]

Cochrane and Jack managed to get the farm back on its feet, but Jack had no luck finding employment and Cochrane's health was poor. They returned to England with Torkington in tow, and the farm was left in Blomefield's charge. And what of Arthur Cochrane's engagement to Josephine Lehmkuhl? All that is known is that he did not marry her.

Haggard and his family moved back to Weston Lodge in late July 1882, and it was in Norwood that 'a little incident occurred which resulted in my becoming a writer of fiction'. At a Sunday morning church service, probably at St Luke's in West Norwood, Haggard and Louie noticed 'a singularly beautiful and pure-faced young lady' sitting in a nearby pew and agreed 'this semi-divine creature ... ought to become the heroine of a novel'. They began work immediately they got home. Louie soon 'ceased from her fictional labours. But, growing interested, I continued mine, which resulted in the story called *Dawn*.'[46]

Haggard said his main object in writing *Dawn* 'was to produce the picture of a woman perfect in mind and body, and to show her character ripening and growing spiritual, under the pressure of various afflictions'. In its writing he had become 'so deeply attached to my heroine that, in a literary sense, I have never quite got over it'.[47] This was perhaps because his 'semi-divine heroine' was based on Lilly Jackson, and several elements of the story duplicate their relationship.

Of all Haggard's books *Dawn* had the most complex gestation, the published version being preceded by two drafts, the first of which was titled 'Angela'. In the autumn of 1882 the Haggards returned to Norfolk, staying at Bradenham Hall while Ditchingham House was made ready, where Haggard worked on 'Angela'. He read a section aloud to Louie, who 'incontinently wept'; Louie was his 'lactometer', he told Aggie Barber. 'I use her to test the literary milk and register her feeling.'[48] The family settled at Ditchingham House in December and, with the birth of their second child imminent, Haggard set aside his unfinished manuscript. On 6 January 1883 Louie gave birth to a daughter, christened Agnes Angela Rider, the first name after Aggie, the second that of Haggard's fictional heroine. Shortly afterwards Aggie arrived at Ditchingham to assist the Haggards with their expanding family. Haggard discussed the manuscript of 'Angela' with Aggie before he commenced on a rewrite with the title 'There Remaineth a Rest', completing the manuscript in three months. There are several autobiographical strands in this manuscript, including a love affair more than reminiscent of Haggard's with Lilly Jackson – an attempt to resolve in writing what Haggard was unable to do in life. Other plot elements mirror Haggard's life in South Africa and his courtship and eventual marriage to Louie.

The hero of the story, Arthur Preston Hyam, falls in love with Angela Caresfoot, whose father refuses permission for them to marry, decreeing they must spend a year apart after which he will reconsider his position. The young couple become secretly engaged and Arthur sails off to Madeira to wait out the year. There he learns Angela has married another man; this after Angela (unknown to Arthur) is deceived into believing Arthur is dead. Deeply wounded, Arthur embarks on an affair with a wealthy older woman, Muriel Carr (shades of Johanna Ford). Time passes, Angela's husband dies, she discovers the deception and writes to Arthur in Madeira, resigned to the possibility he may have married in the interim: 'It is possible that for this world you have passed out of my reach, but in the next I will claim you as my own.'[49] Angela's letter voices Haggard's own thoughts on his love for Lilly:

> Death is the grandest step in life. It solves all enigmas, it is the fulfilment, of which this existence is the prophecy, and to the wise and pure it opens the shimmering portals of an endless day. There will be no marriage there we know, but Arthur there will be an union ten thousand times more mystical and holy, an union of perfect love from which is purged all passion and in which alone the spirit can find its satisfaction.[50]

Muriel intercepts Angela's letter and orders Arthur to leave. Confused and angry, he departs for South Africa and enlists as a volunteer in Wolseley's campaign against the Pedi. Awaiting the final attack on Sekhukhune's mountain stronghold, Arthur receives a packet of letters, including the intercepted missive from Angela, enclosed with a covering letter from Muriel, who confesses that in reading Angela's letter she 'felt that I could not compete with such a woman as this, that I could never hold you from one so calmly faithful, so dreadfully serene'.[51]

Following Arthur's departure, Muriel considered suicide but, on finding herself pregnant (another echo of Haggard's relationship with Johanna Ford), decided she 'did not wish to kill'.[52] Muriel bids Arthur to go and 'be happy with your Angela, your block of virginal marble. Only Arthur sometimes when you are cloyed with unearthly virtue and perfection, remember that a *woman* loved you.'[53] As for Muriel, she plans to go to the United States, returning in a year or two 'with a fresh name and a pretty story of married life but too soon ended, and a baby ... You need not be afraid, nobody will ask awkward questions. I am too rich.'[54]

On reading Angela's letter, Arthur sends a telegram: 'Letter just received. Am not married. Will return instantly. Till we meet God bless you dearest.'[55] There is still a war to be fought, and Haggard's description of the final assault on Sekhukhune's 'Fighting Koppie' draws on information gleaned from his friend Stewart. Arthur is mortally wounded while leading an attack on a cave and dies at sunrise on Christmas Eve. His last words are: 'God have mercy upon me a sinner ... Angela, come to me Angela.'[56] A macabre burial scene is accompanied by a violent thunderstorm and other meteorological portents, the open grave floods and Arthur's body floats to the surface.

In England Angela, having received Arthur's telegram, is convinced her beloved is either dead or dying and, at the moment of his death, hears Arthur's call; she responds: 'I hear, I hear. I am coming.'[57] Dressed in white and putting on a bridal veil, Angela disappears into the falling snow and walks to a deep pool where she prays to God to bring her and Arthur together. Looking into the dark depths, she sees the watery grave of Arthur and 'within it the dead face of her lover all haloed in weird light'.[58] Drawn by 'this dread sight, she bent forward to gaze, the Angel of Death sealed up her senses, and clad in her bridal white, she fell into the open grave: – into her lover's arms.'[59]

Having sent the manuscript to various publishers without success, Haggard consulted Nicholas Trübner, with whom he had become friendly. Trübner recommended Haggard send the manuscript of 'There Remaineth a Rest' to John Cordy Jeaffreson, a neighbour of Trübner's in London's Maida Vale, for an opinion. The 52-year-old Jeaffreson, like Haggard an East Anglian (born at Framlingham in Suffolk), was equally at home in literary and legal circles; he had been a contributor to the *Athenaeum* since 1858 and was called to the Bar in 1859. A prolific novelist, he also wrote non-fiction and published biographies of Byron, Shelley and Lord

Nelson. Jeaffreson paid Haggard the compliment of reading his 'story deliberately and ... with considerable interest'. He correctly surmised that Haggard was young and, like 'most beginners in the really difficult art of novel-writing you have plied your pen under the notion that novels are dashed off. Inferior novels are so written, but you have the making of a good novelist in you.' Jeaffreson advised Haggard to rewrite the book slowly, 'suppressing much, expanding much ... and polishing up every sentence so that each page bears testimony to the power of its producer – the story will be the beginning of such a literary career as I conceive you to be desirous of running.'[60]

To assist Haggard in his rewrite, Jeaffreson appended a detailed critique – a generous gesture on the part of an established literary figure and a kindness Haggard never forgot. There was only one point of disagreement between Haggard and his mentor: the book's ending. Jeaffreson wanted Arthur to survive and the two lovers to be united in this life. Neither Haggard nor Aggie, who was consulted on the matter, thought this desirable. Haggard was invited to dine with Jeaffreson and talk 'all round the literary question over a cigar in my study after dinner'.[61] Cigars were lit, but Jeaffreson was not to be persuaded, and so a happy ending for Arthur and Angela was assured.

Haggard began writing the third and final draft on 15 May 1883 – 'in addition to my legal studies and other occupations and the time taken in attending in London to eat my dinners at Lincoln's Inn ... I wrote nearly two hundred thousand words'[62] – well up to the requirements of the three-volume novel, the standard fictional format of the Victorian era. Aggie was at hand for advice and, when she left Ditchingham at the end of July, Haggard continued their conversation by correspondence. On 5 August 1883 he wrote to her with his thoughts regarding 'a long poem' he wanted Aggie to write on the subject of 'Farewell'.

> Let us suppose a man and a woman, young since it is in youth that the passions strike deepest ... and let these two love one another. Then let circumstances separate them ... Then make the woman weak and let her in spite of the written remonstrance of her absent lover let her herself be forced or frightened with her eyes open into a marriage with some other man, and do not make her an injured angel as it is the fashion to do when a woman plays false with herself and her lover. Let the blow fall upon him as heavily as you will, but in the end let him also marry.[63]

This is self-evidently another reimagining of Haggard's relationship with Lilly. There is more: 'After a time, ten years or so, let these two meet again whilst still in the flush of their beauty and in the June tide of their lives. Then follows the struggle that will ensue when their sleeping or rather imprisoned love rises again in all its strength and takes possession of them when they find that time has only rendered each more thoroughly the perfect counterpart of the other.'[64] Had Haggard met Lilly since her marriage? Quite possibly. Haggard knew her brother Frederick Jackson well and had met 'the other Jackson sisters both at Ditchingham and in London'.[65] When Frederick Jackson returned from hunting in Kashmir, at Haggard's instigation he rented 'a little house some two miles or so'[66] from Ditchingham, and Haggard was a frequent visitor. Even if he did not meet Lilly in person, he would certainly have had news of her, her husband and their two sons, living at 10 Somers Place, near Hyde Park.

When the manuscript, again titled 'Angela', was nearly complete, Haggard sought further assistance from Jeaffreson, who supplied an introductory letter-cum-reference to the publisher Arthur Blackett of Hurst and Blackett. In the letter Jeaffreson spoke of receiving a manuscript 'so good' that he urged its author 'to rewrite it, so that every chapter should be in harmony with its best and strongest parts ... and if the result of his renewed labour answers my anticipation, he has produced a work that will make your reader rub his hands and say "This will do."'[67]

Haggard forwarded Jeaffreson's letter to Blackett with a synopsis of 'Angela'. Blackett's reply was received at Ditchingham with 'jubilation'. Hurst and Blackett agreed to publish the book on the following terms: 'To produce the work at our own expense and risk. To pay you the sum of 40 pounds on the sale of four hundred copies and 30 pounds on the sale of every hundred copies after.'[68] As the title 'Angela' had been used before, an alternative was requested. Haggard 'accepted the offer with gratitude and promised to find another title'. Hurst and Blackett proposed to print 500 copies 'in the three-volume form, leaving me at liberty to make any arrangements I liked for a cheap edition, if one should be demanded'.[69]

In late August 1883 Louie, pregnant with their third child, left Ditchingham with Jock and Angela to visit relatives in London. In their absence Haggard worked long hours to finish the novel, frequently not knocking off 'till about twelve or till my eyes gave out', he told Aggie. The strain on his eyesight was serious enough for Haggard to go to London and consult an ophthalmologist. 'To my relief he told me I was not going blind as I feared, but that the trouble came from the brain which was overworked. He ordered me complete rest and change, during which I was not to read anything.'[70] Lodgings were rented for a month in Southwold on the Suffolk coast. The only occupation Haggard was allowed 'was to walk, or, when this was not feasible, like a child to throw a ball against the wall of the room and see how often I could catch it on the rebound. However, the treatment proved effective.'[71]

Jack Haggard came to Southwold prior to leaving for Zanzibar, where he had been given permission by the Admiralty to take up an appointment as one of four new vice consuls for Zanzibar. (He arrived there in December and brushed up on the local language and his consular duties before taking up his post at the British consular station in the Arab-African town of Lamu on Lamu Island in February 1884.) Haggard read parts of his novel to Jack, who 'took a violent dislike to the name Muriel. He said that every shop girl he had ever met was called Muriel, so I changed the name to please him.'[72] Muriel became Mildred.

Retitled *Dawn* and scheduled for publication in February 1884, the book contained several poems, two by the poet, author and journalist Edmund Ollier, the others written by Aggie, to whom Haggard sent the proofs of *Dawn* for comment, later thanking her 'for the many valuable suggestions you made'.[73] He also shared his thoughts for a 'one-volume sequel to *Dawn* ... I should shew [Angela] after a spell of ordinary married life and becoming the mother of a charming family falling again under the fascination of her love of knowledge and power and unable any longer to keep in check the mighty intellect now only beginning to touch its possibilities'.[74] She-Who-Must-Be-Obeyed was beginning to make her presence felt.

Despite the changes implemented by Haggard as a result of Jeaffreson's critique of 'There Remaineth the Rest', *Dawn* retains plenty of autobiographical material as well as draws on Haggard's personal geography: Bradenham Hall and its surrounding countryside feature and Garsington rectory doubles as Angela's parental home. An in-joke for the Haggard family has Angela's pet raven being named Jack, while Jackson's hunting expedition to Kashmir is borrowed by Arthur – 'I and another fellow killed two tigers, and went after a rogue elephant; but he nearly killed us'.[75]

If one accepts Angela as a Lilly doppelgänger, Arthur's reaction on first meeting her can be read as that of Haggard's first encounter with Lilly, which left him 'trembling in every limb, utterly shaken by the inrush of a new and strong emotion ... never before had he known any such sensation as that which now overpowered him ... the bolt that sped from Angela's grey eyes had gone straight home, and would remain an "ever-fixed mark", so long as life itself should last'.[76] And the following paragraph can stand as testament to Haggard's love-haunted life, proof of Graham Greene's contention that it is in Haggard's books we glimpse 'the emergence of the buried man'.[77]

> Henceforth that love, so lightly and yet so irredeemably given, will become the guiding spirit of his inner life, rough-hewing his destinies, directing his ends, and shooting its memories and hopes through the whole fabric of his being like an interwoven thread of gold ... Time or separation cannot destroy it – for it is immortal; use cannot stale it, pain can only sanctify it ... It alone of all things pertaining to him will defy the attacks of the consuming years, and when, old and withered, he lays him down to die, it will at last present itself before his glazing eyes, an embodied joy, clad in shining robes, and breathing the airs of Paradise![78]

En route to Madeira aboard the *Warwick Castle* for 'his year of probation',[79] Arthur meets the rich widow Mildred Carr, with homes in England and Madeira, and possessing 'a large collection of Egyptian antiquities' inherited from her late husband.[80] Aboard ship we also encounter an example of the anti-Semitism of the period, its first appearance in Haggard's writing: among the passengers are 'two Jewesses ... accompanied by individuals, presumably their husbands, and very remarkable for the splendour of their diamond studs and the dirtiness of their nails'.[81] This is all the more shocking in the light of Haggard's own Jewish ancestry.

In Madeira, Mildred falls 'headlong in love' with Arthur, who meanwhile, like Haggard, is 'suffering from one of his fits of constitutional melancholy ... a physiognomist, looking at the somewhat dreamy eyes and pensive face, would probably have added that he neither was nor ever would be an entirely happy man'.[82]

In England, Angela is deceived into thinking Arthur dead and agrees to marriage in name only to her wicked cousin George Caresfoot, but when, contrary to their arrangement, he insists on his marital rights, Angela succumbs to temporary insanity; the marriage is unconsummated and evil George is savaged to death by a bulldog. The happy ending demanded by Jeaffreson meant there was no need for Arthur to go to Africa, so he remains in Madeira and has an affair with Mildred (he does not impregnate her) and, when Angela's letter arrives, Mildred reads it and does the decent thing: she lets Arthur go. He returns to England and marries Angela.

Dawn was published on 21 February 1884 in 'three nice volumes bound in green'.[83] A 'novel of merit far above the average', according to *The Times*, 'the story arrests the mind and arouses the expectation.'[84] The *Athenaeum* disagreed, accusing Haggard of possessing the 'fatal facility' of chronicling numerous 'repulsive' events but failing to utilise them in illuminating the behaviour and psychology of his characters.[85] 'This might have been an interesting book', opined *Vanity Fair*, 'had it not been for its intolerable length and the unpleasantness of its characters.'[86]

The review in the *Academy* by the literary critic George Saintsbury, one of 'the lords of the reviewing world',[87] was more forgiving: *Dawn* undoubtedly reflected the inexperience of its author, but nonetheless Saintsbury thought it 'well written' with 'considerable interest of plot' and the characters 'not borrowed'.[88] Saintsbury felt the occult elements undermined the novel and advised Haggard to 'train down' if he wanted to be a good writer. (Other than a discussion of spiritualism between Arthur and Angela, the occult elements centre around one of the novel's villains, the occultist Lady Bellamy, and Arthur's lover Mildred, 'a faithful student of the lore of the ancient Egyptians.')[89] Among *Dawn*'s other defects identified by Saintsbury was length: 'It is too long ... It covers too great a stretch of time. There are too many heroines, and they are too beautiful. There are too many minor characters, and they have too much to do. The wicked people (of whom there are several) are too elaborately wicked.'[90]

Jack read *Dawn* in Lamu in July 1884. His long-term fiancée, Etta White, had broken off their engagement earlier in the year and Jack, 'sick to death of her religiosity and preaching and prayers', sent back all her letters 'with alacrity in case she should change her mind'.[91] Jack's unhappiness with *Dawn* reflected his own: '[Rider's] theory of the immortality of the affections is very nice, but what's to become of those forlorn souls who fetch up in heaven without a "Polly", are they to stand off and watch the rest spooning? If so it will be very slow for them.'[92] Haggard also asked his brother Andrew for an opinion. It was a shrewd one: 'There is a little too much of your own personal experiences in the book, and when you write another I would, if I were you, draw a little more upon your own imagination!'[93]

Haggard would always wonder whether Jeaffreson's insistence on a happy ending was correct. Haggard's original intention had been to show Angela's character being tested and ultimately 'perfected by various mortal trials, till at length all frailties were burnt out of it by the fires of death'. At Jeaffreson's bidding, the 'final fires through which the heroine had to pass were those of marriage to a not very interesting young man'. Haggard admits he found young men 'difficult to draw. Young men, at any rate to the male eye, have a painful similarity to each other, whereas woman is of an infinite variety and therefore easier to depict.' This judgement is borne out by the many youthful but wooden male characters populating Haggard's books, forever wandering off into the African hinterland in search of lost relatives, lost loves and lost fortunes. When it came to writing about 'elderly men, such as old Allan Quatermain', Haggard had 'no trouble ... perhaps because from my boyhood my great friends have always been men much older than myself'.[94]

Haggard's final verdict on his first work of fiction was to judge it 'more or less of a failure'.[95] But *Dawn* was not without contemporary admirers. One of its 'most appreciative and indeed enthusiastic readers' was Trübner, who 'paid me the strange compliment of continuing its perusal till within a few hours of his death, a sad event that the enemy might say was hastened thereby'.[96]

Combining literary endeavours with legal studies, Haggard lived 'very quietly' with his family at Ditchingham, for 'we were not well off, and an estate which used to produce sufficient to support a country place of the smaller sort and those who dwelt on it, began to show greatly lessened returns. The bad years were upon us, and rents fell rapidly; moreover the repairs required were legion.' As for the farm in Natal, 'little or nothing came out of the African property, which shared in the depression that followed on the giving back of the Transvaal'.[97] On 29 April 1883 a settlement of farm ownership was signed at Ditchingham House by Haggard, Cochrane and Blomefield (in England to marry a Catherine Arnison), dissolving their partnership. 'Assets after liabilities, amounted to £250.14.6. and this sum was divided among the three signatories.'[98] Blomefield and his wife returned to Hilldrop and rented Haggard's and Cochrane's shares in the farm. Blomefield gave these shares back in 1886 and became a mining assayer. Haggard 'made a present of my share in this property to my brother Jack, who held it for a year or two and then thrust it back on my hands as he found it more trouble and expense than it was worth'.[99] Haggard promised to pay 25 per cent of anything that came from the property to his brother, which he did when the farm was sold in 1895.

Visitors to Ditchingham House were few and 'in the main we had to rely on ourselves and our little children for company'. Haggard remembered this time as 'rather lonely, at any rate for me, since my friends were African, and Africa was far away'.[100] Occasionally some of those friends 'came to see me when they were on visits to England'.[101] He was delighted to see Theophilus Shepstone when he came to England in May 1883 to sort out matters involving his pension with the Colonial Office: 'I don't think they care much for me,' Shepstone told Haggard, 'except perhaps a few personal friends, and with the same exception the feeling is mutual as far as I am concerned.'[102]

In August 1883 Haggard received a letter from Melmoth Osborn, now British Resident Commissioner of the newly established Zulu Native Reserve and ensconced in his official residence in Eshowe – 'one of the loveliest spots in South Africa. I have a very fine forest within half a mile of my house, and a sea view a good sixty miles along the coast.'[103] Osborn had earlier sent Haggard some flowering evergreen clivias from Zululand and in his latest letter detailed the death of Cetshwayo (a false rumour as it turned out) amidst the ongoing Zulu civil war.

Since his restoration in 1883, Cetshwayo had occupied the central territory of Zululand under the watchful eye of the British Resident, Henry Francis Fynn, son of one of the original Port Natal settlers. To the north was his enemy Zibhebhu and to the south the Reserve Territory administered by Shepstone's brother John. Both Zibhebhu and Shepstone demanded the allegiance of all those living in their respective provinces, many of whom were uSuthu loyal to Cetshwayo. As we saw earlier, Zibhebhu and his ally Hamu had begun persecuting the uSuthu, who resolved to strike back. In the ensuing battle of Msebe, thousands of uSuthu were killed at a cost of only ten Mandlakazi. With his people facing starvation, it became imperative to break the power of Zibhebhu and Hamu before the spring planting season. Cetshwayo began assembling an army at Ondini, but Zibhebhu, anticipating an attack, struck first. The Mandlakazi attacked Ondini on the morning of 21 July. Ondini was set on fire and scores of uSuthu leaders killed, including relatives of the king, three of his wives and an infant son. This attack decimated the Zulu leadership and marked 'the end of the old Zulu order ... Zibhebhu succeeded where Chelmsford had failed in July 1879.'[104]

A wounded Cetshwayo found refuge in the Nkandla forest, from where he tried to rally the uSuthu while appealing to the British to intervene in the conflict. The British were prepared to help if the king came under their protection. With the Mandlakazi and the Ngenetsheni destroying crops and livestock as well as taking women and children, Cetshwayo had no choice but to comply, and on 15 October 1883 he was conducted to Eshowe by Fynn and took up residence near the site of his father Mpande's old homestead, kwaGqikazi, under the care of an unsympathetic Osborn.

This was a melancholy time for Cetshwayo: the old Zululand was no more and his enemy Zibhebhu was in the ascendant. The Zulu king died at kwaGqikazi on 8 February 1884. His family forbade a post-mortem and a British military surgeon recorded that the king had died of heart disease. However, the uSuthu were convinced Cetshwayo had been poisoned on the instructions of Zibhebhu.[105] Haggard included an account of Cetshwayo's death in a new introduction to the 1888 edition of *Cetywayo and His White Neighbours*, drawing on information obtained from Osborn, who believed the king had been poisoned. The exact cause of Cetshwayo's death is disputed to this day.

Dinuzulu, Cetshwayo's son and heir, inherited the struggle against Zibhebhu and enlisted the help of the Boers in exchange for land. On 5 June 1884 a combined Boer and Zulu force advanced on the Mandlakazi, who had taken up a position near the mountain of Tshaneni (Ghost Mountain); a rifle shot betrayed their presence and Boer firepower won the day. The Boers established the New Republic over most of north-west Zululand and installed Dinuzulu as a puppet king. The Boers were now in sight of realising their long-cherished ambition: direct access to the Indian Ocean – an ambition the British had long sought to frustrate. When the recently unified Germany began showing interest in the region, Britain finally acted. Zululand was annexed in 1887 and formally incorporated into Natal in 1897.

Dawn's reception among readers and critics, especially the good notice in *The Times*, encouraged Haggard 'to try another novel'.[106] At Ditchingham House on 12 November 1883 Haggard began writing a second novel, 'Eva, or, A Tale of Love and War', and on finishing the first draft, with Jeaffreson's advice still fresh in his mind, he commenced a second.

On 25 March 1884 Louie and Rider's third child was born, a daughter christened Sybil Dorothy Rider Haggard, the middle name derived from the heroine of the new novel. The ever dependable Aggie arrived at Ditchingham House to help Louie with the new baby and play muse to Haggard. A nephew staying at Ditchingham recalled his uncle reading aloud to Aggie what he had already written: 'and on occasion [he would] turn to Miss Barber to ask, "What did he say to her anyway?"' and Aggie 'might make a suggestion'.[107] Perhaps it was at this time writer and muse had a falling out. According to Morton Cohen, 'some Haggards say, there had been a slight tiff between Agnes and Rider. She had read one of his tales in manuscript and told him in no uncertain terms what she thought about it and how he had better improve it. Rider is reputed to have lost his temper – and thrown a book at her.'[108]

In August 1884, with the second draft nearly complete, the Haggards went on holiday with Frederick Jackson and his two unmarried sisters to the seaside resort of Criccieth on Cardigan Bay in North Wales. Earlier in 1884 Jack Haggard had written to his brother suggesting that he, Louie and Jackson stay with him at Lamu for a year: exploration and elephant hunting in the African interior were envisaged. On the Welsh coast Haggard wrote to Jack declining the invitation: 'First there are the children to be considered, then the money question, then the question of the desirability of my, after being called, getting a practical knowledge of law by reading with a barrister.' In addition there was a faint chance 'but still a chance of my being asked to contest a seat at the next election, and I do not think that I should at present be justified in throwing the opportunity away should it arise'.[109] Standing for the Tories against Gladstone's Liberal government would have appealed to Haggard and, though the opportunity didn't materialise, his willingness to make himself available as a candidate is an early indication of Haggard's interest in taking up some form of public service.

In the general election of December 1885 the Liberals failed to obtain an overall majority despite winning the majority of seats. The Irish Home Rule Party held the balance of power, which tipped in favour of the Conservatives and saw Lord Salisbury lead his first government, albeit a minority one, as prime minister. Tory tenure was short, brought down by divisions over Irish Home Rule. The election in 1886 returned Gladstone and the Liberals for a third time and saw the introduction of the first Irish Home Rule Bill.

Though Haggard had dropped out of the proposed East Africa expedition, Jackson went ahead and, on Jack's advice, commissioned a Dundee 30-foot whaleboat from Messrs John Brown of Dundee. Haggard was keen to help Jackson prepare for the trip and together they tested the .500 Express rifle Jackson had used in Kashmir. A paper target was fastened to the brick wall of a cowshed. Jackson never forgot 'the mess that only four shots – two apiece – made of that wall'. Jackson was worried what his landlord might have to say about the 'huge hole' and they agreed to remain silent on the matter. A pair of spotted flycatchers built their nest in the cavity, 'and thereby rendered it less conspicuous'.[110]

In the autumn of 1884 Haggard sent his completed manuscript – now titled 'Found Wanting' – to Hurst and Blackett, who took it on the same terms as *Dawn*, which up to the present time had sold 450 copies, 'earning for Haggard the princely sum of £10'.[111] Haggard decided to prioritise his legal career and in September 1884 stayed in London for a fortnight, knuckling down to his legal studies prior to his final examination. 'I thought it pretty stiff but the *viva voce* exams were the worst,'[112] he told Aggie. Haggard was awarded his certificate on 3 October but chose to wait until the new term in January 1885 before being called to the Bar.

In the same letter to Aggie, he said Hurst and Blackett had requested another title for Haggard's second novel as there was already one in circulation with a similar title to 'Found Wanting'. 'The only thing I could think of was *The Witch's Head* which I don't like,' Haggard told Aggie. 'Have you got such a thing as a title about you?'[113] She didn't. *The Witch's Head* was published on 18 December 1884. Shortly before publication, acting on a suggestion from Louie, Haggard added a poem of Aggie's as an epigraph. 'Swell Out Sad Harmonies' appeared above the name A.M. Barber on the page preceding the contents.

On reading *The Witch's Head*, it is clear Haggard still hadn't taken Andrew's advice to draw on his imagination rather than his personal experience. Once again the romance with Lilly is played out much as it did in life; as is Haggard's marriage to Louie. The central section of the novel is set in South Africa and contains many of Haggard's experiences in Pretoria. However, there was plenty of imagination in the novel's melodramatic storyline and its many subplots involving murder, jealousy, revenge and suicide. The book's hero, the orphaned Ernest Kershaw, grows to adulthood in the care of an unmarried uncle with two other wards, Dorothy and Jeremy, on the East Anglian coast at the house Dum's Ness near Kesterwick (in reality Dunwich, south of Southwold), a village gradually succumbing to coastal erosion and slipping away into the North Sea. At a local ball Ernest meets Eva – the first woman – and falls in love with her the moment she enters. 'It took but a few seconds, ten perhaps, for her to walk up the room, and yet to Ernest it seemed long before her eyes met his own, and something passed from them into his heart that remained there all his life.'[114]

Shortly afterwards, strolling along a coastal path with Dorothy (secretly in love with Ernest), he rescues Eva, who has become stranded climbing down the crumbling cliff face to retrieve a recently exposed wooden box. The box contains the 'head of a lovely woman of some thirty years of age ... covered with rippling brown locks of great length, above which was set a roughly fashioned coronet studded with uncut gems ... this face, all but the lips, which were coloured red, pale with the bloodless pallor of death, and the flesh so firm and fresh-looking that it might have been that of a corpse not a day old.'[115] Despite the book's title, this grotesque find, permanently displayed in a glass case in the dining room at Dum's Ness, has no role in the main story.

At the outset Eva plays with her lover's affections, but when she finds herself beginning to reciprocate Ernest's feelings, she becomes confused and cannot decide whether to become engaged to him or not – 'Eva Ceswick was very loving, very sweet and very good, but she did not possess a determined mind'[116] – an echo of Lilias's sentiments regarding Lilly Jackson: 'it was not in Lilith's gentle and rather stupid character to withstand any particular pressure'.[117] Secretly engaged, Ernest goes to France for a holiday where he befriends a Mr Alston and his young son Roger. Alston, a Shepstone–Osborn amalgam, is on leave from the Transvaal's civil administration. Ernest also encounters his cousin Hugh, heir to the Kershaw fortune, who challenges him to a duel. Ernest kills Hugh and flees with Alston to Pretoria, where the real-life Shepstone has a walk-on part and Mazooku (Haggard's spelling) has a significant role as Ernest's servant.

In Pretoria the Ernest–Eva romance plays out much as it did in reality for Haggard and Lilly in 1878. Eva is pressured into an engagement with another man. Ernest is crushed: 'The cruel news that the mail had brought him ... had, figuratively speaking, destroyed him. He could never recover from it, though he would certainly survive it.'[118] As we saw earlier, Alston suggests Ernest take an *intombi* (Zulu maiden), and a friend on Alston's staff offers to introduce him to 'two charming specimens of indigenous beauty'. In England Dorothy goes 'to see Eva in order to plead Ernest's cause', as did Haggard's sister Mary with Lilly, and an uncle offers Eva 'a home and protection',[119] as Haggard's father offered Lilly. All to no avail.

1. Theophilus Shepstone and William Sargeaunt with staff in Pretoria, 1877. Standing, from left to right, John Sargeaunt, Arthur Cochrane, Captain James Fencott 'Jumbo' James, Captain Robert Patterson. Seated (l-r) Melmoth Osborn, Sargeaunt, Shepstone, H. Rider Haggard and Vacy Lyle. Captain Patterson and John Sargeaunt would be murdered on their expedition to the Victoria Falls, an event Haggard drew on for *King Solomon's Mines*.

RIDER HAGGARD

2. Autographed portrait photograph presented by Haggard to Theophilus Shepstone in 1881.

3. Ida Hector, Haggard's secretary from 1893.

4. Haggard and Masuku during Haggard's 1914 visit to South Africa.

5. Sculptor and subject, Francis La Monaca at work on his bust of Haggard in 1922.

6. Pencil sketch of
H. Rider Haggard in his
youth. Artist unknown.

7. Ella Haggard,
Haggard's mother.

8. William Meybohm
Haggard, Haggard's father.

9. Elizabeth 'Lilly' Jackson.

10. Theophilus Shepstone and his staff on the day of the Annexation of the Transvaal, 12 April 1877. The flag on the left would not be raised until 24 May 1877, Queen Victoria's official birthday. From left to right (standing), Sub-Inspector Frederick L. Phillips, Melmoth Osborn, Colonel Edward Brooke, Captain James Fencott 'Jumbo' James; (seated) Joseph Henderson, Shepstone, Vacy Lyle, Frederick Fynney. Haggard is seated on the ground.

11. Lewis and Johanna Ford.

12. Arthur Cochrane.

13. Masuku in 1914.

14. Mhlopekazi in the 1870s, on the staff of Theophilus Shepstone. He would later become famous as the fictional character Umslopogaas.

15. Mhlopekazi in old age.

16. Louise Margitson and Haggard with his sister Mary behind them. The photograph was taken during their engagement.

17. Haggard (seated) and Arthur Cochrane shortly after their return from Natal in 1881. The knobkerrie that Mazooku (Masuku) gave Haggard is planted in the flowerbed.

18. Haggard's son, Jock.

19. Charles Longman, Haggard's friend and publisher.

Alston, Ernest and Jeremy (who has come to South Africa to find Ernest) take 'a pleasant one-storied house, with a verandah and a patch of flower-garden in front of it',[120] where, on the day of Eva's wedding, Ernest sits looking at his watch. '"Look!" he went on, pointing to his watch, which lay upon the table before him, "by English time it is now about twenty minutes past eleven. They are being married now, Jeremy, my boy, I can feel it. By Heaven, I have only to shut my eyes, and I can *see* it!"' The scene rings true as a recreation of Haggard's feelings and behaviour at 'The Palatial' on the day of Lilly's wedding. Like Haggard in 1878, Ernest goes on a bender: 'He took to evil ways, he forgot his better self. He raced horses, he devoted himself with great success to love-affairs that he would have done better to leave alone ... Eva, pale queen of women, was ever there to haunt his sleep, and though in his waking hours he might curse her memory, when night drew the veil from truth the words he murmured were words of love eternal.'[121]

The South African section of *The Witch's Head* includes the raising of the Border Lances in Pretoria and the panic over the non-existent Zulu impi. When the Anglo-Zulu War breaks out, Ernest and Jeremy, with Mazooku as their servant, join Alston's Horse and are caught up in the battle of Isandlwana. Alston and his son are killed, as were Colonel Weatherley and his son at Hlobane. Haggard gives a detailed description of the Zulu victory, based in part on information from his friend Major Essex. Ernest, Jeremy and Mazooku survive the battle, but Ernest is struck by lightning and blinded. In England Ernest's uncle dies, leaving Ernest the heir to the Kershaw fortune. Ernest, Jeremy and Mazooku return to England, where love blossoms between Ernest and Dorothy and they marry, though not after much self-revealing conversation as to how Ernest will always love Eva/Lilly.

Surely Louie could not have read these passages unaware of their import. For example, when Ernest proposes to Dorothy, one cannot but wonder if the same lines, hopefully not spoken to Louie, are a reflection of Haggard's thoughts at the time: 'I can never give you that passion I gave to Eva, because, thank God, the human heart can know it but once in a life; but I can and will give you a husband's tenderest love. You are very dear to me, Doll, though it is not in the same way that Eva is dear ... Whether I marry or not, I fear that I shall never be able to shake her out of my mind.'[122] Dorothy, being 'an eminently practical little person', agrees to marry Ernest, having 'recognised the "eternal verity" of the saying that half a loaf is better than no bread' and she 'made up her mind to make the best of the position. Since she could not help it, Eva would be welcome to the inward and spiritual side of Ernest, and only she could secure the outward and visible side.'[123]

Ernest becomes a successful member of parliament and, later, 'impatient for the active life of other days', accepts 'the governorship of one of the Australian colonies'.[124] As for Eva/Lilly, she endures an unhappy marriage, and dies young. Was this an act of revenge on Haggard's part?

There is little to recommend *The Witch's Head* other than it is a good example of Victorian popular fiction in the three-volume form. Additional interest accrues when read with Haggard's biography in mind and an awareness of him writing an alternative autobiography. That apart, one element of the book that survives the passage of time is the freshness and energy of Haggard's handling of the African material, something that didn't go unnoticed by contemporary critics. London's *Literary World* acknowledged that the chapters 'on South African life, including a rapid and vigorous sketch of the Zulu War, redeem the book from the commonplace'.[125] 'Only one novel, for a very long time, has kept us out of bed when we were anxious to go thither. That novel is *The Witch's Head*,' declared the *Pall Mall Gazette*, which deemed Haggard a successor to Charles Kingsley 'in the art of truly patriotic and adventurous fiction'.[126] Others concurred: 'That Mr. Rider Haggard has very considerable powers as a novelist was evident from his rather extravagant book *Dawn* and it is still more evident from *The Witch's Head*,' wrote George Saintsbury.[127] 'What with the supernatural Witch's Head, and the love-making, and the fighting, and a tragedy of the first class towards the end, and some very fair dialogue, and a most pathetic and charming Zulu called Mazooku, there is much to be said for the book,'[128] which Saintsbury judged 'far above the average'.[129]

Prior to the appearance of *The Witch's Head*, Haggard wrote a short story, 'Bottles', inspired by an article on Egyptian affairs by his brother Andrew that was published in the October edition of *Blackwood's Magazine* – 'They gave him £20 for it.'[130] Here Haggard's doppelgänger is John George Perrit, nicknamed Bottles because of his nose: 'the end of it was round and large and thick'. As a young subaltern 'quartered in Maritzburg, Natal',[131] Bottles is daily expecting his regiment to be sent back to England, where he intends marrying the beautiful but penniless Madeleine Spenser, to whom he is engaged. Then comes the fateful letter from his fiancée calling off the engagement as she has agreed to marry Sir Alfred Croston – 'he would not take "no" for an answer; and at last, dear, I had to give in ... I do love you, but I can't help myself.'[132]

When his regiment receives its orders for England, Bottles resigns and remains in South Africa. Twelve years later Bottles's eldest brother dies and his surviving older brother, Eustace, tumbles 'into a baronetcy and eight thousand a year, and Bottles himself into a modest but to him most ample fortune of as many hundred'.[133] Bottles returns to England, where Lady Croston is now a widow. Bottles wins back her love, but his brother Eustace insists she possesses a venal nature and will always marry for money, not for love. To prove it, Sir Eustace proposes to her himself and she accepts; Bottles hears all this while hiding behind the blue curtains of a window alcove. Deeply distressed, he commits suicide.

'Bottles' was rejected. The rejection hurt: 'I wonder how people ever get things into magazines. I suppose it must be through being regularly connected with them. I am sure "Bottles" is better than most things that appear in these magazines and behold they will have none of him.'[134]

13

'THE MOST AMAZING STORY EVER WRITTEN'

Time had come to take stock. Haggard had produced three books, *Cetywayo and His White Neighbours* and the novels *Dawn* and *The Witch's Head*. 'The history had cost me £50 to publish, and for the two novels I had received exactly the same sum in all; in short, the net returns were at that time *nothing*.'[1] There was little to no income coming from the Ditchingham estate and, as writing was not proving to be the hoped-for crock of gold, Haggard 'determined to abandon the writing of fiction and devote myself entirely to my profession'.[2] This meant relocating to London, and Louie rented a place in West Kensington, a three-storey house with a pillared portico and basement beneath on the corner of Fairholme and Gledstanes roads. On 26 December 1884 Haggard left Ditchingham House with two nurses and his three children – three-year-old Jock, Angela, nearing two, and the baby Dorothy – for their new home, which Haggard had yet to see and where Louie awaited their arrival. At 1 Fairholme Road the party were welcomed by Louie, one 'dirty cook', a French maid and a 'little dog rather dirtier than the cook'.[3] Early in the New Year, Aggie Barber came to help with the children.

Haggard was called to the Bar on 26 January 1885 and each weekday morning thereafter he departed from Fairholme Road to attend the Probate and Divorce Court on the Strand, where it soon became apparent he couldn't keep his head above water financially by working alone. He was battling to let Ditchingham House and exploring job prospects in the Cape – 'for I don't see how I am to live here'[4] – when he came to an arrangement with Henry Bargrave Deane to work in his chambers at 1 Elm Court, Inner Temple, an arrangement facilitated by a family connection, a cousin of Haggard's having married Deane's sister.

Haggard's resolution to abandon writing didn't last long. The first entry in his 1885 notebook diary, self-evidently post-dated, states: 'Solomon's Mines 77,400 words (about). Begun January. Finished 21 April 1885'.[5] *King Solomon's Mines* was written in the evenings at a small writing desk in the dining room at Fairholme Road and during Haggard's 'somewhat ample leisure in chambers'.[6] Spare time and the generally favourable reviews of *The Witch's Head* seeded the ground for Haggard to return to writing, but in his autobiography he gives another reason: 'I read in one of the weekly papers a notice of Stevenson's *Treasure Island* so laudatory that I procured and studied that work, and was impelled by its perusal to try to write a book for boys.'[7] Lilias gives another version, a story now part of Haggard family tradition:

> Travelling up to London with one of his brothers they started discussing *Treasure Island*, just then making a great success. Rider said he didn't think it was so very remarkable, whereupon his brother replied, rather indignantly: 'Well, I'd like to see you write anything half as good – bet you a bob you can't.'
> 'Done,' said Rider.[8]

Whatever its genesis, when the manuscript of *King Solomon's Mines* was complete, Haggard 'hawked it round to sundry publishers', none of whom 'thought it worth bringing out'.[9] A boy's adventure story was not standard fare for publishers dedicated to supplying the circulating libraries with three-volume melodramas along the lines of Haggard's previous two books. That *King Solomon's Mines* saw the light of day at all is thanks to two giants of the London literary scene in the 1880s: the classical scholar, anthropologist, folklorist, poet, cricket enthusiast and critic Andrew Lang, and the poet and editor William Ernest Henley, model for Long John Silver in Stevenson's *Treasure Island*.

Lang's first contact with Haggard was in March 1885 when Haggard submitted his short story 'Bottles' to the American magazine *Harper's*. Lang, the magazine's London editor, was unable to accept it 'except by permission of the American editor', which Lang thought unlikely as there was a glut of unpublished material from English authors, but he took the opportunity to thank Haggard 'for the great pleasure *The Witch's Head* has given me. I have not read anything so good for a long while'.[10]

Lang's enjoyment at reading *King Solomon's Mines* in manuscript was even greater, prompting him to write to Haggard even before he had finished the book: 'There is so much invention and imaginative power and knowledge of African character in your book that I almost prefer it to *Treasure Island*.'[11] It is probable Lang forwarded the manuscript to 'the rude, boisterous, windy, and headstrong'[12] Henley, the recently appointed editor of Cassell's *Magazine of Art* who had recommended *Treasure Island* to Cassell. The same happened with *King Solomon's Mines*. Henley went to see John Williams, chief editor of the firm, 'with the manuscript of *King Solomon's Mines* under his arm. He threw it across Williams's desk and exclaimed: 'There's a fine thing for you!'[13]

Williams concurred, and Haggard received a letter informing him Cassell 'would publish the book and asking me to call *re* the agreement'.[14] Accordingly, Haggard called at La Belle Sauvage, the imposing home of Cassell in the City off Ludgate Hill, and met Williams, who bade him choose between two possible contracts: one involving Haggard selling the copyright of the book, for which he would receive a one-off payment of £100; the other involving Cassell offering '£50 pounds on account of royalties, to be calculated "at the rate of ten percent of the published price of the book on all copies sold by them during the continuance of the copyright, reckoning thirteen copies to the twelve".[15] In the light of nil profit from his previous writing, Haggard accepted the first contract: '£100 pounds on the nail had great attractions'.[16]

> I had no particular belief in the story which I had thrown off in my leisure hours as a mere *jeu d'esprit*, especially after its rejection in other quarters. Even Mr. Lang's kind expressions of opinion carried no conviction to my mind, for I did not understand all that it meant coming from such a source ... So after a brief moment of reflection I told the business-like editor that I would sell the copyright for 100 pounds, and he departed to fetch the agreement.[17]

In Williams's absence a clerk working unobserved in a corner of the editor's office, who knew the true 'estimate that had been formed of the book by his employers', made his presence known. "'Mr. Haggard," he said in a warning voice, "if I were you I would take the other agreement."[18] When Williams returned with the first agreement, Haggard announced he had changed his mind:, 'I will not sell the copyright; I will take the royalty agreement.'[19] The clerk's advice was sound. In 1911 Haggard recorded that the sales of *King Solomon's Mines* had 'been very great and at present [it] shows signs of increase rather than of diminution'.[20] Haggard had undoubtedly chosen the better of the two contracts on offer, but the arrangement was by no means perfect: the book's copyright remained with the publisher and over time Cassell reaped huge rewards from the various editions and translations published by other firms.

Encouraged by the positive response to *King Solomon's Mines* in manuscript, Haggard sought out a publisher to bring out cheap editions of *Dawn* and *The Witch's Head*. J. & R. Maxwell agreed, and the contract Haggard signed gave him one-third of the profits. There being no canny clerk to advise otherwise, Haggard agreed to let them publish cheap editions of any other books he might write in the next five years on the same terms.

Certain they had a sure-fire hit on their hands, Cassell set about creating an unprecedented advertising and marketing campaign. Under conditions of the strictest secrecy huge posters, each 'as long as a hoarding', were prepared and, a few nights after the publication of *King Solomon's Mines*, were put up after dark 'on hoardings all over London'. As people streamed to work next morning, there was no avoiding the strident message that had suddenly appeared overnight: '*King Solomon's Mines – The Most Amazing Story Ever Written*'.

> They could not get away from it. They went out to their lunch – rich men and poor – and found the same statement staring them in the face. They began to believe it. What was this book? They must know.

> So Cassells put Rider Haggard on the literary map in a night. And a few hours later the machines at the [Belle Sauvage] Yard began to roll to a new song of ecstasy as they flung out copies of *King Solomon's Mines* in thousands.[21]

Not everyone was convinced by the advertising copy, especially publishers who had rejected the manuscript, one of whom was heard to opine: 'There's a silly story of a diamond mine published today ... by a man named Rider Haggard. They offered me this book six months ago and I declined it. Some fool has bought it as you will see – and I'm sorry for him'.[22] The regret was misplaced: *King Solomon's Mines* was an immediate bestseller. Published on 30 September 1885 with an initial print run of 2,000 copies, it quickly went into further impressions and within a year 31,000 copies had been sold. It has never been out of print since. More 'than 650,000 copies, in one form or another, were printed in .... [Haggard's] lifetime: there is no record of receipts, but it is clear it must have amounted to a small fortune'.[23]

Coming in the wake of *Treasure Island* – also a single volume and one which broke the psychological barrier between adult and children's books – Haggard dedicated his 'faithful but unpretending record of a remarkable adventure' to 'all the big and little boys who read it'.[24] It was kitted out with bogus authorities, footnotes and, a vital piece of the adventure's paraphernalia, a sixteenth-century treasure map drawn in blood – a doff of the hat to that in Stevenson's *Treasure Island* – the original of which was contrived by Aggie Barber using an old piece of linen and a bone pen she made herself. Who or what donated the blood is unknown.[25]

King Solomon's Mines was synchronously published at one of those inexplicable-until-afterward moments when the planets align, public taste and global politics combine, and readers are eager and ready to take to their hearts the work that best expresses the zeitgeist. Quite apart from Cassell's innovative advertising campaign, there already existed an avid reading public primed for tales of adventure thanks to *Treasure Island*, and to capitalise on this *King Solomon's Mines* was published as a matching volume. Nor was Haggard an unknown quantity as a writer; his two previous novels were popular with the circulating libraries. Geopolitical events also conspired to create a receptive audience: at the Berlin Conference, which ended in February 1885, the major European powers and the United States had 'laid down the ground rules for dividing Africa's spoils'.[26] The 'scramble for Africa' was well and truly on, and Haggard, right on cue, had produced the inspirational text.

King Solomon's Mines is the story of three quests: a quest for a lost brother, a quest for treasure and the quest for a throne. Hunter-trader Allan Quatermain tells the tale, 'in a plain, straightforward manner', apologising for his 'blunt way of writing' as he is 'more accustomed to handle a rifle than a pen' and therefore unable to 'make any pretence to the grand literary flights and flourishes which I see in novels ... I venture to hope that a true story, however strange it may be, does not require to be decked out in fine words'.[27]

A widower with a son studying medicine in London, Quatermain is no clean-cut hero with jutting jaw. His age is against him for a start: 'It is a curious thing that at my age – fifty-five last birthday – I should find myself taking up a pen to try to write a history.' Haggard would subsequently write fourteen books narrated by Quatermain, twelve featuring his adventures prior to *King Solomon's Mines*. To accommodate these prequels, Haggard revised Quatermain's age in later printings of *King Solomon's Mines* to the point where he would 'never see sixty again.'[28] Whether over 55 or over 60, Quatermain's age is a clever inversion of Stevenson's Jim Hawkins, the 13-year-old narrator of *Treasure Island*. Quatermain's surname is a homage to William Quartermaine, the fondly remembered pig farmer of Haggard's childhood. Quatermain's Zulu name, Macumazahn, meaning 'the man who gets up in the middle of the night, or, in vulgar English, he who keeps his eyes open,'[29] also rendered 'Watcher by Night' and 'He-Who-Sleeps-With-One-Eye-Open', was originally bestowed on Arthur Cochrane in 'those first arduous months when he was alone at Hilldrop.'[30]

Quatermain describes himself as having 'short grizzled hair sticking up straight' and being 'thin, and short, and dark, weighing only nine stone and a half'.[31] A third-person description of the 'very best shot in Africa, who has killed more elephants and lions than any other man alive', is to be found in 'Hunter Quatermain's Story': 'a curious-looking little lame man' with 'large brown eyes, that seemed to notice everything, and a withered face, tanned absolutely the colour of mahogany from exposure to the weather. He spoke ... with a curious little accent, which made his speech noticeable.'[32]

On the voyage to Durban from Cape Town aboard the *Dunkeld*, Quatermain's fellow passengers coincidentally include Sir Henry Curtis and his companion, the naval officer Captain John Good (turned out 'by my Lords of the Admiralty to starve on half pay'[33]), who have journeyed to southern Africa with the aim of finding Henry's brother George, who has vanished into the interior and who was last heard of at Bamangwato in Bechuanaland, about to head north with a 'Kafir hunter named Jim'[34] to find the legendary diamond mines of King Solomon. Quatermain happened to be the last person to see the two before they disappeared into the desert.

As a young man Quatermain had heard of King Solomon's mines from a fellow elephant hunter named Evans, who had 'found far in the interior a ruined city, which he believed to be the Ophir of the Bible ... beyond the Suliman Mountains up to the north west of Mashukulumbwe country'.[35] Decades later, 'up beyond the Manica country at a place called Sitanda's Kraal',[36] Quatermain is bequeathed a sixteenth-century letter and a map scratched on a fragment of linen in the blood of a dying José da Silvestra by his descendant José Silvestre, himself on the brink of eternity after a failed attempt to find the legendary mines.

Sir Henry hires Quatermain to assemble an expedition to find George and the mines. Sir Henry is cast in heroic mould – 'a man of about thirty ... perhaps the biggestchested and longest-armed man I ever saw. He had yellow hair, a thick yellow beard, clear-cut features, and large grey eyes set deep in his head. I never saw a finer-looking man, and somehow he reminded me of an ancient Dane.'[37] Sir Henry's friend Good 'was broad, of medium height, dark, stout, and rather a curious man to look at. He was so very neat and so very clean-shaved, and he always wore an eye-glass in his right eye … He put it in his trousers pocket when he went to bed, together with his false teeth, of which he had two beautiful sets.'[38] Good was also in the 'habit of using strong language when excited – contracted, no doubt, in the course of his nautical career.'[39]

Sir Henry and Good board with Quatermain at his home on the Berea in Durban while their host sets about kitting out the expedition, hiring porters and servants, including Khiva and Ventvögel – named after the servants who died on the Patterson–Sargeaunt mission to Lobengula. Enter the proud, dignified, enigmatic Umbopa, who desires to accompany them:

> Standing about six foot three high he was broad in proportion, and very shapely. In that light, too, his skin looked scarcely more than dark, except here and there where deep black scars marked old assegai wounds. Sir Henry walked up to him and looked into his proud, handsome face.
>
> 'They make a good pair, don't they?' said Good; 'one as big as the other.'
>
> 'I like your looks, Mr. Umbopa, and I will take you as my servant,' said Sir Henry in English.
>
> Umbopa evidently understood him, for he answered in Zulu, 'It is well'; and then added, with a glance at the white man's great stature and breadth, 'We are men, thou and I.'[40]

The men head north. In a hunting interlude on their journey, Khiva is killed by an elephant while saving Captain Good's life.[41] From Sitanga's Kraal on the Lukanga River in Bechuanaland they strike off into the desert, on the other side of which stands the mountain range with two snow-capped peaks, Queen Sheba's Breasts, marked on Silvestra's map, beyond which lie King Solomon's mines.[42] From Sitanga's Kraal, Quatermain, Curtis, Good and Ventvögel step off the real geography of southern Africa into a landscape of Haggard's imagination.

Surviving thirst and hunger in the desert, the adventurers reach the mountains and, in the ascent of Queen Sheba's Breasts, take refuge from the freezing snow and wind in a cave where they discover the mummified body of José da Silvestra, and Ventvögel dies of hypothermia. The following day they descend into Kukuanaland, a seeming land of milk and honey, its ancient buildings, monuments and roads evidence of an earlier civilisation. Resting on the banks of a stream, they are surprised by a small force of Kukuana led by an old chief, Infadoos. Good is caught in mid-toilet, half-shaven, minus his trousers, fumbling with his false teeth, but eye-glass firmly in place. The Kukuana are friendly and Good is about to pull on his trousers when Infadoos begs him not to 'cover up his beautiful white legs' and Good is persuaded, in the best interests of the party, to henceforth 'live in a flannel shirt, a pair of boots, and an eye-glass'.[43]

The Kukuanas are ruled by Twala, a malign and ruthless monarch modelled on white settler perceptions of Shaka, Cetshwayo and Lobengula, who is ably assisted in his reign of terror by the sangoma Gagaoola or Gagool:

> [a] wizened monkey-like figure ... a woman of great age, so shrunken that in size it seemed no larger than that of a year-old child, and was made up of a collection of deep yellow wrinkles. Set in the wrinkles was a sunken slit, that represented the mouth, beneath which the chin curved outwards to a point. There was no nose to speak of; indeed, the whole countenance might have been taken for that of a sun-dried corpse had it not been for a pair of large black eyes, still full of fire and intelligence, which gleamed and played under the snow-white eyebrows, and the projecting parchment-coloured skull, like jewels in a charnel-house.[44]

When Umbopa reveals himself to be Ignosi, true heir to the Kukuana throne, Sir Henry, Good and Quatermain vow to help him regain his throne, and Kukuana chiefs of the old order swear allegiance. Gagool very nearly scuppers their plans when Twala gathers his regiments for a smelling-out ceremony in which the 'dance of Kaffir witches' witnessed by Haggard at Lady Barker's 'Cottage Loaf' in Pietermaritzburg is carried to its fatal conclusion as 'traitors' are identified and dispatched. The corpses pile up, but when Gagool moves towards Ignosi with her fatal wand, Curtis, Good and Quatermain intervene, threatening to shoot Twala and Gagool. Twala bids them put 'away your magic tubes'.[45]

The following day a dance of the maidens is held, the object of which is to choose the perfect sacrifice to the mysterious 'Silent Ones'. The maidens begin their dance, among them 'a beautiful young woman' named Foulata, who dances 'with a grace and vigour which would have put most ballet girls to shame'[46] – attributes conferring on her the status of sacrificial victim. Throwing herself at Good's feet and clasping his 'beautiful white legs', Foulata begs his protection.[47] The stand-off is ended by the fortuitous occurrence of a solar eclipse. In the ensuing panic Quatermain and co. escape with Foulata.

The opposing armies of the two heirs, Twala and Ignosi, square up for battle and an epic reconstruction of the battle of Ndondakusuka in 1856 ensues. Ignosi is victorious and Curtis decapitates Twala in a duel to the death fought with enormous battleaxes.

After the battle a wounded Good is tenderly nursed by Foulata, the 'Kukuana Pocahontas'.[48] Thus begins an interracial romance, much to Quatermain's disapproval, knowing as he does 'the fatal amorous propensities of sailors in general, and of Good in particular. There are two things in the world, as I have found out, which cannot be prevented: you cannot keep a Zulu from fighting, or a sailor from falling in love upon the slightest provocation!'[49]

Gagool survives the slaughter as, according to prophecy, she can only be killed by accident, not design; she also happens to be the only person who knows the location of King Solomon's mines and leads the adventurers north to the mountains known as the 'Three Witches', below which stand the 'Silent Ones', statues of pagan gods from the time of King Solomon who preside over a diamond pit that Quatermain likens to Kimberley's Big Hole.

The mine entrance at the foot of one of the Three Witches gives access to a cavern, 'the hall of the vastest cathedral' filled with stalactites and stalagmites, based on the Wonderfontein caves in the Transvaal, which Haggard visited with John Kotzé, complete with a pulpit 'beautifully fretted over outside with what looked like lace'.[50] Inside they come upon the Place of Death, where a giant skeleton with raised spear presides over a stone table, around which are seated the former kings of Kukuanaland, themselves turned into stalagmites by the slow drip of time. The corpse of Twala sits crouched upon the table, his severed head propped on his knees. While they are lost in contemplation of these horrors, Gagool triggers the opening of a secret door, a sliding mass of stone 'rising from the floor and vanishing into the rock above',[51] the door to Solomon's treasure chamber. Foulata is afraid to enter but agrees, as Good is intent on proceeding: 'Nay, my lord, whither thou goest there will I go also.'[52]

While the adventurers are preoccupied with wooden boxes filled with gold pieces and stone chests brimful of diamonds, Gagool slips away and activates the stone door. Foulata tries to prevent her but is stabbed and mortally wounded. The stone door descends, crushing Gagool. Verdict: accidental death. Foulata dies in Good's arms, telling 'her lord' that 'I love him, and that I am glad to die because I know that he cannot cumber his life with such as me, for the sun cannot mate with the darkness, nor the white with the black.' Quatermain reflects that '[Foulata's] removal was a fortunate occurrence, since, otherwise, complications would have been sure to ensue. The poor creature was no ordinary native girl, but a person of great, I had almost said stately, beauty, and of considerable refinement of mind. But no amount of beauty or refinement could have made an entanglement between Good and herself a desirable occurrence.'[53]

Foulata is not so easily exorcised. The final pages of *King Solomon's Mines* find Quatermain in Durban reading a letter he has just received from Henry Curtis. Among the items of news is mention of Good, who is 'still down on his luck about Foulata. He told me that since he has been home he hadn't seen a woman to touch her, either as regards her figure or the sweetness of her expression.'[54]

Foulata's death is a convenient solution to the racial conundrum and easy to condemn, but, in the context of the time, that Haggard was even prepared to countenance, and relate with sympathy, an interracial romance was a daring departure from the norm. It is worth noting that all the film adaptations of *King Solomon's Mines*, apart from the silent version made in South Africa in 1916, have omitted the Good–Foulata love story. Thereafter every film inserted a white woman, usually blonde, as the romantic interest, and not for Captain Good but either Allan Quatermain or Sir Henry Curtis.[55]

Back in Kukuanaland, the adventurers find a way out of the treasure chamber and escape, Quatermain filling his jacket pockets with diamonds. Once rested from their ordeals, the heroes bid Ignosi farewell and travel back to Natal by an easier route across the desert. On the way Sir Henry is united with his brother at an oasis where George Curtis has been stranded all along because of an injured leg. Thereafter the two brothers sail off home with Good, and the story ends with Quatermain writing up their adventures at his desk in Durban and contemplating a return to England to visit Curtis, Good and his son Harry at Guy's Hospital, and to 'see about the printing of this history, which is a task I do not like to trust to anybody else'.[56]

Even today, especially after reading its predecessors *Dawn* and *The Witch's Head*, one cannot but be struck by the audacity and freshness of *King Solomon's Mines*, the directness of the first-person style, the thrust of the narrative, and Haggard's tight control of his material. The book immediately engages, pulling the reader into a compelling story. If the book retains such power today, one can only imagine its impact on first appearance. *King Solomon's Mines* still satisfies as an adventure, akin to those of Indiana Jones, a character directly descended from Quatermain; but today's reader brings to bear a different perspective, from which *King Solomon's Mines* reads as an adventure story that critiques itself as a product of the colonial period when the British Empire was at its apogee.

Haggard was in Norfolk when *King Solomon's Mines* was published on 30 September 1885, two days after meeting a self-imposed deadline to complete its sequel, 'The Frowning City', prior to the publication of its predecessor.[57] Shortly afterwards, in early October, Haggard learned of the death of Johanna Ford in Pretoria on 30 August at the age of 31. His thoughts and feelings on her death are not known, but this wouldn't be the last he heard of her.

Haggard and his family had left London in July to spend the summer holidays in East Anglia, and as Ditchingham House was let, they rented a farm in Denton not far from Bungay, where Aggie Barber was staying with her mother. The group at Denton were joined by Jack Haggard, back from East Africa for medical treatment following a 'stricture of the bladder' further complicated by a 'form of local mumps, which produced glandular swellings all over his body'.[58] Jack entertained Rider with tales of his African adventures and met Aggie. The roving sailor had finally come to port.

On a shopping trip to Bungay, Haggard bought a copy of the 10 October edition of the *Saturday Review*, 'which contained a two-column notice' of *King Solomon's Mines*. 'With delight my eye fell upon such sentences as "All through the battle piece, 'The Last Stand of the Greys' ... [the] slaying is Homeric ... to tell the truth we would give many novels, say eight hundred (that is about the yearly harvest), for such a book as *King Solomon's Mines*." I went back to the farm that night feeling sure that my book was going to succeed.'[59] The *Saturday Review* ran fiction reviews without by-lines, and consequently Haggard was unaware that the glowing notice came from Andrew Lang. There were some reservations about the comic moments, but Lang had 'only praise for the very uncommon powers of invention and gift of "vision" which Mr Haggard displays' and judged *King Solomon's Mines* the most 'healthily exciting volume' since Stevenson's *Treasure Island*.[60]

Haggard, Lang declared, was not one of the hack writers 'who describe adventures they never tasted in lands which they only know from geography books. He is intimately acquainted with the wild borders of Zululand, Bechuana, and the Transvaal, and he has a most sympathetic knowledge of the Zulu.'[61] Lang judged Haggard to have 'found himself' as a writer with *King Solomon's Mines* and 'added a new book to a scanty list, the list of good, manly, and stirring fictions of pure adventure'.[62]

Lang's praises were repeated across the press. According to the *Athenaeum*, some of the fighting scenes were 'hardly to be beaten outside Homer and the great Dumas'.[63] 'Nothing of the kind has ever been better conceived', raved *Public Opinion*,[64] while the *Spectator* thought *King Solomon's Mines* 'decidedly superior to the best of Jules Verne'.[65] The discovery of the frozen body of José da Silvestra 'in the ice cavern' was singled out as 'an absolute stroke of genius ... We felt when we reached that point that we were in the hands of a storyteller of no common powers; nor did the rest of the narrative, so skilfully and so high is the interest piled up, at all disappoint our expectations.'[66]

There were some contrarians. The reviewer for Boston's *Literary World* thought *King Solomon's Mines* reeked 'with brutality and suffering, and is enough to make the reader as haggard as its author'.[67] The *Dial* acknowledged the bloodiness of the tale and 'the crudeness of many of Mr. Haggard's sentences' but approved of Haggard having demonstrated 'the old distinction between the novel and the romance. In the former the imagination pictures what is: in the latter what is not. The novel dealing with the actual but slightly transposed has come in these days to an almost unmixed realism.'[68]

The term 'romance' was frequently used in opposition to 'realism' at this time and several Victorian authors labelled their more fanciful creations 'romances', but as 'the definition of realism became more precise in the period 1880–1890 with the influence of French theory, so romance was used more programmatically'.[69] Authors such as Haggard and Stevenson, cheered on by Andrew Lang, were conscious of working in opposition to realists such as George Moore, George Gissing and the French realist Émile Zola.

Among contemporary readers the poet and Jesuit priest Gerard Manley Hopkins had no qualms in recommending Haggard's romance for boys: 'I have not read

Treasure Island ... However give 'em Rider Haggard's *King Solomon's Mines*. They certainly will enjoy it; anyone would and the author is not a highflier.'[70] Another reader was Frances Colenso, daughter of the turbulent bishop. While on her way to England aboard the *Anglian*, the captain gave her a copy of *King Solomon's Mines* to read. 'Having a great dislike for the author I only began the book out of politeness to the lender but justice constrains me to acknowledge that it *is* a very clever book and altogether readable. I never saw a more transparent and unpleasant fool than that young man. How *did* he write so good a book?'[71]

Some 'kind hand' sent Robert Louis Stevenson (then living in Bournemouth) a copy of *King Solomon's Mines* 'I know not who did this good thing to me' – it was either Andrew Lang or William Henley – 'and so I send my gratitude to headquarters and the fountainhead'. Stevenson offered brickbats as well as bouquets: 'You should be more careful; you do quite well enough to take more trouble, and some parts of your book are infinitely beneath you. But I find there flashes of a fine weird imagination and a fine poetic use and command of the savage way of talking: things which both thrilled me.'[72] Stevenson – five years Haggard's senior – offered further advice in a subsequent letter: 'You rise in the course of your book to pages of eloquence and poetry ... But you began (pardon me the word) slipshod. If you are to rise, you must prepare the mind in the quiet parts, with at least an accomplished neatness. To this you could easily attain. In other words, what you have still to learn is to take trouble with those parts which do not excite you.'

Stevenson begged to be excused 'the tone of a damned schoolmaster'.[73] Haggard was happy to do so and their correspondence continued. 'Further reflection on "K.S.M." makes me think you are one who gets up steam slowly. In that case, when you have your book finished, go back and rewrite the beginning up to the mark. My case is the reverse: I always begin well, and often finish languidly or hurriedly. P.P.S. How about a deed of partnership?'[74] A partnership with Stevenson never came about, though Haggard did pair up with their mutual friend Andrew Lang to write *The World's Desire*. Haggard and Stevenson maintained an intermittent correspondence over the years but never met in person.

In his *Saturday Review* notice, Lang said that as Haggard, having lived in southern Africa, wrote of what he knew, readers of *King Solomon's Mines* were curious to know what was fact and what fiction. According to Haggard: 'It would be impossible for me to define where fact ends and fiction begins in the work, as the two are very mixed up together.'[75] In his autobiography Haggard describes the book as 'a work of pure imagination, for in my day very little was known of the regions wherein its scenes were laid, many details of which have been verified by subsequent discovery'.[76] For the rest of his life Haggard maintained this somewhat disingenuous stance on the sources and inspirations for his most famous book, especially when it came to the ruins of Great Zimbabwe.

In 'The Real King Solomon's Mines', a 1907 article written for *Cassell's Magazine*, Haggard says he had never heard 'of the great ruins of Zimbabwe or that an ancient civilisation had carried on a vast gold mining enterprise in the part of Africa where it stands',[77] though he acknowledged his imagination may have drawn upon 'chance words spoken long ago that lay dormant in the mind'.[78] Norman Etherington, in his 1977 essay 'South African Origins of Rider Haggard's Early African Romances', points out that 'circumstantial evidence ... clearly indicates that Haggard would have known about Zimbabwe and that important elements in *King Solomon's Mines*, *Allan Quatermain* and *She* were drawn directly from his residence in South Africa in the eighteen seventies'.[79]

On Shepstone's staff in Pretoria, Haggard would have 'made constant use of the maps' by Thomas Baines and Fred Jeppe which 'were crucial to the determination of Transvaal frontiers'. Etherington refers to Baines's 1873 'Map of the Gold Fields of South Eastern Africa', which shows 'Simbabye, ruined cities', and Jeppe's 1877 'Map of the South African Republic', which included the traveller Carl Mauch's route to the Zimbabwe ruins in 1871, featuring a two-inch inset 'view of the ruins'.[80] Baines's map also indicates the 'Supposed Realm of Queen Sheba' to the north of 'Simbabye'.[81] Thomas Baines died in May 1875, three months before Haggard set foot in Natal, but Haggard knew the Baines family – they lived north-west of Bradenham at King's Lynn – and says he doubtless 'heard something of that country from them and others, with the result that it must have been ingrained in my mind that it had once been occupied by an ancient people'.[82]

In 1914, when touring South Africa with the Dominions Royal Commission, Haggard lunched with Julius Jeppe, whom he knew from the Pretoria of the 1870s. Jeppe's uncle was the map-maker referred to by Etherington, Fred Jeppe. Baines, Mauch and other explorers of the African interior were frequent visitors to Jeppe's home in the 1870s, and Haggard must have been aware of their presence in Pretoria, then more of a capital village than a capital city.

Even in Maritzburg Haggard would have heard, if not of Great Zimbabwe, stories of the African hinterland and the Tati goldfields, as the Natal capital was the staging post for many an expedition to the north, such as that made by E.P. Sandeman, recorded in *Eight Months in an Ox-Waggon*, published in 1880 with a pull-out of Jeppe's map.[83] Sandeman's book was surely a candidate for Haggard's library, considering what is known of his reading on Africa in the 1880s.

In 'The Real King Solomon's Mines', Haggard mentions other sources for *King Solomon's Mines*, indicating that the Kukuana are the Ndebele under a different name, of whom he knew something: 'Indeed, I went very near to knowing too much.'[84] This is a reference to the murder of his 'dear friends Captain Patterson and Mr J. Sargeaunt, who were sent ... on an embassy to their king, Lobengula' in 1877.[85]

In 1974 Tim Couzens proposed that the Patterson embassy to Lobengula provided two basic plot elements for *King Solomon's Mines*: the expedition of three white adventurers and the rivalry between a royal heir and his usurper.[86] Etherington suggests as better candidates for the adventurers a trio of 'gold seekers in Mashonaland in the late eighteen sixties', Sir John Swinburne, Captain A.L. Levert and Thomas Baines, who were 'engaged in extensive negotiations with Lobengula at the time of a succession crisis' and 'far more likely models for Sir Henry Curtis, Captain Good and Hunter Quatermain than the untitled and prosaic members of the late Patterson expedition'.[87]

The Ndebele succession crisis was first put forward as an inspiration for *King Solomon's Mines* in Douglas Mackenzie's 1902 biography of his father, the Reverend John Mackenzie of the London Missionary Society, thinking it a 'safe conjecture' that Haggard 'founded one of the most interesting portions of his story ... upon this very incident'.[88] Mackenzie was based at Shoshong in Bechuanaland in the 1870s. His presence there signals another possible source for *King Solomon's Mines*, the travels of two brothers, Frank and William Oates.

In 1873 the naturalist and explorer Frank Oates planned a long expedition to the Zambezi River and beyond to territory unexplored by Europeans.[89] He was accompanied by his brother William, who undertook a shorter trip of about a year. They equipped themselves in Pietermaritzburg and left on 15 May, travelling north via the Transvaal to Shoshong, where they met the Reverend John Mackenzie, whom Frank appointed his executor in the event of any mishap. The brothers parted company at the Tati River and William headed back to England. Frank reached the Victoria Falls at the end of December, becoming the first European to see the falls in all their glory.[90] He died of fever on 5 February 1875, the same day his brother William sailed from England for South Africa, planning to go upcountry and meet Frank coming down. In Pietermaritzburg he learnt of his brother's death in the interior.

All this happened before Haggard's arrival in Pietermaritzburg in September 1875, but it can be assumed that the Oates expedition, kitted out in the city, and its tragic aftermath would have come to his attention and suggested a story element involving two brothers. A passage in *King Solomon's Mines* indicates he knew some of the background. In Chapter IV, 'An Elephant Hunt', the adventurers arrive at 'Inyati, the outlying trading station in the Matabele country ... [where] we with many regrets parted from our comfortable wagon ... requesting a worthy Scotch missionary who lived in this wild place to keep an eye to it'.[91] The missionary can only be Mackenzie. *Matabele Land and the Victoria Falls* by Frank Oates, published posthumously, is another prime candidate for Haggard's library.

Etherington also cites the novel *The Ruined Cities of Zululand* by Hugh Mulleneux Walmsley, published in 1869 and reissued ten years later under the title *Wild Sports and Savage Life in Zululand*, as a possible source for *King Solomon's Mines*. Walmsley was the younger brother of the Natal Border Agent Captain Joshua Walmsley, whom we have encountered in the Prologue. Walmsley's book features a missionary named Wyzinski, based on Alexander Merensky, and 'an encounter with the Amatonga who divided into warring factions when a "good native" accuses the wicked and hideously ugly chief of misrule'.[92] The wife of the chief, 'a preternaturally vengeful old hag, bears a striking resemblance to Gagool'.[93] As we have seen, Haggard took the name (though not the character) of Gagool from the wife of Indabezimbi, who was robbed and assaulted by Boers in 1881; similarly the name Foulata came from the servant at Hilldrop. In these instances Haggard simply made use of their names, but some of the other characters in *King Solomon's Mines* are more directly connected to people Haggard knew.

The physical description of Allan Quatermain – his short stature and shock of grizzled hair – could be taken from life, but if there was a single living inspiration for Quatermain, he remains unknown.[94] The most frequently cited original for the character of Quatermain is the hunter, trader and soldier Frederick Courtney Selous. Haggard always denied this and Selous's biographer Stephen Taylor cautions that it is 'not strictly true to say Selous was Allan Quatermain', but the view persists.[95] When Selous was killed in action in East Africa during the First World War, Haggard noted in his diary that Selous 'was not the original of Allan Quatermain as everybody says'.[96] In 1916 Haggard told Theodore Roosevelt, who assumed Quatermain was Haggard 'clothed in the body of Selous – as many others have done', that the former US president 'was right as to the first but not as to the second, since at the time I conceived Allan Quatermain I did not know Selous'.[97] Selous and Haggard met for the first time four years after *King Solomon's Mines* was published. But Haggard would certainly have heard of him. Selous was one of the signatories to the letter of protest from the Tati goldfields that led to the Patterson–Sargeaunt embassy to Lobengula. Selous's *A Hunter's Wanderings in Africa* was published in 1881. His biographer says Haggard 'drew openly on Selous's book'.[98] But if Selous is rejected as Quatermain's original, then the hero is most likely an amalgam of various hunter-traders whom Haggard encountered in Africa.

There is no real-life counterpart to Sir Henry Curtis. Described as akin to an 'ancient Dane', Curtis embodies the wish fulfilment of Haggard's belief 'that my forefathers were Danes' of heroic mien.[99] When it comes to Captain Good, 'the neatest man I ever had to do with in the wilderness',[100] we are on firmer ground in identifying a real-life counterpart. The Haggard bibliographer J.E. Scott, who knew the Haggard family, states that 'the character of Captain Good is really a study of the author's brother, John G. Haggard, R.N.'[101] Scott notes that Haggard was accused of 'having plagiarised Good's "beautiful white legs" and his false teeth from [Harry] Johnston's *Kilima-Njaro* and [Joseph] Thomson's *Through Masai Land* respectively'.[102] Haggard denied this charge, though to spare Jack embarrassment he refrained from mentioning his brother did indeed have false teeth.

Jack was undoubtedly one of the models for Good: both men were naval officers and, as we have seen, there are several jibes in *King Solomon's Mines* regarding the romantic propensities of sailors. Jack had a reputation as a ladies' man and for using strong language when aroused.[103] But there are other claimants to being Captain Good's inspiration. Four years after Haggard's death, in the *Field* magazine of February 1929, Lord Cranworth claimed Frederick Jackson, who had died earlier in the month, was the original of Good. 'This he owed to his eyeglass and a certain fastidiousness in dress', though there the resemblance ended.[104]

A 1932 correspondence in the *Morning Post* initially confirmed Jackson as the prime candidate for Captain Good. However, a pseudonymous letter published on 19 February claimed that 'another close friend' of Haggard also 'wore a monocle, and was, indeed, the patentee, so to speak, of the undrilled single eyeglass, to which no cord was attached'. This friend was no less than the writer of the letter himself, who long before the publication of *King Solomon's Mines* 'was chaffed by the author of that book, not only on his ability to hold the glass in the socket of the eye under all circumstances, but also on other peculiarities, the careful dressing, &c., which afterwards he tacked on to Captain Good'.[105]

The writer subsequently revealed his identity as James Stanley Little, adding that his claim to be the original of Captain Good had been previously stated in the *Athenaeum* and 'thereafter in numerous Metropolitan South African journals'. Little agreed that Jack was the original model for Captain Good, 'but in the process of painting the picture, very little of Jack Haggard remained, whereas certainly the detached eyeglass, the careful dressing, and several other characteristics, though not the false teeth, were unquestionably taken from me'.[106]

Little's claim has authority. He visited the Cape and Natal in 'the early 1880s and the experience shaped the rest of his life', inspiring him to write books and lecture on South Africa 'from a pro-imperialist standpoint'.[107] Little was a well-known fixture of literary London and a friend of Haggard.[108]

Jack Haggard's romantic inclinations were the motivation for his brother meeting Olive Schreiner, South African author of *The Story of an African Farm*. Schreiner came to England in 1881 with the intention of taking up a medical career and obtaining a publisher for her book; she found the latter in Chapman and Hall, who published it in 1883 under the pseudonym 'Ralph Iron'. In England Schreiner joined the circle of intellectuals that included Havelock Ellis, Edward Carpenter and Karl Pearson. Haggard contacted Olive Schreiner in July 1884, prompted to do so by Jack, who had been so impressed by *The Story of an African Farm* that he wrote to its author and received a 'nice letter' in response. Jack proposed Haggard go and interview Schreiner as a possible marriage prospect for the lonesome Jack in Lamu. Haggard instructed Hurst and Blackett to forward a copy of *Dawn* to Schreiner, then living at St Leonards on the Sussex coast, enclosing a letter from himself. She replied and, in a letter to Havelock Ellis, mentions getting another letter from Haggard. 'Do you know – I half believe it is Lady Florence Dixie.'[109] Ellis expressed his uncertainty as to whether 'Rider Haggard' was a pseudonym or not. 'Interesting if it is Lady F.

Dixie. It looks an assumed name. There should be some distinct traces of Lady F.D. in the novel if it is hers.'[110] A nice irony, if only Haggard had known.

Haggard had outlined his South African past to Schreiner and asked if she knew 'the Lehmkuhl family at the [Kimberley diamond] Fields, one of them married Mr Ford, who now lives in Pretoria? I knew them well.' Haggard requested that he be permitted to call upon Schreiner if she ever came to London. 'Your book [*Story of an African Farm*] made a great impression upon me. I hope that you are writing another. I have got one [*The Witch's Head*] coming out at the end of the year. It deals a good deal with S. Africa, but I have not got a high opinion of it myself ... It has only one merit – it was not so long as *Dawn*.'[111] Schreiner told Haggard *Dawn* had given her 'much pleasure'[112] and informed Ellis that Haggard wasn't Dixie but that she was still sure the writer 'must be a woman. I can't make out what *type* of man would have written such a book.'[113]

In February 1885 Schreiner came up to London. 'I have been delighted to see the favourable reviews of *The Witch's Head*,' she wrote to Haggard. She had been unable to read it as every time she requested it from the local library it was always out on loan, 'which is a promising sign!', adding playfully that 'I can't help sticking to my first opinion that "Rider Haggard" is a woman. A re-reading of *Dawn* makes me hold to it more than ever dogmatically. Your women are not like the women men draw (coming from *one* that is of course a compliment) and I am very keen to prove myself right.'[114] The two met, settling the question of Haggard's gender, and the 'very first thing' Schreiner asked him was 'if I was any relation to a gentleman at large on the East Coast of Africa who had written her a charming letter'. Haggard subsequently wrote Jack a detailed description of Schreiner, whom he described as 'exceedingly good-looking'.

> But what impresses one about the woman is her extraordinary individuality. Every sentence she says & every sentiment she expresses bears its unmistakeable impress. I am bound to say – not without humiliation – that in the presence of that woman I feel what I have never felt before with any other woman, that I have met my intellectual superior. Her insight into human nature is keener & clearer than my own; her reasoning power is stronger & the cast of her mind more original.[115]

Haggard doubted whether Schreiner would marry Jack or anyone else. 'I daresay if she was fond of you she wd have no objection to living with you, but marriage to her would be the emptiest ceremony ... For the opinion of the World she would, I should say, care nothing at all.' Haggard found Schreiner's 'complete & overpowering atheism' repellent. 'She is so sure she is right – that life is a dream & death an eternal sleep.'[116]

In June 1885, prior to the publication of *King Solomon's Mines* in September, Haggard and Schreiner were partnered between the pages of *In a Good Cause*, a fundraising project for the North Eastern Hospital for Children.[117] Subtitled *A*

Collection of Stories, Poems and Illustrations, the volume was organised and edited by Mary Rothes Margaret Tyssen-Amherst, the eldest daughter of the Tyssen-Amhersts of Didlington Hall, a patron of the hospital (later its director), whom Haggard had known since childhood. She approached him to write a story for the book and he obliged with 'Hunter Quatermain's Story', which boasts three illustrations by Samuel Carter, father of the archaeologist Howard Carter. Also among the book's contents is the poem 'Lost' by A.M. Barber – Aggie Barber. Its inclusion was probably facilitated by Haggard, who may have provided an entrée for Olive Schreiner as well; her short story 'African Moonshine' appears under her pseudonym Ralph Iron.[118] Other contributions include a poem from Andrew Lang and another by Oscar Wilde.

14

'IMMORTAL LOVE'

As we have seen, Haggard wrote *Allan Quatermain* – then titled 'The Frowning City' – during the summer of 1885 while on holiday in Norfolk. It was published in August 1887 and preceded by serialisation in *Longman's Magazine* between January and August 1887. Ten thousand subscription copies were sold prior to publication. On the book's title page, a subtitle describes *Allan Quatermain* as 'being an account of his further adventures and discoveries in company with Sir Henry Curtis, Bart., Commander John Good, R.N., and one Umslopogaas'. The subtitle stands above the epigraph 'Ex Africa semper aliquid novi'.[1]

The book opens with Quatermain, Curtis and Good en route to Central Africa, seeking to discover if there is any truth in the stories of a white race said to live in the interior north of Mount Kenia. Their motivations for the expedition differ: Curtis and Good are bored with life in dull, domesticated England; Quatermain is grieving for his son Harry: 'I have just buried my boy, my poor handsome boy of whom I was so proud, and my heart is broken. It is very hard having only one son to lose him thus, but God's will be done.'[2] These lines were invested with tragic irony six years later: 'By one of the saddest of all coincidences, if such things are pure coincidence, *Allan Quatermain* opens with a description of the death of Quatermain's only son. I dedicated it to *my* only son, and shortly afterwards that fate overtook him also!'[3]

Haggard inscribed the book to Arthur John Rider Haggard: 'In the hope that in days to come he, and many other boys whom I shall never know, may, in the acts and thoughts of Allan Quatermain and his companions, as herein recorded, find something to help him and them to reach to what, with Sir Henry Curtis, I hold to be the highest rank whereto we can attain – the state and dignity of English gentlemen.'[4] The death of Jock is yet to come, but Haggard the grim reaper wields his pen to deadly effect in *Allan Quatermain*, killing off two of his best-known heroes, Quatermain and Umslopogaas.

In Lamu, Quatermain, Curtis and Good are hosted by the British consul (the unnamed Jack Haggard), who has received a letter from a missionary living up the Tana River concerning a traveller who had undertaken a three-month journey 'beyond Mt. Lekakisera, which no white man has yet visited' and, after traversing 'over desert and thorn veldt and great mountains', had come to a country 'where the people are white and live in stone houses'.[5] The 'priests of the country put it about he was a devil, and the people drove him away'.[6] Eight months later the explorer turned up at the mission station and died shortly afterwards.

While in Lamu they assemble an expedition and hire some Wakwafi *askaris* (soldiers), one of whom turns out to be an old acquaintance of Quatermain, a Zulu named Umslopogaas, who is based on the real-life Mhlopekazi on Shepstone's staff, complete with 'a great three-cornered hole in his forehead'[7] and his axe, the Woodpecker.

As they canoe up the Tana River, there is a brief but deadly encounter with Masai warriors before the adventurers reach their first destination, 'The Highlands', a mission station run by a Scottish missionary, the Reverend Mr Mackenzie, who lives there with his wife and their 10-year-old daughter, Flossie. The mission is a well-cultivated Edenic paradise centred on a hill where Mackenzie's house sits within a fort. Mackenzie, a 'grey haired, angular man, with a very kindly face and red cheeks',[8] is based on the real-life missionary John Mackenzie of Tati, and the mission station is a duplicate of Alexander Merensky's Botshabelo with its fort, tilled fields and gardens.

Another resident is the cook Alphonse, a comic French character forever fretting for his beloved Annette in France; he is almost as irritating to the reader as he is to Umslopogaas, who subjects Alphonse to a display of skill with his beloved battleaxe reminiscent of that inflicted on Bathsheba Everdene by Sergeant Francis Troy in Thomas Hardy's *Far from the Madding Crowd*. Just as Troy's razor-sharp sword severed a lock of Bathsheba's hair, Umslopogaas's axe clinically detaches 'the tip of one of the little Frenchman's curling mustachios'.[9]

Shortly after the Quatermain party's arrival at the mission, Flossie is kidnapped by the Masai and only rescued after 'a slaughter great and grim'.[10] Mackenzie and his family leave for the coast while the heroes, with the addition of Alphonse, head off into the interior – 'first to Mount Kenia, and thence into the unknown in search of the mysterious white race which we had set our hearts on discovering'.[11]

Bidding them farewell, Mackenzie remarks that it is 'odd that three men, each of whom possessed many of those things that are supposed to make life worth living – health, sufficient means, and position, etc. – should from their own pleasure start out upon a wild-goose chase, from which the chances were they never would return'.[12] Quatermain acknowledges the truth of the remark: 'But then that is what Englishmen are, adventurers to the backbone; and all our magnificent muster-roll of colonies, each of which will in time become a great nation, testify to the extraordinary value of the spirit of adventure which at first sight looks like a mild form of lunacy'.[13]

Subsequent adventures include being sucked into an underground river, scalded by a 'pillar of fire'[14] – a gaseous flame prefiguring that of *She* – and a hair-raising attack by aggressive giant crabs before they are deposited on an inland sea surrounded by a land inhabited by a lost civilisation of white people, the sun-worshipping Zu-Vendi, possibly Persian in origin, ruled by twin queens, one – Nyleptha – who is fair, the other – Sorais – dark. Their complexions stereotypically reflect their natures, one good, the other evil.

Haggard's anthropological history of the Zu-Vendi includes their habits and customs as well as a description of the female mode of dress, consisting

> first of a linen under-garment that hung down to her knee, and then of a single long strip of cloth, about four feet wide by fifteen long, which was wound round the body in graceful folds and finally flung over the left shoulder so that the end, which was dyed blue or purple or some other colour, according to the social standing of the wearer, hung down in front, the right arm and breast being, however, left quite bare. A more becoming dress, especially when ... the wearer was young and pretty, it is quite impossible to conceive. Good (who has an eye for such things) was greatly struck with it, and so indeed was I. It was so simple and yet so effective.[15]

When Curtis falls in love with Nyleptha, the jealous Sorais (much mooned over by Good) declares: 'War – red war!'[16] An epic battle is followed by an equally epic ride in which the wounded Quatermain gallops through the night, Umslopogaas running at his horse's side, in the hope of averting a plot to assassinate Nyleptha in the royal palace. They make it in the nick of time but nevertheless have to fight a desperate battle against the forces of Sorais and the Zu-Vendi priesthood. This is the occasion for one of Haggard's most famous set pieces, Umslopogaas's last stand upon the stair: 'as the fight thickened, the old Zulu's eye seemed to get quicker and his arm stronger. He shouted out his war-cries and the names of chiefs whom he had slain, and the blows of his awful axe rained straight and true, shearing through everything they fell on.'[17]

With a final blow of the Woodpecker, the dying Umslopogaas shatters the sacred stone of the Zu-Vendi, 'a solid mass of black marble', thus fulfilling the ancient prophecy 'that when it was shattered into fragments a king of alien race should rule over the land'.[18] Enter Curtis with his queen. The mortally wounded Quatermain dies a few months later but not before writing the book that will bear his name, the manuscript of which is sent out of the country with Alphonse, who goes to find his beloved Annette.

According to Andrew Lang's biographer, the 'death of Umslopogaas remained one of the scenes in literature that affected him most'.[19] Lang's first reading moved him to compose an epitaph for Umslopogaas in Greek, which, with an English translation, was added to the book's front matter. Lang's wife Leonora told Haggard her husband 'had wasted an entire day' in its composition.[20]

When *Allan Quatermain* was published in August 1887, Haggard was embroiled in a plagiarism controversy, which some critics took as a licence to abuse. J.M.

Barrie, writing under the pseudonym Gavin Ogilvy in the *British Weekly*, compared Haggard to Stevenson as a 'worm to a star',[21] complaining that '2,000 copies of *Allan Quatermain* are in circulation in Mudie's [lending library] and not a single copy of Hardy's *A Pair of Blue Eyes*' and that Mudie's customers 'read *Kidnapped* when the 2,000 copies of *Allan Quatermain* are all out'.[22] Barrie was consoled by the thought that 'a dozen years hence, AQ will be as dead, rotten, and forgotten, as this morning's newspaper'.[23]

By way of contrast, the *Pall Mall Gazette* dubbed *Allan Quatermain* a 'delightful romance ... bloody enough to satisfy the most gluttonous carnivore',[24] commenting that Haggard was becoming the James Fenimore Cooper of the Zulu. A 'dime novel, pure and simple' was the verdict of Boston's *Literary World*, 'though we suppose the boys who get hold of it will devour it'.[25]

One boy who did exactly that was 13-year-old Winston Churchill, son of Sir Randolph, who wrote to its author: 'Dear Mr. Haggard, Thank you so much for sending me *Allan Quatermain*, it was so good of you. I like *A.Q.* better than *King Solomon's Mines*; it is more amusing. I hope you will write a great many more books.'[26] From the outset *Allan Quatermain* 'proved, and has remained, a general favourite', wrote Haggard, much of its popularity due to 'the Zulu in it, old Umslopogaas, being a very popular character with all classes of readers, and especially among boys'.[27]

In an appendix entitled 'Authorities', Haggard acknowledged his source material. 'John G. Haggard, RN, HBM's consul at Madagascar, and formerly consul at Lamu', is thanked for the 'many details furnished by him of the mode of life and war of those engaging people the Masai'. In addition, as Victoria Manthorpe notes, Jack had visited the Watiku tribe and 'discovered that they had Eurasian features rather than Negroid features, and their skins were almost white'.[28] She suggests they 'may well be the origin of the mysterious white tribe' in *Allan Quatermain*.[29]

Haggard expressed his gratitude to his 'sister-in-law, Mrs John Haggard', for putting 'the lines [of 'Sorais's Song'] into rhyme for me and [assisting] in designing the two plans'.[30] As for the 'similarity between the scene of Umslopogaas frightening Alphonse with his axe and a scene in Hardy's *Far from the Madding Crowd*', Haggard, tongue in cheek, expressed regret at the coincidence, 'and [I] believe the talented author of that work will not be inclined to accuse me of literary immorality on its account'.[31]

Haggard and his family returned from Norfolk to West Kensington in the autumn of 1885 and he began work on another book, a 'novel of a very different style'.[32] Vexed by dismissive descriptions of him being a 'mere writer of romances and boys' books', Haggard determined to try his hand at another novel: 'So after I had finished *Allan Quatermain* I set to ... and wrote *Jess*.'[33] The starting date is not known, but a note at the end of the manuscript records the single-volume novel being finished in London on 31 December 1885.[34] *Jess* was serialised in the *Cornhill* magazine between May

1886 and April 1887 and published as a book on 26 March 1887. *Jess* is a hybrid affair, drawing on Haggard's experiences as a civil servant and a farmer in South Africa combined with a melodramatic plot reminiscent of *Dawn* and *The Witch's Head*. There is also a nod to Olive Schreiner's *The Story of an African Farm* though far from sufficient to warrant any accusations of plagiarism.

Two events most likely prompted Haggard to choose South Africa and the Transvaal Rebellion as the backdrop for a novel: one was the death of Johanna Ford in August 1885, the second was the fall of Gladstone. *Jess* is permeated with bitterness at Gladstone's betrayal of the Transvaal, a betrayal compounded by his perceived abandonment of General Sir Charles Gordon in the Sudan. The British public's anger over Gladstone's reluctance to send a relief force to extract Gordon from the besieged city of Khartoum turned incandescent on the news of Gordon's death, when the city fell in January 1885. Gladstone resigned in June 1885 after the Liberals were defeated in a budget vote, leaving the Conservatives under Lord Salisbury to form a caretaker government, which lasted until January 1886 when it was defeated over an agricultural labour question, though politicking around Irish Home Rule was the real cause of the government's demise. The 'Irish question' came to the fore again with Gladstone's return in February, but when his Irish Home Rule Bill was defeated on its second reading, it was back to the polls, where the failure to rescue Gordon and the issue of Irish Home Rule 'broke apart the Liberal Party'.[35] A landslide victory in July saw Salisbury head the first of three Tory governments.

Haggard wrote the greater part of *Jess* in chambers at Lincoln's Inn Fields,[36] bent over his table 'in the dingy room at 1 Elm Court' when not in court, 'where I hung about a great deal, and even for a while reported Divorce and Probate cases for *The Times*', standing in for the newspaper's legal reporter when absent on holiday. Haggard was subject to frequent interruptions while writing in his room 'since young barristers of my acquaintance, with time upon their hands, would enter and scoff at my literary labours. In the evening I placed what I had written in a kind of American cloth music-roll, which either my wife or Miss Barber made for me, and carried it home to West Kensington, so that I might continue my work after dinner.'[37]

Jess incorporates incidents and places known to Haggard, including Hilldrop, which is renamed Mooifontein and relocated close to Wakkerstroom. Captain John Niel, a British officer serving in South Africa and no longer able to afford his commission, buys a partnership in the farm Mooifontein owned by Silas Croft, who lives there with his wards, two nieces: the blonde, blue-eyed Bessie (another incarnation of Lilly Jackson) and her sister, the enigmatic dark-haired and dark-eyed Jess (a New Woman akin to Olive Schreiner with a dash of Aggie Barber, as she still was at the time of writing).

John Niel's arrival at the farm coincides with Bessie being attacked by an ostrich. Niel saves Bessie from being killed and she falls in love with him, but much as Niel is fond of Bessie, he is really in love with Jess, though he just doesn't know it yet, and his love is returned. When Bessie confesses her love for John to her sister, Jess does the noble thing and removes herself to Pretoria (where 'The Palatial' becomes Jess's Cottage). Meanwhile, the evil Frank Muller (half-Boer and half-Brit) proposes to Bessie, who rejects him. Muller subsequently attempts to murder John while on a hunting expedition. When Muller learns of John's engagement to Bessie, he threatens to take her by force – threats brought to naught by the outbreak of the Transvaal Rebellion. John goes to Pretoria to rescue Jess; here the two are caught up in the siege and their love blossoms.

A friend of Muller's, Hans Coetzee, comes to Pretoria to offer a prisoner exchange and meets Jess, who asks for a pass for herself and John to leave the city. Muller learns of this and persuades the Boer leader, Paul Kruger, to grant one. Muller meets John and Jess and their waggon outside Pretoria, and with two of his henchmen they ride to a drift on the Vaal. The drift turns out to be non-existent, and John and Jess are forced to take their waggon across the river. In the course of the crossing they are fired on from the bank by Muller and his men. A Zulu servant and a horse are killed and the waggon founders. Haggard considered 'the account of the passion of John and Jess as they swung together wrapt in each other's arms in the sinking waggon on the waters of the flooded Vaal' among his best pieces of writing.[38] The incident is based on the shooting of Captain J.M. Elliott and the escape of Captain R.H. Lambart while being forced to cross the Vaal in flood.[39]

John and Jess survive the night stranded on a rock. Meanwhile, Muller rides to Mooifontein, where he finds a Union Jack flying above the farmhouse, and has Croft assaulted and arrested. Croft is sentenced to be hanged at dawn as a traitor if Bessie doesn't agree to marry Muller. John and Jess also make for Mooifontein and, when John is arrested by a Boer commando, Jess continues on her own. At Mooifontein, learning of what has happened, Jess kills Muller and flees into the night. Meanwhile, John has been released and makes his way to Mooifontein on foot. Exhausted, he falls asleep in a cave in Lion's Kloof close to the farm, where he is discovered by Jess, who collapses and dies next to him. This cave, thereafter known locally as 'Jess's Cave', was in Tiger's Kloof (Lion's or Leeuwen's Kloof in the book), a favourite picnic spot close to Hilldrop. The novel ends with John's marriage to the less interesting but ever faithful Bessie, and they, together with Silas Croft, return to England and settle in Rutland.

This precis is the bare skeleton of the story, which is fleshed out with several subplots, all with violent outcomes (one is a reframing of the case of Indabezimbi recorded by Haggard and Cochrane before they left Natal in 1881). The violence didn't stop the *Athenaeum*'s reviewer from considering Jess as Haggard's 'most charming creation', a female character superior to Ayesha.[40] *Murray's Magazine* agreed, praising Haggard's 'originality and pathos in the drawing of Jess' and his 'striking command of situations and characters'.[41]

Not everyone was convinced. The *Pall Mall Gazette* thought *Jess* a failure as a psychological study and, despite *Jess* delivering 'a capital story', felt the book was inferior to *King Solomon's Mines* and *She*. Despite *Jess* failing 'to display any spark of the divine genius, it shows that in Haggard we still have a graphic and accomplished story teller'.[42] Modern readers are likely to agree with Boston's *Literary World* in comparing *Jess* to a 'nightmare – grotesque, fantastic, horrible, leaving the mind wearied and depressed'.[43] That was Haggard's own conclusion, albeit for different reasons: 'It is a gloomy story and painful to an Englishman, so gloomy and painful that [Andrew] Lang could scarcely read it, having a nature susceptible as a sensitive plant ... The thing is a living record of our shame in South Africa, written by one by whom it was endured.'[44]

One sensitive reader was quite overcome by *Jess*. 'Nitie has just finished *Jess* and is now lying sobbing on the sofa behind me. Her pocket handkerchief is a *marsh*. She has got a bad headache from crying into the bargain. What higher compliment could you wish for? Confound you!'[45] Nitie, more formally Emily Margaret (née Hancox), was the second wife of Haggard's brother Will – now British chargé d'affaires in Athens – whom he married in January 1887.

Another contemporary fan of *Jess* was Emperor Frederick III of Germany. According to his widow, the Empress Victoria, eldest daughter of Queen Victoria, her husband 'found great pleasure in reading Mr Rider Haggard's books' at San Remo in Italy, where he was being treated for the laryngeal cancer that would kill him in June 1888 after a brief reign of 99 days. 'He as well as the Empress especially admired *Jess*, of which she read out a great part to him aloud.'[46]

The original of *Jess*'s villain, Frank Muller, was the 'rascally attorney' Gerhardus Hendricus Buskes, encountered by Haggard while Master and Registrar in Pretoria and later 'notorious in connection with the treatment of the loyal prisoners at the siege of Potchefstroom ... it is said that before two of these unfortunate men were executed, or rather murdered, he took them into a church and soothed their feelings by playing the "Dead March in Saul" over them.'[47]

Though Jess shares minor aspects of her character with Olive Schreiner and Aggie Barber, she does not appear to have been based on a real person, though there are claims to an original. On Monday, 11 June 1900, the *Natal Witness* carried an advertisement under the banner of Scott's Theatre for the 'last two nights' of the Royal Dramatic Company's production of *Jess*, which had been adapted for the stage by Edwin Chris, 'an Australian actor and author'.[48] At the time of the play's staging, the Anglo-Boer War was erroneously believed to be coming to an end and, to suit the patriotic mood, the producer John Marley added 'a further scene depicting the taking of Johannesburg, and the final raising of the British flag, "for ever and ever" in the Transvaal'.[49] Blanche Ripley was billed as playing Jess but, intriguingly, the anonymous *Witness* journalist mentions there being 'many people who know the original of Haggard's Jess, and of the Boer scoundrel who ended his actual career at

Elandslaagte'.[50] Whether Buskes was killed at the battle of Elandslaagte in 1899 is uncertain.

In February 1886 the Haggard family moved from Fairholme Road to 69 Gunterstone Road, a more commodious three-storey terraced house with basement, also in West Kensington. Haggard staked out the ground-floor front room as his study and, in the bay window overlooking the street, he placed the desk 'on which I wrote *She* in 6 weeks. That stuccoed, suburban residence was a queer birthplace for Ayesha, the immortal.'[51]

The time immediately prior to writing *She* was an unsettling one for Haggard. The literary toast of the town thanks to *King Solomon's Mines*, he still couldn't quite believe his luck, and despite completing two more novels – 'The Frowning City', retitled *Allan Quatermain*, and *Jess* – he was not entirely convinced that his future lay in literature and dutifully showed his face at the law courts each day. His thoughts turned again to the Colonial Service, and in a letter to the Colonial Office he offered his services and outlined his previous experience in Natal and the Transvaal, describing himself as 'a practising barrister' possessed 'of moderate independent means' and 'not unknown as a writer'.[52] Andrew Lang came to Haggard's aid and organised a lunch with his friend and fellow Scot, Arthur Balfour, Secretary for Scotland in Lord Salisbury's minority government, but the Colonial Office 'under Salisbury's premiership was not interested in dispensing patronage to colonial servants of Gladstone's days'.[53]

Haggard's limbo-like existence was rudely brought home to him in court one day when 'watching a case or devilling for somebody, I unconsciously inscribed my name on the nice white blotting-paper before me'. Seeing this, a solicitor behind whispered, 'Are you Rider Haggard, the man who wrote *King Solomon's Mines?*' Haggard nodded a yes. 'Then, confound you! Sir, you kept me up till three o'clock this morning. But what are you doing here in a wig and gown – what are you doing here?'[54]

In contrast to his undemanding employment, Haggard's home life was in a state of flux. On Christmas Day 1885 his brother Jack had announced his engagement to Aggie Barber. Aggie's marriage would end an agreeable domestic and literary arrangement. On New Year's Day 1886, Jack was commissioned as British consul to Madagascar; he would leave a few months later with additional commissions to represent Norway and Sweden. Jack and Aggie were married on 28 January 1886 at St Andrew's Church in Fulham. At this quiet wedding on a sunny midwinter's day, Aggie wore 'a dark blue vicuna costume made up with striped velvet, bonnet and muff to match, white veil, lovely bouquet of white flowers on muff, and on left shoulder another bouquet'. Jack was pale and 'fined down' from his illness. 'I never thought him so good looking before,' remarked a cousin. 'He clapped the ring down on the book with an air, and when the clergyman took it up and gave it to him again said, "What do I do with it?"'[55]

The same question could be applied to the spectacular success of *King Solomon's Mines*. Having resolved to concentrate on law with the intention of finessing this occupation into a parliamentary career, Haggard had written a book on a whim (if not a bet) which found mass acceptance and brought accompanying riches. How to navigate and best exploit this unforeseen El Dorado? Haggard hadn't enjoyed any success in the lucrative magazine market, which, in addition to publishing short stories, had also begun serialising novels prior to their publication in book form. Haggard approached Walter Besant, the novelist, critic, London historian and founder of the Society of Authors, for a recommendation to the *Graphic*. Besant declined: 'recommendations are unfortunately regarded with suspicion'. This wasn't a brush-off. Besant gave Haggard some excellent advice: 'your best plan would be to do what [James] Payn, Wilkie Collins and I myself do – put yourself in the hands of Watt, the literary agent ... I think there can be no doubt that you may follow up a now certain success profitably.'[56]

By the end of the year Haggard was a client of the stereotypically shrewd Scot, 52-year-old Alexander Pollock Watt, widely acknowledged as originating the profession of literary agent. Watt was intensely conscious of the fast-changing environment of publishing in the latter half of the nineteenth century, in which 'more people were reading, and there was more for them to read'.[57] *King Solomon's Mines* appeared on the shelves at the very moment 'a genuine mass market for literature had arisen, and with it the phenomenon of the best-seller'.[58] The increase in literacy, extended leisure time, and improvements in domestic lighting – from candles to paraffin lamps to gas lighting in the 1890s – led to a boom in readers, and an industry came into being in response to their needs, producing books, magazines and newspapers.

Growing demand for reading matter put pressure on the circulating libraries such as Mudie's and W.H. Smith 'to provide more novels at lower costs to readers,'[59] in turn creating a demand for more content from authors. The evolution of different types of publication drove authors to gain greater copyright protection in order to maximise control over their work; writers also sought to enhance their social status, to be regarded as respectable members of society as opposed to 'penny-a-liners', scribblers and hacks – in short, members of a profession requiring regulation and organisation. To facilitate this shift in status, the Society of Authors came into being in 1884 under the direction of Besant.

The mid-1880s marked the beginning of the end for the three-volume novel pioneered by Walter Scott in the second decade of the nineteenth century, a format that became standard for the circulating libraries, the main buyers of books and the main outlet to readers. The circulating libraries preferred the three-volume model as it increased their subscriptions – for the publisher, single and thus cheaper volumes might sell better but did so at greater financial risk. But authors, though mindful of their income, were balking at the creative constraints of the three-volume form, preferring to write books to a length that their subject matter dictated. The time had come for both writers and publishers to chart new territories.[60]

Alexander Watt entered this rapidly changing environment in the late 1870s when 'conditions were ripe for someone ... who had the vision to see that a mediating figure was badly needed'[61] to bridge the gap 'between producers and publishers of literature'.[62] Watt finessed his friendship with the author George MacDonald, for whom he had placed material, into a literary agency with the self-proclaimed task to 'do nothing but sell or lease copyrights, and to make his living doing so, thereby distinguishing himself from "amateur" literary agents – the friends or relatives of writers – who had preceded him'.[63] Publishers were horrified at the idea until they realised a literary agent could be of use to them as well: the go-to person for the product required, precisely tailored to their needs. The author–agent–publisher triad became the norm.

Thanks to Watt, *Allan Quatermain*, *Jess* and *She* would be serialised in magazines prior to book publication. *Allan Quatermain* and *Jess* had been written before *She*, but the last-mentioned title was the first to appear in print after *King Solomon's Mines*. Serialised in the *Graphic* from 2 October 1886 to 8 January 1887, *She* was published on 1 January 1887.

The central thesis underpinning *She* found its first concrete expression in *The Witch's Head* with Ernest describing his love for Eva in terms of eternity: 'it is somehow fixed in my mind that my fate and that woman's are intertwined. I believe, perhaps foolishly enough, that what we are now passing through is but a single phase of interwoven existence; that we have already passed through many stages, and that many higher stages and developments await us.'[64] The concept of intertwined lives spiralling through the ages through reincarnation springs from Haggard's reading of A.P. Sinnett's *Esoteric Buddhism*, in which he discovered the 'most reasonable explanation of the mystery of existence that I have ever yet come in contact with'.[65]

An English journalist, Alfred Percy Sinnett was a disciple of the Russian noblewoman Helena Petrova Blavatsky, better known as Madame Blavatsky, co-founder of the Theosophical Society in 1875. She claimed to have discovered 'an ancient wisdom tradition that underlay all particular manifestations of religion throughout the world', a tradition 'preserved in a secret location in Tibet under the leadership of the "Mahatmas"'. Blavatsky telepathically received instruction from these masters, and their revelations were expounded in *Isis Unveiled* (1877) and *Secret Doctrine* (1888). Thanks to her writings and Sinnett's *Esoteric Buddhism*, published in 1883, 'many Europeans came to believe that the occultist fantasies of Theosophy indeed represented the true teachings of Buddhism',[66] Haggard among them. He read *Esoteric Buddhism* over the winter of 1883/4, enthusing about it to Aggie Barber: 'It offers a clue which the human mind can without violence to its common sense accept as more or less satisfactory of the why & wherefore of things. It presents a panorama of gradual & sure development from small beginnings to infinite ends, of the inheritance in each succeeding incarnation of the good and evil worked in the former incarnation ages since.'[67]

The ideas expressed in *Esoteric Buddhism* didn't come 'into antagonistic contact' with Christianity, according to Haggard, 'since over all this vast system of lives lived by the same individual monads or souls upon different planets & through periods whose lapse must be measured by millions of our years there must be a supreme directing will though Buddhism fails to reach so high'.[68] In his view Christianity 'may well be a sketch map perfectly correct as far as it goes whereas the theories here revealed may also mark out the divisions of a spiritual existence with something approaching to accuracy'.[69]

Haggard was living in a period of great questioning and doubt brought about by the Victorian 'crisis of faith' – a response to the discoveries of science, especially the propagation of Charles Darwin's evolutionary theories in tandem with the new academic discipline of comparative religion, which had exposed Christianity to critical scrutiny as never before. This intellectual ferment was further assisted by the expansion of the British Empire creating a feedback loop that allowed the philosophies and religions of the East, such as Buddhism, Hinduism and Islam, to flow back to Europe.

Hybrid religions sprang up in an attempt to synthesise the new findings in science and religion, the most prominent of which was Theosophy with its distorted view of Buddhism. According to the scholar J. Jeffrey Franklin, Buddhism 'entered the popular discourse in England in the second half of the nineteenth century',[70] and ideas such as reincarnation, 'attended by the doctrine of karma, fully entered popular consciousness in the West, becoming a familiar topic in the literature and the popular press'.[71]

The Victorian contact with Buddhism was largely mediated through Theosophy but, ironically, though *Esoteric Buddhism* was 'virtually unrecognisable as Buddhism', it was this 'non-Buddhism that was instrumental in disseminating a popular understanding of and fascination with Buddhism in the West'.[72] The ideas expressed by Sinnett would permeate much of Haggard's thinking and writing, most especially the sequence of novels featuring Ayesha, She-Who-Must-Be-Obeyed: *She*, its sequel *Ayesha*, and two prequels, *She and Allan* and *Wisdom's Daughter*.

Haggard began writing *She* a month after completing *Jess* in December 1885. A rusted paper clip fastened to the manuscript obliterated the exact starting date, and Haggard could only confirm that he commenced writing *She* in February 1886. The final page is inscribed 'Finished 18 March 1886'.[73]

In his autobiography Haggard is at a loss to explain how his 29-year-old self produced *She*:

The fact is that it was written at white heat, almost without rest, and that is the best way to compose. I remember that when I sat down to my task my ideas as to its development were of the vaguest. The only clear notion that I had in my head was that of an immortal woman inspired by an immortal love. All the rest shaped itself around this figure. And it came – it came faster than my poor aching hand could set it down. [74]

Not all of *She* was written at his desk before the bay window of 69 Gunterstone Road. Haggard recalled a visit to Watt's offices at 2 Paternoster Square near St Paul's, a short walk from the Inns of Court. Finding Watt absent, he sat down to wait and, loath to waste time, 'asked for some foolscap, and in the hour or two that I had to wait wrote the scene of the destruction of She in the Fire of Life'.[75] Haggard delivered the finished manuscript to Watt a few days later, throwing it down on the desk and remarking: 'There is what I shall be remembered by'.[76]

As with *King Solomon's Mines*, a quest lies at the heart of *She*, the search for an immortal white queen living in the heart of Africa, a quest embarked on by Ludwig Horace Holly, his ward Leo Vincey, and their faithful servant Job. There are links to *King Solomon's Mines*: the book's 'editor', though unnamed, is Allan Quatermain, who, in his editorial introduction to *She*, recalls meeting Holly, *She*'s narrator, in a Cambridge street 'some five years ago'; he had coincidentally 'recently read' Quatermain's book describing an adventure in Central Africa 'with much interest'. On the evidence of his book and their fortuitous meeting, Holly decided that Quatermain was the right person to edit and publish 'a real African adventure, of a nature so much more marvellous than [*King Solomon's Mines*] that to tell you the truth I am almost ashamed to submit it to you for fear lest you should disbelieve my tale'.[77]

Holly is a Cambridge academic and an involuntary celibate, having been 'branded by Nature with the stamp of abnormal ugliness, as I was gifted by Nature with iron and abnormal strength and considerable intellectual powers'.[78] Holly's solitude is interrupted by an unexpected midnight visitor on the brink of death, his only friend, M.L. Vincey, bearing a 'massive iron box' and a request that Holly be sole guardian of Leo, his 5-year-old son (the mother died in childbirth). The box is to be opened when Leo turns 25. By way of explanation Vincey details his descent from Kallikrates, an Egyptian priest who broke his vows of celibacy in 339 BC and fled south with Amenartas, a princess of the royal blood. Shipwrecked on the East African coast, they 'were at last entertained by the mighty Queen of a savage people'.[79] The mysterious queen falls in love with Kallikrates, killing him in a jealous rage when he refuses to be unfaithful to his wife Amenartas. The pregnant Amenartas fled north, where she gave birth to a son, thus beginning a lineage ending with the infant Leo.

Holly promises to fulfil his friend's wishes and, prior to young Leo's arrival, hires Job, 'a most respectable round-faced young man, who had been a helper in a hunting-stable' and, being from a large family, was 'well accustomed to the ways of children, and professed himself quite willing to undertake the charge of Master Leo when he arrived'.[80] The real-life model for Job – 'a little touched up'[81] – was the Ditchingham groom Stephen Lanham, who accompanied Haggard and Louie to Natal. Job is described as 'a most matter-of-fact specimen of a matter-of-fact class',[82] and, aside from his unswerving loyalty, the vehicle for some heavy-handed comic relief.

Leo Vincey, a golden curly-haired cherub, grows into a young man handsome as a Greek god, albeit a somewhat empty-headed one, even provoking *She*'s editor to comment that 'there appears to be nothing in his character ... likely to attract an intellect so powerful as that of Ayesha'.[83] On the appointed birthday Leo and his adoptive father open the box to find various artefacts confirming Leo's father's story, including 'the sherd of Amenartas', bearing writing in 'uncial Greek'[84] addressed to her 'little son Tisisthenes (the Mighty Avenger)',[85] which tells of the white queen who enjoys access to eternal life as well as 'a loveliness that does not die',[86] and concludes with a command to her son to 'seek out the woman, and learn the secret of Life, and if thou mayest find a way to slay her'[87] and avenge the death of Kallikrates.

Leo, descendant of Tisisthenes, obeys the ancestral command of his great-great-ad infinitum-grandmother Amenartas and, with a sceptical Holly and the faithful Job, heads for Africa. Sailing down the East African coast in a dhow towing a specially commissioned whaleboat (the double of that ordered by Frederick Jackson on Jack Haggard's advice from Messrs John Brown of Dundee), they encounter a tropical storm. The dhow founders and they take to the whaleboat, eventually making shore with one surviving crew member, Mahomed.[88] Destiny has brought them to the right place and, following a man-made canal into the interior through a land of mosquito-infested swamps, they encounter a party of Amahagger sent to find them by Ayesha, She-Who-Must-Be-Obeyed. Among them is Ustane, a beautiful young woman and latest incarnation of Amenartas, with whom Leo promptly falls in love.

The matrilineal Amahagger are occasional cannibals, and after Ayesha instructs that white men are not on the menu, the darker-hued Mahomed is considered a legitimate *plat du jour*. Such a dish is denied them after the intervention of Holly and Vincey, though not before the Amahagger have demonstrated their method of slaughter – 'hot-potting', a gruesome invention of Haggard's, whereby the victim has a red-hot pot inverted on his head. In the struggle to prevent this happening, Mahomed is shot dead by Holly, 'an awful yet a most merciful accident'.[89]

And so to Ayesha's domain – an extinct volcano wherein lie the ruins of a lost civilisation centred on the abandoned city of Kôr which is situated in the crater's plain. Ayesha and the servile Amahagger inhabit the catacombs burrowed into the surrounding volcanic cliffs. From this point on, *She* is no longer a bracing fresh-air African adventure along the lines of *King Solomon's Mines*, set in wide open spaces with far horizons. In contrast, *She* plays out in the candlelit semi-dark amidst catacombs and caves populated by mummified corpses.

The 2,000-year-old Ayesha, virginal and breathtakingly beautiful, recognises Leo as her lost love, the double of Kallikrates, whose preserved but lifeless body she visits nightly in its catacomb chamber to bestow a good-night kiss. It's not long before her rival Ustane is eliminated, struck dead by Ayesha using her supernatural powers, but such is Ayesha's hypnotic allure that this murderous act doesn't prevent Leo (and Holly, without any hope of fulfilment) falling in love with her. But fate has a trick up its sleeve. Wishing to share the source of her longevity, they are taken by Ayesha to bathe in the volcanic gaseous flame, the 'Spirit of Life', which flares up through a fissure in a deep cavern. When Leo hesitates to step into the flame, Ayesha enters first to reassure him, but this time the flame's effect works in reverse:

> she was shrivelling up; the golden snake that had encircled her gracious form slipped over her hips and to the ground; smaller and smaller she grew; her skin changed colour, and in place of the perfect whiteness of its lustre it turned dirty brown and yellow, like a piece of withered parchment. She felt at her head: the delicate hand was nothing but a claw now, a human talon like that of a badly-preserved Egyptian mummy, and then she seemed to realise what kind of change was passing over her, and she shrieked – ah, she shrieked! – she rolled upon the floor and shrieked!
>
> ... At last she lay still, or only feebly moving. She, who but two minutes before had gazed upon us the loveliest, noblest, most splendid woman the world has ever seen, she lay still before us, near the masses of her own dark hair, no larger than a big monkey, and hideous – ah, too hideous for words. And yet, think of this – at that very moment I thought of it – it was the same woman!

And so Ayesha dies. Or does she? In her final moments she promises: 'I shall come again, and shall once more be beautiful, I swear it – it is true!'[90]

Thereafter matters are quickly wrapped up. Job dies of shock at the sight of Ayesha's transformation, and Leo and Holly return to England. The years pass, and all the while they wait for Ayesha to return. When the sign comes, Holly sends the manuscript of their initial adventure to Allan Quatermain before they go 'away again, this time to Central Asia where, if anywhere upon this earth, wisdom is to be found'.[91] More precisely, Tibet. Where else?

15

'THE LITERATURE OF ANOTHER PLANET'

'Finished'. The final word of Haggard's manuscript of *She* marked the end of an extraordinary burst of creativity. 'Between January 1885 and March 18, 1886, with my own hand, and unassisted by any secretary, I wrote *King Solomon's Mines*, *Allan Quatermain*, *Jess*, and *She*. Also I followed my profession, spending many hours of each day studying in chambers, or in Court, where I had some devilling practice, carried on my usual correspondence, and attended to the affairs of a man with a young family and a certain landed estate.'[1]

Truth be told, Haggard did have some assistance in writing *She*, notably in devising the pseudo-historical Greek, Latin and medieval texts that prop up the tale and were such a 'source of wonder to his old schoolfellows'.[2] The source of their amazement was their former headmaster at Ipswich Grammar School, the classical scholar Hubert Ashton Holden, with whom Haggard became 'very friendly in after life'.[3] The school's academic record had improved dramatically under Holden's headmastership, but his relations with the school governors were fraught and, when he tendered a tactical resignation in 1883, they called his bluff and accepted it. 'He left unthanked and unsung by the governors but almost deified by his loyal colleagues and pupils'.[4] Holden and his family moved to London, taking up residence at 20 Redcliffe Square in South Kensington, where Haggard contacted him and asked if he would compose the ancient Greek inscription on the sherd from Haggard's English text. 'Do you want the Greek to be such as to deceive the learned world into thinking that it is no forgery, but a genuine bit of antiquity?' asked Holden.[5] Yes was the answer, and Holden obliged. The Reverend John James Raven, vicar at Fressingfield, Suffolk, a few miles from Ditchingham, was recruited for the Medieval Latin version of the script and its translation into Old English.

While Haggard composed the bogus texts and commissioned their translations, Aggie constructed the 'sherd of Amenartas'. Researching at the British Museum, she 'copied various characters and signatures from deeds and parchments relating to the periods mentioned in the story, afterwards painting them on to the sherd with a very fine brush'.[6] Haggard attempted to pass the sherd off as genuine to the archaeologist and president of the Society of Antiquaries, Sir John Evans. 'For a long while he peered at it through his eyeglasses and at last put it down, remarking, "All I can say is that it might *possibly* have been forged."'[7]

She first saw the light of day in weekly instalments in the *Graphic* magazine from 2 October 1886 to 8 January 1887. *She: A History of Adventure* was published by Longmans on 1 January 1887. It was the first of many Haggard titles from the publishing house then headed by Charles Longman, 'a solid, ugly man, with few beliefs, less illusions, little imagination and a very hard and practical business head ... about as complete an opposite to Rider as could be imagined'.[8] Opposites famously attract, and Longman became an ardent fan and a good friend of Haggard, a friendship curated by Andrew Lang, a literary adviser to the firm.

Lang read *She* in proof prior to its serial publication in the *Graphic* and, having nearly completed the task, wrote Haggard a letter of congratulation: 'it is one of the most astonishing romances I ever read. The more impossible it is, the better you do it, till it seems like a story from the literature of another planet.'[9] Lang expressed reservations regarding the 'comic element and the horrors', adding a postscript: 'I know I shan't sleep.'[10] On finishing the proofs Lang elaborated further: 'I certainly still think it the most extraordinary romance I ever read, and that's why I want you to be very careful with the proofs, before it goes out in a volume.'[11] Lang spotted the problem with Leo: 'He is not made a very interesting person. Probably he was only a fine animal. Anyhow that can't be helped now and never could perhaps.'[12] He also criticised Haggard's comic dialogue: 'in awful situations [it] lets one down too suddenly ... I hope they find She in Thibet, and all die together'.[13]

Haggard made substantial corrections in preparing the single-volume edition of *She*, including rewriting and toning down the 'hot-potting scene'.[14] When he indicated his intention to dedicate *She* to his friend, Lang acknowledged the prospect was 'a great distinction' but cautioned that if Haggard did so he wouldn't be able 'to review it, except with my name signed thereto and my honest confession. Probably I could do that in the *Academy*.'[15] Haggard went ahead and dedicated *She* to Lang 'in token of personal regard and of my sincere admiration for his learning and his works';[16] and, as promised, Lang reviewed *She* for the *Academy*. As well as praise Lang's review incorporates his earlier caveats and criticisms: finding the humour unsuccessful, balking at the violence, while accurately identifying Holly's writing style as being more like that of Allan Quatermain 'rather than of a Cambridge don'.[17]

Most of the critics took a similar line to Lang, amazed at Haggard's inventiveness but critical of his style. The *Pall Mall Gazette* hailed the former as being 'informed by an energy and intensity of imagination' but, given content so powerful, 'we rebel with a sense of injury against the many defects of execution ... If Dante had been accompanied on his tour through the *città dolente* by a special correspondent of the *Daily Telegraph*, the result would have been just such a book as *She*.'[18]

Literary World declared Haggard had 'made for himself a new field in fiction'; abandoning realism, 'he places the scene of his stories in the unexplored regions of Africa, and there brings his adventurous modern Englishmen into contact with strange peoples living among the stupendous remains of forgotten civilisations'. Readers were encouraged to enter 'Mr. Haggard's fantastic kingdom'.[19]

The reviewer in *Public Opinion* confessed to having 'scarcely met with anything more weird in a long course of promiscuous novel reading. If Flaubert's *Salammbô* came as a surprise to the reading world, Mr Haggard's book is far more fascinating, and is worth sitting up half the night to finish.' Haggard was urged to address issues of style, but on 'the extraordinary character of She the author has lavished a force of imagination, a dramatic instinct, a poetic insight, and an artistic sense of proportion which are truly admirable, and long after the book is finished this strange, lovely ruthless creature haunts the imagination'.[20] The *Spectator* acknowledged the tale was 'a very stirring and exciting one ... vividly and brilliantly told' but sniffily concluded: 'This type of romance is not one that we would place very high in the literary scale, but in its kind it could hardly be rivalled.'[21]

She 'proved a great and immediate success'.[22] Haggard received letters from literary friends assuring him of its merits. Wilkie Collins sent a letter 'highly praising *She*',[23] while Walter Besant congratulated him on producing a book which 'puts you at the head – a long away ahead of all contemporary imaginative writers. If fiction is best cultivated in the field of pure invention then you are certainly the first of modern novelists.'[24] Besant confessed to being astonished by the book, adding that whatever else Haggard might write, 'you will have *She* always behind you for purposes of odious comparison'.[25] A 'thrilled and terrified' Edmund Gosse echoed Besant's forecast: 'I do not know what to say, of hope or fear, about any future book of adventure of yours. I don't know what is to be imagined beyond the death of Ayesha.'[26] Haggard ruefully acknowledged Besant's and Gosse's prescience: 'Quite a large proportion of my critics during many years have mentioned in the course of their reviews of various works from my pen that the one under consideration is not another *She*, or words to that effect. As though a man's brain could harbour a host of *Shes*! Such literary polygamy is not possible. Only one love of this kind is given to him.'[27]

Henry James was appalled by the critical, popular and commercial success of *She*: 'It isn't nice that anything so vulgarly brutal should be the thing that succeeds most with the British race of today,' he wrote to Robert Louis Stevenson. 'More even than with the contemptible inexpressiveness of the whole thing I am struck with the beastly *bloodiness of it* – or it comes back to the same thing – the cheapness of the hecatombs with which the genial narrative is bestrewn. Such perpetual ugliness!'[28]

Leo Tolstoy agreed. Isabel Hapgood, the American journalist and translator, recorded an evening at Tolstoy's Yasnaya Polyana estate when the great writer 'happened to hit upon a couple of Mr. Rider Haggard's books for discussion and, for the benefit of those in the company who had not read it, gave the chief points of *She* in particularly lively style, which kept us all in laughter ... He pronounced *She* and other works of Haggard "the lowest type of literature," and said that "it was astonishing how so many English people could go wild over them".[29]

Reviewing Morton Cohen's biography of Haggard, the writer and critic V.S. Pritchett recalled E.M. Forster speaking 'of the novelist sending down a bucket into the unconscious'. In Pritchett's estimation, 'the author of *She* installed a suction pump. He drained the whole reservoir of the public's secret desires.'[30] Haggard's work, especially *She*, fascinated those pioneering explorers of the human unconscious, Sigmund Freud and Carl Jung, precisely because they saw it as an expression of that unconscious. *She* made such an impression on Freud it even intruded on his dream life. When a female visitor asked him to lend her something to read, he offered *She*, 'a strange book, but full of hidden meaning', which he began trying to explain to her – 'the eternal feminine, the immortality of our emotions' – when she cut him off.[31]

Jung thought Ayesha a classic example of the *anima*, the 'inner feminine character [which] plays a typical, or archetypal, role in the unconsciousness of a man',[32] all the more so from having been produced by Haggard in a 'white heat', bypassing the mediation of the intellect. Anyone seeking 'understanding and insight will find rich fare in *She*', says Jung, 'just because of the simplicity and naiveté of the views which lack deliberate psychological implications.'[33] Jung's disciple Cornelia Brunner in her book *Anima as Fate* interprets *She* as if it were a dream, dreamt by a man coming to terms with and externalising his *anima*. This interpretation gains greater validity if one takes into account Haggard's sense of dislocation and loss of equilibrium in his domestic and professional life both before and during the writing of *She*.

Haggard's bias towards the feminine is well attested. The majority of his books feature strong female characters and twenty-eight of his fiction titles – well over half – feature female names and at least two others began life in manuscript with feminine titles that perforce had to be changed.[34] Real women in Haggard's life also cast their shadow over Ayesha: his strong-willed sister Ella; Aggie, now his sister-in-law – 'her passions are strong, especially her love and hate';[35] Olive Schreiner and her 'extraordinary individuality';[36] the less fiery but nevertheless indomitable Louie, his wife; and Lilly Jackson, whom Haggard 'loved, with an affection which transcends all earthly passion and stretches out hands beyond the grave'.[37] There are phantom presences too: Johanna Ford and their dead child, Ethel; Haggard's own fear of death and the terrors of his childhood, including that hideous rag doll, She-Who-Must-Be-Obeyed, used by his nurse to frighten him 'into obedience'.[38] 'Romance may be the vehicle of much that does not appear to the casual reader,' Haggard noted in his diary in 1917, a day before making a nostalgic visit to 69 Gunterstone Road, the birthplace of *She*.[39] He omitted to add: or to the writer for that matter.

In 1887 *She* earned Haggard the ultimate Victorian seal of approval: a caricature in *Vanity Fair* by Spy (Leslie Ward), and below the cartoon a single word: 'She'. The accompanying biographical sketch by 'Jehu Junior', pseudonym of Thomas Gibson

Bowles, the magazine's founder and editor, concluded that Haggard 'writes plainly, powerfully, and without affectation, and is the most new and fresh, as well as the most successful of our young novelists. He is fond of shooting, amiable, modest, and a lively companion.'[40]

Another determinant of *She*'s success lay in the number of parodies it provoked. An 'Interview with She' by J.M. Barrie appeared in the *St James's Gazette* on 16 February 1887. Andrew Lang immediately responded: 'It is very natural that your Kôr Korespondent ... should have been deceived into thinking that he had enjoyed an interview with She. But, as a matter of fact, Ayesha is really in Thibet, except when, as Madame Blavatsky, she occasionally appears in Anglo-Indian Society.'[41]

An inveterate literary joker, Lang co-wrote an affectionate 120-page parody titled *He* with Walter Herries Pollock, editor of the *Saturday Review*. *He* contained a satirical barb aimed at W.T. Stead, editor of the *Pall Mall Gazette*, who appears as a character named Pell-Melli, 'then conducting one of his numerous crusades, this time against the "Log-rollers" or "Mutual Admiration Society of Authors" of whom he considered Lang and Haggard to be the two most abject'.[42] Stead would not have to wait long for his revenge.

Another spin-off from *She* was a collaboration between Haggard and Lang. The first candidate for consideration was a sequel to *She*, something Haggard already planned on writing himself after an interval of twenty years. A prequel was substituted, then abandoned. As Ayesha proved uncooperative, Haggard and Lang lighted on another female archetype, Helen of Troy, who became the heroine of *The World's Desire*, published after long gestation in 1890 following serialisation in the *New Review*.

A sequel to events recorded in Homer's *Odyssey*, the book homes in on the romance of Helen and Odysseus in Egypt. Lang envisaged one of the characters, Meriamun, powerful queen of the Pharaoh Meneptah, as an earlier incarnation of Ayesha and suggested to Haggard that Meriamun in a vision 'might have a glimpse of Kôr and the Ama-Haggars flitting about', though he left it to Haggard to decide 'how much those *She* references shall stand: the vaguer the better I think'.[43] In the event there are no direct references to *She* in *The World's Desire*, but the vision granted to Meriamun went on to become the template for *Wisdom's Daughter*, the prequel to *She* published in 1923.

Haggard's study at Gunterstone Road was not only memorable as the birthplace of *She*: behind the lace curtains he also 'had the experience with the mummy, which is now at the Norfolk Museum at Norwich'.[44] Barring this tantalising diary entry from March 1917, nothing is known of the incident other than a story handed down in the Haggard family:

On arrival, [the mummy] was placed upright in his study, where on this particular night he was working late. Next morning, it is said, an agitated Haggard announced that the mummy must leave the house immediately and not remain there another night; indeed, it must be sent at once to the museum in Norwich Castle. He would give no reason for his sudden decision but, so it was said, that morning the study was in disarray and grey with mummy dust.[45]

By 1917 Haggard had visited Egypt three times, and his expertise on ancient Egypt had earned him an entry in the Egypt Exploration Society's *Who's Who in Egyptology*.[46] Many of his novels contain Egyptian subject matter or passing references, though *She* was the first to owe such a substantial debt to his interest.[47] Prior to writing *She*, Haggard had already begun collecting Egyptian artefacts, many of them obtained from his brother Andrew, when serving in Egypt. One of these was the mummy Nesmin, son of Ankh-Hap from Akhmim in Upper Egypt, a male adult of the Ptolemaic period, which has been identified as the mummy that Haggard had the experience with referred to in his diary.[48]

A scarab ring inscribed Suten sa Ra – 'Royal Son of the Sun' – from Haggard's collection features in *She*, where it is described as 'a small chocolate-coloured composition *scarabeus*'.[49] Another Egyptian artefact has been proposed as an inspiration for Ayesha: an *ushabti* in the Amherst collection, a small painted wooden figure depicting a slave or servant who would attend their master or mistress in the after-life. However, when the item came up for auction at Sotheby's in 1921, Haggard requested this claim be denied at the sale.[50]

A more likely Egyptian influence on *She*, according to Steve Vinson, may have been two ancient compositions, 'a Greek-language novel ... Heliodorus's *Aithiopika*, or "Ethiopian Story", and an Egyptian-language ghost story from the Ptolemaic period, conventionally called "The First Tale of Setne Khaemwas" or "First Setne"'.[51] Vinson maintains that Ayesha 'owes major aspects of her layered personality to five female characters' from these sources; three of the characters – 'Rhadopis and Arsake from the *Aithiopika* and Tabubue from "First Setne" – are *femmes fatales* who doom the men who come into their power'.[52] If, as Haggard claims, he 'had read everything concerning [ancient Egypt] on which I could lay hands', it is likely he was aware of these texts.[53]

When Haggard returned home after his first visit to Egypt in 1887, he was confronted with the furore provoked by his article 'About Fiction' and accusations of plagiarism with regard to *She* and *Jess*. This will be dealt with in the next chapter, but here we can note Haggard's letter to *The Times* published on 27 April 1887 in which, addressing the charges of plagiarism, he gives 'the real source from which *She* was plagiarised'. Some years previously 'a lady well acquainted with Africa wrote me some notes of native legends'. In one of these she mentioned some caves in the Sneeuberg (Snow Mountain), the highest peak in the Cederberg range in the Western Cape, where it was believed that 'in the last cave there is a spring of water which, if one finds and drinks of it, gives eternal youth'.[54] Haggard says he 'found the germ of *She*'[55] in this story. Possibly he did, but if Ayesha has a precursor in southern Africa, she is usually identified as Modjadji, the Rain Queen of the Lobedu people.[56] Haggard's letter to *The Times* makes no mention of her. Notwithstanding, the connection was made and an anthropological study published in 1943 accepted the linkage without query.[57]

The history of Modjadji goes back to the sixteenth-century Karanga kingdom of Monomotapa (in south-eastern Zimbabwe), whose royal family moved from a patrilineal to a matrilineal mode of succession and relocated to the Molototsi valley near the Soutpansberg range in what is today the Limpopo province of South Africa. The queen, who was (and is) regarded as having rain-making powers, led a life of seclusion; she was not allowed to marry and had children by male relatives. According to tradition, when nearing death the queen named her successor and then took poison. At the time of Haggard's sojourn in the Transvaal from 1877 to 1879, the ruling queen would have been Masalanabo Modjadji II, who had succeeded her mother in 1854.

Exactly when the connection between Modjadji and Ayesha was first made is unclear, but when Modjadji II was captured by a Boer commando in 1894, the *New York Times* reported the incident in a story headlined 'Queen Majajie, or Great She Captured' with a sub-headline declaring 'Her Own Tribesmen Never Saw Her, but Say Her Age Is 300 Years'. The story asks the question: 'Is it Mr. Rider Haggard's "She" who has just fallen into the hands of the Boers?' and concludes: 'It is feared the Queen will not long survive her capture.'[58] Such fears were correct, and in 1895 Modjadji II took poison and died.

In 1914 Haggard, speaking at the African Club luncheon in Pietermaritzburg, made light of any connection between Modjadji and Ayesha, saying he 'did not plagiarise the chieftainess – the chieftainess plagiarised *She*. (Laughter). He only heard of the chieftainess twenty years after the book was written.'[59] But can Haggard's humorous dismissal of the link really be taken at face value? As we have seen, in 1877 and 1878 Haggard accompanied Judge John Kotzé on his court rounds of the recently annexed Boer republic, travelling along the very fringes of Modjadji's kingdom. Haggard had come even closer to her kingdom in March 1877 on the mission to Sekhukhune of the Pedi. Given Modjadji's relationship with the surrounding peoples (including the Pedi and the Zulu), who held her in high esteem as a rain-maker, and given too Haggard's own interest in the indigenous peoples of southern Africa, it seems odd, to say the least, that Modjadji escaped his notice.

Haggard rejected other southern African links to *She*: 'When I wrote *She* ... I had heard only in the vaguest way of the Zimbabwe Ruins and not at all of the famous caves in East Africa, which are also reported to have been her residence.'[60] The caves Haggard refers to are those on Mount Elgon in modern-day Uganda, which were first described by the Scottish explorer Joseph Thomson, author of *Through Masai Land* (1883).

As we have seen, Haggard denied a charge of having plagiarised Captain Good's false teeth from Thomson's book, but though Haggard might not have read *Through Masai Land* at the time of writing *King Solomon's Mines*, he had certainly done so by the time he began work on *Allan Quatermain* in the summer of 1886. To pre-empt any further accusations of plagiarism, when *Allan Quatermain* was published in July 1887 Haggard stated his sources in an appended 'Authorities', where he acknowledged his 'indebtedness to Mr Thomson's admirable history of travel *Through Masai Land* for much information as to the habits and customs of the tribes inhabiting that portion of the East Coast, and the country where they live.'[61]

Allan Quatermain was written before *She* and so Thomson's book can be regarded as a source for the latter. This makes Thomson's descriptions of and comments on the caves of Mount Elgon of particular interest. The caves were used for human occupation and some were 'of such great size that they penetrate far into utter darkness, and even then we have not seen the end of them. In some there are large villages with entire herds of cattle.'[62] Their inhabitants claimed the caves had been created by supernatural forces. Thomson disagreed; they were man-made. But by whom? Thomson concluded that far back in time 'some very powerful race, considerably advanced in arts and civilization, excavated these great caves in their search for precious stones or possibly some precious metal ... Are we to suppose the Egyptians really got so far south?'[63]

Haggard returned to the three-volume format of *Dawn* and *The Witch's Head* for the last time with *Colonel Quaritch, V.C.: A Tale of Country Life*, which he began on 29 July 1886 and signed off on 26 December. It would not be published until December 1888.

Thanks to an inheritance from an aunt, the forty-something Colonel Harold Quaritch, V.C., after serving in India and Egypt – as did Haggard's brother Andrew – retires from the army and takes up residence at the aunt's old house in East Anglia. There Quaritch meets Ida, the daughter of his neighbour Squire de la Molle, whom he has loved since boyhood. The squire – a portrait of Haggard's father – is in financial trouble due to the agricultural depression, and faces the loss of the family home, Honham Castle. Harold Quaritch and Ida de la Molle fall in love, but standing in the way of their marriage is the squire and his financial woes. These are exploited in a complex subplot involving a bigamous lawyer, a libidinous banker, and their wives and mistresses. The squire's factotum George (based on William Haggard's factotum Samuel Adcock) uncovers the lawyer's evil stratagems, and meanwhile Quaritch cracks a coded message written in the De la Molle's family Bible, giving the location of the De la Molle treasure hidden during the English civil war. Fortunes are restored, the villains are vanquished and a happy ending is assured for Harold and Ida.

'Not Rider-Haggard like at all,' according to *Literary World*, but a pedestrian return to sobriety after the heady intoxication of *King Solomon's Mines* and *She*.[64]

The *Illustrated London News* was kinder, lauding Haggard's 'dramatic skill and force' evident in the novel's inventive plotting as a demonstration of his capacity to deal 'successfully with the elements of the usual domestic novel'.[65] Given his previous estimate of Haggard's previous work, W.E. Henley, writing in the *Scots Observer*, was singularly unimpressed, thinking *Colonel Quaritch, V.C.* 'manifestly a potboiler ... unworthy of serious criticism'.[66] Andrew Lang hated it so much 'he called it the worst book ever written'.[67] Even Haggard considered it a 'rather feeble novel'.[68]

16

'BETWEEN SUCCESS AND ATTACKS'

Captivated by ancient Egypt since childhood, Haggard was 'possessed by a great desire to see it for myself'. He travelled to Egypt at the end of January 1887 with the intention of writing 'a romance on the subject of Cleopatra'.[1] No mere holiday this: 'Holidays have never been for me.'[2] Whenever and wherever Haggard travelled, leisure was always subordinate to inquiry, and his investigations would result in a book, sometimes more than one, fiction or non-fiction. Haggard went to Egypt 'seeking knowledge and a holiday'.[3] As their three children were too young to be left alone, he and Louie 'made up their minds to the first separation since they were married six years before'.[4]

Haggard left England – crossing the Channel and travelling on by train to Brindisi – with a sense of accomplishment, of work well done and achievement rewarded. *She* had just been published; *King Solomon's Mines* continued to sell well; *Allan Quatermain* was running in *Longman's Magazine* and *Jess* in the *Cornhill*; *Colonel Quaritch, V.C.* was waiting in the wings; and 'About Fiction', a commissioned piece of literary criticism, was about to appear in the *Contemporary Review*.

On the train south Haggard enjoyed the company of Sir Victor Halston, former Chief Secretary at Malta, who knew his brothers Will and Arthur. The journey was not without incident. In the middle of the night the train came to a halt and everyone had to change carriages as 'something had gone wrong' with the sleeping car. In the confusion, in which 'we had to dress like mad', Haggard mislaid his 'new travelling cap' and Lady Halston 'lost the fur-trimmed skirt of her dress. She had forgotten to put it on!'[5] A change of trains and further confusion awaited them at Modane in the French Alps. Haggard's luggage went astray in Turin and for the remainder of the trip he mourned his missing 'portmanteau, containing, amongst other essentials, all his evening clothes'.[6] Lost luggage would become a hallmark of Haggard's travels. According to Lilias, her father was incapable of travelling without losing his luggage. 'It was always vast in quantity, colossal in weight, and generally composed of the solid skins of crocodiles and such like reptiles. Whether its exotic appearance attracted the luggage thief, or the initials H.R.H. deluded them into thinking it contained the possessions of royalty and vast rewards would be theirs for returning it, no one ever knew.[7]

To compound his woes, Haggard arrived at Brindisi to board the ship to Alexandria suffering from 'violent stomach ache'.[8] Once aboard, he cheered up, as nearly everyone was 'reading either *King Solomon's Mines* or *She*'.[9] Haggard was reading 'a very good book', *The Silence of Dean Maitland* by Maxwell Gray.[10] There were also familiar faces to raise his spirits, including Henry Bulwer's widowed sister Mary Eleanor Caldwell and her daughter Mary (en route via Alexandria to Cyprus, where Bulwer was now British High Commissioner); the Conservative politician Sir Frederick Milner and his wife Adelaide; and the theatrical publisher Samuel French. One passenger was Allan Quatermain come to life: the 31-year-old big game hunter, James Sligo Jameson, grandson of the whiskey distiller and the 'man who shot most of the heads' currently on display at the Colonial and Indian Exhibition in South Kensington, 'on his way to join Stanley'.[11] Jameson had paid £1,000 to join Henry Stanley's blood-soaked expedition to rescue Emin Pasha, the German-born Governor of Equatoria, left stranded there after the debacle in the Sudan. Jameson would die of malaria seven months later. More fortunate was Haggard's cabin mate, who had been 'bitten by a mad dog in India & is just returning after being treated by Pasteur'.[12]

Sailing across the Mediterranean, Haggard enjoyed many a compliment. *In absentia* another mark of approval was being conferred on him in London: election to membership of the Savile Club.[13] The stock exchange of literary London, the Savile had a membership that included writers, journalists, newspaper and magazine editors, and publishers. Here, the rowdy battle between 'the crocodile of Realism and the catawampus of Romance' was fought mercilessly, and 'blows struck at the Savile frequently echoed through the columns of London's dailies and weeklies'.[14]

When Haggard became a member, the Savile was situated at 107 Piccadilly, occupying a 'beautiful little house'[15] that enjoyed a view across Green Park to Buckingham Palace. 'There was a certain table in the corner, near the window, where a little band of us were wont to lunch on Saturdays', among them Andrew Lang, Edmund Gosse, Walter Besant, Alexander Galt Ross, critic for the *Saturday Review*, the Egyptologist the Reverend William John Loftie, R.A.M. Stevenson (cousin of R.L.S.), and the architect Eustace Balfour (younger brother of the more famous Arthur).[16] William Henley, another Savile member, 'would insist upon my telling him stories by the yard about the Zulus and their blood-thirsty battles and customs'.[17] Rudyard Kipling joined Haggard's circle at the Savile in 1889 and remembered his friend telling tales, 'mainly against himself, that broke up the tables'.[18] Other members with whom Haggard was on friendly terms included Max Beerbohm, Robert Bridges, Egerton Castle, Sidney Colvin, Thomas Hardy, Anthony Hope Hawkins, H.G. Wells and George Saintsbury.

In October 1888 Haggard was one of thirty-two members who supported Loftie's proposal of Oscar Wilde for membership of the Savile; among those backing his candidacy were Besant, Gosse, Henley, Ross and Henry James. Wilde was refused membership but was spared being blackballed, as it was the custom at the Savile for the proposer to withdraw the proposal; but, as one of his biographers suggests, considering the status of those backing Wilde's membership proposal, its refusal indicates he had already made some powerful enemies.[19] Wilde joined the Albemarle Club instead, where in February 1895 he would receive the card addressed 'To Oscar Wilde posing Somdomite' from the Marquess of Queensbury, father of Wilde's lover Lord Alfred Douglas.[20] The same year Thomas Hardy's *Jude the Obscure* shocked reviewers and was said to have been burned by the Bishop of Wakefield and noted hymnologist, William Walsham How. Haggard was 'in the little writing-room of the Savile' when Hardy 'entered and took up one of the leading weekly papers in which was a long review of [*Jude the Obscure*]. He read it, then came to me – there were no others in the room – and pointed out a certain passage. "There's a nice thing to say about a man!" he exclaimed. "Well, I'll never write another novel." And he never did.'[21]

On 3 February 1887 Haggard had his first sight of the Egyptian coastline. Egypt had been part of the Ottoman Empire since the early sixteenth century, briefly enjoying semi-independence in the eighteenth century prior to invasion by the French in 1798. The French were seen off by the British in 1801 and Turkish suzerainty restored. In the 1860s the Khedive Ismail set about modernising Egypt along Western lines, borrowing heavily from European banks. He also attempted to abolish the slave trade, which was particularly rife in Egypt's southern satellite, the Sudan. The Suez Canal, constructed by a Franco-Egyptian partnership and completed in 1869, gave the British a direct route to India and an entrée to Egypt; facing bankruptcy, Ismail sold Egypt's shares in the canal to the British government, and it wasn't long before British and French advisers were effectively in control of the country. The British and French presence provoked a nationalist revolt in 1882, determined to end European domination. Despite Gladstone's opposition to imperial expansion, his hand was forced and a British force commanded by Sir Garnet Wolseley was dispatched to Egypt and defeated the rebel army at the battle of Tel-el-Kebir on 13 September 1882. To his great frustration, Andrew Haggard and his regiment arrived too late from India to take part in the fighting, though he was in time to become part of the new order on the staff of the newly appointed Sirdar of the Egyptian Army, Sir Evelyn Wood. Britain was now in charge of what was still, nominally, a province of the Ottoman Empire.

On disembarkation at Alexandria in 1887, Haggard was met by his younger brother, Arthur, then stationed in Egypt with the King's Shropshire Light Infantry. They explored the city's ancient sites before sailing down the Nile to Cairo and driving in a buggy to the Zaffaran (Saffron) Palace in the suburb of Abbassiya, where

Haggard was to stay. Haggard spent the following day sightseeing and in the evening dined as a guest of Arthur's regiment – he was made an honorary member of the mess – kitted out in his brother's dress clothes, which were 'devilish tight around the stomach'.[22]

Haggard had an introduction to the German Egyptologist Heinrich Karl Brugsch, former director of the School of Egyptology in Cairo, and was shown around the collection at the Bulaq Museum, where he gazed with 'awe and veneration at the dead faces of Seti and Rameses'.[23] On Sunday, 6 February, Haggard lunched with the English Egyptologist Bernard Pyne Grenfell and also visited the Scottish physician and Egyptologist James Grant, who 'would not show me his *antiquas* as it was Sunday'. During the week he spent an enjoyable afternoon with Grant and saw the gold signet ring of Meneptah (also known as Merneptah), son of Rameses II, a ring 'that Moses must have looked upon'.[24]

Haggard spent several days in Cairo, all the while in the hope his portmanteau would pitch up and in pleasurable anticipation of travelling south up the Nile. He passed the time shooting duck at dawn with his brother on the Nile marshes (a popular pastime among British officers, topped off with an English breakfast at the recently opened Mena House hotel), dining with Colonel Western, a relative of his brother-in-law, Cissie's husband Maximilian Western; attending a dance given by Lady Alice Borthwick (wife of Sir Algernon Borthwick, owner of the conservative *Morning Post*); and enjoying garrison theatricals: 'Cairo is in many ways a smart place, a sort of miniature London and that is what I do not care for about it.'[25]

Haggard visited the Giza pyramids with the Milners and 'a young fellow' named Brownrigg. They were 'contemplating the second Pyramid' when Brownrigg announced he was going to climb to the top, where he duly executed 'a war dance of triumph'. Coming down was a different matter 'since the thickness of the cap hid the sides of the pyramid from his sight, so that all he saw beneath him was some three hundred feet of empty space', rendering him helpless 'since he could neither find any foothold beneath him, nor could he reascend'. Spread-eagled on the top of the pyramid 'with outstretched arms like one crucified', Brownrigg was rescued by a 'white-robed Arab'. Romantically dubbed 'the Sheik of the Pyramids', he appeared as a character in Haggard's Egyptian romance *The Queen of the Dawn*, published in 1925.[26]

On 11 February Haggard moved to Shepheard's Hotel, the famous imperial watering-hole established in 1841 as a luxurious stopover for those taking the overland route to India. Under its roof, Haggard aided and abetted Arthur's courtship of 'a Miss Calvert, good looking nice and it is confidently hoped well off (isn't there a Calvert's Disinfectant?). He half pulled it off with her last night (thanks to my admirable arrangements) and I started him to tackle the mamma this afternoon. He has absolutely vanished so I hope he is getting on alright.'[27] Arthur married Emily Calvert later that year. With love in the air, Haggard found himself missing Louie:

'I wish to goodness you were here old girl. I don't get on very well without you – at least I mean I miss you – I am no longer a gay young gentleman and somehow don't seem to amuse myself as well as I used to.'[28]

Haggard's luggage arrived on 13 February, and two days later he sailed up the Nile using Cook's Nile Steamboat Service with a small party that included Brownrigg as well as Mr Heath, 'a great man of Lloyds', his wife and their niece – 'a charming and clever girl', together with 'an American Dr. Green and his newly married wife. Very nice. They know Will.' The first halt was at Saqqara, site of the world's first pyramid, the Step Pyramid of the Third Dynasty, from where they rode on donkeys 'to the ruins of Memphis – pausing along the way to see the colossal statue of Rameses which the Royal Engineers are now trying to hoist on its feet again'.[29]

At Asyut on 18 February, they rode to the 'old Necropolis at the back of the Town', where among the rock tombs 'we found fragments countless in number of human bodies and literally marched through the dust, mummy cloth and bones of bygone generations'.[30] Haggard's 'most curious discovery' was the 'mummy (quite perfect) of a girl child between two and three years of age'. Wrapped around the body was some 'finery cloth unfortunately torn which I kept. After taking it I found curiously enough that it had on it marked in some faded pigment a Christian Cross – evidently this poor little thing was an early Christian ... I told them to put some stones over the little body and left it. It was a fair child. The skin was white as ivory.'[31]

On return to Asyut the tourists came across 'a pantomime performance ... of a most indecent and peculiar character but interesting as showing the manners of the people. The women were very good looking – when one of them came up to me and suggested that I should retire with her I thought it time to leave!'[32] Other local attractions were less inviting: 'the state of poverty and degradation of the Fellaheen is something pitiable. It is pitiful to see them fighting like mad things for half a piastre and enduring a frightful thrashing from the dragoman and officials of the boat on the chance of getting their donkey taken.'[33]

Having checked into the Luxor hotel on 21 February, the party took a donkey ride 'to see Luxor in the sunset'.[34] Next day they toured the Valley of the Kings in the Land of the Dead on the west bank of the Nile. The morning of 23 February was spent on the east bank in the Land of the Living, visiting the temple complexes and monuments of Luxor and Karnak – 'my mind is a whirl of temples and gods and tombs'[35] – while the afternoon was devoted to hunting for antiques: 'Bought signet ring', Haggard noted in his diary.[36] This was a large copper-gold ring bearing Akhenaton's name[37] – a 'great find', which Haggard immersed in vinegar in his hotel room: 'a few minutes later it came out clean as a whistle & bright yellow ... It may be very valuable and fits my first finger exactly.'[38]

From Luxor, Haggard's party continued up the Nile to Philae and Aswan, where he 'sneaked and crawled and scrambled down filthy passages where I was nearly murdered by bats'. He was accompanied by Brownrigg and Miss Heath – 'very useful because she is so slim that she can be lowered through the smallest holes'.[39] At Aswan, while investigating some recently discovered tombs, Haggard had what 'nearly proved my last adventure' when he 'crept through a little hole' into a great cavern 'full of hundreds of dead ... most of which had evidently been buried without coffins, for they were but skeletons, although mixed up with them was the mummy of a lady and the fragments of her painted mummy case'. He shouted to attract the others, but the reverberation

> caused the sand to begin to pour down between the cracks of the masonry from above, so that the weight of it, falling upon my back, pinned me fast. In a flash I realised that in another few seconds I too should be buried. Gathering all my strength I made a desperate effort and succeeded in reaching the mouth of the hole just before it was too late, for my friends had wandered off to some distance and were quite unaware of my plight.[40]

This brush with mortality didn't prevent Haggard from spending an afternoon at Aswan happily 'digging at some tombs', where he found a female mummy, 'much decayed', telling Louie that 'she was cutting her wisdom teeth when she died. I am bringing you two of her molars as a present.'[41] Haggard's cavalier attitude towards Egyptian mummies would change over time, and he later opposed their abuse and public display.[42]

On 1 March the party began their return journey down the Nile, visiting Hatshepsut's Temple at Deir al-Bahri and that of Seti I at Abydos before arriving back in Cairo on 6 March. Thoughts of home were never far away, and in a letter to Louie Haggard expressed his desire to give notice to the tenant and return to live at Ditchingham House. 'If I am going in for the writing of books ... it will maybe best to make Ditchingham our headquarters and have a flat in London.'[43] In the same letter Haggard mentioned hearing from his father 'that there have been some hits on *She*' in the press. 'I wish you had sent them to me as I see nothing here.'[44]

Haggard spent his last few days in Cairo shooting quail in the Nile reed beds, shopping in the bazaars and viewing the pyramids by moonlight. In Alexandria on 10 March he boarded the small trading vessel SS *Clutha* – 'a tub of a ship, where a rat had its nest behind my bunk' – sailing for Cyprus two days later. During the short voyage Haggard filled the time reading Lang's *He*, 'very amusing', unlike Émile Zola's *L'Oeuvre* (*The Masterpiece*) – 'an awfully dull book and very long'.[45]

In Cyprus, Haggard was the guest of Sir Henry Bulwer at Government House in Nicosia. Cyprus had been under British control since the secret Cyprus Convention of 1878 in which the Ottoman Empire ceded control of the island to the British in exchange for support against Russia in the event of hostilities.[46] Bulwer was appointed High Commissioner in 1886. Haggard went sightseeing with Mrs Caldwell and her daughter, but even history-soaked Famagusta failed to assuage his homesickness and depression. 'I cannot tell you, dear old girl, how homesick I am ... I miss you very much and get very low and lonely.'[47] On his travels thereafter, Haggard ensured he was accompanied, if not by Louie, then a close relative, such as a daughter or nephew. Despite feeling low, Haggard was enthusiastic about the 'very strong plot'[48] he had worked up for *Cleopatra* and looked forward to commencing writing at Ditchingham, urging Louie once again to get rid of the tenant as the profits from his writing had left them 'a good deal better off',[49] apart from a few outstanding debts. It was a self-revealing heartfelt letter, giving voice to the 'buried man':

> I cannot tell you, my dear, what a pleasure it will be to me if I find myself in a position to give you back the home again which in a way you lost by marrying me. I think that the best thing to me about such a measure of success as I have won is that it has relieved my conscience of a great weight. I do not think I had any business to marry you when I did – it was pulling you down in the world. However, I think that I have now attained, in name if not in fortune, such a position you would not have been likely to exceed if I had not met you, and for that I am very thankful. I dare say that you think me a queer chap for writing like this, more especially as you have always been so gentle and considerate about things, but the matter taken in addition to my other weaknesses and failings, has always pressed upon me, though it is only now after all these years, when I have fought and to some extent won the day, that I can speak of it.[50]

In February *Blackwood's Edinburgh Magazine* ran the first of an occasional series of essays-cum-reviews headed 'The Old Saloon', written anonymously by the Scottish novelist Mrs Oliphant assuming a male persona[51] and proclaiming Haggard 'the new *avatar* of the old story-teller, with a flavour of the nineteenth century and scientific explanation, but at the same time a sturdy and masculine force of invention which disdains these helps even in employing them'. This resurrection was coincident with the 'fancy of the public' turning to the art of storytelling, 'which, perhaps, had fallen a little out of repute, dimmed by the modern art of character-painting and analysis'.[52]

Oliphant's article appeared at the same time as Haggard's 'About Fiction' – an article he claimed to having been 'worried into writing' against his will – in the *Contemporary Review*. He didn't dispute that for a young writer 'suddenly come into some kind of fame to spring a dissertation of this kind upon the literary world over his own name was very little short of madness'.[53] Haggard begins his article by asserting that 'love of romance is probably coeval with the existence of humanity'.[54] While many believe they can write a romantic novel, he cautions that 'with the exception of perfect sculpture, really good romance writing is perhaps the most difficult art practised by the sons of men. It might even be maintained that none but a great man or woman can produce a *really* great work of fiction.'[55] Haggard makes matters worse with an attack on publishers and readers prior to embarking on a critique of contemporary writing, first targeting American authors: 'Their heroines are things of silk and cambric, who soliloquise and dissect their petty feelings.' As for the male characters, 'they are emasculated specimens of an overwrought age, and, with culture on their lips, and emptiness in their hearts, they dangle round the heroines till their three-volumed fate is accomplished.'[56]

Haggard then lets loose on 'the Naturalistic school, of which Zola is the high priest',[57] a school Haggard describes as 'living for lust and lusting for this life ... whatever there is that is carnal and filthy, is here brought into prominence, and thrust before the reader's eyes'.[58] Haggard fervently hopes 'this naturalistic school of writing will never take firm root in England, for it is an accursed thing'.[59] This was particularly so in its portrayal of human sexuality:

> Society has made a rule that for the benefit of the whole community individuals must keep their passions within certain fixed limits, and their social system is so arranged that any transgression of this rule produces mischief of one sort or another, if not actual ruin, to the transgressor. Especially is this so if she be a woman. Now, as it is, human nature is continually fretting against these artificial bounds, and especially among young women it requires considerable fortitude and self-restraint to keep the feet from wandering.

At least Haggard acknowledges the existence of female sexuality, though he recycles the 'virgin–whore' trope and bows before the 'artificial bounds' of conventional morality. According to Haggard, indulgence of sexual feeling 'depends upon the imagination', which can easily be excited by 'a powerful writer'. Sexual passion 'is the most powerful lever with which to stir the mind of man, for it lies at the root of all things human; and it is impossible to overestimate the damage that could be worked by a single English or American writer of genius, if he grasped it with a will.'

As for writers in Britain, 'we are at the mercy of the Young Person, and a dreadful nuisance most of us find her', considering it 'a little hard that all fiction should be judged by the test as to whether or no it is suitable reading for a girl of sixteen'. French naturalism 'is one thing' but the 'unreal, namby-pamby nonsense with which the market is flooded here is quite another. Surely there is a middle path!'[60] Haggard argues that English authors, 'subject to proper reservations and restraints', should be allowed 'to picture life as it is, and men and women as they are',[61] or otherwise an over-moralistic approach will see English fiction continue to 'reflect the conventionalism, not the life, and has in consequence, with some notable exceptions, got into a very poor way, both as regards art and interest'.[62]

Those exceptions – three titles drawn from the previous five years – he lists as *My Trivial Life and Misfortune* by a Plain Woman (1883), *The Story of an African Farm* by Ralph Iron (Olive Schreiner), and *Mrs Keith's Crime*, dealing with infanticide, and published anonymously in 1885 (not so anonymously; it was an open secret that the author was Lucy Clifford, novelist, dramatist and, later, screenwriter).[63] 'These books were written from the heart [and] owe their chief interest to a certain atmosphere of spiritual intensity.'[64] Would another male Victorian writer have selected three books by female authors? In doing so, Haggard displays the fundamental dichotomy that is one of his defining features: on the one hand, loyal to the mores and conventions of his time; on the other, usually unconsciously, out of step with them.

For the 'less ambitious among us', and Haggard modestly includes himself in this category, there is a refuge 'in the paths and calm retreats of pure imagination ...There are still subjects that may be handled *there* if the man can be found bold enough to handle them.' To those who would consider such a path to belong 'in the lower realms of fiction' and 'would probably scorn to become a "mere writer of romances"', Haggard points out that 'many of the more lasting triumphs of literary art belong to the producers of purely romantic fiction', citing as examples *Tales from the Arabian Nights*, *Gulliver's Travels*, *The Pilgrim's Progress*, *Robinson Crusoe* 'and other immortal works'.[65] Haggard concludes that 'when Naturalism has had its day ... and the Society novel is utterly played out, the kindly race of men in their latter as earlier development will still take pleasure in those works of fancy which appeal, not to a class, or a nation, or even to an age, but to all time and humanity at large'.[66]

Light the blue touchpaper and retire. This 'unfortunate article made me plenty of enemies', admits Haggard, and the 'mere fact of my remarkable success made me plenty more ... these foes found a very able leader in the person of Mr. Stead', editor of the *Pall Mall Gazette*.[67] William Thomas Stead, a man of limitless enthusiasm and energy, embraced crusading, controversial journalism (he is credited with being father of the tabloid press) as well as pacifism and spiritualism. At the age of 22 he was appointed editor of the *Northern Echo*, which became a platform for his moral crusades. Stead played a significant role in Gladstone's election victory in 1880 and in the same year moved to London as assistant editor of the evening newspaper the *Pall Mall Gazette*, taking over as editor in 1883. The crusades continued and his famous campaign against child prostitution saw him jailed for three months on a charge of abduction.[68] That Stead should go down with the *Titanic* in 1912, one of the greatest news stories of the twentieth century, was totally in character.

None of Haggard's critics tackled 'About Fiction' directly, they questioned his integrity instead, accusing him of plagiarism primarily in regard to *She*. Stead didn't write the articles himself – that was done by John Cuming Walters of the *Birmingham Daily Gazette* – but Stead was happy to run them and probably contributed some of the editorial comment which stoked the debate and kept the story alive. In an article headlined 'Who is "She" and Where Did "She" Come From? The Strange Case of Tom Moore and Mr Rider Haggard', published in the *Pall Mall Gazette* on 11 March 1887, Walters accused Haggard of plagiarising *She* from *The Epicurean* by Thomas Moore, published in 1827, citing themes as well as specific sentences and paragraphs, and concluding from 'this mass of evidence' that it was 'plain that *The Epicurean* was the fount of Mr Haggard's inspiration'.[69]

She was soon joined in the stocks by *Jess*. Two days before the publication of *Jess* in book form on 24 March, the *Pall Mall Gazette* posed the question 'The Song of "Jess" and Who Wrote It', printing in parallel columns a poem from *Jess* and one published in the *Transatlantic Monthly* of March 1874. They were more or less identical. An explanation was required.

In Haggard's absence Louie wrote to the *Pall Mall Gazette* stating that her husband was in Cyprus and wouldn't 'return home for three or four weeks. When he returns he will reply to your questions or leave them unanswered, as he thinks best.' In the meantime all she could say was that Haggard had never read Moore's *Epicurean* and that the poem in *Jess* was 'sent to Mr Haggard from South Africa in manuscript in a private letter about seven years ago, by a lady now dead, and he has always supposed it to be her own composition, and never to have been published.'[70]

The same edition ran a letter from Charles Longman saying that Haggard had never heard of *The Epicurean* 'until about two months ago', when Longman 'chanced to mention' it when Haggard came to consult him on books about Egypt.[71] James Stanley Little corroborated what Louie said about the poem in *Jess* and suggested that perhaps the 'lady in question copied them from a magazine, and probably unintentionally conveyed the impression that she had written them'.[72]

The *Gazette* knew it had a strong case with regard to the poem in *Jess*: 'the verses put into Jess's mouth were sent to Mr Haggard by a lady, and Mr Haggard put them into his novel, where they would of course pass as his own composition'. Little, executive secretary of the Society of Authors, was rapped over the knuckles for thinking 'so lightly of the appropriation of authors'.[73]

In Cyprus Haggard learnt of the furore in a letter from Louie and another from Longman, who didn't think the matter 'worth while taking any notice of'. Meanwhile the plagiarism controversy ran and ran, the *Pall Mall Gazette* publishing letters for and against Haggard.

Louie knew the identity of 'the lady in South Africa'. She was the late Johanna Ford. On 5 April, the day before Haggard was due to sail back from Cyprus to England via Port Said, he enclosed a letter to be sent to the *Pall Mall Gazette* as well as detailed instructions to Louie on how to proceed in his absence if events so required. He enclosed the key of the dispatch box in his dressing room at Ditchingham House containing keys for the house safe and its drawers: 'the original letter from Mrs F with the poem is amongst other papers in the right hand drawer of the safe'. There was nothing in Mrs Ford's letter 'that will not bear shewing', though he didn't want the name of its writer or any of the letter published other than the part directly bearing on the verses. If matters got to this point, he instructed Louie to contact Andrew Lang and ask him

> to bring with him a couple of gentlemen of standing ... then *in confidence* to produce the letter or so much as necessary to the purpose of shewing that it is a genuine epistle & that the verses were sent to me as an *original composition*. I then want them to sign & publish a declaration to that effect without mentioning names or even that it was a lady. As the person is dead there is an obvious reason for not wishing to drag his or her name into such a controversy.

They could also be shown the verses in the manuscript of *Jess* 'with my notes underneath to the effect that the writer died on a certain date, and I think that you will find in another letter the last Mrs F ever wrote to me ... a sentence to this effect "I am glad you liked my verses"'. He urged Louie not to 'fret about all this business', though it was admittedly 'awkward':

> it will do as much good as harm. What can have induced Mrs F to play such a trick? I think poor soul she must have been a little wicked. Or was it vanity & a desire to impress me? And now I think that is all I have to say about that infernal affair. I shall doubtless hear more about it before I have done with it. I have become public property & I suppose I must take the consequences.[74]

The controversy continued, fuelled by further articles from Walters, one of which presented further comparative quotations from *The Epicurean* and *She* – to a neutral observer they are either unrelated or simply share common literary clichés. Walters also compared verses from *Alciphron*, an epic poem by Moore, offering them as 'proof little short of positive' when compared with a speech by Holly in *She* 'that Mr Haggard has read Alciphron'.[75]

Andrew Lang entered the lists in an unsigned *Daily News* article, 'Literary Plagiarism' – 'It is certainly difficult to understand how anyone, with any sense of what literature is, can read *The Epicurean* and *She*, and then accuse the latter of imitating the former'[76] – concluding that any resemblances were 'remote'. Lang was outed that evening by the *Pall Mall Gazette*, which gleefully pointed out that he was the dedicatee of *She* and went on to repeat the accusations all over again. Impartial outsiders most likely agreed with the *Sheffield Independent* that it was Haggard's turn to feel the sting of 'small literary people ... simply because he has become uppermost on the wheel of popularity'.[77]

The long-awaited response from Haggard appeared on 15 April in the 'Literary and Art Notes' section of the *Pall Mall Gazette*, not exactly prime editorial territory. He put his case briefly and simply: 'My attention has been called to an article that appeared in your issue of March 11 on which it is suggested, or rather asserted, that my book *She* is modelled upon *The Epicurean* by the late T. Moore. I wish to state, by way of comment on this assertion, that until I did so I never read or, directly or indirectly, became acquainted with a single line of Mr Moore's *Epicurean*.'[78] The *Gazette* was 'glad to publish this explicit and straightforward letter' but was not prepared to drop the accusation of plagiarism regarding the poem in *Jess*. Haggard, by that stage in transit between Cyprus and London and unaware of the new development, subsequently wrote another letter to the *Gazette*: 'It is obvious the verses are identical' and detailed how they had come into his possession.

> I put the lines, or rather some of them, into the mouth of Jess, because I knew that my dead friend would have been pleased at my doing so. I have, however, never claimed the authorship of them, and I should have acknowledged it in the book, only to do

so would have been to spoil the *vraisemblance* of the scene. Whether or no my friend was the true author of those lines, I do not now know. If not, I offer a most humble apology for my mistake to their unknown producer.[79]

Haggard was clearly in the wrong, and the poem was omitted from all later editions of *Jess*.[80] But the *Gazette* had more ammunition up its sleeve and in the same article referred to a poem in *Dawn*, 'A Storm on the Strings', written by the book's heroine, Angela.[81] A reader recalled having seen these verses, the product of a member of 'a girls' essay society', and subsequently read them again in *Dawn*. 'According to the new code of literary ethics, does it matter?' the *Gazette* sniped. 'Mr Haggard may have borrowed them. If so, he did not acknowledge the loan, it is true, but what of that? He never said he wrote them: only he said Angela wrote them.'[82]

Haggard moved the battlefront from the *Gazette* to *The Times*: 'On returning from abroad I find myself confronted with a box full of newspaper cuttings, most of which bear in some way or other on my alleged offences against the unwritten laws of literature.'[83] Haggard gave the same explanation as before regarding the verses in *Jess*; as to those in *Dawn*, they 'were written by my sister-in-law, Mrs John Haggard, and published as they appear by her own wish'.[84] Haggard hit out at the *Gazette*, which 'headed the hunt against me' and which, having decided that any similarities between *She* and *The Epicurean* were not a case of 'imitation but of literary coincidence', printed this admission in the 'Literary and Art Notes' section where 'this most modest and retiring withdrawal' was likely to be missed by those 'impressed with the pomp and circumstance of the leading articles, the sensationally-headed paragraphs, and all the artillery of advertised attack'.[85] Haggard repeated his defence with regard to *She*, stating he 'had never read a line of either *The Epicurean* or the poem *Alciphron*' and went on to give 'the real source from which *She* had been plagiarised ... a lady well acquainted with Africa [who] wrote me some notes of native legends'.[86]

Haggard concluded: 'charges of plagiarism are easy to make and difficult to disprove. It is quite impossible for anybody to write anything that does not in some way touch on ground which has already been trodden by others. The human mind is limited and unchangeable: it never thinks a new thought. The most that it can hope to do is to present an old one in a new aspect.'[87] *St James's Gazette* was satisfied with Haggard's explanation and hoped the question of Haggard's plagiarism would 'be allowed to drop'.[88] Not by James Cuming Walters it wouldn't, for he returned to the fray in the *Birmingham Daily Gazette*: 'Mr Rider Haggard is angry – very angry indeed. He has written a book which everyone is reading, and even the books which people formerly refused to read are now being called for. Certain newspapers, too, have conspired to "puff" Mr Haggard by instituting an inquiry into his originality.'[89] Walters repeated his earlier allegations, concluding with a final sting: 'Mr Haggard admits that the germ of *She* is to be found in a legend, and he also admits the charge of inserting lines in his books written by others. So he does not come from the ordeal altogether unscathed; which may account for his present frame of mind.'[90]

The satirical magazine *Moonshine* called for a parliamentary bill 'to Legalise Duelling, so that Mr Stead and Mr Rider Haggard may have an opportunity to settle the question of *She* and *Jess* so'.[91] George Curzon, recently elected a member of parliament and the future Viceroy of India, wrote a letter in defence of Haggard to the *Pall Mall Gazette* and, when it failed to appear, sent a copy to Haggard. The two men did not know each other at the time, but the letter and its subject matter featured in Haggard's dedication of *When the World Shook* to Curzon in 1918.

The *Gazette* was determined to have the last word, which it did in a review of *Allan Quatermain*: 'The book will be a favourite and deservedly so. Nor will the pleasure of the reader be marred by the slightly petulant tone of the page on "Authorities" in which Mr Haggard shows some irritation at the allegations of plagiarism showered on him of late. It is only a page, and most people will skip even that. It is the only page in the book which they will skip.'[92]

After his return to England from Egypt, 'what between success and attacks', Haggard found himself 'quite a celebrity, one whose name was in everybody's mouth. ... it came about that I was much envied and not a little hated by many who made my life bitter with constant attacks in the Press, which, being somewhat sensitive by nature, I was foolish enough to feel. Indeed there came a time when for a good many years I would read no reviews of my books, unless chance thrust them under my eyes.'[93]

Perhaps this was the moment when Haggard felt like throwing in the towel and abandoning writing, provoking a *cri de coeur* from Andrew Lang: 'If you jack up Literature, I shall jack up Reading.'[94] Lang, and Haggard's readers, would no doubt have nodded their approval of the journalist and novelist Robert Barr's judgment: 'my verdict is that if *She* is a plagiarism I hope Mr Haggard will give us some more plagiarisms'.[95]

17

'PASSIONATE AND POETIC'

In May 1887 Haggard 'fled from London to Ditchingham' because 'there were so many distractions and calls upon my time that I could not get on with my work'.[1] Cleopatra beckoned. Haggard dated the first page of his new manuscript 27 May 1887. In the year of *Cleopatra*'s composition all of Haggard's previously published titles were selling well and the annual income from his books totalled £10,680.12s.6d., the equivalent of £1.5 million today.[2] Haggard made no secret of his desire to accumulate wealth: 'I am avaricious,' he told Aggie. 'I should like to make enough money to be able to stop writing at any rate for a time.' Dramatisations of his books added to the coffers: *Dawn*, adapted by C. Haddon Chambers and James Stanley Little with the title *Devil Caresfoot*, enjoyed a successful run in 1887. Haggard was present on the first night – 'it was rather good fun but they have turned Mildred into a comic widow which is a jar'[3] – and negotiations were under way through Watt for dramatisations of *Jess* and *She*.[4] 'I am doing pretty fairly & am glad to say that I am now able to keep Ditchingham going decently.'[5]

Haggard's financial well-being allowed him to obtain a more fashionable London residence, relocating from Gunterstone Road to a five-storey house at 24 Redcliffe Square in Chelsea, 'an elegant but comfortable home surrounded by acres of garden' and two doors along from his Ipswich Grammar headmaster, Hubert Holden.[6] Haggard's study was at the back of the house 'overlooking the grounds', where he wrote on a 'large solidly constructed table' placed in the centre of the room. The Haggards entertained at Redcliffe Square, 'though not to any great extent, for we never were extravagant'.[7]

The total sales of Haggard's books for the first half of 1887 were over 47,000 and Charles Longman worried that Haggard was flooding the market: 'I think it will be for the good of your property not to put another book on the market before the autumn of 1888 if it can be helped.'[8] Haggard 'sold *Cleopatra* for a large sum in cash' to Longmans as well as that of *Colonel Quaritch, V.C.*, a novel Charles Longman liked – it was dedicated to him. 'Some of this money I lost, for really I had not time to look after it, and the investments suggested by kind friends connected with the City were apt to prove disappointing.' Nevertheless Haggard was able to pay off debts and mortgages and renovate Ditchingham House, 'as well as countless farm buildings, and a proportion was absorbed by our personal expenditure'.[9]

Haggard was never particularly astute when it came to financial matters, and selling the copyrights for *Jess*, *Cleopatra* and *Colonel Quaritch, V.C.* was something he would come to regret. In the meantime an earlier agreement came back to bite him. As we have seen, in 1885 he agreed to the publisher J. & R. Maxwell bringing out *The Witch's Head* and *Dawn* in cheap editions, Haggard getting one-third of the profit, an arrangement extended to any further books he wrote over the next five years. This arrangement he soon repented because of the phenomenal success of *King Solomon's Mines* and *She*. Alexander Watt, 'guardian angel of the innocent literati',[10] who was skilled at rescuing authors from themselves, negotiated an escape: Maxwell, now threatening legal action, agreed to have the sole rights to publish two books, which Haggard would write in the next three years. After this episode Haggard came under the banner of Longmans, with whom he published exclusively until 1904 when, to his 'great sorrow', he was forced 'to abandon this arrangement' because publishers owning magazines serialising fiction wanted the book rights as well. Watt managed the situation for a while, selling serial rights to 'the two great illustrated papers', the *Graphic* and the *Illustrated London News*, but 'the competition of the new sixpenny magazines' saw them stop publishing serials, 'or at any rate paying much for them'. Haggard had to go 'to those who would run the serial if, and only if, they were given the book rights also'.[11] From 1904 Haggard's fiction titles were published in Britain by various publishers including Cassell, Ward Lock, Hutchinson, and Hodder & Stoughton. Longmans published his non-fiction titles.

Haggard finished writing *Cleopatra* on 2 August. Longman thought 'very highly indeed' of the result;[12] Andrew Lang less so, recommending Haggard put the manuscript away 'for as long as possible, and then read it as a member of the public. You will find, I think, that between chapters 3 and 8 it is too long, too full of antiquarian detail, and too slow in movement to carry the general public with it.'[13] Lang indicated possible edits. 'Screw it a little tighter, and I think it is undeniably an artistic piece of work.'[14]

Aggie, now Mrs John Haggard and living in Madagascar, was no longer at hand for opinion or assistance, and Haggard turned to Lang, who obligingly rendered the 'Chant of Isis' and 'Song of Cleopatra' into verse from Haggard's prose versions. Haggard didn't follow Lang's advice on editing the text 'since I have always been a very bad hand at making alterations in what I have once put down, unless indeed I rewrite the entire work,'[15] but he kept it in mind. When *Cleopatra* was published on 24 June 1889 (after serialisation in the *Illustrated London News*), he prefaced the text with an 'Author's Note' recommending readers seeking 'a story only' and 'not interested in the Faith, ceremonies, or customs of the Mother of Religion and

Civilisation, ancient Egypt ... exercise the art of skipping and open this tale at its second book'.[16]

Cleopatra's story is told not 'from the modern point of view' but from 'the broken heart and with the lips of an Egyptian patriot of royal blood ... a priest instructed in the inmost mysteries, who believed firmly in the personal existence of the gods of Khem, in the possibility of communion with them, and in the certainty of immortal life with its rewards and punishments'.[17] Harmachis, Haggard's fictional protagonist, is in the genealogical line of the pre-Ptolemaic pharaohs and thus the true Pharaoh in the eyes of those conspiring to overthrow the Macedonian import, Cleopatra. Harmachis, a priest of Isis at Abydos, the centre of the conspiracy, is secretly crowned pharaoh and dispatched to Alexandria to assassinate Cleopatra and trigger a rebellion against the Macedonian usurpers. He gains entry to the pharaonic court as an astrologer. A 'man beautiful to see', he soon becomes the object of Cleopatra's infatuation.[18] Charmion, Cleopatra's lady-in-waiting, genuinely loves Harmachis, but when the ascetic priest spurns her advances, she betrays him to Cleopatra, who averts her own assassination by seducing Harmachis, and the two become lovers. The brief idyll is ended by a command from the Roman triumvir Mark Antony that Cleopatra attend him at Tarsus in Cilicia.

Egypt is under threat, but Cleopatra lacks the finances to wage war against Rome – a problem not without solution. Cleopatra promises to wed Harmachis and defend Egypt together if, in return, he reveals the 'secret of the hidden wealth of the pyramid of *Her*',[19] hiding place of the treasure of Menkaure, an Egyptian king of the fourth dynasty during the Old Kingdom. Entering the pyramid, Cleopatra and Harmachis descend to the tomb chamber and steal the treasure secreted inside the mummified body of the king, thus bringing upon themselves the 'curse of Menkau-ra from which there is no escape'.[20]

Once in Tarsus Haggard falls in line with the historical record, at least as far as Cleopatra is concerned: she and Mark Antony fall in love, while Harmachis, learning of a plan to kill him, flees by ship and spends several years planning his revenge. He returns to Egypt incognito and becomes famous as a healer under the name Olympus.

History continues: Cleopatra and her ships flee the battle of Actium with disastrous results – in Haggard's version because she hears the voice of the 'dead' Harmachis bidding her to do so. In Egypt, learning of the miraculous powers of Olympus, she summons him to court where she persuades Antony to return to her side. The Roman triumvir Octavian and his army draw near. Cleopatra plans suicide, experimenting on slaves to find the least painful poison. Olympus produces the perfect concoction. As per Plutarch, Antony botches his suicide and dies in Cleopatra's arms. Cleopatra takes poison, lingering long enough for Harmachis to reveal his true identity and the fulfilment of the curse of Menkaure. Thereafter he returns to Abydos where, confessing all to the assembled priests, he is sentenced to death and, in the interval between sentence and execution, writes down his story.

Haggard adopts an archaic style for *Cleopatra* – 'hasts' and 'thous' abound in the dialogue set amidst high-flown prose – adhering to this archaism with such dogged consistency that it actually works, creating a stylistic and structural cohesion. But what really impresses is Haggard's knowledge and grasp of Egyptian history, the respect and insight he brings to his recreation of ancient Egypt, its ceremonies and religious rituals. Some of the dramatic scenes – Harmachis's vision of Isis, the robbing of Menkaure's tomb – still make for gripping reading. And Cleopatra? With her seductive powers and her whimsical brutality, she is She-Who-Must-Be-Obeyed placed in a historical context.

Haggard sent the Egyptologist William Loftie the proofs for the magazine serialisation of *Cleopatra*. He thought the book 'an advance in writing on anything else I have seen of yours'.[21] Critics agreed: Henley in the *Scots Observer* judged *Cleopatra* Haggard's highest achievement so far – 'artfully constructed, the most evenly sustained, the most passionate, impressive and poetic'. It was sufficient indeed to rebut critics who dismissed him as a writer of sensation by demonstrating to the contrary that 'there is an artist in Mr. Haggard, though an artist that has still to be developed'.[22]

Haggard dedicated *Cleopatra* to his mother, who first kindled his interest in ancient Egypt and because he thought it 'the best book I had written or was likely to write'.[23]

Haggard continued writing at a furious pace. In mid-September he began work on another African romance featuring an earlier episode in the life of Allan Quatermain, completing it on 10 November 1887. 'Short, stirring and dreadful' was the Boston *Literary World's* assessment of *Maiwa's Revenge*, published in June 1888; the *Athenaeum*, acknowledging the slightness, nevertheless found incidents in the story as exciting as *King Solomon's Mines*, *Allan Quatermain* and *She*, and the tale a striking portrayal of Africa in 'vivid and lifelike colours'.[24]

Maiwa's Revenge, or, The War of the Little Hand is really a novella. A clutch of Quatermain stories make up the book's first half, being set west of Delagoa Bay, where Quatermain has gone hunting elephant in the territory of a chief named Wambe, a clone of Shaka, 'the Zulu Napoleon [who] never allowed a child of his to live'.[25] In the second half Quatermain helps the Maiwa of the title, another strong female character, achieve her revenge on Wambe, who murdered her infant child – she is one of his wives – to protect his supremacy. Quatermain also rescues John Every, prisoner of Wambe and sole survivor of a hunting party murdered by Wambe (another nod to the Sargeaunt–Patterson expedition).[26] There are two battles, and in the assault on Wambe's mountain fortress (borrowed from Sekhukhune's 'Fighting Koppie') Maiwa leads the final charge that decides the battle. The story is recounted after dinner by Quatermain to Curtis, Good 'and myself', the last being Haggard, who records Quatermain's narrative, at the end of which 'we all went to bed, and I dreamed that I had married Maiwa, and was much afraid of that attractive but determined lady'.[27]

Haggard's penchant for violence in books 'whose object is pure amusement' was heavily criticised in the *Church Quarterly Review* of January 1888. The anonymous writer considered the 'repeated introduction of scenes of slaughter ... as a violation of the decency we have a right to demand from all who handle such solemn scenes'.[28] Later in the year Haggard came under fire again, this time in the *Fortnightly Review*, owned and edited by Frank Harris, who in an article headlined 'The Fall of Fiction' laid the blame for its dramatic decline in quality squarely on the shoulders of Haggard, who, having accurately gauged the 'deplorable' taste of a large section of the reading public, deliberately catered to it. 'The taste for novels like Mr Rider Haggard's is quite truly the craving for coarse and violent intoxicants because they coarsely and violently intoxicate.'[29] Thus began another tit-for-tat public correspondence; mercifully short in this case.[30]

On 23 November 1887, less than two weeks after completing *Maiwa's Revenge*, Haggard began work on a contemporary novel, *Beatrice*. He finished the book on 28 February 1888 and it was published on 12 May 1890. Haggard considered *Beatrice* 'one of the best bits of work I ever did'.[31] Like its predecessors *Dawn*, *The Witch's Head* and *Colonel Quaritch, V.C.*, *Beatrice* is a blend of melodramatic incident and convoluted plot. Beatrice Granger, the heroine of the title, is the beautiful younger daughter of an impecunious Anglican vicar in the coastal village of Bryngelly, Wales, a New Woman modelled on Olive Schreiner, and an atheist interested in the works of Charles Darwin, who writes her father's sermons in the style of a freethinker. Beatrice saves Geoffrey Bingham from drowning when the two coincidentally meet while canoeing along the mist-shrouded Welsh coast. Bingham, unhappily married to Lady Honoria Bingham, has taken up law to earn an income, having lost out on an expected inheritance when his elderly widowed father remarried shortly before his death and an heir was born eight months later. The only ray of light in Bingham's life is Effie, his 'dear little six-year-old daughter'.[32]

Recovering from his near drowning, Geoffrey convalesces at the vicarage, and he and Beatrice fall in love, a love unspoken and, when revealed, not acted upon, at least by Beatrice. When Geoffrey receives a brief involving a murder case that he cannot make head or tail of, Beatrice solves the crime using deductive reasoning in the manner of Sherlock Holmes, and as a consequence Geoffrey launches a successful career that will take him to parliament.[33] When Geoffrey comes to stay overnight at the vicarage in Bryngelly to sort out the Reverend Mr Granger's financial difficulties, Beatrice sleepwalks into his room. Geoffrey promptly returns the still-sleeping Beatrice to the room she shares with her jealous older sister Elizabeth, who witnesses the incident and sends an anonymous letter to Lady Honoria. Matters come to a head and Geoffrey begs Beatrice to go abroad with him. She decides on suicide as the best solution to everyone's dilemma. Having arranged matters so that her death will look accidental, she travels to London for one last look at Geoffrey as he gives a key speech in parliament; she then returns to Bryngelly and carries out her plan, paddling her canoe into the offshore breakers. On the same night Lady Honoria is attending a ball where her dress catches fire and she is burned to death. Geoffrey is left to bring up his beloved daughter, Effie.

Beatrice reads like Thomas Hardy-lite, a demonstration of the absurdity of the British divorce laws of the period. This was emphatically not the case, according to Haggard, for the lesson 'illustrated by the tragic story of Beatrice' is this: 'Whatever the excuse of temptation, the man or woman who falls into undesirable relations with a married member of the other sex is both a sinner and a fool, and, in this coin or that, certainly will be called upon to pay the price of sin and folly.'[34] Is Haggard addressing himself?

Longman read *Beatrice* in manuscript and considered it 'a terrible tragedy – unrelieved in its gloom which increases from start to finish. Still there is no denying its power.'[35] Longman preferred Haggard 'best among the caves of old Kôr, or looking back over King Solomon's great road to the old civilisations dead two thousand years ago. But it is a great thing to have several strings and not always harp on the same. And there is the same feeling in all your books – that of a power or Fate or whatever it is behind man controlling his actions and driving him blindly forward.'[36]

Lang, to Haggard's surprise, liked the book: 'it has move, it has go and plenty of it.'[37] Another fan was 'the bestselling of all Victorian novelists', Marie Corelli.[38] '*Beatrice* is *beautiful* – full of poetry and deep thought,' she gushed, 'but I don't believe the public – that with obstinate pertinacity look to you for a continuation ad infinitum of *King Solomon's Mines* and *She* – will appreciate it as they ought and as it deserves.'[39]

Aggie, in a letter wishing her brother-in-law a happy birthday, praised *Beatrice*. Haggard responded: 'I think it is not a bad book however much it may be attacked. I think that women like it however.'[40] Florence Dixie most certainly didn't.

> I have just finished reading your *Beatrice*, and have put it down with a feeling that it is only another book in the many which proclaims the rooted idea in men's minds that women are born to suffer and work for men, to hide all their natural gifts that man may rule alone ... Forgive me – but as you *can* write, why not use your pen to upraise woman, to bid her become a useful member of society – the true companion and co-mate of man.[41]

Dixie enclosed some 'papers which will show you that there are some women, and men too, who feel that the cruel position of woman is unbearable', and offered to send Haggard a signed copy of her new book, *Gloriana; or, The Revolution of 1900*. 'Will you give me the pleasure of accepting a copy if I send you one? If you read it, you will not misunderstand this letter I hope.'[42] To Haggard's credit he included Dixie's letter in his autobiography.

Haggard's mentor John Cordy Jeaffreson thought *Beatrice* 'a fine, stirring, effective story' but 'not the book which will determine your eventual place in the annals of literature. You will write that book some ten years hence, when I shall be resting under the violets.'[43] In his autobiography Haggard mourned: 'Alas! that wondrous work of fiction which Cordy Jeaffreson anticipated never was and never will be written by me.'[44] Jeaffreson's prophecy is not so easily dismissed, as ten years after *Beatrice* Haggard published *A Farmer's Year*, a non-fiction work judged by some to have a claim to being his best book.

Three years after the appearance of *Beatrice*, in the autumn of 1894, Haggard was horrified to receive two letters 'from ladies who alleged their husbands, or the husbands of someone connected with them – one of them a middle-aged clergyman – after reading *Beatrice*, had made advances to young ladies of that name'. He was also told that 'a gentleman and a lady had practised the sleep-walking scene, with different results from those recorded in the book'.[45] Shocked that a book of his had inspired immoral behaviour, Haggard tried to have *Beatrice* suppressed. Longman assured Haggard 'the idea that the character of Beatrice could lead someone into vice is preposterous ... I assure you there is nothing you need regret.'[46] Lang didn't mince his words: 'You Confounded Ass. The thing is Rot. Don't take it *au serieux*.'[47]

Haggard was not to be persuaded. 'I went through the tale carefully, modified or removed certain passages that might be taken to suggest that holy matrimony is not always perfect in its working, etc.', and wrote a short preface to be included in further editions.[48] The incident disturbed Haggard 'a good deal, and more or less set me against the writing of novels of modern life'. (Coincidentally he was working on another at the time, *Joan Haste*.) 'It is very well to talk about art with a large A, but I have always felt that the author of books which go anywhere and everywhere has some responsibilities. Therefore I have tried to avoid topics that might inflame even minds which are very ready to be set on fire.'[49] Haggard's conservatism, thus articulated, is ironically offset by the eroticism of his romances, especially *She* and its sequels; an eroticism eagerly capitalised on by his illustrators.[50]

It is not known precisely when *Mr. Meeson's Will* was written, but Haggard gave the manuscript, entitled 'Meeson v. Addison & Another', to his agent Alexander Watt in April 1888, a gift indicative of Haggard's indebtedness to Watt in extricating him from his contract with J. & R. Maxwell.[51] The fanciful story originated in 'a leg-pull put up by [the] pupils' of Aggie's uncle William Barber, lawyer and member of the Bar at Lincoln's Inn, concerning a man stranded 'on a desert island having his will tattooed on his back by his companion. Counsel's Opinion was sought whether the will was valid since the man could not possibly see what was written on his back when he signed it, which in itself must have been a difficult feat.' Aggie passed on the story to her brother-in-law and it became the kernel of *Mr. Meeson's Will*.[52]

Trapped in a contract to her publisher, the mean Mr Meeson, the popular author Augusta Smithers reaps little financial reward from her work. As nearly happened to Haggard with Cassell vis-à-vis *King Solomon's Mines*, Augusta is duped into selling the copyright of her bestseller *Jemima's Vow* to Meeson's great profit and, as per her contract, has to continue churning out books for another five years along with the other hirelings on Meeson's publishing treadmill. When Augusta requests an increase in payments in order to better nurse her dying 12-year-old sister, Meeson refuses. Meeson's nephew and heir Eustace, present at the meeting, is much smitten with Augusta and, after she has left, intervenes on her behalf, only to find himself disinherited by his choleric uncle. After her sister's death, Augusta emigrates to New Zealand, but there is no escaping Meeson, who is aboard the same ship sailing to his offices in Australia. The ship is wrecked on the shores of Kerguelen Island in the southern Indian Ocean and the only survivors are Augusta, Meeson, two sailors and a child.

Stranded on the deserted island, Meeson repents of having disinherited Eustace and, in the absence of paper on which to write a new will, Augusta volunteers the nape of her neck and shoulders, where the will is tattooed using cuttle-fish ink. Meeson and the two sailors die, and Augusta and the child are rescued. Back in England, Augusta becomes engaged to Eustace. A photograph of the will on her skin is filed and a probate trial follows involving much legal debate as to the validity of such a will. The will is finally declared valid, Augusta and Eustace marry and, having overhauled the business model of Meeson's publishing house, Augusta returns to her pen.

Mr. Meeson's Will was published in October 1888 after its appearance in the bumper summer edition of the *Illustrated London News* in June. Written to fulfil a contractual obligation, *Mr. Meeson's Will* is executed in a devil-may-care spirit. All to the good as it happens, the story moves swiftly and there is none of the banal philosophising or purple prose of Haggard's other contemporary novels. In a preface Haggard describes the single volume as 'a humble skit',[53] and it reads like a parody of the conventional Victorian three-volume novel, an absurd melodrama kitted out with a satire on the worlds of law and publishing, in parts genuinely funny. Haggard gives himself a cameo role as a *Times* court reporter, who 'by-the-way, writes novels ... romances, you know mere romances! and mostly plagiarised from the Book of Genesis and the Egyptian Novelists of the ancient Empire; at least, so I'm told in minor literary circles'.[54]

One work by Haggard from this period of extraordinary productivity remains unpublished. On 23 April 1888 he commenced yet another book, 'Nesta Amor or The Coming of the Lady Isis', completing it on 16 August 1888 and pinning a note on the manuscript: 'There's enough of this to publish but it wants careful revision'.[55] Lang read the manuscript and agreed, but Haggard never found the time to rewrite it.[56]

'Nesta Amor' explores the impact of the arrival of an Ayesha-like character on England, much as Ayesha herself proposed in *She*.[57] Nesta is the daughter of an Englishman who married the daughter of an Arab sheik. Nesta's mother dies giving birth, and her father is later killed by an Arab tribal leader to whom Nesta Amor is betrothed but whom she refuses to marry. She assassinates him instead, takes over the tribal leadership, and embarks on five years of war and conquest until she tires of her martial endeavours, as 'none could stand before me'. Taking up the study of 'dark learning', Nesta develops magical powers and, compelled to seek a non-Arab as a suitable mate, she heads for England.

Aboard ship, Nesta is befriended by Sir Reginald Marville and is employed to teach his wife and daughters Arabic. Intent on Nesta's seduction, Marville keeps her prisoner in his London home, but she escapes into the street and is rescued by a doctor, Ralph Coley, whom she recognises as the mate she seeks. However, Coley is shocked at Nesta's murderous propensities. Thereafter follows a tale of death and destruction, culminating in the ultimate realisation that the secret of the universe is 'Love in Unity! Unity in Love', as expressed by Nesta, now in divine form and revealed as Isis, who ascends on 'glorious wings', abandoning the corpse of Ralph Coley – 'thus the Lady Isis came and thus she passed for aye'.[58]

Critics had frequently ascribed Homeric qualities to Haggard's tales, so it is not surprising he aspired to create an epic of his own. For his subject matter he turned not to the ancient Greeks but to another epic tradition and 'conceived the idea of writing a saga' and, before doing so, 'I would visit Iceland and study the local colouring on the spot'.[59] Haggard's initial research included a call on 62-year-old William Morris at his Thames-side home in Hammersmith, Kelmscott House. The poet, novelist, socialist, and designer associated with the Arts and Crafts Movement had visited Iceland in 1871 and, with the assistance of the Icelandic theologian Eiríkr Magnússon, translated a selection of the Eddas and Sagas into English, notably *The Story of Sigurd the Volsung and the Fall of the Niblungs* (1876). Despite their diametrically opposed political views, Haggard was impressed by the 'fair-haired man with a large head and very pleasant manners',[60] and captivated by the decor, the furniture, and the china from which they drank tea. 'The cups, I think, had no saucers to them, but certainly they were very fine china. No servant came into the room, but then ladies, most artistically arrayed, handed the bread and butter. The walls were severely plain, but on them hung priceless tapestries and pictures by Rossetti and others.' On departing Haggard 'rather wished that Fate had made me a Socialist also'.[61]

Haggard came away with letters of introduction from Morris to friends in Iceland, one of which led to the hiring of Thorgrimmer Gudmunson, a schoolmaster during the island's long winter period and a guide in summer. True to his resolution not to travel alone again, Haggard was accompanied by a friend from the Savile, Alexander Galt Ross, founder member and secretary of the Society of Authors, a frequent contributor to the *Saturday Review* and a friend of Oscar Wilde.[62] Haggard and Ross planned to visit the sites associated with the thirteenth-century *Njal's Saga* and thereafter spend a few days fishing for trout and salmon. Haggard and Ross sailed from the Scottish port of Leith for Reykjavik on 14 June 1888 aboard the trading vessel the SS *Copeland*, a three-masted schooner fitted with two engines, which was licensed to carry passengers.

Disembarking at Reykjavik on 19 June, they made arrangements with Gudmunson, who reappeared two days later 'with a cortege of thin, shaggy ponies, which were to carry us and our belongings'.[63] The ponies were Icelandic horses, a unique breed, small, tough and double-coated. On 22 June, Haggard's thirty-second birthday, he stood above the sky-blue waters of Iceland's largest lake, Thingvallavatn [Lake Þingvallavatn]: 'What man who has read the Sagas can look upon the site of Thingvellii without experiencing the most lively emotion.'[64] The three men overnighted in a 'little wooden church surrounded by graves' after dining on 'a dreadful compound of salt fish and wild duck eggs'. They slept on either side of the altar. 'Smell of church very bad, perhaps owing to bodies about.'[65]

Under Gudmunson's expert guidance Haggard and Ross visited all the sites associated with *Njal's Saga*, including that of Gunnar's hall and the site of his tomb. Back in Reykjavik, Haggard and Ross concluded that 'a pony journey through Iceland is a thing to have done, but oh not a thing to do again'. The rigours of the journey aside, 'the worst part of it is the grub' – a diet of 'coarse black rye bread' and 'raw dried fish' that had to be beaten on 'a big stone before it can be chewed'. All the same Haggard thoroughly enjoyed the journey, especially the experience of walking the hallowed sites of *Njal's Saga* – 'I have got a good plot for my yarn.' He had also bought a pony 'which I think will just suit the children, quiet pretty & lazy – and I shall probably bring another of a better stamp.'[66]

From Reykjavik, Haggard and Ross travelled north to Halsi on the Laxa River for a fortnight's fishing. The two lodged in a farmhouse at the head of the fjord. During their stay an elderly relative of their host living in the loft died. Haggard thought the sound of the family 'singing the national death song over him ... one of the most beautiful and impressive things I have heard'. The song was followed by the 'heavy sound of the coffin being brought down – the lid was lifted to allow us to look on the face of the dead, a fine old face, white as wax ... Not a very cheerful beginning to a day's fishing – but after all that is the way of the world, one to burial and one to sport.'[67]

Haggard and Ross sailed from Reykjavik on 20 July, again on the *Copeland*, now carrying eleven passengers and a cargo of wool, fish and 482 ponies in the holds and on deck, including the two purchased by Haggard. It was not a pleasant voyage: '20th: At sea. Bad weather. 21st: Gale. 22nd: Worse gale. 23rd: Worse gale still. Lay to. 24th: Tried to go about four o'clock. Strained the ship so much that we had to lay to again.'[68] On the morning of 25 July the *Copeland* lay to off the island of Thurso, befogged in a dead calm. Worried the ponies would starve – there was only enough fodder for one more feed and fifteen had already died of exposure – the captain, Charles Thompson, decided to sail on to Leith.

Close to midnight he changed course, assuming Stroma, the southernmost of the Orkney Islands, had been passed in the fog when suddenly 'the curtain of the mist seemed to be drawn up before our eyes, and there – not more than a hundred yards in front of us – we saw a field of breakers, and the current boiling over the rocks; while right ahead something huge loomed up through the heavy air': Stroma. The captain ordered full-steam astern, but 'the way we had on and the tide overpowered the screw, and we glided quickly through the deep, quiet water towards the tip of the breakers ... with a succession of long and grinding, but comparatively gentle shocks, the end came, and the *Copeland* stopped for the last time.'[69] Boats put out from Stroma and a 'handsome-looking man, with wild eyes and flowing hair' boarded the *Copeland* and came running aft, shouting, 'Get off this ... She's only hanging on the rocks; she'll slip off presently and go down by the stern, and drown every man of you!'[70] A boat came alongside and a rope ladder was lowered. Men from other boats retrieved the luggage and ferried it to the island. Of the ponies 360 were saved; Haggard's were not among them.

On 'the rocky shores of Stroma' the first person to arrive on the scene was 'a gentleman in a rusty black coat and a tall hat, a schoolmaster I believe', who came up to Haggard, 'bowed politely, took off the tall hat with a flourish, and said, in the best Scotch, "The author of *She* I believe? I am verra glad to meet you."'[71] The stranded passengers spent six hours on the stony beach before being taken over the Pentland Firth to John o'Groats and on to Wick, terminus of the Highland Railway, where Haggard sent a telegram to his father: '*Copeland* wrecked on Stroma but we are saved.'[72] That night Haggard and Ross 'slept at some inn. I remember that I did not sleep very well ... I realised that I had been very near to death; also all that word means. For some days I did not recover my balance.'[73] Haggard's article 'The Wreck of the Copeland' was published in the *Illustrated London News* of 18 August 1888.

Haggard was back at Ditchingham on 27 July 1888, and on 29 August, two weeks after completing 'Nesta Amor', began work on *Eric Brighteyes*, finishing it on Christmas Day. The plot for this 'yarn' had come to Haggard while he was standing upon the site of Gunnar's tomb. 'Then and there in Rider's mind the story of Eric Brighteyes [and Skallagrim, Eric's faithful and misogynous friend] was born. The tale of Eric and his sword, Whitefire, against whom no man might stand, of Gudruda the Fair and the Witch woman, Swanhild the fatherless, fierce as the winter sea, and the doom which the Norns decreed for them in the days of the Old Gods, before ever the White Christ was preached in Iceland.'[74]

Eric Brighteyes was published to good reviews two years later on 13 May 1891 after serialisation in the *People*. 'Wonderfully fresh and well told,' enthused the *New York Times*, praising the 'unusual crispness and force' of Haggard's prose.[75] Lang thought it one of Haggard's best, 'worth an infinite number of *Cleopatras*, partly because you are at home in the North'.[76] So did his biographer Morton Cohen: 'Haggard here seems to write instinctively, as though his notion that in some previous incarnation he himself had been a viking were true.'[77]

Haggard left a copy of *Eric Brighteyes* at the Savile for Thomas Hardy to collect. 'Many thanks for your thoughtful kindness in sending me a copy,' Hardy wrote from his London home at 12 Mandeville Place, confessing he had been distracted in his reading by 'a wild illustration'.[78] Hardy is referring to the plate by Lancelot Speed depicting Gudruda lying on her bed naked from the waist, impaled by a sword between her breasts. 'Now the light flowed in and struck upon the bed. It fell upon the bed, it fell upon Whitefire's hilt and ran along the blade, it gleamed on a woman's snowy breast and golden hair, and shone in her staring eyes – a woman who lay stiff and cold upon the bed, the great sword fixed within her heart!'[79] What did Freud make of that, let alone the readers of the *Church Quarterly*?

After Haggard completed *Cleopatra* in 1887, he and Lang began their on-off co-authorship, the outcome of which would be *The World's Desire*, published in September 1890. Haggard's bibliographer Scott estimates it was started 'about Jan., 1888'.[80] It was eventually finished on 9 January 1889. As we have seen, one candidate proposed for the collaboration was a sequel to *She*, but Haggard already planned to write that himself. Who came up with the idea of 'the romance of Helen and Odysseus in Egypt after the end of the *Odyssey*'[81] is unclear, though Lang's biographer Roger Lancelyn Green favours Lang as 'more at home among the Greeks of Homer's world than most other moderns'[82] and he had also written the epic poem *Helen of Troy*. According to Haggard, he and Lang discussed the plot, then 'I wrote a part of it, which part he altered or rewrote'.[83] The two men fired off letters to each other about the project, initially titled 'The Song of the Bow', enclosing parts of the work in progress until Haggard, having written a substantial amount, 'sent it to Lang, who promptly lost it so completely and for so long a time that, not having the heart to recommence the book, the idea of writing it was abandoned'[84] – until an undated letter (probably in September 1888) from Lang announced: 'I've found your lost MS!'[85] Lang immediately began work on the manuscript again, and different versions bounced back and forth between the two authors. According to Green, the first four chapters of the published book 'are almost solely the work of Lang, with certain incidents by Haggard rewritten, and a few paragraphs incorporated. After this it is so evenly worked over that no considerable portion can be assigned to either author, though Haggard's style is the most predominant.'[86]

Serialised in the *New Review* from April to December 1890, *The World's Desire* was published as a book on 5 November 1890. Lang described it as an 'experiment in romance'.[87] One that failed was the general consensus. J.M. Barrie in the *British Weekly* thought the book a perfect demonstration of why collaboration in fiction was never a good idea, as it lacked both Haggard's realism and Lang's humour. The *Athenaeum* blamed Haggard, whose touch seemed 'to take away much of the charm which might linger round this dream of old Egypt and of the Golden Helen and the wise Odysseus'.[88] The *Spectator* also sided with Lang: 'We think so well of Mr Lang, that what would please us best would be to be told that his name on the title-page is his principal contribution.'[89]

Allan's Wife, the second title written to fulfil the agreement with J. & R. Maxwell (now Spencer Blackett), was begun on 25 February, completed on 16 April 1889, and published in December. *Allan's Wife*, a novella, is the title tale of a volume padded out with three Quatermain stories, 'Hunter Quatermain's Story', 'A Tale of Three Lions' and 'Long Odds'.[90] Gory hunting tales all, their content was most likely sourced from Frederick Jackson and Jack Haggard: grim fare for today's readers but standard for the time.

Haggard dedicated the book to Arthur Cochrane, addressing him as 'My Dear Macumazahn', Cochrane's 'native name which I borrowed at the christening of that Allan who has become as well known to me as any other friend I have'. In the dedication Haggard indicates *Allan's Wife* is Quatermain's 'last tale – the story of his wife', Stella Carson. We met her earlier at Garsington rectory, the 'little fair-haired girl' Blanche, the daughter of the Reverend Henry Graham.[91]

After his wife leaves the family home, Stella's father takes his young daughter abroad, beyond the bounds of civilisation. Meanwhile, the young Allan has gone to South Africa with his father, a country vicar turned missionary. After a prologue patchwork of near-stand-alone stories (an elephant hunt, a fire fight, Zulu massacres of Boer trekkers), Quatermain, now a young man hunting and trading in the African interior, discovers Stella and her father at Babyans Kraal (Baboon kraal or homestead), situated in the natural amphitheatre of a tall mountain, and home to a troop of baboons. Stella is jealously guarded by her servant-companion, 'the Baboon woman' Hendrika – 'She might have been the missing link'.[92] Allan and Stella fall in love and are married by her father; being far from civilisation, he has been marrying those of his charges who have converted to Christianity. Her father dies, and Stella falls pregnant, subsequently coming down with fever and dying after giving birth to Harry. One night shortly before leaving Babyans Kraal, Allan visits Stella's grave and finds Hendrika 'tearing at its sods with her hands, as though she would unearth that which lay within ... Suddenly she looked up and saw me. Laughing a dreadful maniac laugh, she put her hand to her girdle and drew her great knife from it ... Lifting the knife on high, for a moment she held it glittering in the moonlight, then plunged it into her own breast, and fell headlong to the ground.'[93]

Quatermain and his infant son go to Port Natal. 'Some fifteen years after my darling's death, when I was a man in middle life, I undertook an expedition to the Zambesi, and one night outspanned at the mouth of the well-known valley beneath the shadow of the great peak.' All is derelict, the inhabitants wiped out. He finds Stella's grave, but not before catching a glimpse of a giant baboon, the spirit of Hendrika, 'doomed to keep an eternal watch over the bones of the woman her jealous rage had done to death'. Stella's ghost appears to Allan beneath the orange tree 'where first we had told our love'.[94]

Despite its structural flaws, *Allan's Wife* is another dipstick into the Victorian unconscious. Scholars have suggested lesbianism, necrophilia, and a dash of bestiality.

Cleopatra was published on 24 June 1889. In the dedication to his mother, Haggard expressed the hope his book would 'convey to your mind a picture, however imperfect, of the old and mysterious Egypt in whose lost glories you are so deeply interested'. He sent his mother a first edition of the book, and her letter dated 29 June 1889, 'the last I ever received from her',[95] thanked him for the dedication and the book. 'Thank you greatly for your excellent work, my dear son. It certainly redounds greatly to you, dearest Rider, whatever the critics may say, and I have no doubt they will do their worst. But I think posterity will do justice to your production'.[96] Haggard never knew whether his mother had read *Cleopatra*, as 'by this time her sight was failing much'. So was Ella's health, and in December he 'stood at her death-bed and received her last blessing'.[97]

On Friday, 6 December 1889, when Haggard learnt his mother was dying, he immediately left Redcliffe Square for Bradenham Hall. His mother was still alive when he arrived that night. 'She knew me perfectly – spoke something about my dinner & the children & kissed me with affection.' On Saturday morning the local doctor was of 'the opinion that all things will be ended today. The breath is turning cold & she is sinking into a state of coma. Her face has of course changed greatly, but it has won a strange beauty.'[98] On Saturday night 'we thought that she was dying but she opened her eyes and smiled very beautifully. My father read the prayer for the dying over her and then thanked her for her long life of love and duty as wife, mother and friend. To our surprise she said "Thank you. Thank you."'[99] Ella survived the night. 'Oh what a world is this in which it has pleased the Almighty to place us, & what would it be without some hope for a Beyond! Let those who are Atheists watch such a drama as that now enacting before our eyes – the drama of the loosing of a human soul. Then let them speak.'[100]

On Sunday Haggard went to the morning service at St Andrew's. Around midday his mother sank into a coma. 'About 8 on the Monday morning she opened her eyes and we knew that the last change was at hand. The breath grew ever fainter and at 20 minutes past 8 it ceased, the eyelids fluttered a while and all was done.'[101] Haggard, his father, the family servant Elizabeth Hocking and a nurse were present at her deathbed. 'We buried her on Thursday. She was carried on men's shoulders from the Hall to the Church – all the population followed and preceded her coffin.'[102]

In August 1918 Lilias accompanied her father on his last visit to Bradenham Hall before it was sold and, 'standing in the empty, cheerless room' which had been his mother's, he tried to tell his daughter 'a little of what his mother had meant to him

– of the feeling that with her went something of himself; that there had never been a day when he did not remember her and pray for her. He who spoke so seldom of the things which lay nearest his heart, tried, but could not go on, and turning, walked out of the room and out of the house into the hot August sunshine.'[103] As a memorial Haggard proposed the publication of a new edition of his mother's poem *Life and Its Author: An Essay in Verse* – 'far the best thing she ever did'.[104] William Haggard gave his blessing. The slim volume was published in May by Longmans with a short introduction titled 'In Memoriam' by Haggard.[105]

Prior to his mother's death Haggard had been organising a trip to Athens to see his brother William, first secretary at the British Embassy. He had already purchased tickets, hired a Greek yacht, bought 'some hunting dogs' and sent on ahead 'guns, stores, and cartridges'.[106] The idea for the trip began when Haggard received a letter from William informing him that the Empress Dowager Frederick, the widow of Frederick III of Germany, had told Will when she was in Athens that 'the last pleasure that her husband had on earth was reading [Haggard's] books' and he had expressed the hope he might live to meet their author. Will told the Empress Dowager it would give his brother great pleasure to know he 'had soothed the dying moments of such a man, whereupon she begged me to write and tell you'.[107]

Haggard suggested William ask the Empress Dowager if it would be acceptable to have *Eric Brighteyes* dedicated to her. It was, and Haggard sent her his draft dedication for her approval. The Empress Dowager thought the dedication 'charming' and suggested a minor alteration. On 19 January 1890 she sent Haggard a registered letter from Berlin, 'offering her sincere condolences' on the death of his mother and enclosing a printed draft of the dedication, which saw the light of day when *Eric Brighteyes* was published on 13 May 1891.[108]

Haggard never got to Greece and was peeved with William, who left Athens but arrived too late for their mother's funeral; this meant Haggard's trip had to be cancelled at a cost of nearly a hundred pounds.

18

'I DESCENDED INTO HELL'

In the autumn of 1889 the London literary scene was abuzz with the advent of 23-year-old Rudyard Kipling. Like Haggard, Kipling drew his subject matter from distant, exotic locations (in the minds of their English readers at least) and looked set to depose Haggard as the reigning 'King of Romance'. Members at the Savile were 'all on the qui vive about [Kipling]' as Andrew Lang, a champion of the prodigy, ushered Kipling into the club and its literary circle. 'Rider Haggard appeared really aggrieved at a man with a double-barrelled name, odder than his own, coming up. Literally.'[1] Henry James believed the battle already won: '[Kipling] has killed one immortal – Rider Haggard', he gloated to Robert Louis Stevenson in Samoa.[2] Another Savile member, the poet James Kenneth Stephen, wrote a couple of verses 'deftly exposing the undercurrent of professional jealousies running through the club', which went in part:[3]

> Will there ever come a season ...
> When there stands a muzzled stripling,
> Mute, beside a muzzled bore:
> When the Kiplings cease from Kipling
> And the Haggards Ride no more.[4]

Kipling took to Haggard 'at once, he being of the stamp adored by children, and trusted by men at sight'.[5] The feeling was mutual, Haggard recording that from their first meeting 'we have always liked each other, perhaps because on many, though not on all, matters we find no point of difference'.[6] Personal tragedies in later life would strengthen their bond of kinship.

Despite their disparate ages – Haggard was now 33, Kipling ten years younger – and differences in height – Haggard tall, Kipling short – the two had much in common. Moustaches for one, Kipling's the more luxuriant. Of greater import, neither had gone up to university and each shared similar life experiences: young men in far-off lands – southern Africa and India – eyewitnesses to the operations of the British Empire, and both possessed of an idealised vision of that empire, its future and its responsibilities.

They shared character traits as well, both subject to bouts of depression and an appetite for hard work bordering on the pathological. Another bond was their deep aversion to William Gladstone: Haggard's well-rehearsed grievances over the Transvaal; Kipling's anger at military debacles in Afghanistan. When Kipling's first child, Josephine, was born on Gladstone's birthday, 29 December 1892, Kipling remarked that if the baby had been a boy, he would have dispatched her 'lest she also should disgrace the empire'.[7]

They had even more in common: a lost first love. For Haggard there was Lilly Jackson; for Kipling, Flo Garrard – he would fictionalise his experience in his first novel, *The Light That Failed*. Haggard would have recognised himself in Kipling's story 'The Dream of Duncan Parrenness', the tale of a young man who leaves England for India, having been driven hence by his fiancée 'to get rich, that I might the more quickly marry her'; but she marries another man in his absence.[8] The title character takes up with Mrs Vansuythen of 'the violet eyes and the sweet slow speech' and finds solace in her arms and forgetfulness in drink.[9]

At the time of their meeting Haggard was working on a 'pure Zulu story', *Nada the Lily*: 'I consider it my best or one of my best books'.[10] Lang had alerted Haggard to the potential of a story about 'natives, one with no white men',[11] in an article in the *Scots Observer*, urging Haggard to try his hand at such a tale: 'how delicious a novel *all* Zulu, without a white face in it, would be!'[12] The book's six-month writing period – from 27 June 1889 to 15 January 1890 – is by far Haggard's longest and indicative of the care he took over *Nada the Lily*. The Scottish writer Edward Boyd considered it Haggard's 'greatest achievement, a tremendous story, violent, grim, savage, compelling, and with a rhythm that can only be described as remorseless'.[13]

Eric Brighteyes was the template for *Nada the Lily* and the latter shares many features with its predecessor: a tragically doomed hero in Umslopogaas, similarly accompanied by a faithful but female-shy friend Galazi (counterpart of Skallagrim), caught up in a tragic tale of thwarted love, loyalty and ambition that is played out against the backdrop of the reign of King Shaka, encompassing his assassination at the hands of his brother Dingane, Dingane's defeat by the Boers and the crowning of Mpande, father of Cetshwayo. The story is narrated by the elderly Mopo, a counsellor of Shaka's, to Allan Quatermain, the volume's editor, who bookends the tale with his comments.[14] Mopo's son Umslopogaas is really the son of Shaka, born of Baleka, one of Shaka's concubines and Mopo's sister. Shaka's preferred method of removing potentially aggressive male heirs was to have them killed at birth. Umslopogaas escapes this fate – he is swapped with a stillborn baby – and grows to maturity unaware of his true identity. Nevertheless Shaka grows suspicious and Mopo takes Umslopogaas and his beloved younger sister, the Nada of the title, to Swaziland.

Curiously, given the 'pure Zulu' nature of the book, Nada, 'the most beautiful of Zulu women',[15] is depicted as being more or less white: 'her blood was not all Zulu ... At the least, her eyes were softer and larger than those of our people, her hair longer and less tightly curled, and her skin was lighter – more of the colour of pure copper.' Her grandfather was thought to be 'a Portuguese from the coast ... the beauty of Nada was rather as is the beauty of the white people than of ours, and this might well happen if her grandfather chanced to be a white man'.[16] It has been suggested this racial configuration is intended to make Nada more acceptable to a white readership, and while it is true that Haggard often white-faces his African heroines when they are likely to pair off with white men – Foulata with Good in *King Solomon's Mines*; Mameena with Quatermain in *Child of Storm* – this coupling doesn't apply here and Nada, though pivotal to the tragedy, is absent from most of the narrative.

On the trip to Swaziland, Umslopogaas vanishes, being taken by a ferocious lion from which he is rescued by Galazi, leader of a pack of wolves (read hyenas) on the slopes of Ghost Mountain (Tshaneni) and the possessor of a great club or knobkerrie, 'The Watcher of the Fords'.[17] The two become blood brothers and, from their mountain fastness, roam far and wide with the Wolf Brethren. In their wanderings they encounter the People of the Axe, and Umslopogaas becomes infatuated with the titular weapon of their chief Jizika, and equally fascinated by Jizika's stepdaughter, the sultry Zinita. Having defeated the chief in 'succession by combat', Umslopogaas comes into possession of the axe he will wield in *Allan Quatermain* and marries Zinita, much to Galazi's disgust.

Mopo returns from Swaziland to find his family has been put to death and Zululand is under a reign of terror as Shaka enforces national mourning following the death of his mother Nandi (which is depicted by Haggard as occurring at the hand of Shaka). The opposition to Shaka's tyranny, led by his brothers Dingane and Umhlangana, is harnessed by Mopo for his own ends, intending that Umslopogaas should seize the Zulu throne. Shaka is assassinated and replaced by Dingane, who dispatches any would-be rivals, including his co-conspirators. The wily Mopo avoids the assegai, but Dingane's attention inevitably turns towards Umslopogaas.

Now aware of his true ancestry, Umslopogaas is reunited with Nada; no longer siblings as they thought, they become lovers. A spurned Zinita betrays Umslopogaas and his whereabouts to Dingane, and an impi is sent 'to eat up' the People of the Axe. A desperate battle and a heroic last stand are fought on the slopes of Ghost Mountain, while Nada is hidden out of the way in a cave with a stone door. In the battle all except Umslopogaas are killed; seriously wounded, he manages to reach Nada's cave but is too weak to roll back the stone door. Nada dies and Umslopogaas is doomed to the life of a homeless wanderer.

Part Homeric epic, part Norse saga, *Nada the Lily* is perhaps best classified as a historical novel with an anthropological bent, one drawing directly on Haggard's knowledge of the history and customs of the Zulu people at the time of Shaka and

Dingane. This knowledge was obtained, and acknowledged in a preface, from a number of sources, including David Leslie's *Among the Zulus and Amatongas* and Henry Callaway's *The Religious System of the AmaZulu* as well as accounts from those Haggard knew in Natal: Fred Fynney 'by word of mouth' and his pamphlet *Zululand and the Zulus*, and John Bird's *The Annals of Natal*. Also to hand was George M. Theal's *Kaffir Folk-Lore; or, A Selection from the Traditional Tales Current among the People Living on the Eastern Border of the Cape Colony*.[18] Another volume consulted would have been Nathaniel Isaacs's *Travels and Adventures in Eastern Africa*.

But the overriding influence on *Nada the Lily* is Theophilus Shepstone, to whom the book is fulsomely dedicated. The Shaka of *Nada the Lily* is not Haggard's invention but Shepstone's, mediated through Haggard. In *Cetywayo and His White Neighbours* and *Nada the Lily*, Haggard established 'the popular images of Shaka and the Zulu people'.[19] *Nada the Lily* is framed by a white man to whom the story is told and, consequently, its interpreter and transmitter, producing 'an almost perfect projection of the nineteenth-century colonial mind, with all its conflicting and coexistent attitudes. There is the emphasis on Zulu savagery, a phenomenon which simultaneously attracts and repels the white man while affording him a pseudo-evolutionary pretext to rule.'[20]

Andrew Lang, reading *Nada the Lily* in manuscript, wrote to Haggard: 'It is admirable, the epic of a dying people, but it wants relief. Massacre palls … I like *Eric* better, but this is perhaps more singular. How any white man can have such a natural gift of savagery, I don't know. The Wolves are astonishing.'[21] Lang was even more enthusiastic on finishing the manuscript: 'If all the reviewers in the world denied it, you can do the best sagas that have been done yet: except [*Njal's Saga*] perhaps. Poor Nada! I hope it will be done into Zulu.'[22] Lang warned Haggard there would 'be rows about the endless massacres. I have no doubt a Zulu epic would be like this, but reviewers are not Zulus, worse luck. I think that it is excellent, and quite alone in literature as a picture of a strange life.'[23]

Charles Longman was equally smitten: '*Nada* strikes me with wonder and awe. It is in some ways the greatest feat you have performed … There will of course be a terrible outcry about gore. I never read such a book. It is frightful, and the only justification for it is the fact that it is history, not imagination.' He agreed with Lang that 'the wolf brethren are delightful; I wish you could have given us more of them'.[24] That would fall to Rudyard Kipling: 'it was a chance sentence of yours in *Nada the Lily* that started me off on a track that ended in my writing a lot of wolf stories [*The Jungle Books*]. You remember in your tale where the wolves leaped up at the feet of a dead man sitting on a rock? Somewhere on that page I got the notion.'[25]

As predicted, when *Nada the Lily* was published in May 1892, there was 'a terrible outcry'. The *New York Times* condemned the book's violence as gratuitous and a 'perversion of true literature', accusing Haggard of 'absolutely' gloating over the murder of women and children.[26] 'The most sanguinary work of its size in existence' was the verdict of the *Critic* – 'drenched, sodden, dripping with blood' – in a review headlined 'Rider the Ripper'.[27] Haggard was philosophic about the critical response: 'They for the most part, not having mixed with savages, and never having heard of Chaka and only dimly of the Zulus ... saw little in the book except unnecessary bloodshed. But there it is: a picture, as Lang says, "of a dying people". I hope that hundreds of years hence the highly educated descendants of the Zulu race may read it and learn therefrom something of the spirit of their own savage ancestors.'[28]

Haggard's friends were kinder than the critics: 'this will be regarded as one of the very best of your works', wrote Edmund Gosse.[29] Walter Besant thought it 'the best thing ... since *She*'.[30] '*Nada the Lily* is A1' was Robert Louis Stevenson's succinct critique from Samoa.[31] In the same letter Stevenson mentions Haggard's brother Bazett, who had taken up the post of British Land Commissioner on Samoa in 1890 (after a quarrel with his father and estrangement from his wife Julia): 'we are companions in arms and have helped each other back and forth in some very difficult and some very annoying affairs. This has given a wonderful jog to my sense of intimacy with yourself until I have a difficulty in remembering that I have never seen you.'[32]

Shepstone considered the book's dedication 'a great compliment'.[33] Haggard, assuming the role of *imbongi*, composed a praise poem to his chief and wrote the dedication in ersatz English Zulu. He recalls Shepstone's long association with the Zulu: 'you have crowned their kings and shared their counsels, and with your son's blood you have expiated a statesman's error and a general's fault'. He remembers the mission to the Transvaal 'when you went up among the Boers and took their country for the Queen ... Enemies have borne false witness against you on this matter, Sompseu, you who never erred except through over kindness.' Haggard ends by giving Shepstone his Zulu '"Sibonga" [titles of praise] and that royal salute, to which, now that its kings are gone and the "People of Heaven" are no more a nation, with Her Majesty you are alone entitled'.[34]

When *Nada the Lily* was published in May 1892, Haggard sent a copy to Shepstone, who thanked Haggard for his 'affectionate remembrances, and for your plucky avowal of them, for I do not think that at present it is fashionable to look either upon myself or my work with much approval'.[35] This was the last letter Haggard received from his old chief, friend and mentor. Shepstone died suddenly at the age of 76 on the morning of 23 June 1893, a month after Natal celebrated its fiftieth anniversary with the passing of the Responsible Government Bill.[36]

Andrew Lang's hope that *Nada the Lily* would be translated into isiZulu was realised four decades later when it was translated by F.L. Ntuli as *Umbuso kaShaka* (In the Realm of Shaka) and published in 1930. John Langalibalele Dube, founding member and first president of the African National Congress, wrote the preface to Ntuli's translation, describing *Nada the Lily* as a 'brilliant book' written 'by the late Sir Rider Haggard, an Englishman who was sympathetic towards the Zulu nation, praising the nation for its overwhelming influence, its strength and its honesty. I have no doubt that anyone who reads the first two lines of this book won't willingly put it down until they have finished it, it's a compelling read.' Dube complimented Ntuli's Zulu translation, adding that he hoped the book would 'open the eyes of many who would also like to read books written by some of their own'.[37] Dube served this market himself, writing the first novel in isiZulu, *U-Jeqe, Insila ka Tshaka* (*Jeqe, the Body-Servant of King Shaka*).[38] Dube's version of the Zulu king is more ambivalent than Haggard's heartless tyrant: Shaka is acknowledged as a good leader, responsible for creating the Zulu nation, but also as a man given to excessively violent behaviour.

Reviewing *Umbuso kaShaka*, the poet, novelist and linguist Benedict Vilakazi said the book 'plunges into the Zulu mind which Haggard so successfully portrayed ... On reading *Umbuso kaShaka* one cannot fail to live the great unreturnable past; to roam again the wild pastures of Zululand which are not spotted here and there with the buildings, towns and missions of civilisation and Christianity.'[39]

In 1889, the year Haggard met Kipling, he 'made another great friend',[40] the 48-year-old adventurer John Gladwyn Jebb, managing director of Santa Fé (Chiapas) Copper Mines in the south-east of Mexico. The two met at a dinner hosted by a City connection of Haggard's who had persuaded him to invest in 'certain Mexican enterprises ... that in due course absorbed no small sum out of my hard earnings'.[41] Haggard was 'impressed at first sight by [Jebb's] powerful build, his kindly face, and the peculiar gentleness of his brown eyes ... A man rich in a rare quaintness and originality of mind.'[42]

Jebb and his wife Bertha lived in Mexico, and Jebb regaled Haggard with stories of the country's history, legends, and the 'many strange adventures which had befallen him there'.[43] Jebb wove a potent spell, and the two met frequently thereafter. Jebb urged Haggard 'to come to Mexico and write a novel about Montezuma', adding as bait 'a wonderful and, as I believe, perfectly true tale of hidden treasure which we were to proceed to dig up together'.[44] This trove was the Aztec treasure accumulated by the Spanish conquistadors and left behind when Hernán Cortés and his men were forced to abandon the Aztec capital Tenochtitlan, though not before killing Montezuma in what became known as the 'Noche Triste' in 1520. Ever a candidate for travel with a purpose, here was Haggard being offered by Jebb, a character straight out of one of his own books, the chance to participate in a real-life King Solomon's mines adventure. The lure was irresistible.

The Jebbs returned to Mexico during 1890, and plans were set in motion for Rider and Louie to travel there at the beginning of 1891. This dovetailed with Haggard's desire to move to Ditchingham House on a permanent basis and take on the running of the farm himself.[45] Haggard's income was now substantial enough to support the move, and the plan was for the Haggards to summer in 1890 at Ditchingham and commence the necessary alterations and refurbishments. They would return briefly to Redcliffe Square and, after billeting their children among friends, travel to Mexico to meet up with the Jebbs. On their return from Mexico they would transfer the tenancy of 24 Redcliffe Square to the Jebbs and be reunited with their children at Ditchingham.

In June 1890 the Haggards were installed at Ditchingham and busy with renovations. Haggard put all his energy into the refurbishment of Ditchingham House and the surrounding farm; for once he had no book on the go. Apart from preparing the memorial tribute to his mother in *Life and Its Author*, the article 'The Fate of Swaziland', published in the January issue of the *New Review*, and 'Golf for Duffers', which ran in the *Graphic* at the end of November, were the sum of his creations for the year 1890.

In 'The Fate of Swaziland' Haggard castigated the British government for its less than enthusiastic support of the small southern African country's independence, as guaranteed by the London Convention of 1884, in the face of increasing Boer encroachment.[46] What prompted Haggard to write this article is unclear. Theophilus Shepstone and some of his relatives had considerable interests in Swaziland, but the article doesn't advantage them in any way, though it could be argued that it legitimises their authority and involvement in the country.

'Golf for Duffers' is Haggard's only attempt at a sustained piece of comic writing and was inspired by a visit to Ditchingham by the Gosses in the autumn. Edmund Gosse and his family spent a few days with the Haggards, and they played golf on the links at Bungay. Photographs were taken. Gosse detested the game and one of the photographs is annotated by his son Philip: 'Unique photo of my father playing golf!'[47] While at Ditchingham the Gosses agreed to have 9-year-old Jock stay with them at 29 Delamere Terrace, opposite Regent's Park canal, when the Haggards went to Mexico. From there Jock would then stay with the family of the soldier and opera singer Francis Barrington Foote in Kensington. The girls, Angela (8) and Dorothy (7), were to remain in East Anglia with the Hartcups at Bungay. The Gosses enjoyed Jock's company; Edmund thought him 'a very intelligent boy',[48] and so did their children, Philip and Sylvia. The latter found Jock 'much nicer than she had anticipated, for she found that he could giggle'.[49]

The Haggards were back at 24 Redcliffe Square in early November and busy preparing to leave for Mexico. Haggard's farewell to Jock was a painful one, overshadowed by a grim premonition: 'I knew, almost without doubt, that in this world he and I would never see each other more. Only I thought *it was I who was doomed to die*.' The parting was 'bitter indeed ... I bade him good-bye and tore myself away'. Haggard returned to the house later, expecting Jock to have already been taken to the Gosses, but Jock was still there, about to go. 'Once more I went through that agony of a separation which I knew to be the last. With a cheerful face I kissed him – I remember how he flung his arms about my neck – in a cheerful voice I blessed him and bade him farewell, promising to write. Then he went through the door and it was finished.'[50] Acting on his premonition, Haggard 'made every possible preparation for my death – even to sealing up all important papers in a despatch-box and depositing them in Messrs. Goslings Bank, where I knew they would be at once available'.[51]

Rider and Louie, aboard the *Etruria*, berthed in New York on 10 January 1891. Haggard gave a half-hour interview to the American press that evening at the Victoria Hotel, the first time he had undergone 'examination by eight or ten newspapermen'; ill at ease under such scrutiny, he fidgeted during the interview and gave short uncommunicative answers. Despite this, the *New York Times* reporter penned an amiable portrait of Haggard: '[He] is a tall man, probably six feet high, somewhat loosely put together, with a slight stoop of the shoulders. He has dark hair, but the delicate moustache which adorns his lip is quite light in color. A long pointed nose gives his face a thinnish appearance, but a careful look at him shows that he has a full forehead and that his eyes are well apart. He has an agreeable manner and a pleasant smile.'[52] Journalists excepted, Haggard found 'Americans ... the most hospitable people in the world', so much so that he and Louie were glad to escape New York, 'where literally we were being killed with kindness. To feast with some hospitable host at every meal, from breakfast till a midnight supper, after a week or so becomes more than the human frame can bear'.[53]

The relentless hospitality continued in New Orleans, where the couple made a short stopover. At a dinner party next to 'each napkin lay a little poem anent something I had written'.[54] Haggard was especially thrilled to be shown a 'park in which duels used to be fought in the early days' and a cemetery where the high water table caused the dead to be 'buried in niches in the surrounding walls'.[55] From New Orleans the couple travelled by train to El Paso on the Mexican border, where they had the choice of two different rail routes to Mexico City. They chose wisely: 'the train which left on the same day by the other line ... was twice thrown off the rails by intelligent Mexicans actuated either by spite or the hope of plunder, and some of its occupants were killed'.

Haggard thought Mexico City 'a wonderful city of almost Parisian appearance', but he was more interested in the 'relics of old Mexico' in the museum and 'the mighty volcano of Popocatepetl, which the Aztecs feared and worshipped, towering to the skies'.[56] Preparations for their expedition were well under way at the Jebbs' house on Avenida Bucareli, one of the city's main thoroughfares. Here Haggard's premonition returned 'with terrible strength and persistence',[57] reinforced by one of the first objects he saw in the house, 'the ill-omened effigy of Huitzilopochtli', the Aztec god of war and human sacrifice, 'grinning a welcome across the patio'.[58]

On Sunday morning, 8 February 1891, the two couples were getting ready to go to church when 'Mrs. Jebb called us to their bedroom. She had a paper in her hand.

'Something is wrong with one of your children,' she said brokenly. 'Which?' I asked, aware that this meant death, no less, and waited. 'Jock,' was the reply, and the dreadful telegram, our first intimation of his illness, was read. It said that he had 'passed away peacefully' some few hours before. There were no details or explanations.

Then in truth I descended into hell. Of the suffering of the poor mother I will not speak. They belong to her alone.

I can see the room now. Jebb weeping by the unmade bed, the used basins – all, all. And in the midst of it myself – with a broken heart![59]

Louie 'said little, but spent hour after hour pacing up and down the wide flat roof'. Bertha Jebb, 'listening to the restless beat above her head, many times wished that her husband had never had the idea of this most unlucky visit'.[60]

Haggard sent instructions by telegram to the family in England and wrote a letter to his father:

We have within the last two hours received the awful news of the death of our most beloved son & and I have telegraphed to you asking you to represent me at his funeral as you will readily understand that my dear wife & myself are utterly overwhelmed & can only say one thing 'God's will be done' –

The boy has gone hence before sin and sorrow have touched him leaving us to mourn his memory & to hope for reunion with him in God's own time. So it is – so it must be. With our feelings in this distant place unable even to stand at his grave side, you & all our kin will readily sympathise ... for alas we cannot arrive in time to be of any service. I have given directions that he should be buried near the chancel door at Ditchingham where I hope to be at his side one day.[61]

The letter written, Haggard picked up a Bible and 'opened it at hazard. The words that my eyes fell on were "Suffer little children to come unto me, and forbid them not". The strange chance seemed to cheer me a little.' In the afternoon he went for a walk along the Avenida Bucareli. 'Never shall I forget that walk among the gay and fashionable Mexicans. I did not know till then what a man can endure and live.'[62]

According to Haggard, writing in 1911, Jock 'died suddenly of a perforating ulcer after an attack of measles'.[63] Jock had thrived at the Gosses, skating on the Round Pond in Hyde Park, visiting the London aquarium, enjoying a lively children's party at the Fulham home of the Pre-Raphaelite artist William Holman Hunt, followed by a boisterous return journey on the train. High-spirited outings ended on 16 January, when all the children came down with measles. According to Gosse, it was Jock who 'brought germs of the measles with him and he and our two youngest verily developed the disease ... but we have got through it and are all fumigated now and out of this little state of quarantine'.[64] Jock and Gosse's daughter Sylvia shared their quarantine, kneeling at 'the nursery window-sill' and watching 'dangerous boys poling themselves about on rafts of canal ice'.[65] Everything was under control with 'carbolic baths and different pleasant entertainments of a similar kind'.[66]

All seemed to be well, the measles gone, and then, suddenly, Jock was dead. What happened? According to Jock's death certificate, he died of 'peritonitis following a "perforating gastric ulcer'". Gosse's biographer Ann Thwaite puts forward another cause of death, pointing out that a perforated ulcer is not 'a possible complication of measles and gastric ulcers are extremely rare in small boys',[67] and suggesting instead that Jock's death could have resulted from swallowing 'some of that carbolic bath. Carbolic is a corrosive poison; the effect on the peritoneum would be similar. It is an appalling thought. One hopes it never occurred to Rider Haggard.'[68]

Victoria Manthorpe tells a more complex story. The previous year Jock had been seriously ill on two occasions. Typhoid was suspected but not diagnosed. When Jock arrived at the Gosses', he was carrying the measles virus. 'But the measles took the attention away from other symptoms.'[69] At the time Rider and Louie arrived in Mexico City, Jock had moved from the Gosses, to the Barrington Footes, in Kensington and, according to Alice Haggard, Alfred's wife, Jock was ill with typhoid fever. Lucy Hartcup, Louie's cousin, and Mr Hildyard were called but did not arrive in time. According to Lucy Hartcup, the 'peritonitis had nothing to do with the measles of which the child was practically recovered' nor had Jock had 'typhoid, which always leaves traces behind'; he had suffered from pleurisy and the post-mortem found an 'adhesion of one lung'. Hartcup goes on to say that the gastric ulcer was 'utterly unaccountable as to cause', being 'almost unknown in a child'.[70] Ann Thwaite's conclusion about the cause of Jock's death looks to be correct.

In Mexico the treasure hunt was called off. Haggard's 'nerves broke down entirely, and the rest of the Mexican visit, with its rough journeyings, is to me a kind of nightmare'.[71] To 'try and occupy our minds', Haggard and Louie travelled to a silver mine in which Jebb had an interest near Pinal de Amoles in the Sierra Gorda, over 90 miles north of Mexico City. 'It was a spot of extraordinary loveliness, with its deep valleys and pine-clad heights, but the journey there on horseback was very rough.'[72] They arrived at Pinal de Amoles on a Saturday, 'the night on which the peons get drunk on *mescal* and *agua ardiente* and fight over gambling and women. On the Sunday morning I walked down the street of the village, where I saw two men lying dead with blankets thrown over them. A third, literally hacked to pieces by *machetes*, was seated in a collapsed condition in a doorway, while the village barber tried to sew up his hideous wounds.'[73]

At Santiago de Querétaro, capital of Querétaro province, Haggard felt so ill he thought he was about to die, but an American doctor travelling in the area 'told me that I was suffering from nothing except shock to the nerves'.[74] The diagnosis didn't deter Haggard from being 'taken up a hill and shown the wall against which the unhappy Emperor Maximilian had been butchered some five-and-twenty years before'.[75]

Back in Mexico City, Haggard and Jebb decided to visit the state of Chiapas in south-west Mexico where Jebb had interests in another mine in which, to his 'sorrow', Haggard also had shares. They arranged to meet their wives on the New York-bound streamer during its stopover at the port of Frontera and return to England via the

United States. 'Of course it miscarried ... the whole expedition was of a somewhat crack-brained order, but at the time I cared little what I did.'[76]

From Frontera they travelled into the interior. Haggard and Jebb narrowly escaped being murdered, thanks to having 'in our charge a mule-load of silver of the value of three thousand dollars, which we were conveying to a mine whither went more bullion than ever came out of it'.[77] Local bandits heard about the silver and at night attacked the house where Haggard and Jebb were staying, but gave up after several attempts, being thwarted by the 'furious barking of the dogs belonging to the house' alerting those within.[78]

They continued their 'fearful journey' across plains, mountains, precipices, slides down muddy tracks, falls in flooded rivers and quivering rope bridges, until they arrived at the mine run by an Englishman whose home was plagued with tarantulas. While Jebb was busy at the mine, Haggard botanised in the valley, 'collecting plants and ferns'. Venomous snakes made it necessary 'to be very careful in gathering these floral treasures', but with 'much difficulty I succeeded in bringing a sack load of roots to England, and in the greenhouses here still survive some of the plants I collected in Mexico'.[79]

Back once more in Frontera, travel arrangements went awry because of a corrupt shipping agent, and the two were only finally reunited with their wives in New York before sailing to Liverpool. Haggard came down with influenza during the voyage. After staying a night in London, 'we came to Ditchingham, where I found my two little girls dressed in black and – a grave'.[80]

And silence. The name of the dead child must never be spoken, a 'super-taboo' according to Haggard's nephew Godfrey Cheyne.[81]

> Rider had a dynastic sense. To leave a son, and lands for him to inherit, to perpetuate his name; these were strong prepossessions with him. They were disappointed. Jock was dead and so he must not be mentioned. To come on a book or a toy that once had belonged to my young cousin (whom I never knew) was to strike a hush over the room such as might almost have been observed towards a relative who had been hanged for murder. There was a guilty silence. Jock haunted the house more obtrusively because everyone there pretended they could not see him, and the poor schoolboy wraith seemed to be begging piteously for some notice, so that at last he might be laid to rest.[82]

A 'guilty silence'. Was the guilt Haggard's? Cheyne thought so, citing the 'undeniable note of sadness' running through his uncle's autobiography,

> not only for the ills of the world but also it would seem for some personal sorrow of his own. He speaks more than once of remorse. If he had reasons for remorse he would not be the kind of man to let himself forget it, though he would be the last to disclose what they were. It is only my guess, arrived at by putting one fact with another, that he attached this feeling of contrition for something which had happened in the past.[83]

That 'something' can now be identified with a fair degree of certainty: Haggard's 'utterly reckless' behaviour in Pretoria, his affair with Johanna Ford, and their dead child, Ethel Rider.[84] According to Lilias, multiplying her father's sense of loss was 'undoubtedly the psychological obsession that [Jock's] life had paid the price of the father's sin; that it was required in expiation of transgression, and being so required increased his guilt. That belief (to judge from chance remarks and pencilled passages in his well-worn Bible) he carried with him, an unhealed wound, until the day of his death.'[85]

Louie also kept her silence. She never spoke of those weeks in Mexico, nor did she 'give any indication of what she must have suffered – it was not her way. She had an iron self-control ... a control so rigid that all her life those who were nearest to her seldom knew what her thoughts or feelings were.'[86] The silence was broken once by Haggard, when writing his autobiography, knowing what he wrote would only be read after his death:

> This morning, not an hour since, I stood by my son's grave and read what I had carved upon his cross: 'I shall go to him.' Now that I am growing old these words are full of comfort and meaning to me. Soon, after all these long years of separation, I shall go to him and put my faith to proof. If it be true, as I believe, then surely my spirit will find his spirit, though it must search from world to world. If, with all earth's suffering millions, I am deluded, then let the same everlasting darkness be our bed and canopy.[87]

19

'OCEANS OF GORE'

In the summer of 1891 Haggard's health collapsed. 'Everything, especially my indigestion, went wrong, so wrong that I began to think that my bones would never grow old.'[1] His mind 'reacting upon his body, brought him to a state when he developed bout after bout of influenza, with its aftermath of digestive disturbances, violent headaches and acute mental depression'.[2]

Despite diminished physical and mental resources, Haggard generated sufficient energy to write *Montezuma's Daughter*, working through the summer and signing off the manuscript on 3 September. Drawing on the trip to Mexico, the Spanish conquest and the events of 'Noche Triste' in 1520, the story begins at Ditchingham where the Wingfield family live at Ditchingham Lodge, a real building on the Ditchingham estate below the Vineyard Hills – the Wingfields occupy the original Tudor dwelling prior to the addition of a three-storey Queen Anne frontage. When young Thomas Wingfield's Spanish mother is murdered by her cousin Juan de Garcia, Thomas pursues him to Spain bent on revenge, bidding farewell to his betrothed, Lily Bozard. In Seville he becomes the assistant to Andres de Fonseca, doctor and confidant to the city's elite, and though Wingfield and Garcia cross paths, matters are not brought to a conclusion and Wingfield follows Garcia to Mexico. There Wingfield is captured by the Aztecs, but after saving the life of Guatemoc, cousin of the Aztec ruler Montezuma, he marries Otomie, Montezuma's daughter, with whom he has five children, one of whom is a beloved son. After twenty years in Mexico, Wingfield is caught up in the events of the Spanish conquest; his children are murdered by Garcia and Otomie commits suicide. Wingfield finally brings Garcia to bay and, after exacting his revenge, returns to England and marries Lily. In his old age, after the defeat of the Spanish Armada in 1588, when 'England breathes again',[3] Wingfield writes his life story.

Faithful to the historical record, *Montezuma's Daughter* is inevitably a doom-laden, violent tale. Haggard chronicles the near-endless slaughter, interspersed with scenes of torture and human sacrifice, with a nihilistic fatalism. The repetitive violence and long passages of faux antique speech plunge the book into a gloom only relieved by a gripping climax – a breathless chase up the slopes of the Popocatepetl, culminating in a sword fight on the rim of the fiery crater. The pervading sense of depression did not go unnoticed: *Montezuma's Daughter* 'lacks a spirit which was there before', says Lilias, 'for with the death of Jock some virtue went out of his father never to return. Some spring within him was broken, he had lost his pleasure in writing romances. In his child's grave he buried his youth and much of his ambition.'[4] The tone of *Montezuma's Daughter* reflects Haggard's state of mind as he processed his grief into his writing: 'In this tale the teller loses his children, and I put into his mouth what myself I felt.'[5] Here are the words:

> Ah! we think much of the sorrows of our youth, and should a sweetheart give us the go-by, we fill the world with moans and swear that it holds no comfort for us. But when we bend our heads before the shrouded shape of some lost child, then it is that for the first time we learn how terrible grief can be ... There is no hope but faith, there is no comfort save in the truth that love which might have withered on the earth grows fastest in the tomb, to flower gloriously in heaven; that no love indeed can be perfect till God sanctifies and completes it with His seal of death.[6]

Two decades on, when writing his autobiography, there was no improving on these words: 'they are as true to me now as they were then'.[7]

Other autobiographical aspects of the story would not have been lost on his immediate family. Lily Bozard, Thomas Wingfield's betrothed, was named after Louie's cousin Lily Hildyard, but her first name cannot fail to conjure up Haggard's first love, especially given the arc of the story: the hero leaves his first love, Lily, and goes to South America (life on earth) where he falls in love, marries and has a family. They die, he comes back to England (life hereafter) and is reunited with Lily. Of their initial parting Wingfield writes: 'Can any bitterness equal the bitterness of such good-byes? ... It is a common jest to mock at early love, but if it be real, if it be something more than the mere arising of the passions, early love is late love also; it is love for ever, the best and worst event which can befall a man or woman.'[8]

Even with history as justification, the unrelenting violence in *Montezuma's Daughter* drew fire. While not objecting to bloodshed in romance per se, the *New York Times* critic took exception to *Montezuma's Daughter*, considering it to be coloured crimson throughout – 'oceans of gore are distasteful and Mr. Haggard revels in that kind of inundation'.[9] It wasn't gore but Haggard's depiction of the immuring of a nun that raised the ire of Roman Catholics. James Britten, honorary secretary of the Catholic Truth Society, complained to the *Graphic* regarding Haggard's 'extremely offensive and untrue assertions with regard to the immuring of nuns and the general management of convents'.[10] Despite Haggard taking a conciliatory approach, this sparked a correspondence, which was later transferred to the *Pall Mall Gazette*, between Haggard, Britten, the Jesuit Catholic apologist Herbert

Thurston and others offering proofs and counter-proofs of the phenomenon until the correspondence was terminated by the editor.

At the time of the *Gazette* correspondence, Haggard was working on another Mexican adventure, *The Heart of the World*, which he was contracted to write for serialisation in *Pearson's Weekly* prior to book publication by Longmans. Alarmed at the nun controversy, Charles Pearson wrote to Haggard requesting that his story not contain anything offensive to readers. Haggard reassured him that the story was set in more recent times and he had been 'careful to avoid anything which could possibly give offence to the most susceptible of readers, not altogether an easy task, for strange people have strange manners'.[11]

As well as returning to his pen, Haggard began taking an active interest in local affairs. He became the first chairman of the Ditchingham Parish Council and was elected chairman of the local bench of magistrates, an office which he filled until his death. As a Justice of the Peace, his duties included 'the licensing of public houses, the registering of lunatics, enforcing affiliation orders, coping with petty crime, and the enforcement of school attendance'.[12]

Haggard's retreat from the hurly-burly of literary London did not go unnoticed. The journalist Harry How came to interview Haggard at Ditchingham in December 1891. How was well known for his illustrated interviews with personalities of the day run in the *Strand* magazine. How dubbed Ditchingham 'a distinctly cosy Norfolk village, small and picturesque',[13] a rural refuge in which lived 'Mr. Rider Haggard, barrister, justice of the peace, farmer and novelist', at 35 'tall, somewhat slim, and wears a fair moustache'.[14]

How arrived in the late afternoon at Ditchingham House and spent the evening dining with Haggard. 'There is positively little about Mr. Haggard – whom, perhaps, one might describe as a country gentleman by profession and a novelist by accident – suggestive of the literary man. Literature! We talked of gardening and flowers over the dinner table.' After dinner Haggard showed How around the house, where 'every nook and corner' bore evidence of his travels. There were artefacts from South Africa, Egypt, Iceland and Mexico as well as curios and objets d'art contributed by brothers and friends. Portraits of 'Norfolk worthies' alternated with hunting trophies, including a huge bull buffalo's head shot by Frederick Jackson. In the billiard room at the top of the house, an oil painting of Louie by the portraitist Charles Kerr hung alongside Maurice Greiffenhagen's original drawings for *The World's Desire* – his illustrations from *She* were downstairs – and in a niche of the billiard room stood the desk of Charles Dickens 'bought at the Gad's Hill sale' in 1870.[15]

Haggard's study was 'a perfect treasure-house of curios' presided over by Jack, a tame rat 'liberally supplied with nuts, which he readily cracks'.[16] Here was the gun cupboard, constructed to Haggard's design, and propped in a corner his collection of fishing rods. In a bowl on the mantelpiece were items 'picked up on the battlefield of Isandlwana'.[17] Photographs upon the walls included a print of

Henri Gros's photograph of Shepstone and his band of brothers on the day of the annexation of the Transvaal. Shelves were laden with books and manuscripts; one was filled with American pirated editions. 'No author has suffered more than he in this respect.'[18]

The following morning How and Haggard walked 'through the meadows and newly-planted orchards round the farm', Haggard wearing an 'easy knickerbocker suit' and carrying 'a long Zulu stick surmounted with a huge knob', the knobkerrie given to him by Masuku.[19] Two years' work on the farm had 'worked wonders with the land since Mr. Haggard took it "in hand"'. After cutting some roses and waving 'a good-bye to Angela and Dorothy, his two little daughters ... just off for a ride', the two men entered the house 'delightfully fresh and ready for work after our morning's walk'.[20]

They sat in Haggard's study smoking their pipes while How gathered the material for his profile and was shown the map made by Aggie Barber for *King Solomon's Mines* – 'the original sherd of *She* is over the mantelpiece'.[21] Haggard thought *She* his second best work after *Eric Brighteyes*. 'Amongst his own characters his love leans towards Beatrice.'[22]

Haggard outlined his working regimen: writing 'some three or four thousand words a day, sitting down at a great oaken writing table, with a liberal supply of foolscap paper, about half-past four, working on till dinner-time, and again resuming the thread of his story at night for an hour or two'. The mornings were devoted to the farm and correspondence.

Haggard gave a similar description of his routine to the journalist Frederick Dolman, who also gave a glimpse into Haggard's home life: 'Every morning before breakfast the whole household assembles in the hall for family prayers. Mrs. Haggard and her two little girls, the half-dozen servants and any visitors who may be staying in the house, take their seats in the high-backed chairs, while Mr. Haggard reads a chapter from the old family Bible which always stands on a large table, and afterwards offers a short prayer.'[23]

In the spring of 1892 Louie became pregnant. 'Under the circumstances this might have been welcome and indeed was to Rider, but unfortunately Louie, anyhow at first resented it greatly', wrote Lilias, with whom Louie was pregnant.[24] Her mother was never

> a maternal woman, she had long considered her family complete, and had no desire to start all over again with a nursery. Also there is no doubt she suffered much from Rider's violent grief at the death of his son. Not that she did not always sorrow for Jock, but to allow that sorrow to disrupt the whole course of a successful career, to lose his friends, his health, and his peace of mind struck her as unnecessary, if not wrong. She had done her best to comfort him, but when he persistently turned away from

all the things they had enjoyed together, she, who was still young, went her own way with her many friends.[25]

Grief left a deep impress on Haggard's character. Before the death of Jock he had 'been as careless of risks' as his wife, 'would ride anything, and go anywhere if it offered variety, change or adventure'. Now he was neurotic and 'apprehensive, not so much for himself as for others – and particularly his children'. He became obsessive about their safety, whether boating, riding or swimming, and if they became sick it 'threw him into a frenzy of anxiety'. His behaviour irritated Louie 'almost beyond endurance, inducing an apparent indifference towards their welfare which was far from being the fact, but which Rider, in his super-sensitive and overwrought state, took bitterly to heart'.[26]

With a new life in the offing, Haggard's spirits began to lift and in July 1892, possibly on the advice of his doctor, Bertram Herbert Lyne-Stivens – and much to the relief of Louie – he travelled to the German spa town of Bad Homburg vor der Höhe, accompanied by his sister Ella Maddison Green and her husband the Reverend Charles, renting rooms at 20 Ferdinand Strasse. Bad Homburg, with its mineral baths and casino, sprang to prominence in 1888 when Kaiser Wilhelm II proclaimed the town's schloss an imperial summer residence, and by the time of Haggard's visit the town rivalled Marienbad in popularity as a health spa for English visitors.

Quite coincidentally, several of Haggard's acquaintances were taking the waters, including Sir Henry Bulwer, who had retired from the Colonial Service earlier in the year. The widow of George Pomeroy Colley was showing off her new husband, the businessman, mine owner and politician Wentworth Beaumont (later First Baron Allendale), who married Lady Colley in 1891. Oscar Wilde was in search of solace – 'Oscar has been unbosoming his grievances about [*Salomé*],' Haggard told Louie.[27] The play had been banned three weeks into rehearsals (Sarah Bernhardt was the lead) when the Lord Chamberlain's licenser of plays, Edward Smyth Pigott, troubled by the risqué material, took advantage of an antique law that 'forbade the depiction of Biblical characters'.[28]

Wilde was 'so cast down by the censorship that he thought he must take a rest cure',[29] and so went to Bad Homburg with his lover Lord Alfred Douglas, the first public display of a relationship that would lead to Wilde's downfall.[30] Wilde was placed 'under a regime, getting up at 7.30, going to bed at 10.30, smoking hardly any cigarettes and being massaged, and of course drinking waters'.[31] Haggard was under a similar discipline: 'The great thing the doctors here say is to give up all wine & spirits except some claret and an occasional glass of Marsala.'[32] To augment their glasses of fortified wine, Haggard and the Greens had the occasional mud bath and attended a performance of Richard Wagner's *Tannhäuser*. Charles took a service at the English church and 'preached a most excellent sermon' to the 'large & fashionable congregation'.[33]

Haggard and Bulwer met several times, on one occasion going for a walk. 'He is a most amusing & regular old maid! ... My liver interests him deeply, also my method of treating it. "What," he will say, stopping suddenly. "You mean to say you took *that*. It is madness, positive madness." He has quite won Ella's heart by his politeness ... There is no doubt he is a very charming man, & most kind hearted. I think I like him better than I ever did.'[34]

Haggard saw the Empress Dowager Frederick from a distance at a Sunday church service – 'I really must go & call but I love not royalties'.[35] This is a strange comment given his fawning correspondence with the Empress over the dedication of *Eric Brighteyes*. Haggard dutifully left his card and was invited to lunch – 'I had a long and interesting conversation with her ... She impressed me as a singularly charming and able lady.'[36]

Haggard thought the visit to Bad Homburg had done him 'good on the whole but my digestion & internals have been so seriously deranged by influenza that I fancy they will take a long while to get straight'. After two weeks at the spa he was ready to leave and 'shall be glad to do so for I am thoroughly sick of the place and its endless parade of fashionable people'.[37]

In the early hours of 9 December, the same date on which Haggard's mother had died three years before, Louie gave birth: 'unfortunately Providence made a mistake in the sex', writes Lilias of her own arrival, 'to the dismay of [Haggard's] entire family (who hastily sat down and wrote letters of condolence instead of congratulation) the baby was a girl'.[38] Haggard wrote to his father the same day with news of Lilias's birth: 'It would have been better had it been a boy but we must take what it pleases Providence to send us.'[39] To Aggie he wrote, 'the event has come off resulting in a girl – as a boy happened to be wanted. However she is a dear little baby & seems to be healthy & well developed which is a great thing – so it would be ungrateful to grumble. Indeed I am so fond of children that I would much rather have a girl than nothing at all.'[40] In gratitude to Lily Hildyard's 'sympathetic company' before and after the birth, the baby was named Lilias: another echo of that familiar name.

Following the birth of his third daughter, Haggard's 'health began to improve', thanks in great part to Dr Lyne-Stivens's 'painstaking treatment and great understanding and sympathy'.[41]

Apart from tying up a few literary loose ends and signing contracts for further titles, Haggard attempted nothing new during 1892. 'I wearied of fiction and longed for the life of action to which I had been bred and that, indeed, is native to my character. In truth, the dislike and revolt of my heart in those days still haunts me as a kind of nightmare.' In a dream at this time Haggard found himself guided through a fantastical landscape to an ancient city above 'a Nile-like river' presided 'over by golden guardian figures' and was shown a younger version of himself 'bending over the desk at work, with papers spread before me'. At this sight he was seized by 'terror

... lest this fair place should be but a scented purgatory where, in payment for my sins, I am *doomed to write fiction for ever and a day!*[42]

Haggard would continue to write, but writing would become subservient to a larger vision, one closer to the 'life of action' he yearned for, the nature of which would gradually become apparent over the next five years. First came a change to his working regimen. 'I could no longer endure the continual stooping over a desk which is involved in the writing of books.'[43] Haggard employed a secretary to take dictation, at first employing several on a part-time basis before settling on Ida Hector. Ida was not a writer – 'I once tried to write a novel and miserably failed'[44] – but she was no stranger to literary circles. Her mother was Annie Hector, better known to the public as best-selling novelist 'Mrs Alexander', a pseudonym consisting of the first name of her husband, the explorer and archaeologist Alexander Hector, which she began using after his death in 1875.

Ida, the eldest of four daughters, was born in 1860 and educated at a school in Forest Hill, London, and at a boarding school in Boston, Lincolnshire. When her mother and sisters moved to Paris for 'three or four years Ida received lessons in painting and music', after which the family moved on to Dresden, the capital of Saxony and a cultural hub which attracted a large English population. Ida was considered an excellent translator from French, especially of the writings of the novelist Alphonse Daudet. An accomplished watercolourist, Ida was also 'fond of all outdoor sports in which her sex is permitted to share', never missing 'an opportunity to riding to hounds', and being a keen tennis player.[45]

At the time of her employment by Haggard, the 'tall and graceful' 34-year-old Ida Hector was living in 'her comfortable and luxurious home in Portsdown Road' in Maida Vale,[46] where she enjoyed 'a well-chosen circle of friends'. At the centre of this circle was the top-ranked novelist Eliza Lynn Linton, who had taken Ida's mother under her wing when she first came to London in the 1850s. It was Ida's 'pleasant duty every Saturday afternoon, during the season, to go to Mrs Linton's flat at Queen Anne's Gate in Westminster to "pour tea" at the famous writer's "at homes".'[47]

Ida Hector slipped easily into the Haggard family circle – being a 'good horsewoman' helped – and 'became a lifelong friend of the family'.[48] Haggard called her '"Wisdom's Second Daughter" (Wisdom's first being Ayesha)'.[49] As well as acting as his secretary, Ida, or 'Miss Hector' as the family referred to her, became a 'very faithful friend and companion' to Haggard, 'to whose sound sense and literary judgment' he declared himself 'much indebted'.[50] Miss Hector thought Haggard 'a lonely man' and often helped to break the ice between him and younger generations of the family.[51]

Miss Hector's first task on taking up her duties 'was to purchase a typewriter, and learn to type, in order to get the work done'.[52] Henceforward Haggard did a 'great deal of my work by means of dictation, which has greatly relieved its labour'.[53] Once Miss Hector had taken Haggard's dictation, either for correspondence or a book in progress, she produced a typescript which Haggard proofed and corrected. Their first published 'collaboration' was probably the article commissioned by the *Idler* for the series 'My First Book' at the beginning of 1892. This was followed by the first novel Haggard dictated, *The People of the Mist*.[54] Miss Hector also took dictation for the revisions to *Montezuma's Daughter* for its book publication while Haggard cuddled his new-born daughter.

> He worked mostly in the evenings – his wife's room was next door to his study, and if the baby was fretful she was handed over to her father to keep quiet. Up and down he walked, dictating as he went. The child on his shoulder, her round blue eyes wandering now to the shadow of the copper lamp which glowed like a flower on the ceiling; now to the green chalcedony head of the Aztec god on the wall with gaping mouth and eyes, in which jewels had flashed in the days of Montezuma. Below it hung the sacrificial bowl carved with strange symbols, stained with the blood of human hearts offered upon the altars of the gods.[55]

Montezuma's Daughter, the 'last manuscript Haggard wrote in his own hand',[56] was dedicated to John Gladwyn Jebb, and in the dedication Haggard refers to Jebb owning an 'ancient horror, the veritable and sleepless God of sacrifice, of whom I would not rob you'.[57] There was good reason why. The 'ancient horror' was a statue of Huitzilopochtli, the Aztec god of war, the statue Haggard had first seen at the Jebbs' house in Mexico City; 'its head was sunk almost between the shoulders, while I can only describe the face as devilish'.[58] Following his acquisition of this gruesome artefact, Jebb's life fell apart: 'His health broke, companies with which he was connected collapsed, mines proved unpayable.' Faced with these and other 'catastrophes', Jebb brought the 'peculiar treasure' to London, where it took up residence at 24 Redcliffe Square. Thereafter the house became subjected 'to every sort of unpleasant manifestation ... knockings and crashings, twitching of bedclothes, footsteps, mysterious cold winds'.[59] The Jebbs didn't seem to mind, and a sceptical Louie was happy to visit. She 'stuck it out' for two nights, but on the third 'the horror and terror, the sense of unmitigated evil that descended on her, was so frightful that she lay amid an ever-increasing racket of knocks and bangs absolutely unable to move, until all the clothes were torn off her bed' and she fled to the Jebbs' bedroom, where she spent the rest of the night.[60]

The Jebbs 'decided the idol must go'. A 'hard-headed American friend said he would like to have it, and the little god lived in a city office'. There it 'brought no luck with it, and it was finally given to the British Museum, where the history of this relic of the most bloody ritual came to an end'.[61]

Not so Jebb's history of bad luck. Another business venture collapsed and, finding it hard to live 'in an atmosphere of gloom and London fog and financial strain', he risked everything on a new Mexican mining scheme 'which was to make the whole family's fortune'.[62] Jebb, his wife and their young son headed back to Mexico, but all came to naught and Jebb's health gave out. The family returned to Redcliffe Square, where Jebb died on 18 March 1893.[63]

Another death followed: that of Haggard's father. In a bid to ward off the loneliness he experienced after the death of his wife in 1889, William Haggard hopped from one group of relatives to another while also 'engaging in love affairs which were a strain on his health'.[64] In 1892 he withdrew to Bradenham Hall where he lived 'the life of a recluse', according to his son Alfred, going nowhere and with few visitors; 'the place looks rather neglected ... my father moons about, in a disconsolate way and sees nothing'.[65] When William Haggard came down with jaundice in September, Rider went to see him. 'His appearance shocked me very much – brilliant yellow and much shrunken. His mind however is quite clear but at *the best* it is a complete break up *I should say* though I don't think *this* attack will kill him.'[66]

An 'extraordinary recovery' in November was but a temporary postponement of the inevitable.[67] William Haggard died the following spring as 'the result of a chill which he caught in waiting about for the poll to be declared at an election in cold weather'.[68] The 'doctor stupidly neglected to warn us that the end was near',[69] and consequently no family member was at his bedside on the morning of 21 April 1893 when he died. Haggard got to Bradenham Hall the following day. On a letterhead the nurse had recorded the time of his father's death – 9.50 am – and his last words: 'If I am to get better God will be with me if I die He will also be with me. God is always present is he not?'[70] The ageing servant Elizabeth Hocking had been present at the bedside and William Haggard told her to give his son 'his watch and chain, which I think had been his father's before him. I have it now, still marking the hour at which it ran down under his pillow on that night.'[71]

The administrative power of the English squirearchy had been removed by the Local Government Act of 1888, which allowed for the establishment of elected county councils; and so the last of the squires of Bradenham, William Haggard, was laid to rest beside his wife Ella in the churchyard at St Andrew's in sight of Bradenham Hall.

The same year of 1893 saw the publication of *A Strange Career: The Life and Adventures of John Gladwyn Jebb by His Widow*. Haggard paid tribute to his friend in the introduction: 'He was not suited to the life that fell to his lot, at least not to the commercial side of it, for an adventurer – using the term in its best sense – he must always have been. He was too sanguine, too romantic, too easily deluded by others and too mystical – a curious vein of mysticism was one of his most striking characteristics – for this nineteenth century.'[72] Haggard could almost be describing himself.

20

'SPECULATIVE AND NERVE-RACKING'

Haggard's 'health and spirits began to mend and my energy to return'. A renewed interest in life saw him looking beyond the boundaries of the Ditchingham estate. At 36 and 'still a youngish man', he longed 'to make a change, for this humdrum existence in a country parish, staring at crops and cultivating flowers, was, I felt, more suitable to some aged man whose life's work was done than to myself'. Wearied by the 'unrealities of fiction-writing'[1] and ready to embark in a new direction, Haggard found physical expression for his sense of renewal as well: his fair moustache blossomed into a full beard carefully groomed to a point, endearingly avuncular, impressively aristocratic, appropriate to the patrician-like mien he cultivated from this time forward.[2]

Writing was not abandoned. After its serialisation in *Titbits*, the first novel Haggard dictated to Ida Hector, *The People of the Mist*, was published on 15 October 1894. Describing it as a 'barefaced and flagrant adventure', he dedicated it to two of his godsons in the hope 'that therein they may find some story of healthy amusement'.[3] *The People of the Mist* sees the disinherited Leonard Outram head for Africa with his brother Thomas, placing their faith in the family motto *Per ardua ad astra* – 'through adversity to the stars' – that they will make their fortunes and regain the Outram estate. All the ingredients are in place for a rousing adventure, a perfectly assembled machine, but the vital spark required to get everything moving is missing. As Lilias remarks, some 'spring within him was broken'.[4]

Haggard described *The People of the Mist* as an 'effort of the "primeval and troglodyte imagination"', and much of the adventure takes place in the caves and underground chambers of the mountain kingdom of the People of the Mist.[5] The overall tone and its febrile atmosphere of barely suppressed sex – '"let men see what they are going to buy," and gripping the breast of her white robe he rent it open'[6] – along with graphic descriptions of bondage, slavery and violence somewhat undercut Haggard's claim that the adventure was a 'healthy amusement' for his godsons. Did Haggard really not know what he was writing or, rather, dictating? And Miss Hector?[7]

The People of the Mist has one notable claim to fame: the Outram family motto became that of the Royal Air Force. When the Royal Flying Corps was formed in 1912, its first commanding officer, Frederick Sykes, asked for suggestions for an inspirational motto. A young officer, J.S. Yule, who had recently read *The People of the Mist* proposed 'Per ardua ad astra'. This was passed up the chain of command and, having received the royal assent, was retained by the Royal Air Force on its formation in 1918.[8]

With an eye to the wider world, in the autumn of 1893 Haggard wrote two letters to *The Times* on the topic of King Lobengula, then a figure of great public interest due to the First Ndebele War. He also penned an article on the war for the *Pall Mall Gazette* and was interviewed by the *East Anglian Daily Press* on the origins of the conflict. This increased public profile together with his activities as a parish councillor and local magistrate resulted in Haggard being approached to stand for the safe Conservative parliamentary seat at King's Lynn. He reluctantly declined 'because of the expense and the difficulty of getting backwards and forwards between my home and the borough, since this was before the day of motors'.[9]

Haggard's letters in *The Times* caught the attention of Cecil Rhodes and his cohorts, and led to Haggard being invited by William Arthur Wills to become a co-director in the company publishing the *African Review* – 'the most trustworthy Journal for Investors, and all those interested in the South African Industries'.[10] The weekly publication, co-owned by Wills and Cameron Corlett Cannell,[11] was the London propaganda arm of Rhodes's empire-building project. Haggard, a name synonymous with Africa in the public mind, would be a good man to have onside. Implicit in the agreement was the understanding that Haggard would stand for parliament 'with the general idea of giving my attention to African affairs in the House of Commons'.[12]

From a lowly speculator in the early days of the Kimberley diamond fields, Cecil Rhodes was now the dominant player. The creation of De Beers Consolidated Mines in 1888 gave him a monopoly interest in the diamond industry and he extended his mineral interests to the goldfields of the Witwatersrand when a gold-bearing reef was discovered there in 1886. By the mid-1890s Consolidated Gold Fields of South Africa was paying dividends of 125 per cent to shareholders.[13] Entry into politics was the next logical step, and in 1890 Rhodes became prime minister of the Cape Colony.

Rhodes' proprietorial appetite extended north beyond the Cape Colony, beyond the Limpopo even. To expand the frontiers of white settlement, he founded the British South Africa Company (BSAC) under a royal charter granted in October 1889 – a mutually convenient arrangement that extended British interests with Rhodes bearing the risk. Concessions granted in 1888 by King Lobengula gave the BSAC access to the territory now known as Zimbabwe. Access became invasion and Lobengula's power was broken in 1893.

Haggard had met Rhodes back in 1889, after being invited to meet him at the National Liberal Club on the Thames Embankment when Rhodes was in London smoothing the way for the BSAC. Rhodes 'impressed me a good deal'.[14] Haggard was blissfully unaware that Rhodes was taking his measure to discover where he stood with regard to his brother Alfred, then venturing into territory that Rhodes considered his personal preserve. Alfred had left the Indian Civil Service and returned to England, taking up the post of secretary of the London Hospital, which he resigned in 1888; and then applied to become governor to the King of Siam but was unsuccessful; 'impecunious and nearly forty, he turned his attention to Africa'.[15] In partnership with John Fellowes Wallop, second son of the Earl of Portsmouth, Alfred formed the Austral Africa Exploration Company to seek mining concessions in Matabeleland. Alfred offered his brother Rider the chance of participating and making a profitable investment. Haggard resisted his brother's blandishments and Alfred turned angry 'and I think has never quite forgiven me my backwardness'.[16]

Alfred had reckoned without Rhodes, whose confrères had tricked Lobengula into signing the Rudd–Maguire concession that gave the BSAC the right to a monopoly. Others seeking similar concessions were actively discouraged or bought off. Rhodes was alerted to Alfred's activities when the Austral Africa Exploration Company prospectus was published in Cape Town to coincide with the arrival there of Alfred and Wallop in September 1888. By the end of November they were at Tati in Matabeleland, where a letter from James Maguire, a BSAC stakeholder, ordered them to proceed no further; a force of Ndebele was sent to ensure compliance. Licking his wounds back in Cape Town, Alfred publicly cast aspersions on the Rudd–Maguire concession. Rhodes was unmoved, but he was wary of that other Haggard, H. Rider, fearing his pen might prove mightier than the sword. True to form, Rhodes bought off Alfred with shares in 'a newly minted shell called the Central Search Association, Ltd'.[17] They proved worthless. Alfred ruefully accepted he had been outmanoeuvred.

Whether at Rhodes's direction or not, bringing a well-known writer and commentator on board the *African Review* was an astute strategic move. The arrangement proposed that Haggard contribute articles and edit the literary section of the *African Review* and, together with Wills, 'exercise joint editorial control of the paper', which was advertised as 'conducted by H. Rider Haggard and W.A. Wills'.[18] In return Haggard would receive 500 £1 shares in the holding company, Wills and Cannell Ltd, 'of which he would become a director at the annual salary of three hundred pounds'.[19]

Mining and investment news was the staple content of the *African Review*, accompanied with a wide spread of articles on matters of African interest, including news, features, opinion pieces and profiles of 'African statesmen', among them Sir Hercules Robinson, John Merriman, Ismail Pasha and John Kotzé. A women's page titled 'The Boudoir' featured alternate contributions from 'May' in Paris and

'Martha' in London. A gentlemen's equivalent, 'The Smoking Room', was by-lined 'Chicot'.[20]

Haggard spent a hectic nine months working at the *African Review*'s offices at 10 Basinghall Street in the City of London. According to Lilias, her father and Wills were 'about as well matched as a nightingale and a cock sparrow in the same cage, and what wishful thought induced either of them to start upon a partnership cannot be conceived'.[21] Haggard's brothers were extremely critical of his violent career change, especially at a time when Bazett, Alfred and Andrew were struggling financially. Rider was the only one of his brothers to have achieved substantial success and a measure of stability; he was a financial anchor for his siblings. The family was completely thrown by this new venture and his eldest brother, Will, wrote to Rider expressing his feelings in no uncertain terms:

> It is the worst and most fatal feature in our family, one which has continually prevented our success, that we cannot stick to our professions. I thought that you were a brilliant exception, but it looks as if, just as you had conquered success, you were inclined for the second time in your life to chuck it and go in for a venture in which from the very best point of view you can never achieve an equal success as that which you have attained.[22]

Haggard's arrival at the *African Review* was described as 'an important event ... in the history of Anglo-African journalism'.[23] His acquisition of 'a large proprietary interest in the *African Review*' was a prelude to 'a number of important expansions and improvements', but readers needn't fear, for the 'past political tone of the paper' would be preserved and 'the maintenance of British supremacy in South Africa under all circumstances will continue to be a tenet of our faith'. And beyond South Africa too, in 'the hope that the search-light of civilisation will soon illumine the most barbarous recesses of the interior, and reveal the existence of industrial potentialities before which even the mines of the Cape and the Transvaal will stand in diminished splendour'.[24] The *African Review* was positioning itself 'as a sort of newspaper Agent-General for British Africa – be it North, South, East, or West'.[25]

In furtherance of this role was the parallel creation of the Anglo-African Writers Club under the banner of the *African Review*. The club included 'all the leading Anglo-African and South African journalists and *littérateurs* in London, as well as a sprinkling of well-known authors'. Haggard was elected honorary president. Among those present at the club's inaugural dinner was Will Haggard (about to leave for a new posting in Tunis, but doubtless keeping an eye on his errant brother); Frederick Jackson, about to take up a position as an official in the East Africa Protectorate; and his fellow East African colleague Frederick Lugard, former military administrator of Uganda and soon to be dispatched to West Africa by the Royal Niger Company, another commercial enterprise with a martial air created to extend British influence by securing treaties and concessions with indigenous peoples. Haggard and Lugard were the keynote speakers of the evening. Kipling, unable to attend owing to a previous engagement, promised to 'do his best to come later'.[26]

Items on the menu reflected the accomplishments of those present, for example 'Consommé Ayesha', 'Ris de Veau à la Kilimanjaro 'and 'Glacé à l'Umslopogaas'.[27] Dinner done, cigars lit, and port circulating clockwise, the club got down to business. Apologies were first on the agenda, among them from H.M. Stanley, who declined the honour of being an honorary vice president owing to 'the present exciting time in politics' (Gladstone had resigned in March) during which Stanley was 'wholly at the disposition' of his party, the Liberal Unionists.[28]

The club's chairman, James Smith of the *Cape Argus*, proposing a toast to Haggard, sketched the latter's career in South Africa, including his having been 'one of the two officers who hoisted the British flag over the Transvaal ... we are glad to have in him a staunch supporter of the policy of Cecil Rhodes – (cheers) – who has opened up to civilisation some of the regions in which the scene of not a few of the most tragic pages in Mr. Rider Haggard's writings is laid.'[29] In response Haggard said he had always tried to advance 'what I believe to be the true interest of Africa, the country that I love, with which my youth was connected, and of which I hope never to lose touch while I live'.[30] The discovery of gold in the Transvaal had seen the 'great city' of Johannesburg rise up on the veld, 'peopled by Englishmen and financed by English capital' though without a say in their government, 'but the vote will come, the vote must come, for though a sandbank may hold out the sea for an hour, a year, or a decade, at last the sea will find its level'.[31] Cometh the hour, cometh the man: Cecil Rhodes – 'if there is any man who in this generation can show a greater record, I do not know him'.[32]

Haggard claimed it was for the good not only of southern Africa but 'of the world at large, that Englishmen with English traditions, aspirations, and ideas should dominate in Africa'. He acknowledged this was 'rank Jingoism' but while 'I have a voice to speak, a pen to write, or any power wherewith I may hope to move the hearts of men, I mean to go on sinning, for me at least the English name is the most glorious name in history, and the English flag the most splendid that ever flew above the peoples of the earth'.[33]

Readers of the *African Review* became aware of Haggard's presence by his regular book reviews and occasional opinion pieces. On 5 May 1894 he expressed his views on Swaziland, 'the bride of England',[34] a phrase used by Tibati Nkambule, the Swazi Queen Regent, who was tenaciously fighting a rearguard action against the planned transference of Swaziland to the Transvaal. Haggard reworked the ideas expressed in his article 'The Fate of Swaziland': England's bride was being spurned by her spouse, and once again 'natives, whose interests seem to be guarded by many high sounding but empty and conflicting words, are in reality handed over to the power of white men who covet their country'.[35]

In November the *Review* recorded the arrival of a Swazi delegation in London to protest against the 'impending imposition of Boer administration without Swazi agreement'.[36] The interpreter and organiser of the delegation's arrangements in London was James Stuart, a civil servant from Natal fluent in isiZulu and Siswati. Stuart and Haggard did not meet on this occasion but would in time come to know each other well.

Haggard's book reviews included that of *Travels and Adventures in the Congo Free State and Its Big Game Shooting* by Bula N'Zau (pseudonym of Henry Bailey, meaning 'Elephant Smasher'), a book he read with regret, 'for soon the ancient mystery of Africa will have vanished, and no square mile of that vast continent will remain whereon the wandering Englishman has not "elephant smashed" and triumphantly passed unheard of perils'.[37] Another hunting book reviewed by Haggard was *Tales of a Nomad, or, Sport and Strife* by Charles Montague, featuring hunting expeditions in southern Africa, the final battle in the Pedi war, and sporting adventures in Borneo. The book was dedicated to Haggard 'in token of esteem and also of admiration for his genius'. Charles Montague was Haggard's old friend from Natal and the Transvaal, Charles Stewart, now turned author and using his first two names as a pseudonym. The same year Haggard and Stewart collaborated on an adventure set in Borneo titled 'The Star', either written by Stewart with assistance from Haggard or vice versa. The book, if it was even completed, was never published.[38]

In his review of Edward Sullivan's *Woman: The Predominant Partner*, Haggard addressed what he perceived as 'the real grievance of the British woman of to-day', an overabundance of men, making it impossible for every woman to find a husband and thus fulfil 'the natural mission of women to marry'. If this mission is thwarted, 'they become narrowed, live a half-life only, and suffer in health and body and of mind'.[39] Haggard suggests the civilised life had suppressed sexual desire by laying down 'stricter rules for the game, and, in consequence, too often the individual player must suffer and smile'. He had no remedy to offer other than the operations of time: 'How long will the dam of custom and training resist these pent-up waters of disappointment and empty loss?'[40] He foresees a time when women will conquer 'at the polls' and, as a 'political factor', occupy 'the place that her numbers will give her', but what then? 'Already in the press, in literature, in society appear signs and tokens of an uprising; and though, perhaps fortunately, we of this generation will not see it, all thinking men must wonder as to its ultimate course and direction ... That is one of the many problems of the twentieth century.'[41]

A more substantial offering was Haggard's contribution to *The Downfall of Lobengula: The Cause, History, and Effect of the Matabeli War* by William Wills and Leonard Collingridge and published by the *African Review*, which ran several extracts. The book was the BSAC's history of the war and included a chapter by Haggard, 'The Patterson Embassy to Lobengula'. Haggard drew a parallel with the fate of his friends Patterson and Sargeaunt when reviewing *Man Hunting in the*

Desert: Being a Narrative of the Palmer Search Expeditions, 1882–1883 by Alfred E. Haynes, Captain, Royal Engineers, with an introduction by Walter Besant. Edward Palmer led an ill-advised mission into the Sinai in 1882 to gain Arab agreement to the construction of the Suez Canal. He and his colleagues Captain William Gill and Flag-Lieutenant Harold Charrington were ambushed and murdered.[42]

Through the *African Review* Haggard met Frederick Burnham, a man 'more interesting than any of my heroes of romance'.[43] Five feet four inches tall and sporting the nickname 'He-who-sees-in-the-dark', Burnham was Allan Quatermain made flesh. A veteran scout of the American frontier wars, Burnham had been 'captivated' by Haggard's African romances and was an ardent follower of Rhodes's incursion into Matabeleland.[44] The chance to 'start over on a wild new frontier, the prospect of mineral wealth, and the opportunity to be part of a breathtaking plan to create a new country'[45] saw Burnham and his wife Blanche leave the United States for southern Africa. Here Burnham fought in the First Ndebele War of 1893 and scouted for Major Allan Wilson, who was given the job of capturing King Lobengula. When Wilson's patrol – the Shangani Patrol – was cut off and surrounded by thousands of Ndebele warriors, Wilson sent Burnham with two other scouts to get help, but Wilson and his men were killed in a last stand – a foundation story of Rhodesian white settler society.

Burnham's daughter Nada was born in May 1894, allegedly the first white child born in Bulawayo. She was named after the eponymous heroine of Haggard's novel, which Blanche was reading at the time. When Burnham came to London looking for investors in some Rhodesian mining ventures in late 1894, he naturally gravitated into the ambit of the *African Review*. He met Haggard in January 1895 and presented him with gold beads panned from a stream at Great Zimbabwe.[46] Burnham was not easily drawn, and Haggard was one of the few people to whom he 'imparted any information concerning his many adventures'.[47] Charles Longman offered Burnham 'a handsome sum' to write his autobiography, but despite Haggard's 'entreaties and offers of assistance' Burnham refused.[48]

In London, Burnham reconnected with Cecil Rhodes. They had met during the Ndebele war and 'liked each other from the start, partly because each recognised a fellow gambling dreamer'.[49] After listening to Burnham's sales pitch, Rhodes ceded him and his partners several mineral rights as well as the right to dig for antiquities, stipulating that 'all ancient ruins or buildings shall be preserved intact'. They were also instructed 'not to fight the natives unless absolutely necessary'.[50]

In October 1895 Burnham returned to London, this time with his wife Blanche. Their daughter Nada, now 17 months old, remained in Bulawayo as her mother didn't want 'to subject her to the rigors of the journey'.[51] In January 1896 came news of the Jameson Raid and two months later the outbreak of the Second Ndebele War. The Burnhams returned to Africa and Blanche remained in Mafeking while her husband made for besieged Bulawayo. The infant Nada was weak with fever but expected to recover. Blanche arrived in Bulawayo on 13 May, but her young daughter died a few days later. 'You know the tempest that is raging in my soul,' Burnham replied to Haggard's letter of condolence. 'I am hit awful hard, but for Africa and the Empire I will fight on.'[52]

When Haggard's missionary tale *The Wizard* was published in 1896, this story 'of Faith triumphant over savagery and death' was dedicated to Burnham's daughter Nada, 'who "bound all to her" and, while her father cut his way through the hordes of the Ingubu Regiment, perished of the hardships of war at Bulawayo on May 22nd, 1896'.[53] *The Wizard* was not a popular success: 'possibly many thought they were being offered a missionary story liberally coated with jam, and the British are enormously suspicious of missionary stories'.[54]

Considering Haggard's views on missionaries expressed in his letters home from Africa and the general depiction of clergymen in his fiction as weak, venal and often plain stupid, *The Wizard* – 'the tale of the clergyman who went out from a country parish to preach the teaching of Christ to The People of Fire'[55] – is a marked change of tack, though the application of jam is excessive by any yardstick. Given Haggard's other portrayal of a brave cleric, the pompous Bastin in *When the World Shook*, also an Evangelical, one would conclude Haggard tended in the same direction.

Haggard's change of heart regarding missionaries in *The Wizard* can be traced back to 1893, when he was invited by John Mackenzie, Scottish missionary in Bechuanaland, to speak at a fundraising event in Norwich for the Universities' Mission to Central Africa.[56] That Haggard accepted the invitation was probably influenced by the memory of the Anglican priest Henry Carter Scudamore, a companion of David Livingstone with links to Ditchingham, who had died in the Universities' Mission service in Africa in 1863. Haggard's speech, later published as a pamphlet, invoked the spirit of Livingstone, who had been the inspiration for the founding of the Universities' Mission, quoting a speech that Livingstone had given at Oxford in 1857: 'I shall return to Africa and die there, but I leave it with you to see that the door I have opened for Christianity and civilisation never be closed.'[57] 'We have often heard missionaries disparaged; some of us may at times have joined in the chorus,' Haggard admitted, 'and all missionaries have not been wise', some entering the ministry 'to better their position, to obtain social and political influence – perhaps even to win wealth'; however, Haggard 'after a somewhat searching enquiry' had not been able to find any such 'among the members of the Universities' Mission'.[58]

When *The Wizard* was serialised in the *African Review* during 1896, Haggard had already departed the business world, taking his leave of the *African Review* in early 1895 after only nine months.

> It was the period of the great African boom, and the business machine hummed merrily. We made money, I remember; also we lost money. But it was all much too speculative and nerve-racking for me, while the burden of those companies weighed

upon my mind heavily. The true-bred City man cares little for such things, which to him are all part of the day's work, as writing a chapter of a book might be to me. He is accustomed to take risks, and an adept at getting out of difficult situations.

When Wills announced his departure for South Africa 'for a year or so', leaving Haggard to manage 'all the extremely intricate affairs with which he was connected', the prospect was far too stressful and Haggard resigned. 'There was some difficulty, as under the deed of partnership I was bound for a period', but when Wills realised Haggard was determined to go, he 'kindly signed a dissolution'.[59] Haggard's exit from the *African Review* and all it represented was well timed. At the end of 1895 came the Jameson Raid fiasco.

A decade earlier the discovery of gold on the Witwatersrand sparked a gold rush. A tented camp sprang up on the bare veld but was soon replaced by the more solid structures of Johannesburg. This gold rush was no flash in the pan; the gold-bearing reefs were huge, the main reefs over 30 miles long, and they were deep. The Rand 'seemed, almost literally, a bottomless pit'.[60] The gold deposits were developed by British investors and American mining engineers. Speculators, prospectors, artisans, clerks and shopkeepers – English, French, and German; Jews from Eastern Europe and Afrikaners from the Cape – flocked to the new goldfields and Johannesburg became 'the greatest concentration of Europeans in the whole sub-continent'.[61]

For the Dutch-speaking Transvaal burghers steeped in the Old Testament, Johannesburg was the new Babylon. The mostly rural life of Transvaal was threatened by the huge influx of Uitlanders (foreigners or outsiders) and by the 1890s they outnumbered the burghers and owned more than half the land but were consistently denied citizenship. For the majority of Uitlanders profit was preferable to the vote but by 1895, though there was no appetite for all-out war, there was a desire for outside intervention. Rhodes saw an opportunity to enlarge the sphere of British influence, as he had done to great personal profit in Rhodesia. Prime minister of the Cape Colony since 1890, Rhodes was at the height of his powers, economic and political. Barring his entry into Transvaal was Paul Kruger, president since 1883.

For Rhodes and Joseph Chamberlain, the British Colonial Secretary, the lack of citizens' rights for the Uitlanders was a useful injustice to justify intervention in the Boer republics of the Transvaal and Orange Free State and finally create a British South Africa. Rhodes financed rebellion. Arms were smuggled to Johannesburg, where a so-called reform committee was set up, and a strip of land in Bechuanaland was ceded to the Chartered Company, ostensibly for the building of a railway from the Cape north to Rhodesia but more immediately to allow an armed force to assemble close to the Transvaal border under the command of Rhodes's devoted lieutenant, Dr Leander Starr Jameson, administrator of the Chartered Company. A letter was composed by the reform committee in Johannesburg begging for intervention; the date was to be added later when the time of the rising in the city had been agreed. In London, Chamberlain was kept abreast of developments.

In December 1895 Jameson was teetering on the Transvaal border waiting for the starter's gun. The plotters in Johannesburg couldn't make their minds up. Contradictory messages and changes of plan, cablegrams and telegrams – coded or oblique – flew between Jameson and Johannesburg, Cape Town and London. Christmas passed, the New Year beckoned. Jameson ran out of patience and decided to risk all on the basis, as he said later, that if he 'succeeded I should have been forgiven.'[62] Alas, he didn't succeed. The rising in Johannesburg never happened and Jameson's 'raid' turned into the bungled invasion of a sovereign state. The Boers tracked Jameson's movements almost as soon as he crossed the border, shadowing his force from a distance as it rode to Johannesburg. After a minor skirmish they let him ride into a well-laid trap. After a brief fight he was contained at Doornkop, where the forces arrayed against him left no option but surrender.

For President Kruger, the raid was an opportune moment to display magnanimity in victory: death sentences for the plotters were commuted to fines and Jameson was sent for trial to England, where a very British cover-up erased any involvement on the part of Chamberlain or the Colonial Office. Jameson received a rap over the knuckles for his failed heroics and served eight months of a one-year sentence. Rhodes resigned as prime minister of the Cape.

Haggard saw Rhodes for the last time at the Burlington Hotel a year after the raid in 1896 and recalled him pacing 'restlessly up and down the long room like a lion in a cage, throwing out his words in jerky, isolated sentences, and in a curious high voice that sometimes almost attained to a falsetto. He gave me the idea of being in a very nervous state.'[63] In his autobiography Haggard doesn't damn Rhodes, but he keeps his distance: no jingoistic paeans here. Haggard shared Rhodes's imperial ambitions but was uncomfortable with the methods of their achievement. 'His was one of those big, mixed natures of which it is extremely difficult to form a just opinion. My own, for what it is worth, is that he loved his country and desired above all things to advance her interests; also that he was personally very ambitious ... At least, whatever his faults, he was a great figure in his generation.'[64]

Shortly after Haggard escaped from the City, the *African Review* reported he had accepted 'an invitation from the electors of East Norfolk to contest the seat at the General Election ... he will stand in the Conservative and agricultural interest, and that he will make the absolute necessity of remedial measures for the condition of agriculture the chief point in his programme.'[65] In 1886 Gladstone's insistence on Home Rule for Ireland had caused an exodus of Whig aristocrats – landowners all – from the Liberal Party. They remained independent until 1895 when they went into alliance with the Conservative Party. Gladstone resigned as prime minister and retired from politics in 1894. In 1895 the country went to the polls again.

While at the *African Review* there had been an understanding that Haggard would seek entry to parliament; possibly a condition of the early dissolution of his partnership with Wills was his acceptance of a candidacy. Such speculation is justified by the comment in Haggard's autobiography concerning his subsequent failure to win a parliamentary seat: 'Mercifully the thing miscarried, for had it been otherwise I might have had to bear upon my shoulders much of the burden of the Parliamentary defence of the inspirers and perpetrators of the Jameson Raid, which would have been neither a pleasant nor an easy task.'[66] This would have been necessarily imposed by his support for Rhodes through his involvement with the *African Review*.

Unlike the safe Conservative seat of King's Lynn, the East Norfolk division was 'one of the most difficult in the kingdom from the Conservative point of view'.[67] The constituency had bounced between Conservatives and Liberals for most of the preceding century. In 1892 the Liberal candidate, Robert Price, a surgeon and barrister turned politician, won the seat from the Conservatives with a majority of 440.

Haggard laid out his manifesto, addressing the needs of the rural poor and the agricultural crisis caused by cheap grain imports, in a speech at Norwich on 16 March. He advocated that money raised by the land tax should go to poor relief in districts hard hit and that 'foreign barley coming into this country, unless it be crushed barley to be used as food for cattle, should be subjected to an import duty'.[68] The 'millions of money to be raised by such a tax' should not go into the pockets of the landlords but 'into the pockets of the people' through the creation of an 'Old Age Pension Scheme'.[69] He also motivated for a tax on imported flour – 'let the corn come in free by all means, I say, but do not let it come in free in a manufactured condition. Why should not our millers have the benefit of the grinding of that corn?'[70] Much of this was contrary to Tory policy and 'sounded too much like Protectionist and Socialist doctrine to win Haggard many friends among his fellow-Conservatives'.[71] In taking the side of farmers, Haggard alienated 'another large segment of East Norfolk voters, the wherrymen who made their livelihood ferrying imported wheat up the reedy inlets and rivers to the cities'.[72]

The election campaign, Dickensian in character, began in late April and 'was very severely contested'. Haggard spent much of this time aboard a wherry 'cruising from part to part of that wide and awkward constituency ... Sometimes I had to address three meetings a day, and always there was one or more, besides innumerable visits and much letter-writing.'[73] Arthur Cochrane was recruited to assist at the hustings. Apart from a short period spent working in the City – his experience was similar to Haggard's – what exactly Cochrane had been doing since his return to England from Natal is unknown.[74] During the election campaign he entertained prospective voters by playing the piano and singing comic songs. Haggard would 'speak for half an hour or forty minutes to an audience mainly composed of agricultural labourers, some of whom ... were wont to express their active dislike of me'. One man 'used to follow me about and "baa" like a sheep in the front row. He only stopped when Cochrane began his comic songs.'[75]

Cochrane's performances, the 'most popular part of the proceedings', were also politically necessary as the Liberal Party agent, Lord Wodehouse (son of the Liberal statesman and Colonial Secretary, Lord Kimberley), was 'a master of this form of entertainment' and was said 'to owe much of his popularity' to singing 'a ditty called *The Baby on the Shore*. Alas! in this matter I could not hope to compete.' Meetings over, Haggard, Louie, Cochrane 'and some other ladies' would emerge and 'face the booing without, which sometimes was accompanied by hustling and stone-throwing'.[76]

In July Haggard's speech at Horsford was 'interrupted continually by an organised gang of youths and eventually broke up in disorder'.[77] The same happened at a meeting at the Market Place in Walsham, though he managed to speak there successfully the following day.[78] Scandalous stories were circulated about Haggard, including one depicting him as an 'enemy of the labouring race' who turned off his farmhands at Ditchingham 'to starve during winter' and fired those of different political opinion. This was standard fare, but in Haggard's case there was a 'picturesque addition which I was told proved very effective, namely, that I had been known to murder quite a considerable number of black women'.[79]

The campaign against Haggard did not let up, and polling day on 19 July was 'as bloody as some of his books'.[80] Haggard was touring the constituency in a four-horse coach with Louie, Mrs Hartcup and her sister Jessie Hartcup, Miss Jackson (presumably one of Lilly's sisters), William Wills (another indicator of interest on the part of Rhodes), Cochrane, the coachman and a guard. At the village of Ludham, on the road from Norwich to Great Yarmouth, they were attacked by a mob throwing stones. Mrs Hartcup was hit on the head and required medical treatment. Thereafter they made as quickly as possible for Stalham in expectation of 'a most favourable reception'.[81] Instead they were besieged in the Swan Hotel by 'an infuriated mob'. Telegrams were sent 'off in all directions' for help, and the first assistance came from North Walsham three hours later when a volunteer force of civilians and four or five policemen arrived. At the sight of them advancing four abreast armed with cutlasses, the mob fled 'without offering the slightest resistance'.[82] The incident became known as the Battle of Stalham Bridge. Lord Wodehouse and a drover were subsequently charged with assault and fined £5. This was small comfort to Haggard, who lost the election, though he did reduce Price's majority from 440 to 198.[83] The *Pall Mall Gazette* remarked that when next requiring 'local colour for one of his vivid stories of savage life, [Haggard] will not have to go beyond Stalham or Ludham'.[84] He never stood for parliament again.

> I never was a real Tory ... as a party man I am the most miserable failure. As a politician I should have been useless from any whip's point of view. He would – well, have struck

me off his list as neither hot nor cold, as a dangerous and undesirable individual who, refusing to swallow the shibboleths of his tribe with shut eyes, actually dared to think for himself and to possess that hateful thing, 'a cross-bench mind'.[85]

The Conservatives, allied with the Liberal Unionists, swept the election, and when the 'last government in the Western world to possess all the attributes of aristocracy in working condition' took office in June 1895, Haggard was not of its number.[86] He could take consolation from not having to defend Rhodes and comfort from being spared the cost of financing a seat in the House of Commons, then an unsalaried position, which meant 'the privilege of representing the people in Parliament was a luxury largely confined to the class that could afford it'.[87]

In 1895 'Lilith came for a second time into Rider's life'.[88] If Haggard was not in direct contact with Lilly Archer, he had knowledge of her through his friendship with her brother Frederick Jackson.[89] At the end of 1895 her world collapsed in scandal. Her husband Francis Archer was the sole trustee of the Jackson fortune. Permitted a free hand, he embezzled the Jackson trust as well as those of other clients to pay his gambling debts and 'other expenses incurred by a variety of pleasures'.[90] On 11 December 1895 his crimes caught up with him. Archer was accused of converting a cheque of £493.11s. to his own use and a summons was issued for him to appear in court. When an officer of the court went to Archer's London home to serve the summons, he wasn't there and it was served on Lilly. The same day a warrant was issued for Archer's arrest, but with the help of friends he had already fled the country for East Africa, where his brother-in-law Frederick 'gave him sanctuary'.[91]

Archer was declared a bankrupt, leaving Lilly, their young sons and her unmarried sisters in dire straits. Lilly turned to Haggard for help. Haggard found her family a new home on the Suffolk coast at Snape, south of Aldeburgh, in the Red House, which as the name suggests is an impressive red-brick building.[92] Haggard also made arrangements for the welfare of her sons: Francis, the eldest, was taken out of Eton and articled to a solicitor, while the second son, Geoffrey, was sent to a school in Beccles and in 1901, aged 19, to East Africa 'to train for the Colonial Service with his uncle'.[93]

In the light of Haggard and Lilly's past relationship – and its continual reinvention in his fiction – her sudden reappearance in his life cannot have been easy for all concerned. Lilias acknowledges it was

> not a little difficult, and it was owing to Louie's good faith and common sense that it worked as well as it did. She undertook all the arrangements, and was unwaveringly kind and sympathetic to Lilith, proving a warm-hearted friend to her and her sons. Only a woman of Louie's straightforward and unemotional temperament could have made a success of this risky experiment. As far as her husband was concerned, the past was dead and done with; she trusted him absolutely and what he wished she would do.[94]

Nevertheless it was hardly ideal. 'What Rider felt no one knows, it is doubtful if he realized how bitter can be gift-bread to a woman under such circumstances.'[95]

In early 1899 Lilly received a letter from her husband in East Africa begging her to join him. Haggard, her family and friends advised against it, but Lilly decided to go. Aboard ship and nearing Madeira, she wrote to Haggard acknowledging his letter of farewell and the enclosed photograph of himself, 'which indeed I greatly value. I hope and trust we may meet again and in (for me) happier circumstances. For all your generous help in the time of need, for your friendship and never failing kindness I shall all my life feel the deepest gratitude.'[96] After reading the letter, Haggard wrote the single word 'Finis!' 'under her name and laid it away with other letters belonging to that past which still lived so vividly within his heart'.[97]

So vividly that in 1898 he drafted the plot of *Stella Fregelius: A Tale of Three Destinies*, a contemporary novel with a complex plot involving heirs and lost inheritances centred around the hero Morris Monk's exploration of love and mysticism. The inventor of a wireless telephonic device, the aërophone – anticipating the modern cellular telephone – Morris meets the love of his life, Stella Fregelius, when about to marry his cousin Mary Porson. Morris and Stella accept their situation and together perform a spiritual marriage ceremony in the belief that 'Death will unite us beyond the possibility of parting'.[98] Parting for the last time, Stella bids Morris remember 'that we are wed – truly wed, that I go to wait for you, and that even if you do not see me I will, if I may, be near you always – till you die, and afterwards will be with you always – always.'[99] Stella is killed in a storm. Morris marries Mary, though not before telling her about his relationship with Stella, of which Mary is totally accepting, and the couple go on to have two children. But all the while Morris obsesses about Stella and eventually, after having put himself through a regimen of intense spiritual discipline, he dies – presumably to become united with Stella in the hereafter. The parallels with Haggard's own life and loves are obvious, and one wonders what Louie made of this book when it was written in 1902 and published in 1904,[100] though by this time, according to Lilias, she no longer read her husband's books. *Stella Fregelius* is dedicated to John Berwick, the nom de plume of Aggie Haggard (née Barber).[101]

With City life behind him and political ambitions curtailed, Haggard further cemented his East Anglian roots by buying a house on the Suffolk coast 15 miles from Ditchingham in the village of Kessingland near Lowestoft, changing its name from Cliff House to Kessingland Grange – 'the very easternmost dwelling, I suppose in the whole kingdom' – intending it for use as a summer house by him and his extended family.[102] The house had been created from 'two coastguard cottages, which some later owner had joined together with a long passage, forming a sprawling two-storey house shaped like an E without the middle stroke. It faced east, stood almost on the very edge of the cliff and from its windows nothing was visible except sea and sky'.[103] Prior to being a coastguard station, it was 'a famous resort of smugglers, who used to hide their unlawful treasures in the neighbouring wells'.[104]

Coastal erosion along the East Anglian coastline (a plot element in *The Witch's Head* and *Stella Fregelius*) was a major problem at Kessingland, and Haggard embraced the challenge, sloping the cliff and planting wiry and resilient marram grass to bind the sand and create a more effective barrier to the encroaching waves. The experiment saw the slope increase in height.[105] Haggard set about renovations to the house's interior, which, with 'all its wandering passages, queer cubby-holes, and unexpected rooms ... was like some large, stationary ship, which perhaps gave Rider the idea of naming every bedroom ... after a British admiral'.[106] He proudly exhibited a bust of Nelson, dated 1812, said to have been carved from the timbers of the *Victory*.[107]

Lilias recalled Kessingland Grange as a 'queer mixture': a Victorian drawing room with sacred pictures, 'the morning-room with its set of prim samplers ... the dining-room with its Landseers and old prints of the Kings of England'. Elsewhere the 'atmosphere relapsed into savagery, with the walls decorated with Zulu assegais and native war horns, ox-hide shields and knobkerries'.[108] Charles Kerr's illustrations for *Nada the Lily* were hung up the front staircase, and in the passage leading to Haggard's study hung Maurice Greiffenhagen's illustrations from *Montezuma's Daughter*. Greiffenhagen's 'very fine illustrations to *Jess*' adorned the study walls.[109] These were visual reminders of his most productive period as a writer. Haggard hadn't entirely renounced literature, but he had taken the measure of his literary talents:

> Be it good or be it bad, the best that I can do in the lines of romance and novel-writing is to be found among the first dozen or so of the books that I wrote, say between *King Solomon's Mines* and *Montezuma's Daughter*. Also I would add this. A man's mind does not always remain the same. People are apt to say of any individual writer that he has gone off, whereas the truth may be merely that he has changed, and that his abilities are showing themselves in another form.[110]

21

'ACCURATE OBSERVATION'

In August 1897 Haggard travelled to the Netherlands to research the background for a historical novel set at the time of William the Silent. He visited locations that feature in the book, as well as museums and libraries to study plans of fortifications and towns so as to ensure 'every event in the ghastly story of the persecution of the Dutch was checked and confirmed'.[1] *Lysbeth: A Tale of the Dutch* is set in the Spanish Netherlands of the late sixteenth century during the Dutch Revolt, provoked by the harsh repression of Protestants by the ruling Spanish Catholic authorities. In sympathy with the Dutch burghers of history rebelling against their Spanish overlords, Haggard recreates a grim period of siege and slaughter in a solid historical novel with an authentic sense of place. While there are clichéd racial and religious stereotypes – Catholics bad, Protestants good; Dutch slow and stolid, Spaniards passionate and cruel – *Lysbeth* is one of the best of Haggard's books, with a complex plot executed with attention to atmosphere and style. *Lysbeth* was published April 1901 after serialisation in the *Graphic*.

After his City excitements and his brush with electoral politics, Haggard 'returned to the country and the writing of books; he found 'the thorough change of thought seemed to have rested my mind, with the result that my imagination was fresher than it had been for some years before. Also the work itself was and has remained less irksome to me than during the years 1891 to 1895.'[2] In early middle age Haggard was relaxing into himself, comfortable with his limitations. *Lysbeth* is a confident product of this period; the work of a writer out to please himself as much as the reader. Haggard had also taken a step back from the literary life; writing was no longer his primary focus, and he was haunted by the desire 'to do something in my day more practical than the mere invention of romance upon romance'. He realised 'a great subject lay to my hand, that of the state of English agriculture and of our rural population ... Therefore with a bold heart I gave all my spare time and energy to a study of the matter.'[3]

The 'great subject' was but a step away from his own front door. Haggard farmed 365 acres, 'two-thirds of which were near his house at Ditchingham, a big village of

1100 inhabitants, and a third in Bedingham, a village 5 miles distant'.[4] The 'Golden Age of English Farming' enjoyed by his father was long over.[5] Cheap grain imports had made farming unprofitable.[6] Improved intercontinental transport by land and sea allowed the United States and Canada to penetrate and flood European markets with cheap grain. Better refrigeration methods opened the door to the importation of meat and other perishables, including fruit and dairy from around the world. English farmers simply couldn't compete. France and Germany responded quickly with tariffs and duties, while the British farmer was left to sink or swim.

Aggressive competition was the major component of the agricultural crisis of the 1890s, but bad weather, disease and societal change also played a role. Wet summers and poor crop yields typified the second half of the 1870s. Nor were livestock immune. Cattle were hit by rinderpest in 1877 and foot and mouth disease in 1883; two years later cattle plague struck. Crowning it all, there was a massive exodus of people from the land to urban areas between 1871 and 1881; numbers of agricultural labourers decreased by over a third and farm wages rose as 'labourers were in a stronger position to demand more as rural populations were declining. All farmers were bitterly opposed to the unions and some blamed increased education for both reducing the number of boys available for work and equipping children for something better than fieldwork'.[7]

The agricultural prosperity of Haggard's childhood was gone. His acquisition of Ditchingham House and its estate through marriage to Louie had made that abundantly clear. He had written to *The Times* on 'the land question' in April 1886, expressing his 'dismay over the agricultural economy', and complaining that the privilege of owning a farm cost him £50 a year.[8] When he decided to move permanently to Ditchingham in 1889 and farm his own land at a time 'when many of those who could were getting out of the industry',[9] Haggard was well aware it couldn't be done without the extra revenue derived from his writing. In the mid-1890s 'the farming communities of England were in their worst doldrums'.[10]

A Farmer's Year, Haggard's 'commonplace book for 1898', was serialised in *Longman's Magazine* from September 1898 to October 1899 and published in book form on 2 October 1899. Haggard wrote with the purpose 'of setting down the struggles of those who were engaged in agriculture ... a record of the circumstances of their lives and of the condition of their industry'.[11] He took as his model Thomas Tusser's *Hundredth Good Pointes of Husbandrie*, a 'practical guide to farming written by a professional musician' in the mid-sixteenth century.[12] In stark contrast to Tusser's flourishing agricultural world, Haggard's 'was one of stagnation, collapse and abandonment',[13] and the migration of the labouring classes from the land to the cities 'one of the most significant if the most silent and unnoticed of our time'.[14]

The opening chapter of *A Farmer's Year* sets the scene for what is, in essence, an accounting experiment: a record of the activities and events on an East Anglian farm over the course of a year and the resultant profits and losses, the benefits and deficits in social and financial terms. Haggard begins with the profit and loss account of the preceding year, noting that, despite farming 'with economy and not without intelligence', the loss 'remains heavy'.[15] Embarking on 1898, he expresses the hope his investigation might be useful to those wishing to learn 'something about rural ways of life upon the land in this era of dreadful depression, when the fate of British agriculture hangs quivering in the balance'.[16]

A Farmer's Year is a vivid evocation of a bygone age, detailing the daily, weekly, monthly and seasonal activities of the farm; the methods and practices employed in regard to specific crops and livestock; how to go about building a sod wall; how to thatch and weatherproof a haystack; and the felling of trees. 'I know of no more melancholy sight – indeed, to this day I detest seeing a tree felled; it always reminds me of the sudden and violent death of a man.'[17] There are dissertations on the art of ploughing, hay-making, the necessity for good field drainage, and joy at the splendid sugar beet crop of 1898, courtesy of 'that noble mixture, Bungay compost'.[18] There is a recurring lament that 'notwithstanding the care, knowledge, and intelligence which are put into the working of the land, under present conditions it can scarcely be made to pay'.[19] Haggard's description of the annual rent audit ritual at the King's Head public house in Bungay, 'where the tenants of this estate ... assemble once a year to pay their rent and dine',[20] is a scene straight out of Hardy and, for all the raising of glasses and good fellowship, as dour: Haggard is forced to admit that he doubts his farm 'returns in net profit more than a third of what it produced thirty years ago'.[21]

Beyond the immediate demands of the farm, Haggard addresses pressing social questions; he looks forward to some form of old-age pension and anticipates aspects of a future welfare state. 'Doubtless these ideas are very radical, but there are points upon which some of us grow more radical as we grow older.'[22] The reader of *A Farmer's Year* becomes companion and witness to 'Haggard's personality as he swings over from being a typical conservative to a highly candid radical ... Whatever he sees or feels or does is written down with total candour, and his journal is at once an important and authoritative compendium of farming practice, a private confessional, a history of turn of the century Norfolk and, in its way, an entertainment.'[23]

As 1898 draws to a close there comes a final reckoning: a profit of £422.15s.4d. – 'a round sum which at first sight is enough to make the half-starved farmer almost delirious with joy'. In reality he receives just under £73, 'upon which the farmer would be supposed to exist, that being the living profit left after the satisfaction of outgoings and charges'.[24] Haggard had done better than some of his neighbours, but the conclusion was unavoidable: under current conditions, 'short of the entire stoppage of the industry, it is difficult to see how things could greatly change for the worse'.[25]

As the clock ticked toward midnight on New Year's Eve, Haggard finished his diary: 'the year is dying. In a few minutes its glass runs out and 1899 must come, the last year but one of an eventful and a wondrous century.'[26]

Haggard's dramatic change of subject matter wrong-footed reviewers and readers, something acknowledged by a reviewer in the *Bookman*:

> Mr. Rider Haggard as a farmer ought to be a curious spectacle, as curious, say, as 'She' peeling potatoes at the back door. But he is not. He is, very simply and naturally, in his place. We own we scarcely expected it. We even own that at first we felt disappointed. Our delicious anticipatory creeping of the flesh at the mention of his name was thrown away upon this chronicle of the fields. There is some climbing down to be done before you can appreciate Mr. Haggard among the wheat. But when you are on the ground beside him you will find yourself rewarded. He knows what he is talking about.[27]

'A most delightful and useful book,' declared the *Athenaeum*, displaying 'a breadth of judgment and with a power of accurate observation which are unusual'.[28] The *Literary World* thought *A Farmer's Year* of 'permanent value as portraying the agricultural life of the times'.[29] The *Agricultural Economist* said the scenes of farming life were described with such 'picturesque power that even a townsman will find it hard to skip a sentence'.[30]

Kipling was enthusiastic: 'I don't think there has ever been a better book of the sane, common (which is uncommon) quiet humorous real country life of England. I've been going back and rereading it slowly and leisurely: for the mere taste of it – same as Gilbert White.'[31] Morton Cohen considered *A Farmer's Year* 'one of Haggard's highest achievements, through which one can look at the face of the country as well as into the heart of a man in love with it'.[32]

Though twelve months in the making, *A Farmer's Year* did not absorb all Haggard's writing energy. He was always good at filling gaps of time and in one of these he wrote *Dr. Therne*, 'my only novel with a purpose'.[33] The entry for 20 July in *A Farmer's Year* records Haggard being appalled that the 'Government has given way suddenly on the Vaccination Bill, and that henceforth "conscientious objection" on the part of parents is to entitle them to disregard the law and neglect the vaccination of their children'.[34] Smallpox vaccination was being targeted by a vocal anti-vaccination movement.[35] Between 1853 and 1898 vaccination rates for infants were over 80 per cent, but the compulsory nature of the programme was a cause of continuing public disquiet, and legislation in 1898 introduced a conscience clause 'allowing objectors to avoid the punitive penalties of not vaccinating their child'.[36]

Haggard believed vaccination 'one of the greatest boons that the century has brought to mankind', but the government's retreat placed the onus on magistrates such as himself to judge whether a parent's objection was genuine, an impossible task, and 'one which should not be laid upon the shoulders of any judge'.[37] Haggard was horrified by the potentially catastrophic consequences of the conscience clause and, though not 'a very promising topic for a romance', he felt compelled to write it in view of 'the dreadful things I had seen and knew of the ravages of smallpox in Mexico and elsewhere', fearing 'that they should repeat themselves in this country'.[38]

Haggard began writing *Dr. Therne* soon after his July entry in *A Farmer's Year* and the completed manuscript was in the hands of Charles Longman by the middle of September. 'I sat up last night and read *Dr. Therne*' – it's a short book – 'though the subject is painful and unpleasant there is nothing in the treatment that strikes a jarring note. The question of course is who will read it: you are going quite outside your usual clientele.' Apart from ensuring *Dr. Therne* didn't clash with another forthcoming Haggard title, *Swallow*, Longman felt the book should be published 'as soon as it can be got out'.[39]

Haggard's experiences in Mexico are shared by his character Dr James Therne, who is convinced of the need for vaccination as a public health measure. However, Therne becomes indebted to anti-vaxxer Stephen Strong, a wealthy businessman who funds a parliamentary election bid by Therne on the condition he runs on an anti-vaccination ticket. Therne goes on to become a successful politician and, on his benefactor's death, inherits Strong's fortune. Contrary to Therne's public anti-vaccination stance, he vaccinates himself during a smallpox epidemic, and when his duplicity is exposed, his reputation is ruined. A well-meant piece of propaganda, *Dr. Therne* is a mechanical melodrama, its events and characters transparently manipulated to suit Haggard's purpose. The *Lancet* commended Haggard's courage in writing *Dr. Therne* – published on 28 November 1898 – and thus risking 'losing many readers and creating a fanatical opposition to whatever he may do in a public or private capacity for the sake of telling the truth'.[40] Less sympathetically, the *Spectator* praised Haggard's motives but criticised him for his disservice to the novel form in making it 'a literary maid-of-all-work'.[41]

Swallow, the book referred to by Longman, subtitled *A Tale of the Great Trek*, was dedicated to Marshall Clarke in 'memory of past time and friendship, and more especially of the providential events connected with a night-long ride which once we took on duty together ... across the moon-lit paths of Secocoeni's mountain.'[42] Narrated by the 'dour but not unkindly character' of Vrou Botmar, *Swallow* was regarded by Haggard as being sympathetic towards the Boers. He trusted his portrayal of the narrator would prove that 'time softens a man's judgment',[43] a phrase frequently employed thereafter to excuse the racist views on the Boers expressed in his youth. More novel than romance, the book in its plot harks back to earlier works such as *Jess*, *Dawn* and *The Witch's Head* and incorporates many of their melodramatic elements – yet another disputed inheritance. *Swallow* was serialised in the *Graphic* from 2 July to 29 October 1898 and published in book form on 1 March 1899.

As to time softening judgement, Haggard's characterisation of the Boers in *Swallow*, though an advance on his previous sentiments, remains patronising. The hero of *Swallow* is an Englishman 'whose noble blood told its tale in every feature and movement',[44] and the only Boer character without blemish is Suzanne, the

'Swallow'. Haggard tells the story from a Boer perspective and accurately reflects their grievances of the period – that of the Great Trek – but their point of view is refracted through a British lens that views the Boers as misguided at best, wilfully vicious at worst. Even Haggard's dedication to Marshall Clarke is ambivalent. 'Sympathy with the Voortrekkers of 1836 is easy', he says, 'whether it remains so in the case of their descendants, the present masters of the Transvaal, is a matter that admits of many opinions. At the least, allowance should always be made for the susceptibilities of a race that finds its individuality and national life sinking slowly, but without hope of resurrection, beneath an invading flood of Anglo-Saxons.'[45] When *Swallow* was published in March 1899, the final attempt to stem that flood was but seven months away.

The damp squib of the Jameson Raid had been quickly snuffed out, but it had raised the spectre of a British intervention in Transvaal that was difficult to exorcise. In 1897 Sir Hercules Robinson was replaced as High Commissioner and Governor of the Cape by Sir Alfred Milner. He was determined to restore 'British supremacy in South Africa',[46] his self-appointed task being to bring the Transvaal to submission, if necessary by provoking a war. Milner's vision of the future was clear: 'The *ultimate* end is a self-governing White community, supported by well-treated and justly governed black labour from Cape Town to the Zambesi.'[47]

The British government, especially its Colonial Secretary Joseph Chamberlain, having had their fingers burnt by the Jameson Raid, were happy to let sleeping dogs lie. For them, continuing migration of British subjects to the Rand goldfields and the inevitable increase of British influence in the Transvaal would eventually create an apple ripe for plucking. Until then a 'policy of patience' was all that was required.[48] Caution, not patience, was the watchword. Milner was cautious but he was not patient; he wanted to force a crisis: Kruger must make reforms or make war. Milner set out to manipulate both London and the situation in South Africa to achieve his desired end.

In 1898 Paul Kruger was re-elected as president of the Transvaal for a fourth term. He had taken advantage of his popularity after the Jameson Raid to re-arm the Transvaal with modern weapons; to wield them Kruger could mobilise a well-armed force of over twenty burgher commandos, consisting of 25,000 men; 40,000 if the Orange Free State joined in the fray: an army four times the size of the British garrisons in the Cape and Natal. Milner's object was to persuade London of the dangers of Kruger's Transvaal while luring Kruger to the brink. He had an ally in Johannesburg, 'the leading political mind among the Uitlanders',[49] Percy FitzPatrick. Jameson without the jitters, FitzPatrick was a cool head in the employ of the gold-mining company Wernher-Beit and he set about rebuilding the reform movement.

According to agreements crafted in the Pretoria Convention of 1881 and the London Convention of 1884, access to the franchise was permitted after five years of residence. The discovery of gold and the huge influx of immigrants from 1886 onwards saw Kruger change the five-year period to fourteen. In 1898 only a handful of Uitlanders had the vote. While FitzPatrick stoked unrest in Johannesburg, from Cape Town Milner nudged Chamberlain towards military intervention. Kruger and Milner met in Bloemfontein, ostensibly to avert the growing crisis. Chamberlain would be happy with some concessions from Kruger; but Milner wanted war leading to annexation. A return to the five-year franchise would mean peace, but that would be political suicide for Kruger. The conference ended after four days, Milner content that nothing had been achieved. Kruger was under no illusion: 'It is our country you want.'[50] Milner called for imperial troops to reinforce the Natal and Cape garrisons, while in the Transvaal Uitlander belligerence increased. Kruger offered a retrospective seven-year franchise; then in August he agreed to reinstate the five-year residency requirement.

Milner and his Johannesburg allies knew the 'despatch of British troops would precipitate war'.[51] In London, on the other hand, Chamberlain believed their advent would call Kruger's bluff, not start an all-out war. He requested clarification of Kruger's proposal; if none was forthcoming, it would be interpreted as a sign that the Transvaal was not disposed towards peace. It was a request for clarification, not an ultimatum, and when none came, 10,000 British troops were ordered from India to Natal to join the 4,000 garrison troops already there under Major General Sir William Penn Symons. General Sir Redvers Buller was appointed commander-in-chief. He wouldn't get to South Africa until November, and in the meantime he ordered: 'Do not go north of the Tugela.'[52] Too late, Symons was already north of the river in Ladysmith and advancing on Dundee.

On 9 October the Transvaal delivered an ultimatum to the British, accusing them of massing troops on their borders, and calling for their immediate withdrawal and for those still on the high seas not to be landed in South Africa. If there was no reply within forty-eight hours, the Transvaal would 'with great regret be compelled to regard the action as a formal declaration of war'.[53] The Transvaal had beaten the British government to the draw, for Chamberlain was just about to deliver his own ultimatum. Now there was no need: the Boers had brought the war upon themselves.

With the Anglo-Boer War under way, Haggard's *Cetywayo and His White Neighbours* was rushed into print in an abridged and retitled version, *The Last Boer War* (1899). It was prefaced by an 'Author's Note' written shortly after the Boer ultimatum at a time 'when the melancholy results which its pages foretell have overtaken us. Any who are interested may read and find in this tale of 1881 the true causes of the war of 1899.'[54] A short introduction detailed the negotiations, siding with Milner and highly critical of the Boers: 'it cannot be stated too often or too clearly that this war, which is to come, is a war that was forced upon us by the Boers in their blind ignorance and conceit. The mass of them believe, because they defeated our troops in various small affairs in 1881, that they are a match for the British Empire.'[55]

After a brief setback at the battle of Elandslaagte north of Ladysmith, the Boers quickly gained the upper hand. British troops were besieged at Mafeking, Ladysmith and Kimberley. In December there were Boer victories at Stormberg and Magersfontein in the Cape Colony and at Colenso in Natal in what became known by the British as 'Black Week'. The New Year brought more bad news: Buller's campaign to relieve Ladysmith went into further reverse with the British defeat at Spion Kop. By then Haggard and his family were in Florence, staying with Aggie and her children, where Haggard found it 'a melancholy business ... to spell out the tale of our disasters in the Italian papers'.[56] His brother Jack had been posted from Austria as consul to Nouméa (New Caledonia) in the South Pacific, 'a place impossible for his wife and her four children', and so Aggie had rented a rambling house in Florence 'which had once been a nunnery and had plenty of room for them all'.[57]

The Haggards had been planning to visit Aggie and her family since November, and from Florence Haggard intended embarking on a trip to 'Cyprus, Egypt & the Holy Land', accompanied by his nephew Arthur 'to do Secretary & improve his mind'.[58] Haggard had a personal agreement with Moberly Bell, managing director of *The Times*, to write 'some articles upon the affairs of the Near East'. These articles 'were never written',[59] though Haggard did produce a travel book, *A Winter Pilgrimage*, published in October 1901.

In Aggie's 'vast, echoing house' on a 'narrow street',[60] Haggard had anticipated a sunnier clime, an escape from the East Anglian winter that brought on his chronic bronchitis; instead he got 'the worst winter experienced in Tuscany for many, many years'.[61] The freezing wind of the tramontane was accompanied by rain 'whereof the tropics might be proud' and fogs that would not have discredited 'London in November'.[62] When an influenza epidemic broke out in the city, Dorothy, Angela and young Lilias all came down with the virus and Haggard 'cursed the day he ever came to Florence'.[63]

Convinced Lilias would die, Haggard worked himself 'into such a state that Louie decided the only hope for his peace of mind was to get him off on the proposed trip as soon as possible'.[64] With Arthur as secretary, Haggard set off by train. 'Half-way to Rome, in conformity with my common experience, a train went off the line in front of us, and so at some wayside place we were delayed for hours.' They arrived in Rome over four hours late 'without on this occasion, I am proud to say, losing any of our luggage'.[65] That was still to come. Haggard and Arthur visited the Vatican galleries, the Colosseum and the catacombs. 'What a life ... these poor innocents must have led who crowded into those darksome burrows, to worship while they lived and to sleep when life had left them, often enough by the fangs of a wild beast, the sword of the gladiator, or the torment of the tarred skin and the slowly burning fire.'[66] 'Evil weather'[67] pursued them to Naples, but neither the weather nor the city – 'a den of thieves & other sinners'[68] – marred Haggard's enjoyment of Pompeii and Herculaneum. At Brindisi, as they boarded the mail boat to Port Said, it was discovered their luggage had been sent to Reggio instead. Haggard and Arthur were left with the clothes they were wearing and a typewriter.

Apart from being Haggard's secretary, Arthur had been brought along because of his avowed intention to enter the church. Haggard thought a visit to the Holy Land would be instructive. Sailing across the Mediterranean, Arthur told his uncle he had changed his mind but had concealed the matter 'for fear lest I should refuse to take him on to the Holy Land, but spoke now, perhaps because he did not wish to make the visit sailing under false colours'. Haggard accepted the situation gracefully. 'It all came right in the end ... this dear nephew of mine was perhaps the pleasantest companion with whom I ever travelled.' However, the 'most erratic secretary' was blamed for Haggard's failure to write the articles for *The Times*. 'I could never find him when I wanted him', and when he did, Arthur dropped the typewriter on Haggard's feet. The typewriter was sent home from Cyprus.[69] Haggard made notes from which he produced *A Winter Pilgrimage*, but for a year or two there was 'a certain coolness between me and *The Times*, which had never received the promised articles, for of course I was unable to explain the real reason of my delinquencies'.[70]

At Port Said, Haggard and Arthur transhipped to the *Flora*, the mail boat to Larnaca. They were the only first-class passengers on the ship, evidence of Cyprus being 'a Cinderella among our colonies'[71] and not 'a place of popular resort'.[72] Amidst the graves and ruins of the ancient city of Amathus, Haggard admitted that much 'of our knowledge of the remote past is derived from tombs, and yet to my mind our pleasing habit of violating the dead, whether for purposes of gain or in order to satisfy our thirst for information, is not altogether easy to justify'.[73] He appended his own mea culpa: 'Is it right? I ask who have been a sinner',[74] expressing his regret at removing items from Egyptian graves, including wrappings and mummies, and having participated in forensic examination of ancient corpses 'when younger and more thoughtless'.[75]

In Cyprus they were accompanied by Charles Christian, a British expatriate banker and businessman, 'who was kindly going to conduct us upon our tour'.[76] Christian and his brother Percy were involved in various enterprises, including mining, shipping and construction as well as trading in antiquities and acting as agents for the British Museum. Christian's wife Gladys was the daughter of John Gladwyn Jebb.

Reports that Haggard and Arthur were soon to be reunited with their luggage were exaggerated. 'Cyprus quarantine restrictions forbid shipment,' they were informed by cable from the Alexandria representative of Thomas Cook.[77] Haggard embarked on a titanic struggle with bureaucracy and 'at length the luggage reappeared and with it a very pretty bill'. He would laugh about it later, but 'at the time it was troublesome enough, especially as the remote places of the earth are just where a visitor must dress most carefully'.[78]

Haggard and Arthur's hosts at Government House in Nicosia were the Hart-Bennetts, the dedicatees of *A Winter Pilgrimage*. Haggard had known Ella Hart-Bennett (née Tuck) since childhood, when his mother, 'whose god-daughter she was, wished me to try to marry her'. When she married the colonial official William Hart-Bennett in April 1899, Haggard 'made the speech proposing her health and happiness at the Lodge at Ditchingham'.[79]

From Cyprus the pair sailed to Beirut, where they learnt of the relief of Ladysmith on 28 February 1900. After exploring Beirut and its environs, Haggard and Arthur sailed on a steamer packed with pilgrims travelling to Mecca via Haifa, 'to commence our journey through the Holy Land'.[80] Their dragoman, David, was waiting for them at Haifa. A Christian, former teacher and a dresser at the British hospital in Tiberias, where he became fluent in English, he would take them on a route that included Nazareth, the Sea of Galilee, Mount Tabor, the Plain of Esdraelon, Jenin, Nablus and Jerusalem, from where they would visit Jericho and the Dead Sea.

In Haifa a large group of American tourists – 500 in all – had taken all the good horses. Picking three mounts, the best of a bad bunch, Haggard, Arthur and David rode out of Haifa, along with two baggage animals, a horse and a mule, the former ridden by the owner of the animals and the latter by his assistant, 'both of them perched atop of the great piles of luggage and equipment'.[81] They encountered the Americans at Nazareth and again 'trailing across the plain'. Haggard took a dim view of the riding methods of 'the ladies of the party', most of whom 'rode straddle-legged, after the fashion of men', which struck him as 'inelegant and even unseemly', barring one 'fine-looking girl, however, who sat her pony, a spirited Arab, like a centaur. I never saw any one with a closer or a better grip of a horse, and I imagine that wherever she came from she must have broken many a colt. But perhaps these criticisms are born of the merest prejudice. In every department of life it is nowadays easy to grow old-fashioned.'[82]

Near the site of the ancient city of Capernaum, the party lunched at the monastery of the German Catholic Palestine Society, and close to the Sea of Galilee Haggard found a 'tortoise basking in the sun' and decided to attempt 'the difficult experiment of bringing it home to England'.[83] At Hattin Haggard stood on the supposed site of Jesus's Sermon on the Mount and where, in 1187, the Ayyubid sultan Salah ad-Din decisively defeated the Crusaders and established Muslim dominance over the Holy Land. 'Thus the Mount of the Beatitudes became the Mount of Massacre.'[84] Gazing over this landscape inspired Haggard 'to weave a [tale] of the long war between Cross and Crescent'.[85] The tale, dedicated to his sister Ella, became the historical romance *The Brethren*, set during the time of the Crusades. It was published in September 1904 after serialisation in *Cassell's Magazine*. *The Brethren*, a favourite of Haggard's, was preceded by another book inspired by this trip, *The Pearl Maiden: A Tale of the Fall of Jerusalem*, a story of the early Christians, dedicated to Gladys Christian, which was published in March 1903 after being serialised in the *Graphic*.

Haggard visited all the significant religious sites in and around Jerusalem. The sight of Jews praying at the Wailing Wail under the prying attentions of camera-wielding tourists he found 'grotesque, even to sadness'.[86] He expressed mixed feelings about the spectacle as one who 'in many ways admires and respects the Jew, who, moreover, has the deepest sympathy with him in the cruel sufferings and obloquy which for ages have been and are still heaped upon his ancient, chosen race, such a sight is nothing short of painful'.[87]

After visits to Jericho, the Dead Sea, Bethany and Solomon's Quarries, the time had come to return home. Haggard's travel travails were not quite over. They arrived at Port Said well in time to catch their connection, only to see their ship steaming off into the distance. For reasons unknown, the RMS *Caledonia* had departed six hours early. After an exhausting day at Port Said, a second-class cabin was secured on the Orient Line's *Oroya*, en route to England from Australia, 'leaving behind us an unrecoverable portmanteau, various other packages, and last, but not least, the unhappy Capernaum [the tortoise]'.[88] As their ship got under way, Haggard 'screamed' to the Orient Lines' agent on the quay, 'imploring him to rescue poor Capernaum' and 'forward him by the first opportunity'. A month or two later Haggard went to Ditchingham station to collect Capernaum, finding him 'depressed by his long, cramped wanderings, but still hearty'. The tortoise was released into the garden at Ditchingham House, 'but disliking our climate, which forces him to spend so much of his time underground, continually attempts to return to the Sea of Galilee via the stableyard and the orchard'.[89]

Prior to Haggard and his family leaving for Italy, and unrelated to his personal arrangement with Moberly Bell, *The Times* asked Haggard if he would like to go to South Africa 'as one of their war correspondents', something that didn't strike Haggard 'as an attractive business at my age'.[90] Haggard was 43. Instead, through his agent Alexander Watt, Haggard entered into an arrangement with Arthur Pearson, the owner of *Pearson's Weekly* and the *Daily Express*, that when the war ended he should visit South Africa and write 'a series of articles under the title of "The New South Africa"'. This engagement went unfulfilled as the war continued for another two years, by 'which time the British public was utterly weary of the subject of South Africa.'[91]

In South Africa Sir Redvers Buller had been replaced by Lord Roberts as commander-in-chief. Kimberley was relieved in February 1900, Ladysmith later the same month, and Mafeking in May. Pretoria was captured in June and the Transvaal formally annexed for the second time in October. The war appeared to be over and in November General Lord Kitchener took over the reins from Roberts. The British had secured all their military objectives, but the many Boers remaining in the field now began waging a hit-and-run guerrilla war. The British retaliated by burning farms and relocating non-combatants, women and children, in concentration camps where eventually about 28,000 died in the crowded, unsanitary conditions. This bequeathed a festering legacy that would dog South African politics for the rest of the century and sour relations between Afrikaans- and English-speaking South Africans for even longer. Nor were the indigenous peoples of southern Africa spared. Black refugees were accommodated in segregated camps where 20,000 are estimated to have died.[92] The Boers finally surrendered in May 1902.

Haggard had never been keen on the arrangement to write on the war for Arthur Pearson, and one morning while taking his bath, 'an idea struck me ... that I should like to emulate Arthur Young, who more than a century before had travelled through and written of the state of agriculture in the majority of the English counties'.[93] He envisaged a series of articles followed by a book. Arthur Young was an eighteenth-century agricultural reformer and author of several books based on travels around the English countryside. Haggard had read Young's autobiography and his volume of letters on their first publication in 1898 and felt an intimate connection with Young: they were both farmers sharing 'an overwhelming sense of the vital importance of British agriculture to this country and its citizens'. Both were 'East Anglians and born of the class of landed gentry or "squires"'. Fellow feeling was reinforced by shared sorrow: both had 'suffered a terrible loss that saddened our lives'.[94] Young's beloved daughter Martha had died at the age of 14.

Haggard instructed Watt to tell Pearson that he was prepared to write a series of articles on rural England; otherwise he 'would proceed to South Africa, as I had made all my plans to do'.[95] Pearson agreed and the *Daily Express* commissioned a series of fifty articles, announcing that Haggard was 'undertaking a task as truly patriotic as that of any soldier who goes out to fight for the flag'.[96] Haggard saw himself as part of a tradition of travel undertaken in a spirit of inquiry into country matters, a tradition that had produced Young's *The Farmer's Tour through the East of England*, William Marshall's *General Survey ... of the Rural Economy of England*, William Cobbett's *Rural Rides* and Sir James Caird's *English Agriculture*. As 'everything connected with the land, landowners and husbandmen of England' had since 'undergone great changes', Haggard believed there was a need 'for a new work'.[97] To avoid simply updating that of his predecessors, Haggard adopted 'a new system – that of the interview'. In this way he hoped to preserve 'the individual experience and opinions of many witnesses'.[98] He drew up a ten-point questionnaire on farm rentals, availability of labour, cottage accommodation, the conditions of tenant farmers, landlords and labourers, as well as population movement and its impact on agriculture, in order to 'preserve a large body of incontestable evidence for the benefit of future generations'.[99]

Haggard considered the work that went into *Rural England* as 'the heaviest labour of all my laborious life'.[100] The *Daily Express* described Haggard's task as that of 'a Royal Commission undertaken by a single man'.[101] It was not quite a one-man commission, as Haggard recruited Arthur Cochrane to accompany him and take notes 'while I did the talking'. He also helped 'very much in the preparation of the series of agricultural maps' for the book.[102] Cochrane's role was acknowledged in *Rural England's* dedication to 'the companion of these journeys as of many previous adventures and to all throughout England who have assisted me in my undertaking'.[103] Compiling the book occupied 'the best part of another year of most incessant and careful application, for here every fact must be checked. It was the very antithesis to that involved in the composition of novels, where the imagination has free play'.[104]

Rural England: Being an Account of Agricultural and Social Researches Carried Out in the Years 1901 & 1902 was published in two volumes in November 1902. It consisted of over 1,200 pages packed with tales of profit and loss – usually the latter – amplified where necessary with ledger accounts and statistics, and illustrated with photographs and county maps. Haggard and Cochrane visited twenty-seven English counties as well as the Channel Islands. Traversing the country, Haggard paid homage to a descendant of Isaac Newton's famous apple tree at Woolsthorpe in Lincolnshire; reported favourably on the profitable freehold experiment at Winterslow in Wiltshire; and was suitably impressed by the Dartmoor prison farm in Devon, a 'triumph of the ingenuity and perseverance of man over difficulties of soil, situation and climate'.[105] There were reports on the making of Stilton cheese in Rutland and the manufacture of jam at the Chivers factory in Cambridge. He also dropped in at his birthplace, Wood Farm at Bradenham.[106]

In the book Haggard reviewed various types of farm ownership, from tenancy to freehold. The farms and their activities are recorded in detail, the type of crops planted, their rotation and method of cultivation; the livestock, their care and their culling; the benefits and qualities of different soil types. He conducted interviews with landowners, tenant farmers, small-holders, land agents and labourers (though only a handful of the latter). In the main the labourers' point of view was mediated by their employers. A Mr S. Sweetman wrote to Haggard complaining that his articles 'smacked too much of the Royal Agricultural Society. ... You have told us much about the landlord's losses ... but not much about the common labourer'.[107] Haggard conducted few interviews with labourers and didn't meet with agricultural trade unions, an exclusion that 'resulted in a largely uncritical acceptance of the opinions of the employers about the character and quality of their workforces'.[108]

A constant refrain pertained to the scarcity of labour and the quality of that remaining. The most common reason for the shortage of agricultural labourers was that the working class had moved to towns, where they could earn higher wages and enjoy better standards of accommodation. But it wasn't just about the money; improved levels of education in rural areas had created higher aspirations and a move away from manual labour. Young people were leaving the villages 'where they were born and flocking into the towns'.[109] Haggard mourned the fact that 'some parts of England are becoming almost as lonesome as the veld of Africa'.[110] In a similar vein Thomas Hardy identified 'village tradition' as an unexpected casualty of the migratory rural population: 'a vast amount of unwritten folk-lore, local chronicle, local topography and nomenclature – is absolutely sinking, has nearly sunk, into eternal oblivion'.[111]

General William Booth, founder of the Salvation Army, was convinced of the 'greatness of the evils resulting from the desertion by the rural population of the villages for the towns', earnestly desiring 'that the movement should be checked in the interest of the country at large and its inhabitants'.[112] Haggard interviewed Booth – 'one of the few great men of our time'[113] – at the army's farming colony at Hadleigh, Essex, where he recorded that Booth's 'views and my own seem to be identical in all essentials'.[114]

As a remedy to the migration of the rural population to urban areas, Haggard recommended making loans available to those wanting to buy land, thereby creating a class of new landowners. Haggard was a 'strong believer' in smallholdings: 'wherever small-holdings exist in England there is comparative prosperity, great love of the soil, and a desire to cultivate it'.[115] None of these ideas were popular among the land-owning classes, as Haggard well knew: he wouldn't even find 'standing room upon any of our political platforms ... Therefore, he must be content to remain outside, doing whatever work may come to his hand which he conceives to be clean and, in however humble a measure, useful'.[116]

Haggard made six requests of government: improve rural accommodation; increase financial allocations to agriculture; institute tax reform; review legal issues around land ownership; bolster the power and status of the Board of Agriculture; and lower agricultural transport costs. He cited the example of Denmark, which, despite having 'no advantage over England in soil or climate', had the 'enormous advantage of a Government sympathetic to agriculture',[117] which legislated in its favour.

With the passage of time Haggard's magnum opus has become 'a standard source for historians of rural life'.[118] Both *Rural England* and *A Farmer's Year* are 'recognised as key reading for anyone who wants to know how and why the countryside we see now has emerged'.[119] Contemporary reviewers were more reserved, reflecting political and class perspectives in rejecting Haggard's uncomfortable findings in their desperation to buttress the English urban myth of country life being one long bucolic idyll. The *Edinburgh Review* agreed with much of what Haggard had to say but distanced itself from his conclusions: the 'picture ... is painted in colours altogether too dark'.[120] The *Spectator* acknowledged 'not only [*Rural England*'s] literary charm but the great interest of much of the information' it contained, but vehemently disagreed with Haggard's 'gloomy and dispiriting conclusions',[121] accusing him of failing to distinguish 'his conclusions from his preconceptions ... His judgment seems constitutionally pessimistic.'[122] The *Morning Post* thought 'No gloomier picture of rural England was ever penned'.[123] Conceding Haggard didn't paint a 'cheerful picture', the *Contemporary Review* reassured its readers he wasn't an 'irresponsible alarmist' and that *Rural England* was 'written with a professional charm and whole hearted love of the soil, of growing things, of country sights and sounds, that despite its ballast of facts and figures, carries it into the domain of literature ... It will live for many generations to come.'[124] Kipling considered *Rural England* 'stands with your *Farmer's Year* between Young's *Agriculture of Sussex* and [Gilbert White's] *Selborne*. I take off my hat to you deeply and profoundly because it's a magnum opus and altogether fascinating and warning and chock full of instruction.'[125]

Haggard spent most of 1903 at Ditchingham resting on his laurels almost literally, writing *A Gardener's Year*,[126] a companion to *A Farmer's Year* with a less ambitious focus. It was serialised in the *Queen* in 1904 and published as a book in January 1905, subsequently going 'through two editions and [it] gave pleasure to a good many people'.[127] Among them were the Kiplings in Cape Town, then guests of Cecil Rhodes at the house known as the Woolsack.[128] 'Everything in the book delights my sympathetic soul except your orchids. These leave me cold ... you waste whole pages on Muscisimilifloribunda Venezuelianinis and such like. But I suppose you have fellow maniacs in your ploy.'[129] The garden at Ditchingham House was Haggard's hobby and its 'glory was the orchid houses'.[130]

Haggard continued his agricultural crusade with letters to *The Times*, speeches, articles and press interviews in which he batted away questions about his fiction to foreground his agricultural concerns. When *Rural England* was reprinted in 1906, Haggard wrote a preface for the new edition, there was naught for comfort: 'I must with humiliation report that nothing of consequence has happened';[131] if anything, 'the present state of agriculture ... appears on the whole to have still further disimproved'.[132]

22

'HIGHER AIMS'

At Shepheard's in Cairo in 1887 all the guests had 'sat around one long table'. In 1904 Haggard was not at Shepheard's but at the Gezirah Palace and there were 'two or three hundred people seated on the verandah, all dressed as though for a garden party, and at dinner that night I should say quite five hundred'. Gone was 'the quaint old Cairo of the past. It is a fashion resort of the rich, like Monte Carlo,'[1] where 'wealthy people from England and America, Jews from Johannesburg and successful Germans gather together to spend their superfluous riches, and to display their diamonds and fine clothes. It is all very gay and brilliant, but for the antiquarian, the lover of old Egypt and of the East, the place is spoiled.'[2]

Haggard embarked on his second trip to Egypt on 13 February with his eldest daughter, 21-year-old Angela, as companion and secretary. The trip was jinxed from the start. Even before reaching the English Channel, their P&O liner RMS *Macedonia* (on its maiden voyage to Bombay via Marseilles) ran aground in the Thames estuary and then had to heave-to again 'to bury a Lascar overboard – who, poor fellow, had died of the cold'.[3] In the Channel a 'terrific gale' destroyed the ship's wind gauges and stove in the fore-hatch, flooding the passenger corridors. Worse was to come. The new engines overheated and 'the chief engineer went mad with the strain' and 'rushed from cabin to cabin, telling the passengers to get up as the ship was sinking!'[4] Entering the Mediterranean, the ship nearly ran aground on the coast of North Africa, and in the harbour at Gibraltar an anchor fouled with the mooring chains of a battleship and had to be slipped. After slinging another anchor in the Gulf of Lyons, 'we encountered a very bad *mistral*' and 'crawled into Marseilles at three knots the hour'. Several passengers disembarked at the French port, one explaining, 'for the comfort of the rest of us, that he had the strongest presentiments that [the ship] was going to sink'.[5] As they sailed to Port Said a sandstorm 'turned the day to darkness and covered the decks with a kind of mud'. The ship got 'uncomfortably near the coast of Crete' and began 'shipping seas in the most unaccountable manner'.[6] At Port Said, Haggard was never 'more glad to find myself on land again',[7] as the mad engineer was 'carried ashore raving'.[8] But there were still the 'baksheesh blood-suckers' handling the luggage at the railway station, which cost the 'loss of two articles and a mix-up of the baggage'.[9] No wonder Haggard was a little sour as he dined at the Gezirah.

Cruising upriver on the Nile, Haggard eased back into reveries of the past, 'living again for a time in that lost and ancient world where strangely enough he felt so completely at home, knowing as he himself said, more of its civilisation and its history than he did of that of his own country'.[10] At Luxor Haggard met Howard Carter excavating in the Valley of the Kings. They had met before in the comparatively small world of Egyptology and also enjoyed a childhood connection: their interest in ancient Egypt was inspired by the Tyssen-Amherst collection of Didlington Hall. William Tyssen-Amherst frequently employed the talents of Samuel Carter, a well-known artist and Howard Carter's father. Under Samuel's tuition Howard became a skilled draughtsman who could 'draw and paint with more than ordinary skill'.[11] His skills came to the notice of the Amherst family, and at Margaret Tyssen-Amherst's recommendation the 17-year-old Howard Carter went to Egypt under the auspices of the Egypt Exploration Fund in 1891 to work as an archaeological artist making tracings and drawings. Recording and observation led to conservation and restoration, followed by exploration and excavation. At the time of Haggard's visit Carter had been Inspector of Antiquities in Upper Egypt for the Egyptian government for four years.[12]

Carter took Haggard and Angela around the recently discovered and 'wonderfully decorated'[13] tomb of Queen Nefertari, principal queen of Rameses II, together with the tomb's discoverer, Ernesto Schiaparelli, head of the Italian Archaeological Mission to Egypt.[14] Carter also took them to the tombs 'of Set, Rameses III, and Amenhotep II, all now lit with electricity. The unwrapped body of Amenhotep lies in its sarcophagus, calmly asleep with the electric light blazing full upon his majestic face. Such is the end of royalty – a poor, hideous, dishevelled corpse.'[15]

Carter agreed with Haggard regarding the 'scandal of removing ... the dead and approves of my trying to ventilate it'.[16] Haggard subsequently wrote a series of six articles for the *Daily Mail* on the topic 'Egypt Today: The Land of Cleopatra'. In his final article, 'The Trade in the Dead', Haggard aired his and Carter's concerns about 'the wholesale robbery of the ancient Egyptian tombs and the consequent desecration of the dead', questioning the exposure of royal mummies to public view in the Museum of Antiquities in Cairo.[17] 'Should we English not shudder' if 3,000 years hence 'those who rest in Westminster Abbey were destined to be treated in just this fashion, to satisfy the curiosity of men unborn?'[18] Criticising the trade in mummies which led to tombs being violated and robbed, he recommended that after scientific study the 'royal bodies should be restored to their sepulchres'.[19] If that was not possible, he proposed they be 'placed in the central chamber of the Great Pyramid ... a cavity of no great interest', to be subsequently pumped 'full of cement, so that it may remain inviolate for ever'.[20]

Haggard and Angela travelled back to England via Naples and Spain, visiting Granada, Cordova and Seville, where Haggard harvested background for a historical novel set in Spain at the time of Inquisition, *Fair Margaret*, published in September 1907. On his return to Ditchingham Haggard began work on what would become *The Way of the Spirit*, 'the result of reflections which occurred to me among the Egyptian sands and the empty cells of long-departed anchorites'.[21] Initially titled 'Renunciation', the book was a 'Platonic experiment' investigating the pros and cons of celibacy, long a conundrum of Western Christianity.[22]

The teenage Rupert Ullershaw has an affair with a married woman, Lady Devene, who is later driven to suicide by her husband. Influenced by his ultra-religious mother, Rupert vows to forsake the temptations of the flesh and follow the way of the spirit. After military service in the Sudan and Egypt – drawing on that of Haggard's brother Andrew – Rupert returns a decorated hero and is successfully wooed by his cousin Edith, a shallow young woman more in love with her villainous cousin Dick, but who transfers her affections to Rupert, as being a better match. Rupert confesses to her he had once 'committed a great sin – a love affair – a married woman. She is dead; it is all over, and, thank God! I have nothing more to confess to you.'[23] (Is this Haggard confessing to Louie in 1880?)

Immediately after their wedding, Rupert is sent on a mission to Egypt and the marriage is unconsummated. Various adventures ensue and Rupert returns to England, blind in one eye and minus his right foot, to find Edith has accepted Dick's proposal of marriage in the belief that Rupert is dead. Rupert returns to Egypt and falls in love with Mea, queen of a remnant of the ancient Egyptian civilisation. Owing to his vow and his marriage to Edith, their love also remains unconsummated and the two grow together in spiritual but not physical union. The outside world finally intervenes in the shape of Edith and Dick, who require Rupert's presence to sort out an inheritance. He is given an ultimatum: come back to his wife Edith or remain in Egypt with Mea. In the event Rupert doesn't have to make a choice as both he and Mea die of the plague, and with her last words Mea declares: 'Behold! we who have followed the way of the Spirit inherit the Spirit; and we who renounced, renounce no more. To me it was given to save his life; to me it is given to share his death and all beyond it through light, through dark forever and forever ... make way for [Mea] who comes to her lord's bed!'[24] Once again true love finds its consummation beyond the grave.

Alexander Watt, Haggard's literary agent, thought *The Way of the Spirit* 'perhaps one of your best and finest books, causing one to wonder if renunciation is not perhaps, the more excellent way?'[25] This quandary lay at the core of the book: 'are we not perchance befooled and blind? Driven by impulses that we did not create, but which are necessary to our creation, we follow after the flesh, and therefrom often garner bitterness, who, were our eyes opened, should pursue the spirit and win a more abiding joy which it alone can give.'[26] Lilias, pondering whether her father thought renunciation 'was the more excellent way', concluded it was something he could never decide. 'One wonders if, in his heart of hearts, Rider, with his warm, and all-embracing humanity, really believed that those truly remarkable women – his Beatrice, Jess, Stella and Mea – could, in reality, have withstood the assaults of those natural passions of which he knew the power. Perhaps not, but undoubtedly he would like to think they would.'[27]

Haggard was 'very definitely of the day when self-respecting novelists drew a hard and fast line which must at all costs terminate "compromising situations". Heroes and heroines, in however desperate a state, had to be snatched from a possible infringement of the Seventh Commandment.'[28] These inhibitions did not seem applicable beyond Britain's borders, in the stories Haggard set in Africa, South America, Iceland or ancient Egypt, where sexual relationships are either strongly implied or taken as read (for example, that of Eric and Swannhild in *Eric Brighteyes*). Different countries, different rules?

In Haggard's novels in contemporary English settings, only 'religion or extinction ... were allowed to assuage those broken hearts, often it must be frankly admitted to the detriment of the story'. Lilias once suggested to her father that 'the sorely tried damsels and the highly principled admirers might occasionally have been allowed to stray a little further down the Primrose Path'. 'No', was his response, 'nothing is easier, let me tell you, than to write a book about men and women as they really are; those risky novels you are so fond of making me read do not touch the fringe of it – but it just can't be done, my dear – it just can't be done.'[29] Lilias considered it 'could have been done but Rider's principles and convictions (not to mention his publisher) were certainly not going to allow him to do it'.[30]

Kipling read *The Way of the Spirit* in manuscript and, apart from a criticism of a scene towards the end, which Haggard rewrote, 'simply surrendered myself to the joy of reading and read on. That's better than any criticism.'[31] The book (without serialisation) was published by Hutchinson in March 1906 and, in its dedication to Kipling, Haggard stated: 'Both of us believe that there are higher aims in life than the weaving of stories well or ill, and according to our separate occasions strive to fulfil this faith.'[32]

Thanks to being of Norfolk stock, Haggard received a request to write a book on the royal estate at Sandringham in north-west Norfolk at 'the direct wish of His Majesty' Edward VII, 'practically for nothing'. Requests from royalty and from charities for books on which writers were expected to exercise their talents *pro bono* were the bane of authors' lives, being – especially if a royal command – well-nigh impossible to turn down. Haggard's view was that 'the whole principle of these charity books was extremely bad. People contribute to them because they must ... and they compete most seriously with the work of those who live by writing.' He made 'urgent representations' and 'got out of the writing the book, but was still obliged to spend a fortnight's research and writing composing the introduction',[33] signing it off on 1 September 1904. The book, written by William A. Dutt, was published in November with the title *The King's Homeland: Sandringham and North West Norfolk*.[34]

Haggard didn't begrudge the invitation to be president of the Old Ipswichian Club for 1904–5. He had maintained contact with his old school and his first recorded visit there as an Old Ipswichian was to the Fancy Fair held over two days in July 1889 to raise funds for a new school boiler. Louie ran the club's stall. Haggard spoke at the annual speech day in 1905 and presented the prizes, telling those assembled that 'the room seemed to be full of ghosts' and that it was strange to be back at his old school 'surveying an utterly alien crowd'. Fortunately some 'tradition of me remained in the place' and one of the pupils took Haggard to the room that had been his study and showed him the first two initials of his name, H.R., carved on the mantelpiece. 'Although I was in a great hurry to catch the train, I made shift to add the remaining "H."'[35]

A 'very extraordinary incident' occurred on the night of Saturday, 9 July 1904.[36] Haggard had a dream about his black retriever, 'a most amiable and intelligent beast' named Bob, who 'was trying to speak to me in words, and, failing, transmitted to my mind in an undefined fashion the knowledge that it was dying. Then everything vanished, and I woke to hear my wife asking me why on earth I was making those horrible and weird noises.'[37]

Though this was initially dismissed as 'nothing more than a disagreeable dream', when it became evident the dog was missing 'inquiries were set on foot'[38] and the retriever's body was found 'floating in the Waveney'. Bob had been hit by a train, fallen into the river and drowned, 'undergoing, I imagine, much the same sensations as I did in my dream, and in very similar surroundings to those that I saw therein'.[39] Haggard concluded that the dog, 'between whom and myself, there existed a mutual attachment', had succeeded 'in calling my attention to its actual or recent plight by placing whatever portion of my being is capable of receiving such impulses when enchained by sleep, into its own terrible position'.[40]

Haggard was 'frightened and upset' by the experience and it 'produced a great effect upon me', an enlightenment that allowed him to grasp 'the kinship, I might almost say the oneness, of all animal life'. He had always been fond of animals, especially dogs. 'But up to this date I had also been a sportsman. Shooting was my principal recreation.' Following Bob's death,

> except noxious insects and so forth, I have killed nothing, and, although I should not hesitate to shoot again for food or for protection, I am by no means certain that the act would not make me feel unwell. Perhaps illogically, I make an exception in favour of fishing … I do not think that fish feel much; also I always remember that, if He did not fish Himself, our Lord was frequently present while others did, even after His Resurrection; further, that he ate of the results, and indeed by His power made those results more plentiful.[41]

To relinquish shooting, Haggard's 'one great amusement',[42] was a remarkable gesture for someone of Haggard's class. 'To give it all up for what many of his friends considered some childish dream and the death of an old retriever, seemed to most of them not only foolish but fantastic. But their protests fell on deaf ears – Rider's mind was made up.'[43] The decision came at personal cost: 'I have now no recreation left save that of the garden and of my solitary walks about the farm, which lead, perhaps, to too much thinking.'[44] Haggard didn't impose his choice on others and, though he no longer engaged in shooting, accompanied friends 'who are happy in so doing.'[45]

Out of the blue on 14 January 1905 Haggard received a letter from Alfred Lyttelton, Secretary of State for the Colonies, requesting that he consent to being appointed a commissioner to inspect and report upon the labour colonies established in the United States by the Salvation Army. If they were 'financially sound' and of 'real benefit to the poorer classes', they might 'prove a useful model for some analogous system of settlement from the United Kingdom to the Colonies.'[46] Here indeed was an opportunity for Haggard to pursue 'higher aims', but, unknown to him, the invitation was a trap, one well baited by Lyttelton, who suggested this was a post to which Haggard's 'experience as an observer both of men and agricultural affairs so eminently qualifies you. The remuneration is not very great, but the interest of the question to which the inquiry will relate and the public service which the Commissioner will be able to do may induce you, I hope, to undertake it.'[47]

An acknowledged authority on agriculture, Haggard had become a thorn in the side of Arthur Balfour's government, a Unionist coalition with a cabinet 'largely composed of landed aristocrats or their relations.'[48] Together with the Salvation Army's General Booth, Haggard used his books, articles, public speeches and letters to the press to highlight the government's inertia in dealing with the decline of British agriculture and the plight of the urban poor.[49] Booth's remedy was kibbutz-style farms where unskilled town dwellers could learn agricultural skills and thereafter apply them in the white settler societies of the British Empire. What better than a commission undertaken in an election year to conveniently divert the attentions of these two prominent critics away from the home front?

Haggard and Booth had become the best of friends, 'perhaps, because I was never afraid of him, as seemed to be the case with so many of those by whom he was surrounded.'[50] Both believed smallholdings were the solution to keeping people working on the land. In both England and the United States the Salvation Army had established training camps to provide skills to the urban poor, enabling them to lead productive rural lives.

Haggard's inquiry was to be funded by the Rhodes Trustees, who would provide '£300 (inclusive of all expenses) to defray the expense of sending a Commissioner to the United States.'[51] Haggard would travel as a royal commissioner, an official government representative. On accepting Lyttelton's invitation, he received a detailed brief and the instruction that, after inspecting the Salvation Army's settlements in the United States, he should proceed to Ottawa in Canada and discuss the subject with the Governor General, Lord Grey, who had shown interest in implementing a similar scheme.[52]

Haggard, again with Angela as companion and secretary, sailed for New York on 22 February 1905 aboard the *Teutonic*. The name inevitably recalled the *Teuton* disaster of 1881 off the South African coast and Haggard can only have interpreted it as a sinister omen. But for once the voyage was uneventful (excepting confusions with luggage before embarkation from Liverpool) and on arrival in New York they were met by Colonel Edward John Higgins, chief secretary of the Salvation Army, and installed in a suite at the Waldorf in Manhattan. Here the American press tracked Haggard down in the middle of the night. He eventually removed the handset from the telephone after cutting his foot in rushing to answer it.

Haggard gave an interview to William Griffiths of the *New York Times*, who told his readers the 'one time writer of romances' was now 'a smiling Rhodes Commissioner, come to study the Salvation Army farming forts in Ohio, Colorado and California' as well as 'the vacant lot colony scheme in Philadelphia'.[53] Asked if he had abandoned writing fiction, 'the father of African romance' replied: 'Sociological investigation is expensive ... and one must have means to pursue it independently. Fiction is the means in my case – sociology the end ... no, I have not neglected, far from having abandoned, fiction. As for my sociological work ... it is, one might say, my serious contribution to my people and age.' Haggard said 'he hoped to discover, before leaving America, a working remedy for three major maladies now menacing English progress and civilisation – slumdom, bumdom and rumdom'.[54]

A subsequent interview with the *New York Herald*, run under the headline 'H. Rider Haggard Turned Colonizer' above the subheading 'If he still has a She, he has put a Salvation Army bonnet on her', gives a snapshot of the 48-year-old Haggard:

> Mr. Haggard puts formality at an end by a breezy, poseless, highly English manner. He is very tall and on his very broad shoulders his large enough head sits small in the manner of the 'Farnese Hercules'. He lounges very low in his chair and puffs affectionately at a homely old pipe ... His answers are quick, blunt, brutally final: 'Oh, I don't want to talk about literature!'... 'Hey what?' came out like an explosion. It was fairly detonated. Mr Haggard's speech is quite his own. Giant as he is and cultivated as he is, he has as much trouble with his 'th's' as a baby, a Frenchman or a Dutchman ... the effect is quaintly pleasant ... It was only when he got to the practical side of life that he began to warm up and talk without prodding. He grew earnest, enthusiastic, cogent; but always without arrogance, without self-praise, or over-confidence ... The Rider Haggard of the new crusade is another man from the jaunty romancer of a decade ago.[55]

In Washington, Haggard met Theodore Roosevelt shortly after the latter's inauguration for his second term as president. The White House 'was crowded with people waiting to shake hands with the new Chief of the State, amongst whom I noted a band of Indian chiefs, men with long black hair, copper-coloured skins, and strongly marked features'. Haggard's first impression of Roosevelt was of a 'short, stout man with a fair, fresh complexion and rows of very even teeth, which he shows in their entirety every time he smiles. In manner he is frank and earnest, nor does he mince his words and opinions.'[56] The two had a mutual friend in Kipling.[57]

Discussing land settlement, they found their views were identical. Roosevelt recognised the 'inevitable deterioration of the race which must ensue if the land-dwellers were to become city-dwellers'.[58] Thus began a friendship, maintained by correspondence, lasting until Roosevelt's death in 1919. After this meeting of minds with Roosevelt and an encouraging interview with James Wilson, Secretary of State for Agriculture, Haggard embarked with enthusiasm on a coast-to-coast rail trip to Los Angeles, California, accompanied by a small Salvation Army staff, including Ranson Caygill, treasurer of Industrial Homes, as Haggard's secretary, and his assistant, Staff Captain Harry Wright, as the commissioner's typist, plus Angela, designated 'the Commissioner's Private Secretary'.[59]

At a weekend stopover in El Paso, Haggard recalled passing through the border town with Louie on their way to Mexico in 1891. He spent his time inspecting local farming projects and visiting the Mexican side of town, declining an invitation to attend a bullfight. He grew impatient at the constant attention from people wanting autographs or to discuss his books. 'When we were in the bus [prior to visiting the farming projects] some tourists from Ohio rushed me, wanting to see "R.H." I was so annoyed that I pointed out my Secretary Caygill as the party & they fell on him. He took the point & scraped & bowed while they went on about books &c to the amusement of Angie and the people on the bus, while I did Secretary.'[60]

When their train puffed into Los Angeles at 1.30 on the morning of 24 March, Frederick Burnham was there to greet them. The Burnhams and their two sons, 18-year-old Roderick and 7-year-old Bruce, lived in nearby Pasadena, where the family had settled in 1903 after leaving southern Africa. Burnham accompanied Haggard and Angela to the Westminster Hotel on the corner of Fourth Street and Main Street. The following morning Haggard visited a chiropodist to remove five corns which had made walking painful. Both he and Angela came down with 'California colds'. Later in the day Burnham took them 'by the electric trams' to Pasadena, 'a fine place, very pretty at this season of the year', where Burnham had built 'a charming wooden house on a bluff'. In the afternoon Burnham drove them around Pasadena 'in a splendid motor car belonging to a friend of his, a millionaire, visiting the orange groves & places of interest'. After dinner that evening, Julian Hawthorne, son of the novelist, 'a pleasant, elderly man',[61] came to interview Haggard.

From Los Angeles the Haggard party took the train north to the Salvation Army colony of Fort Romie near Soledad, 150 miles south of San Francisco, and spent three days there – 'a very pleasant place – like stopping at a farm'[62] – interviewing Salvation Army officials and colonists. In San Francisco a visit to the Golden Gate

Bridge was followed by one to Chinatown. Haggard's speech at the California College was greeted with warm applause, though some newspapers declined to report on it 'because I instanced General Gordon, Cecil Rhodes and General Booth as instances of what men could rise to in our generation. They are angry because the whole three are *Englishmen* and say I ought to have quoted *Americans*. They are curiously vain & childish in that way.'[63]

Haggard also ran into John Hays Hammond, 'the great mining engineer, a charming fellow'.[64] Haggard had met Hammond, an associate of Cecil Rhodes, when involved with the *African Review*. The two dined together and, when Hammond heard Haggard was about to travel to Ottawa, he offered to take them as far as Salt Lake City in his private carriage. Hammond gives a colourful description of their journey in his autobiography. The engineer told stories about 'some of the famous holdups' on the track on which they were travelling and, he reported, Haggard went to bed with the scenes 'still vividly present to his mind'. A short while later James, 'my negro cook, came rushing into my room and in great agitation asked what was wrong with my guest'. As Haggard was asleep with his light on, James had gone in to switch it off. Pistol in hand, Haggard leapt 'from his berth and threatened to shoot'. The next day Hammond told Haggard 'it was permissible to defend himself against bandits, but he would have to be careful with James; in addition to being the best cook I had ever had, James was also the best shot'.[65]

At a dinner one night Haggard remarked regretfully that 'he had never encountered a hobo in the flesh'. One was conveniently to hand 'riding the brake beams of our car' and was duly produced 'grimy with dirt and cinders, ragged, and nearly frozen from the cold ride through the snowsheds and alkali desert'. When Hammond introduced Haggard, the hobo's face lit up: '"You don't mean the famous Rider Haggard?" "Yes," I said, "the very same man." "Mr. Haggard," he said, "I've read all your books – some of them several times," and he rattled off their names.'[66] The new guest was invited to dinner – after a shower and in some new clothes – and thereafter was employed by Hammond.

Hammond parted company with Haggard at Ogden, and the train continued on to Salt Lake City, where Haggard and Angela spent a day visiting 'the wonderful Mormon buildings' and met Joseph F. Smith, president of the Church of Latter Day Saints.[67] From Salt Lake City it was on to the Salvation Army colony at Fort Amity in Colorado, where Haggard spent three days studying 'its conditions, its inhabitants, their circumstances and methods of farming'.[68] A photograph shows him standing with a group of children on the bare dusty ground in front of their clapboard school. Then it was back on the train again for two days to Cleveland, Ohio, from where Haggard made a short visit to nearby Fort Herrick, 'devoted to the redemption of inebriates and to the carrying out of certain agricultural experiments'.[69]

Haggard arrived in Ottawa on 13 April. On the long train journey, assisted by Harry Wright, he roughed out a draft report to submit to the Governor General,

Lord Grey. He also gave an address in Ottawa to members of the Canadian Club, a speech he considered one of his best.[70] In it he outlined the 'enormous change that is coming over the Western world; how those, who for countless generations, dwelt upon the land, are deserting the land and crowding into the cities ... The strength of a people, gentlemen, is not to be found in their Wall Streets, it is to be found in the farms and fields and villages.'[71] Haggard said that in Canada there would 'very soon' be 'enormous competition for immigration, for population, and especially for Anglo-Saxon population ... And I venture to say to you: Get them while you can, get them from home, get them from England.'[72] Haggard's speech – and his proposals – were well received. Lord Grey (another associate of Rhodes, a former director of the British South Africa Company and former Administrator of Southern Rhodesia) and the Canadian prime minister, Sir Wilfred Laurier, were prepared to set aside 'ten townships (240,000 acres) for the objects set forth by the said H. Rider Haggard'.[73]

Throughout his North American trip Haggard corresponded with his brother Andrew, then living in Maine. Since resigning his commission, Andrew had 'fallen on evil days'[74] and crossed the Atlantic to pursue a peripatetic, often penniless existence (relieved by occasional loans from Rider), roaming between the United States and Canada. He also continued writing but without great success. In 1883 he married Emily Chirnside, but somewhere in all these wanderings the couple parted company. Increasingly jealous of his sibling's fame, a depressed Andrew was hoping for another loan from his famous brother, who, or so Andrew believed, had a nest egg in the United States thanks to the enormous sales of his books. 'I only wish the riches Andrew supposes had any existence. The fact is I can make precious little out of America although it is true I am famous here.'[75]

Haggard dithered over inviting his brother to Ottawa, as he would be staying with Lord Grey and Andrew would 'feel injured if he isn't there too which I can't arrange for him'. Instead Haggard asked Andrew if he would like 'to come to New York as my guest', before Haggard and Angela departed the United States on 19 April, but he worried 'there will be the same awkwardness as they are going to entertain me at the Lotos Club & they probably won't ask him & if they did, he would not like it. I mean my being the guest of the evening. So altogether it is rather difficult.'[76] Andrew declined his brother's invitation in a sad and bitter letter:

> As to coming to New York to see you sailing away home again after your rapid and triumphal progress – and leaving me behind, well, my dear Rider, it would be too absolutely distressing and I could not stand it. To be alone on the wharf in New York, with no friends, no glory, no excitement, no money, while seeing the smoke from your funnels disappearing. And then all the headlines in the papers – 'Departure of Rider Haggard' – 'Distinguished Novelist Leaves for Europe' – 'Americans are like his Brothers' – that sort of thing greeting me everywhere would be too much altogether – I know our positions are very different – and the cry is why did I ever leave the

Army? Did I blame you for leaving Sir Henry Bulwer for Shepstone, Shepstone for the High Court, the High Court for Ostriches, Ostriches for the Bar and the Divorce Courts, the Bar for Literature? I left the Army because I did not choose to serve in subordinate positions under Kitchener etc., who served under me. Also I got two thousand pounds – gone now! Because *I* have been less fortunate than my rich and successful brother in my change of occupation, *I* must be reproached for leaving the Army.[77]

Andrew married again in 1906, to Ethel Fowler, an English widow he met in Boston. He continued writing histories and biographies, mainly on French subjects. Andrew and Ethel later settled in St Leonard's on the Sussex coast, a popular retirement spot for ex-colonials, as did Haggard's sister Baroness Mary d'Anethan after the death of her husband.

In his cabin aboard the *Majestic*, Haggard drafted his final report, which he delivered on 5 May, and a few days later had 'a brief interview' with Alfred Lyttelton at the House of Commons. Haggard asked if he was satisfied with his work. "'Satisfied?" responded Lyttelton. "I think it splendid," adding, "I wish the Prime Minister would take it up. But *Arthur won't read it – you know Arthur won't read it!*"[78] At long last the penny dropped: Haggard had been gulled. 'I thought to myself then, and am still thinking, that this "Arthur won't read it" was a summary of much of the action, or lack of action, of the Government of that day.'[79]

Haggard's report was published as a Blue Book on 20 June. Two days later, on his forty-ninth birthday, Haggard spent a couple of hours with the editor of the *Review of Reviews*, W.T. Stead, an old foe turned ally, 'devising how we could put pressure on the Govt re my Report!'[80] Their battles in the 1880s had long been put behind them – 'of late years Mr. Stead has quite changed his attitude towards me and has indeed become very complimentary, both with reference to my literary and to my public work. For my part, too, I have long ago forgiven his onslaughts.'[81]

Haggard's report was brimful with information, interview transcriptions, ancillary data and tables, skilfully applied to closely argued conclusions and recommendations. 'Mr. Rider Haggard has done a public service in collecting the information contained in his Report, and in making suggestions which may prove fruitful,' declared *The Times*.[82] Stead's *Review of Reviews* was more direct: 'What more need is there to labour the point? The scheme is business-like, sound and ready.' The *Daily Telegraph* lauded Haggard's efforts, with the caveat that his report 'will possibly remain at the same time the most important and the least read of his varied literary achievements'.[83]

Haggard was deeply wounded by the cynical use and abuse of his talents. 'I confess I did wish that Mr. Lyttelton could have spared me an hour or two in which to talk over its leading points with him, as, for instance, President Roosevelt found himself able to do in the midst of all the tumultuous ceremonies of his inauguration.'[84]

Speaking at the annual general meeting of the Imperial South African Association at Grosvenor House on 14 July, Haggard said that whatever 'the difficulties of writing such a report may involve they are nothing to the difficulties involved in trying to get anybody to read it'.[85] He also discussed the application of the report and its recommendations to South Africa and Rhodesia, urging the settlement of surplus British citizens on 'the waste lands of Rhodesia, so that there may grow up a strong British nation'.[86]

In a bid to goad the authorities into action, Haggard persuaded Longmans to publish his report for public consumption. *The Poor and the Land: Being a Report on the Salvation Army Colonies in the United States and at Hadleigh, England, with Scheme of National Land Settlement* was published in August 1905, thereby placing the report's findings before a larger audience. Again it drew approval in the press, but to little or no avail. There was a brief debate in the House of Commons and Haggard's report was referred to a departmental committee chaired by Lord Tennyson, a former Governor General of Canada and eldest son of the poet. Haggard learned of this from a Conservative agent, who had been told by a cabinet minister 'that my Report was to be sent to a Committee which would "knock the bottom out of it". Then I knew that all was finished.'[87]

Haggard was correct: 'the bottom was knocked out' of his report 'in the most satisfactory official way', and while the departmental committee fully recognised Haggard's 'zeal and ability ... we regret to be obliged to say that we consider his scheme to be open to so many objections that, even if we were prepared to advocate colonisation in principle, we could not recommend that this particular scheme should be adopted ... Moreover, we feel that there are serious objections to placing any such body as the Salvation Army in the position of managers of a colony dependent on money advanced by the Imperial Government.'[88] Lilias was in no doubt that 'prejudice against the Salvation Army had much to do with this decision'.[89] The committee further washed its hands of the matter by recommending Haggard's report be discussed at the next Colonial Conference two years hence.

Haggard had been treated as a statesman in the United States and Canada, but at home he was shown to the tradesman's entrance. 'For me personally this issue was painful. I had worked hard and in all honesty, and, like many better men, I had found myself thrown over'. He didn't receive a letter of thanks from the government nor a copy of the report and evidence of the committee, which he had to buy like 'any other member of the public. All I got was the privilege of paying the bill, for of course the small sum allowed by the Rhodes Trustees did not suffice to meet the expenses of my tour in a high official position through that very expensive country, the United States.'[90]

In the spring of 1907 the Colonial Conference (thereafter known as the Imperial Conference) was held in London. Here it was resolved to grant Dominion status to the self-governing British colonies of Australia, Canada, Newfoundland and New Zealand, and to bring together Natal and the Cape Colony with the Transvaal and the

Orange River Colony (as the Orange Free State was named after its annexation during the Anglo-Boer War) to form the Union of South Africa three years later in 1910.

Also on the agenda was the question of what to do with Britain's surplus population. Australia's prime minister, Alfred Deakin, urged that emigrants be encouraged 'to proceed to British colonies rather than foreign countries' and argued that the British government had an obligation to encourage 'people of British stock' wishing to leave Britain to emigrate to the colonies of Empire with their boundless scope for settlement rather than 'other countries under other flags'. Their presence not only increased the prosperity of those colonies, leading to greater trade with Britain, but also offered 'a guarantee for the control of those great territories by our own people and our own race'.[91] Haggard was not invited to the conference.

23

'SADNESS OF THE WORLD'

Haggard's long and arduous North American trip – he estimated he had travelled 12,000 miles – took a severe toll on his health. He had endured colds, constipation, stomach troubles and neuralgia, and the government's cold shoulder was the final straw. In September 1905, under the supervision of his doctor and friend Lyne-Stivens, Haggard 'retired for a month or five weeks' to a London nursing home at 24 Devonshire Street in Marylebone, the capital's medical district, and underwent 'an operation which the effects of my long journey made necessary'.[1] The operation was performed by one of the top surgeons of the day, William Rose, former professor of surgery at King's College Hospital and an expert on procedures to relieve neuralgia. Haggard was installed in 'a quiet little room at the top' of the home, where he had 'a little chicken & milk pudding for dinner. My tummy feels better.'[2] The room wasn't as quiet as he first thought and later he complained of the constant din: 'the dreadful noise caused by the horse drawn carriages of theatre-goers going home ... the rattle of the mail-carts over the stone-paved road; the continual operations; the occasional rush of the nurses when it was announced that a patient was passing away; and so forth'.[3]

The precise nature of Haggard's operation isn't known, but it was serious enough for Haggard to be given a general anaesthetic for the first time. 'I can still see the face of my friend Dr Lyne-Stivens, and the jovial, rubicund countenance of the late Professor Rose, bending over me as through a mist, both grown so strangely solemn, and feel the grip of my hand tightening upon that of the nurse which afterwards it proved almost impossible to free. Then came the whirling pit and the blackness. I suppose that it was like death, only I hope that death is not quite so dark!'[4] Haggard awoke 'in a state of utter intoxication' to find nurses gathered round him with 'the familiar, hateful autograph books in which, even in that place and hour, they insisted I should write'.[5]

Haggard's time at the nursing home coincided with the publication on 6 October of *Ayesha*, the sequel to *She*.[6] Haggard entertained himself and the night nurse by reading the book 'aloud to her during my long wakeful hours'. Written in 1903, *Ayesha* was published two decades after *She* 'in obedience to my original plan'.[7] The ground for a sequel had been seeded in *She*, which closes with Leo Vincey and Horace Holly en route for Tibet, leaving behind the manuscript of *She* to be published in their absence. Haggard's selection of Tibet in 1886 as a location for Ayesha's resurrection was prescient, for by the time *Ayesha* was published in 1905 Tibet had caught the public imagination thanks to Madame Blavatsky's writings, the sympathetic figure of the Tibetan lama in Rudyard Kipling's *Kim*, and in 1903, the year Haggard wrote *Ayesha*, the British invasion of Tibet – the first major Western incursion into a land which traditionally discouraged outsiders. The invasion opened a door into Tibet, its religion and culture, as never before.

Like its predecessor, *Ayesha* was dedicated to Andrew Lang, who was delighted but doubtful as to the wisdom of resurrecting She-Who-Must-Be-Obeyed, confessing to being 'almost afraid to read' the sequel 'as at 61,00000 one has no longer the joyous credulity of forty, and even *your* imagination is out of the fifth form'.[8] To Haggard's great relief, Lang sent another letter the following day: 'I am Thrilled: so much obliged.'[9]

The thrills commence in a house 'upon the desolate sea-shore of Cumberland'[10] where Leo Vincey and Horace Holly holed up in 1885 'to recover from the fearful shock'[11] of their African experiences and to await news of Ayesha's promised reappearance. Twenty years on, Leo has a vision of Ayesha and dreams of a fiery volcanic mountain crested with a *crux ansata* or ankh, the ancient Egyptian symbol of life and rebirth. Interpreting this as the sign they have been waiting for, they depart for Tibet and are led by further portents into unmapped regions of Central Asia, where they find the mountain of Leo's dream in the land of the Kaloons, a people ruled by an evil Khan and his queen Atene. Atene is a reincarnation of Amenartas, and thus the recurring triangle of Kallikrates, Ayesha and Amenartas take up their places. There is much discussion and speculation on reincarnation in *Ayesha*, which, like its predecessor, draws heavily on Theosophy, referring to theosophical concepts such as the Devachan, an intermediary state between human incarnations.

Leo and Horace are anxious to explore the mountain, an active volcano and the home of Hes (an alternative name for Isis as well as an anagram of She), head of a religious cult protected by a different race from the Kaloons. Escaping the city of Kaloon – and killing the Khan in the process – they encounter a mysterious woman, silent and shrouded, who guides them to the mountain. Of course, this is Ayesha, and on a platform at the edge of the volcano she disrobes, revealing herself as an ancient crone before being revivified to her previous beauty by flames licking up at her from the central vent of the volcano.

Ayesha refuses to marry Leo until a year has passed, as any physical contact between them might prove fatal. During this period of sexual abstinence Leo and Horace grapple with the question of exactly who and what Ayesha is. As in her earlier incarnation, Ayesha possesses spiritual and magical powers but now appears to be semi-divine; true, she is still capable of the temperamental outbursts and vicious caprice of her former self, but she now possesses a gravitas and a greater understanding of the mechanics and meaning of reincarnation. 'I tell thee, Leo, that out of the confusions of our lives and deaths order shall yet be born ... Henceforth I fear no more, and fight no more against that which must befall. For I say we are but winged seeds blown down the gales of fate and change to the appointed garden where we shall grow, filling its blest air with the immortal fragrance of our bloom.'[12]

War with the Kaloons is brewing, and when they invade Ayesha's domain they are annihilated and Atene killed. Leo insists the time has come to marry. Ayesha reluctantly consents but, come their first kiss at the end of the wedding ceremony, Leo is 'slain by the fire of her love'.[13] Leo's body is consigned to the flames of the volcano's crater and Ayesha also 'passes', or at least her physical form disappears. 'Whither had she gone? I know not. But this I know, that as the light returned and the broad sheet of flame flared out to meet it, I seemed to see two glorious shapes sweeping upward on its bosom, and the faces that they wore were those of Leo and of Ayesha.'[14] Once again Haggard sounds the drum of love eternal beyond the grave for those who loved each other on earth but were parted in life: 'in death is love's home, in death its strength; that from the charnel-house of life this love springs again glorified and pure, to reign a conqueror for ever'.[15]

Ayesha was received much as sequels are wont to be: compared with the original and found wanting. As if anticipating a negative response, Haggard states in an 'Author's Note' that he did not regard the book as a sequel, asking that *Ayesha* 'be considered as the conclusion of an imaginative tragedy ... whereof one half has been already published'.[16] Despite the unenthusiastic reviews, Haggard 'met and heard from many people who like *Ayesha* better than they do *She*'.[17] Those looking 'beyond the book as wild adventure, realised that there was a deeper meaning'.[18] One of them was the first British Nobel laureate, Ronald Ross, discoverer of the malarial parasite, who was awarded the Nobel Prize in Medicine in 1902. 'It is really a very great romance because I think it has some very high allegorical meaning. In my opinion this potentiality is what differentiates first-class romance from second-class romance. I do not know what the allegory is, but think that She is the personification of the ancient civilisation or art, and that He is the modern spirit.'[19] The exact nature of the allegory in *Ayesha* also escaped Haggard's brother Arthur, who, despite being 'intensely interested' by the book, was 'not sure that I understand it all, or quite what you are driving at', adding: 'I sometimes wonder if you quite know yourself!'[20]

On discharge from the nursing home, 'very feeble and with much-shattered nerves', Haggard began his convalescence at Dr Lyne-Stivens's home in Mayfair before going down to the Kiplings in Sussex. In 1902 Kipling had purchased 'a real House in which to settle down for keeps',[21] a grey stone Jacobean mansion set amidst the forested slopes of the Sussex Weald four miles from the village of Burwash and accessed by 'an enlarged rabbit-hole of a lane'.[22] Bateman's was a refuge and a sanctuary, a place for Kipling to lick his wounds after the bitter public row with his wife Carrie's brother Beatty and the death of his 7-year-old daughter Josephine in 1899 from pneumonia. At Bateman's he hunkered down and indulged his interest in gardening and farming; there was even a watermill to play with on the River Dudwell running through the property.

Kipling's first-floor study was lined with bookshelves, a glass fronted cabinet held the 'household gods' – golden buddhas and assorted deities from India – and his desk looked out onto the fields. Here Kipling and Haggard spent long afternoons in conversation, writing, and plotting stories. According to Kipling, the two 'found by accident that each could work at ease in the other's company. So he would visit me, and I him, with work in hand; and between us we could even hatch out tales together – a most exacting test of sympathy'.[23]

In the late autumn of 1905 Kipling and Haggard 'compounded the plot of *The Ghost Kings* together, writing down our ideas in alternate sentences'.[24] At Kipling's 'ten-foot table' they sat 'face to face ... discussing, accepting, and rejecting the notions they freely exchanged. One of them would write down the incidents they both fancied and pass the paper across the table to the other, who took up the pen and developed the outline further. Soon they had three pages of outline on which Haggard would build the tale'.[25] Kipling brought the outline to an end, 'finishing with the word *Curtain* and a flourish of the pen'.[26] Then they discussed possible titles. One, 'The Shapes', heavily crossed out, was rejected. 'Above it, Kipling wrote "The Ghost Kings", a title that satisfied them both.'[27] *The Ghost Kings* was published on 25 September 1908 following its serialisation in *Pearson's Magazine*. It is a ponderous romance-cum-novel complete with two star-crossed lovers set in Zululand and beyond.

In 1906 a two-page article headlined 'Mr Rider Haggard on the Zulus', above the subheading 'The Story of a Rebellious People', ran in the *Illustrated London News* on 19 May. This was a somewhat belated response on Haggard's part to what became known as the Bhambatha Rebellion, triggered by the introduction in January 1905 of a poll tax in Natal.[28] Natal's economy, which had expanded during the Anglo-Boer War, contracted in its aftermath and, faced with dwindling coffers, the government 'resorted to cuts in spending and an increase in revenue through a poll tax of £1 on all males'.[29] The rebellion was ruthlessly suppressed by colonial forces under the 'Natal-born and vicious' Colonel Duncan McKenzie.[30] His conduct of the campaign – drumhead court-martials, indiscriminate and extra-judicial killings, looting and burning of homesteads – earned him the nickname Shaka. There was an extra dimension to the brutality: Natal colonials were out to demonstrate to the do-gooding British government how the 'native problem' should be handled. Winston Churchill, Undersecretary for the Colonies in 1906, horrified at the methods employed and mightily frustrated at being restricted by constitutional limitations from interfering, described Natal as 'the hooligan of the empire'.[31] When touring South Africa in 1914, Haggard was shocked at what he learnt of the rebellion, which was 'suppressed with great cruelty', commenting that 'cruelty bred of fear is no new story in South Africa. The white man neglects or oppresses the native and slights his needs until something happens; then in a panic he sets to work and butchers him.'[32]

Haggard's 1906 article concluded with the current situation in Natal, where two peoples stood in opposition: 'a few white folk who ... call themselves lords of the land, and a great mass of black folk ... who in their hearts believe that Africa was made for the Africans'. This situation 'may be "damped" down for a time' but it was not going to go away. 'It will last until the native gets so cramped for room that he has no place left to settle on, except the white man's lands.'[33] Haggard feared the rebellion would turn into a 'dreadful war' in which 'the Imperial Power' might be forced to intervene. 'Moreover, once begun, such a struggle would very possibly become a race struggle, and blaze across South Africa like a grass-fire over its veld and hills.'[34]

When Lilly Archer sailed to East Africa to be reunited with her errant husband Francis in 1899, she was unaware he had contracted syphilis. He died in 1907, leaving her 'penniless and stricken with a fatal disease'.[35] Haggard again took her under his wing. Lilly returned to the Red House at Snape to stay with her sisters and, later, when the disease had reached an advanced stage, she moved to 1 Wentworth Terrace in Aldeburgh with views across the pebble beach to the cold waves of the North Sea.[36] As 'often as they could Rider and Louie went to see her – the ravaged shadow of the woman Rider had loved when they were both young, and whom, as Louie well knew, he still loved, with an affection which transcends all earthly passion and stretches out hands beyond the grave'.[37] Haggard travelled alone by train to be at Lilly's deathbed. 'When he last saw her she was dying, the lovely body ravaged with a ghastly disease, her hair short and grey, and those same blue eyes gazing out of a sunken and emaciated face – and yet he could still say of her, "one of the three really lovely women, whom I have seen in my life".'[38]

Lilly died on 22 April 1909. Haggard and Louie were among the few mourners at the funeral held at the Church of St Peter and St Paul on the hill above Aldeburgh. When the pallbearers carried the coffin to the graveyard through the western door, the arch above struck Haggard as familiar; then he realised it 'was exactly like that other arch through which I had followed her to her carriage on the night when first we met. Also, strangely different as were the surroundings, there were accessories, floral and other, that were similar in their general effect.'[39]

Lilias was aged 17 at the time of Lilly's death and would have had some knowledge of the funeral if not actually present. When she was in her twenties, and acknowledged 'by family and friends to be Rider's "inseparable companion"',[40] he confided to her his feelings on the day of Lilly's funeral:

Almost in a dream he came to the side of the grave and heard from a great distance the words: 'Man that is born of woman hath but a short time to live, and is fully of misery. He cometh up and is cut down like a flower; he fleeth as it were a shadow, and never continueth in one stay – Thou knowest, Lord, the secrets of our hearts – suffer us not, at our last hour, for any pains of death, to fall from Thee.' Rider turned, and left the dead to their sleep.[41]

Not entirely. In old age Haggard attempted an autobiographical reminiscence, determined that prior to his departure 'into the shadows, those shadows which veil the glory of the eternal dawn, I will set down that tale, the tale of my first love and almost of my first adventures'.[42] He got no further than that sentence.

Lilly's death was preceded by another, that of Haggard's first grandchild, the 7-month-old Diana. Haggard's daughter Angela married her cousin Thomas (son of Haggard's brother Bazett and Julia) in 1907. The couple's engagement brought about a reconciliation between the Haggards and Bazett's widow Julia (now married to Samuel Lofthouse, with whom she had had an affair). A year after the marriage Angela gave birth to Diana, who died in February 1909. The same year Haggard supervised the construction of the family vault in the chancel of St Mary's, Ditchingham, capable of accommodating twenty funerary urns on its shelves – 'I could not help reflecting that the next time I went down into that vault it would probably be in a compacter form.'[43]

Less than a year before, in 1908, Haggard's brother Jack died in Spain. In 1904 he had been appointed British consul in Spain for the provinces of Malaga, Almeria, Granada, Jaen and Murcia. He and his family based themselves in Malaga, where Jack died suddenly from sunstroke on 21 May 1908. Spanish law dictated that Jack must be buried in Malaga, 'a contingency of which he had always expressed much horror'.[44] He died without a pension and Aggie was left to raise four children on her own annual income of £115. Haggard came to her assistance.[45]

The death of a beloved brother and a grandchild, Lilly's long decline to an inevitable conclusion – out of this period came *Red Eve*, set against the arrival of the Black Death in Europe. At Bateman's in October 1908 Haggard and Kipling, closeted in the familiar study, hatched 'a tale that Haggard later wrote'.[46] Morton Cohen thought *Red Eve* was Haggard's 'best historical romance',[47] but the presence of Murgh, a character with supernatural powers, sees Haggard venturing into the sword-and-sorcery genre. At the heart of the story are two lovers, merchant's son Hugh de Cressi and the feisty Eve Clavering (the title character, so named for the colour of her apparel), who is coveted by the dastardly French knight Edmund Acours. The crooked path of true love takes Hugh and his companion, the crack archer Grey Dick, through the French wars and thence to Venice, where their fate and that of Acours become intertwined with Murgh, bringer of the Black Death from ancient Cathay. The historical background, the origins and impact of the Black Death, are accurately portrayed and Haggard tells his tale with suspenseful economy

– writing in the third person rules out much of the philosophising that slows down some of his first-person narratives. Many scenes are set in East Anglia, in places well known to Haggard, such as Dunwich, Blythburgh, Walberswick and Southwold.

Kipling had a hand in creating the sinister Murgh. Wanting to 'capture a sense of foreboding in the name', both writers fired off suggestions, Kipling writing them down until getting to the word '*morgue*, and by taking this word through *murth*, *murg*, and *morg*, they arrive at *murgh* and agree that is what they have been searching for'.[48] Kipling made a pencil sketch of the character and Haggard added a few notes: 'Wears gleaming black furs / His hands hid in perfumed gloves / Big quiet large boned man'[49] who presides over scenes of disease and decadence reminiscent of Edgar Allan Poe's *The Masque of the Red Death*.

Written over the winter of 1908/9, *Red Eve* was not published until August 1911.[50] In the interim Haggard had served on the Coast Erosion Commission and the book was dedicated to his fellow commissioner, the geologist James Jehu, 'who was my constant companion during those five years'.[51]

Notwithstanding the short shrift given his land settlement report, Haggard hadn't lost his desire to be of service to his country and, when Balfour's government fell at the end of 1905, he nursed the expectation that his talents might be utilised by the new Liberal government led by Sir Henry Campbell-Bannerman. 'Where is Mr Rider Haggard?' enquired an opinion piece in the January 1906 edition of Stead's *Review of Reviews*, saying that Lord Carrington's appointment as minister of agriculture, coupled with Campbell-Bannerman's 'declaration in favour of land reform and the return of the people to the country', required immediate action. 'Mr Rider Haggard ought to be despatched at once to report on all that has been done in this direction in Denmark, Holland, Belgium and Bavaria.'[52]

In February Haggard told a government committee investigating smallholdings that the growth of such holdings should be promoted as part of a 'settled agricultural policy' and that a 'model for that policy' was to be found in Denmark and he was willing to investigate the matter further *in situ*.[53] His offer was not taken up. In June Haggard gave evidence to the Select Committee on the Housing of the Working Classes Amendment Bill and in the same month he read of plans to create a Royal Commission on Coast Erosion. He wrote to the president of the Board of Trade, David Lloyd George, offering his services and explaining how he had tackled erosion at Kessingland Grange on the Norfolk coast by planting marram grass, which 'might with advantage be more widely followed'.[54] Lloyd George asked Haggard to come and see him, and 'ultimately I found myself a member of the Royal Commission',[55] chaired by a cousin of Winston Churchill, Ivor Guest. The commission was appointed under royal warrant in July 1906 and Haggard served on it for five years.[56]

Haggard's capacity for hard work was fully exploited, and shortly after the coast erosion commission began its work, he was also nominated as chairman of the Unemployed Labour and Reclamation Committee, 'which involved a great deal of extra, but important and interesting, business'.[57] The coastal commission, having sat for almost a year, found there was 'not really very much in the Coast Erosion business, which had been somewhat exaggerated'. Guest and Haggard suggested 'the question of Afforestation should be added to our Reference'.[58] Lloyd George agreed, and the commission was pressed for an interim report on afforestation. A scheme was presented whereby 'enormous areas of waste or poor land in the United Kingdom would in due course have become forests of great value. Needless to say it was *not* adopted ... the venture was too sound and quiet to be undertaken by a Government of party men who look for immediate political reward rather than to the welfare of the country forty or fifty years hence.'[59]

Haggard didn't take this official inaction as personally as he had the rejection of his land settlement report 'since now I shared the responsibility with about a score of distinguished persons who had unanimously made our futile recommendations to the Crown'.[60] Following the 'funeral' of the afforestation scheme, it was back to coastlines. 'I wonder if there is a groin or an eroded beach on the shores of the United Kingdom that I have not seen and thoughtfully considered.'[61]

Haggard chaired two evidence-gathering tours to inspect the coasts of Great Britain and Ireland, and was on his last tour of duty considering the shores of 'the most unsuccessful of all British colonial experiments'[62] in March 1910, when his Egyptian romance *Morning Star* was published by Cassell.[63] The tale of 'an ancient Egyptian Queen who is wooed and, after many strange adventures which include a good deal of the ancient magic, won by a subject who has been her foster-brother, the descendant of a discarded dynasty'. The magical elements in the book include the heroine Tua having a *ka* (or double) who takes her place in a forced marriage while she flees into exile.[64] The book was dedicated to Ernest Wallis Budge, Keeper of Egyptian and Assyrian Antiquities at the British Museum.[65] From Ireland Haggard wrote to Budge: 'I am amusing myself dramatising *Morning Star*.'[66]

There was a compelling motive for this amusement: additional income was needed to fund Haggard's unremunerative public service. Haggard 'was perhaps the country's best-paid writer between 1887 and 1894', according to Philip Waller, 'when his earnings exceeded £10,000 annually. Between 1905 and 1909 these had fallen to a third.' Though he enjoyed a substantial income from his writing, Haggard's public service was a drain on his private purse and he was always on the lookout for other sources of income. Could theatrical adaptations provide one?

Other writers had dramatised some of his books, including *Dawn*, *Cleopatra* and *Jess*, financially benefiting thereby, so why not do so himself? There had been several stage versions of *She*, including a number of pirated productions in the United States. To add insult to injury, those adapting the novel to the stage often substantially altered the source material, in at least one American production of *She* going so far as to substitute a happy ending. Haggard's first attempt at the theatrical form, written in 1888, was to prevent this happening again. 'A Suggested Prologue to a

Dramatized Version of "She"' was specifically 'designed to explain to the spectator, in as few words as possible, such of the antecedent circumstances as are necessary to the right understanding of the tragedy', allowing no room for an alternative outcome.[67]

Other than this dramatic prologue, Haggard's only previous theatrical offering consisted of a single word. In December 1899 his name appeared alongside several other well-known writers in the programme credits as the creators of the play *The Ghost*, performed at Brede Hill School House outside the village of Brede, a few miles inland of Hastings on the Sussex coast, and briefly the home of the American writer Stephen Crane.[68] The play was conceived by Crane for production over the Christmas season. Crane wrote the bulk of the play but asked friends and acquaintances to 'write a mere word ... any word, and thus identify themselves with this crime'.[69] Joseph Conrad provided the line 'This is a jolly cold world', and Henry James the name of Peter Quint from *The Turn of the Screw*. Other contributors included Robert Barr, George Gissing, H.B. Marriott Watson, H.G. Wells, Edwin Pugh, A.E.W. Mason and Haggard. Unfortunately there is no record of the word or phrase Haggard contributed.[70]

Despite the 'Irish Question' being a dominant feature of British politics for decades, Haggard was largely oblivious to the political and social ferment in Ireland at the time: one of growing nationalism, which put Home Rule – if not complete independence – firmly on the agenda. These ambitions were fuelled by a Gaelic revival and the creation of a variety of political and cultural movements, including Sinn Féin and the Gaelic League. The opening of the Abbey Theatre in Dublin in 1904 created the venue for W.B. Yeats's vision of an Irish national theatre. Despite this cultural upheaval, Haggard 'failed to grasp the political situation in Ireland or judge the degree of resentment the people felt towards the British domination of their island'.[71] He was content to allow the Irish to conform to stereotype: 'I found the Irish the most charming and attractive people that I have ever met and the most incomprehensible.'[72] He was 'rather disgusted' at the 'mendicant attitude of mind which again and again I observed among those who gave evidence before us. They all wanted something out of the Government, and generally something for nothing.'[73]

On Saturday morning, 7 May, while dressing in his hotel room at Cork, Haggard learned that King Edward VII had died the previous day. The commission did not leave Cork until later in the day, but 'although the news was well known, I saw no indication of public mourning. No bells were rung, and no flags flew at half-mast. This may have been mere carelessness, or it may have been – something else.'[74] On 12 May Haggard was staying in Dublin at the Plunkett House on Merrion Square and that morning visited the Abbey Theatre, presumably unaware that on the death of the king the Dublin theatres had closed on Saturday, 7 May, as a sign of respect, all except the Abbey. In an earlier visit in April, Haggard had attended a performance of J.M.

Synge's *Deirdre of the Sorrows* at the Abbey and sent Maire O'Neill a letter 'praising her beautiful performance of Deirdre & wishing her every success as an actress'.[75]

The purpose of Haggard's visit to the Abbey in May was to submit the manuscript of his play *Star of Egypt*, adapted from *Morning Star*, for Yeats's consideration. Yeats was in France, so Haggard gave the script to Maire O'Neill. 'She is wild to do the part of Tua if the thing can be fixed up and would I think do it extremely well,' he wrote to Louie. 'She has a great local reputation as an actress in Ireland. The company is coming to London so you will be able to see how she acts.'[76] The theatrical world was not Haggard's accustomed milieu: 'I did laugh at myself discussing plays in the back purlieus of a theatre this morning – quite a new line for me. I only wish I could make some money out of it. I have made up the plot of a patriotic Irish play.'[77]

Haggard left Ireland on Saturday, 14 May, to attend the funeral of King Edward in London, where he viewed the king's body lying in state in Westminster Hall, 'and afterwards watched the noble panorama of his funeral from the upper balcony of the Athenaeum. Thomas Hardy and I sat together.'[78] Meanwhile Yeats had returned to Dublin to find 'a big typed play by Rider Haggard'. He wrote to Lady Augusta Gregory, co-founder of the Abbey, telling her 'it does not come within our scope but he would like to do an Irish play for us, it is rather an embarrassing compliment'.[79] Lady Gregory advised Yeats not to read the play: 'It will give you trouble and make an enemy of him, for you are sure not to like it.'[80]

At the end of May, Yeats was in London delivering a series of lectures while the Abbey Theatre company were performing at the Court Theatre,[81] from where Yeats sent Haggard a note: 'I am very sorry but I have not had a moment to look through [*The Star of Egypt*], rather I had not a moment to listen to it, for my sight makes it necessary to get plays read out to me. I will tell you about it the first possible moment.'[82] He suggested they meet at the theatre between curtain calls.

Whether on this occasion or another, Haggard offered Yeats the script of his 'patriotic Irish play', *To Hell or Connaught*, a story of love and war set at the time of Oliver Cromwell's invasion and colonisation of Ireland. Its title is drawn from a remark attributed to Cromwell reflecting the impossible choice given the indigenous Irish resisting expulsion from their lands and relocation in Connaught. Cromwell's campaign, which included the massacres of Drogheda and Wexford, was brutal, as were many of the policies instituted in the years that followed. Haggard's humanity saw him side with the Irish, and he had no sympathy with the republican and anti-monarchist Cromwell. Haggard had a context with which both he and Yeats might be in accord.

In September Yeats told Haggard that neither of his plays 'would be possible at the Abbey, as I feared when I saw you in London'.[83] Yeats noted *The Star of Egypt* was 'full of wild phantasy' and he was intrigued by Haggard's use of the ka. 'It may interest you to know that a certain Dr Ochorowitz, a Polish man of science, has investigated what looks like a modern case of the Double ... A medium who is one of his patients is haunted by a wonder working image of herself 3 feet high.'[84] Yeats asked if Haggard had considered offering the play to the flamboyant actor-manager Sir Herbert Tree.[85] Haggard did not offer the play to Tree, and neither *The Star of Egypt* nor *To Hell or Connaught* was ever performed.[86]

In the spring of 1910 General Booth approached Haggard to write a report 'upon the social efforts and institutions of the Salvation Army'; he was prepared to pay for it.[87] Spurned 'by the middle and upper classes in the Church of England' as a Methodist offshoot and 'a creed for the lower orders',[88] at best the 'Sally Ann' was a bit of a joke, at worst something more sinister. George Bernard Shaw's *Major Barbara*, performed in 1905, was widely seen as an attack on the Salvation Army, and John Manson's 1906 study, *The Salvation Army and the Public*, had been damning. Booth wanted a more balanced view. Haggard initially turned down the general's request owing to other commitments but then changed his mind, perhaps feeling he should come to the defence of the beleaguered organisation, which he held in high regard. An indication of the wide antipathy towards the Salvation Army is evident in a letter from Arthur Conan Doyle, who, while thinking it 'splendid' of Haggard to write the book, cautioned that by 'lending your honoured name to it you are inducing very many people to support what if this book of Manson's is true, is in many ways (or has become) an evil organisation.'[89]

Refusing payment barring expenses, Haggard 'undertook the task as a labour of love',[90] and in June and July he toured the Salvation Army's shelters, orphanages, workshops, homes and other projects throughout Britain, in the process acquiring a 'most whole-hearted admiration for the Salvation Army and its splendid self-sacrificing labours among the lowest of the low ... Long may it endure and prosper!'[91] He gave the copyright of *Regeneration: Being an Account of the Social Work of the Salvation Army in Great Britain* (published on 16 December 1910) to the organisation, though he didn't suppose it would prove a 'valuable gift, as, to find a large sale, such books must be of the ultra-"sensational" order, which mine was not'.[92]

The Times endorsed Haggard's view of the Salvation Army in an editorial, while the *Spectator* thought Haggard's account of the army's finances should 'satisfy everyone, not only as to what is, but also as to what has been'.[93] Theodore Roosevelt reviewed *Regeneration* for the New York weekly *Outlook*: 'There are few men now writing English whose books on vital sociological questions are of such value as [Haggard's] ... my own limited experience with the Salvation Army has in every respect borne out what Mr. Haggard writes of it.'[94] Andrew Lang was not convinced: 'I daresay the bawling Evangelists mean well, but ...!'[95] General Booth was well satisfied: 'You have not only seen into the character and purpose of the work we are trying to do, with the insight of a true genius, but with the sympathy of a big and generous soul.'[96]

Haggard had long expressed a desire 'to inspect the smallholdings of Denmark'[97] and, during an interval in the work of the Royal Commission on Coast Erosion, undertook 'an agricultural investigation which resulted in my book *Rural Denmark*'.[98] In September 1910 he travelled to Denmark with his widowed sister-in-law Aggie and 19-year-old Lilias, having arranged with *The Times* to either serialise or run extracts from the completed book.

He spent nearly two months in Denmark applying the same modus operandi he had employed in the compilation of *Rural England*: visiting agricultural schools and research institutions, the Royal Veterinary College in Copenhagen, smallholdings and farms; and interviewing farmers and labourers. His travels included a visit to 'a remote estate in the far north-west of Jutland that is named Aagaard', the home of Haggard's putative ancestor Sir Andrew Ogard (or Agard or Haggard) 'of the famous Guildenstjerne family whose seat was at Aagaard in Jutland'[99] and whose name lived on in the form of a star in the Haggard coat of arms. Haggard 'looked on the spot from whence, I believe, we all hailed with some emotion. An ancient manor house buried in trees with the remains of a moated castle alongside situated on a vast plain through which runs a little stream that gives the place its name.' The owners of the estate showed them round the house. In the drawing room was 'a cupboard with the Gyldenstyrne arms – a 7 pointed star in the centre panel' dating back to 1572.

As well as finding ancestral roots, Haggard discovered how farming could be profitable 'in a Free Trade country with an indifferent climate' by 'means of medium or small holdings, for the most part owned and not rented', and a supportive government. Denmark, with a poorer soil and 'an even worse climate' than Britain, exported 'over twenty millions sterling worth of agricultural produce, chiefly to the British Isles, in addition to the amount which it keeps at home for sustenance in a densely populated land'. What Denmark could do, so could the United Kingdom, though not under 'our present system of hired farms, many of which are larger than the tenant can manage, and, as a consequence, indifferently cultivated'.[100]

While in Denmark Haggard and Aggie collaborated on the plot for what became *The Wanderer's Necklace*, the tale of an eighth-century Danish Norseman, Olaf Red-Sword, as well as his various incarnations over time, searching for his true love, Heliodore. With settings in Denmark, Byzantium and Egypt, the book (written in 1913) drew on scenes from Haggard's visit blended with supernatural elements, including reincarnation.

The Royal Commission on Coast Erosion and Afforestation was wound up in 1911 and its third and final report issued on 31 May.[101] 'I missed that commission very much,' Haggard admitted, 'since its sitting took me to London from time to time, and gave me a change of mental occupation and interests. Indeed I do not remember ever being more consistently depressed than I was during the first part of the following winter.'[102] No longer permitted shooting as a diversion, Haggard 'had nothing to do, except the daily grind of romance-writing, relieved only by Bench business, my farm affairs, and an afternoon walk through the mud with the two spaniels, Bustle and Jeekie, and a chat after church on Sunday upon the affairs of the nation with my fellow churchwarden, friend and neighbour, Mr. Carr, the squire of this place'.[103]

Haggard came down with bronchitis in a cold snap during the summer and fell into 'one of those moods of unrelieved depression which had all his life been so great an enemy'.[104] It was not the best of times to begin work on an autobiography, as Haggard did on 11 August 1911, 'for really it seemed as though everything had come to an end'.[105] This statement, from a man of 55, and the title *The Days of My Life* are evidence of Haggard's mental state and the melancholy atmosphere permeating his autobiography: sadness, frustration, and the regret he had been unable 'to gratify a very earnest ambition of my younger years, namely, to enter parliament and shine as a statesman'.[106] For much of its length *The Days of My Life* reads like the work of an elderly man.

If Haggard's depression casts a shadow over 1911, perhaps the year is best remembered for the appearance of Haggard's most atypical and unusual work, a novella entitled *The Mahatma and the Hare: A Dream Story*. As the subtitle suggests, the idea for the story came from a dream; a dream akin to the one Haggard had about his dying retriever Bob, which led him to renounce blood sports. Featuring reincarnation, telepathy, anthropomorphism and astral travelling, *The Mahatma and the Hare* finds Haggard as spiritual seeker and apologist, blending aspects of spiritualism, Theosophy and theism. His initial dream was probably provoked by reading a newspaper story 'about a hare that had been pursued into the sea by hounds'.[107]

In the book, a hare hunted to death recounts a life of suffering mainly inflicted by man, more particularly by a country squire who shot at, chased and finally coursed the hare to death with hounds. The squire 'spent most of the year in killing the lower animals such as me' and, 'when there was no more killing to be done in his own country, he would travel to others and kill there ... "a regular slaughterer" and "a true-blood Englishman".'[108] At the Gates of Judgement (the squire dies of a heart attack during the hunt) and through the intervention of the Mahatma of the title, the hare and his hunter engage in a dialogue on the ethics of hunting and, though no conclusion is drawn, the end of the story makes Haggard's position clear. When the Wardens of the Gates of Heaven ask, 'Who hath suffered most? Let that one first taste of peace,' the waiting souls surge forward but are gently pressed back. Then comes the command: 'Draw near, thou Hare.'[109]

Thomas Hardy thought *The Mahatma and the Hare* 'a strangely attractive book'. He was 'entirely on the side of the hare ... I feel certain that you are too, in spite of your reserve; & that delights me. There is not the least doubt that blood-sport will have to go. To teach boys to love it, in this 20th century, is monstrous.'[110]

The Mahatma and the Hare (published on 16 October 1911) enjoyed 'no great public vogue', thanks in large part to the newspapers neglecting it 'as though it were something improper'. In Haggard's estimate 'they feared to give offence to that great section of their readers who, directly or indirectly, are interested in sport, by extended notices of a parable which doubtless in its essence amounts to an attack upon our habit of killing other creatures for amusement'.[111] Haggard's explanation for the book's neglect is correct; his daughter Lilias, a confirmed countrywoman, does not even mention the title in her biography of her father.

Haggard sent a copy to Lang (also clinically depressed at the time), who, while against the pursuit of hares, observed that 'we are all hunted from birth to death by impecunious relations, disease, care, and every horror. The hare is not hunted half so much or half so endlessly.'[112] Haggard conceded that 'hunted we are, and by a large pack!' though he didn't think 'that this justifies us in hunting other things'.

Haggard told Lang that he found 'the sadness of the world' impressing him 'more and more' as he grew older, especially as he was now engaged on writing 'my reminiscences of my early life in Africa, etc. It is a sad job. There before me are the letters from those dear old friends of my youth, Shepstone, Osborn, Clarke and many others, and nearly every one of them is dead! But I don't believe that I shall never see them more; indeed I seem to grow nearer to them.'[113]

24

'RECOGNITION – WITH A VENGEANCE'

'Many congratulations on your well-deserved honour. Churchill.'[1] Haggard had been gazetted a knight bachelor in the New Year's honours of 1912. The telegram from the First Lord of the Admiralty arrived at Ditchingham House on Tuesday, 2 January. Kipling sent 'heartiest congratulations' from his winter quarters in Switzerland. 'You've done such good work for the State, for so long that in this case the State truly honours itself in honouring you.'[2] Haggard's depression began to lift; 'of a sudden things changed, as they have a way of doing in life'.[3]

Shortly before Christmas, the prime minister, Henry Asquith, had informed Haggard 'the King had been pleased to confer a knighthood upon me'.[4] The honour was in recognition of Haggard's public service, not his literary achievements. Haggard had previously shied at a 'semi-official' approach intimating that a baronetcy might be his if he wished. 'Baronetcies are for rich men who have male heirs, not for persons like myself.' But he accepted the knighthood when offered, on the grounds 'that it is a mistake to refuse anything in this world' and also because the title would be useful in his public service, especially abroad. 'Moreover, it was Recognition, for which I felt grateful; for who is there that does not appreciate recognition particularly after long years of, I hope, disinterested toil?'[5]

Further recognition was to come. On 11 January a letter from Lewis Harcourt, Secretary of State for the Colonies, invited Haggard to be one of the commissioners appointed to the 'Royal Commission to visit the various Dominions and report upon them'.[6] The Colonial Office was responsible for the dependent Crown colonies and the business of the self-governing colonies, the Dominions of white settlement: Australia, New Zealand, South Africa, Newfoundland and Canada.[7] The inquiry was envisaged to take three years and 'entail three visits to the Dominions – six months in Australia and New Zealand, three months in South Africa and another of three months in Canada and Newfoundland'. Harcourt hoped Haggard would accept the position and trusted 'for the sake of the reading public that the Commission will not prevent you from pursuing a good deal of your usual avocations, and might even incidentally provide materials!'[8]

Coming so soon after the knighthood, this was 'recognition – with a vengeance'. Haggard viewed his appointment as an acknowledgement of his 'long years of toil in investigating and attempting to solve the grave problems which lie at the root of the welfare of our country' and felt 'proportionately grateful and honoured'.[9] Honour came with a hefty price tag: the commissioners received no remuneration though their respective governments would pay their representatives' personal expenses. Quite apart from the impact on Haggard's purse, his duties as a commissioner would require a 'long separation from my family' and there was also the question of how to 'carry on my literary work in the intervals of so much public labour'. He and Louie agreed 'such considerations should not be allowed to interfere with the execution of what I look upon as a high and honourable duty'.[10] Charles Longman was elated at Haggard's appointment: 'I would rather have heard this than they had given you a peerage. Anyone can be a peer, but to be one of the six men chosen to represent the United Kingdom on a great Empire inquiry of this sort is a real honour.'[11]

In 1912 the British Empire covered a quarter of the globe, accommodating the same number of its inhabitants, but competition with other industrialised nations was becoming fierce and Britain was falling behind in economic and military spheres. With the United States and Germany snapping at her heels, and internal stressors such as the rise of trade unions, the increasing influence of socialism and the woman's suffrage movement, Britannia was taking strain. 'The weary Titan staggers under the too vast orb of its fate,' Joseph Chamberlain, quoting Matthew Arnold, told the premiers of the white settler societies at the Colonial Conference of 1902. 'We have borne the burden long enough. We think it is time our children should assist us to support it'.[12] This had been a constant refrain, though 'not always so patronisingly worded', at similar conferences since the 1880s.[13] In the aftermath of the Anglo-Boer War, Britain's weariness was tangible. Exactly how the 'children' could come to the assistance of their parent would be the task of the Dominions Royal Commission to discover.

In March, in the midst of Britain's first national coal strike, Haggard travelled to Egypt 'in the hope of shaking off my bronchitis'.[14] Egypt was recommended for its 'dry and tonic' climate during the winter months.[15] He was again accompanied by his daughter Angela. They departed on the Bibby Line's SS *Gloucestershire* on 9 March and spent the first two days buffeted by heavy swells from the Atlantic – 'one night the rolling was quite à la *Macedonia* and there were but few ladies at table'.[16]

In Cairo, Haggard and Angela stayed at the Mena House hotel, a blend of 'Orientalism crossed with Victorian comfort',[17] previously the Khedive Ismail's hunting lodge. The closest hotel to the Pyramids of Giza, it was also a popular health spa where guests could spend time in the desert and 'enjoy its invigorating air from morning till night'.[18] Haggard vetoed going up the Nile to Luxor on the grounds of expense, excessive heat, familiarity with the sites and the attraction of new exhibits at the Cairo Museum; moreover, in Cairo it was easier to maintain contact with home. He feared the coal strike would unseat the government before the official announcement of the commission.

On Tuesday, 26 March, Haggard and Angela went to the Cairo Museum, where the museum's director, the French Egyptologist Sir Gaston Maspero, was 'going to unscrew Meneptah and Seti II his son' specially for them.[19] 'It was a strange thing to look upon the tall form and the withered countenance of the man who is generally believed to have been the Pharaoh of the Exodus, that majesty before whom, perhaps, Moses stood.'[20] Haggard was then contemplating a romance of the Exodus and he discussed a possible plot with Maspero, who had found *Morning Star* 'full of "the inner spirit of the old Egyptians"'.[21] Maspero thought the plot of the proposed book, *Moon of Israel*, 'probable' and consonant with his 'knowledge of those dim days'.[22]

Later there were expeditions south to Saqqara and another to Memphis to 'see a new Sphinx that [Flinders] Petrie has found. It is the second largest in Egypt – 24 feet long and of alabaster!'[23] Viewing the sphinx provided a good excuse to skip the garden party given by the British Consul General, Lord Kitchener.[24]

Haggard and Angela enjoyed their stay in Egypt, but he was not sorry to go. 'Everyone was leaving, the winds have been and remain very cold and upset one's insides! Or perhaps the bites from the mosquitoes and sandflies do that.'[25] Haggard had been plagued by mosquitoes at Mena House and his bronchitis had flared up. By the time they got to Italy, he seemed to have recovered, though Angela was suffering with 'Egyptian tummy ache'.[26] A gale blew them into Brindisi, from where they caught the train to Naples and booked into the famous Parker's Hotel. Here Haggard was relieved to learn the Dominions Royal Commission had received the royal stamp of approval – 'until the announcement of the King's sanction one can never be sure'. Now that he was sure, Haggard shared his thoughts and feelings with Louie:

> It is rather remarkable for a writer of fiction to have attained to a seat on such a commission (though I says it as shouldn't) and shows that the Country must take me pretty seriously. Also it means that whatever happens one cannot be said to have quite *failed* in life. I hope that you are pleased about it dear. I am in a way as it is the end of a long struggle for serious recognition in which I was much hampered by the necessary novel writing.[27]

Naples was full of rumours about the fate of the *Titanic* – 'We hope it is not true. Evidently she has come to grief on ice.'[28] The *Titanic* sank in the North Atlantic on 15 April after collision with an iceberg. One of those who went down with the ship was Haggard's former would-be nemesis, W.T. Stead.

Angela's stomach troubles continued, further travels to Rome and Venice were abandoned, and the two sailed back to England from Naples via Gibraltar. Haggard's bronchitis was held at bay 'until I got back to England, a country in which I am rather doubtful whether I shall ever be able to winter again'.[29]

While Haggard was in Egypt contemplating dead pharaohs, the reading public was enjoying the resurrection of Allan Quatermain in *Marie*, the first of a series of prequels to *King Solomon's Mines* chronicling Quatermain's earlier adventures in Africa. *Marie*, published on 25 January 1912 after serialisation in *Cassell's Magazine*, tells the story of Quatermain's youth on the Cape frontier – borrowing aspects of Theophilus Shepstone's early life – and his first marriage to the titular heroine, Marie Marais. The love story is played out against the backdrop of the Great Trek, the reign of Dingane, the killing of Piet Retief and the battle of Blood River.[30]

Marie was the first of a trilogy, completed by *Child of Storm* and *Finished*, spanning the rise and fall of the Zulu kingdom in the nineteenth century, as engineered by a malevolent sangoma, Zikali – 'The Thing that should never have been born' – as opposed to more prosaic historical forces of which Haggard was fully aware but which he wasn't going to allow to get in the way of a good story.[31] The adventure also marks the first appearance of Hans, Quatermain's Khoikhoi servant and all-purpose factotum, the vehicle for some tiresome humour and frequently the object of racial abuse. However, the schemes of the cunning and wily Hans in *Marie* and other adventures are usually the origin of Quatermain's eventual triumph.[32]

Before his appointment to the Dominions Royal Commission, Haggard was planning to spend 1912 investigating agricultural practices in Ireland, but now there wasn't enough time and so he wrote a story instead. Haggard confessed that, if circumstances allowed, 'I do not think I should write much more fiction, at any rate of the kind that people would buy.' He would prefer to write about 'the land, agriculture, and social matters'. Irish agriculture gave way to *Allan and the Holy Flower*, 'in place thereof I have found myself obliged to edit certain of the reminiscences of Mr. Allan Quatermain.'[33]

> To be honest, these have amused me not a little, perhaps because I always find it easy to write of Allan Quatermain, who, after all, is only myself set in a variety of imagined situations, thinking my thoughts and looking at life through my eyes. Indeed there are several subjects with which I always find it not difficult to deal – for instance, Old Egypt, Norsemen, and African savages. Of these last, however, I prefer to write in the company of the late Allan Quatermain.[34]

As Haggard's alter ego, the new Quatermain was a different character from the rough-hewn hunter-trader of *King Solomon's Mines* and *Allan Quatermain*. The rejuvenated Quatermain was well read, much given to philosophical ruminations and not averse to drug-induced time-travelling adventures with Lady Ragnall, a character based on Haggard's friend Lady Ella Hart-Bennett. With a return to southern Africa in the offing, it was only fitting that Haggard dedicate *Marie* to the man under whose care he first went there in 1875, Sir Henry Bulwer.

The second volume of Haggard's Zulu trilogy, *Child of Storm*, was written prior to *Marie* in 1909. Hearing on a visit to Ditchingham that Haggard was 'completing a Zulu story'[35] similar in style to *Nada the Lily*, Charles Longman asked to read it. Haggard gave him the manuscript, making it clear that if Longman wanted to publish *Child of Storm* it was conditional on buying 'the serial rights straightaway'.[36] Longman enjoyed the book and approached Watt, Haggard's agent, though not before warning his friend 'that the serial issue may be insurmountable'.[37] Thinking Watt might place *Child of Storm* elsewhere, Haggard wrote the prequel, *Marie*, completing it by the end of 1909. Longman was right, the serial issue was insuperable, and both books were published by Cassell.

Child of Storm (published in 1913) was prefaced by a dedication to James Stuart, an authority on Zulu history and culture.[38] Stuart had held magisterial posts all over Natal and had been clerk and interpreter to the Resident Commissioner and Chief Magistrate of Zululand, Melmoth Osborn. Stuart was sent to Swaziland in March 1894 'to interpret during the political crisis then existing in that country'[39] and, as we have seen, accompanied a deputation of Swazi notables to London. It was while in Ladysmith as a magistrate at the turn of the century that the idea of capturing the history, social customs, language and oral literature of the Zulu and other cultures crystallised. Over the next two decades and beyond Stuart recorded over 200 interviews with Zulu, Swazi and white colonials, thereby producing an immense resource on the peoples of Natal, Zululand and Swaziland.

Stuart saw his work as having a number of applications: 'Not only would a systematic record of Zulu life, character, and achievement serve to inspire others to improve it,' he wrote, but 'it would help materially to enlighten the white people among whom the natives live as to what the latter really are ... The gulf between the two races continues to yawn, with nothing to bridge it. And yet it is on this and this alone that mutual trust and sympathy are built up and depend.'[40] Stuart's close contact with the Zulu bred empathy and he was sympathetic towards their political aspirations, urging the authorities that they be consulted about their future government and the form it would take. The ambiguities of his position were thrown into bold relief during the 1906 Bhambatha Rebellion: on one hand, he was supportive of the Zulu; on the other, he was a colonial servant committed to strong governance. During the rebellion Stuart served as a captain in the Natal Field Artillery and as a member of the Greytown court martial that tried many of the rebels. The culmination of Stuart's government career came with his appointment in 1909 as Natal's Assistant Secretary for Native Affairs, but when the four colonies in southern Africa combined to form the Union of South Africa in 1910 he was rendered redundant as the colonial native affairs departments were absorbed into the central administration.

Haggard first met Stuart in London in 1912, ostensibly to discuss a mooted biography of Theophilus Shepstone, who had died in 1893. As he was yet without a biographer, Shepstone's son Arthur wished Haggard to remedy this and, in a bid to persuade him to do so, offered the services of James Stuart to 'help in collecting the necessary material, which is scattered about in all kinds of family records, documents, pamphlets, books and bluebooks'.[41] Stuart's 'intimate acquaintance' with the Zulu, their language, customs and history 'might be of use in those directions in which, owing to your long absence from South Africa, you might feel yourself somewhat out of touch'.[42]

Stuart was writing the official history of the Bhambatha Rebellion, commissioned by the Natal government, but the new Union of South Africa government didn't 'care to associate itself with the Rebellion' and so Stuart had negotiated its publication by Macmillan in London, where he would be in the summer. Arthur suggested that Haggard 'might wish to avail' himself of Stuart's services during this time. Haggard agreed that 'a life of your dear father should be written' but declined the invitation to be its author. He felt his age barred him from undertaking 'so arduous and responsible a business in its entirety'; moreover, 'I have before me a very responsible and important piece of government work which will closely occupy me for some years to come and take me much from home.'[43] He offered to write an introduction and to meet Stuart to discuss the shape and content of the book and point him in the direction of a publisher; he recommended Longmans.[44]

When the 44-year-old Stuart came to Ditchingham in July, he agreed it was impossible for Haggard to contemplate such a biography given his imminent duties with the Dominions Royal Commission. Haggard thought Stuart was 'the man for the task'.[45] At Ditchingham Stuart read the manuscript of *Child of Storm* and made several suggestions which Haggard incorporated. He also gave Haggard a copy of the Zulu 'national anthem' to use in the book, which, according to Stuart, had never been seen in print before.[46]

The Dominions Royal Commission comprised six representatives from the United Kingdom and one from each of the five Dominions. Sir Edgar Vincent (later Lord D'Abernon) was appointed as chairman; he was a former soldier and financial administrator in the Balkans and the Middle East.[47] According to Lilias, the 'enigmatic' Vincent was 'a spoiled child of fortune with his magnificent looks and rapier intelligence; worldly wise, cynical under his tremendous charm, complex where Rider was simple, looking at the world as his oyster and humanity as his plaything'. Notwithstanding, he became Haggard's 'devoted friend'.[48]

Haggard prepared for his task with gusto, and in order to attend the commission meetings at Scotland House on the Victoria Embankment, he rented rooms at 5 Bryanston Street near Marble Arch. The first meeting of the British representatives took place on 16 April 1912 and the first meeting with all the Dominion representatives took place on 13 June 1912, when the way forward was agreed and operations set in motion, including the compilation of questionnaires to be forwarded to various bodies in the United Kingdom and the Dominions requesting information on production, trade and migration, ports and railways.[49] During

October and November witnesses from a variety of organisations were interviewed at Scotland House, and a first interim report was signed off on 28 December 1912.

Earlier in the year, on 22 July 1912, Haggard read in *The Times* 'the news of the sudden death of my dear friend Andrew Lang'.[50] The 68-year-old Lang had died of a heart attack in Scotland the previous Saturday. Lang's health had been failing for some time, and earlier in the year he saw the death omen of his family: 'A black cat, obviously hallucinatory, ran across my study at 10 a.m.'[51] In his autobiography Haggard bade 'farewell for a while' to Lang, 'among men my best friend perhaps, and the one with whom I was most entirely in tune ... For myself I am more lonely, since of those men, not of my kin, whom I knew and loved while I still was young, now Charles Longman and Arthur Cochrane alone are left.'[52]

As globe-spanning duties with the Dominions Royal Commission beckoned, Haggard swiftly brought his autobiography to a close, completing it on 25 September – '"I have spoken!" as the Zulus say'.[53] Having signed and dated the manuscript, he sent it with a note to Charles Longman, instructing that the manuscript be 'sealed up and put away in Messrs. Longman's safe'. Longman complied and the manuscript 'was seen no more till after his death, when it was opened by me in the presence of one of his executors'.[54] The book was dedicated to 'my dear Wife and to the memory of our son whom now I seek. H. Rider Haggard'.[55]

In October 1912 Haggard wrote to Lewis Harcourt enquiring if he would like 'me to send you some confidential letters ... on general topics' such as the 'apparent or prospective prosperity' of the Dominions, 'their people, their statesmen and leading inhabitants, the tendencies of their thought and legislation, the dangers and difficulties in their paths, the real sources of their wealth etc'.[56] Harcourt agreed to the proposal.[57] Haggard also added to his South African schedule a tour of Rhodesia and, once official duties were over, a long-anticipated trip to Zululand.

The first fact-finding mission of the Dominions Royal Commission took them to Australia and New Zealand. On 17 January 1913 there was 'a good send off' from Victoria station, where the commissioners caught the train to Dover.[58] Haggard was not among them, however, having sailed at the end of November 1912 for India, where he planned a month's tour, including a visit to his daughter Dorothy and her husband Major Reginald Cheyne in Ambala, thereafter sailing from Calcutta (now Kolkata) to Ceylon (now Sri Lanka), where he would meet up with his fellow commissioners at Colombo prior to heading for Australia.

To prime himself for the Indian trip, Haggard went to see Kipling at Bateman's, taking with him the proofs of *Child of Storm*, which he read aloud to his friend. Kipling spoke 'of the work in very strong terms indeed, almost overpowering terms: "as terse and strong as a Greek play, not a word that could be improved on or cut out," etc'. Haggard purred at Kipling's approval 'as he is a severe critic of his own and other people's stuff; also because it agrees so thoroughly with my own judgement. But no one else will understand. It takes big men to recognise big work and such are scarce.'[59] Haggard left the proofs with Kipling to read and add comments before returning them, which he did with an accompanying letter: 'it's the best you've done ... It marches straight off from the first and holds like a drug! I'm especially pleased with the characterisation of Mameena, who is a nice little bitch though dusky.'[60]

Haggard sailed for India on the *Arcadia* on 29 November.[61] Arriving in Bombay (now Mumbai) early on 21 December, minus a portmanteau (which was later recovered), Haggard passed through customs 'without much trouble, although there was a certain amount of difficulty over a revolver which I carried. Any importation of arms into India being very carefully watched.'[62] Before leaving by train for Ambala that night, Haggard installed himself briefly at the luxurious Taj Mahal Palace Hotel close to the docks and the railway terminus, where he met up with Colonel Arthur Blowers from the Salvation Army,[63] thanks to whom Haggard saw 'more of Bombay in one day, than the ordinary Globe-Trotter would in three'.[64]

The whirlwind tour took in a Jain temple, a Muslim cemetery and a Hindu cremation site, where half-a-dozen corpses were being burnt: 'in front of us was that of a child reduced to white and glowing ashes'.[65] Afterwards Blowers 'drove to a spot whence we had a good view of Malabar Hill, the fashionable residential quarter of Bombay' where 'my mother was born, and lived many years'.[66] The indefatigable Blowers hired a servant for Haggard, Daya Gopal, 'a queer looking person with a cock-eye and thick neck' who proved himself to be both 'efficient and useful'.[67] With Gopal in attendance, Haggard travelled on the Bombay Baroda and Central India Line via Delhi to Ambala, arriving on 23 December. Haggard 'was delighted' to see his daughter Dorothy, her husband Reginald, and their two children, 6-year-old Reginald and 2-year-old Rider, 'after a separation of three years'.[68]

In Delhi on the same day an assassination attempt was made on the Viceroy, Lord Hardinge, during his ceremonial entry into the city to mark Delhi's replacement of Calcutta as the new capital of India. Hardinge and his wife were in a howdah on the back of an elephant. A bomb was thrown into the howdah by a member of a nationalist revolutionary group, killing the mahout and severely injuring the Viceroy and the elephant.

The Indian Rebellion of 1857 was one of the most traumatic shocks experienced by the British Empire and, when Haggard was 'assured by Anglo-Indians of great experience that another such Mutiny draws near', he adopted a jingoistic stance: 'of the ultimate result I am not afraid. These fawning Hindoos think in blood but lack courage to execute their thought. There may be massacres in isolated places, but the end is sure, unless England be rotten at her heart. If such things should happen, it will be the Home politicians, such as Mr Keir Hardie, and sentimental ignoramuses who are to blame.'[69]

In Delhi the sight of the magnificent Mughal palace, the mosques, and the tombs of past rulers left Haggard wondering 'when the proud British Race in its turn departs from India ... what will be left to show of *our* period of rule'. He was not optimistic: 'Some broken tracks that once were railway lines, some crumbling heaps that once were factories' and, perhaps, 'a few monuments, such as the hideous Memorial which we have thought a sufficient token of our debt and gratitude to the heroes of the Delhi Mutiny, doubtless but one of a hundred mutinies that have been raised against foreign occupiers of this land'.[70]

Dining at the Viceregal Lodge, Haggard was seated next to the Vicereine, Lady Hardinge, minus her husband; he was still recovering from the assassination attempt, which had left her unharmed. She described to Haggard what happened, drawing 'an outline with her finger on my back' of her husband's injuries, which were 'much more serious than has been reported in the press'.[71] Haggard later visited the building from which the bomb was thrown.

From Delhi Haggard travelled south-east towards Calcutta, where he would board ship for Ceylon (Sri Lanka). It was a leisurely trip with stopovers at Agra, Cawnpore (Kanpur), and Benares (Varanasi). At Agra, Haggard admired the 'great red wall Fort' and the Taj Mahal. At sunset, watching 'its white marble blush into loveliness, and then by degrees grow grey and cold in the shadow of advancing night, was to me a sight more moving than any that I can remember of its kind, save one [when] I for the first time saw the full moon shine upon the mighty tumbled pillars of Karnac'.[72] Cawnpore, site of the Bibighar massacre in which 120 British women and children were killed, was the 'saddest of all places I visited in India ... The story is one of those that is apt to dry the very springs of Faith, perhaps because we do not see far enough, for how, our poor hearts wonder, could a merciful God suffer such things to be?'[73]

In the sacred city of Benares Haggard recalled his mother telling him as a boy that this was where 'the Indians burn their dead by the water edge and worship many idols ... the description still holds good'. He cheerfully jostled his way among the thousands of pilgrims thronging the temples to see the cremations taking place on the ghats along the Ganges. Haggard was struck with horror by the Durga Mandhir, dedicated to the warrior goddess: 'it was a dreadful spot, one that affected the nerves, and I was glad to bid it goodbye'.[74] Though critical of Hindu beliefs, he was not totally dismissive: 'who can tell what its flower and fruit may be? Let us look well to our own faith, before we mock that of alien races.'[75] Four miles north-east of Benares, Haggard visited Sarnath with its many Buddhist ruins, among them the Dhamekh Stupa, built on the site at which the Buddha gave his first sermon and from where 'the light of his beautiful if somewhat unsatisfactory dogmas, began to permeate the East'.[76]

In Calcutta, a 'noble city of palaces and history, and possessing a really good Museum',[77] he was struck by the Anglican Cathedral and the clutter of monuments and tablets 'to those who in this way or in that, have died for the Empire. To read them made me proud of my race.' In the cemetery of St John's, 'the old church of Calcutta', Haggard found graves dating back to the eighteenth century: 'How much sorrow has this place seen? Husbands mourning over their young wives, wives over their husbands gone in the prime of manhood, and both over their little children, cut down like flowers in a frost.'[78]

From Calcutta Haggard sailed for Ceylon. A delay of two days, due to low water level in the Hooghly River estuary, allowed him time to catch up with his diary and to reflect on his Indian experiences. He wondered if the British flag would still be flying over India a century on. 'I think that whatever flag streams ... in the breath of the monsoon of 2013, it will not be that of England, and that all those who have toiled, and lived, and died for their King and Country beneath her burning sun, will have laboured but in vain.'[79]

From Colombo Haggard took the train to Ceylon's ancient capital, Anuradhapura, enjoying the 120-mile trip through jungles and 'glades of great beauty', past glimmering lakes and coconut groves.[80] At Anuradhapura he was guided around the ancient Buddhist sites by the Archaeological Survey commissioner Edward Russell Ayrton. Haggard had met him before in 1904 when Ayrton was excavating at the Valley of the Kings in Egypt.[81] Here Haggard had his portrait painted by an unknown artist, sitting beneath a statue of the Buddha and holding his pith helmet in his left hand.

In Kandy he visited the Sri Dalada Maligawa, the Temple of the Sacred Tooth Relic, and 'saw all the treasures of the temple'.[82] From Kandy Haggard travelled four miles to the Peradeniya botanical gardens to stay with Robert Lyne, Ceylon's director of agriculture and previously director of agriculture in Zanzibar. At Lyne's home Haggard met Henry Wyckham, 'whose name is, and always will be, famous in connection with the rubber industry'.[83] Infamous would be the better adjective: Wyckham broke the Brazilian rubber monopoly and destroyed that country's economy by smuggling seeds out of the country in 1876 to the Royal Botanic Gardens at Kew; they were subsequently sent on to Ceylon, Singapore and Malaya to kick-start the rubber industry in the East.

The British civil servant Edward Harding, secretary to the Dominions Royal Commission, kept a personal record detailing the commission's travels in the form of a 'diary-letter' written to his sister Eva and their father the Reverend John Harding: chatty, informed, with often ironic takes on the commissioners. When the RMS *Medina* arrived at Colombo on Saturday, 1 February, and lay to overnight before departing for Australia, he recorded: 'Sir Rider Haggard turned up safely', promising his father that now the commission was complete, he would attempt some 'character sketches' but would 'wait a few days, so as to get a better impression of Rider Haggard'.[84]

Aboard ship, the commissioners were already at work; 'we have divided up the various subjects – and each one sits immersed in a different Blue-book'.[85] Harding was impressed by Vincent, who, of all 'the Commission party', was 'altogether exceptional ... extraordinarily quick, and very fertile in ideas. In fact he has so many that he sometimes forgets one and takes up another while one is still struggling with the first.'[86] Harding suspended judgement on Haggard: 'I think he is of the temperament which has very ordinary Imperial ideas, and thinks they are extraordinary. Perhaps that is the result of being a novelist with a really keen imagination.'[87]

The *Medina* docked at Fremantle on 12 February and the commissioners were driven to Perth, Western Australia's state capital, for lunch and a brief visit to Government House. In Adelaide a few days later, reporters came aboard the *Medina*; 'fortunately Rider Haggard is used to them, and, though he would disclaim it, obviously rather likes them'.[88] As he had in the United States, Haggard the public man distanced himself from Haggard the romancer, but his appointment to the commission was a good public relations move as his reputation as a writer inevitably attracted the attention of the press: 'The last thing Sir Rider Haggard desires to talk about, apparently, is his own work as a novel writer,' reported the *Age* of Melbourne. 'Statistics of immigration, the state of the rural population of the United Kingdom, the resources of the Commonwealth, these and similar matters are at the forefront of his horizon.'[89]

Irritated at the press's persistent focus on him as a writer, Haggard was especially annoyed by a speech at a reception in Brisbane where Robert Martin Collins, 'Father of the Local House of Commons instead of addressing himself to the Imperial matters in hand, dwelt chiefly upon my books while another dilated at length upon the character of Allan Quatermain. This on an official occasion was very trying for me.'[90] There was no escaping the fact that Haggard created interest: 'a pleasant manner and a strong face, mobile and full of expression but on occasion inscrutable, like a sphinx's. He wears his beard trimmed to a point and his sharp features denote an ever-active mind.'[91] Like it or not, Haggard became the public face of the commission.

In Melbourne Haggard received copies of *Child of Storm* (published in January while he was in India) and, with other members of the commission, attended a special performance of William Shakespeare's *A Midsummer Night's Dream* staged by the actor-manager Oscar Asche. At the reception in the theatre foyer after the curtain fell, Haggard met 'Mr and Mrs Asche, the former of whom said he would much like to stage a Zulu play'. Haggard promised to send him *Child of Storm*, 'which I did upon the morrow.'[92]

Together with Mrs Asche, the actress Lily Brayton 'as romantic lead, Asche was unshakeable in his dominance of the popular stage'.[93] In Australia Asche basked in the glory of a returning home-grown hero, having been born at Geelong, Victoria, in 1871. He had gone to London in 1893 and made a name for himself performing Shakespearian roles. He married Lily Brayton in 1898. From 1910 Asche and his wife began touring their productions around the Dominions and in 1911 Asche produced a play by Edward Knoblauch, initially titled *Hajj's Hour*. Asche rewrote the script and turned it into a play with music, *Kismet*, and made a huge success of it, 'the gorgeous oriental scenery and dresses drawing all play-going London'.[94] The couple were touring Australia with *Kismet* and a clutch of Shakespearian productions. Asche probably envisaged repeating the *Kismet* formula with *Child of Storm*. Having read the book, he proposed to undertake the production and 'in order to get local colour ... booked a tour through South Africa on our way home'.[95] Haggard gave Asche an introduction to James Stuart, who was subsequently hired by Asche as adviser to the production on aspects of Zulu culture, to collect genuine Zulu artefacts and commission the making of costumes.

In New Zealand, commission sittings were held over fourteen days in Dunedin, Christchurch, Lyttelton, Wellington and Auckland, 'gathering formal evidence from 76 witnesses plus several official visits'.[96] There was also time for a trip to the hot springs at Rotorua, 'a kind of New Zealand Harrogate with hot and cold springs and Maoris for tourist consumption', according to Vincent.[97] Haggard was saddened by the sight of Maori children diving off a bridge into a river for pennies thrown by visitors – 'a method of earning money that is not ennobling'.[98] The musical entertainment was enjoyed by all the commissioners, even Harding: 'the dancing was really splendid, particularly what are called "Hakas"'.[99] Haggard 'found the entertainment "novel and exciting" and was moved to give a speech on the "Virtues of Barbarism"'.[100]

The commission sailed from Auckland to Sydney aboard the SS *Maheno*, with gale-force winds causing 'much discomfort among various members of the party'.[101] Rough seas didn't prevent Haggard from writing the first of his confidential letters to Harcourt: 'a short précis of my impressions of New Zealand and its people',[102] highlighting the 'extravagant system of Protection' which prevented manufacturing industries from thriving, contrary to 'the advantages of Free Trade'.[103] He thought 'one of the saddest circumstances of rural New Zealand is the dreadful and wholesale destruction of the magnificent native timbers ... much more might have been done to put a stop to the wicked and wilful waste of timber that has taken, perhaps, 1,000 years, or, in the case of the Kauri pine, which is now being ruthlessly exterminated for its selling value, as much as 5,000 years to grow'.[104]

Haggard was struck by a 'peculiar feature' of life in New Zealand which 'I have not met with in any other country', namely the 'terms of good-fellowship and equality whereon white men and aboriginal Maoris live together', further noting that 'English colonists marry Maori wives'. Despite this equable coexistence, the Maoris were 'undoubtedly on the decline, which is to be regretted, as, like the Zulus, they have many fine qualities and would, with proper training and discipline, make brave and loyal soldiers and sailors'. This decline Haggard blamed on their departure from traditional ways of life, disease and alcoholism, with a nod towards Social Darwinism:

'Probably behind all these, however, some deeper and little understood cause is at work, akin to that which brings it about that here the plants and weeds of England end by conquering those of native growth. Although the law has considerable exceptions, as a rule the white man and the aboriginal cannot exist for long together. As the sun of the white man rises the aboriginal withers and disappears.'[105]

After sitting in Sydney, the commission travelled 700 miles by rail to Brisbane for six formal hearings in early April. From where Haggard informed his literary agent Watt that Asche had made up his mind to dramatise *Child of Storm* 'under the title *Mameena* and to produce the same in London somewhere about Christmas time this year'.[106] Haggard agreed with Asche that the dramatisation of *Child of Storm* should be a joint project, and from Cairns in Queensland he sent Asche 'a couple of rough sample scenes ... I wish you would look through them and let me have your views. If you will get out a rough synopsis of your idea of what various scenes and acts should be, I hope to be able to work on it on the way home.'[107]

Returning to England aboard the RMS *Mooltan*, Haggard wrote a long and detailed letter to Harcourt containing his observations of Australia. He was highly critical of the White Australia policy and 'the ideal of White Australia, which has become a kind of national shibboleth'.[108] The immigration of white labour was blocked, according to Haggard, by a combination of racial prejudice and opposition from trade unions. Notwithstanding the latter, it was 'recognised by all the best minds that Australia with its low birth rate ... must have more population, if it is to ensure its future welfare and even its safety'.[109] Haggard's solution was to 'move numbers of persons *with young families* from some of the more overcrowded English *towns*' and settle them on land in Australia. 'Also, boys, in "blind alley" occupations, or orphans ... might be emigrated in large numbers.'[110]

Shortly before leaving Australia, Haggard sent Oscar Asche a partial script titled *Mameena*. 'I have mapped out the play ... and have brought in all the essential points of the drama as far as the stage is understood by me.'[111] Haggard continued working on the script during the return trip via Colombo and the Suez Canal, and by the time he reached England at the end of June he had completed the play and sketched a plot for *Finished*, the final volume of the Zulu trilogy.

Haggard had been absent from home and family for six months. Anticipating his return to South Africa with the Dominions Royal Commission the following year, he resolved not to travel alone but with Louie and Lilias. At Ditchingham he began work on his Danish romance *The Wanderer's Necklace*, which was published on 29 January 1914 with a dedication to the commission chairman, Sir Edgar Vincent: in memory of 'many wanderings overseas I offer these pictures from the past, my dear Vincent, to you, a lover of the present if an aspirant can look upon the future with more of hope than fear'.[112]

25

'LAND OF TROUBLES'

Haggard's visit to South Africa as a royal commissioner was prefaced by a nostalgic fortnight with Louie and Lilias in Madeira. They booked into an annexe of Reid's Palace Hotel, perched on the cliffs of Funchal, from where they 'hunted out the hotel where we put up on our way back to England after disastrous experiences in the shadow of Majuba'[1] – Miles Hotel, now renamed the Carmo, otherwise 'just as it was a generation gone – a large old Portuguese house in a narrow street not far from the cathedral, with a beautiful garden'.[2] Lunching at the Carmo née Miles, Haggard was 'somewhat sad' having 'passed from youth to age since my feet last crossed its threshold'. Told their names appeared in the hotel register of 1881, Haggard and Louie searched through it, but the page 'had been torn out by some autograph hunter', and so they re-entered them at the right place and Haggard added a note explaining 'the circumstances under which we did so'.[3]

While in Madeira, Haggard dedicated the new Allan Quatermain adventure he had written, *The Ivory Child*, to 'The Lady of the New Moon'. The heroine of *The Ivory Child*, Luna Holmes (later Lady Ragnall), had 'a curious white mark upon her breast, which in its shape exactly resembled the crescent moon'.[4] When Haggard outlined the story to Lucy Hart-Bennett the previous autumn, she revealed she had a similar birthmark; hence the dedication.

The *Kinfauns Castle*[5] brought Haggard's fellow commissioners to Funchal on 11 February. A rough passage from Southampton had left 'all except the stalwarts ... more or less *hors de combat*'.[6] On 14 February the ship set sail on the thirteen-day voyage to Cape Town. Edward Harding, the commission's secretary, spent his days 'lolling on deck and watching flying fish' and observing his fellow passengers, such as the Bishop of Lebombo, 'a somewhat rotund and very cheerful looking cleric who is on his way back to his diocese'.[7] Haggard thought Bishop John Latimer Fuller 'the most interesting and informing of our companions'.[8]

Harding passed the evenings playing bridge with 'Sinclair (the New Zealander), Lady Haggard and Mrs. Garnett. Very amusing the games are too. As to Lady Haggard, she improves greatly on acquaintance. She is stout and placid and what might be called an "outdoor person" – very practical and full of common sense – just the reverse of Haggard.'[9] He was perplexed by Lilias, a 'curious mixture of her Father and Mother – she has some of the placidity of the one, and some of the nervousness of the other: the result is rather nondescript ... Anyhow, she is quite good fun.'[10] Another passenger, Sir Hartman Just, a Colonial Office official travelling to Australia and New Zealand on a six-month tour, 'writes topical poems'.[11] One of these, the comic 'Alphabet of the D.R.C.', included Haggard: 'R is for Sir Rider's yarns, queerer and queerer'.[12]

Haggard was busy not on a yarn but a travel diary, daily jotting down notes, as he had done in Cyprus and Palestine, for working up into a book. He had resumed the practice in India and continued when the commission visited Australia, New Zealand, and now Madeira and South Africa. Sailing home, he would use these notes as an aide-memoire to write a fuller diary, published posthumously as *Diary of an African Journey* in 2000.[13]

The Haggard who sailed for South Africa in 1914 was far removed from the callow youth of 1875. Returning to South Africa for the first time since 1881, Haggard was now a household name, a best-selling writer, respected agricultural expert and possessor of a knighthood, reflecting his status as a public servant. Although his return to southern Africa was brought about by official business, once that was done he was looking forward to visiting old haunts, friends and acquaintances. This was a pilgrimage into his past in which the older man would meet the younger.

In 1910, in the aftermath of the Anglo-Boer War, the British colonies of Natal and the Cape along with the former Boer republics of the Orange Free State and Transvaal had united to form the Union of South Africa. The confederation dream of the 1870s was now reality. While the British victory in the war had fuelled hopes among the indigenous peoples that the franchise would be extended to them out of gratitude for the sacrifices they had made in helping defeat the Boer republics, this was not to be. The South Africa Act of 1909, which was passed by the British parliament and which had been drafted by a convention of white South African politicians, reached a compromise on the franchise question so as to allay white fears and concerns. In effect, the Act confirmed the existing arrangements for the franchise in each of the four provinces of the Union: a limited, qualified right to vote for black people in the Cape and, nominally, in Natal, and no voting right at all for black people in the former Boer republics.

The nature of the new Union soon became apparent with the implementation of restrictive and segregatory measures that adversely affected the black majority. The Mines and Works Act of 1911 reserved certain jobs for whites, while the Natives' Land Act of 1913 'massively restricted African landownership'[14] and secured 'a supply of cheap black labour on the *platteland* [rural areas] and in the towns by checking the development of an independent black peasantry'.[15] Godfrey Lagden,

Haggard's friend from Pretoria days, played a major role in drawing up these policies. He chaired the South African Native Affairs Commission (1903–5), whose key recommendation was that 'whites and blacks should be kept separate in politics and land occupation'.[16] Land would be set aside for exclusive black occupation in rural areas and equivalent 'locations' (what became known as 'townships') set up in or adjacent to towns and cities. The 1913 Land Act put this into practice by allocating reserved areas for African occupation in the countryside – mainly existing reserves, tribal areas and black-owned land.

In response to these developments, black people began to organise and mobilise to express their opposition. At the time of the passage of the South Africa Act through the British parliament, an unofficial delegation consisting of Africans and coloureds travelled to London to try to persuade the imperial parliament to reject the draft South African constitution. This deputation was headed by the lawyer William Schreiner, a former Cape prime minister and brother of Olive Schreiner.[17] Among those joining him was the cleric, newspaper editor and educationist John Dube. Mohandas Gandhi, then a Durban lawyer, led a separate Indian delegation to lobby for Indian civil rights in Natal but not the right to vote. Although the Schreiner delegation failed in its objective, the Act of Union and the segregatory intent of the new South African government were the catalysts for the formation of the African National Congress (then styled the South African Native National Congress), headed by John Dube, in 1912.

'It was with pleasure, mingled with a certain melancholy' that Haggard saw once more 'the cloud cap hanging like poured water down the kloofs and steep sides of Table Mountain'. The Haggards were quartered at the Queen's Hotel below Lion's Head in the beachfront suburb of Sea Point.

> Motors fly everywhere; there are electric trams crawling along the sides of Lion's Head and so forth. But the sunshine is the same – the eternal glorious African sunshine – there is the same spirit everywhere which is best represented by the South American word *mañana,* the spirit of 'tomorrow' which makes this land of troubles so restful through them all. To me it feels as though the 33 intervening years had vanished, and once more I were back in the years 1875 to 1881.[18]

Haggard's South African past was ever present. At the Dominions Royal Commission's first official function, a luncheon at a government agricultural show on 25 February, he encountered Hendrik Struben – 'now an old man of 74' – who reminded Haggard that he had 'bought a wagon and a span of oxen from us when we left Newcastle, Natal, in 1881. I used to know him well in Pretoria in the annexation days.'[19] There was a large turnout for the lunch, 'many of them Dutch', and Haggard took a dim view of how the speeches 'were smothered by a hum of conversation'. A reference by the commission chairman, Sir Edgar Vincent, to King George V 'produced not a single cheer'.[20]

In the evening a banquet was hosted by the Union government for the commission in the public dining room of the Mount Nelson Hotel beneath Table Mountain; a strange venue, thought Harding, 'with all the ordinary people finishing their dinners at surrounding tables. It felt as though we were beasts being fed in public.'[21] Haggard was seated opposite Jan Smuts, former Boer general and now South Africa's minister of justice, who gave 'a lively account of how he came to deport the [foreign] labour leaders who reached England yesterday amid much excitement'. These were the leaders of a strike in Johannesburg, which was crushed when Smuts sent in armed troops.[22]

After the first sitting of the commission at the Huguenot Buildings in Queen Victoria Street, Haggard lunched with Louis Botha, the first prime minister of the Union of South Africa. After the Anglo-Boer War, in alliance with Smuts, Botha pursued a policy of conciliation and unification among the Afrikaners and English-speaking whites of South Africa. Once an implacable foe, he was now a loyal friend of the Empire. Botha's vision of the future 'was of a united white South Africa in which it did not matter whether one was Afrikaner or English'.[23]

Botha and Haggard resumed their conversation that evening at Rust en Vrede (Rest and Peace), home of Rhodes's associate Sir Abe Bailey[24] in Muizenberg, a popular resort on the shores of False Bay, where Vincent and Haggard had been invited to stay for a couple of nights. This imposing house in the Cape Dutch style had been designed by Herbert Baker with marble-lined rooms and an arcaded loggia with spectacular views across the bay, but Haggard found the diminutive dwelling next door, Barkly Cottage, of greater interest, 'for in it died Cecil Rhodes. I looked through the window at the little chamber where this remarkable man gave up his breath. A pathetic place.'[25]

Botha elaborated on the 'labour situation at Johannesburg, which he said has a population containing many of the most evil people on the earth, red anarchists and republicans'. He favoured 'the employment of more natives and fewer troublesome and highly-paid whites at nine times the wages of the latter'. He thought 'these skilled natives ... were the worst treated men in South Africa'. There was 'no "down with the kaffir" about General Botha. In every way Botha impresses me enormously. He is indeed a fine man.'[26] The two shared a common bond: both were dedicated farmers and keen proponents of agricultural development.

Guests the following evening included Thomas Cullinan, 'of diamond fame', and the mine owner Henry Nourse, whom Haggard had known in Pretoria.[27] Late in the evening the conversation turned to the Jameson Raid. Bailey said Rhodes had 'planned the whole thing and that Jameson was only a tool. Edgar Vincent led the conversation on, and I, perhaps incautiously, remembering the company I was in, expressed disapproval of the business. Sir Abe Bailey remarked "you are old-fashioned" and I pleaded guilty.' Bailey went on to justify the raid and in answer to another remark of mine to the effect that it was a wretched failure, to allege that on the contrary it was a splendid success since it had 'led to the war which was its whole object' and all that has followed. I said it had cost England £350 million and 20 000 lives. 'What does that matter,' asked A.B., 'lives are cheap' ... If the only argument for this raid is that it led to a great war, it seems to me to be both weak and worthy of a buccaneer ... Altogether the conversation was most instructive, but I cannot say that it raised my opinion of the group who were responsible for the raid.[28]

A stork among cranes, Haggard consoled himself with the thought that 'out of this evil good has come since there seems to be little doubt that racial animosities are beginning to die down'. He was referring to the animosities between Boer and Brit. As to the 'native question', Nourse proposed a solution that Haggard found absurd: 'a plan, which he appeared to think quite feasible, for segregating all the natives, even to the extent of allowing none of them to enter domestic service, although in Cape Town alone there are very many thousands of such servants who are the prop of every household, and indeed of every farm and industry throughout the land'.[29] Haggard expressed his own views in his diary:

The black man is driving a wedge into the fabric of European civilisation, is permeating it through and through ... He is beginning to think for himself and to demand a fair share of the rewards of labour. The white worker on the other hand is falling back, hence his fury and his violence ... Certainly it is true also that the various sections of black folk who inhabit Southern Africa are by no means incapable of advance and adaptation to the civilized needs and ideas. In a time to come once more that these will in effect rule in their own land is not at all incredible.[30]

On Sunday, 1 March, the liberal politician John X. Merriman, a former Cape prime minister who had been passed over for the position of first Union prime minister, called on Haggard at his hotel.[31] A 'strange mixture of philosopher and politician',[32] Merriman was highly critical of Botha and Smuts's policies, but Haggard was more interested in Merriman's views on South Africa's past. 'He knew Shepstone and spoke of him as a "great" man. Had he remained in the Transvaal, he said, all would have gone well and the course of South African history would have been changed. The madness was in moving him and replacing him by a military martinet like Lanyon. All of these mistakes he attributed to Frere with his Indian training and ideas.' Haggard pointed out that the result 'was the re-establishment of Shepstone's policy by means of the expenditure of 20 000 lives and £350 million'. Merriman agreed, 'but it had left the Dutch on top. They were the real rulers of the country.'[33]

Merriman anticipated that 'much of South Africa in the end would become practically native. Mr. Merriman seems generally to think well of the natives and to have considerable appreciation of their powers.'[34] But Merriman had no time for the South African mining magnates, speaking of them with 'bitterness and indignation, stigmatising them as unprincipled, selfish and cruel in their dealings with all, even the natives in their employ'.[35] As for Rhodesia, it was '"a land under a curse" because of the manner of its acquisition'.[36]

Haggard came face to face with his past when he, Louie and Lilias lunched with John Kotzé, now a judge in the Cape provincial division. Haggard enjoyed 'talk of old times, when we used to trek and work together in the Transvaal'. Haggard thought his own memory was 'pretty good, at any rate for those things which happened in my youth', but he conceded Kotzé's was 'certainly better. Several times he corrected my recollection of particular events, even to the words used in connection with them.'[37]

An evening was spent at the Royal Observatory, where Haggard and some of his fellow commissioners were 'shewn the starry heavens through the great telescope'. Haggard was 'crushed and saddened' by the 'majesty of the sight', which he had never seen before. 'The old truisms which we speak about the stars came home to me with the new force of an individual experience. My God! what are they all? My God! didst thou make them all? My God! are these Thee? My God! is Thy name Design or Chance? Answer and tell us.'[38]

Eternal conundrums did not distract from present realities, and at the Wellington Cooperative Winery Haggard was surprised to see 'a white man and a kaffir working together, a sight I never saw in the old days in Africa and one which suggests a great change in sentiment, brought about, I suppose, by the pressure of necessity'.[39] For Haggard 'this meant the approach of equality. Once that was established how could the dwindling white people hold their own against an increasing race, already four or five times as numerous?'[40]

On Friday, 6 March, the commission dined with the Union's Governor General, Lord Gladstone, younger son of Haggard's bête noire, a 'kindly and sympathetic man, but not one of any great force of character, such as one might have expected from his parentage'.[41] Lord and Lady Gladstone were not well liked 'as they insist upon every formality of vice-regal state, such as bowing on entering the presence and so forth. This the South Africans, and especially those of Dutch blood, do not like at all.'[42] To everyone's great relief Gladstone had resigned and was to leave South Africa in July. 'His name is not one of good omen in South Africa and perhaps it is as well that he is giving up the post.'[43]

On Saturday, 7 March, members of the commission lunched at Groot Constantia, one of the grandest of the Cape Dutch homesteads, where Haggard sat next to Annie Botha, wife of the prime minister. Both agreed

> the outlook of the white inhabitants of South Africa in the future ... seemed very doubtful – chiefly because of this native question. The native could no longer be suppressed, or even oppressed: he must follow his destiny and often he was an able and a competent person ... What was to be the end of it? She could not tell but the future was dark and dubious. Perhaps at last South Africa would be the heritage of the black races with an admixture of white blood.[44]

Haggard and Annie Botha shared the conclusion 'that time and experience were wonderful softeners of strong views. Thus today I should not write another *Jess* and she would not think about the English as she had thought even a dozen years ago.'[45]

The commission's sojourn in Cape Town was drawing to an end. It had been a full programme, gathering evidence on harbours and docks, factories, vineyards, pig and cattle farms, and forestry plantations. There had been trips to the Rhodes Fruit Farms in Franschhoek and other farms at Koeberg, Durbanville, Paarl, Wellington and Somerset West, as well as the State Agricultural College at Elsenburg, outside Stellenbosch, but there hadn't been 'nearly so much fuss over the Commission as there was in Australasia', according to Harding, 'in the way of journalists and the like. There have been no interviewers yet ... and anyhow Commissions etc. from home are much more frequent here than in Australia.'[46]

On the evening of 9 March, Haggard and the other commissioners left Cape Town by special train, for a first stopover at Oudtshoorn and then on to Port Elizabeth. Louie and Lilias went ahead by sea. While he was dressing on the train the next morning, the 'iron lid of the washbasin fell on and crushed the top plate' of Haggard's false teeth, 'recently fitted with so much discomfort'. Fortunately he had kept the 'old temporary set with me which the dentist wanted to destroy'.[47]

At Oudtshoorn Haggard renewed his acquaintance with 'that ungainly but profitable fowl, the ostrich'.[48] The town was the centre of South Africa's ostrich feather export industry. The ornate houses of the 'ostrich barons', sporting distinctive white-painted stencilled cast-iron lace-work decoration, stood witness to the fortunes made at the height of the late-Victorian fashion vogue.[49]

In 'heat like the breath of Nebuchadnezzar's furnace', Haggard was driven out to the Cango Caves, which, he was told, were the originals of those in *King Solomon's Mines*. 'This, however, is apocryphal as I never saw them before. My model in the story were certain stalactite caves in the neighbourhood of Potchefstroom, which I had visited when a lad.'[50] One of South Africa's great natural wonders, the Cango Caves extend at least three miles into the mountains, though their exact extent remains unknown. 'Here is every kind of fantastic shape fashioned during thousands or hundreds of thousands of years by the slow drip of the lime-charged water.' What struck Haggard the most was seeing his companions on the tour 'climbing down a precipitous path in single file, each with a lighted taper in the hand', like ghosts 'or a procession of priests and priestesses bearing one of their number to burial in some measureless Egyptian tomb'.[51]

On arrival at Port Elizabeth on Thursday, 12 March, Haggard was met at the station by Louie and Lilias. The next day he lunched with William Charles Scully, the city's resident magistrate[52] and a well-known writer. 'But, as Irishmen are so prone to be, he is an extreme radical ... quite honest in his views with some of which, such as his hatred of the magnates and the state of affairs that they have brought, it is easy to have a certain sympathy'. While discussing his memoir, *The Ridge of the*

White Waters – 'in which he draws a dreadful picture of Johannesburg' – Scully told Haggard that no South African newspaper 'would even mention this book for fear of offending their moneyed supporters and shareholders'. Booksellers wouldn't stock it either; in a Port Elizabeth bookshop Haggard 'was informed loftily that "we do not keep Scully's books"'.[53] Scully was labelled 'a fanatic pro-Boer'[54] by the Anglican archdeacon Augustus Wirgman, who drove Haggard around the city the following day. Motoring along the beachfront, Haggard saw 'mixed surf bathing in progress – an amazing sight'.[55]

While Haggard and the commission travelled on to East London by train, and thence to the Orange Free State, Lilias and Louie sailed from Port Elizabeth for Durban, from where they would go up to Pietermaritzburg. From the train to East London, Haggard saw the 'many kraals, the huts being built of mud and thatched. Round these played scores of children, but alas here civilisation is doing its work. Instead of being naked as in my day, they were nearly all clothed in dirty shirts. The women wear the most horrible garments, broken stays and ill-fitting dresses out of which they burst and bulge. I prefer the fig leaf, or rather *mucha*, costume.'[56]

After hearing evidence at East London, 'a nice town though like all minor South African cities not very interesting',[57] the commission left early for Kimberley on Tuesday, 16 March. Haggard marvelled at the scenery: 'the prospect of water-carved mountains and kloofs and endless plains was in truth stupendous and awe-inspiring'.[58] The train passed Bloemfontein in the night and, when Haggard woke next morning, 'we were running through the deadest and barest veld I ever saw'. A severe drought had brought many farmers to bankruptcy.[59] In Kimberley the commission put up at the Belgrave Hotel, 'like everything else in this place owned by the De Beers Co., who were our hosts here'.[60]

The De Beers chairman, Francis Oats, took some of the commissioners, including Haggard, for a drive around the city, returning in time for a public luncheon, where Haggard was seated next to the Bishop of Kimberley, Wilfred Gore Browne, 'an agreeable cleric ... He said that the Church of England is doing well in South Africa.'[61] After lunch, evidence was taken in the council chamber of the town hall, which was 'hung with truly awful pictures of many mayors'.[62] In the evening 'we were entertained to dinner at the hotel by the De Beers Co. I observed that no diamonds were worn even by the Jewish ladies. I suppose that being so common, they are looked on as vulgar here.'[63]

On Thursday, 19 March, Haggard and another British commissioner, Tom Garnett, with a member of the commission's staff, a Mr Greene, inspected 'the irrigated and irrigable lands on the Modder and Riet rivers about 25 miles from Kimberley' and also visited the Magersfontein battlefield, where an entrenched Boer force had defeated the British forces, inflicting heavy casualties during the 'Black Week' of 1899. Their driver, a Mr Wolhuter, told Haggard that his uncle, fighting on the Boer side, 'shot till his rifle was too hot to hold'.[64]

Back in Kimberley, the commissioners were shown diamond ore being processed, but Haggard found the 'native compound' of more interest: 'Here numberless kaffirs live for four or six months at a time in a state of strict imprisonment. From the day they enter till the day they take their discharge they cannot set foot outside of these walls, or rather outside of the wire fences that ring the mines. They work eight hours a day in the mines reaching the shaft by an underground passage.'[65] Haggard made a note of their wages: 'an average wage of about 3s. a day, out of which they have to pay about 1s. for the cost of their living.'[66] Within the compound there were 'butchers' shops & grocery stores, etc. where they can buy everything they require, down to aerated waters and hop beer and all kinds of clothing.'[67]

Haggard also inspected the 'night quarters where the men sleep in bunks, perhaps 20 or 30 in a compartment, the large room where religious services are held and the hospital where ... we found a good number of cases under treatment'. Some were suffering from scurvy, 'notwithstanding the onions that are served out free with the purchased beef, others from stomach complaints or accidents'. But the 'great scourge' was pneumonia; 'in a recent outbreak of a virulent nature about 20 died out of 30 who sickened. The disease is contracted in the tunnels of the deep mines, but of its real cause little seems to be understood.'[68]

The miners appeared 'happy and contented ... however, it is a strange and unnatural life that these slaves of Vanity endure in order to net their 2s. a day. To isolate thousands of men without their womenkind cannot be good.'[69] The migratory labour system, a marker of the future apartheid state of South Africa, was already well in place, as was the demeaning treatment of black workers: 'Before they take their discharge they are shut up for four or five days for fear lest they should have swallowed any diamonds, a horrid and humiliating business for all concerned, but perhaps necessary.'[70] Oats told Haggard 'that, do what they would, there was still a good deal of IDB (Illegal Diamond Buying).'[71]

On Friday, 20 March, the commission travelled overnight back to Bloemfontein, provincial capital of the Orange Free State and judicial capital of the Union.[72] Haggard visited 'the old graveyard now so full that it has been closed' and found hundreds of iron crosses bearing the names of English soldiers 'who perished in the war, nearly all of them from typhoid. Those crosses stand in rows so endless that the eye grows bewildered in looking at them.'[73] An even sadder sight were the 'countless mounds of brown earth, some of them only two or three feet in length. These cover the bones of unrecorded Boer women and children who died in the concentration camp not far away, but none can tell whose are the mortal remnants that each of them hides from sight, for of these no record was kept.'[74]

Haggard also saw the 'fine monument that has recently been erected to these unfortunates about half a mile from the burying ground ... On it are two figures in bronze of mourning women, very noble and pathetic figures, bronze plaques of children dying in tents, and patriotic sentiments in the Dutch language such as "For

Freedom, Nation and Fatherland".[75] The National Women's Monument, unveiled on 16 December 1913, was erected to the memory of the women and children who died in the concentration camps and elsewhere during the Anglo-Boer War. These camps were part of Lord Kitchener's plan to deny Boer combatants civilian assistance. Thomas Pakenham's observation remains valid: 'The camps have left a gigantic scar across the minds of the Afrikaners: a symbol of deliberate genocide.'[76]

On visiting the site of the concentration camp – 'still bare veld' – Haggard changed his mind about his earlier 'admiration of the monument to the Boer women and children'. He now deeply regretted that

> it should ever have been erected to perpetuate sentiments which I admit to be most natural ... The deaths of all these poor people were most unfortunate but it is difficult to avoid the suspicion that more might have been done to avoid some of them ... Also it does seem sad that as many or more women and children should have perished than were lost by wounds and sickness in the whole war. All these facts this memorial with its noble and pathetic sculptures will commemorate for centuries.'[77]

It is not unusual for inconvenient truths to be suppressed, but Haggard's logic is difficult to countenance.

While in Bloemfontein Haggard sought out the head of police, Colonel Michiel du Toit, who, according to Merriman, had 'witnessed an extraordinary performance by a kaffir witch-doctor, which he, Merriman, supposed quite erroneously to have been the origin of sundry mystic scenes in *She*'.[78] Haggard recorded at length Du Toit's experiences in the Zoutpansberg where he witnessed a sangoma using white smoke from a fire as a screen for visuals produced on request of government buildings in Pretoria and scenes from the 'black water', this after it had been ascertained that the man had 'never seen the ocean or, for the matter of that, Pretoria'.[79] Haggard would use elements of Du Toit's account for the magic performed by the sangoma Zikali in *Finished*.

26

'RETURNED FROM THE DEAD'

On Sunday morning, 2 March, the Dominions Royal Commission's special train zigzagged down Van Reenen's Pass from the highveld escarpment to the Natal coastal plain. The occasional military cemetery at the side of the track provided a salutary reminder that just over a decade ago this land 'of great beauty' had been a bloodily contested landscape. Haggard and his fellow commissioners were steaming their way to one of the most famous sites of the Anglo-Boer War, Ladysmith, 'charming in its hill-surrounded hollow' but a 'hopeless place' to choose to defend as the hollow was commanded by 'many huge and almost impregnable hills'.[1]

Sunday afternoon was spent walking the sites associated with the siege, including the town cemetery, where many of the crosses were 'merely inscribed "Here lies a British soldier"'. Haggard and Vincent 'motored out' to the heights of Platrand, where a Boer attack had been repulsed after bitter fighting on 6 January 1900. The crosses there read, 'Here lies a brave burgher'. Standing among them, Haggard recognised the road to Pietermaritzburg and remembered 'the very spot where I had halted my horse in 1876 and admired the stars with Sir Henry Bulwer as we rode into Ladysmith'[2] on the 1877 tour of Natal with Shepstone.

Aboard the train again, they proceeded to the village of Colenso, unchanged since Haggard was last there in 1881. In the interim it had given its name to the battle fought nearby on 15 December 1899, the first of several attempts by General Sir Redvers Buller to break through the Boer lines and relieve Ladysmith. The local guide said Buller and his staff had ignored advice on the topography from locals – 'it was always the same story, the imperial officers invariably treated the information offered by loyal English having local knowledge with supercilious contempt'.[3] The commissioners were shown other battlefields in the area, but Spion Kop, 'where we met such terrible loss ... we only looked on from a distance'.[4]

At Colenso a coach was detached from the commission train and attached to the mail train that had arrived from Pietermaritzburg bringing Louie and Lilias. The Haggards, together with Newfoundland's commissioner, Edgar Bowring, and Tom Garnett, travelled north through the night to Newcastle. At seven o'clock on

Monday morning 'Louie and I trod the streets of the little town of Newcastle, which we left in 1881. It has grown a good deal, the hotels have changed and there are more trees but, speaking generally, is much the same.'[5] The commissioners were officially received in the small town hall after breakfast. Haggard responded to the speech of welcome and everyone decamped to inspect a nearby coal mine. In the afternoon evidence was taken 'concerning coal and agriculture, which is flourishing here since dipping for cattle was invented, and [we] later visited another coal mine'.[6] The mine was close to the Ingagane River opposite Rooi Point farm. Haggard was shown the place on the riverbank 'to which I used to send a cart to be filled with the coal that outcrops at this place, imagining it was on my property (which it was not). Every little memory of this sort connected with me seems to have been treasured up by the inhabitants of Newcastle.'[7]

Garnett and Bowring left by the night mail for Durban, and the Haggards 'were entertained that evening at a reception which ended in a dance'. Haggard was marched onto a dais where the mayor made another speech of welcome, 'to which of course I had to reply. I escaped early.'[8] Their night 'in a somewhat primitive inn' brought back memories of 'the adventurous journey up to Newcastle' in the first year of their marriage. Lilias was disturbed by the 'bugs in my room, I can see them walking down the wall'. 'Of course there are, my dear,' replied her father placidly, 'dozens of them, but bugs won't give you malaria, and you have a mosquito net which is all that matters – good night'.[9]

The next morning Haggard, Louie and Lilias went to Hilldrop, 'the last place on earth I ever expected to see again. Hilldrop that for me has so many memories ... I looked at all the rooms, including that in which my dear son was born.' In the garden he ate a fruit off one of the old naartjie trees, 'inspected the wagon house where in my book Jess was incarcerated, the stone kraal that we built to hold the ostriches, the new road up the hillside on which I am told the dassies, or rock rabbits, still sit as they used to do'. He walked down the sloping gardens 'past the spring whence we drew water, now nearly hidden in willows, to the spot where we made bricks. Lo! There still lay some of the bricks ... I picked them up with a strange emotion. Well, they are not bad bricks.' And so back to the house, 'presently to step off that well-remembered stoep, I presume for the last time'.[10]

The Haggards left Newcastle early next morning and reached Pietermaritzburg late in the afternoon. From here it was a short journey from the red brick station (where Mohandas Gandhi had famously been ejected from a train in 1893)[11] to the Imperial Hotel in Loop Street, named after the Prince Imperial, who was billeted there in 1879 on his way to the front during the Anglo-Zulu War. Haggard was photographed standing in the hotel's tiled courtyard by a photographer from the *Natal Witness*[12] and shortly afterwards, to his delight, 'my friend, Mr. James Stuart, arrived'.[13] He brought good news: Stuart had succeeded in finding 'my old Zulu servant Mazooku, who was coming to see me on the following morning'.[14]

On Thursday morning, 26 March, Masuku, 'now an old man',[15] came to the hotel 'and oh! he was pleased to see me. He has worn very well, his hair shewing no grey, but I fear has not prospered, as he lost his cattle by the East Coast Fever.'[16] This was one of a series of disasters inflicted on Masuku. Another involved accepting *lobola* (bride wealth) 'of £10 from a suitor of his daughter', which he spent, 'being in difficulties through the death of his cattle ... and owing to very cruel treatment he had received from a white man who, out of revenge for the loss of a lawsuit, destroyed his crops by turning animals into them as they were ripening'. When his daughter then refused to marry, her suitor brought an action against Masuku for the return of the £10, 'which action, rightly or wrongly, the suitor won under some provision of native law'.[17] Haggard settled Masuku's 'complicated business affairs' and paid the amount owed on his behalf, 'so I suppose that in native eyes, Miss Masuku is lobola'd to me!'[18]

With Stuart interpreting, Haggard and Masuku spoke in 'the true Zulu style'. Haggard told Masuku that 'the *inkosikazi* and the maiden', Louie and Lilias, would be staying awhile at Eshowe in Zululand as guests of the district native commissioner, James Young Gibson, and that Masuku 'was to go with them and that I put them "into your hand". He answered in the old way – "*Inkoosi y pagate! Baba!*" (Chief from of old! Father!) thereby signifying obedience to the order. Also that if possible I wished him to accompany me through Zululand afterwards.'[19] Haggard reminded Masuku of how 'he had given me his kerrie when we parted, remarking that I still had and valued it. He remembered but had never thought it possible that such a thing should be preserved for so long.'[20]

Haggard and Stuart went to see Natal's Chief Native Commissioner, Richard Addison, about the tour of Zululand. Haggard had requested the trip be made in a mule-drawn waggonette, the ubiquitous form of transport when he had lived in South Africa, but Addison was unable to find one. A car was hired instead. After arrangements were made, Stuart took Haggard 'outside to where a number of chiefs, headmen and Zulu messengers and policemen were waiting to see officials'. Stuart told them Haggard was 'Sompseu's child' whom he had loved. 'The effect was strange – a volley of enthusiastic salutes. Such is still the magic of that name.'[21] Shepstone's statue stood on the corner of Longmarket Street and Commercial Road, diagonally opposite the city hall. Haggard recognised Shepstone's back 'from 20 yards away', but there was 'something wrong about the eyes and the hair is represented as growing too far back on the forehead'.[22]

Later that morning Haggard met Theophilus's brother John Shepstone – 'now 87 but wonderfully hale and well'[23] – and his daughter Averil and son Percy. 'To the latter old Umslopogaas [Mhlopekazi] had given the hunting knife I sent him years ago by the hand of Osborn, that he might keep it safe lest it should be stolen away. If at any time he came to claim it, good, if not it was to be his.'[24] A walk around the Voortrekker Museum, filled with 'many interesting mementoes of the old Dutch',[25] was followed by dinner with Stuart at the Victoria Club, where Haggard met several old acquaintances, including Henry Koch (Osborn's legal adviser in Zululand) and Henrique Shepstone, Theophilus's eldest son, one of the 'band of brothers' who annexed Transvaal in 1877.

On Friday, 27 March, after taking evidence in the city hall, Haggard was guest speaker at the monthly luncheon of the African Club. A record attendance was expected, especially as 'on this occasion ladies may be brought as guests of members'.[26] Accordingly a larger venue had been commandeered for the occasion, the supper room of the city hall. Haggard, Louie and Lilias sat at the top table with the former city mayor and president of the club, George Macfarlane, facing three long tables occupied by the members and their friends.

Haggard began by saying he wondered 'whether his name was really Rider Haggard or Rip Van Winkle. (Laughter)' as there were 'few left whom he knew' from the 1870s. First he mentioned Shepstone: 'I looked on him very much as a father, and, in truth, he treated me very much as a son.' Shepstone had not been dealt with well, but 'every year that goes by more and more vindicates his honoured name, and higher and still higher lifts his reputation, until that reputation has become, I tell you, a bright and fixed star in the firmament of history. (Cheers.)'[27] Haggard also brought Melmoth Osborn to mind, 'Malimati, with his queer quiet way', and Bishop John Colenso, who was 'attacked, almost crucified, for his opinions', yet now 'there was hardly one who would condemn him today. As time had vindicated Shepstone, so (he would not speak of native policy) time had vindicated Colenso. (Cheers.)'[28]

Having dealt with his earlier years in South Africa and events leading up to Union, Haggard addressed South Africa's future:

> There is the question of the increase of the white population; which is not going on as fast as might be hoped. (Hear, hear.) Then you have the increase of the native population, which is a serious and difficult question. (Hear, hear.) What is to be done with a nation just lifting itself up as it were from sleep and looking for the first time upon the dawn! How are you to lead this people? It is not enough just to rig them up in European clothes ... It is a question of guidance, of the uplifting of these good people – for many of them are indeed very good people. (Hear, hear.) The races must learn to live together and strive together to an end of the common good.

Haggard concluded by wishing South Africa well, and requested that 'as an old Natalian' he be allowed 'to wish the best of all things to this dear and lovely land of yours ... Advance, Natal! God bless Natal, white and black together, and bless her gates of mountain and of sea!' He 'resumed his seat amid enthusiastic cheering'.[29]

On the same day as the luncheon, the front page of the *Natal Witness* ran a photograph of Haggard – 'exactly like that of the mummy of Rameses the Second'[30] – together with a long article on his career and an editorial by Horace Rose in which Haggard was credited with 'giving to the English-speaking world volume on volume of healthy, wholesome and thoroughly entertaining literature, in no page of which is there anything of a degrading or unmanly tendency'. According to Rose, the 'heart of Africa, previously enshrined for the reading public only between the covers of costly books of travel', had been revealed in Haggard's books and placed 'within the reach of all ... Who shall say how many strong and sturdy pioneers have been attracted from the pleasant Homeland to help in winning the African wilds to civilisation as the result of romantic interest aroused in them when as boys they read and revelled in these romances? It has been said that Rider Haggard did more to advertise South Africa to the world when it was less known than it is now than any man of his time.'[31]

On Saturday morning Haggard and his fellow commissioners went on a short train trip 'to the beautiful 24 000-acre farm' of Joseph Baynes, an agriculturalist who had pioneered the dairy industry in South Africa and introduced cattle dipping in order to eradicate ticks and tick-borne diseases. On their return to the city they attended a reception given by the mayor in Alexandra Park, close to where Haggard had responded to the toast to 'The Ladies' at the lunch following the opening of the Alexandra Bridge over the Msunduzi River in 1876. In 1914 there was no danger of the *Natal Witness* misspelling his surname.

That night the Haggards and other members of the commission left by train for Pretoria, passing on Sunday morning 'Rooi Point and Hilldrop. Then appeared all the scenes of the war of 1881, notably the sad Majuba where poor Colley rests with others.'[32] Shortly afterwards 'we emerged on the Transvaal high veld which I had not seen since 1879 when I rode across it on the way to Natal.'[33] The train passed Johannesburg – 'a long range of distant, twinkling lights' – a city that didn't exist in 1879. 'Then darkness and once more the silence of the veld whence it arose and into which perchance it will sink again in a day to be.'[34]

The train pulled into the Pretoria railway station around ten that evening, 'a different arrival indeed to that of my first here by ox wagon in 1877', and the party proceeded to the Grand Hotel in Church Square 'on the site of the old European', the same square where Shepstone's mission had outspanned in 1877. Now 'trams clank and clang beneath the windows, electric lights are flaring and on every side appear huge and costly buildings: government offices, law courts and so forth ... Who would know it for the same that I described in *The Witch's Head* whereon the Boers used to assemble in their wagons at *nachtmaal*.'[35]

After breakfast on Monday, Haggard was interviewed by a journalist on the *Transvaal Leader*, David Pollock.[36]

Sir Rider talks quickly and well. He is restlessly, almost nervously, energetic. His eyes are ceaselessly observant. The moment a thing strikes him as worthy of retention, it is jotted down in a large flat notebook, which the novelist carries ready for action in his hand. For the rest, Sir Rider is tall, with a slight stoop of the shoulders, thin faced and bearded. He does not look his age, which is 58. He looks what he is, a composite of two high avocations – distinguished man of letters and enthusiastic gentleman-farmer.[37]

There was time before the first sitting of the commission for Pollock to call for a taxi and take Haggard to 'The Palatial', now better known as Jess's Cottage. 'Wandering there I felt like one returned from the dead ... We went down a path bordered on one side by a line of great blue gums' that 'Cochrane and I planted with our own hands. Then appeared the house, much altered, for the original building, together with the stable behind it, is now embedded and surrounded by alien masonry, the thatch has been replaced by tin and the stoep has been made or added.' In 'what used to be our sitting room' a woman was 'packing apples, the place one confusion. Looking at it I could not but recall it as it used to be, with its pretty English furniture and the engravings on the walls. Beyond was the sleeping room ... the kitchen, the bathroom and the stable where stood my two fine horses, Black Billy and Moresco.'

The garden was 'a terrible sight, a mere tangle'. Of the vines Haggard and Cochrane planted, 'only one or two survive climbing up trees'. Standing there Haggard 'seemed to forget all the intervening years and grow young again. I saw the walls rising. I saw the sapling gums, the infant vines and the new planted roses and gardenias. The place is a lodging house, not of the highest class, kept by an honest but struggling couple who were delighted to show me everything. I went away with a sad heart. Oh! where are they who used to pass in and out through that humble gate?'[38] At a luncheon for the commission hosted by Pretoria's mayor, Haggard made a heartfelt plea for the preservation of Jess's Cottage 'on account of the historical interest it has acquired. I am glad to say that the matter has been taken up with some enthusiasm by the press and public.'[39] 'The Palatial' was eventually demolished in 1967, and its site is now occupied by Renault Motors.[40]

Proposing the toast to the commission, Judge President Jacob de Villiers devoted part of his speech to Haggard and his books, generally in admiration, but he regretted Haggard 'had not always dealt too tenderly with "the older section of the population"' – a euphemism for the Boers of the 1870s. Haggard defended himself, saying that 'we generally modified the hard and sharp views of youth as we grew older, a statement that was cheered. Still it has not satisfied some people to judge from a long letter I read in a local paper.'[41]

The letter, published in the *Pretoria News* on 1 April and signed pseudonymously 'Dutch Afrikander', responded to Haggard's speech by expressing outrage at 'the heinous literary diatribes against that "older generation" as a whole, of which Sir Rider had been successfully delivered since first he put his facile pen to paper'. The letter was extremely critical of Haggard's depiction of the Boers in *Cetywayo and His White Neighbours* – 'one of the most scurrilous things ever written against your and my countrymen' – and in his fiction, especially *Jess*: 'the embodiment of all the irreconcilable race hatred which its author felt towards what for some inscrutable reason he looked upon as the "degrading peace" of 1881'.[42]

The pseudonymous writer rebutted Haggard's statement that time softened one's views, citing *Marie*, which contained 'the same old "bastard" (cross-bred Englishman-Afrikander) stalking through these newly written pages ... the same irreconcilable racialism'.[43] 'Dutch Africander' is not far off the mark, for apart from Marie Marais and Vrouw Prinsloo all the Boer characters in *Marie* are duplicitous villains, stubborn or stupid.

'Dutch Afrikander' was later revealed as the pseudonym of the famous historian and champion of the Afrikaner, Gustav Preller. In his journal Haggard felt Preller overlooked that in some books, such as *Swallow* and *Marie*, he had 'dealt with [the Boers] very tenderly indeed' and that *Cetywayo and His White Neighbours* was 'a true history' and that 'the Boers in *Jess* ... true pictures of certain of their people at the period' and the villain 'was drawn from life'.[44]

After the luncheon and apparently alone, Haggard visited the Old Cemetery in Church Street. He saw Paul Kruger's tomb – 'massive but not ornamental' – and 'others of those whom I had known, some of them already neglected and in decay like those who lie beneath. It was an even sadder experience than that of Jess's Cottage.'[45] The graves he had gone to visit were those of Johanna Ford and his child by her, Ethel Rider, both interred in the Ford family plot. In his rough note diary Haggard recorded: 'Went graveyards w patience found graves surrounded by stone wall. Monument to A of weeping woman. Gate rotten. Some of the bulbs she planted still growing ... 4 trees of cypress variety planted at corners.' On another page he recorded two inscriptions: 'Ethel Rider B. 16 Sept 79 D. 5 Nov 79 / Johanna Catherine Ford (born Lehmkuhl) / D. Aug 30 1885 in 31st year'.[46]

On Tuesday morning, 31 March, Haggard and other commissioners drove out to the Magaliesberg and saw 'a wonderful example of what can be done with oranges *without* irrigation in this soil and climate'.[47] On the return to Pretoria a detour was made to the 'famous Wonderboom whither we used to ride in the old days. It is one of the few things in Pretoria that does not seem to have changed.'[48] The afternoon was taken up by the Administrator of the Transvaal Johan Rissik's garden party reception, 'one of the most strenuous hours of my life, since I had to talk to dozens of people who remembered me, or said they did, and to rack my brains to remember them'.[49] Haggard formally inspected 'the boy scouts who were on duty. The scoutmaster told me that English and Dutch boys serve together and are the best of friends, which I rejoiced to hear.'[50]

On Wednesday night, 1 April, the commissioners enjoyed a farewell dinner on the commission's train before leaving for Johannesburg, where they 'divided forces, so far as accommodation went' between the Carlton Hotel and the Rand Club.[51] Haggard was allotted a room at the Carlton Hotel, which had been founded by the diamond magnate Barney Barnato. For once Haggard and Harding were in agreement: 'The Carlton is a caravanserai of the approved London type – noisy, large and not too comfortable.'[52] By 1914 Johannesburg had become the largest city in South Africa, but Haggard had little to say about it: 'It is a huge tumultuous city rather more evil and menacing than most and fearfully expensive to live, that is all.'[53] He thought the 'most notable place I visited was the famous Rand Club established in 1887 where I lunched. It was crowded with business men though times are bad.'[54]

After taking 'evidence on agricultural matters' all morning on Friday, Haggard lunched with the Transvaal mining and property magnate Julius Jeppe, 'whom I used to know in our youth'.[55] Jeppe also shared a long connection with Lewis Peter Ford. When gold was discovered on the Witwatersrand in 1886, Ford became a partner on the Randjeslaagte Syndicate and, in partnership with the Jeppe family, developed the townships of Jeppestown and Fordsburg.[56] Jeppe reminded Haggard of 'sundry incidents in the old days: how he served under me in the Pretoria Horse and used to bring my bathwater when we were out at Ferguson's watching the Boer camp'. And how Haggard broke into the post office and abstracted 'my English letters which had arrived by the mail'.[57] Were these letters from Lilly Jackson?

Returning just after five to the Carlton Hotel, where a farewell reception for the commission was in full swing, Haggard was confronted by a 'hard-faced young man' who 'came up to me in the throng of the reception at the door'[58] and said he was the son of George Blomefield, the ward of Haggard's father, who had partnered with Haggard and Cochrane in the Rooi Point farming venture outside Newcastle in 1880. Blomefield junior, a miner, 'proceeded with veiled menaces' to demand that Haggard pay off a mortgage of £500 on some property his mother held at Pretoria or 'give them a farm'[59] on the grounds that his 'father's money had been useful to me'.[60] Blomefield insinuated that Haggard 'had perpetrated some fraud on G. Blomefield which I would pay to have hushed up. It was an attempt at blackmail of a peculiarly disgraceful order when all my father's goodness to George Blomefield (from whom by the way I have heard nothing) is borne in mind.'[61]

The Hilldrop partnership was dissolved in 1883, and Blomefield rented shares in the farm, which he ran for a while before passing them on and becoming a mine assayer. The farm was sold in 1895. In 1912 Haggard had received 'an insolent letter' from Blomefield's wife Catherine 'with a blackmailing note in it'. Another 'of like tenor' came while he was in Egypt. Yet another was waiting for him in 1914 in Johannesburg, 'where this woman (of whom I have heard no good) is living apparently away from her husband'.[62]

The majority of the commissioners left for Cape Town later that evening, prior to disembarkation for England. Thus ended the Dominions Royal Commission's visit to South Africa, during which 26 days were spent on gathering evidence and questioning 141 witnesses. Haggard saw Louie and Lilias 'off to Durban [en route to Eshowe] and started myself in the special train with some of the others for Rhodesia'.[63]

When Haggard awoke on the morning of 4 April, the train was 'running through flat thornveld into the little town of Mafeking, famous for its siege'.[64] Haggard,

Edgar Bowring and Australia's Donald Campbell, shepherded by Mr Greene, were travelling along the line built by Cecil Rhodes to Bulawayo via the Bechuanaland Protectorate.[65] The landscape passing by the window bore stark evidence of the severe drought afflicting the protectorate and Southern Rhodesia, the latter still administered by the British South Africa Company under the royal charter granted to Rhodes in 1889.[66] Bowring and Campbell were now on holiday and keen to see the Victoria Falls; Haggard was on his self-imposed mission, mindful of his promise to send Lewis Harcourt, the Colonial Secretary, his thoughts on Rhodesia. He got off the train at Bulawayo to be hosted by the Chartered Company's manager Frank Inskipp, as he would 'learn more about Rhodesia by staying with him ... than by journeying through this heat to the Falls'.[67]

Bulawayo, the capital of Matabeleland, was built on the site of Lobengula's royal homestead, its name, which translates as 'place of slaughter', commemorating the battle fought by Lobengula to assert his right to be king of the Ndebele. Inskipp's house was built on the site of Lobengula's original homestead, and Haggard walked the area, visiting Lobengula's 'indaba tree' (a *Pappea capensis),* where the king 'used to sit in council and to give judgement ... Here no doubt he received my poor friends Patterson and Sargeaunt and here often the word of death has been uttered.'[68]

On Monday, 6 April, John Jesser-Coope, the Chartered Company's superintendent of farmlands in Southern Rhodesia, drove Haggard to Rhodes's final resting place in the Matopos. After military operations during the Ndebele Rebellion of 1896 proved ineffective, Rhodes turned to diplomacy and camped in the Matopos among the Ndebele, where he held a series of four indabas that led to peace. He bought a large estate at the edge of the Matopos and is buried on the hill Malindidzimu, renamed by Rhodes 'World's View'.[69] Haggard and Jesser-Coope climbed the steep slope of the hill on foot, 'a long trudge in that heat but at last we stood by the lizard-haunted grave; a slab of granite on which is the inscription "Here rest the remains of Cecil John Rhodes"'. Haggard recalled last seeing Rhodes in 'a very different place, a sitting room in the Burlington Hotel in London. God rest him!'[70]

Jesser-Coope told Haggard that it was reading 'my books which sent him to the interior of Africa. Also a young man in the post office, seeing my name on a telegram, told me it was I who had brought him from England to Rhodesia ... so at least I have helped to populate the Empire!'[71]

On Tuesday Haggard was guided around the Rhodesian Museum by the curator, Charles Molyneux. In what must have been a vivid reminder of home, Haggard was accompanied by Walter Scudamore, son of the Reverend John Charles Scudamore, vicar at St Mary's Ditchingham, who was working for the Rhodesian Railways.[72] At lunch Haggard met Alexander Fletcher, the president of the Rhodesian Agricultural Union, a campaigner for responsible government and vocal opponent of the Chartered Company. The afternoon was spent with Molyneux west of Bulawayo exploring the Khami ruins, a large complex of ten distinct ruins dating to the seventeenth century.

Bowring, Campbell and Greene returned from Victoria Falls that evening and next morning the party left for Salisbury (now Harare) – 'a thriving looking town with good shops and a cathedral in course of erection in stone'. Haggard bought 'a little snake-bite outfit containing powdered permanganate of potash and a lancet in a vulcanite case', and a 'pair of canvas gaiters to protect my legs from the tormenting grass seeds and possible snakes at Zimbabwe and Zululand'.[73]

The following day Haggard visited the Agricultural Experimental Farm Station, the Rhodesian Tobacco Warehouse and the 'Mazoe Valley, one of the best farming districts in Rhodesia'.[74] After dinner on the train Haggard bade goodbye to Campbell, Bowring and Greene, who were to travel by the Mashonaland Railway to Beira on the coast of Portuguese East Africa to catch their ship to England. Scheduled to visit the ruins of Great Zimbabwe, Haggard remained on the commission train, which steamed off at ten that evening with Haggard feeling lonely 'as I am now the sole survivor of the commission in these parts'.[75]

The next morning before breakfast Haggard was taken in 'the government motor we had brought with us' to Great Zimbabwe, driving on a dirt road through 'bush-clad valleys and between hills very beautiful to see. Over it we rushed and rocked for an hour or more, passing numbers of nearly naked Mashonas armed with assegai and kerrie, who saluted us in the old fashion by raising the right arm. At length we came to the Zimbabwe Valley, which is surrounded by wild scenery compounded of hills, koppies and bush-clad plains unlike any I have seen before.'[76]

Arriving at Mundell's Hotel – 'some glorified huts and little houses'[77] – Haggard was greeted by Richard Nicklin Hall, curator of Great Zimbabwe. A lawyer, amateur archaeologist and journalist, Hall came to Southern Rhodesia in 1897 and edited the *Matabele Times and Mining Journal* and the *Rhodesian Journal*. In 1900 he was hired by Rhodes to explore the ruins of Great Zimbabwe and appointed curator in 1902. Author of *Ancient Ruins of Rhodesia* (with W.G. Neal) and *Great Zimbabwe*, Hall was removed from his post in 1904 and replaced by David Randall-MacIver, the first professional archaeologist to conduct excavations on the site, whose findings, published in *Mediaeval Rhodesia*, concluded that the ruins were of African origin and constructed after 1300 CE. Randall-MacIver's archaeological peers accepted his conclusions, but the white settler community was outraged and, when Hall published his rebuttal of Randall-MacIver, entitled *Prehistoric Rhodesia*, the settlers vociferously took his side and Hall was reappointed curator.

Haggard took a close interest in the famous ruins and, in his article 'The Real King Solomon's Mines', shared his thoughts on their origins, drawing on the work of Theodore Bent, Alexander Wilmot, R.N. Hall and W.G. Neal, who all erroneously concluded they 'were built by people of Semitic race, probably Phoenicians, or to be more accurate, South Arabian Himyarites, a people rendered obscure by age'.[78] He kept abreast of accounts published by travellers and archaeologists and contributed a preface to Alexander Wilmot's *Monomotapa (Rhodesia)*, published in 1896. As far as Haggard was concerned, Theodore Bent in *The Ruined Cities of Mashonaland* (1892) had proved the ruins were 'undoubtedly of Phoenician origin'.[79]

Haggard's interest in Great Zimbabwe was dealt with in fictional form in *Elissa, or, The Doom of Zimbabwe*. First run as a magazine serial in 1898, it told of how, because of 'the fateful and predestined loves of Aziel the prince, and Elissa the priestess and daughter of Sakon, three thousand years and more ago, the ancient city of Zimboe fell at the hand of king Ithobal and his Tribes, so that to-day there remain of it nothing but a desolate grey tower of stone, and beneath, the crumbling bones of men'.[80] At the heart of this mechanical novella lies the familiar theme of two predestined lovers who meet forever in the hereafter.[81]

While breakfast was being prepared, Haggard and Hall walked 'to the crest of a neighbouring koppie' from where

> the view is really glorious. To the north is a great plain bounded by the Beza Hills, to the north-north-east Imjomi (the Hill of Birds); to the east, Zimbabwe Mount, on which stand the ruins known as the Acropolis, to the south-east, on flatter ground, the great grey circle of the Elliptical Temple, to the south appear broad brown granite slopes. Then (and these are naturally of interest to me) between south and east the two round hills that have been named Sheba's Breasts (the second pair I have seen in Southern Africa) after those described in my tale *King Solomon's Mines*. Down to the Sabi River, which runs far away from north-east to east, is the native path connecting a chain of ancient forts, which to my surprise Mr. Hall called Allan Quatermain's Road.[82]

Hall's *Guide to Great Zimbabwe* states authoritatively that 'Zimbabwe Hill provided the description of the residence of She, while the ruins in the valley contributed "the dead city" of the same romance'.[83] Haggard, on the contrary, insisted that these and 'similar legends I have heard and read elsewhere, are quite apocryphal'.[84] Hall was quite aggrieved, accusing Haggard of being 'responsible for various false ideas about Zimbabwe'. Haggard tried 'to explain to him the differences between romance and history ... with the exception of *Elissa*, which he has not read, I never wrote of Zimbabwe, but rather of a land where the ruins were built by the fairies of imagination'.[85]

During the morning tour of the main site Haggard recited Andrew Lang's poem 'Zimbabwe', standing beneath the famous conical tower.[86] Having 'visited as many of the ruins as our time and strength would allow, we trudged back through the heat to lunch at the hotel',[87] where they rested until three in the afternoon before starting 'forth again to climb the Acropolis'. Hall rejected the easiest path, a recently cleared road, insisting instead on taking a route 'which he declared was "more interesting"'. Hall scrambled up the hill 'over boulder and ancient walls ... plunging at last into a narrow darksome cleft which ran skywards through two cyclopean masses of granite'. Halfway up, 'he turned to beckon to us hesitating weaklings who crawled behind ... in that gloom our learned conductor looked very like Gagool, seeing that he too is aged, shrunken and quite bald'. Haggard 'burst out laughing and nearly came to grief, to say nothing of stinging myself with a peculiarly deadly kind of nettle that grows upon this hill'.[88]

The summit of the koppie gave a spectacular panoramic view of the ruins and Haggard allowed Great Zimbabwe's 'atmosphere to flow into my mind ... a very strange atmosphere, almost uncanny indeed. I do not wonder that the kaffirs flee these spots; when once the sun is down though ... I think that I should like to sleep in them for so perhaps their true past would come back to me.'[89]

Haggard was astonished by the 'vastness' of Rhodesia – 'it seems to stretch on for ever' – as well as its 'semi-tropical nature, for even now in the autumn the heat is great'; qualities that left him wondering whether Rhodesia was a 'white man's land'. In some 'parts yes, or so I suppose. In other and larger parts I should be inclined to answer "no"'. Whatever the drawbacks for white settlement, Haggard was in no doubt Rhodesia was 'a country of great charm and one that I am very glad to have visited. Good luck to it and to its plucky and English-hearted inhabitants. Still, I misdoubt me of that good luck, why I cannot say, but I think that not yet will kind Fortune set her crown on Rhodesia's sun-scorched brow.'[90]

27

'400 MILES THROUGH ZULULAND'

Haggard returned to South Africa from Rhodesia by train to Johannesburg and then on to Durban. Ease of travel on a subcontinental rail network was another indicator of the region's rapid industrialisation, disconcerting for a reawakened Rip Van Winkle in search of his youth. Passing Newcastle, Haggard gazed 'through the early-morning mists at Hilldrop amid its trees on the koppie's flank, I daresay for the last time'.[1]

James Stuart joined Haggard at Pietermaritzburg and in Durban Haggard was reunited with Louie and Lilias at the Marine Hotel on the Durban Esplanade. 'They had a poor time at Eshowe on account of the persistent rain.'[2] In the afternoon Haggard and Louie 'took the tram round Durban to see the Berea', a long ridge overlooking the city and its harbour and a prime residential area. In the 1870s 'there were only a few scattered houses in pretty wildish sort of gardens', one of which became the home of Allan Quatermain. 'Now if the old hunter came to life he would hardly know the Berea.'[3]

On Saturday morning Haggard bade farewell to Louie and Lilias, who were sailing home via the Cape the following day. He was sad at parting, 'but please God we shall meet again in safety'.[4] He and Stuart then left for Zululand on an early train. En route to Gingindlovu, they passed 'the little town of Stanger where once stood the royal kraal, Duguza [kwaDukuza], the place marked by some trees where lie the bones of the mighty Chaka whose death at this very spot I have written of in *Nada the Lily*'.[5]

Many of Haggard's books, notably *Nada the Lily*, exhibited considerable knowledge of Zululand and the Zulu, but Haggard had never set foot there. Now he was about to travel north of the Thukela for the first time. Heading north along the coast, the train ran through the sugar cane plantations carpeting the rolling hills of Natal's subtropical coastal strip.[6] The carriages rattled over 'the long iron bridge built above the old ford'[7] on the Thukela River. Haggard saw the battlefield of Ndondakusuka, where 'Cetywayo conquered his brother Umbelazi with great slaughter', which was the inspiration for many of his battle scenes and which 'I have tried to describe in *Child of Storm*'.[8] Haggard was now in Zululand.

After a lunch of beer, bread and cheese at the small hotel at Gingindlovu, Haggard and Stuart were taxied 'on an excellent road' up through the 'grass-clothed hills' 16 miles to 'the hot but beautifully situated town of Eshowe'.[9] Following the annexation of Zululand in 1887, Eshowe was chosen as the capital and seat of the resident commissioner and chief magistrate, the first of whom was Melmoth Osborn. At the residency Haggard was welcomed by his hosts, James Young Gibson and his wife Harriette. Gibson, author of *The Story of the Zulus*, had only recently been appointed district native commissioner. At dinner that evening the 'arguments' between Stuart and Gibson at dinner 'on obscure points of Zulu history were prolonged and at times rather hot. Rival experts are always apt to grow fierce about their own subjects.'[10] Haggard acknowledged he was 'particularly fortunate' to be accompanied on his trip through Zululand by Gibson and Stuart, 'the greatest living experts in the Zulu history and language. From them I heard all sorts of things which would never come to the ears of the ordinary traveller.'[11]

The residency, a bungalow with a verandah and corrugated-iron roof set in a well-treed garden, had been built and laid out by Melmoth Osborn, 'who lived in it for five years before his retirement'.[12] Osborn's successor was Haggard's former comrade Marshall Clarke, who had died in Ireland in 1909.[13] Another presence from Haggard's past was Osborn's son Jack, briefly Haggard's ward in 1879, who 'breathed his last in this house ... it almost seems as though I felt them about me now'.[14] Present in life was Masuku and, when Haggard awoke next morning, 'there he was laying out my things just as he used to do nearly 40 years ago ... It was as though all the intervening years had faded away and we were young again.'[15]

On Sunday Haggard attended services at the Anglican Cathedral of St Michael and All Angels. At the evening service the Bishop of Zululand, Wilmot Lushington Vyvyan, spoke on the 'desecration of Sunday by the continual playing of golf, tennis, etc., which it seems has become almost a vice in South Africa, tacking into his dissertation a few remarks about the future state of man'.[16] Haggard and Vyvyan knew each other: 'he and I ate our dinners together at Lincoln's Inn, after which he became a bishop and I a writer and other things'.[17]

Braving the enervating humidity on Monday morning, Haggard and Stuart walked to the site where Cetshwayo died in 1884, the homestead 'that is (or was) called Jazi' or, more correctly, kwaGqikazi, meaning 'finished' or 'finished with joy', which gave its name to the final volume of Haggard's Zulu trilogy, *Finished*. There had been around fifty *imizi* in Cetshwayo's time, but now there were only 'two or three huts and in front of them a patch of kaffir corn ... Once there was a large hut here and in that hut at the very spot on which I stood to the left of the entrance died our old enemy (or friend?) Cetywayo, the last King of Zululand – poisoned.'[18]

Haggard and Stuart questioned their guide, Umnikwa, about Cetshwayo's death. He thought the king was 'killed with strychnine and that he was ill three days', which suggested 'some native poison' was used and not strychnine. 'Who did the deed? ...

No one knows or will ever know (at least no one will ever tell, least of all that quiet, secret-faced native. He had become useless and was put out of the way – by someone. The rest is darkness.'[19]

On Gibson's office wall a large map of Zululand gave graphic evidence of the plight of the Zulu people under colonial rule. Since 1875 about two-thirds of the country' had been 'appropriated by Boers and other white men. If this goes on what is to become of the poor Zulus. And what will happen if they are continually crowded together. I imagine that which happens to a thin glass bottle when compressed air or water is driven into it. Truly their case is sad and they have been ill-treated.'[20]

On Tuesday afternoon Haggard attended a 'war dance' arranged in his honour at the Eshowe golf club, 'attended by all the population of Eshowe and many natives'.

> Perhaps 200 danced, men and women, but the thing, except for a girls' dance, had not the fire of that I saw nearly 40 years ago, which I described in 'A Zulu War Dance' ... The pervading umbrellas marked the change. Old things are dying out and new ones draw near. It is a time of transition and therefore a bad time. Still I enjoyed the dance though the sun was terribly hot and the dresses, or in the case of the women, the lack of them, were appropriate and striking, as were the swelling chants and the advance and retreat of the lines of dancing men and women.[21]

The dance was hosted by the Native Affairs Department official Harcourt Tyrrell. His 3-year-old daughter Barbara, later a respected ethnological artist, recalled the event in her autobiography:

> Adults were seated in deck chairs facing the dancing area, VIPs in the front row; the shadowy figure of the Great Man, Haggard ... The scorching Zululand sun beat down and up again from hot earth, baking us in our unaccustomed, uncomfortable, starched white 'best' ... A dance of brown people watched by white people, of almost unclad people and heavily overclad people ... Ropes of beadwork tossing wildly around brown bodies, and ostrich feathers against blue sky. A dance of praise for the honoured visitor.[22]

On 22 April Haggard, Stuart and Gibson drove back down to Gingindlovu, stopping along the way while Stuart photographed the graves of those who fell in the battle of Gingindlovu on 2 April 1879 during Chelmsford's advance to relieve Eshowe. 'The spot which is by the roadside is surrounded by long grass and looks rather desolate.'[23] At the station they met Masuku – he had walked there from Eshowe before dawn – and took the train north 80 miles to the rail terminus at Somkeli, arriving shortly after dark and putting up at Redgrove's Hotel, 'the dirtiest in which I ever slept'.[24]

The hired car for the Zululand trip was waiting for them at Somkeli, 'driven oddly enough by a young fellow of the name of [H.M.] Edwards the grandson of old Marsdon, the miller at Bungay where he was born. He is a nice young man and seems to be getting on well in South Africa.'[25] The car was an Overland, manufactured by the Willys-Overland Motor Company in Toledo, Ohio. On Thursday at 'about nine o'clock we packed ourselves (including Mazooku) and our belongings into the motor and started for Hlabisa, about 20 miles away',[26] to be greeted there at noon by the magistrate, Albert Harrington. A map of the district in his office indicated the discrepancy in land ownership between whites and blacks. 'The white population, I was told, is about 100, and the native population about 16 000, yet the whites are supposed to require twice as much land as the natives! This is typical of what is going on all over South Africa.'[27]

An indaba had been organised for the local *inkosi*, indunas and headmen to meet the newly appointed commissioner. 'They were a wonderfully fine looking set of Zulus of all shades of colour, from jet black to light yellow.'[28] As a representative of the British monarch, Gibson was met with the royal salute 'Bayete' and, following an exchange of formal compliments, came the complaints: boundary alterations, the encroachment of white farms, the spread of tsetse flies and 'the new land law which prevents them from living on farms unless they pay rent in labour' and another law 'that they may not kill the game as the white man does'.[29] 'All is done decently and in quiet; the chiefs speaking in order of seniority and never interrupting each other ... Mr. Gibson replies most sympathetically, his remarks being punctuated with exclamations of respectful assent. So, in the end, after he has promised to represent their troubles in the proper quarter, whatever that may be, the meeting breaks up, apparently in a very good humour and we depart amidst a volley of salutes.'[30]

After another indaba at Xedeni (Qudeni), the party 'travelled on over a bad road, very steep in places and always running uphill', arriving 'thoroughly tired' after 20 miles at Nongoma 'on its healthy hilltops', where Gibson had been a magistrate in the 1890s. At over 2,600 feet above sea level, the climate was markedly different from 'the hot and fever-stricken Somkeli, and indeed of Gingindlovu, both of which are little removed from ocean level'.[31] At Nongoma they slept at a trading store-cum-hotel – 'very clean and comfortable' – run by Charles Adams, whose father had accompanied David Livingstone and Bishop Charles Mackenzie of the Universities' Mission to Central Africa up the Zambezi and Shire rivers in 1861.[32] Strolling over to the magistracy next morning, Haggard and Gibson inspected the remains of the British fort once under the command of the late Jack Osborn,[33] which gave a panoramic view of the surrounding countryside, including the Ngome forest, one of the largest indigenous forests in Zululand, where Cetshwayo was captured in 1879.

There is a photograph of the morning's indaba at Nongoma.[34] On the shaded stoep of the courthouse Haggard sits alongside Gibson and Lieutenant William Matravers of the South African Mounted Rifles, all three hatted and helmeted; only the clerk of the court, Edgerton Tritton, is bareheaded. Before them, beyond the shade of the stoep, is a group of local chiefs with their leader Umpikanina, son of Ziwedu, Cetshwayo's half-brother, who was placed under Zibhebhu in the 1879 Wolseley settlement of Zululand – 'a fine-looking man, very like the rest of his royal race. He sat in front of all the other chiefs by virtue of his rank and was clothed in a military helmet and mackintosh cloak.' In the photograph Umpikanina has taken off his pith helmet and is holding it in his hands. Hats and shade: indicators of colonial status and authority.[35] The main grievance concerned the 'taking away of ancestral lands. Said one old chief: "If you can exercise any power as to these lands which have been given away to the white men, you would indeed be ruling us for our good."'[36]

Approaching Mahlabatini, the Overland got bogged down on 'a most fearsome hill' so steep the 'petrol could not get to the engine'. Everyone got out, the luggage was removed and, with the help 'of some native boys, foot by foot we did get the car up backwards, propping it with stone every few yards to prevent it running down again ... and to our great gratitude, the motor, which was strained, crawled up to Mahlabatini before dark'.[37]

They departed early on Saturday morning for 'our longest day's journey'. An hour later they came to the 'great hill-surrounded plain of Ulundi ... cradle of the Zulu race' and site of the battle that brought the Anglo-Zulu War to an end.[38] As they were unsure of the exact site, Masuku was sent 'to inquire at a neighbouring kraal [and] returned with an old Zulu named Simpofu', who had fought in the battle 'and was able to tell us everything'.[39] At Ulundi on 4 July 1879 in a clinical square action – repeating rifles versus assegais – the British defeated the Zulu. Zulu losses were estimated at around 1,500 dead; British casualties were 13 dead and 69 wounded. Martini-Henry cartridge cases and rusted bully-beef tins still lay scattered around the battlefield.

At midday they met George Whitefield Kinsman, the magistrate at Babanango, waiting on the road with horses to 'carry us to the site of Dingaan's old kraal Umgungundhlovu, now a farm called by the cheerful name of Moord-Plaats (Place of Murder)'.[40] Dingane's homestead, uMgungundlovu, was constructed in 1829 in the Emakhosini Valley, or Valley of Kings, the burial place of many of the Zulu kings. After a simple lunch – 'bread and a tin of potted meat' – they mounted up, Haggard on 'a wooden and not too sure-footed animal (it was the first time I had ridden for many years) and we set out'.[41] After a ride of several miles they came to the Hill of Slaughter, 'known as Kwa Matiwane (at or the place of Matiwane) from an unfortunate chief who threw himself on the mercy of Dingaan and in return was here massacred'.[42] This was also the site of 'the massacre of Retief and his party (100 souls in all counting the 30 servants)' in 1838, an event depicted in *Marie*.[43]

Riding the 'hateful hill', Haggard was in his element, sensing the place had 'an evil air' and 'the impression of being horror-haunted'. The entrance to the royal homestead was 'marked by two large euphorbia ... through this gate the Boers were dragged out to slaughter ... they were hauled across the Umkumbane rivulet and up these stony slopes where their necks were twisted and (according to certain accounts) the barbarity of impalement was inflicted on some of them'.[44] Frustrated at not being able to find Retief's grave and 'hoping to find some relics of the massacre', Haggard stumbled on a cairn that 'had been torn open by man or beast and there all about were scattered human bones'. Out came Stuart's camera to photograph 'the mortal remains of some of Retief's people and, for aught I know, of Retief himself'.[45]

Back in the Overland, they motored through 'glorious country, high and healthy with deep and wooded ravines between the hills', arriving as darkness fell at Sir Charles Saunders's 'charming house, Imfulazane, where we received the warmest of welcomes and what we needed much after our exhausting day – something to drink. It seemed strange to reach this refined, English home in the heart of Zululand', where 'the air was so sharp that good fires both in the drawing and my bedroom were very welcome'.[46]

Saunders had succeeded Clarke as Chief Magistrate and Civil Commissioner for Zululand at the time of the incorporation of Zululand into Natal in 1897 and in 1902 he sat on the Zululand Lands Delimitation Commission, which resulted in certain areas being set aside for Zulu occupation and 'the remainder, especially the rich coastal sugar lands, [being] opened up for white settlement'.[47] Haggard was apparently unaware of Saunders's role in this land theft and listened attentively as his host 'spoke feelingly of the harsh treatment [the Zulu] have received and are receiving and declared that "constant pin-pricks" such as land-snatching and the poll tax were the direct cause of the 1906 "rebellion"'.[48]

A day later on the way to Nkandla, the Overland and its five occupants came to the banks of the uMhlathuze River, a formidable barrier despite the water being low. Foot down on the accelerator, Edwards charged at the ford and got 'stuck fast right in the middle of the river'. Their predicament was witnessed by 'a pretty young witch-doctress in full professional array with the regulation bladders in her hair ... accompanied by her father, a wizened old fellow and one or two other people'. Haggard told her 'she was very pretty, which seemed to please her enormously notwithstanding her spiritual attainments, for she smiled, nodded and even seemed to blush beneath her light copper-hued skin'. She sat down and 'began a course of incantations on our behalf, swaying herself to and fro'.[49] The luggage was removed and, with Haggard 'steering and everybody else pushing', they got across.

Haggard helped Stuart empty the water from his Gladstone bag, pointing out that his had 'remained dry' despite being deeper in the water. This was 'because I had told Miss Nombe (that was her name) that she was beautiful whereas he had done nothing of the sort. Therefore, she had brought her Lord of the Spirits to my particular assistance and incidentally rescued the motor from its very awkward predicament'.[50] 'Miss Nombe', as Nombi, is a central character in Finished.

Next morning at the Nkandla Hotel, Haggard looked out on 'to the range of mountains beyond which lie the Inkandhla forest'. Later that morning Haggard, with Stuart translating, spoke at an indaba attended by '70 or 80 chiefs and their indunas', telling them that he was the 'child of Sompseu (Sir T. Shepstone) and of Mali-mati (Sir M. Osborn)', from whom he had learned the history of the Zulu people and 'had learned to love them'. He had written of them in books 'and striven to make their name known about the world'. Now he was grown old, he wanted to 'look once more upon the faces of the Zulus'.[51] He came 'as their friend' that he 'might see them with my eyes and hear their thoughts and help them in any way I could ... and that in the time unborn the good sun of peace, happiness and plenty would shine upon them from day to day and year to year'. This was well received and one person asked 'by what name they must remember me. Stuart told them "Sir Rider Haggard" but at this they shook their heads and smiled, saying that their "tongues could not go round" those words – was there no other name?' Haggard said yes, there was. 'In the land years ago I had been called Lundanda, or, with my title of praise, Lundanda u Ndand Okalweni (The tall one who walks on the mountain tops). Possibly this means "with his head in the air" or "absent-mindedly". "Ah!" they answered, "*now* we hear, *now* we understand, *now* we shall never forget."'[52]

Thomas Jackson, magistrate at Nkandla, had recently read *Child of Storm* and 'would scarcely believe that Zululand was not familiar ground to me'.[53] Even if the ground was unfamiliar, one place in Zululand had great emotional significance for Haggard, the battlefield of Isandlwana. Friends and acquaintances had died there in 1879 and he had written of the battle in fact and in fiction.[54] On the way to Isandlwana, Stuart and Gibson argued over the meaning of the mountain that gave the battlefield its name. Gibson was adamant the name meant 'like a little house'; Stuart, 'on the contrary, says that the true interpretation thereof is "the second stomach of an ox". When such learned doctors disagree, as they did with vigour, I may be pardoned if I cling to the old rendering "the place of the little hand".'[55]

> At length the strange, abrupt, lion-like mount of Isandhlwana appeared before us, standing solitary and, in a way, terrible upon the plain; its sheer brown cliffs of rock rising like the walls of some cyclopean fortress. Between it and another low and stony hill there lies a nek of some 500 yards in width. All about this nek stand monuments and little cairns built of rough stones marking where the bones of the dead were buried when our forces returned to Isandhlwana in 1880, a year or so after the disaster ... It was sad for me to stand by the piles of stones which cover all that is left of so many whom once I knew; Durnford and Pulleine and many other officers of the 24th, George Shepstone and the rest. Coghill I knew also very well but he died with Melvill by the river bank.[56]

The sun had set when they left the battlefield and the crescent of the young moon was rising 'above the hill. It looked like a plume of faint, unearthly fire burning upon Isandhlwana's rocky brow. This must be a quiet place for man's eternal sleep. But the scene which went before that sleep!'[57]

That night they slept near the battlefield at the trading store run by Charles Parr, who gave Haggard some 'cartridge cases and the head of one of Durnford's rockets'.[58] On Tuesday morning, 28 April, they walked down the Fugitives' Trail which led to

Fugitives' Drift on the Mzinyathi (Buffalo) River, so named after those, like 'Lucky' Essex, who fled the battlefield and the pursuing Zulu warriors. 'At first the cairns are many but by degrees they cease. All were slain by now save those who were marked for another space of life ... Peace to the brave, white and black together, for be it remembered our men did not die alone. "Is this a victory of which you tell me?" asked Cetywayo, as he surveyed his thinned regiments, "Wow! I name it defeat."'[59]

The battlefield of Rorke's Drift was viewed from a distance on the way to Nqutu, where another indaba was held at the Nqutu magistracy. The senior *inkosi* was Manzolwandle kaCetshwayo, a son of King Cetshwayo. Haggard said 'how glad I was to meet him, which seemed to please him very much, if I might judge from his face and the warmth of his salute'. Haggard was pleased at being addressed 'as "Father" and "Chief from the dead days" by the head of the race of Zulu and Senzangacona'.[60]

After lunch with the magistrate John Farrer and his wife, 'we entered our motor for the last time and trekked on over a wide, open country where, by contrast, the roads seemed almost heavenly, to the little town of Dundee in Natal, which we reached before nightfall. So ended my journey of over 400 miles through Zululand ... one of the most interesting journeys out of the many I have made in various lands in the course of my life.'[61]

Early on the morning of Wednesday, 29 April, Haggard, Gibson, Masuku and Stuart caught the Durban mail at Glencoe near Dundee, and at the station in Pietermaritzburg around half past three in the afternoon Haggard said goodbye to Masuku.

> His last salute to me of '*Inkoos! Baba!*' (Chief! Father!) was given in a somewhat quavering voice for I believe he loves me dearly ... I felt very sad as I watched him disappear with his bundle in that crowded station – good fortune go with him! He proved a perfect treasure on our Zululand journey. Stuart is kindly going to try to arrange a new home for him on the corporation lands of Maritzburg, far from his persecuting white man, where I hope he will grow old and die in peace. Whoever forgets me I am sure that Mazooku never will in whatever land memory remains to him.[62]

Haggard's southern African journey was coming to its end. Durban was a fitting place for his departure as Haggard's relationship with the region really began when he stepped ashore there aged 19 in 1875. On that occasion he landed by boat after disembarking from the coastal steamer *Florence*, anchored in the open seas beyond the harbour bar. Haggard's departure in 1914 would be an altogether different affair, boarding the Union-Castle line's *Gaika* at the passenger terminal in the city's impressive modern harbour facility. In the few days remaining before sailing he had a packed schedule ahead of him, including a visit to the Roman Catholic Mariannhill monastery, and tours of the harbour and various municipal facilities for Africans and Indians.

On Thursday, 30 April, Haggard was 'fortunate enough to have a long interview' with the founding president of the African National Congress, John Dube. The interview took place shortly before Dube left for Cape Town as head of a Congress delegation to voice their objections to the 1913 Natives Land Act; should that fail, it was on to London to make their case before the British government and the king. Throughout Haggard's South African journey he was sensitive to the tensions between the government and white settler society, on the one hand, and the majority disenfranchised black population, on the other, and was keen to canvass the opinions of people of differing views. 'I am an educator, that is my business,' Dube told Haggard. 'I have been thrust into a semi-political position by my people.' The aim of the Congress was 'to unite the natives for political purposes, to consider proposed legislation affecting their interests and to make representations to those in authority. We want an organisation to speak for us as we have no representation in the Union parliament.'[63]

Dube set out his objections to the Land Act: 'You must remember that we natives today only hold as native reserves 10 million morgen (20 million acres) out of the 400 million morgen (800 million acres) in the Union.'[64] Dube objected to the fact that 'natives are not now allowed to lease land or to farm on shares with Europeans. In fact they may not become rent-paying tenants or squat on farms except on condition that they labour for the farmer. The law lays down the duration of such labour but its provisions are frequently evaded by unscrupulous whites to the disadvantage of my people.'[65] Dube told Haggard that in recent times

the white people have been tightening the screw more and more. They used to be more sympathetic. This attitude has evoked a like feeling among the natives whose sentiments towards the whites are now harsher than they used to be. They say: 'If the whites declare they cannot live with us let them go away and live in their own country.' Your people could do more to bring about a better understanding if they chose. They have the power in their hands, and can take us Natives into their confidence. The whites are so far away from us. We have no means of communication with the authorities or public opinion except through the magistrates who have little time in which to attend to native grievances.[66]

Haggard read the notes of the interview back to Dube, who acknowledged his views had been 'correctly set down'.[67] Haggard was impressed 'most favourably' by Dube and thought the case he advanced a hard one to answer. 'Thus, there is no doubt that this new Land Act inflicts great hardships on the native community and if an attempt were made to enforce it everywhere I do not know what would happen.' But he thought Dube had 'little hope' of success either with the Union parliament or the King. 'But what will be the end of it all? Seven million of black folk, I think that is about the number including the population of the protectorates, cannot be permanently neglected (or is oppressed the word?) by one million and a quarter of whites. Compressed steam will escape somehow and somewhere.'[68]

Haggard was right. In Cape Town Dube's delegation found there was no time to petition the Union parliament as they only had until 19 June 'to ask the King to disallow the act'.[69] In London they were stonewalled. Lewis Harcourt at the Colonial Office exhibited 'a complete lack of interest',[70] and their cause faded into obscurity, overwhelmed by international events: following the assassination of Archduke Ferdinand and his wife Sophie on 28 June in Sarajevo, Europe was sliding inexorably towards the First World War.

On the evening after meeting Dube, Haggard wrote a letter to the Governor General, Lord Gladstone,[71] outlining his impressions of Zululand and the Zulu: 'I think that the Zulus are in a most unhappy position. Some two-thirds of their land are in the hands of white people: often they are rent-paying squatters on the territory which their fathers occupied. They have no head whatsoever, they "wander and wander". They are a people whom we have broken and not mended.'[72]

Maurice Evans, author of *Black and White in South-East Africa*, told Haggard the Land Act was 'utterly preposterous and unworkable in its present form and that before passing it the government should have awaited the report of the [Beaumont] commission which is now sitting'.[73]

> Generally he takes a most gloomy view of the outlook. So do I. The white man has a very heavy bill to pay to the native and certainly he will be called upon to pay it in this coin or in that. Those who persistently sow the wind must expect to reap the whirlwind. Possibly in the end South Africa will become more or less black; the increasing miscegenation that is going on and the very small increase in the white population suggest that this may be so ... After all, so far as I am aware, no white race has succeeded in establishing itself permanently in Africa.[74]

Having attended the Sunday morning service at St Paul's Anglican church, a short walk from his hotel, the Marine on the Durban Esplanade, he spent the rest of his last full day in Durban 'writing letters home and others of thanks to people who had been kind to me'.[75] On his final evening in Durban, Haggard dined with Stuart, who 'brought me some splendid Zulu curiosities – head-rings, an *iziqu* with horns, some old hoes, i.e. made by native smiths which are now so rare'.[76] The next morning was spent shopping, 'buying a large pilgrim basket to take the overflow of my luggage, which seems to have swollen (luggage undoubtedly possesses a reproductive quality of its own)', and Stuart helped him pack. 'The curiosities we accommodated in a whisky case.'

After lunch at the Durban Club on the Esplanade overlooking the inner harbour, Stuart drove Haggard down to the Point and 'deposited myself and my luggage upon the *Gaika*'. Haggard bade goodbye to Stuart and 'presently saw my last of Durban Bluff and the Berea. So ended my visit to South Africa – the last I think that I shall ever make.'

And so to South Africa that farewell, which is the dominant word in life. It is a fair land of which the charm still holds me, and whose problems interest me more than ever, if that be possible. How will they work out I wonder, when I have gone to sleep – or maybe to dream elsewhere? Well, my name will I believe always be connected with the country if it remains a white man's home and even if it does not – perhaps![77]

Sailing up the east coast of Africa, Haggard diligently gathered information about people and places while working up his rough diary notes into an expanded record of his travels. Coincidentally, Lieutenant William Matravers, present at the Nongoma indaba in Zululand, was also on board the *Gaika*, returning to England on leave for the first time after thirteen years. Haggard was interested to hear of 'the fate of his predecessors and companions in office': one died of fever, another was 'drowned with a friend in a lake and one was killed by lightning'.[78]

The Archbishop of Cape Town, William Carter, and his wife Hester, having travelled overland from the Cape on their way to Madagascar via Zanzibar on church business, boarded the *Gaika* at Lourenço Marques, capital of Portuguese East Africa.[79] Archbishop Carter – 'a most interesting companion' – was positive about the reconciliation of the two white factions – Boer and British – but perturbed at the inadequate protection of non-white political rights in the South Africa Act which had led to union. The two had 'sundry long talks upon various subjects, ranging from the Zulus, among whom he was bishop for a number of years, to religion. I find that on all these matters his views coincide with my own.'[80] Whether his companionship was as congenial to the archbishop is uncertain. Carter thought Haggard 'one of those very keen men who want to know about everything'.[81] At Beira this required taking a launch up the Pungwe River in the unrealised hope of catching sight of the 'famous crocodile that is known locally as "Lloyd George"'.[82]

Anchored at Pemba Bay off Port Amelia (now Pemba) not long after a cyclone had 'wrecked the place',[83] Haggard saw 'some hundreds of natives' on the shore 'just landed from a steamer, having returned from the Johannesburg mines whither no more of them may go on account of the awful death rate among them there'.[84] In 1913 South Africa banned all labour recruitment north of the 22-degree parallel in a bid to lower the high death rate among 'tropical' Africans and also to fend off criticism of South Africa by Mozambican and Portuguese business interests. 'The natives of these parts seem to be very willing to earn money in distant places. Thus, a ship we saw at Mozambique was taking 1 500 of them to the cocoa plantations of Messrs. Cadbury on the other side of Africa. They are, I am told, apprenticed for three years and Messrs. Cadbury undertakes to ship them, or the survivors of them, home again at the expiration of that time.'[85]

In Zanzibar Haggard went sightseeing with the Carters and called upon the Sultan, Khalifa bin Harub Al-Said, 'who had signified his desire to see me'.[86] The Sultan sat chatting with Haggard in 'a long low room of the palace', plying his guest with cigarettes, 'which he insisted upon lighting matches for himself' and 'sent for sherbet'.[87] Meanwhile a fellow passenger managed 'to get himself shewn through the women's part of the palace by the distribution of some cash. A eunuch led him and his guide and, under pretext of exhibiting the beauty of the rooms, took him past one in which he saw 15 gaudily dressed young women of various shades of colour who, he was informed, were the Sultan's ladies.'[88]

Next stop on Haggard's African trek was the British East Africa Protectorate (now Kenya), where he finally acknowledged a degree of weariness: he was still far from home and within a matter of weeks would be joining other members of the Dominions Royal Commission for the next stage of their inquiries in Canada. Nevertheless he summoned up sufficient energy to maintain an interest in his surroundings, enthusing about game sightings and probing away endlessly at the thorny problems of land and agriculture in Africa.

At Mombasa he took advantage of the *Gaika*'s three-day stopover to travel by train to Nairobi through the Tsavo National Park. 'Were it not for this great reserve by now all would be gone, as doubtless all are destined to go since soon or late the destroying white man will have them upon this pretext or the other ... I have seen the Transvaal veld black with game and 35 years later I have travelled through it without finding so much as a duiker buck and that is what will one day happen in East Africa, or so I fear.'[89] Nor did he hold out much hope for the European population in East Africa. He thought the future of the region lay in 'the development of the native peoples. Already I believe most of the exports are produced by these, not by the whites, and it is reasonable to suppose that this will be more and more the case in future years.'[90]

Haggard signed off his African diary at Suez on 29 May, adding a postscript in Naples on 3 June on learning Ella Hart-Bennett had drowned during the sinking of the *Empress of Ireland* 'in the terrible catastrophe of the St. Lawrence River, in which she was a passenger on her homeward journey from the Bahamas.'[91] She had stayed with the Haggards at Ditchingham in the autumn of 1913 and it was 'hoped she would again this year, and since then we have exchanged epistolary jokes for she was a merry and a witty woman.'[92] In Madeira he had dedicated *The Ivory Child* to her, 'The Lady of the New Moon'.[93] But when the book was published in 1916, it was without a dedication.

28

'ARMAGEDDON HAS FALLEN'

Haggard was back at Ditchingham in early June and in July the Kiplings were installed at Kessingland Grange, let to them for the summer for the second year running. Haggard sent Kipling the manuscript of *The Wanderer's Necklace*, published back in January, and that of his Irish play, 'To Hell or Connaught'. Kipling enjoyed the romance but not the play. 'That's because I'm an envious dramatist I suppose. Besides I love not Irish dramas being a low minded Englishman.'[1]

There were no summer holidays for Haggard, as he was sitting on the Dominions Royal Commission's sessions in London hearing evidence on telegraphic and cable communication throughout the Empire and getting ready for the commission's third scheduled journey to Newfoundland and Canada. They sailed from Liverpool on 17 July aboard the *Alsatian* with Sir Alfred Bateman as acting chair; Edgar Vincent – Lord D'Abernon since 10 July – planned to join them at Quebec. The Allan Line's luxurious SS *Alsatian* had been launched a few months earlier and was 'furnished in Jacobean oak ... with old engravings on the walls, open fire places in the great saloons'.[2] These provided comfortable retreats for passengers as their ship laboured through the fog. Fog 'always upset Rider's nerves, the result of that old adventure off the shores of Stroma.' He filled the 'weary hours reading histories of Canada, and re-reading Gibbon and Carlyle'.[3]

At St John's, Newfoundland, on 29 July, the commissioners heard 'that there is a grave peril of a European war ... I am *very* anxious and wonder whether Armageddon has come at last?'[4] Undeterred, the commission went about its work, hearing evidence, attending official dinners, and visiting mines, paper mills and orphanages. In Halifax, Nova Scotia, on 5 August 'we learned that England had declared war against Germany'. The commissioners continued working, though it was 'very hard to have to sit here taking evidence on canned lobsters and such matters when the Judgement Day of nations has dawned upon the world'.[5]

At a 'pretty heated' meeting of the commissioners, the 'Dominion members wanted to go on, and the UK ones to go back, if they could go back'.[6] A compromise was reached to carry on for the present and to telegraph D'Abernon for clarification on the international situation. A telegram from the chairman, crossing paths with that of the commissioners, suggested postponement and return. This led to a 'two hours' wrangle', which left the secretary, Edward Harding, 'quite exhausted and the members more "jumpy" than before'.[7] Further instructions were requested.

On 10 August a telegram from the British government recalled the commission after completion of its 'work in the maritime provinces, a week hence'.[8] When Bateman communicated the contents of this telegram next morning, another stormy scene followed. The outcome was that the last sitting would be held at Charlottetown, Prince Edward Island, on 17 August, after which the commissioners would 'return to Quebec, and thence sail for England, taking our chance of a German cruiser on the way'.[9]

From the beginning of the Canadian tour the commissioners had been instructed not to give speeches at public events, to prevent inflaming existing divisions between English-speaking and French-speaking Canadians over British demands, prior to the war, for Canada to contribute to the Royal Navy in the light of the German naval challenge. A public dinner hosted by Halifax's mayor was 'a somewhat slow affair, for it is dull work listening to toasts to which no answer is vouchsafed'. Finally Bateman was 'forced to murmur a few words, in which he complained of the breach of the contract as to the matter of public speaking'.[10] When Bateman sat down, 'from all round the room there arose a veritable storm of cries of "Haggard! Rider Haggard!"' Haggard remained seated until Bateman, 'growing disturbed, motioned me to rise'.[11] Haggard 'spoke for about three or four minutes only, but "with my heart", as the Zulus say'.[12] According to the Canadian *Daily Telegraph*, he was 'deadly pale' and spoke with 'repressed fervour'.[13] 'I doubt if those present, indeed if those in this country realise the state and appreciate the peril in which this Empire stands tonight,' said Haggard.

> I know Canada is glad to give her aid, and I know that England is glad to accept your help, but do you understand that *you* are all England? Do you understand that if we fall you fall? Do you understand that if Germany and her allies become the masters of England they become masters of the world; and that in two or three years there will be no British Empire? If you realise that, every man of you must go, must play his part with us to the end. For today we stand at desperate straits with Fate.
>
> The Angel of Death appears in a dawn of blood; the Armageddon which has been so long foretold has at length fallen upon us. In our country we have a party which for years and years has tried to drive down our throats the untruth that a large Navy is not necessary to England. Through thick and thin, in face of ridicule of every kind, those who fought against the little Navy struggled on, driving home the fact that a mighty fleet was necessary to the life of the Empire. If it had not been for them England today would have had no sufficient Navy and what then?
>
> We believe that through the aid of God we shall conquer, and that through us the world shall be free. If our belief is vain, good night to England – and good night to all who are England. But it is not in vain.[14]

For some, Haggard's speech was 'the extreme of pessimism, to others a "trumpet-call"'.[15] One guest said that in 'a few words of intense earnestness and conviction [Haggard] pierced all present with a sudden realisation of the world tragedy upon which the curtain has risen'.[16] Harding thought the speech 'in the worst of taste. But Haggard prides himself on his diplomacy'.[17]

The commissioners sailed on 20 August aboard the SS *Virginian*, not knowing 'by what route we are to sail, or whether or not we are to be escorted by warships. Our funnel is ... painted black, and the stewards are pasting brown paper over the cabin window-lights. Pleasant preparations for an ocean journey!'[18] Off the coast of Ireland Haggard wrote: 'It has been a strange and depressing voyage, rushing through ice and reek in this dumb shrouded ship. It has been perhaps the worst so far of any of the hazardous voyages I have made.'[19] It had not been improved by the death of a young woman on board 'from the effects of quinsy', who was buried at sea. 'She had been a governess and housekeeper in Canada and was coming home to be married.'[20]

Back at Ditchingham, Haggard 'found all well and the harvest up'.[21] In an atmosphere of general uncertainty the Dominions Royal Commission was put on hold on the basis that nothing more could be done and no report produced until after the war, which was famously expected to be over by Christmas.

Haggard met Charles Longman during September to discuss writing a history of the war – 'if we should all live so long' – and found his friend 'very depressed. He said nothing could be sold and no money collected and it was difficult to know how to meet outgoings.'[22] The underlying cause of Longman's depression was fears for his son Freddie, serving with the Royal Fusiliers 'somewhere at the front, and he knows not what is happening to him. But there we are all in the same boat.' Haggard's nephews, Bazett's sons George and Mark, were both in Belgium, George interned as an enemy alien, Mark 'fighting in the Welsh regiment' and leaving his 'poor young bride ... in a sad state of anxiety'.[23] George escaped from Brussels in November after bribing a sentry and using a forged passport.

With Armageddon under way, Haggard felt it was both inopportune and inappropriate to proceed as if everything was normal and asked his agent Watt to postpone the book publication of *Allan and the Holy Flower*, currently being serialised in the *Windsor Magazine*. However, publication went ahead and the book came out in March 1915. Haggard fared no better with Oscar Asche in requesting 'the production of *Mameena* be put off'.[24] A global conflagration wasn't going to stop Asche from sticking to the theatrical motto 'the show must go on'. *Mameena* was being 'most carefully rehearsed', Asche reported, with James Stuart 'putting us right as regards details'.[25]

Stuart had arrived in London in early August with Mandhlakazi kaNgini and Kwili kaSitshidi; all three would assist in the staging of *Mameena* at the Globe Theatre on Shaftesbury Avenue.[26] Mandhlakazi and Kwili were taken sightseeing –

London Zoo, Hampton Court, St Paul's Cathedral, Madame Tussaud's, and a magic show performed by Maskelyne and Devant.[27] For Mandhlakazi, the highlight of the visit to London was seeing the Royal Family arriving at Buckingham Palace: 'We took off our hats and greeted the King.'[28] Meanwhile, rehearsals were 'being pushed vigorously', according to Stuart; 'my advice is followed in 9 cases out of 10, there are occasional differences where Zulu custom is overridden in order to attain what is thought to be a better dramatic result.'[29]

All the speaking roles for Zulu characters were played by white actors in black-face. Herbert Grimwood played the sangoma Zikali while Asche took the role of Saduko, the husband of Mameena, who was played by Asche's wife Lily Brayton.[30] Black British actors were hired to perform as Zulu in the crowd scenes and those involving Zulu dances and ceremonies. 'Their figures, hair, colour &c are exactly what is wanted, but they require a lot of drilling.'[31] Mandhlakazi and Kwili trained both white and black members of the cast, teaching them how to 'perform marriage ceremonies, and sing ... to grind maize and other foodstuffs on a grinding-stone. We taught the men to dance war-dances ... We taught them about the throwing of the bones by witch-doctors, to sing praises, to pay homage and shout "Bayete!" ... They were taught for six weeks, and they learned well.'[32]

Haggard sat in on a rehearsal while in London for a meeting of the Dominions Royal Commission. The rehearsal went 'very well under the direction of, so far as the native business is concerned, James Stuart ... Whether the public will patronise any play in the midst of all this excitement remains, however, to be seen.'[33]

Mameena opened on 30 September and the first night 'was a tremendous success', according to Asche. 'London had never before seen what appeared to be real Zulus in all their war rig-out. At the end of the wedding dance, in which over eighty dancers sang and danced till the curtain fell – and then was raised time after time – even the jaded first-nighters got up on their feet and sang the time and stamped with their feet in rhythm.'[34] Haggard conceded individual scenes were 'beautiful' and 'the incidents interesting, but the drama as [Asche] conceives it is nowhere. However, it is of no use arguing with actor-managers. I should imagine that its career will be short.'[35]

The critic William Archer considered that the story existed 'simply for the sake of some extraordinary illustrations of Zulu life. Mr Asche has got together a large company, if not of Zulus, at any rate of unimpeachable Africans, who give wonderfully spirited representations of the epileptic dances of a Zulu wedding, of the weird ceremonies of witch-hunting, and of the other incidents of South African life.'[36] Likewise the *Daily Telegraph*: 'The story is not of any overwhelming force, and such as it is we like it better in the pages of Sir Rider Haggard than on the stage of Mr Oscar Asche.' The threadbare plot aside, all the critics raved about the spectacular and scenic qualities of the production: 'We were given many engaging scenes, with noble outlines of mountain and crag against sky and cloud, to which stage devices gave rare beauty.'[37]

The box office for the first week after opening was excellent, but then war-time street-lighting restrictions were imposed 'and for some considerable time the theatres suffered terribly'.[38] Haggard saw *Mameena* again on 24 November – 'much improved and a fine spectacle, if not the play I should have liked to make of it'. At interval Asche told Haggard he was 'obliged to withdraw the play after another five weeks' when the lease on the theatre expired, 'with the intention of reviving it in happier days, as I suggested that he should'.[39]

Mameena should have been an enormous success, 'but the times are too much to fight against'. Dark streets became even less inviting with the implementation of restrictive licensing laws prohibiting the sale of alcohol after 9.30 p.m., 'which keeps people away'; add to this the 'general lack of cash, and lastly the ever-increasing lists of killed, which put so many into mourning of all classes, especially those who patronise theatres. Also there is the all-prevailing anxiety that at present does not predispose to entertainments, since to it the country is not yet accustomed.'[40]

Mameena closed on 14 January 1915, by when theatregoers 'had become accustomed to the new regulations ... and we got some of our losses back. In all we played *Mameena* 133 times, and lost about £8 000 over it.'[41] *Mameena*'s career, as Haggard had predicted, was short; its unprofitable brevity and Haggard's general unhappiness with the production deterred him from further involvement in the theatrical world. His reasons for entering it in the first place had been unashamedly mercenary, motivated by the need for another income stream to support his family and assorted dependent relatives and fund his largely unpaid public service. The new medium of cinema came to his rescue, and by 'the middle of the Great War Haggard's income had bounced back: he was receiving £9,000 from cinema royalties ... His comforts thereafter derived as much from this source as from book sales.'[42]

In 1915 H. Lisle Lucoque, an Englishman (his French name notwithstanding), set up Lucoque Films with offices in Wardour Street, Soho, and negotiated with Haggard's literary agent Watt to buy the film rights to six of Haggard's novels over seven years.[43] The first Haggard title to go into production was *She*.[44] On 2 October 1916 Haggard went to Lucoque's offices in Wardour Street to view it for the first time – 'fair, considering all things, though somewhat distressing to an author'.[45] *She*, starring the French actor Alice Delysia, who had made a career in English musical theatre, was co-directed by Lucoque with Will Barker. Lucoque would go on to make films from three more of Haggard's books. *She* was followed by *Dawn* in 1917. 'It is not so bad, but as I have remarked before to an author these cinema performances of his books are full of woe and grief. The women as usual are better than the men, but I doubt if Angela would know herself.'[46]

In October 1916 Lucoque set a up co-production deal with I.W. Schlesinger of African Film Productions in Johannesburg to come to South Africa and make films of *King Solomon's Mines* and *Allan Quatermain* 'with massive casts and grandiose sets worthy of Italian and recent Hollywood epics'.[47] In this respect Giovanni Pastrone's epic *Cabiria* (1914) was ground-breaking: it 'established a benchmark for epic filmmaking in the years to come'[48] and became a key influence not only on D.W. Griffith's Babylonian sets for *Intolerance* (1916) but also those built in South Africa for *King Solomon's Mines* (1918) and *Allan Quatermain* (1919), both directed by Lucoque.

King Solomon's Mines premiered at the Johannesburg Empire cinema on Christmas Day 1918. The writer of the screenplay is unknown, which is a pity, for of all the film versions of *King Solomon's Mines*, this anonymous scriptwriter's is the most faithful to Haggard's book. It is particularly notable for being the only film adaptation to include the interracial romance between Foulata and Captain Good.

Haggard first saw *King Solomon's Mines* at the trade screening in London on 12 May 1919 at the Alhambra in Leicester Square. The cinema was packed and Haggard was later told by the African Film Production staffer Charles Holder Nesse 'that it was the most successful trade show that had ever been held in London'.[49] 'Nearly thirty-five years have gone by since the story was written by me and it is remarkable that it should still have so great a hold upon the imagination of the world. My belief is that it will live.'[50] In the *Bioscope*'s assessment, *King Solomon's Mines* struck 'a new note in film productions' and was mounted 'on a scale approached hitherto only by the Italian and American film spectacles'; 'the picture possesses distinctive characteristics as a pure African production' and was 'a thorough novelty, as refreshing as it is interesting'.[51] The film broke box office records at the New Gallery Kinema in London's Regent Street.[52]

Haggard attended a private viewing of *Allan Quatermain* on 29 October 1919. 'It is not at all bad, but it might be a great deal better. I wonder if the cinema business will ever be adequately handled in this country. It has great possibilities but it ought to be in the hands of artists and strictly upright men.'[53]

In 1914, immediately on his return to England from Canada, Haggard put his back into the war effort. Three army officers had been put up at Ditchingham House, and the district around Ditchingham was 'full of soldiers'.[54] On 4 September Haggard gave a recruiting speech in Bungay at the local drill hall – 'we got seventy-five recruits'[55] – and had 10,000 copies of his speech printed under the title *A Call to Arms: To the Men of East Anglia* and sent 'to various press agencies for distribution'.[56] Haggard was glad to record 'that all our unmarried servants volunteered'.[57]

On 18 September Haggard's daughter Angela telephoned him with the news that her brother-in-law, Haggard's nephew Mark Haggard, had died of his wounds in France on 15 September. 'It is a great shock, for I was fond of him ... He said before he left that never would he live to be taken prisoner by the Germans. Well, he has not lived. All honour to him who has died the best and greatest of deaths! But his poor young wife, whose marriage I attended not a year ago! R.I.P.'[58] On 25 September Angela telephoned again with news that Reginald Cheyne and his wife

Dorothy were coming back from India. 'No doubt Cheyne will be delighted, for he is the keenest of all soldiers, but I confess I am not so pleased. We seem to have enough of our family in this war.'[59]

The 'first batch of Canadian troops arrived' in October, among them Haggard's godson and nephew Lance Rider Haggard, 'who has pluckily thrown up his billet in Canada where I missed him, and come over as a private, for which I honour him. I hope he will get through the war unscathed.' Lance Haggard would become a captain in the Princess Patricia's Canadian Light Infantry, raised in honour of the daughter of Canada's Governor General, the Duke of Connaught. Six of Haggard's nephews, as well as his son-in-law Reginald Cheyne, would serve in the war. 'Old, gentle-born families like our own bear a large share in the national defence. Would that I were not too old and full of ailments to take my share! I should like to carry a rifle again!'[60]

Haggard had kept a diary from the beginning of his work on the Dominions Royal Commission. It now became a 'war diary' in which he recorded 'his reactions to the war news, his own activities, and whatever seemed to him at the time of any lasting value'.[61] The habit proved addictive and Haggard continued the diary until his death in 1925. Entries in Haggard's 'War Diaries' are at times fretful and reactionary: 'One of the effects of the war is that numbers of elder women, being better off, are drinking a great deal, while the young ones rejoice wholeheartedly at the presence of so many soldiers in their midst and are to be met with them in every lane.'[62] Even the war wasn't up to scratch: 'This war lacks the grandeur and picturesqueness of those of old time. There are no great battles, only one long hideous slaughter in the trenches. In the same way, where is now the majesty of Nelson's battles on the sea? In the place of them we have mines and sneaking submarines.'[63]

But Haggard's diaries are also big-hearted and free-thinking. He may have been politically and temperamentally conservative but, as he said of himself, he was no party man and he opposed the government's censorship policy on war news, believing that 'a clear and connected account of what was going on should be published day by day'.[64] He discussed the matter over lunch at the Athenaeum with General Sir Ian Hamilton, whom he had known since Newcastle days. Hamilton passed on the idea to Lord Kitchener, Secretary of State for War and famously antipathetic towards journalists, who 'only "snorted"'.[65]

Haggard declined an approach from the *Evening Standard* for a series of articles on the war, giving the spurious excuse that he was a royal commissioner, but confiding to his diary that it was really 'because I am too outspoken a person in these days of censorship. If I wrote at all I should say what was in my mind, and that would never do.'[66]

Haggard's patriotism triumphed over his loathing of 'charity' books and, at the invitation of the best-selling novelist Hall Caine,[67] he contributed a brief statement titled 'The Desolation of Belgium' to *King Albert's Book*, published in December

1914. The volume was intended as 'a tribute to the Belgian King and people from representative men and women throughout the world' and was to be sold for the benefit of the *Daily Telegraph*'s Belgian Fund.[68]

The subject of war, a topic formerly 'more or less taboo in England', was now unavoidable and Haggard crowed at the irony that for years he had been

> violently attacked for writing stories that deal with fighting rather than with sexual complications [in fact he had written both]. Once or twice I remember I have been provoked to answer that I was not in the least ashamed for trying to inculcate in the mind of youth the ancient and elementary fact that their hands were given them to defend their head – also their King and Country. A lesson I hope has been learned by some of my young readers.[69]

At a sitting of the Dominions Royal Commission in early November, it was decided to suspend meetings until the end of the war. The last meeting of the commission was held on 11 November. The members signed off on the Newfoundland report and decamped for lunch to 'a queer old room' at Ye Olde Cheshire Cheese in Fleet Street, 'one of Dr Johnson's haunts, where we ate lark-pudding and toasted cheese. I wonder if we shall all live to meet again and finish our work?'[70]

The next day Haggard saw Charles Longman and learned that 'poor Freddie was killed by a shell', a circumspect way of saying he had been blown to bits. 'I did not like to pursue the subject, seeing that it distressed him beyond bearing.'[71] Ditchingham House did not escape unscathed: 'Poor Gussie Williams, the son of Williams, the carpenter ... has been killed. He was a nice fellow, a reservist, and leaves a widow and two children, one an infant born three days before he left.'[72]

In anticipation of being in demand for war work and to make it easier to attend his various committees, Haggard took a flat at Montagu Mansions in Marylebone.[73] He accepted an invitation to join the Belgian Agricultural Restoration Committee, a 'small committee of which the object will be to restore Belgium after the war'.[74] The Royal Agricultural Society, of which Haggard was a member, had begun a similar venture which eventually absorbed this smaller committee, and Haggard was appointed to the executive committee of the Royal Agricultural Allies Fund 'on the re-stocking of devastated countries'.[75]

These committees were small beer compared to being a royal commissioner and Haggard felt sidelined by the authorities. Another committee membership added to his list was the 'Land Settlement at home and in the Colonies after the war' committee under the auspices of the Royal Colonial Institute, chaired by its president, Earl Grey.[76] Situated at 25 Northumberland Avenue, the Institute was an avowedly non-political patriotic body dedicated to promoting knowledge of the British colonies and their welfare, and it wielded considerable influence on government policy with regard to the Empire. It was the perfect home for Haggard and he was reunited there with an old friend from the Pretoria of the 1870s, Godfrey Lagden, now Sir Godfrey Lagden, who had retired from the Colonial Service in 1907.

In the New Year Haggard came down with a 'severe attack of influenza and bronchitis' and, in order to recover and 'fight the depression which it always left as its aftermath',[77] the Haggards took a furnished house at St Leonards on the Sussex coast. The Kiplings' home was only thirty miles away and on 22 March they came to visit. Neither Kipling nor his wife Carrie looked as 'well as they did at Kessingland', where they summered in 1914. 'He is greyer than I am, and, as he says, his stomach has shrunk, making him seem smaller. I expect that anxiety about the war is responsible.'[78] The Kiplings' son John, 'not yet eighteen, is an officer in the Irish Guards, and one can see that they are terrified lest he should be sent to the front and killed, as has happened to nearly all the young men they know.'[79] Haggard asked Kipling how he occupied his mind 'amidst all these troubles. He answered – like myself – writing stories, "I don't know what they are worth. I only know they ain't literature."'[80]

The Haggards moved back to Ditchingham in the spring and in April Haggard attempted to abstain from alcohol, prompted to do so by the King, who ruled on 6 April that 'nothing alcoholic is to be drunk in any of his houses'.[81] This was a belated response to the Defence of the Realm Act, passed in August 1914 (Dora, as it was popularly known), which reduced the opening hours of public houses in the belief that consumption of alcohol would impede the war effort. Haggard followed the King's lead as 'an experiment and to see how it agrees with me',[82] but gave up after a fortnight as it 'thoroughly disorganised my liver. Henceforth, I shall obey the Pauline maxim and take a little wine for my stomach's sake. Nearly fifty-nine is too old for these violent changes of the habits of a lifetime.'[83]

On 22 June, Haggard's fifty-ninth birthday, he received a 'patent anti-gas respirator' as a gift from Louie's cousin Rose Hildyard. 'Such are the birthday gifts in this year of Count Zeppelin 1915.'[84] He also received a letter from Watt enclosing one from Cassell requesting that their authors avoid mentioning the war. 'What it means exactly I cannot pretend to say – that the public is "sick of the war" I suppose. If so I'm not certain that attitude is healthy, although personally the last thing I want to read or write fiction about is the war.'[85]

A few days later Haggard bought a Lee–Mitford bolt action repeating rifle from William Carr at Ditchingham Hall. His intention was to join a local Volunteer Corps. A muscular leg injury sustained when 'jumping out of the way of a taxi-cab' in London rendered him 'too lame to do much drilling', but he was 'still man enough to fight Germans from ditch to ditch until knocked out. I would sooner die putting up a fight than any other way. Alas! that such a thing should happen when one has grown old and useless. How I envy all my nephews who can go to the front.'[86] As Haggard's eyesight was not good enough for sighting rifles, he went to Norwich 'to be fitted with glasses for rifle shooting' and to buy cartridges, though these proved impossible to obtain as the government had forbidden the sale of ammunition and rifles to volunteers.[87] On 14 July Haggard drilled on Bungay common with the Ditchingham and Bungay Volunteer Defence Corps, 'whereof I am a platoon Commander'. He was aware of the comic potential: 'a lot of determined old gents stumping about and doing their best to execute manoeuvres which they did not understand'.[88]

Haggard's attempts to find war work better suited to his talents were consistently frustrated. 'I feel sore, and not altogether for my own sake, since I know well enough I could do good work for the nation, if only I were given the chance.'[89]

In mid-July Haggard was a weekend guest of Lord D'Abernon at Esher Place in Surrey. D'Abernon told Haggard that the Canadian government was 'anxious' that the Dominions Royal Commission 'go to Canada at once to finish our investigations there'[90] and that Andrew Bonar Law, recently appointed Secretary of State for the Colonies, was in favour. Mingling with D'Abernon's titled cronies, rich businessmen, politicians and their wives, Haggard felt out of his social depth:

> It was curious to me to watch all these brilliant and exalted folk, Mrs Winston Churchill – a very handsome young woman – among them, playing every kind of game (golf and tennis in the day time and bridge at night) there in that soft lap of luxury and wealth, with its wonderful gardens, priceless pictures and the rest, at this somewhat dark hour in a struggle to which only light and casual allusion was made from time to time, and to wonder what would happen to these and their kind, and indeed all of us, if we should chance to go down in the war.[91]

Haggard subsequently met Bonar Law and Lord Selborne, president of the Board of Agriculture, as a member of the Royal Colonial Institute's 'After the War' deputation and spoke 'on Overseas Land Settlement of soldiers and sailors at the end of the war'.[92] Another speaker, Sir John Taverner, a former Australian Agent General, suggested Haggard 'be sent round the Dominions to find out the minds of their governments on this and kindred matters'.[93] Bonar Law nodded approval. Nothing more was heard of the matter until early October when, visiting his widowed sister Ella Maddison Green at Ledbury, Herefordshire, Haggard was taken aback to read in the *Yorkshire Post* that Bonar Law had received promises from the Dominion governments 'to cooperate in making provisions for settling returned soldiers to the land' and had gone as far as appointing a 'small Commission, of which Sir Rider Haggard is chairman, to visit the Dominions with a view to drawing up a scheme'.[94]

This was news to Haggard. At the end of the month, at a meeting of the 'After the War' committee (shortly to be renamed the Empire Land Settlement Committee), when it became clear, pace the *Yorkshire Post*, that the government would not be driving the initiative, 'the question arose as to whether the Royal Colonial Institute should not undertake the work and send me to the various Dominions to interview the Governments'.[95] In the absence of government support for the idea, the Institute decided to send Haggard on the tour as its representative 'in a private and unofficial capacity', with instructions to 'determine what lands would be available for returning servicemen'.[96]

On 7 October Haggard recorded that Kipling's son John, 'whom I have known since a child',[97] was reported wounded and missing on the 2nd. 'Poor Kipling, I know how great have been his anxieties about this boy ever since he joined the Irish Guards about a year ago; now they must be terrible.'[98] In London shortly before Christmas, Haggard met Kipling, who had 'heard nothing of John' and had evidently lost hope. Kipling told Haggard of John's affection for him and asked 'me what I had done to make his children so fond of me. I answered I didn't know except that young people like those who like them – a fact, I think, to which I owe the affection of many of my nieces and nephews.'[99]

As the Kiplings strove to uncover the circumstances of their son's death, Haggard came to their aid. On 27 December Haggard interviewed Bowe, 'a young wounded soldier of the Irish Guards'. He had been forty yards from John Kipling 'when they entered the wood near Givenchy where the latter vanished'. It was the belief of Bowe and his companion, another soldier named Frankland, that John 'was either blown absolutely to bits by a large shell ... or taken and murdered in the German lines'.[100] Haggard took a signed statement from the two men, minus these suppositions, which he sent to Kipling. 'There is still a faint hope he is a prisoner.'[101]

Shortly after the meeting Bowe remembered some other details: namely, that he had in fact seen Kipling after the wood was taken, heading for the rear and 'trying to fasten a field dressing round his mouth which was badly shattered by a piece of shell. Bowe would have helped him but for the fact the officer was crying with the pain of the wound and he did not want to humiliate him by offering assistance.' Haggard did not pass on this information to Kipling as being too painful 'but, I fear, true'.[102]

Sir Harry Wilson, secretary of the Royal Commonwealth Society as well as of the Royal Colonial Institute, telephoned Haggard on 10 December to tell him that, though Bonar Law would 'not help officially about Land Settlement in the Dominions ... there is no doubt it will be arranged for me to go to Australasia'.[103] Practical arrangements remained vague. Haggard was fully aware the government 'were anxious to avail themselves of any promise he might get from the Dominion Governments, but were prepared to disclaim anything to do with the mission should it prove a failure'.[104] The Colonial Office was not officially opposed to Haggard's tour but feared his findings could cause trouble 'with the Government of the Dominions at a critical time, or stir up the passions of Labour by advocating the settling in them of migrants'. These fears led to the Colonial Office writing 'to the various Governors to caution them against me'.[105]

The New Year of 1916 brought Haggard's marching orders from the Institute. He was instructed to visit South Africa, Australasia and Canada, 'a long and arduous business! I can only hope the mission will be fortunate and fruitful. At any rate it is my duty to take the risks, go ahead and do the work to the best of my ability. Here is my war offering!'[106]

And so began a fuss over who was to be Haggard's secretary. Haggard initially approached Arthur Cochrane, who for once was not available. Then A.R. Uvedale Corbett applied for the job. Corbett would later tell Haggard 'a curious story'. Corbett happened to be in the offices of the Empire Settlement Committee, when Haggard's letter arrived 'stating that Cochrane had failed me'. Corbett suddenly recalled that a year or two previously he had consulted a 'certain "wise woman" who reads the future by cards' and she had told him he would journey 'by sea and land with a tall man who was the first expert of his day on the questions which were the objects of the journey'. The journey would be 'extraordinarily successful' but that 'nothing must be believed or accepted that was not in writing'. Further, that they 'should be nearly wrecked in a terrible storm but that he must not be frightened as the ship would live through'. Corbett immediately 'determined to apply for the secretaryship'.[107] His selection was initially disallowed as he didn't have a passport. One was quickly granted.[108]

Prior to his departure on 10 February, Haggard ceaselessly promoted his mission. Guest of honour at the Authors' Club dinner on 3 February, he spoke on the 'After-War Care of Sailors and Soldiers', while *The Times* ran two of his letters headlined 'Soldiers as Settlers' and 'Soldier Settlers: The Future of Rural England'. At Haggard's send-off luncheon on 1 February, held by the Institute at the Cecil Hotel, with frontages on both the Thames Embankment and the Strand, Lord Curzon, who was in the chair, 'spoke most handsomely of me', declaring 'I was a "great Empire servant" going on a great errand'.[109] Kipling declared: 'You're in for the deuce and all of a big job.'[110]

29

'A SECOND ST. PAUL'

Thursday, 10 February 1916, Paddington station, London terminus of the Great Western Railway. Haggard stands beneath Brunel's daring span of glass and sky in dread of the abyss of time and distance about to yawn between him and those he loves as he takes the first step of his journey around the world. There are goodbyes and handshakes from the huddle of well-wishers, and last kisses from Louie and his daughters.

> I wondered if we should ever meet again. Oh! it is a sad world so full of partings. I enter on this great undertaking without illusions, for estimating the risks of my non-return at from thirty to forty per cent. The seas are very dangerous in these times and it will indeed be fortunate if we get back to England without accident by torpedo or otherwise. Still I take the chance gladly because I hope to do good work for the Empire.[1]

Haggard's diary and his letters home during his 'great undertaking' are invested with a valedictory tone; good health was no longer guaranteed – he was suffering from lower back pain – and on this long journey, his final turn around the Empire, he would turn 60. Aboard the *Kenilworth Castle*, warmer climes relieved Haggard's lumbago, and on 22 February a wire brought news of the German surrender in the Cameroons. 'So now only East Africa remains.' He thought the East African campaign a sideshow, as the war 'must be settled in Europe', though, like Kipling, he was sceptical about the calibre of Britain's current leaders.

> Am I justified in writing that these men, Haldane, Lloyd George, Churchill, Asquith, for instance, to say nothing of the galaxy of minor lights, are responsible? I think I am. They knew what was coming; they must have known what was not hid even from common people without secret sources of information, like myself ... And what did they do – they, the Trustees of the Nation? Did they preach a crusade – did they warn our blind and ignorant population? Not they.[2]

The *Kenilworth Castle* docked in Cape Town harbour on the morning of 28 February. Letters were awaiting Haggard from Lord Buxton, Lord Gladstone's successor as Governor General, and John Merriman, both 'cautioning me to be very careful as this country is in a volcanic state, owing to racialism, & British settlement must not be mentioned *publicly*'[3] as it would be 'instantly seized on by the Nationalist Party'.[4]

Several fault lines fractured Afrikaner politics after the Union of South Africa, pitting the prime minister and former Boer general, Louis Botha, and his ally Jan Smuts against the Afrikaner nationalist General J.B.M. Herzog. Botha was committed to a policy of reconciliation between the English- and Afrikaans-speaking South Africans and was forced to tread carefully to keep fellow members of his South African Party on side. This was a delicate balancing act given talk of British immigration to South Africa as well as financial support for the Royal Navy.[5] The advent of the First World War 'could not have come at a more inconvenient time' for Botha.[6] Memories of the suffering inflicted by the Anglo-Boer War were still fresh and the Union in its vulnerable infancy was unsteady on its feet. Botha's 'great task of reconciliation' seemed a vain hope if he was to take his country into war on the side of the British, especially when 'many of the white population were openly anti-British and thus pro-German'.[7]

The day Britain declared war on Germany, Botha sent a telegram pledging South Africa would defend itself if imperial forces were withdrawn to the Western Front. In return came a request for the Union Defence Force to invade German South-West Africa. This was a step too far for many Afrikaners: there was mutiny among sections of the defence force and the burghers of the Transvaal and Free State were called to arms. Martial law was declared in October and the rebellion was soon quelled by government forces skilfully led by Botha, though not before martyrs had been made. With internal dissent snuffed out, Botha's attention turned to German South-West Africa. His campaign was a 'tactical triumph'[8] and, with the German surrender on 9 July 1915, another 'huge territory had been added to the British Empire'.[9] But it was mainly English-speaking South Africans who were celebrating: Botha knew he had alienated many of his own people.

Haggard's presence went unreported by the local press though they were aware of his visit. Merriman told Haggard that the editors of *Die Burger* and other Nationalist newspapers were preparing to 'dig up' his anti-Boer sentiments expressed in *Jess* and other books 'if I publicly advocated Land Settlement'.[10] There was a smidgen of good news: the board of the British South Africa Company had agreed to offer 500,000 acres of land in Rhodesia free 'to approved soldier settlers from overseas' as well as provide 'expert advice and supervision'.[11] And, as ever, the weather was 'warm and beautiful; no wonder one loves South Africa and its sunshine'.[12]

At a low-key dinner held to welcome him, Haggard met familiar faces from his visit two years earlier, including Louis Botha – 'does not look very well, worried' – and Mrs Botha – 'ill with her heart'. Merriman was as 'evergreen and amusing as ever'.[13] Botha was 'sympathetic' to Haggard's mission, 'if somewhat helpless in the grip of circumstance ... He is deeply anxious to get British population into the Union but dare say nothing openly.'[14] Haggard's admiration for Botha continued to grow: 'I believe him to be entirely whole-hearted and reliable: earnest in the Empire cause.'[15] But Haggard was distinctly averse to General Hertzog: 'a dangerous face; that of a fanatic, brooding, intense and rather cruel. A thin dark-eyed man.'[16] A vehement opponent of Botha's reconciliation policies, Hertzog would have been equally unimpressed by Haggard, seeing him as the worst type of English jingo given his role in the annexation of the Transvaal and his anti-Boer prejudice.

Haggard's fortnight in the Cape flew by in a cascade of meetings with politicians and ministers. Sir Thomas Watt, minister for the interior, promised Haggard a letter relaxing immigration regulations in favour of men wounded in the war 'and seemed inclined to include all soldiers who had served'.[17] There was little to no time for leisure, although Haggard managed to snatch a half-hour alone to inspect the San rock art in the South African Museum and spent an evening with John Kotzé and his family. 'The judge is well but very white,' and his wife Mary, whom Haggard hadn't seen since 1879, 'a handsome old lady but deaf. The unmarried daughters are curiously early-Victorian in appearance. They were all very glad to see me and it is strange that we should meet again after all this time – more than a generation.'[18]

For their first three days in Cape Town, Haggard and his secretary Corbett were put up at Government House, where they had the use of an office. On 1 March they moved to the Mount Nelson Hotel, 'fairly comfortable, but food indifferent as is usual in South Africa'. That evening Haggard dined with Corbett and Merriman. In a letter to Louie, Haggard enclosed a story he thought would amuse Lilias about a woman

> who appeared last night in this hotel in a dress so low and short that really at a distance it looked almost as though she was wearing a *moocha*! ... I thought she must have a pink tight underneath and sent Corbett to ascertain but it was only Nature's 'tight'! Then I went to talk to her to satisfy myself. But that didn't take her in for she said to Corbett afterwards in the course of some midnight motor drive that they took together, 'I know why Sir Rider came to speak to me; it was to see whether I was wearing a net!'[19]

Haggard made overnight forays from the Mount Nelson. One night was spent with the Merrimans at their Cape Dutch homestead Schoongezicht near Stellenbosch – 'a wonderfully peaceful place, except for the sounds of acorns falling continually on to the stoep from the oaks that overhang the old house'.[20] With Merriman and the leader of the Unionist Party, Sir Thomas Smartt, Haggard motored out 'to the pretty Dutch town of Stellenbosch', the Afrikaner Oxbridge, 'where are many educational establishments and much disloyalty'.[21] From Smartt and Merriman he gathered that 'of the Boers, the lower sort hate us & most of the others are lukewarm & would be "glad to see us get a good beating to take the conceit out of us"'.[22] As in 1914,

Haggard was aware of a bigger picture: while 'this handful of 1 300 000 whites are at enmity ... the menace of the bush Native population with whom they are mixing their blood so freely, presses down on them like cloud on the crest of Table Mountain ... Altogether the usual African hell's broth is on the boil, though whether it will boil over remains to be seen.'[23]

Haggard also stayed with Archbishop William Carter at Bishopscourt, the official residence of the Anglican Archbishop of Cape Town on the eastern side of Table Mountain, 'beautifully furnished as an English home with long, large rooms and a lovely garden'.[24] From here he, the archbishop and his wife Hester strolled to the recently opened National Botanical Gardens at Kirstenbosch: 'devoted to indigenous trees and flora ... in 20 years it should be a wonderful place'.[25] The next day was Ash Wednesday and after breakfast 'the A.B. & I had a long talk about various points of theology & the mystery of things in general'.[26]

Haggard and Sir William Beaumont enjoyed a catch-up conversation at the Mount Nelson – they had last seen each other in Newcastle in 1881 – reminiscing about those they knew in 1875 and later. Most were dead or retired like Beaumont. 'Everybody seems to have retired in one sense or another, except myself, whose lot it is to go on working rather harder than usual. So we parted, I reminding him as he went down the steps of how he had been married in my frock coat.'[27]

Haggard kept abreast of news of the war: 'Winston Churchill is at it again.' Churchill had resigned from public office after the Gallipoli disaster and, while remaining a member of parliament, served on the Western Front in the Royal Scots Fusiliers. 'Weary of the trenches, where he has suddenly bloomed into a colonel', Churchill returned to parliament 'and made a violent onslaught on the present administration of the Admiralty ... So far as one can judge his object must be advertisement, at least it is difficult to see what other end he hopes to serve.'[28]

Prior to his sailing for Australasia on the morning of 13 March, Haggard received a letter by special messenger from Lord Buxton: 'You certainly have made the most of your time & I feel certain that your visit will be fruitful of result. You can certainly feel that your visit (thanks to your tact & industry) has helped to soothe & not to ruffle.'[29] Haggard was 'glad to be through with the business without contretemps ... So for the fourth time in my life I bid farewell to the shores of South Africa leaving them as usual peopled by problems and political trouble.'[30]

Haggard and Corbett sailed for Hobart, capital of Australia's island state, Tasmania, aboard the SS *Turakina*.[31] Corbett 'by payment of £20 has got a large double cabin to himself in which we can work',[32] and the ship was 'very comfortable with some nice people on board',[33] among them several soldiers from the New Zealand Expeditionary Force returning from Gallipoli – 'they are fine young men, among whom are 10 Maoris and some of them have been badly hit'.[34] Haggard was asked to 'make a little speech' at a tea party organised by the New Zealand soldiers 'to celebrate the engagement of one of their number to a young lady'.[35] Later in the voyage he invited them all forward to listen to his talk upon 'The War and its lessons'. 'I never heard "God Save the King" more heartily sung than it was at the conclusion of the lecture.'[36] He subsequently gave another talk on Zulu history.

Otherwise he passed the time pacing the decks or reading in a deckchair. Watching 'the albatrosses sail – sail day and night eternally' inspired Haggard to plot a 'new story to be called "The Fatal Albatross" set 'in some of the desolate islands we are passing. Or it might be called "Mary of Marion Isle".'[37] When the temperature dropped in the Southern Ocean and he was no longer able to sit on deck, Haggard took refuge in his 'bitterly cold' cabin, where he fell into a depression. 'This kind of solitary confinement is not gay,' he wrote to Louie. 'All one's failures and failings rise before one in melancholy procession till one is sick of contemplating them. In short it is a lonesome job and there is another fortnight of it ahead. No wonder everyone on this boat makes love furiously.' A day later the sun shone and, 'wrapped in a multitude of garments', he was able to sit on the deck. 'I see I have been writing some melancholy stuff ... The truth is, my dear, that I have as many moods as a woman – yes as She herself.'[38]

The 'apparently endless voyage' ended on 3 April 1916 when the *Turakina* docked at a storm-lashed Hobart. Once ashore, it was another round of polite diplomacy, visiting Government House to see Sir William Ellison-Macartney, Governor of Tasmania and Western Australia, who didn't rate Haggard's chances of achieving anything very high. 'I daresay he is right. However one can only try.'[39] And try he did, with the result that the Tasmanian premier, John Earle, promised Haggard a letter 'formally undertaking to provide land for and to look after a minimum of 300 soldiers (and their families)'.[40]

Haggard left Hobart on 8 April aboard the SS *Loongana* for Melbourne, where 'my round begins again – new interviewers, new ministers and the same old arguments.'[41] Haggard found the burden of work hard for one man to carry. 'Speech making, diplomacy, interviews, bores, endless arrangements, and negotiations fill the day very full, to say nothing of the constant strain of thought. I hope I shall pull through the job all right, but it is very, *very* tough.'[42]

And so passed Sydney, Brisbane and Fremantle in Australia, and Wellington and Auckland in New Zealand: a treadmill occasionally interrupted by batches of letters from Louie, Lilias and the farm steward at Ditchingham, John Longrigg. Louie and a family party had attended the premiere of *She* at the Empire in Leicester Square. 'The Empire was absolutely packed and I think Mr Lucoque was satisfied with the reception it received and certainly it was *very* good on the whole.'[43] News from Norfolk was not so cheerful: 'the most *terrific* gale with a blizzard' had brought down the 'big elm ... right across the drive smashing the old beech tree' as well as the 'fir tree my father planted on the front lawn'.[44] At Bradenham Hall, where Will Haggard was recovering from gout, the devastation caused by the gale was 'heartrending. There are over 200 trees down.'[45]

Aggie Haggard was at the Hall with her eldest son, Andrew, suffering from a 'nervous breakdown after a fearful doing in the trenches but is otherwise well'. Haggard's brother Alfred was 'very ill again and in bed, with a nurse ... I gathered she thought badly of the case.'[46] Alfred Haggard had cancer. At Ditchingham House a prize grey mare died while foaling, and the shortage of labour thanks to the conscription tribunal refusing to exempt the milkmen – 'we must have women'[47] – had Longrigg talking of selling the cows.

The letters reinforced Haggard's feelings of homesickness, not helped by a feverish cold and other unspecified aches and pains. 'I ought to see a doctor but dare not do so ... fearing lest it might be cabled home that I am ill.'[48] But it wasn't all bad news: Louie had discovered the joy of gardening and filled her letters – warm, affectionate, often humorous – with details of the Norfolk spring and the new blooms to be seen around the grounds at Ditchingham. 'I am amused at your Mum taking to kitchen gardening,' Haggard wrote to Lilias. 'Does she boss Mason [head gardener at Ditchingham] or does he boss her? Or do they take it turn and turn about?'[49]

In Brisbane Haggard had news of the Easter Rising in Ireland while a telegram from Louie told of the death of his brother Alfred. '*Requiescat!* He was I think, intrinsically the ablest of us, yet the lack of some qualities and the over-plus of others made his abilities of no avail.'[50] Haggard also learned that Henry James had died. 'He was a kind old boy ... and if personally I did not find his novels entertaining it is my own stupid fault. I wonder how many of them will be widely read twenty or ten years hence?'[51]

On 2 May Haggard recorded that the Irish Rebellion had collapsed. 'The wicked thing is that the Government, the Irish Administration and the Irish Party must all have known what was coming ... Yet they did nothing, and by the help of Censorship kept the truth hidden from the public.'[52] Haggard also blasted government censorship for the lack of information about the surrender of Kut-al-Amara to the Turks on 29 April 1916, 'the most abject capitulation in Britain's military history.'[53]

The 'terrible storm' prophesied by Corbett's 'wise woman' struck when Haggard and Corbett were sailing between Australia and New Zealand aboard RMS *Manuka*. The cyclone 'blew like all the infernal regions let loose for over 20 hours, after which it became an ordinary gale again!' At the storm's height the *Manuka* was suspended between two giant waves, 'the delicate question being whether she would turn turtle or break her back, for there was nothing underneath her.'[54] Fortunately the ocean surged up to fill the vacancy.

In Auckland Haggard attended a memorial service at St Mary's Cathedral for Lord Kitchener, drowned in the North Sea on 5 June when the HMS *Hampshire* taking him to Russia struck a mine and sank with the loss of 737 lives. Bishop Alfred

Averill 'preached a good sermon, all about Kitchener and his career', but Haggard 'could not help thinking of the seven hundreds of good men and true who went to doom with him. But of these we heard little or nothing.'[55] On his own account Haggard took solace from a comment made by Sir Francis Bell, New Zealand's immigration minister, who dubbed him 'a second St. Paul engaged in converting the Dominions to the Gospel of Imperialism!'[56]

On 13 June Haggard and Corbett boarded the SS *Niagara* bound for Canada via Suva, in Fiji, and Honolulu, in Hawaii. 'This is a fine boat and I have a very nice cabin,'[57] he wrote, blissfully ignorant that the *Niagara* was once advertised as 'the Titanic of the Pacific', quickly changed to 'Queen of the Pacific' after the sinking of the *Titanic*. A fellow passenger, a New Zealander named Johnson, told Haggard that reading *She* had saved his life. As a teenager he had a 'very bad fever ... and it was feared he would die'. All attempts to make him perspire failed until he was given a copy of *She*. 'He read with avidity and when he came to the end of the book burst into a profuse sweat, which carried off the fever – whether because it terrified him or for some other reason I do not know.'[58]

Haggard's own reading on the voyage included Frederick Scott Oliver's *Ordeal by Battle*, promoting national service, and a re-reading of *Natural Law in the Spiritual World* (first published in 1883) by the Victorian evangelist and biologist Henry Drummond, which united faith and science in a theory of theistic evolution. Haggard was particularly captivated by *Thy Rod and Thy Staff* by A.C. Benson, academic, novelist, diarist, memoirist and author of the unofficial British national anthem 'Land of Hope and Glory'. Published in 1912, *Thy Rod and Thy Staff* is Benson's account of his nervous breakdown and subsequent recovery.[59] Benson shared similar dilemmas regarding love, sexuality, death and depression, which stimulated Haggard to write a 'sermon for my own private benefit'. Benson spoke 'with some horror of all the sexual business. Doubtless he is right in a way; it is, at any rate in highly civilised conditions, the source of our worst woes.' But 'not withstanding its elemental coarseness [sexuality] has its splendid side'. Aside from the dawn of morning, is 'there anything in the world we know more full of wonder and of beauty than the face of the woman fate-stricken with Love, upon whom Passion has laid his most burning wand?'

Haggard was also struck that Benson, 'like myself, has strong leanings towards belief in reincarnation', which would explain many things 'whereof the bewildered contemplation drives us almost to madness; sins I think among the rest. Also loves and hates.' Regarding hate, Haggard thought he had none, he was by nature forgiving and had never hated anyone 'except perhaps the late Mr Gladstone, and him only in an impersonal way for national reasons'.[60]

'My dearest old girl,' Haggard wrote to Louie on 22 June. 'It's my birthday – I wonder if you've remembered it – & a pretty lonely one. I don't know anyone well on this big ship so haven't many to talk to.' Haggard was now off Hawaii en route to

Honolulu. 'Sixty blessed years and am definitely an old man now. Which of course doesn't make for cheerfulness. However there it is and meanwhile I thank heaven that I can still do my work such as it is. But I'm tired of this eternal travelling and to tell the truth, rather homesick!'[61] Haggard entered similar sentiments into his diary along with reflections on his life's course.

> For me the world is largely peopled with the dead: I walk among ghosts, especially at night. Well ere long I must join their company; ten more years the Psalmist would give me, but with my weakened health I cannot expect as much, even though I should escape accidents. My work, for the most part, lies behind me, rather poor stuff too – yet I will say this: I *have* worked. My talent may be of copper not of gold – how can I judge of my own abilities? – but I have put it to the best use I could.[62]

By evening Haggard had perked up and penned a chatty letter to Lilias, including an outline of the plot for 'Yva' (published as *When the World Shook*), his only foray into the realm of science fiction. A central plot device was a gyroscope set at the centre of the earth around which the planet revolves.

Haggard enjoyed the stopover in the Hawaiian capital, so much so that he wished he had an official invitation to stay longer. When the *Niagara* sailed, 'a native band played very well upon the wharf ... but the real joy was a native woman who in a rich and thrilling voice sang the famous South Sea farewell song. I don't know when anything has stirred me so much ... It was the very spirit of mournful, resigned "goodbye": it had in it all woman's love, all life's futility and sadness.'[63]

When he reached Victoria on the southern tip of Vancouver Island on 28 June, his brother Andrew was waiting on the quay, 'looking thin and of course older, but otherwise just the same as ever'.[64] Andrew came aboard with his wife Ethel and 'a whole crowd of distinguished citizens to greet me'.[65] Two days were spent with Andrew and Ethel before Haggard was back 'in the thick of it again', meeting officials, making and listening to speeches.[66]

In Vancouver Haggard learned that the Dominions Royal Commission had decided to come to Canada in the autumn, a pointless exercise in his view, 'and contrary to what we had arranged'. Haggard was aware that 'my being so generally known is not always pleasing to my colleagues when we are travelling in the Dominions' and hoped this meant they would 'not be too anxious for me to journey through Canada again in their company'.[67]

Travelling on the Grand Trunk Pacific Railway to Ottawa, via Prince Rupert, Edmonton, Calgary and Regina, Haggard was told a mountain and a glacier were to be named after him in the Canadian Rockies – Sir Rider Mountain and the Haggard Glacier. 'It is a curious world. Here they give my name to a towering Alp; in Norfolk they would not bestow it on a "pightle"! Truly no man is a prophet in his own country.'[68] He saw the mountain from the train: 'a wonderful and magnificent Alp, some ten thousand feet high and measuring many miles round its base'.[69]

20. The Haggard brothers. Left to right, Alfred, Andrew, Rider, William and Jack.

21. Haggard in the early 1890s.

22. Haggard in the late 1890s.

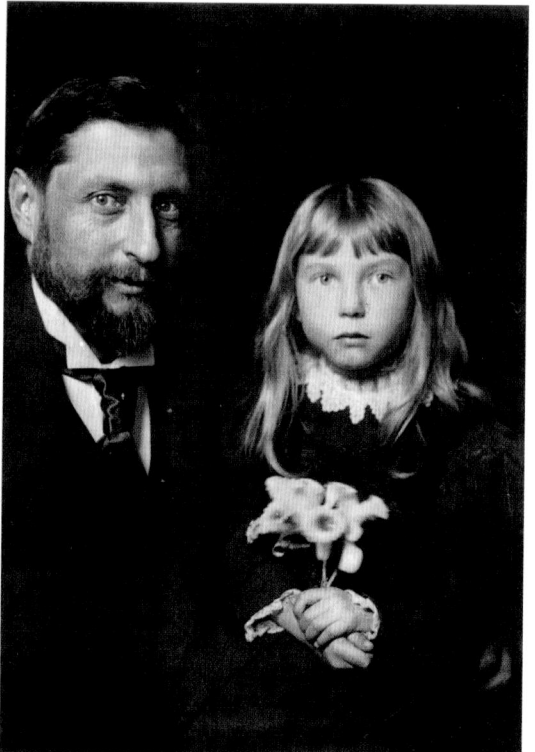

23. Haggard and Lilias, his youngest daughter and first biographer.

24. Haggard (far right) and his daughter Angela with friend and dragoman at the temple of Karnak, Egypt, 1904.

ISANDHLWANA, WITH MONUMENT TO THE 24TH REGIMENT.

25. Haggard (left foreground) contemplating the memorial to the 24th Regiment (South Wales Borderers) at Isandlwana a few weeks after its unveiling in March 1914. J.Y. Gibson is standing to his right and the driver, H.M. Edwardes, is behind him.

THE CAR HAD STUCK FAST IN MHLATIEZE RIVER, WHEN SIKOUYANA AND HIS DAUGHTER NOMBI, DRESSED AS A ZULU DIVINER, CAME TO HELP TO EXTRICATE IT.

26. The Overland stuck fast in the uMhlathuze River during the 1914 trip to Zululand. From left to right, Haggard, Sikouyana and Nombi. The latter would become a major character in *Finished*.

27. John Langalibalele Dube, founding president of the African National Congress, who Haggard interviewed in 1914. John and Angelina Dube with their children in the mid-1930s: (from left) Nomagugu, Joan Lulu, James Sipho and Douglas Sobantu.

28. John Langalibalele Dube.

29. Haggard in Egypt, at the temple in Abydos in 1924. 'Surely such a spot should be holy if there is aught so upon the earth.'

30. Bradenham Hall, Norfolk, where Haggard grew up.

31. Government House, Pietermaritzburg, where Haggard lived and worked when on the staff of the Lieutenant-Governor of Natal in the 1870s, as it is today.

Jess' Cottage
Pretoria.

32. 'The Palatial', the dwelling built by Haggard and Cochrane in Pretoria in the late 1870s, as it was in 1914. Later known as 'Jess's Cottage'.

33. Hilldrop farmhouse depicted in the lower right corner of the Haggard memorial window at St Mary's, Ditchingham.

34. Hilldrop today.

35. Ditchingham House.

36. Rear of Ditchingham House. Haggard's study is above the garden seat and the shrubbery.

37. 1 Fairholme Road (to the right) at the corner with Gledstanes Road, West Kensington, where Haggard wrote *King Solomon's Mines*.

38. Exterior of 56 Gunterstone Road in West Kensington, showing the front room wherein Haggard wrote *She* and the incident with the mummy occurred.

The Canadian capital of Ottawa marked the last stop of Haggard's imperial apostolic journey. At his farewell luncheon, where he spoke, the heat was such that Haggard's white shirt was blackened by the dye from his waistcoat, but despite his discomfort his speech was well received. When he sat down 'amidst loud cheers ... my heart was grateful as I reflected this was my last speech and that I had successfully accomplished the work I set forth to do throughout the Empire'.[70]

An hour later Haggard was on the train to New York, where, after setting up at the City Club, he took another train to visit Theodore Roosevelt at his home, Sagamore Hill, on the north shore of Long Island. Here he 'enjoyed a solid three hours of the most delightful intercourse I have perhaps ever had with any man'.[71] After lunch the two walked up to a summer house in the extensive gardens, where they sat and talked in 'an almost mysterious sympathy with each other', agreeing on 'the fundamental truth of Christianity, the highest revelation as yet vouchsafed to man', and discussed 'the mystery of faith, and the difficulty of its attainment'.[72]

They parted with 'real affection and understanding'. Roosevelt said he wouldn't visit England again or other countries where he would hear criticism of his country, 'which I know to be just and I cannot defend'. If he went anywhere, it 'will be to wild lands'. In response Haggard said he would like 'to end my days in Africa'.[73]

Haggard and Corbett docked at Liverpool aboard the SS *St Louis* on 30 July and caught the train to London, steaming into Euston station around eleven that night. Here 'I found Louie and Angie waiting to meet me, both well and glad enough I was to see them safe and sound after this long absence, during which one has run so many risks – oh! glad indeed and thankful to Providence'.[74] After a night at the York and Albany Hotel and an interview with a Reuters journalist the following morning, Haggard reported to the Royal Colonial Institute and was instantly 'whisked off to the House of Commons where a conference was sitting of representatives of the Colonies'. They gave Haggard 'a fine reception, all the gathering clapping when I came in'.[75]

Haggard, Louie and Angela travelled home to Ditchingham on a train packed with soldiers, to be 'greeted by a Zeppelin Raid, several of these accursed machines being on the bomb in the neighbourhood'.[76] In London, to his great relief, Haggard had been told he had 'leave to skip' the Dominions Royal Commission's Canada tour but would be required to attend sittings in London when the commission returned from Canada in November. 'I do not think I could face Canada again at present. Indeed I must have a little rest and look to my affairs.'[77] Haggard was prescribed 'rest and strychnine tonic' by Dr Gilbert Ransome in Bungay and instructed not 'to travel again at present. That mission has taken it out of me.'[78]

In his study at Ditchingham House Haggard corrected the proofs of his Royal Colonial Institute report. *The After-War Settlement and Employment of Ex-servicemen* was published on 26 August. This slim 68-page volume consisted of the letters and telegrams from the High Commissioners of the Dominions of South Africa, Rhodesia, East Africa and Canada, and 37 pages written by Haggard with several appendices.

30

'ONE OF THE HELLS'

Haggard's energies were diminishing and, mindful of her husband's well-being, Louie went to Budleigh Salterton on Devon's south coast where Dorothy and her children were staying, to find a house for the winter months. Tribulations at Ditchingham continued. Haggard was angry and upset when a tribunal rejected an application in mid-August for some of the milkmen on the farm to have their war service deferred or excused. The 'line taken was that I as a "gentleman" could shift for myself while others were helped'. To make matters worse, a letter to the tribunal from Louie stating that if the men went they would 'be obliged to sell the cows unless we could find milkers was publicly described as "unpatriotic". A 'strange term to be used in view of what I was and am doing for the country ... there is a great jealousy of "gentlemen" who farm, although in my case I have done this for reasons the reverse of "unpatriotic" and have never made anything out of the business.'

The tribunal's judgment was the final straw: 'I shall give up farming. I can no longer be exposed to all this pettiness for what brings me in nothing at all. The incident throws a lurid light on the difficulties that those who would help forward reforms in matters to do with English land.'[1] William Simpson, a land agent and auctioneer in Bury St Edmunds who had advised Haggard since the early 1880s, agreed it was 'wisest to wind up my agricultural affairs ... I have done my best, but the fact is that the adventure is scarcely possible for a gentleman in East Anglia. Too many forces are arrayed against him.'[2] These included the British army: the soldiers who took possession of Kessingland Grange in May were busy 'turning it into some kind of fortress'[3] and, in spite of warnings, digging pits between the house and the cliff edge 'which will probably result in the Grange going into the sea as the water will gather in them and let down the cliff ... and I shall be exposed to losses I cannot afford'.[4]

Meanwhile, the Colonial Office was showing signs of 'stirring about the appointment of an Imperial board' and Haggard wondered whether he would be offered a seat. While not 'particularly anxious for more arduous, unpaid labour', he felt 'they *ought* to do so *if* they mean business'.[5] The Germans certainly did, and on the night of 2 September the Ditchingham area was heavily bombed. Haggard was enjoying a smoke when just after eleven Lilias called down from the top floor, 'Dad, I hear a Zeppelin.' Haggard told them to come down to the cellar, but instead Lilias and Bertha Jebb, there on a visit, looked out of the window to see a Zeppelin approaching. 'Louie also saw it out of the bathroom window.' As they were coming down the stairs heading for the cellars, a bomb exploded 'two hundred yards from the house and sixty or so from the stockyard pond, where it made a large hole but by some miracle did not kill the horses ... The next bomb fell in the little shrubbery over the Norwich road just by our front gate' while other bombs fell over Bungay Common. 'It was hellish – the whirr of the machine above, the fearful boom of the bombs, and the crashing of glass in the greenhouses and one pane in the garden door, also one of the kitchen windows. The accursed thing went over spawning shells, and we sat for hours in the cellar.'[6]

Not surprisingly, Haggard was having trouble sleeping, and on a visit to Bradenham Hall on 9 September he slept well 'for the first time for a month ... in Hocking's old room'. He had asked Will that he not be installed in 'either of the front spare rooms because they have such painful recollections for me. I watched my mother's long death scene in the one and saw my father lying dead in the other.' Writing in bed before breakfast, he recorded:

> It is odd at the end of life coming back to houses in which one has spent its beginnings, for then such become one vast and living memory. Every bit of furniture, every picture on the walls, every stone and tree brings forgotten scenes before the eye, or finds tongues and talks. Scenes in which dead actors played, voices that stir the air no more! Where are they all, oh where do they hide from the search-light of our love? Well, ere long the play of our generation will be finished and we too shall learn or cease to be eager and curious for ever and a day.[7]

In London he spent time drafting a sub-report of the Dominions Royal Commission on 'the Agriculture and Forestry of the Empire, a very difficult task in the limits allowed, especially as I am asked to make it interesting'. Here Louie joined him and, with Angela and Bertha Jebb, they went to see the documentary *The Battle of the Somme*. Haggard was most impressed by a scene showing 'a regiment scrambling out of a trench to charge and ... one man who slides back dead. There is something appalling about the instantaneous change from fierce activity to supine death.'[8] This scene had a huge impact on the British public, who didn't know the death had been faked for the camera.[9]

In mid-October Ditchingham House was closed and the Haggards moved down to Devon to stay at Thornsett, the house Louie had found in Budleigh Salterton, 'a pleasant place ... comfortable and well furnished'.[10] Haggard spent the winter there, going up to London when necessary on the direct line to Paddington. At a Royal Colonial Institute dinner in mid-November he received an illuminated address in recognition of his work on their behalf and had conferred on him an honorary life-fellowship for his public service.[11] A letter from Bonar Law read aloud at the function indicated he was in 'communication with the authorities in the Dominions as to setting up a Central Board to deal with all these matters of emigration which we had raised'.[12] A few days later Haggard heard that 'favourable replies' were coming from the Dominions in response to a telegram sent by Bonar Law, suggesting 'an Imperial Board to arrange emigration to the Dominions'.[13]

Things were looking up, and Haggard went for a walk and, 'happening on St Thomas' [Church]' just off Regent Street, 'found there was a service and attended it. One lady and I formed the congregation! It was a restful, hallowed place.'[14] Haggard was a regular visitor and became a friend of the church's vicar, the Reverend Philip T. Bainbrigge, to whom he dedicated *Love Eternal*, published in 1918.

Haggard's diary entry for 25 December 1916 at Thornsett gives a poignant snapshot of a wartime Christmas:

> A sad, sad Xmas for many. I had not the heart to drink healths after dinner. That old custom reminds one of too much. Angie and Dolly here, so all the girls were present. They had just gone home when there was a ring and who should come in but Reggie, who had got his leave and motored from Exmouth. He was an impressive and war-torn figure, his khaki clothes covered with trench-mud, haggard, exhausted, almost unable to speak from bronchial laryngitis or some other form of throat common at the front. I don't remember anything that has, in a flash as it were, brought the war more home to me than his sudden appearance in that quiet drawing room in search of his wife whom he must have passed on the road.[15]

The New Year of 1917 brought news of the death of Frederick Courtney Selous, killed in German East Africa while fighting with the Royal Fusiliers. 'He was an odd but most gallant man, with a frame and constitution of iron – a mighty hunter before the Lord ... God rest him! He is one of the last of his sort, an African hunter of the Allan Quatermain stamp!' – though 'not the original of Allan Quatermain as everybody says'.[16]

On 12 January the Dominions Royal Commission rose 'for about three weeks' and Haggard returned to Budleigh Salterton with Edward Harding to work on the introduction to the final report, a 'tricky piece of hack writing, of which the chief objects are to avoid giving offence and to conceal certain unpalatable facts. Moreover, one feels that it is to great extent a labour in vain, since few read these documents and fewer still follow their advice.'[17] The final report was signed off the following month, 'rather a sad function after five years of corporate work', and all involved dined at Claridge's.[18]

On 22 January Haggard heard from Lord D'Abernon, who had recommended him as chair of the proposed Emigration Board, that a chairman had already been appointed. Haggard was disappointed: 'I should have liked to run that show.'[19] The war continued to exact its toll on the Haggard family: on the evening of 25 January news came that Will's son Hal, 'my nephew and godson', had been 'terribly wounded' while serving on the Dover Patrol in the Channel, 'one of his feet has been amputated and the other operated on; also that he was much cut about in other ways'.[20]

At the end of January Haggard learned that Lord Tennyson was to chair the Empire Land Settlement Committee and he would be one of its thirty-five members. The next day Haggard received his official appointment to the committee. 'I have accepted, though of course I should have liked the chairmanship.'[21]

On 17 March Haggard lunched with Kipling and spent the afternoon with him at Brown's Hotel in Albemarle Street, the Kiplings' pied-à-terre when in town.[22] Kipling was 'thin and aged' – suffering from duodenal ulcers, which remained undiagnosed until 1933. The Kiplings still didn't know what had happened to their son 'but are trying to win news from the Germans by means of messages dropped from aeroplanes. The truth is that business has knocked them both out and when I said so he did not deny it.'[23]

The two friends met several times over the next few days and Haggard dined one evening with Kipling and his wife, bringing with him the completed manuscript of 'Yva' – 'I am rather proud of having been able to do this work in the midst of so many distractions and anxieties, especially as I think it good of its sort'[24] – and he read 'them the "Gyroscope" theme'.[25] Haggard subsequently sent the manuscript to Kipling, who declared it 'a remarkable work of imagination – really a new thing'.[26] When asked if he had any criticisms, Kipling said very few, 'it's as fresh and convincing as the work of a boy of 25 and it held me like a drug. That's your d----d gift!'[27]

Snow fell heavily in the early hours of 31 March, but by the time Haggard stepped out from the Norfolk Hotel where he was staying in North Kensington, the snow had turned to slush and the streets become rivers. Haggard lunched with Charles Longman and his wife Harriet, both still desolate at the death in action of their son Freddie. In the afternoon Haggard visited Louie's cousin Cecil Hildyard, who had recently moved with his wife to a new home in West Kensington, and he went for a stroll with Cecil to look at 69 Gunterstone Road, which he hadn't seen for over thirty years. They left when a servant came out, suspicious at their behaviour, worried they 'contemplated burglary'.[28] Perhaps looking at his old study prompted Haggard to consider extending the story of Ayesha beyond its sequel, an idea he eventually abandoned as 'my hands are too tied by the contents of She and Ayesha ... there I think the venture better end.'[29]

But Ayesha was determined to return, and Haggard subsequently wrote *She and Allan*, published in January 1921, bringing together She-Who-Must-Be-Obeyed with Haggard's two other most popular heroes, Allan Quatermain and Umslopogaas. Readers of Haggard's earlier romances who thought they were in for a rip-roaring adventure found themselves plodding through familiar tropes from Haggard's African romances and much philosophising from Ayesha and Quatermain.

The first meeting of the Empire Land Settlement Committee was held on 12 April 1917. With the prospect of being required to reside in London for longer periods while working on this and other committees, Haggard signed the lease on a flat in 26 Ashley Gardens, a prestigious Victorian flat block, one of five built in the 1890s with stone-striped red brick, adjacent to the similarly constructed Roman Catholic Westminster Cathedral.[30] On 20 April, 'after an absence of six months', the Haggards returned to Ditchingham.[31]

The King's birthday honours on 4 June brought the Dominions Royal Commission chairman Lord D'Abernon a GCMG and Edward Harding a CMG. 'The five-year-long labours and journeyings of the rest of us are not acknowledged,' noted Haggard.[32] D'Abernon told Haggard he had no idea he was due for a gong and was given to understand his submission of names of the commissioners for honours would be passed but was 'simply "shelved" without his knowledge'. Haggard thought it all 'rather a shameless affair'.[33]

Throughout the summer of 1917 Haggard shuttled between Ditchingham and London for meetings of the Empire Land Settlement Committee, signing off on a final report on 11 July. 'So there is an end of my public work – at any rate for the present.'[34] The report was published in August and Haggard was pleased to see passages he had written 'approvingly quoted in the papers' while *The Times* carried a 'sympathetic article upon the subject'.[35]

On 8 September 1917 a Mr Burch of the Sundays River Settlement Company in the Cape came to visit Haggard at Ditchingham, to ask if he would be interested in coming to South Africa to write a report on the settlements. Haggard was interested in principle, but only after the end of the war. 'I confess that I should like to have a house there in which to spend the winter since, as I grow old, the longing for South Africa where I spent my youth has become very strong with me. Also the climate of this country at that season of the year no longer suits me with my bronchial tendencies.'[36]

Recurrent poor health strengthened Haggard's intimations of mortality, reinforced by the family belief that male Haggards seldom lived beyond 60.[37] Haggard's literary star had faded, his public career had reduced him to a committee man; horizons were no longer limitless, and there was a sense of an ending. Haggard began putting his affairs in order. On 10 September Frank Leney, curator of the Castle Museum in Norwich, came to Ditchingham House and 'departed with a motor-car full of gifts'. These included all Haggard's bound handwritten manuscripts. 'Otherwise, within a very short period of a man's decease, there would be no one left would take the slightest interest in them ... Still it makes me rather sad to part with them.'[38] The same month Haggard sold all his livestock, including shire horses and cattle, making between £7,000 and £8,000. It was a 'tiring and anxious day' for Haggard, but 'on the whole the sale was successful and I consider I am well out of the business'.[39]

Reminiscence was the order of the day. On 12 October 1917 Haggard lunched with Arthur Spurgeon, manager of Cassell, and the publisher's chief editor, Newman

Flower: 'it was an interesting meal, at which I gave them my recollections of Cassell's before their time here, not altogether complimentary all of them, for in those days the firm treated authors like the dirt beneath their feet'.[40] Cassell took *The Ancient Allan* and *When the World Shook* (still titled 'Yva') 'at a fair price, not so much, of course, as one used to get in pre-war days, but still a good sum ... This is something at my age, and after publishing books for so long, and I am thankful for it.'[41]

The war ground on. The dead and wounded in Haggard's family and the losses of his friends – Rudyard Kipling, Charles Longman, Maurice Greiffenhagen and Godfrey Lagden[42] – were in the forefront of his mind at Charing Cross station on 15 October when seeing off his son-in-law Reginald Cheyne, returning to the front. The station was a 'curious and melancholy spectacle when a [troop] train is departing. Dozens of officers, from Generals down, with their kit', men from other ranks from both services, 'also their womenkind come to say them goodbye'.

> They are wonderfully brave, these women – mothers, wives, sweethearts, daughters! A quiver of the lip, a breaking of the voice – that is all! Though occasionally as I walked up and down seeking for Reggie, I saw a pair in each other's arms in a compartment of the train. How many farewells have this station and Waterloo witnessed during the past three years – farewells, hundreds of them, for the last time on earth! The thing is terrible; if there is haunted ground anywhere it should be this prosaic railway station.[43]

A Zeppelin raid on London kept Haggard and Louie awake at Ashley Gardens, and at 'half-past two we were roused from bed by fire engines and motor-bicycles rushing about furiously, blowing blasts on sirens'. In the morning he walked down Piccadilly to inspect the damage done by a bomb dropped near Piccadilly Circus; many of the shops were wrecked including the famous Swan and Edgar store. Broken glass lay everywhere and a 'huge hole' in Regent Street was cordoned off 'so that buses must go around by other routes'.[44]

A short break at Budleigh Salterton visiting his daughter Dorothy and her children was a relief from 'the strain of London'. The relief was short-lived, for there Haggard heard from his brother Arthur that his son Lance was 'reported "Missing; believed killed"'. Haggard had last seen his nephew on the evening of 17 January when he 'came to say goodbye to me ... before returning to France no longer a private but an Acting Major in the Princess Patricia's Canadian Regiment'.[45] Lance was killed in an attack on a farmhouse at Vimy Ridge. 'Soon there will be few young men of the upper classes left in England.'[46]

The final instalment of Haggard's Zulu trilogy, *Finished*, was published on 10 August 1917. Roosevelt was 'very proud' at the dedication and would never forget Haggard's last visit – 'one of the most enjoyable afternoons I have spent with any friend'.[47]

Haggard's friendship with Roosevelt was well known in government circles, and he was approached in November by General Frederick Maurice, Director of Military Operations at the War Office, to use his influence with the former president. In particular he was asked to write a letter, asking Roosevelt what additional help the United States could provide in the prosecution of the war in the event of Russia pulling out as a consequence of the October Revolution. Haggard complied, making it clear in the letter that he wasn't writing in his personal capacity but on behalf of the War Office. This all struck him 'as rather curious and I do not quite understand what it means ... I am not sure R will answer the letter.'[48] The letter was never sent for fear President Wilson might be offended if he heard the British had made secret overtures to Roosevelt.

By then Haggard, suffering from bronchial catarrh, had taken up winter quarters at St Leonards, where Louie had rented a serviced flat on the Grand Parade. There in December Haggard signed the contract for the purchase of 'a quaint little house' known as the North Lodge and Paygate on Upper Maze Hill, 'in which, all being well, we hope to spend the winters in future, for the sake of the climate, which I find helpful to my chest'.[49] The Lodge was the old tollgate of the town and 'the public roadway runs under the stone arch that in its upper part forms the long room which I hope to take as a study'.[50] St Leonards would become an annual refuge from the cold Norfolk winters and the fogs of London. There was a good train service to the capital, and Kipling was happy his friend was 'so near to us'.[51] North Lodge was in need of extensive repair and Haggard wasn't to spend a night under its roof until October 1918. The architect and surveyor Percy Hunter Oxley was employed to do the necessary renovations. Haggard was inspecting progress one day when Oxley 'silently handed me a telegram' he had just received announcing the death of his son and only child in action. 'It was a painful business, since the unhappy man burst into tears and then went on talking about pipes and painting.'[52]

The New Year of 1918 brought an invitation from the Agricultural Wages Board for Haggard to be one of several investigators appointed on its behalf to report on agricultural wages. Haggard would 'have been delighted at any other time of the year' but doubted whether his health would bear 'prowling about the country in winter on such a job ... I am not proud and would gladly help, but will my "pipes" stand it?'[53] Haggard thought he would hear nothing further, but the matter went ahead and he was allocated Cornwall, Devon and Somerset, which were to be investigated over a three-month period commencing on 28 January. Haggard enlisted Arthur Cochrane to accompany him and requested a 'motor-car to travel in as my chest will not stand up to these draughty stations.'[54]

Haggard and Cochrane – 'at the business of agricultural research after a lapse of twenty years'[55] – began their investigations in Cornwall, headquartered at the Red Lion Hotel in Truro. Haggard's fears for his health were well founded and within two days he had 'contracted a bad cold which may or may not be influenza. If it is anything of the sort, I dare not attempt motor driving in this weather.'[56] A local doctor diagnosed emphysema and bronchial catarrh, stating in a certificate: 'I consider Sir Rider Haggard is running a grave risk in going about the country in a motor-car and stopping at casual Inns. I have told him definitely that in my opinion he ought to give up his investigations and stop at home at St Leonards.' Haggard concurred and sent in his resignation. 'The fact is I should never have taken on the job in winter; I ought to have known I should break down with my constitutional delicacy, but in a sense my eyes were bigger than my stomach.'[57]

Haggard's novel *Love Eternal*, dedicated to the Reverend Philip Bainbrigge, was published on 4 April 1918. Written against the backdrop of the First World War and its many bereaved families, including Haggard's, it was another variation on the Haggard–Lilly romance, played out between the book's hero Godfrey Knight, much drawn to metaphysics, and the free-thinking materialist Isobel Blake. Godfrey's father disapproves of the relationship and he is sent to learn French in Switzerland, where his mediumistic talents are recognised by Madame Riennes, a Madame Blavatsky clone complete with a faithful American colonel, Josiah Smith. Godfrey eventually rejects spiritualism and Theosophy, but his relationship with Isobel is further frustrated by his army service in the First World War. They eventually marry and, as they walk together down the aisle, Isobel whispers to Godfrey: 'Do these words and vows and ceremonies make any difference to you?' To which he replies: 'They do not to me. I feel as though all the rites in the world would be quite powerless and without meaning in face of the fact of our eternal unity.'[58] Married bliss is short-lived as Isobel dies soon afterwards. Her dying words are: 'Good-bye, my darling ... good-bye, and remember what I have told you, that near or far, living or dead, we can never really be apart again, for ours is the Love Eternal given to us in the Beginning.'[59]

A sympathetic notice in *The Times* acknowledged that the book 'should prove a comfort to many and is especially suitable to these days of ours'. However, the reviewer took issue with the quality of the writing, and Haggard was stung at being told he was not a 'literary artist', though the critic was 'good enough to add that I make what I want to say clearly understood. This, to my view, doubtless quite an inartistic one is the real point of all writing! ... It is a part of the Stevensonian, Meredithian and Henry Jamesian tradition to decry simple straightforward English. Meanwhile if what I have said in my own humble fashion does bring any comfort to bruised and sorrowing hearts, well, I have my reward.' Haggard conceded *Love Eternal* 'was rather hurriedly written' and he would have 'liked to see another set of proofs but there was no time'.[60]

A heavier blow landed on 17 April 1918. Haggard's eldest brother Will sold Bradenham Hall, 'where the family has lived for over a century and where we all were born. Could he know of it, it would break my father's heart, especially as I have a strong suspicion that the estate has gone to one of those speculators who are roving about the country buying up properties and, after cutting down every stick of timber, peddling them in lots for what they will fetch.' Haggard did not hold anything against his brother at this stage and could well understand his decision: 'he gets nothing out of the estate; indeed I believe it costs him money and there is no prospect of his son being able to live there, in short he is freeing himself from an intolerable burden'. This did not lessen 'the sadness of the break', despite Haggard considering Bradenham Hall 'a haunted house, in which ever since I saw my beloved mother die there, I have not cared to stay. Yet it was her home for nearly fifty years, and there was spent most of my childhood.'[61]

Haggard spent 22 May at Bateman's with Kipling, one of the few friends 'left to me who in this respect grow lonely in my old age'.[62] Kipling was unwell, suffering 'from fits of pain in his inside'.[63] Their conversation revolved around 'the soul and the fate of man'. When Haggard remarked 'that this world is one of the hells', Kipling responded 'that he did not *think*, he was *certain* of it', describing how it has 'every attribute of hell, doubt, fear, pain, struggle, bereavement, almost irresistible temptations springing from the nature which we are clothed, physical and mental suffering, etc., etc., ending in the worst fate that man can devise for man, Execution!'[64] As to life after death, Kipling was content to 'let the matter drift'; all he desired was a 'good long rest'.[65] However, 'like myself he has an active faith in the existence of a personal devil and thinks (I gathered) that much which is set down to God, is really attributable to the personality who at present cannot be controlled *even* by God, at least not altogether'.[66]

They spoke of their personal weaknesses and failings: Haggard on his growing sense of 'utter insufficiency, of complete humiliation both in the case of those things that I had done and left undone and of the knowledge of sin ingrained in my nature which became more and more apparent to me as I approached the end of my days'.[67] Kipling said the same applied to him and that human beings 'were subject to different weaknesses and temptations at the various periods of life'.[68]

When Haggard suggested Kipling must find some consolation in his fame, he 'thrust the idea aside with a gesture of disgust – "What is it worth – what *is* it all worth?"' – adding that anything which 'any of us did *well* was no credit to us: "We are only telephone wires." In his own case he cited the poem 'Recessional'; in Haggard's, *She*. "'*You* didn't write *She* you know," he said, "something wrote it through you!"'[69]

Kipling was delighted to have had 'a good mental and spiritual clean out'[70] and asked Haggard 'how much older I was than himself. I told him – ten years. "Then you have the less time left in which to suffer," he answered, or words to that effect. I think he was alluding chiefly to the great loss which has overtaken both of us in life.'[71]

At the end of May Haggard was back at Ditchingham House, 'looking beautiful, notwithstanding "war conditions". The pink mays on the lawn which I planted about thirty years ago are lovely and so are the copper beeches and indeed all the trees. The garden too flourishes though vegetables are growing in the flower beds.'[72] Further economies were required due to the rising cost of coke to heat the greenhouses: Haggard's beloved orchids had to go – 'rather sad when they have taken twenty-five years and considerable expenditure of money to collect, as the hobby of a hard-working man'.[73]

The bells of St Mary's rang out on King's George V's birthday on 3 June, joined by 'the drumming of the big guns at the front ... rather like beating an accompaniment to cheerful music on a coffin!'[74] In July 'the constant drumming' of the guns interfered with Haggard's work,[75] and the sudden unexpected percussion of German bombs was an even greater strain: 'When those bombs explode I confess that my heart jumps and flutters ... Also one grows no younger and does grow a great deal *thinner*. My clothes almost slip off me as do the rings off my fingers.'[76]

The war struck English class distinctions, and social and gender divides, a mortal blow. The result was a minefield for a man of Haggard's generation and status. On 17 June a son of the Scottish landscape painter John MacWhirter (a friend of Haggard's who had died in 1911) came for lunch. He was a private soldier serving in the ranks. Meanwhile, down in the kitchen Lieutenant Mason was having lunch with his mother and his father, the Ditchingham House gardener. 'The thing is awkward and I am glad the two did not meet.'[77]

Other customs were changing as well. Haggard lamented the loss of 'courtesy that used to prevail'; few 'among what are known as the working classes, unless they are very old friends ... will condescend to take the slightest notice' if met. Haggard had 'never been one for the bowing and scraping habit, still there are degrees in haughtiness, as in undue familiarity at the other end of the scale. A little courtesy, especially when it is known it will be reciprocated, harms no one and oils the wheels of life.'[78]

Two days after Haggard's sixty-second birthday, on 22 June, his brother Will came to visit, depressing Haggard with 'melancholy tales about the sale of Bradenham'. Will brought bundles of old letters, 'some of them written by me as long as forty-three years ago', including the farewell letter to his mother written when he sailed for southern Africa in 1875 and another written from Mexico City in 1891 on the death of Jock – 'Its perusal affected me much'.[79]

Haggard was glad not to have known beforehand about the sale of Bradenham Hall 'since then one might have felt it a duty to try to save the place for the family which would have stripped me bare'.[80] Indeed, Will had done everything in secret, fearing his siblings would pressure his brother into buying the property, thus forcing Will to drop the price below the market value of £18 per acre.

On 20 August Haggard paid 'a heart-breaking visit to that abomination of desolation, an ancient home that is being broken up'. Articles familiar from his childhood were 'scattered about and labelled with the tickets of the sale', including 'the ancient clock' whose 'chimings ... were the first and last sounds that one's forefathers heard for generations'; according to the caretaker, it had '"stopped last night", appropriately enough at midnight'.[81] There was a picnic in the garden 'under the great beech tree where my father always sat in summer'. After visiting his parents' graves, Haggard bade goodbye to Bradenham Hall, 'where, if I can help it, I shall never go again'.[82]

There was great family bitterness over Will's decision to sell all the contents of the family home; no arrangements were made for family members to take items of sentimental value or personal interest. Haggard confessed his own temper was 'permanently damaged'[83] and accused Will of having brought about what 'I believe will be a permanent family split'.[84]

Haggard appointed an agent to bid on his behalf at the auction, held over three days from 26 to 28 August. Sale prices were inflated by the Rider Haggard name: the dealer claimed items with a connection to the famous author 'would be of great value in the future!' As a result many of the lots Haggard placed bids for 'went for the most part beyond my means'. He did manage to buy his father's desk and its three-corner chair, the bed in which he slept as a boy, his childhood butterfly cabinet now containing only a 'dilapidated moth', and 'the remains of my mother's favourite blue Copeland breakfast service ... like the rest of my family I find it hard to forgive my brother for having ordered the sale of these relics.'[85]

On 21 October Haggard spent his first night at North Lodge, St Leonards, where rumours were spreading that the war was coming to an end – 'no one knows; but the feeling is there like that of spring while winter still endures'.[86] On 11 November Haggard was able to write: 'There is Peace ... the guns or maroons are firing and I hear the cheers of Victory!'[87]

A few days earlier he received a letter from Kipling about *Moon of Israel*, published on 31 October 1918. 'What *is* your secret, old man? It goes, and it grips and it moves with all the first freshness of youth and – I got into a row with my wife because I had to finish it in bed with the electrics turned on. It's *ripping* good and I'm d----d jealous.' Haggard thought Kipling's opinion 'worth a ton of professional criticism, because it comes from a great writer who knows what creation is and its difficulties'.[88] He laughed at the idea Kipling was 'jealous of *me* who am written down as the deadest of letters. Also I wish that I could rise to his high opinion of my work.'[89]

Three days after peace was declared, Haggard went down to Bateman's to find Kipling was 'much better than when I last saw him ... he puts it down to the war news'. At Kipling's request Haggard brought his 'War Diary' and 'read passages out of it until I was tired'. Excited by what he heard, Kipling urged Haggard to carefully preserve the manuscript so it could be published fifty years hence when it would be safe to do so. Haggard was taking precautions for its preservation and intended making two typed copies, depositing one with Longmans and keeping the other himself as well as the original 'in different places'.[90]

They spoke of their dead sons, Kipling saying that Haggard was lucky to have lost his son

> early when I still had youth to help me to bear up against the shock and time in which to recover from it, at any rate to some extent (which I never have done really). 'If he had lived to see the war,' he added, 'he would now have been dead or mutilated, perhaps leaving a family behind him.' Mayhap he is right, I often think so myself. I pointed out that this love of ours for our lost sons was a case of what is called 'inordinate affection' in the Prayer book ... 'Perhaps,' he answered, 'but I don't care for ordinate affection, nor do you.'[91]

A long talk with Kipling was 'one of the greatest pleasures' Haggard had left in life: 'I don't think he talks like that with anyone else, indeed he said as much to me. He is a very shy bird, and as he remarked, has no friends, except I think myself, for whom he has always entertained affection, and no acquaintance with literary people. "But then," he added, "I don't think I am really 'literary', nor are you either." I suggested that our literary sides were "bye-products". "Yes," he repeated, "bye-products."'[92]

A few days later in London Haggard spoke at his club Windham's 'peace dinner' on the British armed forces, and then at a Masonic dinner he 'dwelt on the atrocities of the Germans'.[93] On another evening he dined with Reginald Cheyne, his son-in-law, who came to 'say good bye before starting for India. He is grown deaf from ailments contracted in the trenches.'[94] The London streets were lit again at night. 'After more than four years of an abysmal darkness with the knowledge that often enough Death was floating overhead, I feel as though I should like to pass the rest of my days in a lake of light – as though night and day I could never be satisfied with brilliance.'[95]

At the request of Dennis Crane, 'a gentleman who runs Government propaganda', Haggard wrote an article in support of the coalition government in the coming general election. The outcome was a landslide victory for the government headed by David Lloyd George, who had replaced Asquith as prime minister in December 1916. Louie travelled alone to Ditchingham to cast her vote. 'I am afraid of the journey in this horrible damp, as it would probably bring back my bronchitis. I confess that I feel somewhat "out of it". It is galling when, whatever may be the case with the physical, one's mental qualities are as good or better than ever to feel a "dead letter" of no account.'[96] Such feelings most likely spurred him to go up to London on 18 December to attend a meeting of the Empire Land Settlement Committee, where he suggested the Royal Colonial Institute 'take the matter up privately and send me or some other person to the Dominions to see what can be done'.[97]

Christmas Day was spent with his daughter Dorothy, who was hosting a children's party 'where we played games. It was happy and yet sad to an old man. One remembers so many Christmas parties as far back as fifty years or more ago and oh! where are the children that played at them?'[98] Haggard cheered up two days later when informed he was to receive from His Majesty the rank of a knight commander of the Most Excellent Order of the British Empire (KBE). 'Of course, I am gratified, though what I have always wished to become is a Privy Councillor ... However one must not look a gift-horse in the mouth, and it is a recognition of my work for the Empire ... I hope sincerely too that it may lead to my being offered more honorary work to do before I grow too old for it.'[99]

31

'I SINK INTO OLD AGE'

In the New Year's honours list of 1919 Haggard received the KBE he had been informed was coming his way. Kipling sent a congratulatory note: 'I am glad to see you took it because if anyone was a Knight of the Empire – by land and sea and shipwreck – you're It!'[1]

The New Year found Haggard grappling with the 'Theory of the Universe' following the first experimental test of Albert Einstein's theory of relativity, published in 1915. Haggard attributed his lack of understanding to his 'dense stupidity' but noticed that when questioning his scientific friends on the matter 'they generally turn the conversation'.[2] Kipling was entirely dismissive of Einstein's theory, owing in part to his rabid anti-Semitism – 'another little contribution toward assisting the world towards flux and disintegration'.[3] Later in the year when Kipling came for lunch at North Lodge, he blamed 'all our Russian troubles, and many others, to the machinations of the Jews'. Haggard disagreed. 'I am inclined to think that one can insist too much on the Jew motive – the truth being that there are Jews and Jews ... For my part, I would be inclined to read Trade Unions instead of Jews, for surely they are the root of most of our embarrassments and perplexities.'[4]

Haggard suggested he, Kipling and the conservative author and cleric William Inge, the Dean of St Paul's, collectively write a letter to *The Times* 'setting out this Bolshevist business clearly and trying to arouse the country to a sense of all its horrors'. Kipling said he would mull it over but was afraid 'it would be set down as a "Northcliffe" stunt'.[5] Alfred Harmsworth, First Viscount Northcliffe, who founded the *Daily Mail* in 1896 and became owner of *The Times* in 1914, was well known for his press campaigns. Kipling was not alone in thinking them stunts.[6]

After the war Haggard's life fell into a repetitive pattern: May to October at Ditchingham, October to April wintering in warmer climes at St Leonards; train trips to London from either location to attend social events, deliver speeches, sit on committees and attend meetings of the Royal Colonial Institute. There were frequent meetings with Kipling and annual attendance at the royal garden party. Haggard's desire for public service remained, but while the spirit was willing, the flesh was weak, his physical energy and stamina being in decline. He continued writing fiction, including the prequel to *She*, *Wisdom's Daughter*, and four more Allan Quatermain adventures, *She and Allan*, *Heu-Heu, or, The Monster*, *The Treasure of the Lake* and *Allan and the Ice Gods*.[7]

The casualty lists of war had been taken down, but not so those of time. Deaths of relatives, friends and contemporaries feature regularly in Haggard's diary. In January 1919 Haggard was 'desolated' to learn of the death of Theodore Roosevelt from a pulmonary embolism, aged 60.[8] He was distressed 'both for myself, who have lost a friend, and for the world's sake'.[9] Kipling was also 'awfully heavy hearted ... He was the best friend we had out there and I can't see who takes his place.'[10]

Now in his sixties, Haggard thought of himself as an old man; post-war portraits, photographs and film footage show a frail figure. But there was nothing tentative about his opinions and he fully utilised his 'Isaiah-like gift of promiscuous fulmination'[11] in letters to friends and the press, as well as in his diary and many a public speech. But his voice was out of step with the times; conservative, often reactionary. Haggard's views coincided with those of the nationalist right in Britain and coloured his responses to political events in the last years of his life: including his 'anti-Bolshevik' activism, his criticism of contemporary art and poetry, his views on women and women's rights. In the post-war period Haggard was left bemused, disenchanted and alienated in uncharted waters. He remained a man of the late nineteenth century, the time of his greatest fame as a writer.

In the years leading up to his death his life is fragmented, with no clear direction shown: some committee work there, peripheral involvement with the film industry, opening or attending exhibitions, sitting on a variety of committees, even a suicide and a ghost story. But some themes can be separated from the tangle, such as his political involvement with the right.

In April 1919 Haggard met Sir Reginald Hall, Conservative MP and former Director of Naval Intelligence, and founder of the organisation National Propaganda committed to combating Bolshevism in Britain – a chimera that 'threatened the peace and troubled the dreams of Conservative souls'.[12] Out to counter anything 'subversive', National Propaganda (later renamed the Economic League) had been founded by Hall and a group of industrialists. Hall hoped Haggard would join their crusade, but the latter feared it would take up too much of his time: 'if only I could manage to live somehow, I would not grudge that if thereby I could help my country in this hour of peril'.[13]

Haggard met Hall's assistant, Captain Richard Kelly, to discuss 'anti-revolutionary propaganda and how it should be managed'. At the time a 'most poisonous leaflet ... aimed at the seduction of the Royal Navy', produced 'probably with German or Bolshevist money', was being 'left in lavatories in seaports'. A counter-leaflet was prepared, also 'to be left about in lavatories'.[14]

In January 1920 Haggard was invited by the editor of *The Times*, Henry Wickham Steed, to come and see him 'in connection with the Bolshevist peril'.[15] Also present was Lieutenant Colonel G. Maitland Edwards, a former member of the British headquarters staff attached to the Russian Army after the Revolution. Steed proceeded to unfold 'a mighty plan for fighting Bolshevism in this country by means of elaborate propaganda'. A council was to be formed, which the government would approve, and Haggard was invited to be its president. He declined, voicing his concern that this might be a 'Northcliffe stunt'. Steed assured him it wasn't and that 'there was the gravest uneasiness among capitalists about the advance of these doctrines and that any amount of money would be forthcoming to fight them'. Steed said the object of the council was to 'split the Labour Party in two and to separate the Constitutional sheep from the Bolshevist goats, one that is in my opinion perfectly legitimate and proper'.[16]

After a renewed invitation, Haggard agreed to be president of the Anti-Bolshevik League, renamed the Liberty League at his request, with Edwards as organiser and treasurer, and Captain Arthur de Courcy Bower as secretary. When Haggard asked whether he would 'have the unqualified support of *The Times*', Steed responded in the affirmative. 'Apparently all the money will be forthcoming and the impression left on my mind is that the real backer of the business is Lord Northcliffe.'[17]

A letter, drafted by Haggard, was published in *The Times* on 3 March announcing the foundation of the Liberty League, signed by, among others, Haggard, Kipling, Lord Sydenham, a former colonial administrator, Sir Henry Bax-Ironside, former ambassador to Bulgaria, Major General Sir John Hanbury-Williams, former head of the British military mission with the high command of the Russian armed forces, and Edwards. The letter described the aim of the League as combating 'the advance of Bolshevism in the United Kingdom and throughout the Empire'.[18] Readers were requested to send donations to Edwards at 17 Bruton Street, Mayfair. An editorial urging readers to support the initiative described Haggard as 'a man whose record of unostentatious political service needs no emphasis', and Kipling as a 'poet, seer ... patriot ... [and] national possession'.[19]

Less than two months after its founding and before there had even been a committee meeting, Haggard was informed that the Liberty League was in dire financial straits due to criminal activity. Haggard was reticent about what exactly happened: 'all men are not honest. However I hope not much harm has been done as luckily the business was discovered in time.'[20] At the first meeting of the League's committee on 29 April, Haggard explained 'the circumstances of the disastrous conspiracy of which we have been the victims'. A finance committee was appointed and the meeting adjourned to allow Steed to see Lord Northcliffe and 'ascertain what he is prepared to do, bearing in mind that our troubles are rooted in the action of *The Times*'.[21] By 7 May the Liberty League worries were 'overpowering ... We seem plunged in an atmosphere of deception or worse.' Haggard told Steed that if Lord

Northcliffe didn't come to their assistance, 'we must wind up the League'. Steed said *The Times* had acted in good faith.[22]

On 10 May Haggard received a letter from Northcliffe repudiating 'all that *The Times* has done about the Liberty League'.[23] Northcliffe said he had been away 'from England for nearly three months, and the name of the Liberty League was first brought under my notice on Friday last'. As for Bolshevism in England, in Northcliffe's opinion 'it does not exist. I presume I am in as close touch with Labour as any person in this country, for I have to deal with some 50 trade unions and I do not believe there is any more Bolshevism among them than there is at the Universities of Oxford and Cambridge.'[24] The Liberty League quietly merged with National Propaganda and disappeared from view. The financial scandal was suppressed.

Four years later, a news story in the *Daily Chronicle* on 15 September 1924 revealed, if not quite all, at least most of it. On the previous day Captain Arthur de Courcy Bower was fined for being drunk and disorderly and 'damaging a woman's dress by ink splashing in the West End' (a form of violence against women trending at the time), close to the London Hippodrome. Bower, according to a police witness, 'had a remarkable record', including breaking the bank at Monte Carlo by winning over £200,000. Once a wealthy man, he had become 'a great gambler, lost all his money, and then resorted to drink'. In 1904 he had served a period of imprisonment for a bankruptcy offence. The anonymous *Daily Chronicle* 'representative' said Bower's name would be recalled 'with mixed feelings by a number of eminent persons' and went on to detail the creation of the Liberty League and the role of Haggard as its president and the other signatories of the letter to *The Times*. The League's organiser, Maitland Edwards, had 'to go abroad on a special mission almost as soon as the formation of the League had been announced', leaving Bower 'in complete charge of its affairs'. He sent out appeals for financial aid to a long list of well-to-do people which 'elicited a big response'. All seemed set for success, but information came to light that 'caused consternation among Sir Rider Haggard and those identified with him'. A forensic audit of the organisation's finances revealed that in 'the two months of its existence the League had received donations amounting to over £2,500'. Bower had managed to pay this amount to himself using fraudulent cheques. By this time Bower had disappeared.[25]

There was a sequel. On 14 October 1924 Haggard attended a council meeting at the Royal Colonial Institute, where it was decided unanimously 'to strike the name of Colonel Maitland Edwards off the list of Fellows'. Edwards had involved the Institute in a settlement scheme that came to an end 'under circumstances strangely resembling those that marked the decease of the Liberty League'. He was assisted 'by two other persons whom he succeeded in persuading the Council to elect as Fellows of the Institute – with horrid results. The loss on this occasion, however, was heavier ... £6,000 or £8,000 have vanished.'[26]

From Bolshevism to the birth rate. In April 1919 Haggard was sitting alongside Marie Stopes on the National Birth Rate Commission, which was intended to address the dramatic decline in the birth rate among the British middle class. Though not totally opposed to birth control, Haggard was far from an advocate. In his view birth control by 'artificial means' saw women once more eating of 'the fruit of a forbidden Tree of Knowledge, but this time it was also a Tree of Death' and eating of its fruit led to 'race-suicide'.[27] Haggard claimed the 'maternal instinct was not highly developed in modern women', but though it was 'never intended that civilized woman should become but a breeding machine, and if able to do so without injury to her health, he believed a married woman should enrich the world by four or five children'.[28] He recommended a slew of state remedies, including subsidised motherhood and, as 'a desperate, ultimate resort', that the state undertake 'the care and the upbringing of all children according to their degree, even holding out a kind hand to those not born in wedlock'.[29]

A seat on a proposed royal commission to investigate 'the present crisis in agricultural matters' was better suited to his sphere of expertise. He approached Lord Ernle, the Board of Agriculture president, who said 'my name was one of the first that had occurred to him ... Whether I shall be nominated I cannot say, nor do I greatly care. At best the job would be anxious and responsible.'[30] He later learned he was not on the list of those chosen to serve; 'on the whole I daresay I am well out of it'.[31]

Haggard's advocacy of the overseas emigration of servicemen and surplus population continued. The activities of the Royal Colonial Institute's Empire Land Settlement Committee had led to the Emigration Bill of 1918, which proposed the creation of a Central Emigration Authority. The bill pleased neither its supporters nor the opponents of emigration and its withdrawal in October 1918 'seemed to herald a return to laissez-faire policies'.[32] But in January 1919 Lord Milner, long an advocate of imperial emigration, was appointed Colonial Secretary with Leo Amery as his undersecretary, and their combined impetus led to the creation of the Overseas Settlement Committee with Amery in the chair. The committee would work closely with the Institute.

Seeking new challenges, on 5 February 1919 Haggard took the train to London to see Amery to discuss 'the whole problem of emigration'. Amery was 'quite alive to its importance' and indicated the government wanted 'to make use of me in some capacity in connection therewith'.[33] Amery subsequently told Haggard he would be asked to serve if an advisory committee was set up on emigration.

Three years on, in February 1922, Haggard was a member of a deputation to Winston Churchill, then Colonial Secretary, concerning inter-imperial migration. Churchill had 'grown much more stout and solid than when I saw him last, and has a very large bullet-shaped head ... Somewhat to my astonishment, he knew me again and came to shake hands with me.'[34] Churchill 'promised all sorts of things in furtherance of the cause of Empire Migration', but Haggard doubted whether 'these would in fact ever be translated into performance under the present circumstances of the Government and the state of our national finances'.[35] However, a new bill was being drafted and at the end of April 1922 the Empire Settlement Bill was read for a second time in the House of Commons, 'putting migration from this country upon a sound, continuous basis. Although my share in the business is now forgotten, I look upon this advance with some pride since surely I have had some part in bringing it about.'[36]

On 6 April 1920 Haggard opened 'The South African Week' exhibition at the Albert Hall in London, a trade fair for 'South African products, including gold and other minerals, grain, hides, tobacco, ostrich feathers, &c. Cinematograph films depicting orange growing, diamond mining, and ostrich farming will be shown twice daily.' Other attractions included showings of the film version of *King Solomon's Mines*.[37] Haggard spoke of the 'great responsibilities of the producers of films which have such an enormous influence upon the young. Many of these films, especially those that come from America, I am convinced do much harm.'[38]

The previous year Haggard finally wreaked revenge on the American film-makers who had plundered his books without payment, winning 'after a year and a half of effort … £2000 of the amount due to me, or rather the amount on which we compromised from the American pirates, the Fox Company, for their purloining and exhibition of *Cleopatra*'.[39] Receiving damages for someone else's 'shameless plagiarism' must have been a sweet victory.[40]

In 1920 there was more talk of Haggard being plagiarised, this time in France. While visiting the First World War battlefields, Haggard heard about 'the *She* and *L'Atlantide* controversy'.[41] *L'Atlantide*, a fantasy novel by Pierre Benoit, published in February 1919, had been awarded the French Academy's Grand Prize. When Henry Magden writing in the *French Quarterly Review* accused Benoit of plagiarising *She*, Benoit sued for damages. He told the court the accusation was false as he neither read nor spoke English and at the time *She* had not been translated into French. He lost the case and had to pay costs.[42]

The visit to the battlefields took place in October 1920, when Haggard accompanied Louie, Jessie Hartcup and his niece Joan Haggard, Jack's daughter, whose fiancé had died in the war. In Belgium they stayed at the Hotel de Flandre in Bruges and on 11 October the party drove around the nearby battlefields.

First we went to Passchendaele and found the new British Cemetery there, which I was told contained 4000 graves: at any rate there are a vast number … In Plot 8, Row A, Grave No. 19 lie the remains of my nephew and godson Lance. On his grave lay two pieces of rusted shell. I took one of these and Joan took the other. Afterwards it occurred to me that these might be the missiles which caused his death. I wish to see no more battlefields.[43]

The same month *L'Atlantide* was published in English translation under the title *Queen of Atlantis*. Haggard and Louie saw the film version of the book in February 1923. As well as being reminiscent of *She*, it also bore similarities in Haggard's opinion to *The Yellow God* – 'all I can say is that the coincidences are very remarkable' and consequently 'a film of *The Yellow God* would probably now be impossible'.[44] Fortunately this was not the case with Haggard's other books. In 1921 H. Lisle Lucoque, now operating under the banner of Reciprocity Films, formed another partnership with I.W. Schlesinger's African Film Productions to make a film of Haggard's novel *Swallow*. The film, which departed completely from the original story, was directed by Leander de Cordova, a colleague of Lucoque's, and was released in 1921.

In April 1921 came the release of *Stella*, the film version of *Stella Fregelius*, starring Molly Adair and H. Manning Haynes. Haggard doesn't appear to have seen the film, though he did read *The Times* review, which drew attention to the 'terrible anti-climax' of the happy ending – there is an unhappy one in the book.[45] He also had a private viewing of the Italian film of *Beatrice*: for 'an author the experience as usual is somewhat heart-breaking'.[46] He questioned why a 'poverty-stricken Welsh clergyman' should be represented as inhabiting a costly palace from the upkeep of which an archbishop would blench' and why the book's hero, Geoffrey, 'getting on for forty with a powerful legal stamp of face, be impersonated by an oily-haired person of about 22'.[47]

Although he reaped its profits, Haggard was no fan of the film industry. In September 1921 he complained that the 'Press of England seems literally to have gone mad over the cinema star, Charlie Chaplin, and so have other people'.[48] Chaplin was welcomed on arrival at Southampton by the port city's mayor and 'hideous pictures' were published of 'this very undistinguished-looking person, surrounded by crowds with folly stamped on every face'.[49] Even *The Times* joined in the adulation, running a leading article under the headline 'A Clown of Genius'. Haggard was not amused, considering of weightier interest the death of Sir Peter Freyer, 'a great surgeon and a great benefactor of the human race, which owes to him the operation on the prostate gland and the prevention of much misery'. Freyer didn't get an editorial but 'only a short notice in small type. However he takes with him into the grave the gratitude of thousands.'[50] Given the silence around some of his own clinical conditions, possibly Haggard was among them.

On 27 July 1923 a day after attending the royal garden party, Haggard went to the Wardour Street offices of the newsreel and documentary production house Pathé News to see the footage filmed of him in the gardens at Ditchingham two weeks previously. 'It was very good, especially of my poor old spaniel, Jeekie, but as the bright sunlight seemed to turn my hair snow-white, it made me look even older than I am.'[51]

The war had wrought great societal upheaval in Britain, and Haggard was not immune. On returning to Ditchingham in May 1919 after wintering on the south coast, he encountered problems with the servants, or rather the lack of them. 'The domestic servant question is becoming most difficult in England. The women will not go into service, and when they make an engagement often do not keep it.'[52]

Adding to his woes, Kessingland Grange was in a ruinous state following its wartime occupation by the military. The damage was such that unless he received adequate compensation, Haggard thought demolition might be the better option. The cost of repair was estimated to be £492.8s.8d. Haggard was offered 'about half by Government'. He objected to no avail and so wrote to the member of parliament for Lowestoft, intimating that he 'thought of publishing my moving tale in *The Times*'. Negotiations were 'mysteriously reopened and to save further trouble and worry I have been advised to accept an offer of £429.15.11, in satisfaction of all claims'. He was still out of pocket, 'but on the whole I think myself fortunate to have got so much'.[53] Haggard cut his losses elsewhere by selling his two remaining farms at North Walsham, making £600 more than the reserve – about £20 per acre. 'I am glad to be rid of them as all property has become a burden nowadays.'[54]

In late September a national strike was called in response to Lloyd George's government's attempt to impose wage reductions on the railwaymen. Haggard was in London at the time, obliged to walk the pavements at one stage because the buses were full and there were long bus queues. The 'streets presented an extraordinary sight with thousands of pedestrians thronging the roadway and making dashes for every passing bus off which they were pushed again by the conductors'. He believed the 'hardship and inconvenience' inflicted by the strike would 'turn the country against the strikers ... So long as one class paid for everything, the masses did not mind, but when directly they have to bear their share of the trouble and contribute their quota of the blackmail, it may be a different story.'[55] The strike ended on 6 October.

On 13 October 1919 Haggard was back at St Leonards for the winter, but there was no escaping the servant problem. Parnell, an ex-soldier engaged nine months earlier as an odd-job man, left without notice 'and then returned to ask for his wages and saying that the work was "too hard for him"' while the man 'who used to come in the morning cannot return because he "has signed on with the Unemployment Office"'.[56] Three servants remained, one each for Haggard, Louie and another resident at North Lodge, possibly Ida Hector.

Haggard maintained his lifelong interest in the supernatural in correspondence with the physicist and Christian spiritualist Oliver Lodge.[57] In January 1919 in nearby Hastings, he and Louie attended a lecture by Arthur Conan Doyle, well launched on his post-war spiritualist crusade. The Doyles came to supper at North Lodge. 'What he told us, both at the lecture and privately, was interesting but I cannot say that it carried much conviction to my mind. It may all be true, but "the spirits" seem to be singularly reticent upon many important points.'[58]

In November 1919 Haggard was shocked to read his 'dear friend' the Reverend Philip Bainbrigge, 'from whom I have received more spiritual help and comfort than from anyone else in my lifetime', had died. Haggard had last seen him after a service a month before, when he said he 'was much worried about many things, financial and others, and that it seemed to him he "could do nothing right"'. Haggard offered to help and they agreed to lunch at the Athenaeum later in the week, but Bainbrigge cried off as his doctor 'had ordered him away at once'.[59]

A year after Bainbrigge's death Haggard received a letter from Mrs Bainbrigge saying her husband's ghost had been seen by the Reverend Clarence May, a curate at St Thomas's Church, 'coming out of the little chapel where the Reserved Sacrament was and, it seems, still is kept'. It was suggested the appearance may have been connected with the current vicar's intention to remove the Reserved Sacrament.[60] Haggard met May and the sacristan at St Thomas's and took their statements. 'There seems to be little doubt that he *did* appear.'[61] He was 'inclined to think that this manifestation, partly in the nature of the appearance of a shadow, haunting a place with which the Earthly interest of the personality was identified, something after the Egyptian Ka, were real'.[62]

The casualty lists of time continued. 'Shakespeare talks of "troops of friends" as an accompaniment of age, but mine are nearly all gone ...'[63] On 18 September 1920 there was the death of Egerton Castle, a stalwart member of the Society of Authors, who, with 'the exception of Edmund Gosse' and Haggard himself, was the last 'of the group of us who used to lunch together on Saturdays at the Savile Club between 1886 and 1890. Now from Besant and Lang down, all, or nearly all, have gone.'[64] There were few people now living who knew Haggard when he began writing. 'Indeed as Arthur Cochrane, who has been staying here on his return from one of his periodical visits to South Africa, and I were saying yesterday, hardly any whom we knew in our youth remain; we have almost no surviving friends.'[65]

In January 1922 Haggard went to the private viewing of 'the works of recently deceased R.A.s' at the Royal Academy in Piccadilly, among them Sir William Blake Richmond's portrait of Haggard's friend and co-author, Andrew Lang, the 'picture which pleased me most to see again'.[66] Haggard was a regular at private viewings of the annual summer exhibition at the Academy, and the previous year his near-life-size portrait by Maurice Greiffenhagen was hung in a prominent position in Room III. Not wishing to appear self-obsessed, he 'did not venture near enough to examine it closely' but noted in his diary that all 'the Academicians rave about it'. Haggard thought it 'an imposing work of art, though melancholy', Greiffenhagen having made 'the most of my wrinkles ... I never set up for a beauty, but this picture with its harshness and accentuated realism will give posterity a queer side of my appearance at my present age. There was a crowd round it all day.'[67] In the portrait Haggard looks directly at the viewer, his gaze invested with bleak sadness, perhaps reflecting Greiffenhagen's loss of his son in the war as much as Haggard's world-weariness and depression. 'D'Abernon does not like it and it horrified Lilias.'[68]

In March 1922 the Italian painter and sculptor Francesco La Monaca produced a bust of Haggard, part of his exhibition at the Bromhead, Cutts and Company's Fine Art Gallery, 18 Cork Street, featuring thirty-four busts in bronze and marble of eminent English figures of the time, including George Bernard Shaw, Sybil Thorndike, and Randall Davidson, the Archbishop of Canterbury. According to Haggard, 'most judges' thought the bust 'a fine and vital work of art'.[69] Otherwise Haggard was silent: Monaca's style was uncomfortably close to that of Jacob Epstein, whose work he did not admire.[70]

On 29 March 1921 Haggard's 'dearest sister' Ella Maddison Green, who had opened his 'childish eyes' to 'the blessed kingdom of Romance'[71] and who was eldest of the Haggard siblings, died suddenly of a heart attack at the age of 75.

In May 1923 Haggard went down to St Leonards (the Haggards had left the place for the summer in mid-April) to visit his brother Andrew, who was dying. Andrew and his wife Ethel had been living in Paygate, the small cottage attached to North Lodge, since returning from Canada in 1920. Haggard was saddened to see 'one who all his life till late years has been full of vigour, reduced to such a state, literally coughing himself to death with chronic bronchitis, to say nothing of other complaints'. Haggard thought it better 'he should pass away than continue to suffer so much'.[72] Haggard was back at Ditchingham when Andrew died on 13 May. He praised his brother's record as a soldier and 'his many books on French history for which he had an extraordinary flair'. A study of Victor Hugo had been published a few weeks before his death. 'Very glad am I to have been able to free his last years from anxiety of a certain sort.'[73] Andrew had 'a more or less military funeral' at St Leonards on 17 May, but Haggard was not well enough to attend.

Despite lamenting the death of relatives and friends, Haggard made a new friend in Ronald Ross, discoverer of the malarial parasite and winner of the Nobel Prize in Medicine in 1902. Haggard and Ross had been in correspondence with each other since 1905. 'He is an able and many-sided man, and once he wrote an admirable romance, now out of print, called *The Child of Ocean*. I wrote to congratulate him upon it and that is how our epistolary connection came about.'[74] They first met in person in March 1917 when Haggard went to Hampstead to a reading of Ross's poetry at Inverforth House. This marked the beginning of a friendship centred on their mutual enthusiasm for fishing, the one blood sport Haggard permitted himself.

Haggard's health continued fragile. In May 1921, two days after returning to Ditchingham, Haggard was 'thoroughly overhauled by the doctor', who found 'nothing organically wrong with me but says I am slack and run down in every way, and must take things quietly without hammering about. I suppose the truth is that age has got a grip of me; we all wear out at last and therefore I must not complain.'[75]

The onset of winter brought on Haggard's usual afflictions, including a 'bad attack of gout with unpleasing complications, which makes sleep difficult and walking an agony'.[76] In early November, up in London to attend a meeting of the Empire Land Settlement Committee of the Royal Colonial Institute and en route to St Leonards for the winter, Haggard was examined by Sir Thomas Horder, physician to the King, who didn't 'find much seriously wrong with me – nothing organic so far as he can discover'.[77]

For the next two years Haggard underwent a regimen of biannual injections 'for my bronchial ailments and leg trouble' by Dr Archibald Cowan Guthrie at his rooms in Harley Street.[78] In November 1922, in London for another round of injections, he read that Kipling was going into a nursing home for an operation. Haggard was 'in the dark as to what is or was the matter with him'.[79] On 13 December he visited a recuperating Kipling at Bateman's and found 'him infinitely better than expected'; the cause of the operation was not cancer as feared 'but simply due to some constriction inside'.[80]

Attendance at the royal garden party at Buckingham Palace in the summer was an annual ritual. That of July 1921 turned out to be an 'agreeable entertainment' with the 'weather not too hot and very fine'. There were thousands of guests 'including many of the most distinguished in the land' wandering 'about the sun-scorched grounds'.[81] Haggard spent much of the afternoon hunting through the crowd trying to find Louie (she was coming later from a wedding), rather like 'Orpheus hunting Hades for Eurydice. It was quite useless. I never found her.' He found refuge chatting to Kipling, who enthused about the 'War Diaries' and said he wished Haggard would make him his literary executor 'with discretion to publish such portions of it as he wished (I suppose that rightly he expects to live much longer than I shall)'.[82]

Prior to the event in 1922 Haggard went to English's, the hatters, to have his top hat 'ironed up'. Its age raised doubts, but after closer inspection it was proclaimed serviceable. 'Lord! Sir Rider. We have had some relics in here this morning!'[83] Haggard attended the garden party with Louie and Lilias, along with some 5,000 others 'wandering about the Palace grounds, all the women in their best'.[84] He thought the women of the Victorian era more beautiful, crediting this response to his age and the change in fashions. The following year Haggard's sentiments were much the same: 'Of course it may be one of the illusions which we develop in age, but certainly I think the ladies of forty years ago were as a whole both better-looking and fresher in their air.'[85]

En route to St Leonards in the autumn of 1923 Haggard and Louie attended a royal afternoon party in the Palace chambers. They chatted with Edmund Gosse and his wife – 'really, he is a wondrous evergreen'. He saw Winston Churchill in the crowd. The first volume (there would be six) of Churchill's account of the First World War, *The World Crisis*, had just been published, exciting 'much comment, not all of it complimentary, indeed I see the *Daily Herald* says outright that it makes his further employment as a minister impossible'.[86] Churchill looked 'worn and much older'.[87]

Lower down the social register on the annual calendar was the Fur, Feather and Vegetable Show, held on the front lawn of Ditchingham House, 'a small local function organised by Lilias' which became 'an annual fixture in south Norfolk'.[88]

On 22 June 1922 Haggard recorded his sixty-sixth birthday: 'I am now quite an old man.'[89] Arthur Cochrane forgot the birthday and wrote two weeks later, having just 'dipped my pen into the inkpot made from one of old Moresco's hoofs', which brought back memories of their time in Pretoria and Newcastle. Cochrane blamed his forgetfulness on being

> hard at work chasing the elusive guineas needed to keep the bodies of my wife, self and family in being whilst we are on the globe ... I wonder how long the road is for you and I, and who shall see the end of it first. This beastly weather brings one down to the realities of life, but I suppose we shall have a few warm days before the winter with its darkness comes upon us. The place to live in is *Africa*.[90]

On 20 August 1922 Haggard and his brother Arthur 'motored to Bradenham'[91] to visit St Andrew's Church and see the litany stool presented by Haggard and Louie in memory of their three nephews killed in the war. Haggard 'was glad to see this church again which I have known from infancy and to occupy the pew where I have often sat with my mother'.[92] The church was unchanged. 'The same bees hive in the roof, the same red carpets stamped with a *fleur de lys* are on the chancel floor.'[93]

Arthur wanted to visit Bradenham Hall, Haggard didn't, but Arthur prevailed and, as Haggard feared, he found the place 'a wilderness and a desolation'. He had been right about the estate being bought by a speculator:

> All the trees in the plantation have been felled; even the oak planted to commemorate my father's and mother's marriage has been hacked down ... I went over the empty rooms of the house where the places upon which well-remembered pictures hung are shown by marks on the wall. It was a melancholy experience and those empty, echoing rooms offered a strange and indeed a terrible contrast to what they were as I remember them, filled with the life and noise of young people, most of them now dead, and with my father's voice ringing through the house.[94]

At the end of the year, Christmas at St Leonards – 'no joyous festival to the old' – prompted memories of Haggard's childhood Christmases at Bradenham Hall and 'the throng of merry youngsters – brothers and sisters, nine of them, most of whom are dead – twisting the holly garlands to decorate the oak of rooms that today are the home of the spider and the bat. Where are they now? A few remain, bent, scarred and weary from struggling with the world, while the rest are dust – like the holly wreaths they wove. And whither they have gone we follow apace.'[95]

St Leonards might be an agreeable winter refuge, but it wasn't virus proof, and in early March 1923 Haggard and Louie fled to London, driven away 'by the influenza. First the housemaid got it and now the cook is down with worse symptoms and I think the parlour maid looks queer.' Haggard went to Garland's Hotel and Louie to the Empress Club. 'It is a great nuisance and of course puts a stop to my book.'[96] He was writing another Allan Quatermain adventure, *Heu-Heu, or, The Monster*. While in London, *Wisdom's Daughter*, the prequel to *She*, was published on 9 March.[97]

At Garland's, Haggard was 'laid by the heels ... by a sharp attack of gout and the doctor tells me that henceforward practically I should become a teetotaller, which is not cheering'.[98] The attack lasted several days and on 12 March, with 'the help of sticks, cabmen and porters', Haggard limped back to St Leonards, in the hope the influenza had departed, 'thus finishing a somewhat disastrous and expensive trip to London'.[99] Ronald Ross commiserated on the gout but assured Haggard he wouldn't 'find teetotalling unpleasant: I am always much more cheerful and energetic when dry – like gunpowder'. Ross had just read *Wisdom's Daughter*: 'the great thing in this book, to my mind, and indeed all the Ayesha books is the character of that lady – it is at once human, feminine, and yet Olympic. She is a *figure*: she stamps herself on one's memory once for all.'[100]

Haggard spent 20 March at Bateman's. With Haggard recovering from his gout and Kipling 'suffering from sundry minor consequential troubles' from another operation, 'we were a pretty pair of old crocks, I lying with my leg on the couch in his study and he bending over the fire'.[101] They read and discussed *Wisdom's Daughter*. Kipling thought it '------ good prose ... "a philosophy of life" and an epitome of all the deeper part of my work'.[102] Kipling was convinced the book 'represented the whole sum and substance of your convictions along certain lines' and thought Haggard should 'take the whole book up again for your own personal satisfaction – and go through it from that point of view'. This was not for literary reasons, 'but as a means of re-stating and amplifying your ideas and convictions through the mouth of your chief character [Ayesha narrates *Wisdom's Daughter*] ... Damn it man – you have the whole tragedy of the mystery of life under your hand, why not frame it in a wider setting?'

Haggard agreed that *Wisdom's Daughter* contained some of his philosophy: 'The Eternal War between the Flesh and the Spirit, the eternal loneliness and search for unity.' But he didn't think he could attempt 'the mystery of life' with Ayesha, 'unless I scrapped everything concerning her and began afresh, which can't be done'.[103] He proposed instead the Wandering Jew as the vehicle for his ideas over several volumes – 'how about the fight of the Norse Gods against the White Christ for one. The plot of Germany against the world with the rise of Bolshevism for another (the last). The Crusades for one perhaps.'[104] Kipling responded, saying his friend wasn't 'choosing any small canvas for your latter years to expiate in, are you, when you turn your mind towards the Jew'.[105] He went on to sketch an outline for a trilogy – 'Kipling's vivid and merciless imagination painting in a few swift words scene after scene'.[106]

In December Haggard let the house at St Leonards prior to going to Egypt with Lilias early in the New Year. The festive season was spent at Ditchingham, and on Christmas morning the family walked to St Mary's. The weather 'was frosty and beautiful and the walking good'. There was 'a small congregation ... largely composed of what are called the "gentry". I wonder what proportion of the inhabitants of this land continues to take any *genuine* interest in the Christian religion ... I wonder who will go to church at Ditchingham on Xmas Day 2223 and to worship at what altars.'[107]

32

'OLD PHARAOH'

Howard Carter 'has made a marvellous discovery in the Valley of the Kings at Thebes ... a sealed cache of several chambers full of all the funeral furniture, also the chariots and throne of Pharaoh Tutankhamen'.[1] When Carter's momentous find was announced in November 1922, Haggard contacted *The Times* about going to Egypt 'to write about this business', but the newspaper already had a journalist on the spot and Haggard conceded he was unsuited to the 'complicated system of news dissemination'[2] now involved in covering a major news story. The discovery aroused huge interest and Lord Carnarvon, Carter's patron and partner, feared constant press attention would hamper their work, so when *The Times* proposed an exclusive arrangement, Carnarvon accepted.[3] He had misjudged the near-hysterical public interest and there was furious protest from other newspapers, not least the Egyptian press, which understandably felt a sense of ownership. Carnarvon's and Carter's relationship with the press was permanently soured.

Five months after the tomb was opened, Lord Carnarvon died at the Continental Hotel in Cairo. Already in poor health, his body was unable to cope when pneumonia set in after a mosquito bite on his cheek turned septic. Even before his death, the idea of a mummy's curse was being bandied about, and Haggard received a telegram from the *New York World* asking for his opinion on the 'efficacy of magical curses against despoilers placed around ancient mummies' apropos Lord Carnarvon's illness.[4] Haggard had no intention of making a 'public fool' of himself by replying and, when Carnarvon died on 5 April, he acknowledged there would 'be a lot of foolish talk about magical influences directed by the Ka of the indignant Pharaoh into whose rest he had broken'. Haggard couldn't resist his own explanation: as Carnarvon was one of the first to enter the tomb in the absence of disinfection or time for 'the air to purify', if he 'had any abrasion, some evil germ may have attacked him there'.[5] Haggard broached the subject in a talk on 'Ancient Egypt' given to the Rotarians in Hastings. Paying tribute to Carnarvon, he said stories that his death had been brought about 'by magic' were 'nonsense, and dangerous nonsense'. As a Christian, one could not believe that God would permit a dead Pharaoh 'to murder people by magical means thousands of years after his own death'.[6]

Inspired by the Tutankhamun discovery, Haggard invited Ronald Ross to join him on a trip to Egypt in the new year. Ross declined, being 'engrossed in my mathematics and my book on operative analysis'.[7] On 10 January 1924 Haggard and Lilias sailed for Egypt aboard the P&O's SS *Malwa* on the Tilbury–Australia run 'with a party of friends and relations'.[8] The sea route to Egypt was chosen 'in the hope of providing a bracing and restorative environment'.[9] The Bay of Biscay obligingly brewed up a storm and the *Malwa* sailed into 'head gales and violent seas which did us some damage'.[10] Storms notwithstanding, the choice was the right one as Haggard's spirits 'rose every day they travelled eastwards. Anxieties and depressions were laid aside, his health improved, and he was, as always, an extraordinarily amusing companion.'[11]

As well as Lilias, Haggard's party included his niece Joan Haggard and Helena Rotenberg, 'a middle-aged matron and family friend'.[12] Others were to join the group in Cairo prior to sailing down the Nile to Luxor and returning to Cairo for a week or two before travelling on to Palestine. At the end of a passage 'extremely cold with much rain',[13] the *Malwa* docked at Port Said on the morning of 23 January and the party travelled by train to Cairo, where they stayed for one night at the Continental Hotel in the Place de l'Opéra overlooking the Ezbekiyyeh Gardens. Here they met up with the rest of the party, including Evelyn Samuel, Ralph Calvert, Percy Calvert, brother of Emily Haggard, Arthur Haggard's wife, and Arthur's son Geoffrey and his wife Mardie, fresh from their honeymoon in Naples.

Since Haggard's last visit in 1912 Britain had granted Egypt independence. As a consequence, the future of excavations at the Valley of the Kings hung in the balance. The excavation was a whirlpool of clashing interests: political, academic and archaeological – Britain, France, the United States and Egypt itself all clamouring for control over monuments and artefacts. The row threatened 'not only the progress of Carter's enterprise, but also the future of archaeological work in Egypt generally'.[14] Carter continued clearing and cataloguing the items of Tutankhamun's tomb on the basis that Carnarvon's concession remained in force until November 1924.

After a night at the Continental, the Haggard party steamed down the Nile on the SS *Victoria*, visiting tombs and temples 'much as I did 36 years ago'.[15] On the donkey ride from the steamer to the ruins of Abydos, Haggard noticed men armed with rifles 'stationed every mile or so' for 'the protection of our party', he was told. 'If so it looks to me as though interference with foreign travellers were considered quite possible in the Egypt of today!'[16]

Luxor was the scene of a 'curious little incident', recounted by Lilias. A fortune-teller came aboard the *Victoria*, 'a high-class Arab wearing the green turban which denoted that he had made the pilgrimage to Mecca'. He sat down on the deck and poured out from a bag 'a little pile of silver sand, smoothed it flat and with the aid of various dots and lines drawn with his finger on the surface, proceeded to tell the fortunes of the chattering crowd which gathered round. Rider stood behind him watching.' Haggard's experiences with sangomas in southern Africa had led him to 'respect their powers of divination' – and to keep his distance. When it was Geoffrey Haggard's turn to have his fortune told, Haggard murmured:

> 'Leave the man alone, my boy – you may hear something you don't like.' The Arab caught the tone if not the sense of the words, and suddenly swept his hand across the sand, wiping out the little maze of lines he had been tracing. Then he looked up at Rider – the evening sun pouring in across the covered deck, lighting the harsh, dark face which reflected a sudden malignancy – and said in a low voice: 'You call me a common cheat – is it not so? – Then what of the son whom you always think?'

Haggard made no comment 'but walked away and stood looking out over the river to where the road ran over the desert to the Valley of the Kings. That mysterious rocky cliff where lay the tombs of Egypt's Pharaohs.'[17]

By the time the party reached Luxor the stresses and strains of group travel were making themselves felt: donkey rides had jarred Haggard's spine and Percy Calvert's backside having been rubbed raw he now had to be conveyed in a carriage or use Haggard's blow-up boat cushion. Lilias and Joan lamented the 'lack of chocolates and the insufficiency of the tea',[18] while Geoffrey's wife Mardie was sullen and silent – 'everybody has given up trying to talk to her'.[19] Petty squabbling broke out.

Howard Carter invited Haggard and Lilias to see Tutankhamun's tomb. Haggard thought the burial chamber 'small and, for a Pharaoh, rather a mean tomb and the paintings on the burial chambers seem to have been hastily and poorly executed'. However, the gilt shrines 'are wonderful, and the gold on them glitters as though it were laid on yesterday'.[20] By way of contrast Carter was 'very worn and tired ... he is much harassed by his continual row with the Egyptian Government'.[21]

The trip to Palestine was abandoned as too expensive and it was decided to spend a longer time in Cairo, from where Haggard and Lilias would return to Luxor for a fortnight, the climate there being 'charming – warm and genial'.[22] The change of plan caused further rifts among the party – a comedy of manners, which Haggard outlined in a letter to Louie, concluding: 'Women are very odd fish!'[23]

Haggard was oppressed by the crowds of tourists in Egypt but, thankfully, it was 'still possible to separate oneself' from them, as he did on the return journey to Cairo, sitting alone in the pillared hall of a temple at Abydos

> in the silence that was broken only by the hum of bees that hive upon the wall and the twitter of the building birds. Everywhere soared great columns as firmly set as when Seti looked upon them, and saw that they were good. Everywhere rose the sculptured walls where kings made offerings to painted gods, or goddesses led them by the hand

into some holy presence ... Surely such a spot should be holy if there is aught so upon the earth.[24]

Cairo was much changed since Haggard's last visit: 'one everlasting hooting of motor-horns, varied by the shouts and songs of political processions. Inside the hotel a cosmopolitan crowd chatters and brays continually; in short, there is no peace.'[25]

Again staying at the Continental, the younger members of the party were up for a good time: Joan, Geoff and Mardie went on several nights to the Cairo Music Hall and on another to a hotel dance. Joan bumped into an old friend, one George, and they dined together every evening followed by dancing and night clubs. Joan fell out with Evelyn Samuel, who had her eye on Ralph Calvert. At dinner one evening Haggard witnessed Joan lash out verbally at Evelyn. 'That tongue of hers will land her in a law court one day, for, like her father [Jack], she can be pretty venomous and says things that can't be put on paper.'[26] According to the gossip, Evelyn Samuel continued to pursue Ralph Calvert and anyone else in trousers. 'These women are so different to what women used to be – of romance there is none, of other things too much. Dignity too is utterly lacking.'[27]

On 14 February Geoff and Mardie left for Ceylon and married life in the Empire. Haggard was surprised when the previously mute Mardie 'said goodbye to me with a good deal of affection last night, embracing me warmly – although she has scarcely spoken to me on the voyage. A queer child! Geoff too is queer – like most of our breed.'[28]

Escaping the noise, dust and demands for baksheesh in Cairo, Haggard and Lilias left for Luxor by train with Helena Rotenberg and Evelyn Samuel. 'The change to this hotel with its ancient, peaceful garden full of tall palms and birds, is complete and most welcome.' On the evening of 20 February they 'rode on donkeys to see the temples of Karnac in the light of the full moon – just as I did in 1887 with others, nearly all of whom are now dead. It is a wondrous sight ... one of the most solemn and beautiful in the whole world.'[29]

Alas, even Luxor was not what it used to be. 'Floods of Americans touring in shiploads invade the hotels and make them dreadful, so that one must fly to one's bedroom. The costumes they wear are often strange and, indeed, in the case of stout, elderly women, sometimes to my old-fashioned tastes, positively indecent.'[30] The time in Luxor was also 'much interfered with'[31] by Lilias coming down with influenza, much to Haggard's concern, 'though it always seems to be my lot when I take my daughters abroad to have them go sick'. Lilias would not allow her father into her room for fear she was infectious. 'Helena however, who says she is flu proof, looks after her well: – indeed Helena is a dear.'[32]

The party returned to Cairo at the beginning of March, booking into the Mena House hotel, where Haggard had stayed with Angela in 1912: still a 'charming place and restful compared to most in Egypt'. Haggard enjoyed sitting in his room watching 'the mighty mass of the great Pyramid, gradually devoured of the night ... by degrees till it becomes but a blacker blot upon the blackness. Then it is gone, yet being gone, its presence is still felt, something palpable lost to the eye.'[33]

On Saturday, 15 March, on a final shopping expedition in Cairo on their way to Port Said, the city was 'crowded with thousands of people in a state of great excitement owing to the opening of the first independent parliament by the Egyptian King, indeed we had to reach the station by a roundabout route, as many of the roads were blocked.'[34] At dawn on Monday, aboard the steam passenger ship *Yorkshire*, Haggard bade farewell to Egypt, as he did not expect to go there again, nor did he wish to do so: 'for the country has changed much since I first knew it. If the old Pharaohs and their courts and people could behold it now in all its hateful and brazen vulgarity, I think they would go mad! ... Only those with sufficient imagination and powers of abstraction to enable them to withdraw from the present, to forget what they see and bury themselves in the depths of the dead past, should dare to visit them.'[35]

Haggard was 'very glad to be home again' at Ditchingham in early April, no longer enjoying 'foreign travel as I did in years bygone and hat[ing] continuous packing and movement from place to place, as is common in those who grow old even in this restless age.'[36] Advancing years didn't prevent him from writing to Lord Curzon, asking to serve on a committee being set up 'to consider problems connected with Eastern Africa'. When the Colonial Office approached him in June, he said he would 'be honoured to serve in any capacity that may be desired.'[37] Privately he hoped his age would prevent him from being sent abroad. The committee was to investigate the possible union in East Africa of Kenya, Uganda and Tanganyika. As with South Africa's union, this meant juggling the interests of the indigenous populations and Indian immigrants with those of the European settlers. Haggard attended the first meeting of the East African Committee chaired by Sir Hilton Young; 'the inquiry promises to be interesting, also I fear long.'[38] The inquiry outlived him, finally issuing a report in 1929 concluding 'that any drastic changes would be premature' and that the passage of time would see a 'much closer association' develop 'between the East African territories.'[39]

On 23 April Haggard and Louie went to a neighbour who had installed a 'wireless broadcasting set' – the British Broadcasting Corporation had begun broadcasting in November 1922 – and sat around the radio wearing headphones listening to the King open the British Empire Exhibition at Wembley, the first radio broadcast by a reigning monarch. Haggard heard the Prince of Wales fairly well and 'several times I caught the words "your Empire" but of the King's reply I could distinguish little, except an allusion to the "unfavourable weather". Still that is marvellous enough, or would have been held so when I was a boy.'[40]

A month later Haggard and Louie attended the exhibition – 'the most ambitious show of its kind ever staged.'[41] Part shrine, part shop window, the exhibition was a massive trade fair showcasing the fifty-eight countries constituting an Empire 'of four hundred million people and covering fourteen million square miles'.[42] The Empire Stadium and surrounding concrete pavilions and 'palaces' dedicated to the arts, engineering and other assorted industries were constructed over an area of 220 acres. Kipling advised on the naming of the streets and avenues, and buildings were designed to reflect their exhibits and exhibitors: the South African pavilion was built in Cape Dutch style, while Australia opted for imperial neoclassical. The Canadian pavilion boasted a Prince of Wales sculpted in Canadian butter. Howard Carter went to court over the use of copyrighted material in the construction of a facsimile recreation of the tomb of Tutankhamun.[43] On 26 April the Football Association cup final kicked off at the Empire Stadium, which was built in a blend of Mughal and Roman architectural styles. Newcastle United beat Aston Villa 2–0 in the first cup final played in what would become known as Wembley Stadium.

Haggard thought the exhibition and its setting 'a wonderful place, though tiring and hard to get at'.[44] The head of the South African Publicity Service 'enabled us to get into the South African pavilion and examine it quietly when the public was shut out, because the King and Queen with the Italian Royal Party were to go over it a little later'.[45] Unknown to Haggard, James Stuart was present working behind the scenes. Stuart had married in 1916 and in the same year accompanied the South African Native Labour Corps to France. He returned to South Africa in 1917, continuing to build up his archive of oral evidence until 1922, when he and his wife Ellen moved to England. Stuart's reputation as a 'native expert' saw him in charge of the Zulu section of the Aldershot pageant and, when the Zulu *imbongi* (praise singer) succumbed to stage fright at the Wembley Empire Exhibition, Stuart put on 'black-face' and took his place – a deception that went undiscovered.[46]

On 22 June Haggard marked his sixty-eighth birthday, as did the newspapers: 'Their interest in an individual seems to increase as he grows older. It is, I think, of a sporting sort, because the public is supposed to be astonished that one is alive.'[47] Haggard was alive enough to produce two books during the course of the year, both set in ancient Egypt: *Queen of the Dawn*, published in April 1925, and *Belshazzar*, published posthumously in 1930.

In October, again in London, Haggard chaired the Authors' Club dinner for Sir Joseph Cook, the High Commissioner for Australia, where he received a 'warm, and I might say, almost affectionate reception, who am one of the original members that is now entering on its thirty-fourth year'.[48] On 14 October he lunched at the Athenaeum with Kipling, who 'pointed out to me that in the *Book of Revelation* it is prophesied that the Beast will only be allowed to dominate a third of the earth and that Bolshevist Russia already occupied a fifth of the third so that there would not be very much more left to go mad and bad, begging me to consult the Bible on which he was good as to believe me an authority! I propose to do so tonight.'[49]

Haggard had barely arrived back at Ditchingham when he received a wire from Stoll Pictures 'requesting me to be in Town by *11 tomorrow morning!*' to see the

Austrian film version of *Moon of Israel* – entitled *Die Sklavenkönigin*, (The Queen of the Slaves) – 'after informing me yesterday that it could not be seen for another fortnight.'[50] Haggard was required to rewrite the inter-titles for the English version of the film. They had been translated from English to German and back again into English 'with results that could only be called ludicrous.'[51] The screenplay was 'in parts very fine, except where it leaves my story, replacing it with introduced incidents or modifications. Then it comes utterly to grief.'[52] The epic film, featuring over 5,000 extras and lavish sets, was directed by Mihaly Kertész, better known as Michael Curtiz, director of *Casablanca*.

There were also objections to the film from the British Board of Film Censors regarding 'soldiers being shown with arrows sticking in them ... too much of the heroine's back being visible in some scene (which I never noticed) and ... the warmth of the embrace which in the moment of her death, the heroine gives to her husband, the Prince of Egypt ... What Pharisees and humbugs we are in England! No wonder the foreigners make a mock of us on this matter.'[53]

After attending an East African Committee meeting on 3 November, Haggard met Louie and Miss Hector and went to see *Moon of Israel* at the Pavilion cinema in Shaftesbury Avenue – 'on the whole it is a really wonderful production and I cannot conceive how effects such as that of the crossing of the Red Sea are obtained. Everybody seems to like it very much so I hope that it will be successful.'[54]

The general election had been held a few days earlier on 29 October. Haggard prayed that 'things may go as we wish ... everything that is evil in the land is at the back of these Socialists who love the Russian anarchists because they have reduced that great empire to a condition which they hope to see re-duplicated in Britain and her empire also.'[55] The Conservatives won a huge majority, the Liberals were all but destroyed and the Labour Party lost more than forty seats. Haggard's prayers had been answered.

The same day as the election, Will's wife Nitie died suddenly of a heart attack. 'The strange thing is that this was nearly his own fate a few weeks ago, but now she is gone and he is left.'[56] Haggard attended the funeral at Hartlip in pouring rain on 1 November 1924. 'It was a sad business and I don't think that the expedition did me any good.' Will, already suffering from atherosclerosis and digestive problems, was in bed with gout and 'much broken by this blow and no wonder'.[57]

On Guy Fawkes Day, 5 November, Haggard and Louie attended the 'great luncheon given by Longmans Green & Co., at Stationers' Hall near St. Paul's cathedral in celebration of their bicentenary'.[58] Haggard sat on the right hand of his friend Charles Longman, and among the many invited guests were Arthur Conan Doyle, Edmund Gosse, Andrew Lang's widow Leonora, Henry Newbolt, Lloyd Osbourne, and Sidney and Beatrice Webb. Haggard prefaced his toast to the publishing trade with a brief history of Longmans before concluding that it was a difficult thing 'to talk about an old friend in his presence', a friend he had known for 'a matter of forty years in business and in pleasure'. He recalled their 'mutual attachment to our late great friend Andrew Lang' and proposed the toast to publishing, 'coupling it with the name of my very dear friend Charles Longman, and in hoping that in some way my own may go down with his to generations that know us not'.[59] Duty done, Haggard turned to Longman, put his hand on his shoulder and said: 'God bless you, and again God bless you!'[60] Longman was brought to tears. 'For all his gruff manner he had a very soft heart!'[61]

The sequel to this emotion-laden occasion was, to use Haggard's word, a 'catastrophe'. He was returning to St Leonards while Louie was staying on in London. Hurrying to find a taxi to Charing Cross station, Haggard was 'seized by a most fearful attack of indigestion that almost stopped my heart from beating'. He managed to get to St Leonards, where he put up at the East Sussex Club; a member who was a doctor assisted him in undressing and sent for medication. Haggard was better the next morning 'but still had wind'. He attributed the attack to the lunch, where he ate 'some oysters and then a sort of lobster stew, after which I drank a glass of champagne and a liqueur brandy'. The heat of the hall followed 'by the cold of the street and the excitement of speaking may have had something to do with it. The fact is however, that I am no longer at all robust and I do not know how long I shall be able to take London engagements in winter.'[62]

On 25 November he felt well enough to come up to London for a night in order to attend a dinner of the Delphian Coterie, a Conservative society, and open a debate on 'The Good and Bad of Imagination'. The debate 'went off extremely well, Ronald Ross and others taking part in it'. Lilias was present and recalled her father speaking 'with a vividness and warmth which stirred and held' his audience.

> Imagination was power which came from they knew not where ... Perhaps it was existent but ungrasped truth, a gap in the curtain of the unseen which sometimes presses so nearly upon us ... it might be that those who possessed it were gates, through which the forces of good and evil flowed down in strength upon the world; instruments innocent of their destiny. For it seemed to him as he grew old that the spirit of man was like those great icebergs which floated in Arctic seas – towering masses of glittering blue-green ice, which yet hid four-fifths of their bulk beneath the water. That it was the hidden power of the spirit which connected the visible and the invisible; which heard the still small voice calling from the infinite.[63]

According to Lilias, it 'struck some of those who watched Rider that night that he was not very far from the full knowledge of those mysteries of which he spoke'.

It was his last public speech. 'Taken ill again after the dinner', Haggard returned to Ditchingham, where it was 'apparent that there was some un-diagnosed internal mischief which made him unable to stand any strain or exertion'.[64] In the preceding months he had 'changed in some intangible fashion', a change Lilias first noticed after his return from Egypt: 'his face had settled into that brooding sadness so noticeable in the portrait painted by Maurice Greiffenhagen'.[65] Leaving Ditchingham for the rest of the winter was ruled out. 'A nurse was installed and through the dark and cheerless days of December, he fought a losing battle with pain, weakness and depression.'[66]

Haggard's spirits can only have been lowered further by the death of his sister-in-law Emily, Arthur's wife, on 17 December. Christmas Day, 'a mild, open Xmas with the sun shining', was not a pleasant one for Haggard. A month earlier, following various 'preliminary illnesses and symptoms ... including an almost total loss of appetite and on the top of an attack of gout', he was hit by a bladder infection, which

> has made an invalid of me and there are symptoms that I do not altogether like. I had to sit through a Xmas Day dinner at which my grandsons, as children do on these occasions, did justice to their creature cravings ... I begin to think that my active career is at an end and that I must resign from all public work. Nor indeed at present am I fit to do any of whatever kind. I wished to begin a new romance, but I cannot face it. On Xmas Day I did manage to get to the second service in a motor-car, and to sit it out ... the first time I have been able to enter a church for six weeks![67]

Illness and discomfort didn't entirely prevent Haggard from writing. He managed to complete his Egyptian romance *Belshazzar* and early in the New Year he was busy critiquing the screenplay for a new film version of *She* planned by Lucoque. 'I consider it impossible' was his comment on Scene 26, featuring the death of Kallikrates at the hands of Amenartas utilising a snake. 'For heaven's sake stick to the version that Amenartas gives on the Sherd. Let her blast him.'[68] As to Scene 52, Haggard begged the 'bath scene be omitted. It is quite unnecessary and not in too nice taste.'[69] In a second letter Haggard objected to 'some abominable scenes of torture' introduced by the scriptwriter, to 'which I wish to state outright I cannot have my name associated'. He also thought they would fall foul of the censor.[70] Haggard said he was 'willing to pass the scenario *as it now leaves me*' and signed off wishing 'every success to the venture'.[71]

On 16 January Haggard learned that Arthur Cochrane, his 'oldest remaining and nearest friend, with whom in my youth in Africa I lived as a brother', had died.[72] Cochrane had experienced 'some years of failing health ... the loss to me is great, though of late decades his domestic circumstances tended to separate us to a certain extent, we always remained close in spirit.'[73] He recalled their first meeting in Pretoria in 1877, building 'The Palatial' together, and their 'rather wild agricultural venture' in Natal.[74]

Excepting his candid letters from Hilldrop in 1879 and 1880, Cochrane remains a shadowy figure in Haggard's life. He was a faithful companion we never really meet. Cochrane married shortly after his return to England in 1881. The marriage appears to have been an unfortunate one. In October 1924 Haggard was in London and 'thought of going to see Cochrane but the thought of those stairs & of Mrs C at the top of them put me off it'.[75] This observation explains Haggard's above-mentioned reference to Cochrane's domestic arrangements as being a source of separation.

> He was not a brilliant man, but extraordinarily hard-working and conscientious, also of an affectionate nature – at any rate towards myself … These qualities never did more than suffice to earn him a livelihood, mostly as a director of small South African companies and as an expert who visited that country on sundry occasions to make reports upon landed properties, which were always full, valuable and accurate. I grieve that I am not well enough to attend his funeral. God rest him – as I'm sure he will.[76]

The bell next tolled for Haggard's younger brother, Arthur, 'killed ostensibly by some virulent form of kidney disease, but really, as I believe, by his ceaseless labours for year upon year on behalf of the Veterans Club and Association which he founded'.[77] Arthur's death was followed by the 'sudden removal' of Haggard's friend and neighbour William Carr, 'who died of heart-stoppage'.[78] Haggard attended the Bungay Petty Sessions, of which he was still chair, to pay tribute to his friend but was not well enough to go to the funeral.

Hearing his friend was 'under the weather', Kipling wrote to Haggard on 15 February sending 'condolences and congratulations. In a hell-broth of a winter like this bed's the best and soundest place there is; and, anyhow, all England is one filthy ditch at present. So lie up in peace: only send me a line when you feel like it.'[79] This was the first of a series of chatty letters written to cheer up his old friend. One letter urged Haggard to deposit his 'War Diaries' in the British Museum for later publication; another bade Haggard

> be glad you're in bed – even if those damnable nights are long and even Ecclesiasticus who is my refuge, doesn't help always. I've had a touch of it and done a deuce of a lot of thinking – the sum and substance of which is that I wish I had a straight and high record as you have of work done. But I never took on Commissions and now I rather regret it. Dictate me another letter some time when you're in a better (or a worse!) temper. Let me hear you cuss the present state of things.[80]

Haggard responded: 'My dear boy, you almost bring tears to my eyes (they are very near them when one is weak) by some of the things you say. For instance when you compare my humble record with your own, by which it is not fit to stand – but comparisons are odious.' In his 14-page letter dictated to Ida Hector, he attempted an appraisal of his life and work: he had tried to do his best to serve his country in 'the teeth of much official opposition (Lord! how officials hate the outsider with ideas) … to the full extent of my small opportunities which, generally, I have had to *make*'.

So far as royal commissions were concerned, 'the effort seems to have been utterly wasted, that is, if anything earnest is ever wasted in the end. When they had served the Government purpose they were chucked aside on the national rubbish heap at Whitehall.' Those efforts that succeeded, if indeed they had, were 'done off my own bat – such as the "Rural England" work and my mission on behalf of the RCI [Royal Colonial Institute] during the war'. The latter was 'bitterly opposed by the Colonial Office at the time', but nevertheless out of his findings 'sprang the present [Empire Settlement Act] which is imperfect and insufficient enough, but still a beginning'.[81]

From the political to the personal: 'Lying in bed here day after day, one dissects oneself with thoroughness and alas – a somewhat miserable anatomy appears.'[82] Haggard wrote his own post-mortem:

> Lack of sufficient principle, or it seems to me, rashness, want of a steady aim (except where the country was concerned of which at heart I have always been the servant) and of character, liability to be swept away by primary impulses ... But the Powers that made me thus, perhaps to excite strength of repentance and opposition, did give me one great gift which probably I don't deserve – that of attracting the affection of which you speak[83] – though this has sometimes been of a kind that leads to disaster.[84]

Nevertheless he was feeling 'somewhat better'.

> I got up yesterday and sat in the old study next door for a little while, but of course my limbs are like sticks and the sight of *meat* is abhorrent to me. You would laugh to see me being fed by the nurse with milk pudding from a spoon just like a baby. Also my rings fall off my hands and there was a deuce of a hunt for one of them the other night – finally retrieved from the seat of my pajamas.[85]

One of these rings Haggard proposed giving to Kipling for his past birthday – 59 on 30 December 1924 – 'to use as a seal, for it is too massive to wear, copper I think with a little gold in it, probably a memorial ring of Akhenaton'.[86] After the letter was dictated and typed up, Haggard signed it and dictated a postscript: 'The truth is I have fought against this illness too long: I ought to have gone to bed much earlier. But I kept at it sitting on that E. African Committee ... and the thing grew and grew until it bowled me over.'[87]

Kipling thanked Haggard 'a hundred times' for the ring: 'that it has been yours and that you've given it to me *does* mean a lot to this teacher of the alphabet'.[88]

Haggard's diary lay untouched from 3 February until 26 March 1925 owing to his 'suffering many unpleasant things on which I will not dwell'. He took it up to record the death of Lord Curzon on 20 March, 'over whom a service was celebrated yesterday with much pomp in Westminster Abbey ... May this great servant of his country forever rest in honour and in peace.'[89]

Haggard's strength was failing and in April it was decided he 'must go to London for further examination and possible operation'.[90] On a 'grey spring morning' an ambulance came to Ditchingham House to collect him.

> [Louie] was in his room helping with the last-minute preparations. The nurse had dressed him and left him in a chair, but he looked down at his overcoat as if something was missing, he got up, walked to the table where there was a bowl of daffodils, and

taking one pulled it through his button-hole – then turned with rather a sad little smile to his wife. How many hundred times had she seen him do that. The last little action of a morning ritual in his dressing-room; for every day the gardener brought in a buttonhole, a rose or carnation in summer, an orchid in winter. Rider was never without a flower. The little incident broke her control –

'Rider,' she said, 'do you really want to go, dear? You have only got to say if you don't and we will send the ambulance back – are you quite, quite sure ...?'[91]

Haggard went. In a nursing home at 3 Devonshire Terrace in Bayswater, he received another news-filled letter from Kipling, who had spent a 'wholly absorbed evening' reading *Queen of the Dawn*. 'How the *dickens* do you do it? ... it held me as a drug might, but it was a *good* drug.' Kipling commiserated with his friend being confined to a nursing home, where the

> man who lives by his imagination pays for his gift a thousandfold in such places ... But there is this – and just this to be said – when the big Machine of Fate is felt and realized to have us in its hold, one gets a blessed incuriousness and content on the matter – on all matters: and the odd feeling that somewhere at sometime the self-same thing has happened before and that, try as one may, one can't put a foot wrong. I *know* that that will come over you as you go up to the table – if you've got to, and it beats any known anaesthetic.[92]

Haggard underwent surgery on Saturday, 9 May. The doctors said the operation was 'entirely successful' and Haggard lay, 'pain more or less kept at bay, quiet and speaking little for three days'.[93] Ida Hector kept Kipling informed of Haggard's condition and her bulletin of Wednesday, 13 May, made him 'feel a little easier. Seeing that the operation was last Saturday and he is reported as reading and smoking on Tuesday, there seems to be a chance of the luck turning.'[94] But 'a new abscess gathered' and Haggard 'lapsed into semi-consciousness'. On Thursday 'about midday, without speech or any struggle except to protest noiselessly against some effort to feed him, he died'.[95]

Haggard's son-in-law Reginald Cheyne was with him the night before. 'The window-blind was up, and the blaze from a large building on fire was visible in the distance. Rider rose up in bed, and pointed to the conflagration with arm outstretched, the red glow upon his face. "My God!" said Cheyne to himself, "an old Pharaoh."'[96]

Haggard's obituary in *The Times* described him as

> one of the most striking, picturesque versatile men of his day and generation. Romantic writer; agricultural expert; Imperial politician; deeply interested in the affairs of Church and State; much of a mystic, and not a little an ascetic also, so much so that an intimate said of him that a turn of the wheel might have sent him into a Trappist monastery; Haggard was nevertheless keenly alive to mundane affairs,

especially when they bore the charm of a speculative or adventurous colouring. But with all his many-sided interests and activities, he remained first and foremost a patriotic Englishman of whom his fellow countrymen had every reason to be proud.

This prefaced a brief biography detailing his literary career and achievements as well as his advocacy of agricultural issues and land settlement. Though 'a Conservative' in politics, he 'could not be considered a thorough-going party man. A strong believer in the humanizing and civilizing mission of the English peoples, he was ever ready to aid all movements and agencies which had for their object the strengthening and consolidating of the Empire.'[97]

Haggard's funeral service was held at St Thomas's in Regent Street.[98] The Reverend Clarence May was one of the officiating clergy, and among members of the Haggard family attending were Louie and her three daughters: Dorothy with her husband Colonel Reginald Cheyne, Angela and her husband Thomas Haggard, and Lilias. Also present was Mrs John Haggard (Aggie), her daughter Joan and several nephews and nieces. Others present included Ida Hector; Alexander Galt Ross, who had accompanied Haggard to Iceland in 1888;[99] Sir Frederick and Lady Jackson; Haggard's friend from Pretoria days, Sir Godfrey Lagden, representing the Royal Colonial Institute; friends from the 1880s such as Charles Longman, Leonora Lang and James Stanley Little. Alexander Strahan Watt represented Haggard's literary agent A.P. Watt; Algernon Rose, the Authors' Club; and Sir Anthony Hope Hawkins, the Society of Authors.[100]

The service was followed by cremation at Golders Green Crematorium. Haggard's ashes were interred in the vault in the chancel of St Mary's at Ditchingham. A slab of black marble above the vault bears the epitaph he composed:

> Here lie the ashes of Henry Rider Haggard
> Knight Bachelor
> Knight of the British Empire
> Who with a Humble Heart Strove to Serve his Country.

In the north aisle of the church there is a memorial window dedicated to the 'memory of a beloved father ... by his younger daughter Lilias'. A framed piece of calligraphy explains various features of the window: the centrepiece of the Risen Christ is flanked by the angels Michael and Raphael while 'below in the centre is a view of Bungay ... On the left the Pyramids ... On the right Hilldrop, Sir Rider's farm in South Africa. These views he loved.'[101]

APPENDIX: MHLOPEKAZI

Mhlopekazi, under the corrupted form Umslopogaas, featured in three of Haggard's books: *Allan Quatermain* (1887), *Nada the Lily* (1892) and *She and Allan* (1921). In the last title Umslopogaas refers to himself by his real name.[1]

Umslopogaas is depicted as being a Zulu, but in reality Mhlopekazi was a Swazi. Accounts of how he came to Natal vary. His obituary in the *Natal Witness* says he was a son of 'Mswazi, King of Swaziland, and in his youth belonged to the Nyati Regiment – the crack corps of the country'.[2] According to H.C. Lugg, Mhlopekazi came to Natal in 1859 during the reign of Mswati, Ngwenyama Mswati Dlamini, Swaziland's monarch between 1840 and 1868, 'as an emissary' for the king and thereafter 'entered the service of Sir Theophilus Shepstone'. His duties included leading 'his master's saddled horse Nqakamatshe down to the office daily'.[3]

His obituary records that, 'being a "Prince of the Blood" and a warrior of some renown, Umhlopekazi [*sic*] appears to have commanded a considerable amount of respect from the first' and was soon taken into Shepstone's staff, 'accompanying that gentleman as a kind of aide-de-camp in his travels and mission through the Cape Colony, Basutoland and the Transvaal'. On 'one occasion, when Sir Theophilus and Sir Marshall Clarke were in the Basutu country on an unofficial errand, Umhlopekazi was instrumental in saving the life of the latter. A plot was on foot to murder Sir Marshall Clarke, which the Chief discovered, and killed the would-be assassin'.[4]

William Lucas says Mhlopekazi was 'born to the great Swazi Royal House' and was 'a man of war in his boyhood ... [his] frame studded with well-won scars, not the least the historic three-cornered gash beneath the red handkerchief we were all so familiar with'.[5] Mhlopekazi was a favourite subject for talks given by Lucas, an architect by profession. The *Natal Who's Who of 1906* lists Lucas's hobbies as 'delivery of occasional sermons and addresses'.[6] In one of the latter given on 1 January 1898, Lucas recalls Mhlopekazi as 'a tall, broad man, quite 6ft 3ins., but gaunt, with lean, wiry-looking limbs and a great three-cornered hole in his forehead who, removing his hand, placed to hide a yawn, revealed a powerful-looking face with a humorous mouth, a short woolly beard, tinged with grey and a pair of brown eyes, keen as hawks'.[7]

Mhlopekazi was aware of his pseudonymous fame. In a conversation with Melmoth Osborn, he asked whether Haggard received any remuneration for these stories which featured him. Being told 'yes', he suggested some of this might be passed his way. Haggard sent him a knife with his name engraved upon it. On another occasion Mhlopekazi was asked if he was proud of his name being in books. 'No,' he answered, 'to me it is nothing. Yet I am glad that Indanda [Haggard] has set my name in writings that will not be forgotten, so that when my people are no more a people, one of them at least, will be remembered.'[8]

In 1890 Mhlopekazi received the Victoria Medal, 'given to certain Zulu Chiefs on the occasion of her late Majesty's completing her sixtieth year of queenship, and to Umslopogaas among them'.[9]

Mhlopekazi was present at the unveiling of the statue of Sir Theophilus Shepstone in Longmarket Street, Pietermaritzburg, on 23 October 1896. He died a year later on 24 October 1897, aged 80, and was buried in the Native Cemetery on Pietermaritzburg's Town Hill.[10]

Some of this information is contradicted in testimonies recorded by James Stuart. 'Mhlopekazi, (Shepstone's) *induna*, was not given him by the king but seems to have become attached to Somsewu on his own account. Mhlopekazi was only a *young man (ijara)*. He was not an *inxusa* [ambassador] of the Swazi.'[11] According to another informant, 'Mhlopekazi came and konza'd [paid allegiance to] Somtseu. He came from Swaziland.'[12]

The Swazi played a sophisticated diplomatic game with the Natal authorities, and with Shepstone in particular, one involving a degree of espionage. Shepstone was intent on playing kingmaker to the thrones of the Zulu and the Swazi, creating pliant chiefs among their subsidiary peoples. The Swazi successfully penetrated 'the inner sanctum of Shepstone's household'[13] – most of his staff were Swazi, and 'may even have gained an inkling of his ambitions to preside over a confederation of south-east African states'.[14]

The Swazi even went so far as to attempt to forge an alliance with Shepstone, through marriage between him and Mswati's sister Tifokati. They didn't expect Shepstone himself to marry Tifokati 'but specifically suggested a proxy in the shape of his chief *induna* Ngoza – this would have a symbolic significance as well as opening 'a channel of communication into the heart of the Shepstone camp'.[15] The Swazi tried to revive this arrangement 'after Ngoza fell from grace. Once this had happened Mhlopekazi was despatched to enter Shepstone's service, and soon rose to fill Ngoza's place as the chief *induna* in Shepstone's entourage.'[16]

Umslopogaas/Mhlopekazi was also memorialised by the sculptor Mary Stainbank. When studying sculpture in London (1922–6) at the Royal College of Art, she created a sculpture of Umslopogaas for her 'monument' project. The sculpture, titled *Umhlobogazi*, does not appear to have survived but is recorded in a photograph.[17]

NOTES

Note on abbreviations: titles of books by Haggard are given without authorial attribution.

CC	–	Cheyne Collection
Cetywayo	–	*Cetywayo and His White Neighbours*, by H. Rider Haggard
Cloak	–	*The Cloak That I Left*, by Lilias Rider Haggard
DAJ	–	*Diary of an African Journey*, by H. Rider Haggard
Days	–	*The Days of My Life*, by H. Rider Haggard
DSAB	–	*Dictionary of South African Biography*
HRH	–	Henry Rider Haggard
JSA	–	*The James Stuart Archive*, 6 vols., ed. C. de B. Webb and John Wright
KSM	–	*King Solomon's Mines*
LHD	–	Lady Haggard's Diary
NRO	–	Norfolk Record Office
PD	–	*The Private Diaries of Sir H. Rider Haggard*, ed. D.S. Higgins
RR	–	*Rudyard Kipling to Rider Haggard*, ed. Morton Cohen

INTRODUCTION

1. *Days*, vol. 1, p. 246.
2. *Allan and the Ice Gods*, p. i.
3. V.S. Pritchett, 'Haggard Still Riding', *New Statesman*, 27 August 1960, p. 277.
4. *Days*, vol. 1, p. 245.
5. *Dawn* was first titled 'Angela'; *Witch's Head* began life as 'Eva: A Tale of Love and War'.
6. Olive Schreiner to Havelock Ellis, 29 October 1884, Olive Schreiner Letters Online, www.oliveschreiner.org.
7. *Cloak*, p. 31.
8. Tania Zulli, *Colonial Transitions: Literature and Culture in the Later Victorian Age*, Bern: Peter Lang, 2011, p. 68.
9. Ibid, p. 70.

10. Neil E. Hultgren, 'Haggard Criticism since 1980: Imperial Romance before and after the Postcolonial Turn', *Literature Compass*, https://doi.org/10.1111/j.1741-4113.2011.00827.x, accessed 3 April 2023.

11. Guy, Jeff, *Theophilus Shepstone and the Forging of Natal: African Autonomy and Settler Colonialism in the Making of Traditional Authority*, Pietermaritzburg: University of KwaZulu-Natal Press, 2013, p. 229.

12. Graham Greene, 'Rider Haggard's Secret', in *Collected Essays*, London: Penguin, 1971, p. 159.

13. Ibid, p. 160.

14. *Days*, vol. 2, pp. 85–6.

15. Greene, 'Rider Haggard's Secret', p. 158.

16. Ibid, p. 159.

PROLOGUE

1. Quoted in Ruth Gordon, *Shepstone: The Role of the Family in the History of South Africa, 1820–1900*, Cape Town: Balkema, 1968, p. 238.

2. John Laband, *Rope of Sand: The Rise and Fall of the Zulu Kingdom in the Nineteenth Century*, Johannesburg: Jonathan Ball, 1995, p. 135.

3. The Boer victory over the Zulu at the battle of Blood/Ncome River in 1838 broke Dingane's power and provoked a civil war in Zululand. Dingane attempted to create a new Zulu kingdom north of the Phongolo River but was assassinated by a Swazi patrol in early 1840. Mpande became king.

4. Mpande married Ngqumbazi during Shaka's reign, his royal brother paying the bride price, *ilobolo*, to the bride's family on his behalf.

5. Laband, *Rope of Sand*, p. 136.

6. Ibid.

7. *JSA*, vol. 4, interviewee: Mtshapi ka Noradu, p. 61.

8. Norman Etherington, 'South African Origins of Rider Haggard's Early Romances', *Notes and Queries*, October 1977, p. 437.

9. Laband, *Rope of Sand*, p. 142. John Dunn (1835–1895), a hunter-trader in Zululand until 1854 when he became assistant to the British Border Agent at Nonoti, Lower Tugela. After the civil war of 1856 he befriended Cetshwayo and settled in Zululand. However, he fought on the side of the British in the Anglo-Zulu War of 1879 and after the war was appointed one of the thirteen chiefs presiding over a partitioned Zululand. Dunn appears in Haggard's *Child of Storm*. See Chapter XIII, 'Umbelazi the Fallen'.

10. HRH, 'Haggard on the Zulus: The Story of a Rebellious People', *Illustrated London News*, 19 May 1906, pp. 710–1.

11. Ian Knight, *The Anatomy of the Zulu Army from Shaka to Cetshwayo, 1818–1879*, London: Greenhill Books, 1995, p. 192. Figures for combatants from Gilbert Torlage, 'Impi Yaba Ntwana: The War of the Children', *Soldiers of the Queen*, no. 74, September 1993, p. 3.

12. John Laband, *The Eight Zulu Kings: From Shaka to Goodwill Zwelithini*, Johannesburg: Jonathan Ball, 2018, p. 173.

13. HRH, 'Haggard on the Zulus', pp. 710–1.

14. John Dunn, *Cetywayo and the Three Generals*, ed. D.C.F. Moodie, reprint, Durban, 2006 [1886], p. 6.

15. Torlage, 'Impi Yaba Ntwana', p. 4.

16. Figures from Torlage, 'Impi Yaba Ntwana', p. 5.

17. C.M. Doke and B.W. Vilakazi, *Zulu-English Dictionary*, Johannesburg: Witwatersrand University Press, 1958, quoted in Adrian Koopman, *Zulu Names*, Pietermaritzburg: University of Natal Press, 2002, p. 251.

1. 'I TOO MUST DIE'

1. India was then under the control of the East India Company, which administered the subcontinent for the British Crown via the three presidencies of Bengal, Madras and Bombay, each possessing a civil service and an army.

2. The Doveton and Bazett families were both associated with the island of St Helena where Ella's uncle Sir William Webber Doveton had been Treasurer and member of its council during Napoleon Bonaparte's imprisonment in exile from 1815 to 1821.

3. Rottingdean School became St Aubyn's preparatory school in 1895 and closed in 2013.

4. Ella Doveton diary, 31 May 1838, John George Haggard Papers, MSS. Brit. Emp. s. 465, Oxford, Bodleian Libraries.

5. Ibid, 30 May 1838.

6. Ibid, 9 December 1837.

7. *Days*, vol. 1, p. 27.

8. Ella Doveton diary, 8 September 1838.

9. Ibid, 27 September 1838.

10. Ibid, 7 September 1838.

11. Ibid, 3 September 1838, quoted in Victoria Manthorpe, *Children of the Empire: The Victorian Haggards*, London: Gollancz, 1996, p. 32.

12. *Days*, vol. 1, p. 15.

13. *Cloak*, p. 25.

14. *Days*, vol. 1, p. 15.

15. *Cloak*, foreword by Sir Godfrey Haggard, p. 16.

16. *Days*, vol. 2, p. 136.

17. *Days*, vol. 1, p. 1.

18. According to Haggard's daughter Lilias, 'the English tongue found the double A (of Aagaard) awkward to deal with, and it first became Ogard, then Hoogard and finally Haggard'. *Cloak*, p. 23.

19. *Days*, vol. 1, p. 1.

20. *Cloak*, p. 23. The star is in fact silver. The Amyand and Meybohm lines are also

represented on the Haggard coat of arms. The star is still engraved on rings presented to members of the Haggard family when marking significant life events.

21. *Days*, vol. 1, p. 3.
22. *Cloak*, p. 24.
23. *Days*, vol. 1, p. 3.
24. *Cloak*, p. 24.
25. Ibid.
26. Ibid.
27. Ibid.
28. Margrit Schulte Beerbühl, *The Forgotten Majority: German Merchants, Naturalization and Global Trade 1660–1815*, New York: Berghahn, 2015, p. 155.
29. *Cloak*, pp. 23–4.
30. Manthorpe, *Children of the Empire*, p. 232, n. 7.
31. See http://www.thepeerage.com/p64836.htm, accessed 9 September 2019.
32. Ellen Maria Haggard to her cousin Ella Maddison Green, 31 August 1917, quoted in Manthorpe, *Children of the Empire*, p. 232.
33. *Days*, vol. 1, p. 25.
34. Susanna Wade Martins, *Norfolk: A Changing Countryside, 1780–1914*, Chichester: Phillimore, 1988, p. 5.
35. C.S. Armstrong (ed.), *Under the Parson's Nose: Further Extracts from the Diary of the Revd B.J. Armstrong M.A. (Cantab), Vicar of East Dereham 1850–1888*, Dereham: Larks Press, 1912, entry for 26 October 1853.
36. Quoted in Martins, *Norfolk*, p. 22.
37. Ella Haggard, *Life and Its Author: An Essay in Verse*, London: Longmans, 1890, HRH introduction, p. 7.
38. *Cloak*, pp. 25–6.
39. *Days*, vol. 1, pp. 8–9. The tenants installed at Bradenham on this occasion, the Gellibrands, were likely known to the Haggards; they were 'partly Russian' and had 'resided 22 years at St Petersburg'. Armstrong, *Under the Parson's Nose*, entry for 23 June 1855.
40. *Cloak*, p. 26. The farm was demolished in the 1950s.
41. Ibid.
42. Ibid, p. 26.
43. *PD*, pp. 243–44. On 22 September 1856 the infant was formally received into the Anglican Church and was added to the church register under the names he was christened with, which appear on his birth certificate, Henry Rider.
44. *Days*, vol. 1, p. 25.
45. Ibid, p. 29.
46. Ibid.
47. Ibid, pp. 29–30.
48. Ibid, p. 17. Sir Roger de Coverley, character created in the eighteenth century by Joseph Addison, whose adventures appeared in the *Spectator*.

49. Ibid, pp. 17–8.
50. Ibid, p. 16.
51. Ibid, p. 16.
52. Ibid, p. 17.
53. *Colonel Quaritch, V.C.*, p. 327.
54. *Days*, vol. 1, p. 16.
55. *Cloak*, foreword by Godfrey Haggard, p. 17.
56. 'Notes on the family of William Meybohm Rider Haggard (1817–1893) and Ella Haggard (née Doveton) (1819–1889) by Andrew Haggard (1892–1976)', p. 7, Jack Haggard Papers, National Maritime Museum, Greenwich.
57. *Days*, vol. 1, pp. 20–1.
58. *Cloak*, p. 29.
59. *Days*, vol. 1, p. 23.
60. Ibid, p. 18.
61. Ibid.
62. Ibid.
63. Morton Cohen, *Rider Haggard: His Life and Works*, London: Hutchinson, 1960, p. 21.
64. *Days*, pp. 19–20.
65. Manthorpe, *Children of the Empire*, p. 30. Thacker remained close to the family and was servant to Andrew Haggard on campaign in Egypt and the Sudan; 'his letters to the Haggards, while not lacking in deference, are unusual'. Ibid.
66. See Michael Mason, *The Making of Victorian Sexuality*, Oxford: OUP, 1994, p. 71.
67. *DAJ*, p. 134. In his autobiography Haggard says one of the most beautiful women he ever saw was 'a village girl from Bradenham who was reported to be the daughter of a gentleman'. *Days*, vol. 1, p. 42.
68. *Days*, vol. 1, p. 24.
69. Ibid, p. 26.
70. Ibid, p. 24.
71. Ibid, p. 27.
72. Ibid.
73. Ella Haggard, *Life and Its Author*, HRH introduction, pp. 8–9.
74. Tom Pocock, *Rider Haggard and the Lost Empire*, London: Weidenfeld and Nicholson, 1993, p. 10.
75. Shirley M. Addy, *Rider Haggard and Egypt*, Accrington, Lancashire: AL Publications, 1998, p. 2.
76. *Ushabti* (meaning 'answerer'), a small painted wooden figure depicting a slave or servant who would attend their master or mistress in the after-life.
77. See Addy, 'Didlington Hall: A Guide to the Egyptian Collection', in *Rider Haggard and Egypt*, Appendix 1a, p. 36.
78. Mary married Lord William Cecil and carried out her own excavations in Egypt.
79. Defrauded by his lawyer, Lord Amherst had to sell most of his book collection in 1906. 'He died, so it was said, a broken man in 1909. Lady William Cecil held on to the

Egyptian collection until her death in 1919, but the family then sold it entire in 1921 ... The dilapidated Didlington Hall was razed to the ground after military use in World War II: it constitutes one of the most significant of England's lost country houses.' Roger Luckhurst, *The Mummy's Curse: The True History of a Dark Fantasy*, Oxford: OUP, 2012, p. 191. Howard Carter assisted in the sale of the Egyptian collection.

80. Arthur Haggard went to Pembroke College and Jackson to Jesus College.

81. *Days*, vol. 1, p. 36.

82. Ibid, p. 11. A thaler was a large German silver coin. Haggard tells the same story in *A Winter Pilgrimage*, vol. 1, p. 20, identifying the book as *Robinson Crusoe* and dating the incident as taking place 'in or about 1867'.

83. HRH, 'Books That Have Influenced Me', *British Weekly*, May 1887, pp. 66–7.

84. Ibid, p. 66.

85. *Days*, vol. 1, p. 12.

86. Ibid, p. 9.

87. Ibid.

88. Ibid.

89. Ibid, pp. 9–10.

90. HRH, 'Childhood Reminiscences: An Unpublished Manuscript', *Columbia Library Columns*, New York, November 1981, p. 18.

91. Ibid.

92. Ibid.

93. Ibid.

94. *Days*, vol. 1, pp. 28–9.

95. Armstrong, *Under the Parson's Nose*, entry for 20 July 1869.

96. *Cloak*, pp. 27–8.

97. Ibid, p. 28.

98. Ibid, p. 29.

99. Having read of a woman who died in the early nineteenth century planting her initials in daffodils which could still 'be clearly read', Haggard was inspired to do the same 'upon the bank of the Sunk Path'. *Gardener's Year*, p. 131.

100. *Days*, vol. 1, p. 28..

101. Ibid, p. 29.

102. *Days*, vol. 1, p. 5.

103. Ibid.

2.   'LOVE'S SWEET DREAM'

1. Stephen Inwood, *A History of London*, London: Macmillan, 1998, p. 576.

2. *Days*, vol. 1, p. 6.

3. Ibid, pp. 6–7.

4. Ibid, p. 7.

5. Ibid.

6. Ibid, p. 5.
7. Ibid, pp. 5–6.
8. Ibid, p. 7.
9. *Cloak*, p. 29.
10. HRH, 'On Going Back', *Longmans Magazine*, XI, November 1887, p. 61.
11. Ibid, p. 63.
12. Ibid.
13. *Days*, vol. 1, p. 7.
14. *Allan's Wife*, pp. 12–4.
15. HRH, 'On Going Back', p. 62.
16. Ibid, p. 62.
17. Ibid, p. 64. Quartermaine died in 1872. His gravestone and that of his wife Jayne are to be found in St Mary's churchyard.
18. Haggard similarly renders the surname in the 1887 article as well as in his autobiography. Nor can the misspelling be explained as a misprint. 'Quatermain' is how the name appears in the handwritten manuscript of *King Solomon's Mines*. Rider Haggard Papers, MC 32, Norfolk Records Office.
19. HRH, 'On Going Back', p. 61.
20. Ibid, pp. 64–5.
21. Ibid, p. 65.
22. Ibid.
23. *Love Eternal*, pp. 18–9.
24. Ibid, p. 193.
25. *Days*, vol. 1, p. 30.
26. Ibid.
27. Ibid, p. 31.
28. Ibid, p. 27.
29. See *Cloak*, p. 30; Cohen, *Rider Haggard*, p. 24.
30. John Blatchly, *A Famous Antient Seed-Plot of Learning: A History of Ipswich School*, Ipswich: Ipswich School, 2003, p. 189.
31. *Days*, vol. 1, p. 32.
32. Blatchly, *Famous Antient Seed-Plot*, p. 185.
33. Ibid, pp. 185–6.
34. Ibid, p. 186.
35. Ibid, p. 188.
36. *Days*, vol. 1, p. 33.
37. Ibid, p. 31. A style of hat 'with a four-inch crown and very wide brim ... closely associated with piety.' Ruth Goodman, *How to Be a Victorian*, London: Penguin, 2013, p. 55.
38. *Days*, vol. 1, p. 31.
39. Ibid.
40. Ibid, p. 32.
41. Ibid, p. 34.

42. Haggard later received a letter from King 'the gist of which was to ask me what land and climate I could recommend to him to ensure a quick road to the devil. I think I replied that West Africa seemed to fulfil all requirements, but whether he ever reached either the first or the second destination I do not know. Poor fellow! I am sorry for him. He was clever and handsome, and might have found a better fate. I have heard, however, that he made a disastrous marriage, which often takes men to a bad end than does or did even the hinterland of West Africa.' *Days*, pp. 34–5. King doesn't appear to have followed Haggard's advice, nor does he appear to have married. He died in Japan in 1918. Armine King was identified by John Blatchly using the biographical details given by Haggard in his autobiography.

43. An anonymous 'Old Boy', *East Anglian Daily Times*, 15 May 1894.

44. *Days*, vol. 1, p. 32.

45. Wallace Mortimer Morfey, 'Guts Sanderson', *The Ipswichian*, 1990, p. 42. His surname is spelt incorrectly as 'Saunderson' in *Days*.

46. *Days*, vol. 1, p. 32.

47. Ibid.

48. Ibid, p. 33.

49. Ibid, p. 28.

50. Sir John Edwin Sandys (1844–1922), orator of St John's College, Cambridge, for 43 years.

51. *Days*, vol. 1, p. 28.

52. At some time in 1872 Haggard took the Army entrance examination not because he wished 'to become a soldier but in order to keep a friend company, and was duly floored by my old enemy, Euclid, for which I am very thankful. Had I passed I might have gone on with the thing and by now been a retired colonel with nothing to do, like so many whom I know.' *Days*, vol. 1, p. 28.

53. Ibid, p. 35.

54. Ibid.

55. Ibid.

56. Ibid.

57. Ibid, pp. 35–6.

58. Ibid, p. 36.

59. Ibid.

60. Ibid.

61. *Love Eternal*, p. 206.

62. Quoted in T.G. Otte, *The Foreign Office Mind: The Making of British Foreign Policy*, 1865–1914, Cambridge: CUP, 2011, p. 13.

63. Ibid.

64. Ibid.

65. Victoria Manthorpe, *Children of the Empire: The Victorian Haggards*, London: Gollancz, 1996, p. 65.

66. *Days*, vol. 1, p. 36.

67. Ibid.

68. Ibid.

69. Inwood, *History of London*, p. 412.

70. Ibid, p. 571.

71. Peter Ackroyd, *London: The Biography*, London: Chatto and Windus, 2000, p. 573.

72. *PD*, 13 January 1922, p. 235.

73. *Days*, vol. 1, p. 37. Haggard incorrectly gives her name as Lady Paulet.

74. Alex Owen, *The Darkened Room: Women, Power and Spiritualism in Late Victorian England*, Philadelphia: University of Pennsylvania Press, 1990, p. 54.

75. Professional magicians such as Harry Houdini and John Nevil Maskelyne went to great lengths to expose the mechanisms used by mediums and their assistants to produce apparently supernatural effects.

76. Andrew Martin, *Ghoul Britannia: Notes from a Haunted Isle*, London: Short Books, 2009, p. 47.

77. Brian Inglis, *Natural and Supernatural*, quoted in ibid, p. 51.

78. *Days*, vol. 1, p. 38.

79. Ibid.

80. Lady Caithness, who believed she was a reincarnation of Mary Stuart, Queen of Scots, owned a palace in Nice which became a centre of Theosophy. She also organised the Parisian branch of the Theosophical Society.

81. Owen, *The Darkened Room*, introduction.

82. Ibid, p. 42.

83. Ibid, p. 54.

84. *Days*, vol. 1, p. 37.

85. Ibid.

86. Ibid.

87. Ibid.

88. Owen, *The Darkened Room*, p. 51.

89. Ibid, p. 48. See Lorna Gibb's novel *A Ghost's Story*, London: Granta, 2016; this 'autobiography' of Katie King is an informative and historically accurate view of the magical and erotic aspects of spiritualism.

90. The Reverend W. Stainton Moses, quoted in Owen, *The Darkened Room*, p. 51.

91. Ibid, p. 52.

92. *Days*, vol. 1, p. 38. Cook and Showers were later exposed as frauds.

93. *Days*, vol. 1, p. 40.

94. Ibid, p. 39.

95. Ibid, p. 41.

96. Ibid.

97. Ibid, p. 42.

98. Ibid.

99. *Cloak*, p. 31.

100. *Days*, vol. 1, p. 42.

101. *Cloak*, p. 202.

102. *Days*, vol. 1, p. 42.

103. Ibid.

104. *Cloak*, p. 31.

105. Higgins's article 'Identifying Haggard's Secret Love', originally published in *London Magazine*, February 1987, appears as an appendix to the revised edition of his biography published in 2013. Some biographers have rendered Lilly as Lily, but the former spelling is correct and is the way she was referred to in letters by her brother Frederick Jackson. See Higgins's appendix to revised edition, p. 395.

106. Ibid, p. 395.

107. Ibid.

108. *Dawn*, p. 179.

109. *Witch's Head*, p. 45.

110. Ibid, pp. 85–6.

111. Haggard travelled to Tours via Paris. He had last been in the French capital in 1871 shortly after the end of the Franco-Prussian War and the suppression of the Paris Commune. A young Frenchman he knew took him to 'a spot backed by a high wall where shortly before he had seen, I think he said, 300 communists executed at once. He told me that the soldiers fired into the moving heap until at length it grew still. On the wall were the marks of their bullets.' *Days*, vol. 1, pp. 43–4. The massacre would find an echo in many a sanguinary episode in Haggard's fiction. *Days*, vol.1, pp. 43–4.

112. Richard Burton, quoted in F.M. Brodie, *The Devil Drives: A Life of Sir Richard Burton*, London: Eyre and Spottiswoode, 1967, p. 29.

113. *Days*, vol. 1, p. 44.

114. HRH, 'Books That Have Influenced Me', *British Weekly*, May 1887, pp. 66–7. Edward Bulwer-Lytton (1803–1873), politician and author, best known for *The Last Days of Pompeii* (1834), *Rienzi* (1835), *A Strange Story* (1862) and *The Coming Race* (1871).

115. *Days*, vol. 1, p. 44.

116. Bulwer to Ella Haggard, 22 June 1875, CC.

117. HRH to Lilly Jackson, undated letter, CC.

118. Ibid. The 'season' referred to was the spring and summer period when Britain's upper classes flocked to London to socialise and match-make at parties, balls and other events.

119. Ibid.

120. Ella Haggard to Alfred Haggard, quoted in Manthorpe, *Children of the Empire*, pp. 67–8.

121. Ella Haggard to Bulwer, 24 June 1875, CC.

122. Bulwer to Ella Haggard, 29 June 1875, CC.

123. *Days*, vol. 1, p. 44.

124. Ibid.

125. John Laband, *Rope of Sand: The Rise and Fall of the Zulu Kingdom in the Nineteenth Century*, Johannesburg: Jonathan Ball, 1995, p. 191.

126. 'A Tale of Three Lions', in *Allan's Wife*, p. 199.

127. *Cloak*, p. 32.
128. Ella Haggard, quoted in *Cloak*, p. 33.
129. This stanza is quoted by Allan Quatermain in *Allan and the Holy Flower*, p. 204.
130. The poem is signed 'Ella Haggard' and dated 16 July 1875, CC.
131. *Days*, vol. 1, p. 49.
132. Ibid.
133. Ibid.
134. *Dawn*, p. 199.

3. 'A MASS OF CONTRADICTORY EVIDENCE'

1. Direct telegraphic communication between South Africa and London was not achieved until December 1879.
2. HRH to father, 18 August 1875, CC. Penny readings – one penny was the price of admission – consisted of readings of prose poetry and drama. They were popularised by Charles Dickens, who gave penny readings to promote literacy, especially among the poor.
3. Ibid.
4. Ibid.
5. Martin Meredith, *Diamonds, Gold and War: The Making of South Africa*, London: Simon and Schuster, 2008, p. 135.
6. Richard Cope, *Ploughshare of War: The Origins of the Anglo-Zulu War of 1879*, Pietermaritzburg: University of Natal Press, 1999, p. 102.
7. HRH to father, 18 August 1875, CC.
8. T.V. Bulpin, *Discovering Southern Africa*, Cape Town: Bulpin, 2001, p. 50.
9. Sir Henry Barkly (1815–1898) was Governor of Cape Colony from 31 December to 31 March 1877, when he was succeeded by Sir Henry Bartle Frere. During his career he was also Governor of British Guiana, Jamaica and Mauritius.
10. HRH to father, 18 August 1875, CC.
11. Ibid.
12. Ibid.
13. Ibid.
14. Ibid. Jones was the second person to hold the title of Bishop of Cape Town, the senior Anglican bishop in southern Africa. The position was elevated to an archbishopric in 1897 and Jones became the first Archbishop of Cape Town.
15. HRH to father, 18 August 1875, CC.
16. *Days*, vol. 1, p. 50.
17. Andrew Duminy and Bill Guest (eds.), *Natal and Zululand: From Earliest Times to 1910*, Pietermaritzburg: University of Natal Press and Shuter & Shooter, 1989, p. 147.
18. *Days*, vol. 1, p. 58.
19. See Jeff Guy, *The Destruction of the Zulu Kingdom*, David Philip, Cape Town, 1982, p. 51, n. 12. In general such names were a descriptive honorific but they could also be

ironic in intent. According to Shepstone's son Arthur, 'there was a great hunter of the name of Somtseu and Sir T.S. got his name from that man'. On a hunting trip during his first visit to Port Natal in 1838, Shepstone had a close encounter with elephants in which he was lucky to escape with his life and thereafter he steered well clear of the animals.

20. See Norman Etherington, 'The "Shepstone System" in the Colony of Natal and beyond its Borders', in Duminy and Guest, *Natal and Zululand*.

21. Shepstone had one claimant to the Ndebele throne in his household, his name variously given as Kuruman, Kruman and Nkulumane, who worked as a stable hand and gardener.

22. John Laband, *Rope of Sand: The Rise and Fall of the Zulu Kingdom in the Nineteenth Century*, Johannesburg: Jonathan Ball, 1995, p. 166.

23. HRH to father, 18 August 1875, CC.

24. Durnford was a friend and supporter of Bishop Colenso. Haggard met Durnford in Pietermaritzburg and describes him in *The Witch's Head* as 'a handsome soldier-like man, with his arm in a sling, a long, fair moustache, and a restless, anxious expression of face'. *Witch's Head*, p. 244. Durnford was wounded in action during the Langalibalele Rebellion and lost the use of his left arm, hence the sling.

25. Quoted in Jeff Guy, *The Heretic: A Study of the Life of William Colenso, 1814–1883*, Pietermaritzburg and Johannesburg: University of Natal Press and Ravan Press, 1983, p. 212.

26. Meredith, *Diamonds, Gold and War*, p. 64.

27. Ibid, p. 157.

28. Ibid.

29. A 'singular type of Africander Talleyrand, shrewd, observant, silent, self-contained, immobile.' Bartle Frere's assessment of Shepstone quoted in *Days*, vol. 1, p. 133. Sir Garnet Wolseley thought Shepstone 'a very cunning underhand fellow ... in dealing with him I always felt I was dealing with a hard, unfeeling man, who had he been a Roman Emperor, would never have hesitated to commit any amount of cruelty in the coolest manner if by so doing he gain his ends.' Sir Garnet Wolseley, *Sir Garnet Wolseley's South African Journal, 1879–1880*, ed. Adrian Preston, Cape Town: Balkema, 1973, p. 270.

30. The *Natal Witness* (now the *Witness*), first published in 1846 and now the oldest continuously published newspaper in South Africa.

31. Wolseley, *Sir Garnet Wolseley's South African Diaries*, p. 248.

32. Ibid, p. 250.

33. Ibid, p. 249.

34. Ibid.

35. Ibid, p. 251.

36. HRH to mother, 15 September 1875, CC.

37. It has been claimed the name of the city derives from Pieter Retief alone, his second name was Mauritz and early records refer to the city as Pieter Mauritzburg. The Zulu name for the city is uMgungundlovu, meaning 'Place of the Elephant', a name originally belonging to the royal homestead of King Dingane kaSenzangakhona and given to the

newly created city in 1838 after the defeat of Dingane's army by the Voortrekkers at the battle of Blood (Ncome) River.

38. Graham Dominy, *The Last Outpost on the Zulu Frontiers: Fort Napier and the Imperial Garrison*, Urbana: University of Illinois Press, 2016, p. 113.

39. Ibid, p. 109.

40. *Natal Witness*, 3 September 1875.

41. HRH to mother, 15 September 1875, CC.

42. *Days*, vol. 1, p. 51.

43. Ibid. Another English expatriate considered Government House one of Maritzburg's few outstanding buildings, set in a 'nice garden and boasting a rather pretty porch, but otherwise reminding one except for the sentinel on duty of a quiet country rectory'. Lady Barker, *Life in South Africa*, Philadelphia: Lippincott, 1877; reprint, New York: Negro Universities Press, 1969, pp. 25–6.

44. *Natal Witness*, 3 September 1875.

45. HRH to mother, 15 September 1875, CC.

46. Ibid.

47. *Natal Witness*, 3 September 1875.

48. The ironic tone was adopted by the *Natal Witness* in its coverage of local politics during the tenure of editor Walter Smith, lawyer and legal partner of Bishop Colenso's son Frank.

49. HRH to mother, 15 September 1875, CC.

50. Ibid.

51. Ibid.

52. Ibid.

53. *Natal Witness*, 30 March 1914. Haggard and previous biographers spell Masuku as Mazooku. I have retained this rendering in quoted material. Masuku kaMadubana was interviewed by James Stuart on 6 May 1914. JSA, vol. 2, p. 239. Circumstantial evidence indicates this was probably Haggard's servant Masuku.

54. In *Witch's Head*, p. 279, Masuku is described as being the 'son of Ingoluvu, of the tribe of the Maquilisini, of the people of the Amazulu'.

55. HRH to mother, 15 September 1875, CC.

56. HRH to father, 18 August 1875, CC

57. Ibid. Kafir or kaffir, derived from an Arabic word meaning 'unbeliever' or 'infidel' (hence Kafiristan, the land of the unbelievers), subsequently applied to black Africans. Its use is now highly abusive and actionable under South African law.

58. HRH to mother, 16 April 1876, quoted in *Days*, vol. 1, p. 56. Robert Gray, the first Bishop of Cape Town, visited Forncett St Mary in 1852 and asked Colenso to accept the headship of the newly created diocese of Natal.

59. *DAJ*, p. 66.

60. HRH to mother, 15 September 1875, CC.

61. Ibid.

62. Ibid.

63. HRH to mother, 26 July 1876, CC.

64. *Natal Witness*, 10 December 1875.

65. HRH to mother, 1 December 1875, CC.

66. Ibid.

67. Arthur J. Wood, *Natal Past and Present: A History of the Natal Mounted Police 1874–1894 and the Natal Police 1894–1913*, Ilfracombe: Stockwell, 1961, p. 100.

68. HRH to mother, 1 December 1875. CC. Hounds being unsuited to subtropical summers, it was 'necessary to start at 4.30 a.m., in order to avoid the midday heat'. Ibid, p. 100.

69. Bruno Martin and Michael Cottrell, *The Natal Old Main Line from Durban to Pietermaritzburg*, Montclair: KwaZulu-Natal Railway History Society, 2015, p. 16.

70. Ibid, p. 4.

71. *DSAB*, vol. 2, p. 617.

72. *Natal Mercury*, quoted in Martin and Cottrell, *The Natal Old Main Line*, p. 177.

73. Ibid.

74. Barker, *Life in South Africa*, p. 37.

75. Ibid.

76. Betty Gilderdale, *The Seven Lives of Lady Barker*, Auckland: Bateman, 1996, p. 100.

77. Ibid, p. 198. The *Times* editor John Thadeus Delane and the Duke of Somerset also recommended Broome take the post.

78. Wolseley, Sir Garnet, *Sir Garnet Wolseley's South African Diaries (Natal), 1875*, ed. Adrian Preston, Cape Town: Balkema, 1971, p. 120.

79. Gilderdale, *Seven Lives*, p. 202.

80. Wolseley, *Sir Garnet Wolseley's South African Diaries*, p. 176.

81. Ibid, p. 183.

82. Gilderdale, *Seven Lives*, p. 157.

83. Gilderdale, p. 170.

84. Subsequently published in book form as *A Year's Housekeeping in South Africa* and in the United States as *Life in South Africa*.

85. Haggard later saved Cox's life. A blow received playing polo severed Cox's external carotid artery. A 'serious operation was performed on him by doctors which necessitated his being kept under chloroform for five hours, but great difficulty was experienced in tying this artery'. Cox appeared to recover and 'at last was allowed to eat a snipe', which Haggard 'went out and shot for him'. Haggard remained uneasy about his colleague and checked on him throughout the night; at dawn he 'found him still lying asleep, but with blood spurting from his head in a little fountain. I pressed my thumb on the artery and held it there until assistance came. Another operation was performed, and ultimately he recovered, though one of his eyes was affected.' *Days*, vol. 1, p. 72.

86. Barker, *Life in South Africa*, p. 37.

87. Ibid.

88. Ibid.

89. *Natal Mercury*, 4 January 1876. See Martin and Cottrell, *The Natal Old Main Line*, Appendix 1, p. 178.

90. Ibid, p. 180.

91. Ibid.

92. Ibid.

93. Ibid.

94. Barker, *Life in South Africa*, p. 38.

95. HRH to mother, 14 February 1876, CC.

96. Ibid.

97. Marina King, *Sunrise to Evening Star: My Seventy Years in South Africa*, London: Harrap, 1938, p. 150.

98. Ibid, pp. 130–1.

99. *Natal Witness*, 10 March 1876.

4.   'THE FIRST THING I EVER WROTE'

1. HRH to mother, 16 April 1876, CC.

2. Ibid.

3. Lady Barker, *Life in South Africa*, Philadelphia: Lippincott, 1877; reprint, New York: Negro Universities Press, 1969, p. 24.

4. Ibid, p. 74.

5. Ibid, p. 74.

6. Ibid, p. 72.

7. Ibid. p. 72.

8. Ibid, p. 73.

9. Ibid, p. 74.

10. Ibid. Sakabula feathers are the long floppy tail feathers from the male Longtailed Widow in breeding plumage. The isiZulu name for the bird is iSakabuli, corrupted variously as saccaboola, saccabula and sakabula.

11. Ibid, pp. 74–5.

12. Ibid, p. 75.

13. Ibid, pp. 75–6.

14. Ibid.

15. *Days*, vol. 1, p. 57.

16. Colenso was still legally Anglican Bishop of Natal. William K. Macrorie was styled Bishop of Maritzburg; he preached in his own cathedral, St Saviour's, a short walk from St Peter's.

17. *Natal Witness*, 18 April 1876, p. 3.

18. Ibid.

19. HRH to mother, 16 April 1876, CC.

20. Ibid.

21. A reference to the Zulu attacks on the Voortrekker encampments on the orders of Dingane following the killing of Piet Retief and his men in 1838.
22. *Natal Witness*, 2 May 1876, p. 3.
23. Ibid.
24. While staying at the homestead of the Mchunu *inkosi*, Phakade kaMacingwane, Colenso was given his Zulu name Sobantu, 'Father of the People', neatly complementing Shepstone's Somsewu, 'Great Father'. Colenso also met Langalibalele, whom he thought 'much more genial and good-natured' than Phakade, and boasting 'that dignity and grace in his actions which so commonly amidst the savage nations, proclaim the king' (John William Colenso, *Ten Weeks in Natal, A Journal of a First Tour of Visitation among the Colonists and Zulu Kafirs of Natal*, Macmillan, 1855, p. 124). Totally unexpected was the theological discussion that took place when Langalibalele brought up the subject of a supreme being, the *umKulunkulu*, which Colenso enthusiastically equated with the God of Christianity.
25. John Sanderson, *Memoranda of a Trading Trip into the Orange River (Sovereignty) Free State, and the Country of the Transvaal Boers*, reprint, Pretoria: State Library, 1981, p. 234.
26. HRH, 'Lost on the Veld', *Windsor Magazine*, 1903, p. 187.
27. HRH to father, 13 May 1876, CC.
28. Ibid.
29. Ibid.
30. Ibid.
31. HRH, 'A Zulu War Dance', *King Solomon's Mines*, ed. Gerald Monsman, Appendix B, item 3, p. 259. I have used this version of Haggard's article 'A Zulu War Dance', which appeared originally in the *Gentleman's Magazine*, July 1877, throughout this chapter. A revised version was added as an appendix to the 1882 edition of *Cetywayo and His White Neighbours*. There are also several quotations from the article in *Cloak*, substantially edited and rewritten. Pagadi's Kop, the highest mountain in the area, has since reverted to its precolonial Zulu name, Ntanyana, meaning 'thin protuberance that looks like a throat': an odd name to give to the highest peak in the area. Perhaps it is a reference to the smaller hill below the summit, which looks like the Adam's apple on the human throat. Or possibly it's an example of the Zulu custom of not drawing attention to oneself.
32. Ibid, pp. 260–1.
33. Ibid, p. 261.
34. Ibid, p. 262.
35. Ibid, pp. 261–2.
36. Ibid.
37. Ibid.
38. Ibid, p. 263.
39. *King Solomon's Mines*, ed. Denis Butts, Oxford: OUP, 1992, p. 28. This edition is used throughout unless otherwise indicated.
40. *King Solomon's Mines*, ed. Monsman, pp. 262–4.

41. Ibid, p. 264.
42. Ibid, pp. 264–8.
43. *Cloak*, p. 44.
44. Ibid.
45. J.E. Scott, 'Hatchers-Out of Tales', *New Colophon*, part IV, October 1948; reprint, *Haggard Journal*, no. 64, Easter 2002, p. 3.
46. Email from Morton Cohen to author, 21 December 2002.
47. Ibid. 'I believe that I never saw any South African notebooks or diaries. I worked exclusively with the material that is now in the Norfolk Records Office. I think it is very likely that Lilias Haggard held those notebooks back ... and then perhaps destroyed them.'
48. *Natal Witness*, 2 June 1876, p. 3.
49. *Cloak*, p. 56.
50. *Days*, vol. 1, p. 49.
51. *DAJ*, p. 115. According to isiZulu linguist Adrian Koopman, Haggard's Zulu name Lundanda uNdandokalweni, meaning 'the tall one who travels on the heights', is derived thus: *lundanda* means 'tall person', and the verb *ndanda* (to glide along, move lazily) has been chosen as a play on words; *khalweni* means 'on the ridge'. With modern spelling and word division, the sentence behind the name would be *undanda okalweni* ('the tall one who walks on the ridge'). The phrase *Ondande ngokhal' olude* ('He who glided along the long ridge') occurs in the praises of King Shaka.
52. See *DAJ*, p. 200.
53. *Days*, vol. 1, p. 57.
54. Ibid, vol. 1, p. 71.
55. HRH to mother, 7 June 1876, CC. Inaugurated in 1851, the show was granted 'royal' status in 1905 and is held annually as the Royal Show.
56. Hilton School, a private school (now Hilton College), founded in 1872 with the object of educating boys to be gentlemen 'in the very best sense of the word, a boy who was honest and upright and true as steel', according to the school's first headmaster the Reverend William Orde Newnham; quoted in Robert Morrell, *From Boys to Gentlemen: Settler Masculinity in Colonial Natal 1880–1920*, Pretoria: University of South Africa, 2001, pp. 52–3.
57. Ibid.
58. *Natal Witness*, 2 June 1876, p. 3.
59. *Days*, vol. 1, p. 120.
60. HRH to mother, 7 June 1876, CC.
61. Ibid.
62. Ibid. The man in question was probably wearing a suit, plus shirt and tie.
63. HRH to mother, 6 July 1876, CC.
64. Barker, *Life in South Africa*, p. 79.
65. Charles Ballard, 'Traders, Trekkers and Colonists', in Andrew Duminy and Bill Guest

(eds.), *Natal and Zululand: From Earliest Times to 1910*, Pietermaritzburg: University of Natal Press and Shuter & Shooter, 1989, p.131.

66. Carolyn Hamilton, *Terrific Majesty: The Powers of Shaka Zulu and the Limits of Historical Invention*, Cape Town: David Philip, 1998, p.133.

67. Norman Etherington, 'Christianity and African Society in Nineteenth-Century Natal', in Duminy and Guest, *Natal and Zululand*, pp. 286–7.

68. Ibid, p. 288.

69. HRH to mother, 7 June 1876, CC. Some sources give Cowley's forename as Edward.

70. Edward C. Tabler (ed.), *Trade and Travel in Barotseland: The Diaries of George Westbeech and Captain Norman Macleod*, Berkeley: University of California Press, 1963, p. 105.

71. Ibid, p. 109.

72. Ibid.

73. Ibid, p. 111.

74. HRH to mother, 7 June 1876, CC.

75. Ibid.

76. Ibid.

77. HRH to mother, 6 July 1876, CC.

78. Ibid.

79. Ibid.

80. Ibid.

5.   'A STRANGER IN STRANGE LANDS'

1. Richard Cope, *Ploughshare of War: The Origins of the Anglo-Zulu War of 1879*, Pietermaritzburg: University of Natal Press, 1999, p. 94.

2. O.C. Weeber. The landdrost was 'the chief officer in a district who acts as Magistrate and Civil Commissioner with the assistance of a Landdrost clerk, who is at the same time Public Prosecutor, Postmaster, and Distributor of Stamps'. Fred Jeppe, *Transvaal Book Almanac and Directory for 1877*, reprint, Pretoria: State Library, 1976, p. 35.

3. Simon Haw, *Bearing Witness: The Natal Witness, 1846–1996*, Pietermaritzburg: Natal Witness, 1996, p. 107.

4. John Laband, *Zulu Warriors: The Battle for the South African Frontier*, London: Yale University Press, 2014, p. 68.

5. Jeff Guy, *Theophilus Shepstone and the Forging of Natal: African Autonomy and Settler Colonialism in the Making of Traditional Authority*, Pietermaritzburg: University of KwaZulu-Natal Press, 2013, p. 472.

6. The boundary dispute between the Boers of the Transvaal and the Zulu went back to the 1850s, a complex mix of lies, deception and land cessions with little documentation, and what there was had been frequently forged. Not in doubt was that Boers were increasingly settling on land the Zulu considered to be theirs.

7. HRH to mother, 6 July 1876, CC.

8. Ibid.

9. Cope, *Ploughshare of War*, p. 104.

10. Letter to father, 3 November 1876, CC.

11. Ibid.

12. Ibid.

13. Ibid.

14. Sir Garnet Wolseley, *Sir Garnet Wolseley's South African Journal, 1879–1880*, ed. Adrian Preston, Cape Town: Balkema, 1973, p. 270.

15. HRH to father, 24 November 1876, CC.

16. Ibid.

17. HRH to mother, 26 July 1876, CC.

18. Quoted in Betty Gilderdale, *The Seven Lives of Lady Barker*, Auckland: Bateman, 1996, p. 240.

19. HRH to father, 3 November 1876, CC.

20. Letter quoted in *Days*, vol. 1, p. 61.

21. HRH to mother, 2 December 1876, CC.

22. HRH to mother, 13 December 1876, CC.

23. Ibid.

24. *Days*, vol. 1, p. 172. 'An honest man's the noblest work of God' – Alexander Pope, 'An Essay on Man'.

25. Ibid, p. 106.

26. *DSAB*, vol. 3, p. 154.

27. Cecil Cowley, *Schwikkard of Natal and the Old Transvaal*, Cape Town: Struik, 1974, p. 2.

28. Shelagh O'Byrne Spencer, *British Settlers in Natal: A Biographical Register*, vol. 8, Pietermaritzburg: University of KwaZulu-Natal Press, 2016, p. 206.

29. *Natal Witness*, 1 December 1876, p. 3. This observation was emphasised a few days later: 'We have no very high opinion of the Boers but even they are entitled to be invaded by a force of respectable numbers.' *Natal Witness*, 5 December 1876.

30. *Cloak*, p. 48. The quotation is from a diary which, according to Lilias, her father kept during 'this first trip into the Transvaal'. *Cloak*, p. 48. The diary is no longer extant.

31. E.F. Sandeman, *Eight Months in an Ox-Waggon*, reprint, Johannesburg: Africana Book Society, 1975 [1880], p. 48.

32. HRH, quoted in *Cloak*, p. 48.

33. Ibid.

34. Ibid.

35. Ibid.

36. The fort was rebuilt in 1874 by Major Anthony Durnford.

37. Sandeman, *Eight Months in an Ox-Waggon*, p. 60.

38. Haggard, quoted in *Cloak*, p. 49.

39. HRH to mother, 25 December 1876, CC. Lilias includes this letter, substantially rewritten, in *Cloak*, p. 49.

40. Ibid. At the time 'miasmas' were thought to be the cause of malaria.

41. Ibid.

42. Ibid.

43. HRH, quoted in *Cloak*, pp. 49–50.

44. Ibid, p. 50.

45. Ibid.

46. Ruth Gordon, *Shepstone: The Role of the Family in the History of South Africa, 1820–1900*, Cape Town: Balkema, 1968, p. 256.

47. John Nixon, *The Complete Story of the Transvaal*, reprint, Cape Town: Struik, 1972 [1885], p. 39.

48. HRH, quoted in *Cloak*, p. 50.

49. Ibid.

50. Bulwer to William Haggard, 2 January 1877, CC.

51. Letter from father to HRH, 20 December 1876, CC.

52. Ibid.

53. Ibid.

54. Letter to Ella Haggard from William Haggard, 25 January 1877, CC.

55. HRH, quoted in *Cloak*, p. 50.

56. Ibid. The attack Haggard refers took place on 2 January 1877 when a force led by Mbilini waSwati, an exiled Swazi prince and claimant to the Swazi throne who had pledged allegiance to Cetshwayo, attacked the farm of a Boer called Labuschagne and killed fifty Africans. As a result of these attacks 'some 60 Boer families trekked from the border area'. Huw Jones, *The Boiling Cauldron: Utrecht District and the Anglo-Zulu War, 1879*, Bisley, Gloucestershire: Shermershill, 2006, p. 119.

57. HRH, quoted in *Cloak*, pp. 50–1.

58. Kotzé, John, *Biographical Memoirs and Reminiscences*, Cape Town: Maskew Miller, [1934], p. 475.

59. Born in 1817, Stander was wounded at the battle of Boomplaats in 1848, fought to prevent British incursion north of the Orange River. The Boers were defeated, Stander's land was confiscated and he moved to a farm on the Vaal River. Here on 12 August 1865 in his farmhouse below Stander's Kop, he fought off Basuto raiders with his sons, the eldest of whom was killed while 'his wife and baby, accompanied by a servant, fled into the winter's night and waded through the Vaal river.' R.N. Currey, *Vinnicombe's Trek: Son of Natal, Stepson of Transvaal*, London: James Currey; Portsmouth: Heinemann; Pietermaritzburg: University of Natal Press and Shuter & Shooter, 1989, p. 107.

60. Cowley, *Schwikkard of Natal*, p. 49.

61. Ibid, p. 50.

62. Ibid, p. 12.

63. Ibid, p. 15.

64. Ibid, p. 40.

65. Ibid, p. 50.

66. Ibid.

67. Ibid.

68. Fannin Papers, Campbell Collections.
69. Cowley, *Schwikkard of Natal*, p. 51. Shepstone's birthday was not until 8 January.
70. Ibid.
71. Ibid, p. 52.
72. Ibid, p. 53.
73. *Days*, vol. 1, p. 76. Square-face, an imported Dutch gin also called Geneva or Hollands. 'The only gin in use is the Schiedam, sold in square green glass bottles, and generally known as square-face or square rigger.' Sandeman, *Eight Months in an Ox-Waggon*, p. 97.
74. Ibid, pp. 74–5.
75. See Appendix, p. 473.

6.   'ONE OF THE HARDEST JOURNEYS IMAGINABLE'

1.   HRH, quoted in *Cloak*, p. 51.
2.   *Cetywayo*, p. 139.
3.   Cecil Cowley, *Schwikkard of Natal and the Old Transvaal*, Cape Town: Struik, 1974, p. 53.
4.   HRH to mother, 21 January 1877, CC.
5.   Ibid.
6.   Ibid.
7.   Ibid.
8.   Cowley, p. 33.
9.   Anon., *Rosmarine: A Story of Twenty-Five Years and a Sequel, with a preface by Sir H. Rider Haggard*, London: Mowbray, 1913, p. 11.
10. Ibid, p. 14.
11. John Kotzé, *Biographical Memoirs and Reminiscences*, Cape Town: Maskew Miller, [1934], p. 407.
12. HRH, quoted in *Cloak*, p. 51. Founded in 1851, the Good Templars promote abstinence from alcohol and drugs.
13. Anthony Trollope, *South Africa*, reprint, Manzini: Bok Books, 1987, vol. 2, p. 53.
14. *Cetywayo*, pp. 139–40.
15. HRH, 'Camp Life in Pretoria', p. 3, The Brenthurst Library, Johannesburg, MS 251, Memorandum.
16. Ibid, p. 4.
17. According to Morcom, 'prior to annexation – a period of 11 weeks – Pretoria was treated to no less than fifty-nine social functions given either in honour of or by the Special Commissioner. There were dinners, dances, picnics, whist drives, "moonshine" parties.' Morcom, quoted in Gordon, *Shepstone*, p. 259.
18. *Cetywayo*, p. 142.
19. HRH, 'Camp Life', p. 6. Haggard gives the number of Boers at 450; other estimates vary between 600 and 800.
20. Ibid, p. 7.

21. Ibid, pp. 7–8.

22. Kotzé, *Biographical Memoirs*, p. 306.

23. HRH, 'Camp Life', p. 12.

24. Ibid, p. 14.

25. Shepstone Papers, Miscellaneous, Transvaal, '"Family Notes by Morcom" vol. 92, 30 April 1877, p. 41, Pietermaritzburg Archives Repository.

26. HRH, 'Camp Life' p. 16.

27. Ibid, p. 17.

28. Ibid, p. 19a.

29. Ibid, p. 20.

30. Morcom family letter, in Shepstone Papers, Miscellaneous, Transvaal, '"Family Notes by Morcom"', vol. 92, 30 April 1877, p. 41, Pietermaritzburg Archives Repository. Morcom's description still applies; the tree is estimated to be over a thousand years old.

31. HRH, 'Camp Life', p. 21. Anthony Trollope visited the tree later in the year and thought it 'a graceful green tree – but not very wonderful'. Trollope, *South Africa*, vol. 2, p. 62.

32. Quoted in Betty Gilderdale, *The Seven Lives of Lady Barker*, Auckland: Bateman, 1996, p. 244.

33. HRH, 'The Transvaal', *Macmillan's Magazine*, May 1877, p. 71.

34. HRH, 'Camp Life', p. 26. 'Dopper' is 'a nickname for a member of the strictly Calvinist Gereformeerde Kerk in Suid-Afrika', one of the family of Dutch Reformed churches of which the Nederduits Gereformeerde Kerk in Suid-Afrika (Dutch Reformed Church) has the largest membership'. Jean Branford and William Branford, *A Dictionary of South African English*, Cape Town: OUP, 1991, p. 195.

35. HRH, 'Camp Life', p. 26.

36. Ibid, pp. 27–8.

37. Ibid, p. 28.

38. Richard Cope, *Ploughshare of War: The Origins of the Anglo-Zulu War of 1879*, Pietermaritzburg: University of Natal Press, 1999, p. 128.

39. *Days*, vol. 1, pp. 96–7. The incident features in *Finished*, the concluding volume of Haggard's Zulu trilogy, pp. 22–3.

40. HRH, 'Camp Life', p. 34.

41. *Days*, vol. 1, p. 97.

42. Ibid.

43. *Cetywayo*, p. 158.

44. Cope, *Ploughshare of War*, pp. 128–9.

45. Ibid, p. 125.

46. Ibid.

47. *Days*, vol. 1, p. 83.

48. *Cetywayo*, p. 159. Message dated 16 February 1877.

49. Ibid.

50. HRH to father, 16 March 1877, CC.

51. The article 'A Visit to the Chief Secocoeni' was published in *Gentleman's Magazine*,

September 1877, above the initials H.R.H. All quotations from the article are from the original magazine version of the article reprinted in *A Guide to the Non-Fiction of Rider Haggard* by Roger Allen, where the article is reproduced unpaginated. Subsequent unreferenced quotations in this chapter are from this source.

52. Shepstone to Bulwer, 20 March 1877, NRA 28118, A 96, Pietermaritzburg Archives Repository.
53. Cockle's Anti-Bilious Pills, a universal panacea of the time.
54. Report to the Colonial Office, 3 February 1879, by Frere, quoted in *Days*, vol. 1, p. 133.
55. Kotzé, *Biographical Memoirs*, p. 296n.
56. *Days*, vol. 1, p. 133.
57. Kotzé, *Biographical Memoirs*, p. 523.
58. Ibid, p. 524.
59. Ibid.
60. Joseph O. Vogel, 'Merensky and Nachtigal in Southern Africa: A Contemporary Source for *King Solomon's Mines*', *Journal of African Travel Writing*, no. 4, 1998, pp. 20–30.
61. Botshabelo looks much the same as it did in 1877. The buildings and stone walls are all intact as is the beautiful red-brick church with its roof of thatch. Fort Wilhelm remains an anachronistic but impressive sight.
62. *Cetywayo*, p. 160.
63. Ibid.
64. African horse sickness remains endemic to Africa, but in the 1870s there was no cure nor was the mechanism of infection understood. The disease was finally brought under control with the advent of an effective vaccine in 1934.
65. The Salons River, a tributary of the Olifants.
66. Despite the remote location and adverse conditions, including 'danger from surrounding tribes', the three-year-old mine had already 'reduced the price of cobalt – the blue dye used to colour such things as willow-pattern plates – by one half in the English market, bringing it down from somewhere about £140 to £80 a ton'. HRH, 'A Visit to Secocoeni'.
67. *Days*, vol. 1, p. 84.
68. Ibid, p. 88.
69. *Cetywayo*, p. 161.
70. HRH, quoted in *Cloak*, p. 63.
71. Ibid.
72. HRH, *Memorandum of the Circumstances Connected with the Plot to Murder the Late Melmoth Osborn, Sir Marshall Clarke, and H. Rider Haggard*, privately printed, McLean, VA: Alfred Tella, 2003. Haggard was prompted to write the memorandum, having written 'an article on Dr Leyds' mendacious work called "The First Annexation of the Transvaal" and the receipt of a letter from my old friend, Sir Marshall Clarke, both of which circumstances have revived old memories in my mind, that have caused me to record this curious incident of bygone history in black and white. Perhaps some day it may be of interest to those who come after us.' HRH, *Memorandum*, p. 8.

73. Ibid, p. 4. Their names are given in *Days* as Sekouili and Nojoiani. The name of Scowl is given to a Zulu servant in *Child of Storm*.

74. Ibid. According to the account in *Days*, 'one of my companions I think it was Osborn, said with a laugh, "Oh! Let the young donkey have his way. Who knows he may be right!" or words to that effect.' *Days*, vol. 1, p. 90.

75. *Days*, vol. 1, p. 90. This episode features in *The Witch's Head*, see pp. 233–4.

76. HRH, *Memorandum*, p. 5.

77. Ibid, p. 7.

78. Ibid.

79. Ibid.

80. Ibid, p. 7.

81. Ibid, p. 6.

82. Ibid.

83. Ibid.

84. Ibid, p. 5.

85. Shepstone to Bulwer, 3 April 1877, NRA 28118, A 96, Pietermaritzburg Archives Repository.

86. Ibid.

87. HRH to mother, 30 October 1877, CC.

88. HRH, *Memorandum*, p. 7.

89. Ibid.

90. 'It is said ... that when Mr. Osborn, Clarke & another went to see Sikikuni' that Ferreira 'endeavoured to get Sikukuni to murder the party: in fact that upon three occasions he endeavoured to accomplish their murder but failed each time.' Sir Garnet Wolseley, *Sir Garnet Wolseley's South African Journal, 1879–1880*, ed. Adrian Preston, Cape Town: Balkema, 1973, p. 117.

91. *Days*, vol. 1, p. 89. In *Finished* there is an oblique reference to the ambush conspiracy when Allan Quatermain mentions the Boers 'intriguing against the British through Makurupiji'. *Finished*, p. 61. The conspiracy also provides a plot element in *Finished*, when a character named Rodd colludes with the Pedi (referred to as Basutho) to have Quatermain killed. The first section of the novel is set in the Lydenburg district and draws on Haggard's travel experiences on the trip to Tsate.

92. Ian Knight, *Zulu Rising: The Epic Story of iSandlwana and Rorke's Drift*, London: Macmillan, 2010, p. 122.

93. Ibid.

94. Cope, *Ploughshare of War*, p. 127.

95. Kotzé, *Biographical Memoirs*, p. 327.

96. Ibid.

97. *Cetywayo*, p. 165.

98. Cope, *Ploughshare of War*, p. 126.

99. Kotzé, *Biographical Memoirs*, p. 328.

100. *Cetywayo*, p. 166.

101. *Days*, vol. 1, p. 104.

102. Ibid, p. 105.

103. Proclamation in Appendix to Alfred Aylward, *The Transvaal of Today: War, Witchcraft, Sport and Spoils in South Africa*, Edinburgh: William Blackwood and Sons, 1881, pp. 296–297.

104. Ibid, pp. 297–299.

105. Ibid, pp. 299–300.

106. *Cetywayo*, p. 167.

107. Ibid.

108. *Finished*, p. 19.

109. *DAJ*, p. 129. According to Kotzé, Osborn, though 'a man of courage ... was of retiring disposition, and when reading the proclamation his hands trembled so, that his assistant ... Haggard, had to hold the document for him.' Kotzé was not present at the annexation so his account is based on what he was told later, possibly by Haggard.

110. Fred Jeppe, *Transvaal Book Almanac and Directory for 1877*, reprint, Pretoria: State Library, 1976, p. 82.

111. *Cetywayo*, p. 173

112. Morcom family letter, in Shepstone Papers, Miscellaneous, Transvaal, '"Family Notes by Morcom" – in Shepstone's Camp at Pretoria before and after the Annexation', vol. 92, 'Notes', 2 May 1877, p. 97. Pietermaritzburg Archives Repository.

113. Morcom family letter, in Shepstone Papers, '"Family Notes by Morcom"', vol. 92, 'Notes', 9 May 1877, p. 111.

114. *Cetywayo*, p. 174. The presence of a British battalion rendered the twenty-five Natal Mounted Police under Lieutenant Frederick Phillips superfluous and they returned to Natal.

115. The 'natives' included representatives of chiefdoms in the Transvaal. The Swazi had also been invited but objected to pledging fealty to the crown. See Philip Bonner, *Kings, Commoners and Concessionaires: The Evolution and Dissolution of the Nineteenth-Century Swazi State*, Johannesburg: Ravan, 1983, pp. 148–9.

116. *Days*, vol. 1, p. 106.

117. *Cetywayo*, p. 175.

118. HRH to mother, 17 June 1877, CC.

119. HRH to father, 13 March 1877, CC.

120. Ibid.

121. Ibid.

122. *Days*, vol. 1, p. 21.

123. Ibid.

124. Ibid.

125. Ibid, p. 22.

126. Ibid.

127. Ibid, p. 100.

128. Ibid, pp. 99–100.

129. Ibid, p. 100.

130. Ibid.

131. *Cloak*, p. 70.

132. Ibid.

133. Ibid, p. 69.

134. *Witch's Head*, p. 75.

135. HRH to father, 1 June 1877, CC.

136. Ibid.

137. Ibid.

138. Ibid.

139. Ibid.

140. Ibid.

141. Ibid.

7.   'PLEASANT RECOLLECTIONS'

1.   Ford to daughter Muriel, 12 May 1913, Peter Smits Collection (in private hands).

2.   J. Kotzé, *Biographical Memoirs and Reminiscences*, Cape Town: Maskew Miller, [1934], p. 433.

3.   Smits, 'Lewis Peter Ford: An Almost Forgotten Pioneer of Johannesburg', MS, Peter Smits Collection.

4.   Ford to daughter Muriel, 12 May 1913, Peter Smits Collection.

5.   Ibid.

6.   Ibid.

7.   Smits, 'Lewis Peter Ford', Peter Smits Collection.

8.   Kotzé, *Biographical Memoirs*, p. 207.

9.   Ibid, p. 405.

10.   Ibid, p. 406.

11.   Ibid, p. 414.

12.   Ibid, p. 422.

13.   Ibid, p. 429.

14.   Despite his youth Kotzé was a highly competent judge and his judgments were held in high regard. In 'the early years of the ZAR, qualifications and training were not considered a prerequisite for entrance to the legal profession. Instead, measures were put in place to exclude unwanted persons from the profession, namely an undefined "ability" as well as objective proof of White Afrikaner morality in the form of membership of the Dutch Reformed Church.' L. Wildenboer, 'For a Few Dollars More: Overcharging and Misconduct in the Legal Profession of the Zuid-Afrikaansche Republiek', *De Jure* (Pretoria), vol. 44, no. 2, 2011, pp. 353–4.

15.   Kotzé, *Biographical Memoirs*, p. 431.

16.   'He is 28 years of age, and the ordinary stamp of Cape Africander, speaks English with a Dutch idiom, and does not strike one as likely to inspire the beholder with respect

for the court of which he might perchance be the chief presiding officer.' Shepstone Papers, Miscellaneous, Transvaal, '"Family Notes by Morcom" – in Shepstone's Camp at Pretoria before and after the Annexation', vol. 92, 30 April 1877, p. 114, Pietermaritzburg Archives Repository. In 1879 Morcom was appointed Attorney-General of the Transvaal by Sir Garnet Wolseley. Kotzé opposed the appointment on the grounds Morcom 'was not a properly qualified lawyer' for the position. Kotzé, *Biographical Memoirs*, p. 697.

17. HRH to mother, 17 June 1877, CC.

18. Ibid.

19. Philip Bonner, *Kings, Commoners and Concessionaires: The Evolution and Dissolution of the Nineteenth-Century Swazi State*, Johannesburg: Ravan, 1983, p. 148.

20. Richard Cope, *Ploughshare of War: The Origins of the Anglo-Zulu War of 1879*, Pietermaritzburg: University of Natal Press, 1999, p. 154.

21. Shepstone to Carnarvon, 11 December 1877, quoted in Peter Delius, *The Land Belongs to Us: The Pedi Polity, the Boers and the British in the Nineteenth-Century Transvaal*, Johannesburg: Ravan Press, 1983, p. 232.

22. Quoted in Cope, *Ploughshare of War*, p. 166.

23. Ibid, p. 178.

24. Ibid, p. 187.

25. *Days*, vol. 1, p. 137.

26. Kotzé, *Biographical Memoirs*, p. 458.

27. *Farmer's Year*, p. 86.

28. HRH to mother, 16 September 1878, CC.

29. Kotzé, *Biographical Memoirs*, pp. 459–60.

30. Ibid, p. 460.

31. HRH, 'Lost on the Veld', *Windsor Magazine*, 1903, p. 192. The same story is found in *Days*, vol. 1, pp. 137–40.

32. HRH, 'Lost on the Veld'.

33. Ibid, pp. 192–3.

34. Ibid, p. 193.

35. Ibid, p. 194.

36. See *Queen Sheba's Ring*, pp. 47 and 51.

37. Kotzé, *Biographical Memoirs*, p. 463.

38. Ibid.

39. Ibid, p. 464.

40. Ibid.

41. Ibid, pp. 464–5.

42. Ibid. The korhaan is the blue korhaan (*Epeudotis caerrulescens*). The red-winged partridge is the red-winged francolin (*Sceleroptila levaillantii*).

43. Ibid.

44. Ibid.

45. Ibid.

46. Delius, *Land Belongs to Us*, p. 139. African children or *inboekselings* (apprentices)

were often captured in Boer raids, and were as valuable as ivory in terms of trade. Haggard himself recorded seeing *inboekselings* in the south of the Transvaal, probably at Wakkerstroom, where he was struck by the number of black children standing around certain houses. '[I] learnt a few hours later that they were part of loads which were disposed of on the outskirts of the town the day before.' *Cetywayo*, p. 128.

47. Sandeman, E.F., *Eight Months in an Ox-Waggon*, reprint, Johannesburg: Africana Book Society, 1975 [1880], p. 203. Florida Water, an alcohol-based perfume.
48. Kotzé, *Biographical Memoirs*, p. 467.
49. Ibid.
50. Ibid, p. 469.
51. Ibid.
52. Ibid.
53. Ibid.
54. *Farmer's Year*, p. 85.
55. Kotzé, *Biographical Memoirs*, p. 472.
56. Ibid. They were marooned on the Elandsberg, a spur of the Drakensberg.
57. Ibid, pp. 472–3.
58. Ibid, p. 473.
59. Ibid, p. 474.
60. *Jess*, p. 143.
61. 'I cannot say that the hotels along the way were very good ... We were a week on the road from Newcastle and pulled off our clothes but once – when we were under the hospitable roof of Mrs Swickhard [*sic*], who keeps a store about half way at a place called Standers Drift.' Anthony Trollope, *South Africa*, reprint, Manzini: Bok Books, 1987, vol. 2, p. 4.
62. HRH to mother, 13 October 1877, CC.
63. *Days*, vol. 1, p. 137.
64. Maré was reinstated as landdrost after the retrocession of the Transvaal in 1881.
65. HRH to mother, 13 October 1877, CC.
66. Kotzé, *Biographical Memoirs*, p. 479.
67. In 1880 Sir Garnet Wolseley referred to Buskes as 'this old villain'. Wolseley, *Sir Garnet Wolseley's South African Journal, 1879–1880*, ed. Adrian Preston, Cape Town: Balkema, 1973, p. 263.
68. Kotzé, *Biographical Memoirs*, p. 480.
69. Ibid, pp. 481–2. See *King Solomon's Mines*, p. 264.
70. Ibid, p. 483.
71. HRH to mother, 13 October 1877, CC.
72. Ibid. In the 1860s Bell facilitated the white settlement of New Scotland, which saw 300 Scots occupying farms along the Transvaal–Swaziland border. Thereafter he had been Justice of the Peace for New Scotland and captain of the local volunteer corps. A Swaziland border commissioner and a sub-commissioner of Native Affairs, he was also a member of a commission investigating charges of slavery in the Transvaal.

73. HRH to mother, 13 October 1877. CC.
74. Ibid.
75. Ibid.

8. 'A CRUSHING BLOW'

1. HRH to mother, 30 October 1877, CC.
2. Ibid.
3. Ibid.
4. HRH report to Shepstone, 8 January 1878, TAB SS vol. 321, R 4611/78, National Archives Repository, Pretoria.
5. Ibid.
6. Ibid.
7. Ibid.
8. John Kotzé, *Biographical Memoirs and Reminiscences*, Cape Town: Maskew Miller, [1934], p. 501.
9. HRH, Unpublished report or draft for an article, Pretoria, 8 January 1878, in Shepstone Papers, Pietermaritzburg Archives Repository.
10. Kotzé, *Biographical Memoirs*, pp. 424–5.
11. L. Wildenboer, 'The Judicial Officers of the Transvaal High Court, 1877–1881', *Fundmina*, vol. 25, no. 2, 2019, p. 270. Apart from being an acting Attorney General, Ford also acted as a judge on two occasions. He was chancellor of the Anglican diocese of Pretoria from 1879 to 1889.
12. HRH to mother, 11 February 1878, CC.
13. Kotzé, *Biographical Memoirs*, p. 495.
14. See Huw Jones, *A Biographical Register of Swaziland to 1902*, Pietermaritzburg: University of Natal Press, 1993, p. 558.
15. HRH to mother, 22 July 1878, CC.
16. Stewart was fluent in isiZulu and had Swazi connections owing to earlier hunting expeditions.
17. HRH to mother, 16 September 1878, CC.
18. Ibid.
19. HRH to father, 20 October 1878, CC.
20. HRH to mother, 4 March 1878, CC.
21. Ibid.
22. His name is given variously as Ubekana, Makebani and Kabana in contemporary sources.
23. *Days*, vol. 1, pp. 112–3.
24. Ibid. Haggard gave a similar account of the incident in an interview by Harry How in 1892. See *Strand Magazine*, January 1892, pp. 10–1.
25. Kotzé, *Biographical Memoirs*, p. 487.
26. Ibid.

27. Ibid, p. 488. Kotzé also took issue with Haggard over another 'serious slip' in the novel *Finished*, where President Burgers is said to have been bribed with a pension prior to annexation. See Kotzé, *Biographical Memoirs*, p. 389n.

28. Ibid, p. 488. There is an allusion to the hanging in *Allan Quatermain*. While waiting for the dawn, the signal for a battle to commence, Quatermain reflects that such a time is 'most oppressive to the spirits. I once remember having to get up before dawn to see a man hanged, and I then went through a very similar set of sensations.' *Allan Quatermain*, p. 84.

29. *DAJ*, p. 61.

30. HRH to father, 31 March 1878, CC. Haggard had suggested the taxation of bills of costs prior to his being made acting Master and Registrar in a letter to Osborn, dated 5 December 1877, TAB SS vol. 258, R4625/77 170-171, National Archives Repository. See L. Wildenboer, 'For a Few Dollars More: Overcharging and Misconduct in the Legal Profession of the Zuid-Afrikaansche Republiek', *De Jure* (Pretoria), vol. 44, no. 2, 2011, p. 356, n. 125.

31. HRH to father, 7 April 1878, CC. According to the official record, Haggard's appointment ran from 3 August 1877, incorporating the period while he was acting in the position.

32. Ibid.

33. Ibid.

34. HRH to mother, 13 April 1878, CC.

35. HRH to mother, 11 February 1878, CC.

36. 'The Patterson Embassy to Lobengula', in W.A. Wills and L.T. Collingridge, *The Downfall of Lobengula*, London: Simpkin, Marshall, Hamilton and Kent, 1894; reprint, Bulawayo: Books of Rhodesia, 1971, p. 227.

37. Ibid, p. 228.

38. Ibid.

39. Kotzé, *Biographical Memoirs*, p. 451.

40. Rowland J. Atcherley, *A Trip to Boerland*, quoted in Joy Collier, *The Purple and the Gold: The Story of Pretoria and Johannesburg*, Cape Town: Longmans, 1965, p. 55.

41. Collier, *The Purple and the Gold*, p. 54.

42. Kotzé, *Biographical Memoirs*, p. 451.

43. Ibid.

44. E.F. Sandeman, *Eight Months in an Ox-Waggon*, reprint, Johannesburg: Africana Book Society, 1975 [1880], p. 127.

45. Ibid.

46. Ibid, pp. 128–9.

47. Ibid, p. 129.

48. HRH to father, 2 June 1878, CC.

49. HRH to father, 1 June 1877, CC.

50. HRH to father, 2 June 1878, CC. See M. Emms, 'Henry Rider and the Elusive Jess Cottage', *Africana: Yearbook of the Africana Society of Pretoria*, no. 30, 2013, p. 37.

51. HRH to mother, 22 July 1878, CC.

52. HRH to father, 2 September 1878, CC

53. HRH to father, 22 September 1878, CC.

54. HRH to mother, 18 November 1878, CC.

55. *DAJ*, p. 241.

56. HRH, notebook diary for 1878, CC.

57. Ibid.

58. *Days*, vol. 1, p. 116.

59. *Cloak*, p. 72.

60. Ibid, p. 73.

61. Ibid.

62. *The Witch's Head*, p. 219.

63. *Cloak*, p. 72.

64. *Days*, vol. 1, p. 116.

65. *Witch's Head*, p. 128. Alston repeats this advice later in the book: 'go in for an Intombi. It is not too late yet, and there is no mistake about the sort of clay of which a Kafir girl is made.' Ibid, p. 178.

66. A letter written by the 19-year-old Shepstone to Henry Fynn in 1836 reveals Shepstone had a relationship with a woman of colour named Meeta with whom he may have fathered a child. In the letter he asks Fynn to pass on a gift to her with the instructions: 'Please tell her and let her kiss the seal three times – as I have done. Oh what a foolish fellow I am, this is my weak point, pray excuse me.' Quoted in J. Weir and N. Etherington, 'Shepstone in Love: The Other Victorian in an African Colonial Administrator', in *Orb and Sceptre: Studies on British Imperialism and Its Legacies, in Honour of Norman Etherington*, ed. Peter Limb, Melbourne: Monash University ePress, 2008, DOI: 10.2104/os080002, pp. 2–3.

67. The relationship between Haggard and Johanna Catherine Ford was first brought to light by Victoria Manthorpe in *Children of the Empire: The Victorian Haggards*, London: Gollancz, 1996, see pp. 89ff.

68. Josephine Lehmkuhl was born in 1861.

69. HRH, notebook diary for 1878, CC.

70. Kotzé, *Biographical Memoirs*, pp. 518–9.

71. Ibid, pp. 520–1.

72. Ibid, p. 523.

73. HRH to father, 2 September 1878, CC.

74. Ibid. William Emil Hollard practised as an attorney during the 1870s and 1880s. On various occasions he was 'accused of crimes such as theft, prison-break, murder and fraud, although never convicted of any of them'. Wildenboer, 'For a Few Dollars More', pp. 356–7.

75. Wills and Collingridge, *Downfall of Lobengula*, p. 228.

76. Ibid.

77. HRH to mother, 18 November 1878, CC.

78. HRH to father, 20 October 1878, CC.

79. HRH to mother, 18 November 1878, CC.

80. *Days*, vol. 1, p. 116.

81. *Witch's Head*, pp. 233–4.

82. *Cloak*, p. 73.

83. *Dawn*, p. 200. The origin of the quotation is unknown.

84. *Cloak*, p. 72.

85. *Dawn*, p. 199.

86. *Cloak*, p. 85.

87. Kotzé, *Cases*, p. 67.

88. HRH to mother, 22 July 1878, CC.

89. T.V. Bulpin, *Lost Trails of the Transvaal*, Cape Town: Bulpin, 1974, p. 171.

90. Alfred Aylward, *The Transvaal of Today: War, Witchcraft, Sport and Spoils in South Africa*, Edinburgh: William Blackwood and Sons, 1881, p. 86.

91. Ibid, p. 86.

92. Ibid.

93. Ibid.

94. Ibid, p. 90.

95. Haggard described *De Volkstem* as 'a newspaper of an extremely abusive nature', adding that the *Natal Witness* 'has an almost equally unenviable reputation'. *Cetywayo*, p. 176.

96. Kotzé, *Cases*, pp. 72–3.

97. Adrian Greaves and Ian Knight, *The Who's Who of the Anglo-Zulu War 1879*, Barnsley: Pen and Sword, 2006, vol. 2, p. 118.

98. Ibid.

99. Ibid.

100. *Cetywayo*, p. 183. Some aspect of Weatherley's erratic and impulsive character probably explains the brief entry in Haggard's diary on 11 February 1878: 'Had row with Weatherley. Received his apology.'

101. Ibid.

102. Ibid, p. 183.

103. Ibid, pp. 183–4.

104. Ibid, p. 184.

105. Ibid.

106. Ibid.

107. Ibid, p. 186. Kotzé gives a figure of 'about 500 signatures ... some genuine many of them fictitious'. Kotzé, *Biographical Memoirs*, p. 512.

108. *Cetywayo*, p. 186.

109. Ibid. There was ill-feeling between the sons and their mother, knowing which Weatherley 'did not pay the same attention that a more suspicious or vigilant husband would perhaps have done'. Kotzé, *Cases*, p. 95.

110. Kotzé, *Cases,* p. 67.

111. Henry William Alexander Cooper (1842–94) was the son of British immigrants to the

Cape. In 1866 he became legal agent in Fraserburg in the Karoo. From there he wrote gossipy articles in an early form of Afrikaans under the pseudonym Samuel Zwaartman for the *Cape Argus* and *Het Volksblad*. After being involved in amorous adventures with a local hairdresser, Cooper came to the Transvaal and was admitted as a lawyer and advocate, subsequently becoming a magistrate in Lydenburg before returning to Pretoria and building a thriving practice.

112. Kotzé, *Cases*, p. 98.

113. Kotzé, *Biographical Memoirs*, p. 513.

114. Kotze dismissed Colonel Weatherley's 'summons for a divorce *a vinculo*'. Kotzé, *Cases*, p. 67.

115. HRH, notebook diary for 1878, CC.

116. Ibid.

117. Kotzé, *Cases*, p. 73.

118. Greaves and Knight, *Who's Who of the Anglo-Zulu War*, vol. 2, p. 119.

119. HRH, notebook diary for 1878, entry 4 December. CC.

120. Kuruman, also known as Nkulumane. Haggard had 'a recollection of hearing the late Sir Theophilus Shepstone tell Captain Patterson the story of this Kruman, who I think was at one time in his employ as a gardener, but of whose rights to the chieftainship of the nation a section of the Matebeli people were advocates'. Wills and Collingridge, *Downfall of Lobengula*, p. 229.

9.   'DISASTER IN ZULULAND'

1.   HRH to mother, 16 September 1878, CC.

2.   Anon., *Rosmarine: A Story of Twenty-Five Years and a Sequel, with a preface by Sir H. Rider Haggard*, London: Mowbray, 1913, p. 10.

3.   Entry from *DSAB*, vol. 1, pp. 457–8.

4.   Bousfield and his wife Charlotte had two sons and six daughters.

5.   J. Kotzé, *Biographical Memoirs and Reminiscences*, Cape Town: Maskew Miller, [1934], p. 555. In Britain city status was traditionally bestowed on towns boasting a diocesan cathedral (or a bishop), hence Bousfield's pronouncement. This arrangement ceased in the late 1880s.

6.   HRH to father, 13 April 1878, CC.

7.   HRH to father, 6 July 1876, quoted in *Days*, vol. 1, p. 61.

8.   *Days*, vol. 1, pp. 69–70.

9.   Ibid, p. 70.

10. Quoted in Richard Cope, *Ploughshare of War: The Origins of the Anglo-Zulu War of 1879*, Pietermaritzburg: University of Natal Press, 1999, p. 237.

11. Quoted in ibid, p. 222.

12. Quoted in John Laband, *Zulu Warriors: The Battle for the South African Frontier*, London: Yale University Press, 2014, p. 220.

13. Cope, *Ploughshare of War*, p. 233.

14. Cochrane, now a clerk on Shepstone's staff, was with his new master in Utrecht, where Shepstone had gone to await developments after the announcement of the ultimatum.

15. HRH, 'An Incident of African History', *Windsor Magazine*, 1900, p. 112.

16. Ibid, p. 113.

17. Ibid.

18. *Days*, vol. 1, pp. 117–8.

19. Ibid, vol. 1, p. 118.

20. *Cloak*, p. 44.

21. HRH to father, 28 January 1879, CC.

22. Bradstreet and Hitchcock died in Durnford's last stand at Isandlwana. A few days before the battle Bradstreet's wife Maud helped her friend Elizabeth Hitchcock deliver a baby girl, Georgina. When they heard their husbands were dead, the 'two women decided to set off for the safety of friends living across the mountains in the Orange Free State; it would be a week before they found a safe refuge there. The baby survived on a diet of water strained through mealie meal.' Ian Knight, *Zulu Rising: The Epic Story of iSandlwana and Rorke's Drift*, London: Macmillan, 2010, p. 516.

23. HRH to father, 31 January 1879, CC.

24. Ibid. Haggard's brief account is broadly accurate. Colonel Henry Pulleine was in charge of the British camp beneath the mountain of Isandlwana. Durnford and his column (the rocket battery and Natal Native Contingent cavalry) arrived after Lord Chelmsford's departure. Durnford outranked Pulleine and, as per military protocol, assumed command. However, when he left the camp with his men to find and attack a reported Zulu force, there was confusion as to who exactly was in charge at Isandlwana. Durnford, being killed in the battle, provided a convenient scapegoat. See Knight, *Zulu Rising*, pp. 314ff.

25. Shepstone to Osborn, 24 January 1879, quoted in Ruth Gordon, *Shepstone: The Role of the Family in the History of South Africa, 1820–1900*, Cape Town: Balkema, 1968, p. 280.

26. HRH to father, 31 January 1879, CC.

27. *Cetywayo*, p. 192.

28. *Days*, vol. 1, p. 120.

29. Both officers were posthumously awarded the Victoria Cross.

30. *Days*, vol. 1, p. 120. Essex gave evidence to the court of inquiry into the battle of Isandlwana.

31. Kotzé, *Biographical Memoirs*, pp. 559–60.

32. *Days*, vol. 1, p. 126. Volunteers 'always tried to insist upon the right to elect their own officers ... so that they might choose men in whom they had confidence to be their masters when the lives of all of them were at stake'. HRH, 'An Incident of African History', p. 114.

33. Betty Gilderdale, *The Seven Lives of Lady Barker*, Auckland: Bateman, 1996, p. 252.

34. Quoted in ibid, p. 253.

35. Weatherley's Border Lances became better known as the Border Horse.

36. *Days*, vol. 1, p. 127.

37. Weatherley was mounted on a horse which Haggard had previously owned, a handsome animal 'not unlike the fancy horses depicted by Vandyke'. *Farmer's Year*, p. 224.

38. *Days*, vol. 1, p. 126.

39. A vivid eyewitness account of the Border Horse action, including the death of Weatherley and 'his cripple son' Rupert, is given in Ron Lock and Peter Quantrill (eds.), *Zulu Frontiersman: Major C.G. Dennison*, London: Frontline Books, 2008, pp. 50–8. These events feature in *Witch's Head*.

40. Bridget Theron, 'Theophilus Shepstone and the Transvaal Colony, 1877–1879', *Kleio*, no. 34, 2002, p. 117.

41. Ibid, p. 123.

42. Quoted in ibid, pp. 124–5.

43. Shepstone to Lanyon, 2 September 1878, quoted in Theron, 'Theophilus Shepstone', p. 125.

44. Shepstone Papers, A96, vol. 71, letters dispatched 1869–1880, 19 September 1878, Pietermaritzburg Archives Repository. In September 1878 members of Shepstone's staff presented him with a silver punchbowl inscribed 'In remembrance, Transvaal 12 April 1877' – the day of the annexation. The punchbowl came with eleven silver goblets, each inscribed with the names of those present at that date, including Haggard. Shepstone thought it 'a magnificent souvenir of our close and pleasant companionship in the Transvaal and will I am sure long be cherished by my family as the memorial of an achievement won by the co-operation of fellow workers who fully trusted each other'.

45. Theron, 'Theophilus Shepstone', p. 126. Another account suggests Shepstone did not return to Pretoria but travelled down from northern Natal to Pietermaritzburg with Mhlopekazi in attendance, lingering at Standerton during February at Mrs Schwikkard's, where he wrote letters of farewell.

46. Cope, *Ploughshare of War*, p. 254.

47. Ibid. Frere died in 1884.

48. HRH, 'An Incident of African History', p. 115.

49. Ibid.

50. Ibid.

51. *Cetywayo*, p. 193.

52. *Days*, vol. 1, p. 127.

53. Ibid, p. 128.

54. Ibid.

55. Ibid, pp. 128–9.

56. *Cetywayo*, p. 195.

57. Ibid.

58. *Days*, vol. 1, pp. 130–1.

59. Ibid, p. 131.

60. Ibid, p. 132.

61. *Cetywayo*, p. 196.

62. *Days*, vol. 1, p. 140.

63. Ibid, vol. 1, p. 132.

64. HRH to mother, 15 April 1879, CC. Frere knew Ella Haggard from his time in the Bombay Presidency. He and William Haggard both attended the East India Company College, which, in 1862, became Haileybury and Imperial Service College.

65. *Days*, vol. 1, p. 136.

66. *Cloak*, p. 85.

67. John Laband and Paul Thompson, *The Illustrated Guide to the Anglo-Zulu War*, Pietermaritzburg: University of KwaZulu-Natal Press, 2004, p. 139.

68. Ibid, p. 177.

69. HRH to father, 19 May 1879, CC.

70. HRH to Administrator of the Transvaal, 29 May 1879, SS R1547/79, no. 158/79, Transvaal Archives Repository.

71. Ibid.

72. Letter from Osborn to Haggard, 31 May 1879, SS R1547/79, no. 158/79, National Archives Repository.

73. In his autobiography Haggard refers to the farmhouse as Hilldrop. In correspondence Cochrane refers to it as Hill Drop. Rooi Point (Red Point) is variously given as Rooipoint, Rooipunt and Roypoint.

74. HRH to father, 19 May 1879, CC.

75. Ibid.

76. HRH to father, 19 May 1879, CC.

77. Ibid.

78. Ibid.

79. Ibid.

80. *Cloak*, p. 85.

81. Quoted in *Days*, vol. 1, pp. 142–3.

82. Kotzé, *Biographical Memoirs*, pp. 627. Henry (Hendrik) Cloete (1851–1920), a barrister at Inner Temple, 1877; advocate of the Supreme Court of the Cape Colony 1878; appointed to the Transvaal Bar in 1879.

83. Ibid, p. 628.

84. Lagden, 1879 diary, A 951, Historical Papers and Research Archive, University of the Witwatersrand.

85. *Days*, vol. 1, p. 143.

86. HRH to father, 13 June 1879, CC.

87. Ibid.

88. Cecil Cowley, *Schwikkard of Natal and the Old Transvaal*, Cape Town: Struik, 1974, p. 94.

89. HRH to father, 13 June 1879, CC.

90. Ibid.

91. HRH to father, 13 June 1879, CC. Louis Napoleon, the Prince Imperial, was killed while out on a patrol, accompanied by Captain Jahleel Brenton Carey, six irregular

cavalry troopers and an African scout. After dismounting for a brief rest halt in a deserted Zulu homestead, they were ambushed by a Zulu scouting party. Two troopers, the African scout and the Prince Imperial were killed. Carey was court-martialled and found guilty of misbehaviour before the enemy. In his autobiography Haggard had a better grasp of what actually happened and recalled the death of the Prince Imperial somewhat differently from his letter written close to the event: 'it has always seemed to me that the most of the blame should have fallen, not upon the unfortunate officer and his companions who were with the Prince, but on whoever allowed him to go out on picket duty of so peculiarly dangerous a nature'. *Days*, vol. 1, p. 145.

92. HRH to father, 13 June 1879, CC.
93. HRH to mother, 3 July 1879, CC.
94. Ibid.
95. Ibid.
96. Sir Garnet Wolseley, *Sir Garnet Wolseley's South African Journal, 1879–1880*, ed. Adrian Preston, Cape Town: Balkema, 1973, pp. 162–3.
97. Haggard's friend Stewart fought with a volunteer unit, either Ferreira's Horse or the Swazi.
98. Sekhukhune remained in a Pretoria gaol until August 1881 when, under the treaty signed between Britain and the Transvaal after the First Anglo-Boer War, he was set free. In August 1882 he was assassinated by his half-brother Mampuru. Ferreira was awarded a CMG for his services. He went on to command the Mounted Police during the First Anglo-Boer War (1880–1) and became a significant figure in the early days of the Johannesburg goldfields. After the Second Anglo-Boer War (1899–1902) he retired to farm near Louis Trichardt in the northern Transvaal, where he died in 1921. Haggard claims to have 'read in the papers that [Ferreira] was involved in some disreputable proceedings connected with gun running of which I forget the details'. HRH, *Memorandum of the Circumstances Connected with the Plot to Murder the Late Melmoth Osborn, Sir Marshall Clarke, and H. Rider Haggard*, privately printed, McLean, VA: Alfred Tella, 2003, pp. 7–8.

10. 'MY OWN SWEET LOVE'

1. Victoria Manthorpe, *Children of the Empire: The Victorian Haggards*, London: Gollancz, 1996, p. 84.
2. HRH to father, 8 August 1879, CC.
3. *Days*, Vol. 1, p. 162. Green turtles kept in ponds or 'tanks' at Georgetown, the island's capital, were transferred live to ships and thence to London restaurants to be rendered into soup.
4. Ibid, p. 163.
5. Ibid.
6. Broome had been confirmed as Lieutenant Governor in recognition of his prompt response in sending troops to South Africa following the British reverse at Isandlwana.

7. Barker to Macmillan, quoted in Betty Gilderdale, *The Seven Lives of Lady Barker*, Auckland: Bateman, 1996, p. 256.

8. Ibid.

9. HRH to father, 8 August 1879, CC.

10. Ibid.

11. Ibid.

12. Andrew Haggard to father, 11 August 1879, CC.

13. Ibid.

14. Quoted in *Cloak*, p. 89. These lines are from a letter no longer extant which Lilias Rider Haggard combines with the one already quoted.

15. From 'One of the Old Brigade' (Donald Shaw), London in the Sixties, 1908, quoted in https://www.victorianlondon.org/houses/lanes.htm, accessed 17 November 2020.

16. Haggard probably joined the club during his time in London while at Scoones. Windham's was founded in 1828 as a 'place of meeting for a Society of Gentlemen all connected with each other by a common bond of literary or personal acquaintance'. https://www.victorianlondon.org/entertainment/windhamclub.htm, accessed 4 June 2023.

17. *Days*, vol. 1, p. 163.

18. Ibid.

19. Ibid, p. 162.

20. Quoted in Manthorpe, *Children of the Empire*, p. 90.

21. Ibid, p. 90.

22. Judith Hickey, *Journal: Agnes Marion Haggard (née Barber)*, privately published, 2013, p. 5.

23. Margaret Fairless Barber (1869–1901) published under the pseudonym Michael Fairless. She is best known for her bestselling religious allegory *The Roadmender* published posthumously in 1902.

24. Sketch written 16 September 1879; see Hickey, *Journal*, illustrative material, p. 18.

25. Hickey, *Journal*, p. 6.

26. Shepstone Papers, A96, vol. 7, Pietermaritzburg Archives Repository.

27. The name is isiXhosa in origin and means 'tamed'.

28. Shepstone to W. Haggard, 7 October 1879, CC.

29. *DAJ*, p. 134.

30. Ibid.

31. *Days*, vol. 1, p. 146.

32. Founded in 1835, Mount St Bernard Abbey in Leicestershire was the first permanent Catholic monastic foundation since the dissolution of the English monasteries in the sixteenth century.

33. *Days*, vol. 1, p. 147.

34. Ibid, p. 148.

35. Ibid.

36. Osborn to William Haggard, 10 October 1879, CC.

37. Osborn to HRH, 10 October 1879, quoted in *Days*, vol. 1, p. 168.

38. HRH to Beach, 29 October 1879, CC.

39. The post had been filled by Richard Kelsey Loveday since 1 July 1879.

40. HRH to Herbert, 29 October 1879, CC.

41. Cochrane to HRH, 14 August 1879, CC.

42. Ibid.

43. Cochrane to HRH, 22 September 1879, CC. Cochrane didn't attend Ethel Rider's christening in Pretoria. Henry Cloete stood in as his proxy.

44. Ibid.

45. Ibid.

46. Cochrane to HRH, 30 September 1879, CC.

47. Ibid.

48. Cochrane to HRH, 8 October 1879, CC.

49. Ibid.

50. Ibid.

51. Cochrane to HRH, 16 October 1879, CC.

52. John Bramston to HRH, 7 November 1879, CC.

53. HRH to Chatto and Windus, 3 November 1879, CC. The two articles mentioned appear to have been the only articles published by Haggard, despite comments by Kotzé and Lilias Haggard implying he published numerous articles at this time. In Haggard's article 'My First Book' published in *The Idler* in 1893 he refers to his two articles discussed above as if they were the only two published items prior to his first book *Cetywayo and His White Neighbours*.

54. The article, or a later version, finally saw the light of day in 1900 in the *Windsor Magazine* under the title 'An Incident of African History'.

55. Cochrane to HRH, 8 November 1879, CC.

56. Cochrane to HRH, 21 November 1879, CC.

57. *Days*, vol. 1, p. 163.

58. Lilias Rider Haggard, *Too Late for Tears*, Bungay, Suffolk: Waveney Publications, 1969, p. 17.

59. Ibid, p. 143.

60. Ibid, p. 153.

61. Ibid.

62. Ibid.

63. Ibid, pp. 153–4.

64. Ibid, p. 154.

65. Ibid.

66. D.S. Higgins, *Rider Haggard: The Great Storyteller*, London: Cassell, 1981, p. 41.

67. The Philosopher's Walk was 'a wide gravel path with the east wall of the stable courtyard one side and the orchard the other, with a big border of flowers and shrubs between' and at its end was 'the graceful figure of the Philosopher leaning on his staff, silent, remote, eternally youthful, against the dark background of the laurels'. *Cloak*, pp. 165–6.

68. *Cloak*, p. 90. Lilias adds that 'the extent of the girl's knowledge of Rider is illustrated by the fact that in the letter announcing her engagement to her guardian she spelt his name Ryder!'

69. *Days*, vol. 1, p. 164.

70. Cochrane to HRH, 8 November 1879, CC.

71. HRH to Louie, 29 November 1879, CC.

72. Ella Haggard to William Haggard, quoted in Manthorpe, *Children of the Empire*, p. 94.

73. HRH to Louie, 29 November 1879, CC.

74. Louie to Ella Haggard, 2 December 1879, CC.

75. Louie to HRH, 2 December 1879, CC.

76. Shepstone to William Haggard, 27 December 1879, CC.

77. Osborn to HRH, 14 April 1880, quoted in *Days*, vol. 1, p. 169.

78. Jeff Guy, *The Destruction of the Zulu Kingdom: The Civil War in Zululand, 1879–1884*, Pietermaritzburg: University of Natal Press, 1994, p. 76.

79. Allan Quatermain summed up the settlement thus: 'Sir Garnet Wolseley set up his Kilkenny cat Government in Zululand ... In place of one king, thirteen chiefs were erected who got to work to cut the throats of each other and of the people.' *Finished*, p. 293.

80. Louie to HRH, 2 December 1879, CC.

81. HRH to Louie, 12 December 1879, CC

82. HRH to Will Haggard, 21 December 1879, quoted in *Days*, vol. 1, p. 166.

83. Both popular farces of the period, *Two Heads* was written by F. Lennox Horne and *Ici* by Thomas J. Williams, who were active in the 1860s and 1870s.

84. Programme. Alfred Tella Collection, since dispersed.

85. Ibid.

86. William Hartcup to Louie, 13 January 1880, CC.

87. Quoted in Manthorpe, pp. 100–101.

88. Ibid.

89. *Cloak*, p. 95.

90. Ibid, p. 96.

91. Ibid.

92. Ibid.

93. Ibid, p. 96. Lilias Rider Haggard identifies Louisa Hildyard as being the aunt proposed as female guardian to Louie. I have opted for her sister Hannah Hamilton, who was unmarried and already had a long association with Louie.

94. Quoted in ibid, p. 97.

95. Quoted in Manthorpe, *Children of the Empire*, p. 96.

96. W.H.C. Hamilton to William Hartcup, 8 March 1880, CC.

97. Ibid.

98. Quoted in Manthorpe, *Children of the Empire*, p. 97.

99. Ibid, p. 97.

100. Ibid, p. 98.

101. Letter dated 27 March, quoted in ibid, p. 98.
102. Ibid.
103. Ibid, p. 99.
104. Ibid, p. 100.
105. Ibid, p. 99. In 1881 Cissie was committed to St Andrew's Hospital, a psychiatric institution in Northamptonshire, where she remained until her death in 1916.
106. Manthorpe, *Children of the Empire*, p. 87.
107. Ibid, p. 99.
108. *Cloak*, p. 95.
109. Cochrane to HRH, 8 November 1879, CC.
110. Cochrane to HRH, 27 November 1879, CC.
111. Note in Lehmkuhl genealogy, p. 14, Peter Smits Collection.
112. *Cloak*, p. 95.
113. Cochrane to HRH, 14 April 1880, CC.
114. Ibid.
115. Cochrane to HRH, 9 June 1880, CC.
116. Cochrane to HRH, 4 May 1880, CC.
117. Ibid.
118. Cochrane to HRH, 30 May 1880, CC.
119. Cochrane to HRH, 4 May 1880, CC. Tucker was Alfred Tucker, owner of the Masonic Hotel in Newcastle.
120. Cochrane to HRH, 30 May 1880, CC.
121. Ibid. Loo is a card game.
122. Ibid.
123. *Farmer's Year*, p. 86.
124. Cochrane to HRH, 18 June 1880, CC.
125. Quoted in *Days*, vol. 1, p. 173.
126. Ibid, pp. 173–4.
127. Cochrane to HRH, 7 August 1880, CC.
128. Ibid.
129. Haggard recalled Colley 'wished to sell a shotgun which I wished to purchase ... We had a difference of opinion as to the price of the article. Finally I interviewed him one morning when he was taking his bath, and he suggested we should settle the matter by tossing. This I did with a half-sovereign, he giving the call but who won I forget.' *Days*, vol. 1, p. 51.
130. Government House, Pietermaritzburg, to HRH, 10 August 1880, CC.
131. *Cloak*, p. 98.
132. Ibid. William Scudamore was vicar of St Mary's from 1839 until his death in 1881.
133. Ibid.
134. Ibid, p. 99.
135. Quoted in *Cloak*, p. 99.
136. Anonymous account of wedding, CC.

137. *Cloak*, p. 99.
138. *Days*, vol. 1. p. 165.
139. Ibid, vol. 1, p. 153.
140. Ibid.
141. Ibid. A monk named Basil makes a brief appearance in *The Lady of Blossholme*, pp. 283–4.
142. Cochrane to HRH, 27 August 1880, CC.
143. Ibid.
144. *Cloak*, p. 99.
145. Invoice from Whiteleys, CC. William Whiteley set up his 'small fancy drapery shop' in Westbourne Grove in 1863, later becoming Whiteleys department store, the 'Universal Provider' and rival to Harrods in Knightsbridge on the south side of Hyde Park.
146. Invoice from Jolly & Son, CC.
147. Manthorpe, *Children of the Empire*, p. 101.
148. LHD, typescript transcribed from original, p. 1, CC.
149. Ibid.
150. Ibid, pp. 1–2.
151. Ibid. *HMS Pinafore,* the popular comic opera, with music by Arthur Sullivan, libretto by W.S. Gilbert, first performed in 1878.

11.   'LAND OF MURDER AND SUDDEN DEATH'

1. LHD, 28 December 1880, p. 2, CC.
2. Ibid.
3. The Transvaal Rebellion is also known as the First Anglo-Boer War, the First Boer War, the First War of Independence and the Anglo-Transvaal War. For a discussion of the nomenclature, see John Laband, *The Transvaal Rebellion: The First Boer War, 1880–1881*, Harlow: Pearson Longman, 2005, pp. 4ff.
4. Ibid, p. 27.
5. Roy Jenkins, *Gladstone*, London: Papermac, 1996, p. 501.
6. Brian Bond (ed.), *Victorian Military Campaigns*, London: Hutchinson, 1967, p. 211.
7. Ibid, p. 212.
8. LHD, 28 December 1880, p. 2. CC.
9. *Days*, vol. 1, p. 175.
10. LHD, 31 December 1880, p. 3, CC.
11. Ibid.
12. The incident is recorded by Haggard in Appendix 1, 'The Potchefstroom Atrocities, &c', in *Cetywayo and His White Neighbours*, p. 294.
13. *Days*, vol. 1, p. 176.
14. HRH to father, 30 January 1881, CC.
15. *Days*, vol. 1, p. 177.
16. Fort Amiel, Newcastle, established in 1876, was a strategic base for military operations

until 1902 and is now a national monument. A room is devoted to Haggard memorabilia, including furniture from Hilldrop and an axe belonging to Mhlopekazi/Umslopogaas.

17. Shepstone Papers, A96, vol. 7, Pietermaritzburg Archives Repository.
18. LHD, 10 January 1881, p. 4, CC.
19. Ibid, p. 5.
20. Louie to William Haggard, 19 January 1881, CC.
21. *Days*, vol. 1, p. 178.
22. Ibid, vol. 1, p. 180.
23. Louie to William Haggard, 19 January 1881, CC.
24. Ibid.
25. LHD, 14 January 1881, p. 5.
26. Ibid.
27. *Days*, vol. 1, p. 181.
28. Louie to William Haggard, 19 January 1881, CC.
29. Ibid.
30. LHD, 21 January 1881, p. 6.
31. *Days*, vol. 1. pp. 179–80.
32. LHD, 24 January 1881, p. 6.
33. Ibid.
34. Ibid.
35. *Cecil Cowley, Schwikkard of Natal and the Old Transvaal*, p. 83.
36. HRH to father, 30 January 1881, CC.
37. Quoted in *Days*, vol. 1, p. 181.
38. Elwes's death is the subject of a painting by Elizabeth Thompson, Lady Butler, first exhibited in 1882 and titled 'Floreat Etona' (Let Eton flourish). 'The two Eton boys whom I show, Elwes and Monck, went forward (Elwes to his death) with the cry of "Floreat Etona" and I gave the picture these words for its title.' Quoted in Laband, *Transvaal Rebellion*, p. 2.
39. *Cetywayo*, p. 227.
40. HRH to father, 30 January 1881, CC.
41. *Days*, vol. 1, p. 183.
42. HRH to mother, 8 February 1881, CC.
43. Ibid.
44. *Days*, vol. 1, pp. 184–5.
45. *Cetywayo*, p. 232.
46. Ibid, p. 233.
47. *Days*, vol. 1, p. 183.
48. Ibid, p. 184.
49. Ibid.
50. Ibid, p. 185.
51. LHD, 14 February 1881, p. 7.
52. Ibid, p. 8.

53. Ibid, p. 9.
54. *Days*, vol. 1, p. 177.
55. Ian Castle, Majuba 1881, *The Hill of Destiny*, Osprey, London, 1996, p. 87.
56. After the rebellion, mistrusted by Boers and British alike, Merensky moved back to Germany with his family.
57. Under his editorship circulation rose sufficiently to make it viable to publish on a daily basis. Previously it had come out on Tuesdays, Thursdays and Saturdays.
58. Simon Haw, *Bearing Witness: The Natal Witness, 1846–1996*, Pietermaritzburg: Natal Witness, 1996, p. 115.
59. Louie to Ella Haggard, 7 March 1881, CC.
60. *Days*, vol. 1, p. 198.
61. Louie to Ella Haggard, 7 March 1881, CC.
62. LHD, 14 July 1881, p. 22, CC.
63. HRH, *My Stallion Moresco*, privately printed, McClean, VA: Alfred Tella, 1998, p. 3. Previously unpublished article written by Haggard on 16 May 1893 at the request of a publisher on the topic of 'my favourite pet'. He wrote the article dipping his pen in 'an inkstand made from one of his front hoofs'.
64. Ibid.
65. Charles Gubbins (1855–1911), Newcastle district surgeon and acting resident magistrate when William Beaumont was absent from Newcastle. His wife Maud was the widow of Robert Bradstreet, killed at Isandlwana with the Newcastle Mounted Rifles.
66. LHD, 14 March 1881, p. 11, CC.
67. Ibid.
68. Ibid, 23 March 1881, pp. 11–2.
69. Ibid.
70. *Days*, vol. 1, p. 194.
71. *Cetywayo*, p. 253.
72. LHD, 29 March 1881, p. 12, CC.
73. Ibid, 30 March 1881.
74. Lease agreement, CC.
75. Quoted in *Days*, vol. 1, p. 189.
76. Marshall Clarke was besieged in Potchefstroom where he had been sent as Special Commissioner in November 1880 to prevent Boer tensions turning into open rebellion. He was captured during the siege and held prisoner until April 1881.
77. Louie to Ella Haggard, 4 May 1881, quoted in *Days*, vol. 1, p. 189.
78. *Days*, vol. 1, p. 196.
79. Ibid.
80. Ibid.
81. Ibid, p. 197.
82. Ibid, pp. 196–197.
83. Ibid, p. 198.

84. Ibid. 'Tulip' is a common name for various wild bulbous plants of the Homeria group fatal to cattle and sheep.
85. HRH to mother, 3 May 1881, CC.
86. Ibid.
87. Ibid.
88. Ibid.
89. HRH to father, 24 May 1881, CC.
90. *Days*, vol. 1, p. 196.
91. LHD, 13 May 1881, p. 16, CC.
92. HRH to father, 24 May 1881, CC. Spice subsequently died at Hilldrop. Her bones were later interred at Bradenham Hall under a slab engraved 'To the memory of / SPICE / A Terrier Dog / Born in England 1874 / Died in Natal South Africa from the effects of an encounter with an Ant-bear / Her bones were brought home and interred here in 1883'.
93. Wood to Jack Haggard, 18 May 1881, CC.
94. HRH to father, 24 May 1881, CC.
95. LHD, 23 May 1881, p. 17, CC.
96. HRH to father, 24 May 1881, CC.
97. Shepstone to Haggard, 16 June 1881, quoted in *Days*, vol. 1, p. 192.
98. Brian Roberts, *Ladies of the Veld*, London: John Murray, 1965, p. 79. Her brother was John Sholto, the Ninth Marquis of Queensbury, father of Lord Alfred Douglas, Oscar Wilde's beloved Bosie.
99. Florence Dixie, *In the Land of Misfortune*, London: Bentley, 1882, p. 62.
100. Ibid.
101. HRH to Shepstone, 3 June 1881, CC.
102. Quoted in *Days*, vol. 1, p. 192.
103. Ibid, p. 191.
104. LHD, 11 June 1881, p. 18, CC. In celebration of Haggard's twenty-fifth birthday, Rider and Louie went into Newcastle where they left Jock with Louise Schwikkard and went off to the annual horse races then in progress; next evening attending the race ball which Louie 'much enjoyed as I had good partners'. Entry for 22 June 1881, p. 19.
105. *Days*, vol. 2, p. 41.
106. HRH to Blake, 28 June 1881, CC.
107. LHD, 14 June 1881, p. 18, CC.
108. Captain Augustus Morris, later Lieutenant Colonel, was present at the catastrophic replay of Majuba, the battle of Spion Kop in the Anglo-Boer War.
109. LHD, 15 June 1881, p. 19, CC.
110. HRH to father, 30 July 1881, CC.
111. Guy, *Destruction*, p. 98.
112. Ibid, p. 114.
113. Dixie, *In the Land of Misfortune*, p. 396.
114. Roberts, *Ladies on the Veld*, p. 151.
115. LHD, 11 July 1881, p. 21, CC.

116. Ibid, 24 July 1881, p. 22.

117. HRH to father, 30 July 1881, CC.

118. HRH to Shepstone, 2 August 1881, Shepstone Papers, Pietermaritzburg Archives Repository.

119. LHD, 1 August 1881, p. 23, CC.

120. Ibid, 11 August 1881, p. 24. There are no tigers in Africa. The term 'tiger' was used to describe any large cat. The kloof features in *Jess* but renamed Lion's Kloof.

121. Ibid.

122. LHD, 16 August 1881, p. 25, CC.

123. *Cetywayo*, p. 301.

124. Indabezimbi's name was used for a sangoma who becomes Allan Quatermain's ally in *Allan's Wife*.

125. Joseph Mipping and Co. auction catalogue, CC.

126. *Days*, vol. 1, p. 201.

127. LHD, 23 August 1881, p. 25, CC.

128. *Days*, vol. 1, p. 201.

129. Ibid, pp. 201–2. A kerrie or knobkerrie is a stick cut from a single piece of wood with a heavy knob on the end.

130. LHD, 27 August 1881, p. 26, CC.

131. Ibid.

132. HRH, *Farmer's Year*, p. 303.

133. See Cecil Cowley, *Schwikkard of Natal and the Old Transvaal*, Cape Town: Struik, 1974, pp. 118–9. Otto Schwikkard became an assistant director of transport during the Anglo-Boer War and was awarded a CMG for his service. He died aged 96 in 1949.

134. LHD, 29 August 1881, p. 26, CC.

135. Ibid, 30 August 1881, p. 26. The quotation 'limp lank long Lily love' is from the poem 'A Maudle-in Ballad, to the Lily' that appeared in June 1881 edition of Punch, a parody by Oscuro Wildegoose of the poetry of Oscar Wilde, who had just published *Poems*.

136. Ibid, 31 August 1881, p. 27.

137. *Days*, vol. 1, p. 202.

138. LHD, 2 September 1881, p. 27, CC.

139. *RR*, p. 99.

140. LHD, 5 September 1881, p. 27, CC.

141. Ibid, p. 30.

12.   'WRITE A BIT, DON'T YOU?'

1. *Days*, vol. 1, p. 203.

2. Ibid, p. 200.

3. LHD, 3 December 1881, p. 33, CC.

4. D.S. Higgins, *Rider Haggard: The Great Storyteller*, London: Cassell, 1981; rev. edn, 2013, p. 53.

5. *Cloak*, p. 115.

6. Andrew Haggard's novel *Ada Triscott* was published in 1890 following the success of *Dodo and I* the previous year.

7. *Cloak*, p. 117.

8. Ibid, pp. 117–8.

9. Ibid, p. 118.

10. Ibid, p. 117.

11. Elizabeth Hocking, 'a handsome, vigorous, black-eyed, raw-boned Cornishwoman who spent most of her active life in the service of the family.' *Days*, vol. 1, p. 5.

12. Ibid.

13. *Days*, vol. 1, pp. 203–4.

14. Ibid, p. 204.

15. Ibid.

16. HRH, 'My First Book', *Idler*, April 1893.

17. *Days*, vol. 1, pp. 204.

18. Ibid, p. 205.

19. Ibid.

20. Quoted in Norman Etherington, *Rider Haggard*, Boston: Twayne, 1984, p. 7.

21. *Cetywayo*, p. 43.

22. *Cetywayo*, p. 12.

23. Ibid, p. 16.

24. Ibid, p. 13.

25. Ibid, p. 21.

26. Ibid, p. 57.

27. Ibid, p. 77. From mid-1880 the post of Lieutenant Governor of Natal was upgraded to Governor.

28. Ibid, p. 168.

29. Ibid, p. 96.

30. Ibid, p. 100.

31. Ibid, pp. 269–70.

32. *Vanity Fair*, 29 July 1882, quoted in Lloyd Siemens, *The Critical Reception of Sir Henry Rider Haggard: An Annotated Bibliography 1882–1991*, English Literature in Transition 1880–1920, Special Series no. 5, 1991, Greensboro: University of North Carolina, 1991, p. 7.

33. Quoted in *Days*, vol. 1, pp. 205–6.

34. *Spectator*, 19 August 1882; *Saturday Review*, 12 August 1882, quoted in Siemens, *Critical Reception*, p. 7.

35. HRH to Agnes Barber, 6 September 1882, H. Rider Haggard Collection, Correspondence, Box 2: 14, 43, 8, 4, Columbia University, Rare Book and Manuscript Library.

36. *British Quarterly Review*, October 1882, quoted in Siemens, *Critical Reception*, p. 7. Financially *Cetywayo and His White Neighbours* 'proved a total failure', selling only 154 copies. *Days*, vol. 1, p. 207. This left Trübner 'out of pocket to the extent of £82.15s.5d.

Against this, of course, we hold the £50 advanced by you, but we fear that we are never likely to recover the balance, £32.15s.5d.' Quoted in *Days*, vol. 1, p. 207. The outstanding amount was recovered three years later when, as Haggard put it, 'I became known through other works of a different character [when] the edition sold out. Perhaps the public bought it thinking it was a novel; at any rate, I have come across a letter from a melancholy youth who made that mistake.' Ibid.

37.   This was the third civil war in Zululand. The previous two were in 1840 and 1856.

38.   Aggie's father Fairless Barber died in 1881 aged 46. His wife Maria, 'never a strong woman was devastated by his death. Finding the house [Castle Hill House, Rastrick] too large and her daughters married or away, decided to leave Yorkshire and settle at Glenwood, Bungay in Suffolk, where she died on 26 October 1890.' Hickey, *Journal*, p. 13.

39.   Quoted in *Days*, vol. 1, p. 206.

40.   Carl Rudolph Sohn, German portrait painter invited to England by Queen Victoria to paint her portrait as well as those of other relatives and members of the royal household.

41.   *The Times* quoted in Stephen Coan, 'Royal Interpreter', *Witness*, 2 May 2005, p. 9.

42.   Jack to father, 22 November 1882, Jack Haggard Papers, item 65, Bodleian Library.

43.   Ibid.

44.   Ibid.

45.   Ibid.

46.   *Days*, vol. 1, p. 209. In the *Idler* Haggard gives a different account: 'the face of a girl whom I saw in a church at Norwood gave me the idea of writing a novel. The face was so perfectly beautiful, and at the same time so refined, that I felt I could fit a story to it. When I next saw Mr Trübner I consulted him on the subject. "You can write, it is certain you can write. Yes, do it, and I will get the book published for you," he answered. Thus encouraged I set to work.' HRH, 'My First Book', p. 282.

47.   Ibid.

48.   HRH to Agnes Barber, 6 September 1882, Columbia Collection.

49.   HRH, 'There Remaineth a Rest', MS 4692/4, p. 516, NRO.

50.   Ibid, p. 518.

51.   Ibid, p. 524.

52.   Ibid, p. 525.

53.   Ibid, p. 527.

54.   Ibid.

55.   Ibid, p. 532.

56.   Ibid, p. 544.

57.   Ibid, p. 549.

58.   Ibid, p. 552.

59.   Ibid.

60.   Jeaffreson to HRH, 27 April 1883, quoted in *Days*, vol. 1, pp. 209–10.

61.   Jeaffreson to HRH, undated, quoted in *Days*, vol. 1, p. 215.

62. *Days*, vol. 1, p. 213. As well as passing examinations, to qualify as an English barrister one must also attend twelve formal dinners.
63. HRH to Agnes Barber, 5 August 1883, Columbia Collection.
64. Ibid.
65. Higgins, *Rider Haggard*, p. 62.
66. Frederick Jackson, *Early Days in East Africa*, London: Edward Arnold, 1930, p. 1.
67. *Days*, vol. 1, p. 214.
68. Quoted in *Days*, vol. 1, p. 214.
69. Ibid, pp. 214–5.
70. *Days*, vol. 1, p. 213.
71. Ibid, p. 214.
72. HRH to Agnes Barber, 30 January 1884, Columbia Collection.
73. HRH to Agnes Barber, 21 February 1884, Columbia Collection.
74. Ibid, pp. 63–4.
75. Ibid, p. 128. Haggard uses Jackson's surname for Tom Jackson, 'one of the best elephant hunters in Africa', in *Benita*, p. 62.
76. *Dawn*, p. 125.
77. Graham Greene, *Collected Essays*, London: Penguin, 1971, p. 159.
78. *Dawn*, pp. 125–6.
79. Ibid, p. 191.
80. Ibid.
81. Ibid, p. 196.
82. Ibid, p. 355.
83. *Days*, vol. 1, p. 217. *Dawn* had no dedication, an omission remedied when it was reissued in a new edition in 1894: 'After many years I dedicate this my first story to THAT UNKNOWN LADY, once seen but unforgotten, the mould and model of Angela, the magic of whose face turned my mind to the making of books.' In 1893 Haggard edited *Dawn* for a new edition, cutting 'some of the mysticism and tall writing, for which it is too remarkable, and was pleased to find that it still interested me'. HRH, 'My First Book', p. 284.
84. *Days*, vol. 1, p. 218.
85. *Athenaeum*, 22 March 1884, quoted in Siemens, *Critical Reception*, p. 8.
86. *Vanity Fair*, 12 April 1884, quoted in Siemens, *Critical Reception*, p. 8.
87. Phillip Waller, *Writers, Readers, and Reputations: Literary Life in Britain, 1870–1918*, Oxford: OUP, 2008, p. 155. According to Waller, the 'lords of the reviewing world before the Great War were the bookmen and belletrists Andrew Lang, Edmund Gosse, and George Saintsbury'. Ibid, p. 155.
88. *Academy*, 22 March 1884, quoted in Morton Cohen, *Rider Haggard: His Life and Works*, London: Hutchinson, 1960, p. 81.
89. *Dawn*, p. 191; *Academy*, 22 March 1884, quoted in Siemens, *Critical Reception*, p. 8.
90. *Academy*, 22 March 1884, quoted in Cohen, *Rider Haggard*, p. 81.
91. Manthorpe, *Children of the Empire*, pp. 121–2.

92. Quoted in ibid, pp. 127–8.

93. *Cloak*, p. 119.

94. *Days*, vol. 1, pp. 216–7.

95. Ibid, p. 218.

96. HRH, 'My First Book', p. 287.

97. *Days*, vol. 1, p. 220.

98. Cohen, *Rider Haggard*, p. 61.

99. *DAJ*, p. 134.

100. *Days*, vol. 1, p. 221.

101. Ibid, p. 222.

102. Shepstone to HRH, 26 May 1883, quoted in *Days*, vol. 1, p. 222.

103. Osborn to HRH, 2 August 1883, quoted in ibid, p. 224.

104. Jeff Guy, *The Destruction of the Zulu Kingdom: The Civil War in Zululand, 1879–1884*, Pietermaritzburg: University of Natal Press, 1994, p. 204.

105. The uSuthu wanted to bury the king with his ancestors in the Mahlabatini plain. Permission was refused and Cetshwayo was laid to rest in the Nkandla forest.

106. *Days*, vol. 1, p. 218.

107. Admiral Vernon H. Haggard, Haggard's nephew, interview with Morton Cohen, in Cohen, *Rider Haggard*, p. 137n.

108. Ibid.

109. HRH to Jack, 28 August 1884, quoted in Higgins, *Rider Haggard*, p. 66.

110. Jackson, *Early Days in East Africa*, p. 2.

111. Higgins, *Rider Haggard*, p. 67.

112. HRH to Agnes Barber, 5 November 1884, Columbia Collection.

113. Ibid.

114. HRH, *Witch's Head*, p. 45.

115. Ibid, p. 62.

116. Ibid, p. 75.

117. *Cloak*, p. 72.

118. *Witch's Head*, p. 200.

119. Ibid, p. 212.

120. Ibid, p. 188.

121. Ibid, pp. 233–4.

122. Ibid, p. 313.

123. Ibid, p. 285.

124. *Witch's Head*, p. 342.

125. Quoted in Siemens, *Critical Reception*, p. 10.

126. *Pall Mall Gazette*, 15 January 1885, quoted in Cohen, *Rider Haggard*, p. 83.

127. *Academy*, 17 January 1885, quoted in Cohen, *Rider Haggard*, p. 83.

128. Siemens, *Critical Reception*, p. 9.

129. *Academy*, 17 January 1885, quoted in Cohen, *Rider Haggard*, p. 83.

130. HRH to Agnes Barber, 5 November 1884, Columbia Collection. *Blackwood's* was considered the pre-eminent literary magazine and referred to as the *Maga*.

131. 'Blue Curtains', in *Smith and the Pharaohs*, p. 96.

132. Ibid, p. 99.

133. Ibid, p. 102.

134. Letter to Agnes Barber quoted in Higgins, *Rider Haggard*, p. 66. 'Bottles' was published unsigned under the title 'The Blue Curtains' in the *Cornhill Magazine*, vol. 7, no. 39, 1886, pp. 310–36. According to Scott, 'considerable alterations were made in the text' for its publication in the collection *Smith and the Pharaohs* (1920).

13. 'THE MOST AMAZING STORY EVER WRITTEN'

1. *Days*, vol. 1, pp. 219–20.

2. Ibid, p. 219.

3. HRH to Agnes Barber, 26 December 1884, Columbia Collection.

4. HRH to Jack Haggard, 20 February 1885, Brenthurst Library (transcription in CC).

5. D.S. Higgins, *Rider Haggard: The Great Storyteller*, London: Cassell, 1981, p. 71.

6. *Days*, vol. 1, p. xix.

7. Ibid, vol. 1, p. 220.

8. *Cloak*, pp. 121–2. Lilias records Haggard as writing *King Solomon's Mines* at Gunterstone Road. This is incorrect as Haggard and his family moved in early 1886 from 1 Fairholme Road to 69 Gunterstone Road, where he wrote *She*.

9. *Days*, vol. 1, p. 226.

10. Lang to HRH, 28 March 1885, quoted in *Days*, vol. 1, p. 227.

11. Ibid, p. 227.

12. Henry James, quoted by A.C. Benson in David Newsome, *The Edge of Paradise: A.C. Benson the Diarist*, Chicago: University of Chicago Press, 1980, p. 91.

13. Newman Flower, *Just as It Happened*, quoted in Higgins, *Rider Haggard*, p. 77.

14. *Days*, vol. 1, p. 231.

15. Ibid.

16. Ibid, pp. 231–2.

17. Ibid, p. 232.

18. Ibid.

19. Ibid.

20. Ibid, p. 233. The identity of the clerk is unknown. Years later 'this gentleman wrote reminding me of the incident and forwarding a book that he had published'. Ibid. Alas, Haggard doesn't provide a name.

21. Flower, *Just as It Happened*, p. 78, quoted in Phillip Waller, *Writers, Readers, and Reputations: Literary Life in Britain, 1870–1918*, Oxford: OUP, 2008, pp. 669–70.

22. The opinion of a fellow diner recorded by Max Pemberton in *Sixty Years Ago and After* (1936), quoted in Morton Cohen, *Rider Haggard: His Life and Works*, London: Hutchinson, 1960, p. 67.

23. Simon Nowell-Smith, *The House of Cassell*, London: Cassell, 1958, p. 136.

24. *King Solomon's Mines*, p. 6. Unless otherwise stated, quotations are from the OUP edition, ed. Dennis Butts.

25. Both items are held by the Norfolk Record Office.

26. Cohen, *Rider Haggard*, p. 90.

27. *King Solomon's Mines*, p. 6.

28. This revision first appeared in the 1912 edition of *King Solomon's Mines*.

29. *King Solomon's Mines*, p. 47.

30. *Cloak*, p. 110. The name Macumazahn is neither Zulu nor Sotho; the best estimate of its provenance is that it is of obscure Nguni origin.

31. *King Solomon's Mines*, p. 54.

32. HRH, 'Hunter Quatermain's Story', in *Allan's Wife*, p. 164.

33. *King Solomon's Mines*, p. 19. Haggard and his family sailed on the *Dunkeld* from Durban to Port Elizabeth in 1881.

34. Ibid, p. 16.

35. Ibid, pp. 21–2. Mashukulumbwe is a real place.

36. *King Solomon's Mines*, p. 23. Sitanda's Kraal is a real place.

37. Ibid, p. 11.

38. Ibid, pp. 12–3.

39. Ibid, p. 53.

40. Ibid, pp. 48–9.

41. This incident is probably drawn from the death of Quabeet in F.C. Selous, *A Hunter's Wanderings in South Africa*, London: Bentley, 1881, pp. 332–4.

42. For discussion on Haggard's sexualisation of landscape, see Anne Mclintock, 'Maidens, Maps and Mines: *King Solomon's Mines* and the Reinvention of Patriarchy in Colonial South Africa', in Cheryl Walker (ed.), *Women and Gender in Southern Africa to 1945*, Cape Town: David Philip, 1990.

43. *King Solomon's Mines*, p. 119.

44. Ibid, p. 147.

45. Ibid, p. 178.

46. Ibid, p. 179.

47. Ibid, p. 183.

48. Andrew Lang, quoted in *King Solomon's Mines*, ed. Gerald Monsman, p. 246.

49. *King Solomon's Mines*, ed. Butts, p. 248–9.

50. Ibid, p. 264. On 11 March 1914 Haggard visited the Cango Caves in the Swartberg near Oudtshoorn. The caves extend at least three miles into the mountains. Locals informed Haggard he had used them as the model for 'those written of in *King Solomon's Mines*. This however is apocryphal as I never saw them before. My model in the story were certain stalactite caves in the neighbourhood of Potchefstroom, which I had visited when a lad.' *DAJ*, p. 78.

51. *King Solomon's Mines*, p. 271.

52. Ibid, p. 261.

53. Ibid, p. 300.

54. Ibid, p. 319.

55. Namely Anna Lee, *King Solomon's Mines* (1937), Deborah Kerr, *King Solomon's Mines* (1953), Sharon Stone, *King Solomon's Mines* (1986) and Alison Doody, *King Solomon's Mines* (2006). See Stephen Coan, '*King Solomon's Mines* on Film: Modernity in Reverse', 2020, https://journals.openedition.org/erea/10648. 'Most subsequent novels and films developed further Haggard's idea of primitive Africa and far outdid the author in their racist representations.' Okaka Opio Dokotum, *Hollywood and Africa: Recycling the 'Dark Continent' Myth, 1908–2020*, Grahamstown: NISC, 2020, p. 67.

56. *King Solomon's Mines*, p. 320.

57. Haggard began writing the sequel on 17 July 1885.

58. Victoria Manthorpe, *Children of the Empire: The Victorian Haggards*, London: Gollancz, 1996, p. 135.

59. *Days*, vol. 1, pp. 233–4.

60. Lloyd Siemens, *The Critical Reception of Sir Henry Rider Haggard: An Annotated Bibliography 1882–1991*, Greensboro: University of North Carolina, 1991, p. 9.

61. Lang, quoted in *King Solomon's Mines*, ed. Gerald Monsman p. 245.

62. Ibid.

63. Quoted in Cohen, *Rider Haggard*, pp. 94–5.

64. Ibid, p. 95.

65. Ibid, p. 94.

66. Quoted in *King Solomon's Mines*, ed. Gerald Monsman, pp. 247–8.

67. Siemens, *Critical Reception*, p. 11.

68. Quoted in *King Solomon's Mines*, ed. Gerald Monsman, p. 249.

69. John Sutherland, *The Longman Companion to Victorian Fiction*, Harlow: Longman, 1988, p. 543.

70. Claude Colleer Abbot (ed.), *Letters of Gerard Manley Hopkins to Robert Bridges*, Oxford: OUP, 1970, pp. 236–7.

71. Frances Colenso to her mother, June 1889, Colenso Papers, A204, vol. 4, Frances Colenso letters, Pietermaritzburg Archives Repository. My thanks to Shelagh Spencer for drawing my attention to this item.

72. Quoted in *Days*, vol. 1, p. 235.

73. Ibid, p. 236.

74. Ibid, pp. 236–7.

75. Letter to the American *Book Buyer*, quoted in Higgins, *Rider Haggard*, p. 71.

76. *Days*, vol. 2, p. 96.

77. HRH, 'The Real King Solomon's Mines', in *The Best Short Stories of Rider Haggard*, ed. Peter Haining, London: Michael Joseph, 1981, p. 19. Great Zimbabwe was 'discovered' by Adam Renders in 1868, the ruins were explored by Carl Mauch in 1871 but it was not until 1891 that J. Theodore Bent, explorer-archaeologist, did a detailed examination of the ruins at the behest of Cecil Rhodes and the British South Africa Company. Bent subsequently published *Ruined Cities of Mashonaland* in 1892.

78. Ibid, p. 20.

79. Norman Etherington, 'South African Origins of Rider Haggard's Early Romances', *Notes and Queries*, October 1977, p. 437.

80. Ibid.

81. Ibid.

82. Ibid.

83. Jeppe's 1879 map (updated from the 1877 edition).

84. HRH, 'The Real King Solomon's Mines', p. 20.

85. Ibid.

86. For a much expanded version of this essay, see Tim Couzens, 'A Tale of Two Mysteries: The Patterson Embassy to Lobengula', *Brenthurst Archive*, vol. 2, no.1, 1995.

87. Etherington, 'South African Origins', p. 437.

88. W.D. Mackenzie, *John Mackenzie: South African Missionary and Statesman*, London: Hodder and Stoughton, 1902, pp. 137–8.

89. Oates was the uncle of the Antarctic explorer Lawrence Oates who would provide the twentieth century with the ultimate example of British sangfroid when, on leaving the tent of the doomed Scott Antarctic expedition, he uttered his famous last words: 'I may be some time.'

90. Oates left no description of what he saw, which is especially regrettable as all previous European travellers had visited the falls in the dry season.

91. *King Solomon's Mines*, pp. 50–1.

92. Etherington, 'South African Origins', pp. 437–8.

93. Ibid, p. 438. Monsman says Walmsley's book provided 'a thematic background for Haggard's adventure into an unknown African interior, as well as details for Haggard's stalactite cave, sorcerer's dance, and sinister chieftain'. While the first observation might be correct, the 'details' Monsman refers to have their origins in Haggard's experience in Natal and the Transvaal. See Monsman (ed.) *King Solomon's Mines*, p. 290.

94. The adolescent Haggard was reported to have 'a shock of rather rebellious hair'. See p. 31 above.

95. Stephen Taylor, *The Mighty Nimrod: A Life of Frederick Courtenay Selous, African Hunter and Adventurer, 1851–1917*, London: Collins, 1989, p. 89.

96. *PD*, 6 January 1917, p. 93. Haggard got to know Selous in later life and there was a portrait of the hunter at Ditchingham House, which Selous visited on at least one occasion. 'He was an odd but most gallant man, with a frame and constitution of iron – a mighty hunter before the Lord ... God rest him! He is one of the last of his sort, an African hunter of the Allan Quatermain stamp.' Ibid, p. 94.

97. Ibid, p. 74.

98. Taylor, *The Mighty Nimrod*, p. 88. Dan Wylie considers some of Haggard's 'phrases so close to those of Selous as to border on plagiarism'. Dan Wylie, *Death and Compassion: The Elephant in Southern African Literature*, Johannesburg: Wits University Press, 2018, p. 93.

99. *Days*, vol. 1, p. 255.

100. *King Solomon's Mines*, p. 55.

101. J.E. Scott, *A Bibliography of the Works of Sir Henry Rider Haggard, 1856–1925*, Bishop's Stortford: Elkin Mathews, 1947, p. 36.

102. Ibid.

103. That Foulata's name was derived from the African servant at Hilldrop present at the time of Jack's visits adds another layer of speculation.

104. Letter to the *Field*, 29 February 1929, p. 247. The eyeglass is visible in photographs of Frederick Jackson. Cutting in Jackson and Archer Scrapbook, 'Was Jackson the Captain Good of *King Solomon's Mines*?', GBR/0115/RCS/RCMS 114, 9, Cambridge University Library.

105. Letter to *Morning Post*, 19 February 1932.

106. Letter to *Morning Post*, 28 March 1932.

107. Sutherland, *Victorian Fiction*, p. 378.

108. Little dedicated his 1888 novel *Whose Wife Shall She Be?* to Haggard. A by-product of *King Solomon's Mines*'s success was that Haggard had his portrait painted by Little's brother George Leon Little. He would later illustrate Haggard's *Farmer's Year*. See Jim O'Brien, 'Rider Haggard and the Brothers Little', *Rider Haggard Society Journal*, no. 124, November 2017, pp. 5–7.

109. Olive Schreiner to Havelock Ellis, 22 October 1884, Olive Schreiner to Havelock Ellis, 22 October 1884, HRC/CAT/OS/2b-xiv, Olive Schreiner Letters Project transcription, line 15, Harry Ransom Research Center, University of Texas at Austin.

110. Havelock Ellis to Olive Schreiner, 23 October 1884, in Olive Schreiner, *My Other Self: The Letters of Olive Schreiner and Havelock Ellis, 1884–1920*, ed. Yaffa Claire Draznin, New York: Peter Lang, 1992, p. 156.

111. HRH to Olive Schreiner, 21 October 1884, HRC/CAT/OS/2b-iii, Olive Schreiner Letters Project transcription, Harry Ransom Research Center, University of Texas at Austin.

112. Olive Schreiner to HRH, 14 November 1884, CC. Ten years on, Schreiner's opinion of Haggard's work had changed dramatically: 'To read one of Haggard's novels would be as agonizing to me as to sit in a room & hear Ta-ra-ra-boom-de-ai played over & over. They are not art to me … They may be written with the highest & noblest motives; but they were not necessities; they were made up!' Olive Schreiner to Constance Lytton, 3 February 1895, Lytton 01229/10, Olive Schreiner Letters Project transcription, line 50, Harry Ransom Research Center, University of Texas at Austin.

113. Olive Schreiner to Havelock Ellis, 29 October 1884, HRC/CAT/OS/2b-xxHRC/ CAT/OS/FRAG/NFPm, Olive Schreiner Letters Project transcription, line 21, Harry Ransom Research Center, University of Texas at Austin.

114. Olive Schreiner to HRH, 6 February 1885, CC.

115. HRH to Jack Haggard, 17 February 1885, quoted in Phyllis Lewsen, 'Olive Schreiner: Selected Documents', *Brenthurst Archives*, vol. 1, no. 1, 1994, p. 8.

116. Louie also called 'on Miss Schreiner (who is up here for a week) & likes her'. Ibid, p. 9.

117. In 1907 the hospital was renamed the Queen's Hospital for Children.

118. 'Hunter Quatermain's Story' was collected in *Allan's Wife* (1889); Olive Schreiner's 'African Moonshine' in the posthumous collection *Stories, Dreams and Allegories* (1923).

14. 'IMMORTAL LOVE'

1.   'There is always something new out of Africa' from Pliny the Elder's *Naturalis Historia*.
2.   *Allan Quatermain*, ed. Dennis Butts, Oxford: OUP, 1995, p. 7.
3.   *Days*, vol. 1, p. 275.
4.   *Allan Quatermain*, p. 3.
5.   Ibid, pp. 20–1.
6.   Ibid, p. 22.
7.   Ibid, p. 25.
8.   Ibid, p. 40.
9.   Ibid, p. 59.
10. Ibid, p. 89.
11. Ibid, p. 100.
12. Ibid, pp. 100–1.
13. Ibid, p. 101.
14. Ibid, p. 117.
15. Ibid, p. 128.
16. Ibid, p. 223.
17. Ibid, p. 259.
18. Ibid, p. 143.
19. Roger Lancelyn Green, *Andrew Lang*, Leicester: Ward, 1946, p. 124.
20. *Days*, vol. 1, p. 274.
21. *British Weekly*, 5 August 1887, quoted in Lloyd Siemens, *The Critical Reception of Sir Henry Rider Haggard: An Annotated Bibliography 1882–1991*, Greensboro: University of North Carolina, 1991, p. 14.
22. Quoted in Cohen, *Rider Haggard*, p. 233.
23. *British Weekly*, 5 August 1887, quoted in Siemens, *Critical Reception*, p. 14.
24. *Pall Mall Gazette*, 18 July 1887, quoted in Siemens, *Critical Reception*, p. 15.
25. *Literary World*, 23 July 1887, quoted in Siemens, *Critical Reception*, p. 11.
26. Quoted in *Days*, vol. 1, p. 275.
27. *Days*, vol. 1, p. 274.
28. Victoria Manthorpe, *Children of the Empire: The Victorian Haggards*, London: Gollancz, 1996, p. 123.
29. Ibid, p. 123. The Watiku, better known as the Bajuni, occupy the coastal areas of Kenya.
30. *Allan Quatermain*, p. 284.
31. Ibid.
32. *Days*, vol. 1, p. 244.
33. Ibid, p. 265.

34. This date was added to the revised and illustrated edition of 1896 below Haggard's dedication: 'To my wife'.

35. Barbara Tuchman, *The Proud Tower*, London: Papermac, 1997, p. 38.

36. Haggard shared rooms with a son of the judge Robert Malcolm Kerr. Charles Henry Malcolm Kerr, another son of the judge, would illustrate several of Haggard's books: *Allan Quatermain* (1887); *She: A History of Adventure* (1888); *Allan's Wife and Other Tales* (1889); *Nada the Lily* (1892); *The Witch's Head* (1893); *The Wizard* (1896); *Black Heart and White Heart and Other Stories* (1900).

37. *Days*, vol. 1, pp. 244–5.

38. *Days*, vol. 2, p. 207.

39. *Cetywayo*, p. 101.

40. *Athenaeum*, 19 March 1887, quoted in Siemens, *Critical Reception*, p. 12.

41. *Murray's Magazine*, April 1887, quoted in Siemens, *Critical Reception*, p. 12.

42. *Pall Mall Gazette*, 15 March 1887, quoted in Siemens, *Critical Reception*, p. 14.

43. *Literary World*, Boston, 16 April 1887, quoted in Siemens, *Critical Reception*, p. 14.

44. *Days*, vol. 1, pp. 264–5.

45. Will Haggard to HRH, 31 December 1887, CC.

46. The Empress in a letter to Haggard's brother Will, first secretary at the British Embassy at Athens, quoted in *Days*, vol. 2, p. 3.

47. *Days*, vol. 1, p. 109. Buskes is identified by name, and this incident detailed in 'The Potchefstroom Atrocities &c', an appendix to *Cetywayo and His White Neighbours*.

48. *Natal Witness*, 11 June 1900.

49. Ibid.

50. Ibid.

51. *PD*, entry for 31 March 1917, pp. 101–2.

52. HRH draft letter, 25 January 1886, CC.

53. Cohen, *Rider Haggard*, p. 127.

54. *Days*, vol. 1, pp. xix–xx. 'Devilling' means working as a junior assistant for a barrister.

55. Fanny Haggard to Ella Maddison Green, 29 January 1886, in Judith Hickey, *Journal: Agnes Marion Haggard (née Barber)*, privately published, 2013, p. 21.

56. Letter to Haggard from Besant, 28 October 1885, quoted in Higgins, *Rider Haggard*, pp. 85–6. Besant had been with A.P. Watt since 1883. Rudyard Kipling signed with Watt in 1890 also on Besant's recommendation. James Payn (1830–93) was editor of the *Cornhill Magazine* and a prolific best-selling popular novelist. Wilkie Collins (1824–89) was the author of *The Woman in White* and *The Moonstone*. Besant was a good man to have onside; through the Society of Authors, this 'avatar of the versatile man of letters' 'professionalised British letters'. John Sutherland, *The Longman Companion to Victorian Fiction*, Harlow: Longman, 1988, p. 61.

57. Mary Ann Gillies, *The Professional Literary Agent in Britain, 1880–1920*, Toronto: University of Toronto Press, 2007, p. 23.

58. Phillip Waller, *Writers, Readers, and Reputations: Literary Life in Britain, 1870–1918*,

Oxford: OUP, 2008, p. vi. The term 'bestseller' was coined in the United States in 1889. See ibid, p. 668.

59. Gillies, *The Professional Literary Agent in Britain*, p. 16.

60. Waller, *Writers, Readers and Reputations*, p. 34. For a discussion of this issue, see ibid, pp. 26ff, 668.

61. Gillies, *The Professional Literary Agent in Britain*, p. 25.

62. Ibid, p. 26.

63. Ibid, p. 12.

64. *Witch's Head*, p. 315.

65. HRH to Agnes Barber, 30 January 1884, Columbia Collection.

66. Stephen Batchelor, *The Awakening of the West: The Encounter of Buddhism and Western Culture, 543 BCE – 1992*, London: HarperCollins, 1994, p. 270.

67. HRH to Agnes Barber, 30 January 1884, Columbia Collection.

68. Ibid.

69. Ibid.

70. J.J. Franklin, *The Lotus and the Lion: Buddhism and the British Empire*, Ithaca, NY: Cornell University Press, 2008, p. 12.

71. Ibid, p. 89.

72. Ibid, p. 86.

73. *Days*, vol. 1, p. 245.

74. Ibid, pp. 245–6.

75. Ibid, p. 246.

76. Ibid.

77. *She*, ed. Daniel Karlin, Oxford: OUP, 1991, p. 3.

78. Ibid, p. 8.

79. Ibid, p. 11.

80. Ibid, p. 19.

81. *Days*, vol. 1, p. 175.

82. *She*, p. 30.

83. Ibid, p. 6.

84. Ibid, p. 31.

85. Ibid, p. 30.

86. Ibid.

87. Ibid, p. 31.

88. The shipwreck draws on that of Frederick Jackson in 1885. Jackson gave a detailed account of the shipwreck in a letter to Haggard's father, dated 5 July 1885, CC. See also Frederick Jackson, *Early Days in East Africa*, London: Edward Arnold, 1930, pp. 54–7.

89. Ibid, p. 100.

90. Ibid, p. 294.

91. Ibid, p. 4.

15.   'THE LITERATURE OF ANOTHER PLANET'

1. *Days*, vol. 1, p. 246.
2. An anonymous 'Old Boy', *East Anglian Daily Times*, 15 May 1894. See above p. 31.
3. *Days*, vol. 1, p. 32.
4. John Blatchly, *A Famous Antient Seed-Plot of Learning: A History of Ipswich School*, Ipswich: Ipswich School, 2003, p. 185. All the masters bar one left at the same time as Holden.
5. John Blatchly, 'Sir Henry Rider Haggard: Storyteller Supreme', *Old Ipswichian: Journal of the Old Ipswichian Club*, vol. 7, October 2006, p. 39.
6. Scott, *Bibliography*, p. 38.
7. *Days*, vol. 1, p. 248.
8. *Cloak*, p. 135.
9. Andrew Lang to HRH, 12 July 1886, quoted in *Days*, vol. 1, p. 247.
10. Ibid.
11. Andrew Lang to HRH, 25 July 1886, quoted in *Days*, vol. 1, p. 247.
12. Ibid.
13. Ibid.
14. For details of the revisions, see H. Rider Haggard, *The Annotated She: A Critical Edition of H. Rider Haggard's Victorian Romance with Introduction and Note*, ed. Norman Etherington, pp. xix–xxiii; and H. Rider Haggard, *She: A History of Adventure*, ed. Andrew M. Stauffer, pp. 343–56. The Stauffer edition of *She* uses the text of the *Graphic* serialisation. An illustrated edition of *She* with plates by Maurice Greiffenhagen and Charles Kerr was published in 1888, and later editions with further revisions were published in 1891 and 1896. The 1896 edition includes a sonnet to Ayesha written by Andrew Lang.
15. Lang returned the compliment, dedicating *In the Wrong Paradise* (1886) to Haggard.
16. *She*, dedication page.
17. *Academy*, 15 January 1887, quoted in *She*, ed. Stauffer, p. 285.
18. *Pall Mall Gazette*, 4 January 1887, quoted in *She*, ed. Stauffer, pp. 281–2.
19. *Literary World*, 7 January 1887, quoted in *She*, ed. Stauffer, p. 282.
20. Ibid, p. 283.
21. *Spectator*, 15 January 1887, quoted in *She*, ed. Stauffer, pp. 286–7.
22. *Days*, vol. 1, p. 249.
23. Sotheby's Catalogue, 12 February 1951, p. 18, item 120.
24. Besant to HRH, 22 January 1887, in *Days*, vol. 1, p. 249.
25. Ibid.
26. Haggard met Gosse in 1885, rallying to his support the following year when the critic John Churton Collins pilloried Gosse's *Seventeenth Century Studies: A Contribution to the History of English Poetry*. Though no authority on the subject himself, Haggard told Gosse, 'I do know what conduct one gentleman has a right to expect from another.' Quoted in Ann Thwaite, *Edmund Gosse: A Literary Landscape, 1849–1928*, London:

Secker and Warburg, 1984, p. 288. The two became good friends and on at least one occasion Gosse and his family stayed at Ditchingham House.

27. *Days*, vol. 1, pp. 249–50.
28. James to Stevenson, 2 August 1886, in Leon Edel (ed.), *Henry James Letters*, Cambridge, MA: Harvard University Press, 1980, vol. 3, p. 128.
29. Isabel Hapgood, 'Count Tolstoy at Home', *Atlantic Monthly*, November 1891, p. 606. In the same interview 'we got upon the subject of English things and ways. The count's eyes flashed. "The English are the most brutal nation on earth!" he exclaimed. "Along with the Zulus, that is to say. Both go naked: the Zulu all day long, the Englishwomen as soon as dinner is served."' Ibid, p. 611.
30. V.S. Pritchett, 'Haggard Still Riding', *New Statesman*, 27 August 1960, p. 277.
31. Analysing a dream provoked by his visitor, Freud cites *She* and also *Heart of the World*, Haggard's romance set in Central America – 'numerous elements of the dream are taken from these two fantastic romances'. S. Freud, *The Interpretation of Dreams*, London: Penguin, 1992, p. 453.
32. C.G. Jung, *Memories, Dreams, Reflections*, London: Fontana, 1993, p. 210.
33. Cornelia Brunner, *Anima as Fate*, Dallas, TX: Spring Publications, 1986, p. xiii. See also Sue Austin, 'Desire, Fascination and the Other: Some Thoughts on Jung's Interest in Rider Haggard's *She* and on the Nature of Archetypes', *Harvest: International Journal for Jungian Studies*, vol. 50, no. 2, 2004.
34. *Dawn* was first titled 'Angela'; *Witch's Head* began life as 'Eva: A Tale of Love and War'.
35. Sketch written 16 September 1879; see Judith Hickey, *Journal: Agnes Marion Haggard (née Barber)*, privately published, 2013, for illustrative material, p. 18.
36. Ibid.
37. *Cloak*, p. 202.
38. Ibid, pp. 28–9.
39. *PD*, entry for 31 March 1917, p. 101.
40. *Vanity Fair*, 21 May 1887, p. 329.
41. Roger Lancelyn Green, *Andrew Lang*, Leicester: Ward, 1946, p. 122. *He* inspired a young barrister, Henry Chartres Biron, to write *King Solomon's Wives* by Hyder Ragged, published in April 1887. Lang sent Biron a congratulatory letter with a parody of his sonnet on *She* titled 'Twosh'. Parodies were also published in *Punch*, among them *Hee-Hee!* by the pseudonymous Walker Weird, credited as being the author of *Solomon's Ewers* and *Adam Slaughterman*. See Lindy Stiebel, 'The Reception of *She* in Its Day', in Tania Zulli (ed.), *She: Explorations into a Romance*, Rome: Aracne, 2009, p. 144.
42. Green, *Andrew Lang*, p. 122. Log-rolling is a term used to criticise mutual admiration and assistance along the lines of 'you roll my log and I'll roll yours', particularly applied to writers and politicians. *He* was published on 23 February 1887 as a shilling paperback and included Lang's sonnet to Ayesha and a dedication to 'Dear Allan Quatermain' signed 'Two of the Ama-Logrolla'. Ibid, p. 121.
43. Ibid, p. 133.
44. *PD*, entry for 31 March 1917, p. 103.

45. Tom Pocock, *Rider Haggard and the Lost Empire*, London: Weidenfeld and Nicholson, 1993, p. 70. Tom Pocock was told this story by the late Commander Mark Cheyne, Haggard's grandson. See also M. Shirley Addy, *Rider Haggard and Egypt*, Accrington, Lancashire: AL Publications, 1998, p. 2. The mummy of Nesmin is now held in the store of Liverpool Museum and has been the subject of two Egyptological studies. For a catalogue of Haggard's collection of Egyptian antiquities, see Addy, *Rider Haggard and Egypt*, p. 85. Details of the mummy are on pp. 104–5.

46. Haggard's entry in the 1995 edition notes that 'his novels were extremely popular, several of them being based on Ancient Egyptian themes; he had a small but choice collection of Egyptian antiquities'. Quoted in Addy, *Rider Haggard and Egypt*, p. 1.

47. Haggard's other novels and stories dealing directly with Egyptian subject matter are *Cleopatra, World's Desire, Way of the Spirit, Morning Star, Moon of Israel, Ancient Allan, Smith and the Pharaohs, Wisdom's Daughter* and *Queen of the Dawn*.

48. See Addy, *Rider Haggard and Egypt*, pp. 2, 91. Addy suggests the mummy was sent to Haggard by his brother Andrew and tells a similar story of Haggard's experience to that above which she was told by Haggard's grandson, the late Commander Mark Cheyne, who in turn heard the story from his aunt Lilias Rider Haggard.

49. *She*, p. 26. The ring is thought to have been obtained for Haggard by the Egyptologist William John Loftie (1839–1911), Anglican priest and author of numerous works on art, architecture, Egypt and the history of London. In March 1888 Loftie designed Haggard's Egyptian letterhead using hieroglyphics which, translated, read: H. Rider Haggard, the son of Ella, lady of the house, makes an oblation to Thoth, the Lord of writing, who dwells in the moon'. Percy Muir (1894–1979) of the book dealers Elkin Mathews later created a bookplate from Haggard's letterhead which was inserted in titles from Haggard's library sold at auction by his firm. See Elkin Mathews Catalogue 102, May 1946; also M. Shirley Addy, 'Rider Haggard's Egyptian Bookplate', *Rider Haggard Society Journal*, no. 141, July 2023, p. 4. There was an auction of Haggard's manuscripts at Sotheby's on 12 February 1951.

50. See Addy, *Rider Haggard and Egypt*, Appendix 1A, p. 36, 'A Guide to Didlington Hall: The Egyptian Collection'. For details of sale see Scott, *Bibliography*, p. 39.

51. Steve Vinson, 'They-Who-Must-Be-Obeyed: Arsake, Rhadopis and Tabubu; Ihweret and Charikleia', *Comparative Literature Studies*, vol. 45, no. 3, 2008, p. 289.

52. Ibid, p. 289. Haggard refers to 'First Setne' in his introduction to *Morning Star*, in which the name of a character is derived from this source; similarly in his novella *Smith and the Pharaohs*.

53. *Days*, vol. 1, p. 254.

54. Quoted in Ayresome Johns, *'She' and 'Jess': The Great Plagiarism Debate*, London: Ferret Fantasy, privately published, 1997, p. 57. The caves are probably the Stadsaal Caves.

55. Ibid.

56. Rendered in earlier orthography as the Lovedu.

57. See E.J. Krige and J.D. Krige, *The Realm of the Rain Queen: A Study of the Pattern of Lovedu Society*, London: OUP, 1943, p. 3.
58. *New York Times*, 27 November 1894, p. 4.
59. *Natal Witness*, 28 March 1914, quoted in *DAJ*, p. 318.
60. Ibid.
61. *Allan Quatermain*, p. 284.
62. Joseph Thomson, *Through Masai Land*, London: Sampson Low, 1884, p. 301.
63. Ibid, p. 302. *She* can be credited with inspiring Joseph Thomson to write his own African adventure, *Ulu: An African Romance* (1888). According to Thomson's female co-author, E. Harris-Smith, the idea they should write a novel together originated while they were discussing *She*, 'which had stirred Joe's indignation by depicting Africa as it is not – the theatre of a thousand incidents and adventures appropriate only to a Baron Munchausen or the heroes of the Arabian nights. "I've a great mind to write a novel myself," he exclaimed, "that shall be a protest against all this impossible stuff. Yes, I will, if you will help me!"' J.B. Thomson, *Joseph Thomson: African Explorer*, London: Sampson Low, 1896, p. 190.
64. *Literary World*, 8 December 1888, quoted in Lloyd Siemens, *The Critical Reception of Sir Henry Rider Haggard: An Annotated Bibliography 1882–1991*, Greensboro: University of North Carolina, 1991, p. 18.
65. *Illustrated London News*, 15 December 1888, quoted in Siemens, *Critical Reception*, p. 18.
66. *Scots Observer*, 22 December 1888, quoted in Siemens, *Critical Reception*, p. 18.
67. *Days*, vol. 1, p. 266.
68. HRH to Mrs John Haggard, 28 August 1887, Columbia Collection.

16. 'BETWEEN SUCCESS AND ATTACKS'

1. *Days*, vol. 1, p. 254.
2. Ibid, p. 264.
3. Ibid, p. 256.
4. *Cloak*, p. 131.
5. HRH to Louie, 29 January 1887, CC.
6. *Cloak*, p. 130.
7. Ibid.
8. Ibid, p. 131.
9. Ibid.
10. Ibid. *The Silence of Dean Maitland* (1886) by Maxwell Gray, pseudonym of novelist, poet and feminist Mary Gleed Tuttiett (1846–1923). This tale of an errant cleric and his comeuppance was her most popular book and was subsequently adapted as a stage play and filmed three times.
11. HRH to Louie, 2 February 1887, CC. The Colonial and Indian Exhibition in South

Kensington was opened by Queen Victoria in May 1886 and ran for six months, attracting over five and a half million visitors.

12. Ibid. Louis Pasteur produced the first vaccine against rabies, first used on a human patient in 1885. In 1886 he treated 350 patients, only one of whom died.

13. Lang to HRH, 1 February 1887, in *RR*, p. 9.

14. *RR*, p. 15. 'The crocodile of Realism and the catawampus of Romance', quoted from Andrew Lang's essay 'Realism and Romance', *Contemporary Review*, November 1887.

15. Henry Newbolt, quoted in *RR*, p. 9. The building is now the Park Lane Hotel, 107 Piccadilly.

16. *Days*, vol. 1, p. 273.

17. Ibid, p. 276.

18. Rudyard Kipling, *Something of Myself*, London: Macmillan, 1981, p. 85.

19. See Montgomery Hyde, *Oscar Wilde: A Biography*, London: Methuen, 1975, p. 142.

20. Richard Ellmann, *Oscar Wilde*, London: Penguin, 1988, p. 412.

21. *Days*, vol. 1, pp. 272–3. Hardy's decision to cease writing novels was not solely based on the negative response to *Jude the Obscure*. See Claire Tomalin, *Thomas Hardy: The Time-Torn Man*, London: Penguin, 2006, pp. 259ff.

22. HRH to Louie, 6 February 1887, CC.

23. Ibid.

24. HRH to Louie, 11 February 1887, CC.

25. HRH to Louie, 6 February 1887, CC.

26. *Days*, Vol. 1, pp. 261–3. Recalling the incident, Haggard said it 'still makes my back feel cold and my flesh creep. I have tried to reproduce it in *Ayesha* [the sequel to *She*], where Holly falls from the rock to the ice-covered river far beneath.' *Days*, vol. 1, pp. 261–2. See *Ayesha*, pp. 67ff.

27. HRH to Louie, 11 February 1887, CC. F.C. Calvert and Co. produced disinfectant products, including toothpaste.

28. Ibid.

29. HRH to Louie, 17 February 1887, CC. The transcription of this letter is dated 17 February and datelined Assiout, but it was clearly written after the letter dated 18 February as an attached note. I have retained the date of the transcription.

30. HRH to Louie, 17 February 1887, CC.

31. Ibid.

32. Ibid.

33. HRH to Louie, 18 February 1887, CC.

34. HRH diary, 21 February 1887, quoted in M. Shirley Addy, *Rider Haggard and Egypt*, Accrington, Lancashire: AL Publications, 1998, p. 7.

35. HRH to Louie, 24 February 1887, CC.

36. Addy, *Rider Haggard and Egypt*, p. 7.

37. See the description in ibid, p. 91. The cartouche was engraved with the ka-name of King Ikhnaton, 'Live Rē-Harakhte Living-in-Righteousness', according to Aylward M. Blackman, quoted in ibid, p. 103.

38. HRH to Louie, 24 February 1887, CC.

39. HRH to Louie, 2 March 1887, CC.

40. *Days*, vol. 1, pp. 260–1.

41. HRH to Louie, 2 March 1887, CC.

42. On 15 December 1889 Haggard was present at 'one of the last, great mummy unrollings in the United Kingdom' at the Botanic Lecture Theatre, University College London. Ernest Wallis Budge did the unwrapping before an audience of a 'great many amateur Egyptologists of the day' including Haggard and the artists Edward Poynter and Lawrence Alma-Tadema. They 'watched as Budge hacked away at the wrappings of one Bak-Ran, before distributing portions of the bandages to an appreciative audience'. This was the penultimate public unrolling in the United Kingdom. Johnson, *Going Forth by Night*, p. 9; 'The Unrolling of the Mummy', *New York Times*, 12 January 1890, p. 13; and 'Unrolling a Mummy', *Illustrated London News*, 28 December 1889, p. 831.

43. HRH to Louie, 6 March 1887, CC.

44. Ibid.

45. HRH to Louie, 13 March 1887, CC.

46. On his return to England, Haggard wrote 'Our Position in Cyprus', published in the July edition of the *Contemporary Review*.

47. HRH to Louie, 19 March 1887, CC.

48. Ibid.

49. Ibid.

50. Quoted in *Cloak*, p. 133.

51. They appeared between 1887 and 1892. Mrs Oliphant, Margaret Oliphant (née Wilson) (1828–97) was a popular, prolific and critically approved novelist, Queen Victoria's favourite.

52. *Blackwood's Edinburgh Magazine*, vol. 141, February 1887, pp. 291–315; *She*, ed. Stauffer, pp. 288–9.

53. *Days*, vol. 1, p. 264.

54. 'About Fiction', p. 1, Ayresome Johns, *'She' and 'Jess': The Great Plagiarism Debate*, London: Ferret Fantasy privately published, 1997, p. 1. 'About Fiction' is also published in an appendix to KSM edited by Gerald Monsman, p. 269.

55. Ibid, p. 2.

56. Ibid, p. 4.

57. Ibid.

58. Ibid.

59. Ibid, p. 5.

60. Ibid.

61. Ibid, p. 6.

62. Ibid, p. 7.

63. Lucy Clifford (1849–1929) was the widow of the mathematician and philosopher W.K. Clifford. A prominent literary figure, she introduced Rudyard Kipling to her

publisher Frederick Macmillan. She was a friend of Henry James and the only female beneficiary in his will.

64. Johns, 'She' and 'Jess', p. 8. In an article 'Books Which Have Influenced Me', published in the *British Weekly*, May 1887, pp. 65–8, Haggard said his two favourite novels were *A Tale of Two Cities* by Charles Dickens and Edward Bulwer-Lytton's *The Coming Race*. He added he had 'always been stirred more by poetry than by prose, except, indeed, by some passages where prose, in the hands of a perfect master, surpasses even the dignity of worthy verse'. He cited poems from Matthew Arnold ('Dover Beach'), Andrew Lang ('Homeric Unity') and Edmund Ollier ('Florimel') as being particularly inspiring as well as the 'Ode to Mother Carey's Chicken' by Theodore Watts. 'And there is one immortal work that moves me still more – a work that utters all the world's anguish and disillusionment in one sorrow-laden and bitter cry, and whose stately music thrills like the voice of pines heard in the darkness of a midnight winter gale: and that is the book of Ecclesiastes.'

65. Johns, 'She' and 'Jess', p. 8.

66. Ibid.

67. *Days*, vol. 1, p. 265.

68. To demonstrate it was possible to purchase a child prostitute, Stead set up a situation where he 'bought' Eliza Armstrong aged 13 for £5. Hence the charge of abduction.

69. Quoted in Johns, 'She' and 'Jess', p. 13.

70. Ibid, pp. 19–20.

71. Ibid, p. 20.

72. Ibid.

73. Ibid.

74. HRH to Louie, 5 April 1887, CC.

75. Quoted in Johns, 'She' and 'Jess', p. 29.

76. Ibid, p. 31.

77. Ibid, p. 34. Havelock Ellis to Olive Schreiner: 'Two or three people have written to tell me that Haggard's *Bess* [*sic*] is taken entirely from S.A.F. [*The Story of an African Farm*] Is it? Did you see the article in [the *Pall Mall Gazette*] showing that he took the whole of *She* from an old book written 70 years ago. They say there are some bits almost copied from S.A.F.!!' Havelock Ellis to Olive Schreiner, 6 April 1887, in Olive Schreiner, *My Other Self: The Letters of Olive Schreiner and Havelock Ellis, 1884–1920*, ed. Yaffa Claire Draznin, New York: Peter Lang, 1992, p. 437.

78. Datelined 'Kyrenia, Cyprus, March 30'; see Johns, 'She' and 'Jess', p. 48.

79. Ibid, p. 50. This letter and the previous one were both written by Haggard while still in Cyprus.

80. The *Pall Mall Gazette* named the writer of the poem, identified in the *Philadelphia Press* in a letter by a reader published on 27 March, as R.C.V. Meyers, a resident of Philadelphia. According to Scott, the poem 'If I Should Die Tonight' first appeared in the *Anglo-American Times*, 31 January 1874. It was reprinted over the years in various publications credited to different authors. Jackson in 'The Author of the Poem',

pp. 187–92, identifies the writer as Meyers (1848–1917). D.S. Higgins traced the poem back to publication in 1873 in the 'American *Christian Herald* (subsequently *The Outlook*) ... crediting them to Miss Belle Smith', a teacher and librarian. The jury is still out. See Higgins, *Rider Haggard: The Great Storyteller*, London: Cassell, 1981; rev. edn, 2013, p. 112n, and J.E. Scott, *A Bibliography of the Works of Sir Henry Rider Haggard, 1856–1925*, Bishop's Stortford: Elkin Mathews, 1947, pp. 41–2.

81. *Dawn*, pp. 157–8.
82. Johns, *'She' and 'Jess'*, p. 52.
83. Ibid, p. 55.
84. Ibid.
85. Ibid.
86. Ibid, pp. 56–7.
87. Ibid, p. 57.
88. Ibid.
89. Ibid, pp. 58–9.
90. Ibid.
91. Ibid, p. 61.
92. Ibid, p. 80. Oscar Wilde wrote in his essay 'The Decay of Lying', *Nineteenth Century*, January 1889: 'As for Mr. Rider Haggard, who really has, or had once, the makings of a perfectly magnificent liar, he is now so afraid of being suspected of genius that when he does tell us anything marvellous, he feels bound to invent a personal reminiscence, and to put it into a footnote as a kind of cowardly corroboration.'
93. *Days*, vol. 1, pp. 266–7.
94. Lang in an undated letter quoted in *Days*, vol. 1, p. 273.
95. In *Detroit Free Press*; see Johns, *'She' and 'Jess'*, p. 75.

17. 'PASSIONATE AND POETIC'

1. *Days*, vol. 1, p. 268.
2. For Haggard finances, see D.S. Higgins, *Rider Haggard: The Great Storyteller*, London: Cassell, 1981, p. 121.
3. HRH to Mrs John Haggard, 18 August 1887, Columbia Collection.
4. In a final agreement with William Rose he gave the actor-producer sole rights for the theatrical adaptation of *She* in the United Kingdom, Haggard getting 50 per cent of the profits. The play was produced in 1888 and was highly successful. With Sophie Eyre in the title role, *She*, dramatised by William Sidney and Clo Graves with a prologue by William Rose, premiered at the Gaiety Theatre on the Strand.
5. HRH to Mrs John Haggard, 18 August 1887, Columbia Collection.
6. Bullock, Geoff, 'Rider Haggard's Residences', *Haggard Journal*, no. 119, March 2016, p. 7. In a letter to Randolph Churchill dated 25 March 1888, Haggard indicates that after 10 April he would move from Gunterstone Road to 24 Redcliffe Square. Lord

Randolph Churchill, Correspondence and Papers, GBR/0012/MS Add. 9248/2852, Cambridge University Library.

7. *Days*, vol. 1, p. 267.
8. Longman to Haggard, 16 July 1887, CC.
9. *Days*, vol. 1, pp. 266–7.
10. Morton Cohen, *Rider Haggard: His Life and Works*, London: Hutchinson, 1960, p. 123.
11. *Days*, vol. 1, pp. 268–9.
12. Ibid, p. 268.
13. Quoted in ibid, p. 269.
14. Ibid, p. 270.
15. Ibid, pp. 270–1.
16. *Cleopatra*, pp. vii–viii.
17. Ibid, p. viii.
18. Ibid, p. 256.
19. Ibid, p. 257.
20. Ibid, p. 157.
21. Loftie to HRH, 13 November 1888, quoted in M. Shirley Addy, *Rider Haggard and Egypt*, Accrington, Lancashire: AL Publications, 1998, p. 117. Loftie corrected the proofs of *Cleopatra* and also suggested a few textual alterations.
22. Henley, *Scots Observer*, 7 April 1887, quoted in Lloyd Siemens, *The Critical Reception of Sir Henry Rider Haggard: An Annotated Bibliography 1882–1991*, Greensboro: University of North Carolina, 1991, p. 21.
23. *Days*, vol. 1, p. 271.
24. *Literary World*, 4 August 1888; *Athenaeum*, 3 September 1888, quoted in Siemens, *Critical Reception*, p. 19.
25. *Maiwa's Revenge*, Preface, p. vii.
26. Sir William Sargeaunt died in July 1888.
27. *Maiwa's Revenge*, p. 123.
28. Quoted in Higgins, *Rider Haggard*, p. 121.
29. *Fortnightly Quarterly*, 1 September 1888, quoted in Higgins, *Rider Haggard*, pp. 126–7. Frank Harris (1856–1931) was a journalist, novelist, editor, and dedicatee of Oscar Wilde's play *The Ideal Husband*. At the outbreak of the First World War Harris returned to the United States where he had spent much of his early life. His journalism was critical of the role of Britain in the war, something Haggard commented on in his diary: 'Frank Harris, the malicious man who did me so much harm years ago, has been distinguishing himself by reviling his own country and belauding the Germans.' *PD*, entry for 16 March 1915, p. 23.
30. Harris's article also provoked Haggard into writing a preface, an ironic piece on plagiarism, to *Mr. Meeson's Will*.
31. *Days*, vol. 1, p. 279.
32. *Beatrice*, p. 19.

33. Beatrice's use of the deductive method is so striking, it immediately conjures up Arthur Conan Doyle's detective. The first Sherlock Holmes story, 'A Study in Scarlet', was published in *Beeton's Christmas Annual* for 1887 while Haggard was writing *Beatrice*, so perhaps use of the method can be regarded as a form of homage. See *Beatrice*, pp. 134ff.

34. *Beatrice*, 'Advertisement' in prelims to 1894 and subsequent edition.

35. Quoted in *Days*, vol. 1, p. 279.

36. Ibid.

37. *Days*, vol. 2, p. 9.

38. John Sutherland, *The Longman Companion to Victorian Fiction*, Harlow: Longman, 1988, p. 77.

39. Quoted in *Days*, vol. 2, p. 10. Haggard and Marie Corelli 'corresponded on various occasions' over the years and 'once she asked me to stay with her but for some reason or other I did not go – perhaps because she rather alarmed me with her enthusiasms'. When she died in 1924, Haggard recalled that 'nearly a generation ago there had been a craze for making absurd couplets about well-known people. One of the best of these ran: Why was Rider Haggard / Because he must Marie Corelli'. *PD*, 22 April 1924, p. 270.

40. HRH to Mrs John Haggard, 24 June 1890, Columbia Collection.

41. Quoted in *Days*, vol. 2, p. 11.

42. Ibid, p. 11.

43. Ibid, p. 12.

44. Ibid.

45. Ibid, pp. 13–4.

46. Ibid, p. 14.

47. Ibid, p. 15.

48. Ibid.

49. Ibid.

50. Haggard remained sensitive about *Beatrice* and, when an Italian company produced a silent film version of the book in 1921, Haggard insisted the last paragraph of the preface mentioned above be shown on the screen before each performance. The final paragraph referred to reads: 'Whatever the excuse of temptation, the man or woman who falls into undesirable relations with a married member of the other sex is both a sinner and a fool, and, in this coin or in that, certainly will be called upon to pay the price of sin and folly.' *Beatrice*, p. iii. The film, also known as *The Stronger Passion*, was directed by Herbert Brenon and starred Marie Doro and Sandro Salvini.

51. Spencer Blackett, a son of Henry Blackett of Hurst and Blackett who published *Dawn* and *The Witch's Head*, bought J. & R. Maxwell in 1887.

52. Judith Hickey, *Journal: Agnes Marion Haggard (née Barber)*, privately published, 2013, p. 4.

53. *Mr. Meeson's Will*, p. x.

54. Ibid, pp. 234–5.

55. MS, CC.

56. *Days*, vol. 1, p. 278.

57. 'Two thousand years have I waited for the day when I should see the last of these hateful caves and this gloomy-visaged folk, and now it is at hand, and my heart bounds up to meet it like a child's towards its holiday. For thou shalt rule this England – '
'But we have a queen already,' broke in Leo, hastily.
'It is naught, it is naught,' said Ayesha; 'she can be overthrown.' *She*, pp. 254–5.

58. Quotes from MS, CC. The storyline is summarised from notes made by Dorothy Cheyne in 2010.

59. *Days*, vol. 1, p. 278. Haggard may have been inspired to look to Scandinavia by Meredith Townsend, former editor and a co-owner of the *Spectator*, who wrote to Haggard saying 'it would be worth living to read your account of a Berserk, a white Umslopogaas, with a vein of pity in him for women only'. Quoted in Higgins, *Rider Haggard*, p. 124. Townsend was born at Bures, Suffolk, on 1 April 1831 and, like Haggard, educated at Ipswich School.

60. *Days*, vol. 1, p. 284.

61. Ibid, p. 285.

62. Alexander (Aleck) Ross was a founding member and honorary secretary of the Society of Authors. Both Haggard and Ross sat on the council of the Society in 1890 and Haggard also served on the management committee. Ross's younger brother Robert was Oscar Wilde's lover, friend and future literary executor.

63. *Days*, vol. 1, p. 285.

64. From Haggard's diary, quoted in *Cloak*, pp. 140–1.

65. Ibid, pp. 141–2.

66. HRH to Louie, 2 July 1888, CC.

67. Haggard's diary, quoted in *Cloak*, p. 144.

68. Haggard's diary, quoted in Higgins, *Rider Haggard*, p. 124.

69. HRH, 'The Wreck of the Copeland', p. 194.

70. Ibid.

71. *Days*, vol. 1, p. 293.

72. HRH to William Haggard, telegram, 25 July 1888, CC.

73. *Days*, vol. 1, p. 294.

74. *Cloak*, p. 144.

75. *New York Times*, 31 May 1891, quoted in Siemens, *Critical Reception*, p. 23.

76. Lang to HRH, undated, quoted in *Days*, vol. 2, p. 5.

77. Cohen, *Rider Haggard*, p. 130.

78. Hardy, Thomas, *The Collected Letters of Thomas Hardy*, ed. Richard Little Purdy and Michael Millgate, Oxford: Clarendon Press, volume 1, 1979, p.235.

79. *Eric Brighteyes*, p. 273. The illustration by Lancelot Speed is on the preceding page.

80. J.E. Scott, *A Bibliography of the Works of Sir Henry Rider Haggard, 1856–1925*, Bishop's Stortford: Elkin Mathews, 1947, p. 62.

81. Ibid.

82. Ibid.

83. *Days*, vol. 1, p. 280.

84. Ibid, p. 281.

85. Ibid.

86. Roger Lancelyn Green, *Andrew Lang*, Leicester: Ward, 1946, p. 129. According to Green, the poems and songs are by Lang 'though the Israelitish hymns appears to be versified from Haggard's prose, as the Duologue of the Bow and the Snake may also be'.

87. Ibid, p. 131.

88. *Athenaeum*, 6 December 1890, quoted in Siemens, *Critical Reception*, pp. 22–3.

89. *Spectator*, 14 February 1891, quoted in Siemens, *Critical Reception*, p. 24. Robert Louis Stevenson sent Lang an unfinished satiric poem on *The World's Desire* and in October 1889 Rudyard Kipling, three weeks after his arrival in England, sent Lang a ten-stanza verse parody in the style of Brett Harte's 'Plain Language from Truthful James', written, according to Cohen, 'in the context of the Savile Club gossip about Lang and Haggard's year-old collaboration on a romance about Odysseus' latter-day wanderings'. *RR*, p. 25. The poem is given on pp. 26–7. Stevenson's poem appears in *Days*, vol. 2, p. 8.

90. 'Hunter Quatermain's Story' first appeared in *In a Good Cause*; 'A Tale of Three Lions' was serialised in *Atlanta* in late 1887 and 'Long Odds' appeared in *Macmillan's Magazine* in February 1886.

91. HRH, 'On Going Back', *Longmans Magazine*, November 1887, p. 63.

92. *Allan's Wife*, p. 79.

93. Ibid, p. 154.

94. Ibid, p. 159.

95. *Days*, vol. 1, p. 271.

96. Ibid, pp. 271–2.

97. Ibid, p. 272.

98. HRH to Louie, 8 December 1889, CC.

99. HRH to John Haggard, quoted in Higgins, *Rider Haggard*, p. 134.

100. HRH to Louie, 9 December 1889, CC.

101. Ibid.

102. Ibid.

103. *Cloak*, p. 148.

104. HRH to father, 25 December 1889, CC.

105. Ella Haggard, *Life and Its Author: An Essay in Verse*, London: Longmans, 1890, pp. 6–7. The book also includes extracts from some of Ella Haggard's other poems including 'Myra: or, The Rose of East: A Tale of the Afghan'.

106. Higgins, *Rider Haggard*, p. 134.

107. Will added that 'the Prince of Wales and his family read *Cleopatra* on their way out here, and think it your best book'. Quoted in *Days*, vol. 2, pp. 1–2.

108. Ibid, p. 3.

18. 'I DESCENDED INTO HELL'

1. John Addington Symonds to Horatio Brown, quoted in *RR*, p. 17.

2. Quoted in *RR*, p. 17. Stevenson responded to James: 'Kipling is by far the most promising young man who has appeared since – ahem – I appeared. He amazes me by his precocity and various endowments. But he alarms me by his copiousness and haste.' Quoted in Charles Carrington, *Rudyard Kipling: His Life and Work*, London: Macmillan, 1955, p. 187.

3. *RR*, p. 18.

4. Ibid. Kipling wished he had written the verse himself. 'It ran joyously through all the papers. It still hangs faintly in the air and, as I used to warn Haggard, may continue as an aroma when all but our two queer names are forgotten.' The last two lines remain frequently quoted. Rudyard Kipling, *Something of Myself*, London: Macmillan, 1981, pp. 92–3. The poem was dedicated to Kipling on publication in Stephen's 1891 collection *Lapsus Calami* (A Slip of the Pen).

5. *RR*, p. 85.

6. *Days*, vol. 2, pp. 26–7.

7. Kipling to W.E. Henley, quoted in Andrew Lycett, *Rudyard Kipling*, London: Phoenix, 2000, p. 345. The two were also Freemasons: Haggard was first initiated into the fraternal order in Pretoria and subsequently received into the Lodge of Good Report No. 156 in London in December 1887. Kipling was initiated into the Lodge of Hope and Perseverance No. 782 in Lahore in April 1885 and maintained an active participatory interest in Masonry throughout his life. Haggard, claiming he was never able to learn anything off by heart, felt obliged to abandon 'the active pursuit of Masonry' in 1890. *Days*, vol. 1, p. 28.

8. Kipling, 'The Dream of Duncan Parrenness', in *Life's Handicap*, p. 400. First published in the *Civil and Military Gazette*, 25 December 1884; collected in *Life's Handicap* in 1891.

9. Ibid, pp. 401–2.

10. *Days*, vol. 2, p. 16.

11. Morton Cohen, *Rider Haggard: His Life and Works*, London: Hutchinson, 1960, p. 187.

12. *Scots Observer*, 16 February 1889; see Cohen, *Rider Haggard*, p. 187.

13. Edward Boyd, introduction to *Nada the Lily*, London: Collins, 1957, p. 14.

14. As with *She*, Allan Quatermain is not named but internal references identify him as the editor.

15. *Nada the Lily*, London: Macdonald, p. 21.

16. Ibid, pp. 61–2.

17. Tshaneni (also known as Ghost Mountain) is in the Lebombo range that borders north-eastern KwaZulu-Natal. Haggard never visited the area.

18. Haggard owned the first 1882 edition in which he made 'numerous marginal notes in pencil'; Elkin Mathews Catalogue 102, May 1946, p. 6.

19. Carolyn Hamilton, *Terrific Majesty: The Powers of Shaka Zulu and the Limits of Historical Invention*, Cape Town: David Philip, 1998, p. 124.

20. Edward Boyd, introduction to *Nada the Lily*, pp. 14–5.

21. Quoted in *Days*, vol. 2, p. 17.
22. Ibid.
23. Ibid, p. 18.
24. Ibid.
25. Quoted in Cohen, RR, pp. 31–2.
26. *New York Times*, 15 May 1892, quoted in Lloyd Siemens, *The Critical Reception of Sir Henry Rider Haggard: An Annotated Bibliography 1882–1991*, Greensboro: University of North Carolina, 1991, p. 24.
27. A reference to Jack the Ripper, the unidentified murderer who killed several women in the Whitechapel area of London in 1888. Haggard met Charles Warren, London's Metropolitan Police Commissioner in charge of the Jack the Ripper investigation, in 1887 in Pretoria.
28. Quoted in *Days*, vol. 2, p. 18.
29. Gosse to HRH, quoted in D.S. Higgins, *Rider Haggard: The Great Storyteller*, London: Cassell, 1981; rev. edn, 2013, p. 150.
30. Besant to HRH, quoted in Higgins, *Rider Haggard*, p. 150.
31. Quoted in *Days*, vol. 1, p. 239.
32. Ibid. The companions in arms engaged in a literary joust: Stevenson, his wife Fanny and friends entertained themselves writing *An Object of Pity; or, The Man Haggard*, 'A Romance / By Many Competent Hands', a satire on expatriate life in Samoa with Bazett as the hero; Bazett responded in kind with *Objects of Pity; or, Self and Company* 'by a Gentleman of Quality'. Both titles were printed and Stevenson sent them in July 1893 to Ditchingham where Haggard was 'unable to make head or tail of them'. *Days*, vol. 1, p. 241. The comic aspect of Bazett's involvement in the social and political life of Samoa was offset by bouts of malaria and general poor health, not helped by excessive drinking, and not long after Stevenson's death in December 1894, Bazett returned to England.
33. Quoted in *Days*, vol. 2, p. 19.
34. See *Nada the Lily*, London: Macdonald, pp. v–vii.
35. Shepstone to HRH, 13 July 1892, quoted in *Days*, vol. 2, p. 23. The fashion has not substantially changed, but there have been some scholarly reassessments, notably Jeff Guy's *Theophilus Shepstone and the Forging of Natal* and Thomas McClendon's *White Chief, Black Lords*. A full biography of Shepstone has yet to be written.
36. Haggard had Shepstone's letter bound with the manuscript of *Nada the Lily*, which he later donated to the Norfolk Record Office.
37. Translation from isiZulu by Dumisani Zondi.
38. First published in 1930. An English translation, *Jeqe, the Body-Servant of King Shaka* by J. Boxwell, was published by the Lovedale Press in 1951 and reissued as a Penguin Modern Classic, edited by Stephen Gray, in 2008.
39. Benedict Vilakazi's review appeared in *Ilanga lase Natal*, 6 October 1933, quoted in Tim Couzens, *The New African: A Study of the Life and Works of H.I.E. Dhlomo*, Johannesburg: Ravan Press, 1985, p. 345, n. 350. Benedict Vilakazi (1906–47) was a

poet, novelist and critic. He collaborated with the linguist Clement Martyn Doke on a Zulu-English dictionary, first published in 1948 and now in its fourth edition.

40. *Cloak*, p. 151.

41. *Days*, vol. 2, p. 40.

42. Mrs Jebb, *A Strange Career: The Life and Adventures of John Gladwyn Jebb*, Edinburgh: Blackwood, 1894, p. xv. Jebb's widow, unidentified in the book, was Bertha Jebb.

43. Ibid, pp. xv–xvi.

44. *Days*, vol. 2, p. 40

45. 'My farming began in the year 1889, when, letting off the rest of it in small parcels, I took about a hundred and twenty acres on the occasion of the tenant giving up the farm.' The 'land was in so scandalous a condition' that it took eight years of 'cleaning and manuring' to recover its fertility. *Farmer's Year*, p. 32.

46. HRH, 'The Fate of Swaziland', *New Review*, January 1890, p. 66.

47. Quoted in Ann Thwaite, *Edmund Gosse: A Literary Landscape, 1849–1928*, London: Secker and Warburg, 1984, p. 334. 'Golf for Duffers' was reprinted in Roger Allen, *A Guide to the Fiction of Rider Haggard*, privately published, 1998. Haggard joined the Waveney Valley Golf Club (later the Bungay and Waveney Valley Golf Club) shortly after it came into existence in January 1889. He was on the club's committee from 1890 to 1894 and was a vice president in 1903; it was proposed to invite him to be president in 1915, but shortly thereafter the club was suspended for the duration of the First World War. Louie joined the club shortly after her husband and at the autumn meeting of 1890 presented the Handicap prize won by her friend Jessie Hartcup. The following year Louie won the same prize, plus the Ladies' Medal. Closely involved with the club's ladies' section, Louie became its president in 1929, being succeeded in 1934 by Jessie. The Silver Rose Bowl presented by Louie in 1914 remains the first of the club's Ladies' trophies.

48. Quoted in Thwaite, *Edmund Gosse*, p. 336.

49. Ibid, p. 335.

50. *Days*, vol. 2, p. 42.

51. Ibid. Goslings was a private bank. It merged with Barclays in 1896.

52. *New York Times*, 11 January 1891, quoted in Cohen, *Rider Haggard*, p. 133.

53. *Days*, vol. 2, p. 50.

54. Ibid.

55. Ibid, p. 51.

56. Ibid.

57. Ibid, p. 43.

58. Ibid, p. 56.

59. Ibid, p. 43.

60. *Cloak*, p. 155.

61. HRH to William Haggard, 8 February 1891, CC.

62. *Days*, vol. 2, p. 46.

63. Ibid, p. 46n.

64. Quoted in Thwaite, *Edmund Gosse*, p. 336.
65. Ibid.
66. Ibid.
67. Ibid.
68. Ibid.
69. Victoria Manthorpe, *Children of the Empire: The Victorian Haggards*, London: Gollancz, 1996, p. 168.
70. Quoted in ibid, p. 169.
71. *Days*, vol. 2, p. 57.
72. Ibid.
73. Ibid, pp. 57–8. This incident features in *Heart of the World*, p. 34.
74. Ibid, p. 58.
75. Ibid.
76. Ibid, p. 59.
77. Ibid, p. 62.
78. Ibid, p. 63. The attempted robbery was recreated in Haggard's South American romance *Heart of the World*, published in 1896, where Haggard made use of many of the locations visited during his trip with Jebb. See *Heart of the World*, pp. 63ff.
79. Ibid.
80. Ibid, p. 71.
81. *Cloak*, p. 16.
82. Ibid.
83. Ibid, p. 21.
84. Ibid. Cheyne also records Haggard's 'non-rational belief' hinted at in his autobiography and says that it was 'easily to be gathered from his conversation that he was dogged by evil luck – not directly evil to himself but to those he loved and whom he had befriended'.
85. Ibid, p. 156. At the 2007 annual Rider Haggard Society dinner held that year at the Bungay and Waveney Valley Golf Club, the Society donated a new trophy to the club, the Jock Haggard Trophy, to be awarded to junior golfers for one year. According to the programme for the evening, 'The Trophy is in memory of Rider Haggard's son Arthur John "Jock"'. The trophy was carved by Haggard's great-grandson Jonathan Cheyne and was presented by HRH's great-great-grandson Benjamin Cheyne. During the course of the dinner Haggard's granddaughter Nada Cheyne read from *Nada the Lily* and the author Louis de Bernières read 'Golf for Duffers'.
86. *Cloak*, p. 155.
87. *Days*, vol. 2, pp. 43–4.

19. 'OCEANS OF GORE'

1. *Days*, vol. 2, p. 83.
2. *Cloak*, p. 157.
3. *Montezuma's Daughter*, p. 13.

4. *Cloak*, p. 159.

5. *Days*, vol. 2, p. 44.

6. *Montezuma's Daughter*, pp. 313–4.

7. *Days*, vol. 2, p. 44.

8. *Montezuma's Daughter*, p. 53.

9. *New York Times*, 26 November 1893, quoted in Lloyd Siemens, *The Critical Reception of Sir Henry Rider Haggard: An Annotated Bibliography 1882–1991*, Greensboro: University of North Carolina, 1991, p. 25.

10. Quoted in 'They Walled Up Nuns Didn't They? H. Rider Haggard's *Montezuma's Daughter* and Anti-Catholicism in Victorian England', chapter 2 of Rene Kollar, *A Foreign and Wicked Institution? The Campaign against Convents in Victorian England*, Cambridge: James Clarke, 2011, p. 27.

11. Quoted in D.S. Higgins, *Rider Haggard: The Great Storyteller*, London: Cassell, 1981, p. 158.

12. Susanna Wade Martins, *Norfolk: A Changing Countryside, 1780–1914*, Chichester: Phillimore, 1988, p. 22.

13. *Strand Magazine*, January 1892, p. 3.

14. Ibid, p. 4.

15. Ibid, p. 5. Charles Kerr, the artist mentioned above.

16. Ibid, p. 7.

17. Ibid, pp. 7–8.

18. Ibid, p. 8.

19. Ibid.

20. Ibid, p. 9.

21. Ibid, p. 10.

22. Ibid, p. 17.

23. Article by Frederick Dolman in *Young Man*, partially reprinted under the heading 'How Mr. Haggard Works', *Review of Reviews*, January 1894, p. 31.

24. *Cloak*, p. 157.

25. Ibid, pp. 157–8.

26. Ibid, p. 158.

27. HRH to Louie, 24 July 1892, CC.

28. Richard Ellmann, *Oscar Wilde*, London: Penguin, 1988, p. 351.

29. Ibid, p. 356.

30. Marie Corelli was also in Bad Homburg around this time, intent on obtaining an introduction to the Prince of Wales. She also met Wilde. See Phillip Waller, *Writers, Readers, and Reputations: Literary Life in Britain, 1870–1918*, Oxford: OUP, 2008, p. 801.

31. Wilde's wife Constance to her brother Otho, 9 July 1892, quoted in Rupert Hart-Davis (ed.), *Selected Letters of Oscar Wilde*, Oxford: OUP, 1979, p. 316.

32. HRH to father, 2 August 1892, CC.

33. HRH to Louie, 24 July 1892, CC.

34. Ibid.

35. Ibid.

36. *Days*, vol. 2, p. 4.

37. HRH to father, 5 August 1892, CC.

38. *Cloak*, p. 158.

39. HRH to father, 9 December 1892, CC.

40. HRH to Mrs John Haggard, 10 December 1892, Columbia Collection.

41. *Cloak*, p. 159.

42. *Days*, vol. 2, p. 88.

43. Ibid, p. 83.

44. Dolman, 'Mrs. Alexander's Daughter', one of four articles (three by other writers) under the heading 'Clever Daughters of Clever Parents' in *Ladies, Home Journal*, February 1894, p. 3.

45. Ibid.

46. Portsdown Road; Randolph Avenue since 1939.

47. Dolman, 'Mrs. Alexander's Daughter', p. 3.

48. *Cloak*, p. 157.

49. Morton Cohen, *Rider Haggard: His Life and Works*, London: Hutchinson, 1960, p. 137n.

50. *Days*, vol. 2, p. 83.

51. *Cloak*, Foreword by Godfrey Cheyne, pp. 18, 20.

52. J.E. Scott, *A Bibliography of the Works of Sir Henry Rider Haggard, 1856–1925*, Bishop's Stortford: Elkin Mathews, 1947, p. 73.

53. *Days*, vol. 2, p. 83.

54. A minor character in the book is named Ida.

55. *Cloak*, p. 159.

56. Scott, *Bibliography*, p. 70.

57. *Montezuma's Daughter*, p. v.

58. *Days*, vol. 2, p. 55.

59. *Cloak*, p. 161.

60. Ibid.

61. Ibid. Haggard suggested it come to Ditchingham and be erected 'in the shed used for pig-killing on the farm' as it evidently required blood in copious amounts. The statue inspired *The Yellow God*, in which the statue of the title deity does indeed come to live in a city office, to baleful effect.

62. Ibid, p. 162.

63. Haggard had contact with another adventurer, the archaeologist and explorer Percy Harrison Fawcett (1867–1925), who spent (and lost) his life searching for lost cities in South America. Fawcett stated as having in his possession 'an image about ten inches high, carved from a piece of black basalt. It represents a figure with a plaque on its chest, and about its ankles a band similarly inscribed. It was given to me by Sir H. Rider Haggard, who obtained it from Brazil, and I firmly believe it came from one of the

lost cities.' Fawcett, *Exploration Fawcett*, p. 12. I have been unable find any reference on Haggard's part to either the statue or Fawcett. Haggard did partially fund an expedition by J.G.H. Carmichael to find a lost city in south-west Mexico, where at the approach of the Spanish conquistadores, the Aztecs had hidden treasure worth $3 million. Carmichael headed off to Mexico, where he was struck down by fever and deserted by his Indian carriers. His health broken, Carmichael died shortly after his return to England. See *Days*, vol. 2, pp. 128–9.

64.   Victoria Manthorpe, *Children of the Empire: The Victorian Haggards*, London: Gollancz, 1996, p. 180.

65.   Letter from Alfred Haggard, quoted in ibid, p. 180.

66.   Haggard to Mrs John Haggard, 7 September 1892, Columbia Collection.

67.   *Days*, vol. 2, p. 120.

68.   Ibid.

69.   HRH to Jack Haggard, 5 May 1893, inserted in letters from HRH to Agnes Barber, Columbia Collection.

70.   Haggard added a note dated 24 April 1893: 'The nurse told me that he added after the word "present" "He is in this room".' CC.

71.   *Days*, vol. 2, p. 120.

72.   Mrs Jebb, *A Strange Career: The Life and Adventures of John Gladwyn Jebb*, Edinburgh: Blackwood, 1894, pp. xxii–xxiii.

20.   'SPECULATIVE AND NERVE-RACKING'

1.   *Days*, vol. 2, p. 84.

2.   Haggard first appeared in a photograph with his beard in *Black and White*, 11 August 1894.

3.   *People of the Mist*, Dedication.

4.   *Cloak*, p. 159.

5.   *People of the Mist*, Dedication.

6.   Ibid, p. 93.

7.   *People of the Mist* draws heavily on the stories of Frederick Jackson, especially his encounters with slavers and his exploration of the interiors of what are now Kenya and Uganda, including Mount Elgon and its caves. He recounts these exploits and much else in *Early Days in East Africa*, London: Edward Arnold, 1930. He was later Lieutenant Governor of the East African Protectorate and Governor of Uganda. He retired in 1917.

8.   See Geoff Bullock, 'Rider Haggard and Royal Air Force Connections', *RAF Historical Society Journal*, http://www.raf.mod.uk/history/theroyalairforcemotto.cfm.

9.   *Days*, vol. 2, p. 110.

10.   From an advertisement on the unpaginated endpapers of W.A. Wills and L.T. Collingridge, *The Downfall of Lobengula*, London: Simpkin, Marshall, Hamilton and Kent, 1894; reprint, Bulawayo: Books of Rhodesia, 1971.

11. William Arthur Wills was born in Liverpool in 1863 and educated at Dulwich College. In 1887, having trained as a geologist, he headed to the Witwatersrand goldfields in the Transvaal where he made a systematic study of the Rand reefs and in 1890 established the *South African Mining Journal* in Johannesburg. After returning to London in 1892, he founded the *African Review* with his brother Walter Wills and Cameron Cannell; Leonard Thomas Collingridge came on board as printer and publisher.

12. *Days*, vol. 2, p. 111.

13. See Martin Meredith, *Diamonds, Gold and War: The Making of South Africa*, London: Simon and Schuster, 2008, p. 303.

14. *Days*, vol. 2, p. 116.

15. Victoria Manthorpe, *Children of the Empire: The Victorian Haggards*, London: Gollancz, 1996, p. 158.

16. *Days*, vol. 2, p. 115. There was another letter in *The Times* in December on the death of Haggard's friends Patterson and Sargeaunt at the hands of Lobengula. The Ndebele king was the real reason for Haggard's rejection of Alfred's investment overtures: 'I held that Lobengula would never grant [Alfred] what he wanted unless it was wrung from him by force of arms. Indeed I am convinced to this day that no one except Cecil Rhodes, with his vast command of money, could have dispossessed this tyrant and annexed those great territories.' *Days*, vol. 2, p. 115.

17. Robert I. Rotberg, *The Founder*, Johannesburg: Jonathan Ball, 2002, p. 277.

18. From an advertisement in Wills and Collingridge, *Downfall of Lobengula*.

19. D.S. Higgins, *Rider Haggard: The Great Storyteller*, London: Cassell, 1981, p. 158.

20. Chicot was the pseudonym of Keble Howard (itself a pseudonym for John Keble Bell), critic, journalist, playwright and novelist. His novel *Lord London* (1913) based on the life of Lord Northcliffe was suppressed by Northcliffe, who ordered his newspapers not to advertise or review any books from its publisher, Chapman and Hall.

21. *Cloak*, p. 168.

22. Quoted in *Cloak*, p. 169.

23. *African Review*, 28 April 1894, p. 539. Thereafter, until Haggard's resignation, the weekly's masthead carried the information that it was 'Conducted by H. Rider Haggard & W.A. Wills'.

24. Ibid.

25. Ibid.

26. Ibid, p. 541.

27. Ibid, p. 545.

28. Ibid, p. 541. When Gladstone resigned as prime minister in March, a general election looked imminent but Lord Rosebery kept the Liberals in power for another fifteen months until the election of 1895. Stanley entered politics as a Liberal Unionist candidate for North Lambeth in 1892 after the resignation of the former incumbent. Stanley lost the by-election by 130 votes. He remained politically active and was elected to parliament as member for North Lambeth in August 1895.

29. Ibid.

30. Ibid, p. 542.

31. Ibid.

32. Ibid.

33. Ibid.

34. Quoted in an article, 'The Bride of England', *African Review*, 5 May 1894, p. 577.

35. Ibid.

36. Huw Jones, *A Biographical Register of Swaziland to 1902*, Pietermaritzburg: University of Natal Press, 1993, p. 112.

37. *African Review*, 9 June, 1894, p. 762.

38. Correspondence with Longmans and a letter to Stewart from Haggard indicated that, should the book be published, it would be under Haggard's name with an acknowledgement to Stewart and the royalties split: three-quarters to Haggard and the remaining quarter to Stewart.

39. *African Review*, 17 September 1894, p. 407. There were in fact more women than men. There had been more women than men in England for nearly a hundred years. See Samuel Hynes, *A War Imagined: The First World War and English Culture*, London: Bodley Head, 1992, p. 379.

40. Ibid, p. 408.

41. Ibid.

42. *African Review*, 23 June 1894, p. 842. Norman Etherington cites the Palmer mission as the inspiration for *Queen Sheba's Ring*. See Norman Etherington, *Rider Haggard*, Boston: Twayne, 1984, p. 111. Colonel Charles Warren, who met Haggard in Pretoria in 1877 and is famous as having been Commissioner of Police at the time of the 'Jack the Ripper' murders in the late 1880s, subsequently headed a recovery expedition to find the remains of Gill and Charrington, which were interred in St Paul's Cathedral.

43. HRH, quoted in Steve Kemper, *A Splendid Savage: The Restless Life of Frederick Russell Burnham*, New York: Norton, 2015, p. 2.

44. Ibid, p. 117.

45. Ibid, p. 120.

46. Haggard refers to these beads in his introduction to *Monomotapa (Rhodesia)* by Theodore Wilmot, p. xvi. See Kemper, *A Splendid Savage*, p. 138.

47. *Days*, vol. 2, p. 122. Burnham provided Haggard with information for 'Major Wilson's Last Fight', Haggard's account of the Shangani Patrol, published in Andrew Lang's *The Red True Story Book* in 1895.

48. Ibid. Burnham later published two memoirs, *Scouting on Two Continents* (1926) and *Taking Chances* (1944).

49. Kemper, *A Splendid Savage*, p. 183.

50. Ibid, p. 184.

51. Ibid, p. 193.

52. Ibid, p. 205. Burnham fought on, infamously assassinating the Mlimo, the Ndebele's spiritual leader whose prophecies and pronouncements had fuelled the rebellion in March.

53. The dedication was also included when *The Wizard* was republished in 1900 in the same volume with *Elissa, or, The Doom of Zimbabwe* (previously published as a serial in the *Long Bow* between 2 February and 8 June 1898) and *Black Heart and White Heart* (previously published in *African Review*, January 1896) under the title *Black Heart and White Heart and Other Stories*.

54. *Cloak*, p. 171.

55. Ibid.

56. It is not known if Haggard met Mackenzie in South Africa, but Haggard sent him a copy of the second edition of *Cetywayo and His White Neighbours* in 1888 and the two subsequently corresponded.

57. *An Heroic Effort*, London: Butler and Tanner, 1893. Reprinted in D.E. Whatmore (comp.), *Rider Haggard's Good Deeds*, Pamphlet One: *Deeds for the Church*, Cheltenham: D.E. Whatmore, 1995, p. 11.

58. Ibid, p. 12.

59. *Days*, vol. 2, pp. 119–20.

60. Pakenham, *Boer War*, p. 47.

61. Ibid.

62. Quoted in Longford, Elizabeth, *Jameson's Raid*, Jonathan Ball, Johannesburg, 2012, p. 275.

63. *Days*, vol. 2, p. 117.

64. Ibid, pp. 117–8.

65. *African Review*, 16 March 1895, p. 419.

66. *Days*, vol. 2, p. 111.

67. Ibid.

68. Speech quoted in *Days*, vol. 2, p. 112.

69. Ibid.

70. Ibid.

71. Morton Cohen, *Rider Haggard: His Life and Works*, London: Hutchinson, 1960, p. 157.

72. Ibid.

73. *Days*, vol. 2, p. 113.

74. 'Cochrane has chucked his city employment, found it did not pay & was too risky to dabble in.' HRH to Mrs John Haggard, 3 June 1890, Columbia Collection.

75. *Days*, vol. 2, pp. 113–4.

76. Ibid, p. 113. 'The Baby on the Shore' was written by comedian and actor George ·Grossmith, famous for his comic songs and his performances in the operettas of Gilbert and Sullivan; co-writer with his brother Weedon of *The Diary of a Nobody*.

77. *Norfolk Chronicle*, quoted in Cohen, *Rider Haggard*, p. 157.

78. J.E. Scott, *A Bibliography of the Works of Sir Henry Rider Haggard, 1856–1925*, Bishop's Stortford: Elkin Mathews, 1947, p. 190.

79. *Farmer's Year*, p. 164.

80. *Pall Mall Gazette*, 24 July 1895.

81. Ibid.

82. Ibid.

83. Price retained his seat until his retirement shortly before the 1918 general election when it went to a Unionist candidate.

84. *Pall Mall Gazette*, 24 July 1895.

85. *Days*, vol. 2, p. 111.

86. Barbara Tuchman, *The Proud Tower*, London: Papermac, 1997, p. 3.

87. Ibid, p. 14.

88. *Cloak*, p. 190.

89. There is a possibility Haggard and Lilly may have met at the 1886 wedding of Haggard's sister Mary to Baron Albert d'Anethan; she certainly sent a gift. See Manthorpe, *Children of the Empire*, p. 149. Mary converted to Roman Catholicism in 1900. Her husband Baron Albert d'Anethan in 1886, a Belgian politician and diplomat, whom she met in Rio de Janeiro when visiting Will in 1885, was a Catholic.

90. Higgins, *Rider Haggard*, p. 165.

91. Manthorpe, *Children of the Empire*, p. 181.

92. Later the home of twentieth-century composer Benjamin Britten and his partner, the tenor Peter Pears.

93. Manthorpe, *Children of the Empire*, p. 181. Geoffrey Archer subsequently became Governor of Somaliland, Governor of Uganda and Governor General of the Sudan. He died in 1964. While Governor of Somaliland he attended the 1921 Cairo conference, bringing with him two young lions en route to the London Zoo. They escaped at the welcoming reception at the British Residency but were caught by Archer and an African servant and thus prevented from devouring the Governor's pet marabou stork.

94. *Cloak*, pp. 190–1.

95. Ibid, p. 190.

96. Ibid.

97. Ibid. The letters referred to by Lilias are no longer extant.

98. *Stella Fregelius*, p. 234.

99. Ibid, p. 242.

100. *Stella Fregelius* was serialised in *T.P.'s Weekly* between November 1902 and April 1903. Haggard revised this text for the book, published 3 February 1904.

101. See Scott, *Bibliography*, p. 97. Agnes Haggard (née Barber) wrote three novels under the pseudonyms John Berwick and Agnes Marion: *The Tangena Tree* (1889), *Secret of Saint Florel* (1896) and *A Philosopher's Romance* (1897); a volume of poems was published posthumously in 1963.

102. *Farmer's Year*, p. 447. Differing dates are given by different biographers for the purchase of Kessingland Grange. The year 1895 is that on the sale documents supplied to David Critchlow by the Suffolk Record Office. See *Rider Haggard Society Journal*, March 2020, p. 2. The house was subsequently sold by auction in 1928.

103. *Cloak*, p. 193.

104. *Farmer's Year*, p. 205.

105. *Gardener's Year*, p. 136.
106. *Cloak*, p. 193.
107. Kipling described the house as being 'for all practical purposes the side of a ship'. Quoted in *RR*, p. 80.
108. *Cloak*, pp. 193–4.
109. Ibid, p. 194. Places were also found for Kerr's illustrations from the serialisation of *The Wizard* in the *African Review* as well as those by Frank Sydney Wilson for *Joan Haste* and G.P. Jacomb-Hood for *Lysbeth*.
110. *Days*, vol. 2, p. 12.

21. 'ACCURATE OBSERVATION'

1. *Cloak*, p. 213.
2. *Days*, vol. 2, p. 131.
3. Ibid.
4. *Farmer's Year*, Ronald Blythe introduction, p. ix.
5. Morton Cohen, *Rider Haggard: His Life and Works*, London: Hutchinson, 1960, p. 159.
6. 'The price of grain in Norwich fell from about 65 shillings a quarter in 1872 to below 55 shillings for the rest of the century, reaching its lowest in 1894 at 25 shillings.' Susanna Wade Martins, *Norfolk: A Changing Countryside, 1780–1914*, Chichester: Phillimore, 1988, p. 43.
7. Ibid, p. 45. Between 1861 and 1901 over a half a million people left the agricultural sector.
8. Cohen, *Rider Haggard*, p. 161.
9. *Farmer's Year*, Ronald Blythe introduction, p. ix.
10. Cohen, *Rider Haggard*, p. 161.
11. Ibid, p. 132.
12. *Farmer's Year*, Ronald Blythe introduction, p. vii.
13. Ibid, viii.
14. Ibid, Author's Note, p. xiv. See appendix to *Farmer's Year*, 'The Rural Exodus'.
15. Ibid, p. 41.
16. Ibid, p. 44.
17. Ibid, p. 140.
18. Ibid, p. 383.
19. Ibid, p. 129.
20. Ibid, p. 49.
21. Ibid, p. 50.
22. Ibid, pp. 71–2. Haggard's duties on the local bench included visitations to the Heckingham Workhouse, now 'an infirmary for the aged poor, rather than the last shelter to which the destitute are driven by necessity', conjuring up the memory of when he sat on its board some years earlier and proposed children and infants there be given

fresh not skimmed milk and was opposed on the grounds that 'the children were not fed upon new milk in their own homes, to which I replied that even if they were starved at home, it was no reason why they should be starved when in the public charge'. His motion was passed with a majority of one vote. See *Farmer's Year*, pp. 426–7.

23. Ibid, Ronald Blythe introduction, pp. x–xi.

24. Ibid, p. 443.

25. Ibid, p. 446. A conclusion supported by the Agricultural Summary in *The Times* of 26 December 1898, where Haggard read that 'this year 76,079 acres have been entirely lost from the previously cultivated area, as against a loss of 13,546 acres in 1897. Further, this cheerful fact is recorded – that in 1898 the aggregate of all corn crops, cereal and pulse together, is absolutely the lowest on record.' Ibid.

26. Ibid, p. 458.

27. *Bookman*, quoted in Cohen, *Rider Haggard*, p. 165.

28. Ibid.

29. Ibid.

30. Quoted in Lloyd Siemens, *The Critical Reception of Sir Henry Rider Haggard: An Annotated Bibliography 1882–1991*, Greensboro: University of North Carolina, 1991, p. 29.

31. Gilbert White was the author of *The Natural History of Selborne*. Kipling to HRH, 12 November 1899, in *RR*, pp. 41–2.

32. *RR*, p. 41.

33. *Days*, vol. 2, p. 139.

34. *Farmer's Year*, p. 279.

35. The vaccine was created by Edward Jenner in 1796.

36. David Baxter, 'Opposition to Vaccination and Immunisation: The UK Experience; From Smallpox to MMR', *Journal of Vaccines and Vaccination*, vol. 5, 2014, doi:/10.4172/2157-7560.1000254, p. 3.

37. *Farmer's Year*, p. 279.

38. *Days*, vol. 2, pp. 139–40.

39. Quoted in D.S. Higgins, *Rider Haggard: The Great Storyteller*, London: Cassell, 1981, p. 169.

40. Ibid.

41. *Spectator*, 3 December 1898, quoted in Siemens, *Critical Reception*, p. 27.

42. *Swallow*, p. vi.

43. Ibid, p. v.

44. Ibid, p. 131.

45. *Swallow*, pp. v-vi.

46. Thomas Pakenham, *The Boer War*, London: Abacus, 1995, p. 14.

47. Ibid, p. 118.

48. Ibid, p. 18.

49. Ibid, p. 48.

50. Quoted in ibid, p. 68.

51. Ibid, p. 89.
52. Quoted in Pakenham, *Boer War*, p. 113.
53. Quoted in ibid, p. 103.
54. *The Last Boer War*, p. 1.
55. Ibid, p. 12. Quatermain manqué Frederick Courtney Selous was sympathetic to the Boers, a stance attacked in the press by Haggard. Selous confessed to being 'an appreciative reader of Mr Rider Haggard's works', adding astutely that he had always thought 'the personal humiliation [Haggard] endured at the time of the recession of the Transvaal to the Boers in 1881 had somewhat clouded his judgement concerning the people'. Stephen Taylor, *The Mighty Nimrod: A Life of Frederick Courtenay Selous, African Hunter and Adventurer, 1851–1917*, London: Collins, 1989, p. 256.
56. *Days*, vol. 2, p. 134.
57. *Cloak*, p. 175. Jack Haggard remained in Nouméa until 1904 when he was appointed a consul to Spain.
58. HRH to Mrs John Haggard, 5 November 1899, Columbia Collection.
59. *Days*, vol. 2, pp. 137–8.
60. *Cloak*, p. 176.
61. *Winter Pilgrimage*, p. 27.
62. Ibid, p. 28.
63. *Cloak*, p. 176.
64. Ibid. The 'brethren of the *Misericordia* at their work of mercy' held a morbid fascination for Haggard: sinister in appearance, cloaked in black from head to foot in a garb reminiscent of the Ku Klux Clan, this Catholic lay order 'for more than five centuries have laid out the dead, or carried the sick of Florence to where they might be succoured. Their very appearance indeed is ominous of death and sorrow; when they come upon the sight thus swiftly it even shocks.' *Winter Pilgrimage*, pp. 50–1.
65. *Winter Pilgrimage*, p. 65.
66. Ibid, p. 68.
67. Ibid, p. 70.
68. HRH to Mrs John Haggard, 6 February 1900, Columbia Collection.
69. *Days*, vol. 2, p. 138.
70. Ibid, p. 137.
71. *Winter Pilgrimage*, p. 12.
72. Ibid, p. 96.
73. Ibid, p. 153.
74. Ibid, p. 155.
75. Ibid, p. 156.
76. Ibid, p. 196.
77. Ibid, p. 193.
78. Ibid, p. 194.
79. *DAJ*, p. 278. Ella Hart-Bennett's maiden name was Tuck (pers. comm., Victoria Manthorpe). Ella was a close friend of Haggard's sister Mary and had accompanied her

to Japan in 1893 when Mary, by then Baroness d'Anethan, went with her husband when the Baron took up his post as Belgian Minister to the Imperial Court in Tokyo. Ella stayed until October 1896. Ella was no stranger to Japan, having visited it with her father Charles Tuck in 1882. She subsequently wrote a book based on her diary of this trip, *An English Girl in Japan* (1904), which she dedicated to Mary. See also Mary d'Anethan, *Fourteen Years of Diplomatic Life in Japan* (1912).

80. *Winter Pilgrimage*, vol. 2, p. 37.
81. Ibid, p. 51.
82. Ibid, p. 68.
83. Ibid, p. 83.
84. *Brethren*, Author's Note, p. 11.
85. Ibid.
86. *Winter Pilgrimage*, p. 251.
87. Ibid, p. 253.
88. Ibid, p. 270.
89. Ibid, pp. 270–1.
90. *Days*, vol. 2, p. 134. War correspondents such as Leo Amery, Winston Churchill, George Warrington Steevens and Edgar Wallace were younger men in their twenties and thirties, though the *Telegraph*'s Henry Nevinson was a year older than Haggard and the Australian journalist Edith Dickenson was 50.
91. *Days*, vol. 2, p. 134.
92. Giliomee and Mbenga, p. 220.
93. Ibid, pp. 134–5.
94. Ibid, p. 137.
95. Ibid.
96. *Daily Express*, 17 April 1901, quoted in Mark Freeman, *Social Investigation and Rural England 1870–1914*, Woodbridge, Suffolk: Boydell, 2003, p. 92. The articles were also published in the *Yorkshire Post*.
97. *Rural England*, vol. 1, p. xxvii.
98. Ibid, p. xxxi.
99. *Days*, vol. 2, p. 142.
100. Ibid, p. 141.
101. *Daily Express*, 1 October 1901, quoted in Freeman, *Social Investigation*, p. 93.
102. *Days*, vol. 2, p. 141.
103. *Rural England*, Dedication, p. v.
104. *Days*, vol. 2, p. 141.
105. *Rural England*, vol. 1, p. 188.
106. Ibid, vol. 2, p. 502.
107. Quoted in Freeman, *Social Investigation*, p. 97. See also *Rural England*, vol. 1, p. 492 for a section of Sweetman's letter.
108. Freeman, *Social Investigation*, p. 96. Haggard's reporting of the outspoken views of a Cambridgeshire publican, Tom Stone, in the *Daily Express* in August 1901, who said St

Neots' 'labourers were lazy, ignorant and unintelligent', led to protests outside Stone's house. Freeman, *Social Investigation*, p. 99.

109. *Rural England*, vol. 1, p. 539.
110. Ibid, p. 540.
111. Quoted in ibid, p. 283.
112. Ibid, p. 504.
113. Ibid, p. 494.
114. Ibid, p. 504.
115. *Rural England*, vol. 2, pp. 546–7.
116. *Days*, vol. 2, p. 108.
117. Ibid, p. 570.
118. Freeman, *Social Investigation*, p. 92.
119. *Farmer's Year*, Ronald Blythe introduction, p. vii.
120. Quoted in Cohen, *Rider Haggard*, p. 174.
121. Siemens, *Critical Reception*, p. 132.
122. Quoted in Cohen, *Rider Haggard*, p. 174.
123. Siemens, *Critical Reception*, p. 31.
124. Ibid.
125. *RR*, p. 49. When Haggard's complimentary copy of *Rural England* arrived at Ditchingham house from Longmans and the 'two great volumes ... portly, blue and beautiful' were placed upon a table for the family to admire, his daughter Dorothy, a 'young lady with a turn for humour, "My word, Dad!" she said, "if *I* had written a book like that, *I* should spend the rest of my life sitting to stare at it!"' *Days*, vol. 2, p. 141.
126. *Days*, vol. 2, p. 154.
127. Ibid.
128. The Kiplings summered in the Cape from 1899 to 1908 as guests of Rhodes at the Woolsack, a house specially built for them on his estate at Groote Schuur.
129. Kipling to HRH, 31 January 1905, quoted in *RR*, p. 59. Haggard changed Kipling's mind with regard to orchids by sending him some as a gift and by 1909 Kipling, if not quite a fellow maniac, was at least appreciative: 'The orchid flowers are superb. They are now ornamenting the dining room.' Ibid, p. 68.
130. *Cloak*, p. 182.
131. *Rural England*, 2nd edn, vol. 1, p. vii.
132. Ibid, vol. 1, p. ix.

22. 'HIGHER AIMS'

1. *Daily Mail*, 'Egypt Today: The Land of Cleopatra', 23 April 1904, quoted in M. Shirley Addy, *Rider Haggard and Egypt*, Accrington, Lancashire: AL Publications, 1998, p. 42.
2. *Pall Mall Magazine*, 1906, 'Thebes of the Hundred Gates', quoted in Addy, *Rider Haggard and Egypt*, p. 53.
3. *Days*, vol. 2, p. 155. 'Lascar' was a general term for a sailor of Asian origin.

4.   Ibid, pp. 155–6.

5.   Ibid, p. 156.

6.   Ibid, p. 157.

7.   Ibid.

8.   Ibid, p. 156.

9.   *Daily Mail*, 'Egypt Today: The Land of Cleopatra', quoted in Addy, *Rider Haggard and Egypt*, p. 41.

10. *Cloak*, p. 183.

11. T.G.H. James, *Howard Carter: The Path to Tutankhamun*, London: Tauris, 2001, p. 18.

12. Carter maintained frequent contact with Lord and Lady Amherst as well as their daughter Mary. In the 1900s he arranged the permits which allowed Mary, by then Lady William Cecil, to excavate near Aswan, where she uncovered thirty-two 'Tombs of the Nobles', also known as the 'Cecil Tombs'.

13. James, *Howard Carter*, p. 93.

14. *Days*, vol. 1, p. 157. Haggard describes the visit in 'The Debris of Kings', *Daily Mail*, 4 June 1904. See Addy, *Rider Haggard and Egypt*, p. 49.

15. Quoted in Addy, *Rider Haggard and Egypt*, p. 11. Carter had electricity installed in the Valley of the Kings in 1903.

16. Haggard notebook, 1 March 1904, MS 4694/2/12, NRO, quoted in Tom Pocock, *Rider Haggard and the Lost Empire*, London: Weidenfeld and Nicholson, 1993, p. 124.

17. *Days*, vol. 2, p. 158.

18. Quoted in Addy, *Rider Haggard and Egypt*, p. 51.

19. Ibid.

20. Ibid, p. 52. Haggard dealt with this subject in fictional form in a novella, *Smith and the Pharaohs*, serialised in the *Strand* from December 1912 to February 1913. As well as *Daily Mail* articles, Haggard wrote longer pieces for *Pall Mall Magazine, Travel Magazine* and *Windsor Magazine*. The trip also provided material for a romance set in ancient Egypt, *Morning Star*, published in March 1910. *Queen Sheba's Ring*, published in September 1910, also draws on material from this trip, according to Pocock, *Rider Haggard*, p. 126.

21. *Way of the Spirit*, p. 9.

22. Ibid. *Renunciation* by Dorothy Summers, published in 1905, was in circulation and so Haggard changed his title to *The Way of the Spirit*.

23. *Way of the Spirit*, p. 95.

24. Ibid, p. 344.

25. *Cloak*, p. 185.

26. *Way of the Spirit*, p. 257.

27. *Cloak*, p. 185.

28. Ibid.

29. Ibid.

30. Ibid.

31. Kipling to HRH, 2 December 1904, in *RR*, p. 56.

32. *Way of the Spirit*, dedication, dated 14 August 1905. Charles Longman shied at the prospect of serialisation: 'The basis of the book is sexual relationship and its renunciation – it cannot be put in the background, and it is this particular relation which I think it better not to discuss in magazines. I have been a good deal tempted – but there it is – we all have our cranks, and that, I suppose, is mine.' Quoted in *Cloak*, p. 184.

33. *PD*, p. 27.

34. William Dutt was author of *Highways and Byways in East Anglia* and *The Norfolk Broads*. The issue of 'charity books' was taken up by the Society of Authors, which eventually adopted a policy whereby members could only contribute to books which had the Society's official approval. The policy caused Kipling to resign from the Society in 1917. See Andrew Lycett, *Rudyard Kipling*, London: Phoenix, 2000, p. 627.

35. *Days*, vol. 1, p. 33. John Blatchly has Haggard being lent a knife to complete the carving on a desk, not a mantelpiece. Desk or mantelpiece, the 'result remains in the school museum today'. John Blatchly, 'Sir Henry Rider Haggard: Storyteller Supreme', *Old Ipswichian: Journal of the Old Ipswichian Club*, vol. 7, October 2006, p. 40.

36. HRH to *The Times*, 21 July 1904, quoted in *Days*, vol. 2, p. 160.

37. Ibid. This letter and other correspondence 'testifying to the facts of the case ... and other matter' were published in the *Journal of the Society for Psychical Research*, October 1904.

38. Ibid.

39. Ibid, p. 161.

40. Ibid, pp. 161–2.

41. Ibid, p. 163.

42. *Cloak*, p. 197.

43. Ibid, p. 198.

44. Ibid.

45. *Days*, vol. 2, p. 164.

46. Ibid, pp. 173–4. See *The Poor and the Land*, p. xxxix.

47. Letter quoted in *Days*, vol. 2, p. 173.

48. A.N. Wilson, *After the Victorians*, London: Arrow, 2006, p. 48.

49. Booth's book *In Darkest England and the Way Out* (1890) shocked Victorian society with its revelations of life in city slums.

50. *Days*, vol. 2, pp. 216–7.

51. Ibid.

52. Ibid, p. 175.

53. William Griffiths, 'Rider Haggard and His American Mission', *New York Times*, 12 March 1905. In Philadelphia, en route to Washington, Haggard inspected the garden allotments utilising land earmarked for future development, a scheme supervised by the Vacant Lots Association, and was 'entertained at lunch by the Franklin Inn Club, a society of gentlemen connected with literature'. *Days*, vol. 2, p. 176. The Franklin Inn Club was founded as a literary society in 1902.

54. Ibid.

55. *New York Herald*, 19 March 1905, quoted in Morton Cohen, *Rider Haggard: His Life and Works*, London: Hutchinson, 1960, pp. 240–1.

56. Ibid.

57. Kipling first met Roosevelt during a winter holiday in Washington in 1895. See Rudyard Kipling, *Something of Myself*, London: Macmillan, 1981, p. 121.

58. *Days*, vol. 2, p. 177.

59. *The Poor and the Land*, p. 45.

60. HRH to Louie, 18 March 1905, CC. En route to Los Angeles, the party became stranded at Yuma, 300 miles from their destination. Heavy rains had washed away an embankment and several sections of track; but for the train being eight hours behind schedule 'it would have been on this very spot at the exact time & doubtless its great weight would have brought the embankment down & then ...' HRH to Louie, 22 March 1905, CC.

61. HRH to Louie, 25 March 1905, CC.

62. HRH to Louie, 30 March 1905, CC.

63. HRH to Louie, 2 April 1905, CC.

64. HRH to Louie, 30 March 1905, CC.

65. John Hayes Hammond, *The Autobiography of John Hayes Hammond*, vol. 2, New York: Farrar, 1935, vol. 2, p. 523.

66. Ibid.

67. HRH to Louie, 7 April 1905, CC.

68. *The Poor and the Land*, p. 67.

69. Ibid, p. 2.

70. In 1911 Haggard gave instructions that the speech be appended to his autobiography, *The Days of My Life*, 'as it gives the essence of his views on the subject of the settlement of the surplus town population of Great Britain on the unoccupied land of the empire, a subject to which he devoted so much time and energy'. Charles Longman, editor's note, *Days*, vol. 2, p. 261.

71. Ibid, p. 271.

72. Ibid.

73. *The Poor and the Land*, p. xxxiii.

74. *Cloak*, p. 188.

75. HRH to Louie, 30 March 1905, CC.

76. HRH to Louie, 11 April 1905, CC. The Lotos Club, its membership primarily drawn from the arts, was founded in 1870.

77. Quoted in *Cloak*, pp. 188–9.

78. Ibid, pp. 191–2. Haggard's italics.

79. Ibid, p. 192.

80. *Days*, vol. 1, 265. Stead left the *Pall Mall Gazette* in 1889 and started up the *Review of Reviews* in 1890.

81. Ibid.

82. *The Poor and the Land*, p. 145.

83. Ibid, p. 146.

84. *Days*, vol. 2, pp. 193–4.

85. Minutes of meeting, author's collection, p. 3.

86. Ibid, p. 5.

87. *Days*, vol. 2, p. 195. General Booth was so 'indignant about the treatment my Report received ... he refused to give evidence before the committee'. Ibid, p. 202.

88. Ibid, p. 196.

89. *Cloak*, p. 187.

90. *Days*, vol. 2, pp. 196–7.

91. Charles Drazin, *Mapping the Past: A Search for Five Brothers at the Edge of Empire*, London: Heinemann, 2016, pp. 306–7.

23. 'SADNESS OF THE WORLD'

1. *Days*, vol. 2, p. 204.

2. HRH to Louie, 13 September 1905, CC.

3. *Days*, vol. 2, p. 204.

4. Ibid, pp. 204–5.

5. Ibid, p. 205.

6. Following serialisation in *Windsor Magazine* from December 1904 to October 1905.

7. *Days*, vol. 2, p. 205.

8. Ibid, p. 206.

9. Ibid.

10. *Ayesha*, p. 21.

11. Ibid, p. 19.

12. Ibid, p. 261.

13. Ibid, p. 293.

14. Ibid, p. 301.

15. Ibid, pp. 297–8.

16. Ibid, p. vii.

17. *Days*, vol. 2, p. 205.

18. *Cloak*, p. 207.

19. Quoted in ibid, p. 208. Haggard wrote to Ross in November 1889 praising his romance *The Child of Ocean*. Ross replied while on active service as junior medical officer with the 9th Madras Infantry in Burma; thereafter the two kept up an intermittent correspondence and Ross sent Haggard a copy of his romance *The Spirit of Storm*, published in 1896.

20. Ibid.

21. Rudyard Kipling, *Something of Myself*, London: Macmillan, 1981, p. 176.

22. Ibid, p. 178.

23. Ibid, p. 193.

24. *Days*, vol. 2, p. 208.

25. *RR*, p. 62.

26. Ibid.

27. Ibid, p. 63.

28. Bhambatha was chief of the Zondi living in the Greytown area north of Pietermaritzburg. Though he gave his name to the rebellion, he remains an obscure figure.

29. P.S. Thompson, *An Historical Atlas of the Zulu Rebellion of 1906*, Howick: Brevitas, 2001, p. 2.

30. Jeff Guy, *The Maphumulo Uprising: War, Law and Ritual in the Zulu Rebellion*, Pietermaritzburg: University of KwaZulu-Natal Press, 2005, p. 27. McKenzie was knighted for his services in 1907.

31. Jeff Guy, *Remembering the Rebellion: The Zulu Uprising of 1906*, Pietermaritzburg: University of KwaZulu-Natal Press, 2006, p. 42.

32. *DAJ*, p. 197.

33. This line quoted from *Cetywayo*, p. 68.

34. *Illustrated London News*, 19 May 1906, p. 712.

35. *Cloak*, p. 202. D.S. Higgins says it was 'almost certainly' while writing *The Way of the Spirit* that Haggard was 'informed that Archer, Lilly's husband was dying in Africa of tertiary syphilis', which, if correct, adds another layer of autobiography to the novel and its subject matter. See D.S. Higgins, *Rider Haggard: The Great Storyteller*, London: Cassell, 1981, pp. 187–8.

36. Victoria Manthorpe, *Children of the Empire: The Victorian Haggards*, London: Gollancz, 1996, p. 214.

37. *Cloak*, p. 202.

38. Ibid, pp. 31–2.

39. *Days*, vol. 1, p. 43.

40. Victoria Manthorpe, *Lilias Rider Haggard: Countrywoman*, Cromer: Poppyland, 2015, p. 83.

41. *Cloak*, p. 203. Quotation from the Burial Service in the Book of Common Prayer, taken from the Book of Job.

42. Quoted in Higgins, *Rider Haggard*, rev. edn, p. 399.

43. HRH to Ella Maddison Green, quoted in Tom Pocock, *Rider Haggard and the Lost Empire*, London: Weidenfeld and Nicholson, 1993, p. 151. Cremation was legalised and regulated by the 1902 Cremation Act but could still be a sensitive matter in Anglican circles. Haggard was something of a pioneer in this regard.

44. Aggie Barber to Ella Maddison Green, 30 May 1908, quoted in Judith Hickey, *Journal: Agnes Marion Haggard (née Barber)*, privately published, 2013, p. 29.

45. In 1922 Aggie had Jack's bones smuggled back to England disguised as a sack of potatoes.

46. *RR*, p. 64.

47. RR, p. 64.

48. Ibid.

49. Ibid, p. 65.

50. After serialisation in the *Red Magazine*.

51. *RR*, p. 225.

52. Quoted in Higgins, *Rider Haggard*, p. 194.

53. Ibid, pp. 194–5.

54. *Days*, vol. 2, p. 209.

55. Ibid.

56. Haggard only missed one day's sitting of the commission, in September 1910, 'and that was because the steamer from Denmark could not get me there in time'. Ibid, p. 211.

57. Ibid.

58. Ibid.

59. Ibid, p. 212. 'Many years later, after the 1914–18 war, some of their recommendations were adopted; if had been done [earlier], the young trees would have been fit for felling by 1940 when we so sorely needed the timber after all imports stopped'. *Cloak*, p. 200.

60. *Days*, vol. 2, pp. 212–3.

61. Ibid, p. 213.

62. A.N. Wilson, *The Elizabethans*, London: Arrow, 2012, p. 7.

63. Published on 10 March after serialisation in *Christian World News of the Week*. In Ireland the commission travelled from Dublin to Wexford, Tramore and Dungarvan, the Shannon and the Fergus, and along the coasts of Clare and Connemara.

64. *Ka*, the spirit or 'double' of a person; the *ka* was believed to be part of an individual's personality before and after death. Haggard had used the device before in his collaboration with Andrew Lang, *The World's Desire*. '[Haggard] made better use still of the Ka in his *Morning Star* which is one of the best re-creations of Ancient Egypt ever written.' Roger Lancelyn Green, *Tales of Ancient Egypt*, London: Puffin, 2004, Introduction, p. xx.

65. Quoted in M. Shirley Addy, *Rider Haggard and Egypt*, Accrington, Lancashire: AL Publications, 1998, p. 14.

66. Ibid, p. 119.

67. 'A Suggested Prologue to a Dramatized Version of "She"', *Harper's Weekly*, 3 March 1888, pp. 297-8. Reprinted in *Mameena and Other Plays: The Complete Dramatic Works of H. Rider Haggard*, ed. Stephen Coan and Alfred Tella, Pietermaritzburg: University of KwaZulu-Natal Press, 2007, p. 49.

68. A large fifteenth-century stone manor with later Elizabethan alterations, Brede Place was described by the architect Edwin Lutyens as 'the most interesting and haunted inhabited house in Sussex'. Quoted in Joseph Braddock, *Haunted Houses*, London: Batsford, 1956, p. 101. Local villagers refused to work there after dark and Lady Churchill, after a night spent in the house, refused to enter Brede Place again, though her son Winston had no such qualms.

69. Gordan, 'The Ghost at Brede Place', p. 593.

70. The programme of *The Ghost* has survived but not the script. See Miranda Seymour, *A Ring of Conspirators: Henry James and His Literary Circle, 1895–1915*, London: Scribner, 2004, pp. 30–3.

71. Peter Beresford Ellis, *H. Rider Haggard: A Voice from the Infinite*, London: Routledge 1978, p. 187.

72. *Days*, vol. 2, p. 213.

73. Ibid, p. 214.

74. Ibid.

75. HRH to Louie, 27 April 1910, MC 32/39/11, NRO.

76. HRH to Louie, 12 May 1910, MC 32/39/24, NRO.

77. Ibid.

78. *Days*, vol. 2, p. 214.

79. Yeats to Gregory, 19 May 1910, quoted in *Mameena and Other Plays*, Introduction, p. 13.

80. Gregory to Yeats, 22 May 1910, quoted in Coan and Tella, *Mameena and Other Plays*, Introduction, p. 13.

81. Court Theatre, later the Royal Court, in Sloane Square, Chelsea.

82. Yeats to HRH, 31 May 1910, Lockwood Collection, State University of New York at Buffalo. Attesting to Yeats's poor eyesight, this letter (dated 31 May 1910) is written in another hand (presumably to Yeats's dictation) and only signed by him.

83. Yeats to HRH, 8 September 1910, Lockwood Collection.

84. Yeats was a devotee of the occult, an interest sparked by his teenage reading of A.P. Sinnett's *Esoteric Buddhism*, which so influenced Haggard. See Brenda Maddox, *George's Ghosts: A New Life of W.B. Yeats*, London: Picador, 2000, p. 195. Julien Ochorowitz (1850–1918) was a psychologist and co-director of the Institut Général Psychologique of Paris as well as a psychical researcher. In 1908–9 he conducted a series of experiments with the Polish medium Stanisława Tomczyk. Her spirit guide or control was known as Little Stasia. According to Tomczyk, Little Stasia was not the spirit of a dead person but her own double.

85. Sir Herbert Beerbohm Tree (1853–1917) was noted for his lavish Shakespearian productions.

86. The texts of the two plays are published in *Mameena and Other Plays*.

87. *Days*, vol. 2, p. 216.

88. Pocock, *Rider Haggard*, p. 132.

89. Quoted in Morton Cohen, *Rider Haggard: His Life and Works*, London: Hutchinson, 1960, p. 246.

90. *Days*, vol. 2, p. 216.

91. Ibid.

92. Ibid.

93. *Spectator*, 25 March 1911.

94. Quoted in Cohen, *Rider Haggard*, pp. 246–7.

95. Quoted in *Cloak*, p. 202.

96. Booth to Haggard, 10 December 1910, quoted in *Days*, vol. 2, p. 218.

97. *The Poor and the Land*, p. xviii.

98. *Days*, vol. 2, p. 220.

99. *Days*, vol. 1, p. 1.
100. *Days*, vol. 2, pp. 220–1. Returning to Ditchingham in November, Haggard began work on *Rural Denmark and Its Lessons*. Four extracts were run in *The Times* in February and March 1911 prior to the book's publication in April.
101. The two previous reports were issued in 1907 and 1909.
102. *Days*, vol. 2, p. 225.
103. Ibid, pp. 225–6. William Carr was the owner of Ditchingham Hall.
104. *Cloak*, p. 213.
105. *Days*, vol. 1, p. 226.
106. *Days*, vol. 1, Introduction, p. xx.
107. Higgins, *Rider Haggard*, p. 206.
108. Ibid, p. 216.
109. Ibid, p. 247.
110. Thomas Hardy, *The Collected Letters of Thomas Hardy*, ed. Richard Little Purdy and Michael Millgate, Oxford: Clarendon Press, vol. 4, 1984, pp. 191–2.
111. *Days*, vol. 2, pp. 166–7.
112. Quoted in *Days*, vol. 2, p. 73.
113. Quoted in *Days*, vol. 2, p. 74.

24. 'RECOGNITION – WITH A VENGEANCE'

1. Telegram from Winston Churchill to HRH, CC.
2. Kipling to HRH, 3 January 1912, in *RR*, p. 74. Kipling always refused state honours, not wanting to be seen as politically aligned; academic and literary honours were another matter and he accepted the Nobel Prize in Literature in 1907.
3. *Days*, vol. 2, p. 226.
4. Ibid. Asquith was elected head of the Liberal Party in 1908 and took over as prime minister in 1908 after Henry Campbell-Bannerman's resignation due to ill health.
5. *Days*, vol. 2, p. 226.
6. Ibid, p. 227.
7. Australia, New Zealand, South Africa, Newfoundland and Canada were designated as Dominions following the 1907 Imperial Conference.
8. *Days*, vol. 2, p. 227.
9. Ibid, pp. 227–8.
10. Ibid, p. 228.
11. Quoted in *Days*, ibid. Haggard's fellow British representatives were Sir Alfred Bateman, a career civil servant specialising in commerce; railwaymen Joseph Tatlow and William Lorimer; and cotton manufacturer and engineer Tom Garnett. See E.J. Harding, *Dominions Diary: The Letters of E.J. Harding, 1913–1916*, ed. Stephen Constantine, Halifax: Ryburn Publishing, 1992, Introduction, for a comprehensive overview and assessment of the work of the commissioners.
12. Amery, *Life of Joseph Chamberlain*, vol. 4, p. 421, quoted in Harding, *Dominions Diary*,

p. 18. The quotation is from Matthew Arnold's 'Heine's Grave' in *New Poems*, published in 1867.

13. Ibid, p. 18.

14. *Days*, vol. 1, p. 230.

15. J.M. Bentley and C.G. Griffinhoofe, *Wintering in Egypt: Hints for Invalids and Travellers*, 2nd edn, London: Simpkin, 1895, p. 4.

16. HRH to Louie, 12 March 1912, CC.

17. Adrian Mourby, *Rooms with a View: The Secret Life of Great Hotels*, London: Icon, 2017, p. 221.

18. Bentley and Griffinhoofe, *Wintering in Egypt*, p. 122.

19. HRH to Louie, 26 March 1912, CC.

20. *Days*, vol. 2, p. 230.

21. *Moon of Israel*, p. x.

22. Ibid.

23. HRH to Louie, 31 March 1912, CC. Sir William Matthew Flinders Petrie (1853–1942), Egyptologist and archaeologist.

24. On Tuesday, 2 April, a visit to the 800-acre Pyramids Estates resulted in an article, 'An Egyptian Date Farm, the Financial Aspect', in *The Times*, 11 October 1912.

25. HRH to Louie, 9 April 1912, CC.

26. HRH to Louie, 12 April 1912, CC.

27. Ibid.

28. HRH to Louie, 16 April 1912, CC.

29. *Days*, vol. 2, p. 230.

30. The name of Marie Marais was possibly inspired by 'Sarie Marais', an Afrikaans folk song thought to have been composed during the Transvaal Rebellion. The first lines of the song mention Sarie Marais living 'near the Mooi River before this war began'. Mooi River features prominently in the book.

31. The name Zikali was probably taken from Zikhali kaMatiwane, *inkosi* of the Ngwane. In the early 1820s, during the time of Shaka, the Ngwane fled Zululand, eventually settling in a valley of the upper Thukela in the Drakensberg. The Ngwane would supply 157 mounted men, known as Zikhali's Horse, and 243 foot soldiers to fight on the British side during the Anglo-Zulu War. It is possible Haggard met Zikhali in 1876 during the tour of the Natal hinterland. Zikali appears in *Marie*, *Child of Storm* and *Finished*. Zikali also appears in *She and Allan* and *Heu Heu, or, The Monster*; there are references to him in *Allan and the Holy Flower*, *The Ivory Child*, *The Treasure of the Lake* and 'Magepa and the Buck'.

32. The other books featuring Hans are *Allan and the Holy Flower*, *The Ivory Child*, *Heu-Heu, or, The Monster*, *She and Allan* and *The Treasure of the Lake*.

33. *Days*, vol. 2, p. 85.

34. Ibid, pp. 85–6. Haggard began writing *Allan and the Holy Flower* after returning from Egypt. It was published in 1915 by Ward, Lock after serialisation in *Windsor Magazine*.

35. HRH to Watt, quoted in D.S. Higgins, *Rider Haggard: The Great Storyteller*, London: Cassell, 1981, p. 202.

36. Ibid.

37. Ibid.

38. Stuart was born in Pietermaritzburg on 30 January 1868 and grew up among Zulu speakers. He was educated at Hilton College and sent to England where he attended St John's College, a private school in Hurstpierpoint, Sussex. He returned to Natal in 1886 and farmed at Eshowe, Zululand.

39. *Natal Who's Who of 1906*, p. 190.

40. Quoted in Carolyn Hamilton, *Terrific Majesty: The Powers of Shaka Zulu and the Limits of Historical Invention*, Cape Town: David Philip, 1998, pp. 141-2. Stuart was not above berating his white settler audience for their ignorance of their fellow inhabitants. 'Cannot the Zulus tell you something about the Native Question? Why then, I pray, don't you ask them?' Ibid, p. 149.

41. Copy of letter from A.J. Shepstone to HRH, 30 December 1911, Stuart Papers, file 19, p. 172, Campbell Collections, University of KwaZulu-Natal.

42. Ibid.

43. Ibid, p. 178; copy of letter from HRH to A.J. Shepstone, 23 January 1912, Stuart Papers, file 19, p. 178, Campbell Collections, University of KwaZulu-Natal.

44. *A History of the Zulu Rebellion, 1906* was published by Macmillan in 1913.

45. HRH to A.J. Shepstone, 13 July 1912, CC.

46. See *Child of Storm*, p. 184.

47. When Governor of the Imperial Ottoman Bank in Constantinople in 1895, Vincent spearheaded a move to purchase South African mining shares, causing a run on the bank, which subsequently crashed, though not without Vincent making a huge profit. Vincent married society beauty Helene Venetia Duncombe in 1890 and became a Conservative member of parliament in 1899.

48. *Cloak*, p. 215.

49. Representing the Dominions was the Canadian minister of trade and commerce, George Foster; the South African Sir Jan Willem Stuckeris Langerman, president of the Rand Chamber of Mines and managing director of the Robinson Group of Mines; the New Zealander John Robert, a lawyer and parliamentarian; the Australian Donald Campbell, journalist, engineer and parliamentarian; while the businessman and politician Edgar Rennie Bowring represented Newfoundland.

50. *Days*, vol. 2, p. 72.

51. Roger Lancelyn Green, *Andrew Lang*, Leicester: Ward, 1946, p. 207.

52. Ibid, p. 80.

53. Ibid. Haggard also found time to write two short stories, 'Barbara Who Came Back', published in the March and April issues of the *Pall Mall Magazine*, and 'Magepa the Buck', published in the *Pears' Christmas Annual* of 1912. Higgins, *Rider Haggard*, p. 212.

54. *Days*, vol. 1, preface by Charles Longman, p. vii.

55. Dedication to *Days*, vol. 1, p. v.

56. HRH to Harcourt, 30 October 1912, CC.

57. The complete letters have been compiled by D.E. Whatmore in *Rider Haggard's Good Deeds*, Pamphlet Four: *Letters to the Right Hon. Lewis Harcourt*, Cheltenham: D.E. Whatmore, 1996.

58. Harding, *Dominions Diary*, p. 39.

59. Note by Haggard dated 9 November 1912 on the back of an undated letter from Kipling, in *RR*, p. 75.

60. *RR*, p. 74.

61. Steaming across the Mediterranean to Port Said, Haggard sketched out a structure for an appendix on religion to his autobiography, working it up into a full essay, 'A Note on Religion', while the 'liner was lying in the heavy heat of Aden'. Tom Pocock, *Rider Haggard and the Lost Empire*, London: Weidenfeld and Nicholson, 1993, p. 168.

62. India Diary, 24 December 1912, p. 1, CC.

63. In 2008 the hotel was attacked by terrorists and, in a battle lasting three days, 127 people were killed.

64. India Diary, 24 December 1912, p. 1, CC.

65. Ibid, p. 3.

66. Ibid.

67. Ibid, p. 4.

68. Ibid, p. 6.

69. Ibid, p. 14. James Keir Hardie (1856–1915), trade unionist and socialist, founding member of the Labour Party and campaigner for home rule in India.

70. Ibid, p. 3.

71. Ibid, p. 5.

72. Ibid, p. 6.

73. Ibid.

74. Ibid, p. 12.

75. Ibid, p. 8.

76. Ibid, p. 12.

77. Ibid.

78. Ibid, p. 15.

79. Ibid, pp. 16–7.

80. Ibid, p. 2.

81. Ayrton began his career as assistant to Flinders Petrie and had excavated in Egypt since 1902, almost exclusively in the Valley of the Kings. He joined the Archaeological Survey of Ceylon in 1911. A year after meeting Haggard, he drowned while on a shooting expedition. He was 31.

82. India Diary, p. 7, CC.

83. Ibid, p. 10.

84. Harding, *Dominions Diary*, p. 62.

85. Vincent, quoted in Harding, *Dominions Diary*, p. 63n.

86. Harding, *Dominions Diary*, p. 64.

87. Ibid, p. 65.

88. Ibid, p. 107.

89. *Age*, 18 February 1913, quoted in Pocock, *Rider Haggard*, p. 171.

90. Quoted in Higgins, *Rider Haggard*, p. 214.

91. *Lyttelton Times*, 1 March 1913, quoted in Pocock, *Rider Haggard*, p. 171.

92. Quoted in Higgins, *Rider Haggard*, p. 214.

93. Brian Singleton, *Oscar Asche: Orientalism, and British Musical Comedy*, Westport, CN: Praeger, 2004, p. 191.

94. Hesketh Pearson, *The Last Actor Managers*, London: White Lion, 1974, p. 67.

95. Oscar Asche, *His Life*, London: Hurst and Blackett, 1929, p. 142. In his autobiography Asche mistakenly says he met Haggard in Brisbane, adding that it was Haggard who 'persuaded me to dramatize his book, "A Child of Storm", an Allan Quartermain [*sic*] story with a Zulu setting'.

96. Harding, *Dominions Diary*, p. 105, note 133.

97. Quoted in ibid, p. 105, note 134.

98. Ibid, 108, note 137.

99. Ibid, p. 108.

100. Ibid, note 139.

101. Ibid, p. 114.

102. HRH to Harcourt, quoted in Whatmore, *Rider Haggard's Good Deeds*, Pamphlet Four, p. 3.

103. Ibid, p. 4.

104. Ibid, p. 5.

105. Ibid.

106. Quoted in Higgins, *Rider Haggard*, p. 214.

107. Ibid.

108. HRH to Harcourt, quoted in Whatmore, *Rider Haggard's Good Deeds*, Pamphlet Four, p. 7.

109. Ibid, p. 15.

110. Ibid.

111. Quoted in Higgins, *Rider Haggard*, pp. 214–5.

112. *Wanderer's Necklace*, Dedication.

25. 'LAND OF TROUBLES'

1. *DAJ*, p. 44.

2. Ibid.

3. Ibid.

4. *Ivory Child*, p. 35.

5. This was the second ship to carry the name *Kinfauns Castle*. Haggard and his family travelled back to England in 1881 aboard the first, owned by Donald Currie and sold

to the Russian Volunteer Fleet in 1883. The second *Kinfauns Castle* was built for the Union-Castle Line and launched in 1899.

6. E.J. Harding, *Dominions Diary: The Letters of E.J. Harding, 1913–1916*, ed. Stephen Constantine, Halifax: Ryburn Publishing, 1992, p. 177. The British commissioners on board the *Kinfauns Castle* included Sir Edgar Vincent, Sir Alfred Bateman, Tom Garnett, William Lorimer and Joseph Tatlow, plus Donald Campbell (Australia), Sir John Robert Sinclair (New Zealand) and Sir Edgar Bowring (Newfoundland), together with Alfred Bridgman (staff) and various commissioners' wives. Sir Jan Willem Stuckeris Langerman (South Africa) would join them on arrival at Cape Town while Sir George Eulas Foster of Canada was absent due to pressure of business.

7. Ibid. p. 182. John Latimer Fuller was the second Bishop of Lebombo in Portuguese East Africa (now Mozambique).

8. *DAJ*, p. 51.

9. Harding, *Dominions Diary*, p. 183.

10. Ibid, pp. 183–4.

11. Ibid, p. 184.

12. Ibid, p. 185.

13. Publication of the diary at the time was probably ruled out by the outbreak of the First World War in August 1914.

14. Harding, *Dominions Diary*, p. 214, note 309.

15. H. Giliomee and B. Mbenga, *New History of South Africa*, Cape Town: Tafelberg, 2007, p. 233.

16. Martin Meredith, *Diamonds, Gold and War: The Making of South Africa*, London: Simon and Schuster, 2008, p. 497. The report was delivered in 1905.

17. Olive Schreiner, in a letter written in 1908: 'I believe that an attempt to base our national life on distinctions of race and colour, as such, will, after the lapse of many years, prove fatal to us.' Quoted in Martin Plaut, *Promise and Despair: The First Struggle for a Non-Racial South Africa*, Johannesburg: Jacana, 2016, p. 209.

18. *DAJ*, pp. 51–3.

19. Ibid, p. 53. Hendrik Willem Struben (1840–1915) was a member of the Volksraad at the time of the Transvaal annexation in 1877. He played an important role in the discovery of gold on the Witwatersrand and was the first president of the Chamber of Mines. The purchase of Haggard's waggon is referred to in his *Recollections and Adventures*, Cape Town: Maskew Miller, 1920, p. 166.

20. Ibid

21. Harding, *Dominions Diary*, p. 191. The Mount Nelson, one of the celebrated colonial hotels, opened in 1898 and was built by the Castle Line to surpass its rival, the Grand, built by the Union Line. Both hotels were intended to extend the luxurious accommodation found on their ships and to replicate the standards of first-class hotels in Europe.

22. *DAJ*, p. 53. In July 1913, a dispute over the recognition of trade unions and conditions of service ended in violence in the centre of Johannesburg. Many died before Botha

and Smuts intervened. Less than six months later, workers at coal and gold mines and on the railways were involved in renewed strike action. Smuts sent in troops and two people were killed. The strike leaders surrendered and Smuts deported nine non-South Africans without trial.

23. Richard Steyn, *Louis Botha: A Man Apart*, Johannesburg: Jonathan Ball, 2018, p. 133.

24. Abe Bailey (1864–1940), gold magnate and politician. As a member of the British South Africa Company, he acquired extensive land and mining properties in Rhodesia. He was knighted for his work in promoting the unification of South Africa in 1910.

25. *DAJ*, p. 54.

26. Ibid.

27. Ibid, p. 55. Sir Thomas Cullinan (1862–1936), diamond magnate. In 1902 he established the largest single diamond property in the world, the Premier (Transvaal) Diamond Mining Company near Pretoria. In 1905, the largest diamond found – the 'Cullinan', weighing 3,023 carats – was discovered there. Henry Nourse (1857–1942) went to the Kimberley diamond fields in 1870 and in 1874 helped to raise the Kimberley Light Horse. In 1877 he went to the Transvaal and became a captain in Ferreira's Horse, operating against Sekhukhune in the north-eastern Transvaal and later in the Anglo-Zulu War (1879). During the Second Anglo-Boer War (1899–1902), he commanded Nourse's Horse in the defence of Pretoria. He founded Nourse Mines in 1886.

28. Ibid, pp. 55–6.

29. Ibid, pp. 56–7.

30. Ibid, pp. 57–8.

31. John X. Merriman (1841–1926), liberal Cape politician and last prime minister of the Cape Colony. He refused a cabinet post in Botha's administration but supported the South African Party during the rest of his parliamentary career.

32. *DAJ*, p. 60.

33. Ibid, p. 61.

34. Ibid, p. 62.

35. Ibid, p. 61.

36. Ibid, p. 62.

37. Ibid, p. 62.

38. Ibid, pp. 62–3.

39. Ibid, p. 69.

40. Ibid, p. 73. Haggard predicted a successful future for the South African wine industry: 'there is no doubt but that the Cape, where the sun always shines and the rain falls in winter thus making sure of a good set of grapes and a fine season for the vintage, ought with skilled direction and viticulture, to produce wines which will equal or almost equal those of Europe'. Ibid, p. 70.

41. Ibid, p. 74. Herbert John Viscount Gladstone (1854–1930), British politician and younger son of the Liberal prime minister W.E. Gladstone. He was Home Secretary in 1906–10 before his appointment as the first Governor General of the Union of South

Africa. On his own authority he chose Botha in preference to Merriman as the Union's first prime minister after consultation with leading South African politicians.

42. Ibid, p. 60. Harding was told 'that neither (the G.G.) nor the "Governess" is exactly popular in S. Africa ... he is known as "Lord God" and she as "Lady God"'. Harding, *Dominions Diary*, p. 199.

43. *DAJ*, p. 60.

44. Ibid, pp. 72–3.

45. Ibid, p. 73.

46. Harding, *Dominions Diary*, p. 191.

47. *DAJ*, p. 76.

48. Ibid.

49. Harding, *Dominions Diary*, p. 197, n. 284.

50. Ibid, p. 78. The map in the Cango Caves leaflet (2018) featuring the cave route open to the public names one of the caves 'King Solomon's Mine'. Thanks to Stephen Gray for the leaflet.

51. Ibid, p. 78.

52. William Charles Scully (1855–1943) was a magistrate, author, poet and botanist. He immigrated to South Africa with his parents from County Wicklow, Ireland, in 1867. He prospected for diamonds at Kimberley in 1871, sharing a tent with three brothers – Frank, Herbert and Cecil Rhodes. After prospecting for gold in the Transvaal, he embarked on a career as a civil servant in 1882. His books include *The White Hecatomb and Other Stories*, *By Veld and Kopje*, *Ridge of the White Waters*, *Reminiscences of a South African Pioneer* and *Daniel Vananda*.

53. *DAJ*, p. 79.

54. Rough Note Diary, MC 32/51, p. 33, NRO.

55. *DAJ*, p. 80.

56. Ibid.

57. Ibid, pp. 80–1.

58. Ibid, p. 81.

59. Ibid, pp. 92–4.

60. Ibid, p. 94. Kimberley accounted for over 95 per cent of global diamond production at the time.

61. *DAJ*, p. 94. Francis Oats (1848–1918), mining engineer, prospector and leader of the diamond industry, became a director of De Beers.

62. Ibid.

63. Ibid.

64. Ibid, p. 95.

65. Ibid, p. 96.

66. Ibid, p. 97.

67. Ibid.

68. Ibid.

69. Ibid.

70. Ibid.
71. Ibid, p. 95. Illegal diamond buying is a plot element in *Finished*.
72. Pretoria was the administrative capital of the Union of South Africa and Cape Town the legislative capital.
73. *DAJ*, p. 98.
74. Ibid.
75. Ibid.
76. Thomas Pakenham, *The Boer War*, London: Abacus, 1995, p. 495.
77. *DAJ*, pp. 98–9.
78. Ibid, p. 100.
79. Ibid, p. 101. A colleague in Pretoria who didn't believe Du Toit's story subsequently visited the sangoma and was shown 'friends of his own walking about the streets of a town in Holland so clearly that he recognised them at once'. Ibid, p. 102.

26. 'RETURNED FROM THE DEAD'

1. *DAJ*, p. 105.
2. Ibid, p. 107.
3. Ibid.
4. Ibid, p. 108. On 25 January 1900 British forces were pinned down on the top of the mountain Spionkop (also Spioenkop). The final accounting rendered 350 men dead, 1,000 wounded and 350 taken prisoner. The Boers lost 75 dead and 100 wounded.
5. Ibid, p. 109.
6. Ibid.
7. Ibid.
8. Ibid.
9. *Cloak*, pp. 222–3.
10. *DAJ*, pp. 109–110.
11. While travelling first class by train from Durban to Pretoria in 1893, Mohandas Gandhi was instructed by a white passenger to remove himself to a third class carriage on arrival in Pietermaritzburg. Gandhi, who had purchased a first class ticket, refused and was ejected from the train. This incident was a pivotal moment in Gandhi's life, motivating him to fight against the racist treatment of Indians in South Africa and then in India.
12. Imperial Hotel, Loop Street, opened in 1878. Substantially altered since, but the inner tiled courtyard remains.
13. *DAJ*, p. 111.
14. Ibid, p. 112.
15. Ibid, p. 291.
16. Ibid, p. 112. East Coast Fever or tick fever swept away a large proportion of the cattle in Natal during the 1900s.
17. *DAJ*, pp. 291–2. *Lobola* or *ilobolo*, translated as 'bride wealth', the payment (traditionally

in the form of cattle) the prospective groom agrees to pay the bride's father. Only when agreement on the amount is reached does the engagement become official.

18. Ibid, p. 210.

19. Ibid, p. 112. *Inkosikazi*, 'chief or first wife'. *Inkoos! Inkoos y umcool! Inkoos y pagate* should be rendered as *Nkosi! Nkos' enkulu! Nkos' ephakade!*, meaning 'Chief! Great chief! Chief from olden times!' Louie and Lilias stayed in Eshowe while Haggard visited Rhodesia.

20. Ibid, p. 113.

21. Ibid, p. 113–4.

22. Ibid, p. 115. In a stroke of historical irony Longmarket Street was renamed Langalibalele Street in 2005. Commercial Road is now Chief Albert Luthuli Road.

23. Ibid, p. 114.

24. Ibid. Haggard also met William Lucas, a local authority on Umslopogaas/Mhlopekazi. See Appendix.

25. Ibid, p. 115. The original Church of the Vow built by the Voortrekkers to commemorate their victory over the Zulu at the Battle of Ncome or Blood River on 16 December 1838. A place of worship until 1861, thereafter it was used for commercial purposes until it reopened in 1912 as the Voortrekker Museum.

26. *Natal Witness*, 24 March 1914.

27. *DAJ*, p. 320.

28. Ibid, p. 321. Haggard may have changed his mind since the 1870s when he and the majority of white settlers had vehemently opposed Colenso's stance towards the indigenous peoples, but reactionary views were still the norm among whites in Natal in 1914, though, as Jeff Guy points out, 'time had softened the reality of Colenso's presence, [and] colonial Natal was able to incorporate the Bishop into its gallery of quaint Victorians who, gaitered, waistcoated or bonneted, trip through the pages of the colony's histories or, when the circumstances demand it, defend civilisation with grit and determination'. Jeff Guy, *The Heretic: A Study of the Life of William Colenso, 1814–1883*, Pietermaritzburg and Johannesburg: University of Natal Press and Ravan Press, 1983, p. 352.

29. Ibid, pp. 321–2.

30. Ibid, p. 111.

31. *Natal Witness*, 27 March 1914. Horace Rose (1876–1965), author and editor of the *Natal Witness* from 1904 to 1925. He won the Hodder and Stoughton book competition with *Golden Glory* (London, 1915).

32. Ibid, p. 117.

33. Ibid, p. 127.

34. Ibid, pp. 127–8.

35. Ibid, p. 128. See *Witch's Head*, pp. 161–2.

36. David Pollock was a cousin of Walter Pollock, co-author with Andrew Lang of *He*, the parody of *She*.

37. David Pollock, 'Sir Rider Haggard's Return', *Transvaal Leader*, 31 March 1914, in *DAJ*, Appendix 2, p. 312.

38. *DAJ*, pp. 129–30.

39. Ibid, p. 130. Edward Harding was sceptical: 'We had the usual scramble of evidence and entertainments for the 2½ days we spent in Pretoria. Haggard was in his element, and made lots of speeches ... In one of his speeches he suggested [Jess's Cottage] might be bought up as a municipal – or even a national – possession. Not having read *Jess* I feel quite cold – nor did I notice a very strong feeling in the way of adopting the suggestion.' E.J. Harding, *Dominions Diary: The Letters of E.J. Harding, 1913–1916*, ed. Stephen Constantine, Halifax: Ryburn Publishing, 1992, p. 225.

40. In March 1967 it was announced 'The Palatial' was to be demolished to make way for a block of flats. A number of people expressed the wish that it be preserved and Hermann Moritz Rex, who was sympathetic, was asked to prepare the April edition of *Pretoriana* as a 'special Haggard-house edition'. Through the course of his research Rex became 'thoroughly acquainted with one of the most vitriolic Boer-haters that I ever came across ... My sense of honour, as an Afrikaner, as a descendant of the Boers that Haggard slandered and as heir of their ideals, left me no other choice than to completely distance myself from any effort, in whatever form, of honouring Rider Haggard.' Rex recorded what happened in a pamphlet, *Die strydvraag oor die bewaring en restorasie van die woonhuis van Henry Rider Haggard in Pretoria* (The Dispute over the Conservation and Restoration of the Dwelling-House of Henry Rider Haggard in Pretoria).

41. Ibid, p. 130.

42. Letter from 'Dutch Afrikander' to *Pretoria News*, 1 April 1914.

43. Ibid.

44. *DAJ*, p. 130.

45. Ibid, p. 131.

46. Rough Note Diary, MC 32/51, p. 144, NRO.

47. Oddly, Haggard doesn't mention his nephew Gerald Haggard, his brother Alfred's second son, who was killed in action at Naauwpoort in the Magaliesberg on 4 April 1901 during the Anglo-Boer War. Originally interred on a farm close to the battlefield, Gerald Haggard's remains were later exhumed and reburied at the cemetery in Krugersdorp.

48. *DAJ*, p. 132.

49. Ibid.

50. Ibid. After the garden party Haggard was taken to see Rider Haggard Street sited not far from 'The Palatial', 'somewhat in embryo at present but may become a fine thoroughfare if Pretoria continues to increase'. Ibid, p. 130. Rider Haggard Street is now a small back street close to Pretoria station.

51. Harding, *Dominions Diary*, p. 229.

52. Ibid.

53. *DAJ*, p. 132.

54. Ibid, p. 133.

55. Ibid.

56. Ford returned to England in 1888 owing to illness. After he came back to South Africa in 1889, his health gave way again and he left the country for good. During the 1890s he

was involved in a number of commercial African enterprises, notably in developing areas of East Africa. He died in 1925.

57. Ibid.

58. Rough Note Diary, MC 32/51, p. 61, NRO.

59. *DAJ*, p. 134.

60. Rough Note Diary, MC 32/51, p. 62, NRO.

61. *DAJ*, pp. 134–5.

62. Ibid, p. 134. Worried he hadn't heard the last of the matter, Haggard wrote a letter to his lawyer in Pietermaritzburg, Robert Morcom, brother of William Morcom, the lawyer on Shepstone's mission to annex the Transvaal and also the agent for the sale of Rooi Point farm in 1895. William Morcom died in 1910.

63. *DAJ*, p. 135. Mafeking is now called Mahikeng.

64. Ibid, p. 143.

65. The British annexed the territory occupied by Tswana- and Sotho-speaking peoples in 1885 as a Crown Colony to prevent the Transvaal linking up with German South-West Africa. The region south of the Molopo was incorporated into the Cape Colony in 1895, thereafter becoming part of the Union of South Africa. The area north of the Molopo, the Bechuanaland Protectorate, remained a High Commission territory until it gained independence as Botswana in 1966.

66. Southern Rhodesia became a Crown Colony in 1922 after its white settlers voted not to join the Union of South Africa. From 1953 until its dissolution on 31 December 1963, Southern Rhodesia was part of the Central African Federation with Northern Rhodesia and Nyasaland. When the latter two gained independence as Zambia and Malawi in 1964, it became known as Rhodesia. In November 1965 the government of Ian Smith declared its independence from Britain (UDI) and in 1969 it became a republic. A long-running bush war between the white regime and insurgents was ended by the Lancaster House agreement in 1979, and the subsequent fully democratic general election in what is now Zimbabwe saw Robert Mugabe become president.

67. *DAJ*, p. 144.

68. Ibid, pp. 144–5.

69. Sir Leander Starr Jameson, who died in 1917, is also buried there. Matopos, a range of hills with distinctive bare smooth granite domes, acquired its name from Lobengula's heir, Mzilikazi, who described the hills as looking like an assembly of elders, calling them the *amaTobos*, 'the bald heads', corrupted by white settlers to Matopos.

70. *DAJ*, p. 148. Jesser-Coope, a participant in the Jameson Raid, had blasted Rhodes's final resting place out of the granite.

71. Ibid, p. 150.

72. Walter's father was the Reverend John Charles Scudamore, vicar of St Mary's, Ditchingham, from 1888 to 1936. His father William had been vicar of St Mary's from 1839 until his death in 1881.

73. *DAJ*, p. 155. The Cathedral of St Mary and All Saints, designed by the architect Herbert Baker; construction began in 1913.

74. Ibid, p. 153.

75. Ibid, p. 155.

76. Ibid, p. 156.

77. Ibid.

78. *The Best Short Stories of Rider Haggard*, ed. Peter Haining, London: Michael Joseph, 1981, p. 21.

79. HRH, preface to Alexander Wilmot, *Monomotapa (Rhodesia), Its Monuments, and its History from the most Ancient Times to the present Century*, Fisher Unwin, London, 1896, p. xv.

80. *Elissa*, pp. 243–4.

81. *Elissa* ran in *The Long Bow* between February and June 1898. It was published in book form in 1900 in *Black Heart and White Heart and Other Stories*.

82. *DAJ*, pp. 156–7.

83. Ibid, p. 157.

84. Ibid. Similar observations by Hall are to be found in *Guide to Rhodesia for the Use of Tourists and Settlers*, Salisbury, 1914, p. 287.

85. *DAJ*, p. 159.

86. A photograph of Haggard reciting Lang's poem can be found in Hedley A. Chilvers, *The Seven Wonders of Southern Africa*, Johannesburg: SA Railways and Harbours, 1929, p. 316. Andrew Lang's poem 'Zimbabwe', originally titled 'Ophir', was written at Haggard's request. See Andrew Lang, *New Collected Rhymes*, London: Longmans, 1905.

87. *DAJ*, p. 161.

88. Ibid.

89. Ibid, p. 162.

90. Ibid, p. 167. Re Rhodesia not being 'a white man's land', Elspeth Huxley points out when people 'argued as to whether Kenya was, or was not, a white man's country, they were not then making a political judgement. They were making a medical judgement.' One school of thought was that people 'of European stock would not be able to establish a healthy, self-perpetuating population on the equator, and at an altitude of over 5,000 feet, because the actinic rays of the sun, combined with the rarefied atmosphere, would sap the vitality of the European stock and lead to its degeneration.' Huxley's conclusion could equally be applied to Rhodesia: 'I do not think it occurred to anyone that politics, not health, would decide the issue.' Elspeth Huxley, *Out in the Midday Sun: My Kenya*, London: Chatto, 1985, p. 54.

27. '400 MILES THROUGH ZULULAND'

1. *DAJ*, p. 177.

2. Ibid.

3. *Natal Mercury*, 18 April 1914. See *DAJ*, p. 212, n. 7.

4. *DAJ*, p. 178.

5. Ibid, p. 179. Stanger was established in 1873 and named after William Stanger, first

Surveyor General of Natal. The Zulu name is kwaDukuza, meaning 'secret place' or 'place of concealment'. It is the site of the homestead of King Shaka, established in 1826, where he was subsequently assassinated (see *Nada the Lily*, Chapter 21, 'The Death of Chaka'). The town was renamed Dukuza in 1998.

6. Sugar was the colony's distinctive crop; to cultivate and harvest it, indentured Indian labourers had been brought to Natal in the 1860s after agitation from farmers who claimed Shepstone's system of native reserves made it difficult to source African labour.

7. *DAJ*, p. 179.

8. Ibid.

9. Ibid. Originally a Norwegian mission station; a British force was besieged there during the Anglo-Zulu War.

10. Ibid, p. 180.

11. Ibid, p. 209.

12. Ibid, p. 179. Osborn died in 1899.

13. Marshall Clarke, Haggard's friend and colleague in the 1870s, was Resident Commissioner and Chief Magistrate of Zululand from 1893 to 1898. He was a more enlightened administrator than Osborn and, perhaps not coincidentally, a friend of Bishop Colenso's daughter Harriette. He died in 1909.

14. *DAJ*, p. 180.

15. Ibid. Masuku remained in Eshowe after Louie and Lilias departed for Durban.

16. Ibid.

17. Vyvyan originally embarked on a legal career and was admitted to Lincoln's Inn in May 1883. While reading law, he became involved in missionary work among the London poor and in 1887 began studying for the ministry. He became Bishop of Zululand in 1903.

18. *DAJ*, p. 180. Nothing remains of the homestead today. On a tiny traffic island in a quiet suburban street sits a small granite slab bearing the legend 'A memorial to King Cetshwayo kaMpande who died on this spot in 1884'.

19. Ibid, pp. 180–1. A character named Umnikwa guides Allan Quatermain to kwaGqikazi and relates the history of the homestead as given by Haggard in his diary. See *Finished*, p. 297.

20. Ibid, p. 181.

21. Ibid, pp. 181–2.

22. Barbara Tyrrell, *Her African Quest*, Cape Town: Lindlife, 1996, pp. 2–3. In a 2012 interview marking her hundredth birthday Tyrrell said the dance was her earliest memory and remembered Haggard talking to her father 'and I thought "what's an author?"' See Stephen Coan, 'The Art of a Life Lived Well', *Witness*, 15 March 2012, p. 13.

23. *DAJ*, p. 182. Chelmsford laagered his force on an elevated position to form a fortified square – he'd learned his lesson at Isandlwana – and the attacking Zulu soldiers stood little chance against the volley of fire from the square, losing an estimated 1,000 men; the British lost two officers and eleven men.

24. Ibid, p. 183.

25. Ibid.

26. Ibid.

27. Ibid, p. 184.

28. Ibid.

29. Ibid.

30. Ibid, pp. 184–5.

31. Ibid, p. 186.

32. See Tim Jeal, *Livingstone*, London: Hutchinson, 1973, p. 236.

33. Jack Osborn was a Sub-Inspector of the Zululand Police in charge of a garrison of fifty men.

34. The photograph appears in Haggard's article, 'A Journey through Zululand', *Windsor Magazine*, December 1916. Reprinted in *DAJ*, p. 187.

35. Ibid.

36. *DAJ*, p. 189.

37. Ibid.

38. Ibid, p. 190.

39. Ibid. Simpofu's name is given to a minor character in *Finished*, pp. 223–4.

40. *DAJ*, p. 192.

41. This contradicts Lilias's comment on 'how rapidly her generally fastidious parent had reverted to the ways of his youth. He rode the small veld ponies with real enjoyment.' *Cloak*, p. 223, A photograph of Haggard on horseback when visiting Dingane's royal homestead of uMgungundlovu appears in his article 'The Hill of Death', *Windsor Magazine*, December 1919, p. 53.

42. *DAJ*, p. 192. Matiwane kaMasumpa of the Ngwane was one of several people executed by Dingane as they were perceived to be threats to his authority following the assassination of Shaka.

43. Ibid, See *Marie*, p. 228–9.

44. Ibid, p. 193.

45. Ibid, pp. 194–5.

46. Ibid, pp. 196–7.

47. *DSAB*, vol. 4, p. 535.

48. *DAJ*, p. 197.

49. *DAJ*, pp. 198–9.

50. Ibid, p. 199

51. Ibid.

52. Ibid, p. 200.

53. Ibid.

54. Haggard gives a factual account of the battles of Isandlwana and Rorke's Drift in *The True Story Book*, edited by Andrew Lang, London: Longmans, 1900. See 'The Tale of Isandhlwana and Rorke's Drift', p. 132. The battle of Isandlwana also features in *The Witch's Head*, and *Finished*, and the short story 'Magepa the Buck', published in *Pear's*

Christmas Annual (1912) and *Princess Mary's Gift Book* (1914) before being collected in *Smith and the Pharaohs*.

55. *DAJ*, pp. 200–1. The argument wasn't resolved but Stuart's interpretation is the correct one.

56. Ibid, p. 202. Haggard's friend Lt Nevill Coghill together with Lt Teignmouth Melvill died attempting to save the 24th Regiment's Queen's Colour. They were each posthumously awarded the Victoria Cross.

57. Ibid, pp. 202–3. Relics of the battle could still be found – 'broken medicine bottles, a good many fragments of bully-beef tins, pieces of the bones of men and animals ... the remnants of two Martini cartridges; the one I found on the nek had not been fired, probably it came from the pouch of some slain soldier, a slate pencil and such sundries'. Ibid. p. 202.

58. Ibid.

59. Ibid, pp. 204–5. 'Wow': correctly in Zulu, *hau!* Cetshwayo is recorded as saying: 'A spear has been thrust into the belly of the nation. There are not enough tears to mourn for the dead.' See Ian Knight, *Brave Men's Blood: The Epic of the Zulu War, 1879*, London: Greenhill Books, 1990, p. 82.

60. *DAJ*, p. 206. Manzonwandle (current orthography) regarded himself as the true heir of his father and 'the colonial authorities manipulatively persisted in considering him "a good trump card" to be used against Dinuzulu'. John Laband, *The Eight Zulu Kings: From Shaka to Goodwill Zwelithini*, Johannesburg: Jonathan Ball, 2018, p. 196.

61. *DAJ*, pp. 208–9. 'Battered, bruised, with its steering gear bent and its starting machinery out of action, that American-made motor car did limp into Dundee, in Natal, where I bade it farewell. I wonder what it cost to put it in repair again?' HRH, 'A Journey through Zululand', *Windsor Magazine*, December 1916. The Berea Livery and Bait Stable in Durban from whom the Overland had been hired estimated the depreciation in value of the car at over £50. There was considerable correspondence with the Natal Native Affairs Department regarding the payment of the final account. See *DAJ*, pp. 224–5, n. 119.

62. *DAJ*, pp. 210–1.

63. Ibid, p. 227.

64. Ibid.

65. Ibid, pp. 227–8.

66. Ibid, p. 229.

67. Ibid, p. 230.

68. Ibid, p. 230. Haggard forwarded his interview with Dube and his thoughts on it, as expressed in his diary, to Lewis Harcourt, British Colonial Secretary.

69. Heather Hughes, *First President: A Life of John Dube, Founding President of the ANC*, Johannesburg: Jacana, 2011, p. 184.

70. Ibid, p. 186.

71. Haggard had offered to write the letter to Lord Gladstone, or been requested to do so, when they met at the dinner in Cape Town on 6 March 1914.

72. *DAJ*, p. 231.

73. Ibid, p. 238.

74. Ibid, p. 239.

75. Ibid. Owing to his industry, Haggard was unable to see Frederick Phillips, commander of 'the famous 20 policemen' at the time of the annexation of the Transvaal. 'I am sorry as he and I, I think, alone remain of those who were with Shepstone at Pretoria in 1877 ... He is now an elderly man and has retired. However, I wrote him a note.'

76. Ibid. *Iziqu* – Zulu awards for bravery 'which answer, more or less, to our Victoria Cross'. Ibid, p. 208.

77. Ibid.

78. Ibid, p. 246.

79. After a long and bitter war of liberation Portuguese East Africa gained independence and was renamed Mozambique in 1975. Lourenço Marques was renamed Maputo in 1976. The Archbishop of Cape Town, William Marlborough Carter (1850–1941), was Bishop of Zululand 1891–1901, Bishop of Pretoria 1902–8, and Archbishop of Cape Town 1908–30. Haggard knew the archbishop's brother Thomas Carter, who opened the European Hotel in Pretoria in 1878 and who was killed by lightning the following year.

80. *DAJ*, pp. 249–50.

81. Quoted in O.J. Hogarth and R.L. White, *The Life of Archbishop Carter: 'Eton's Gift to South Africa'*, privately published, 1952, p. 48.

82. *DAJ*, p. 252.

83. Ibid, p. 257.

84. Ibid.

85. Ibid. The indentured labourers were probably being taken to the Portuguese colony of São Tomé and Príncipe. See Catherine Higgs, *Chocolate Islands: Cocoa, Slavery, and Colonial Africa*, Athens: Ohio University Press, 2012, pp. 130–60.

86. *DAJ*, p. 257.

87. Ibid, p. 259.

88. Ibid, p. 260.

89. Ibid, p. 266.

90. Ibid, p. 270.

91. Ibid, p. 278. On 29 May 1914 the *Empress of Ireland* collided in fog with a Norwegian collier while en route to Liverpool and sank in minutes with a loss of 1,014 lives out of the 1,477 people aboard. The sinking of the *Empress of Ireland* constitutes Canada's worst civil maritime disaster, and the world's third worst civil maritime disaster after the *Titanic* and the *Lusitania*.

92. Ibid.

93. Ibid. The American edition of *The Ivory Child* was titled *The Lady of the Heavens*.

28. 'ARMAGEDDON HAS FALLEN'

1. *RR*, p. 80.

2. Haggard, quoted in E.J. Harding, *Dominions Diary: The Letters of E.J. Harding, 1913–1916*, ed. Stephen Constantine, Halifax: Ryburn Publishing, 1992, p. 236, n. 347.

3. *Cloak*, p. 245.

4. *PD*, 29 July 1914, p. 3.

5. Ibid, 5 August 1914, pp. 3–4.

6. Harding, *Dominions Diary*, p. 248.

7. Ibid.

8. Ibid.

9. Ibid, p. 251.

10. *PD*, p. 5.

11. Ibid, pp. 4–5.

12. Ibid, p. 5.

13. Harding, *Dominions Diary*, p. 257, n. 375.

14. Quoted in *Cloak*, p. 246. Phrases from the speech were used for a Canadian recruitment poster in 1915: 'If England falls you fall! Every man of you must go, as we, too, must go!

15. Harding, *Dominions Diary*, p. 256.

16. Quoted in *Cloak*, p. 246.

17. Harding, *Dominions Diary*, p. 256.

18. *PD*, p. 6.

19. Ibid, p. 6.

20. Ibid.

21. Ibid, p. 6.

22. Ibid.

23. Ibid, pp. 6–7. Mark Haggard married Doris Elizabeth Vaughan Schuldam on 15 October 1913.

24. Ibid, p. 7.

25. Oscar Asche, *His Life*, London: Hurst and Blackett, 1929, p. 157.

26. Now the Gielgud Theatre.

27. John Nevil Maskelyne (1839–1917), a British magician specialising in stage illusions. His initial partner was George A. Cooke but when Cooke died in 1904 Maskelyne teamed up with magician David Devant (1868–1941).

28. Stuart to his mother, 21 August 1914, Stuart Papers, MS STU 1.04, file 8, Campbell Collections.

29. Quoted in *Mameena*, p. 28.

30. Herbert Grimwood (1875–1929), stage and film actor.

31. Stuart to his mother, letter dated 21 August 1914. Campbell Collection, MS STU 1.04, File 8: for E.R. Dahle's translations of Chapters 11 and 12 of *uHlangakula*; see *Mameena*, Appendix, p. 378. Edwardian Britain boasted a 'widespread population of African birth or descent', many of whom were 'resident at the centre of the world's largest empire, participating in the affairs of the leading industrial nation'. Jeffrey P. Green, *Black Edwardians: Black People in Britain, 1901–1914*, London: Frank Cass, 1998, p. 1. Hundreds of black people worked in the entertainment industry. Though it

is not possible to identify with certainty any of the black members of *Mameena*'s cast, two likely candidates are Napoleon Florent and Joseph Bruce, both of whom appeared in other Asche productions, including *Kismet* and *Chu Chin Chow*. See Stephen Bourne, *Black in the British Frame: Black People in British Film and Television 1896–1996*, London: Cassell, 1998, pp. 43–4.

32. Quoted in *Mameena*, p. 31. According to Asche, Mandhlakazi and Kwili were not allowed to appear on stage as 'the result of the behaviour of some white women at the South African Exhibition at Earl's Court, and which had prejudiced the safety of white women in South Africa'. Asche, *His Life*, pp. 159–60. See *Mameena*, p. 28; and Ben Shephard, *Kitty and the Prince*, Johannesburg: Jonathan Ball, 2003, p. 82. Edwardian Britain boasted a 'widespread population of African birth or descent', many of whom were 'resident at the centre of the world's largest empire, participating in the affairs of the leading industrial nation'. Jeffrey P. Green, *Black Edwardians: Black People in Britain, 1901–1914*, London: Frank Cass, 1998, p. 1. Hundreds of black people worked in the entertainment industry. Though it is not possible to identify with certainty any of the black members of Mameena's cast, two likely candidates are Napoleon Florent and Joseph Bruce, both of whom appeared in other Asche productions, including *Kismet* and *Chu Chin Chow*. See Stephen Bourne, *Black in the British Frame: Black People in British Film and Television 1896–1996*, London: Cassell, 1998, pp. 43–4.

33. *PD*, pp. 7–8.

34. Asche, *His Life*, p. 159.

35. *PD*, 4 October 1914, p. 9.

36. William Archer, *The Nation*, 5 November 1914.

37. *Daily Telegraph*, undated cutting from the London Theatre Museum.

38. Asche, *His Life*, p. 159. From 1 October 1914 bright street lights in London were either extinguished or dimmed by being painted with black paint. These blackout restrictions were extended to the rest of the country in February 1916. On 17 October, Haggard was in London on Dominions Royal Commission business and staying at the Garlant Hotel, Suffolk Street, close to Charing Cross Station. At 'about six o'clock I went for a walk down Piccadilly, and when I reached the Ritz Hotel came back again, as I could scarcely see my way about. Many lights are put out altogether, and most of the others are blacked or veiled, while even the shop fronts no longer look gay ... It is strange too to see the great search-lights wheeling about the sky in their quest for hostile aircraft.' *PD*, p. 10.

39. *PD*, 25 November 1914, p. 15.

40. *PD*, 25 November 1914, pp. 15–6.

41. Asche, *His Life*, p. 159.

42. Phillip Waller, *Writers, Readers, and Reputations: Literary Life in Britain, 1870–1918*, Oxford: OUP, 2008, p. 12.

43. Alexander Watt died on 3 November 1914 and his son Alexander Strahan Watt took over the agency.

44. There had been earlier films based on Haggard's books: Georges Méliès's 1899 short *La*

Danse du feu, also known as *Pillar of Fire*, was inspired by the famous scene from the end of *She*. Versions of *She* were shot in the United States in 1908, 1911 and again in 1917. A film of *Mr. Meeson's Will* (retitled *The Grasp of Greed*) was made in the United States in 1916. There were two American productions of *Jess*, under Haggard's original title in 1905 and a Fox production titled *Heart and Soul* starring Theda Bara in 1917. That Haggard derived any income from these productions is unlikely.

45. *PD*, 2 October 1916, p. 85.

46. Ibid, 12 January 1917, pp. 94–5.

47. Neil Parsons, *Black and White Bioscope: Making Movies in Africa, 1899–1925*, Pretoria: Protea, 2018, p. 136.

48. Mark Cousins, *The Story of Film*, London: Pavilion, 2004, p. 48.

49. *PD*, 12 May 1919, p. 167.

50. Ibid.

51. Parsons, *Black and White Bioscope*, p. 143.

52. Now Burberry's flagship store in London's Regent Street.

53. *PD*, 31 October 1919, p. 178.

54. *PD*, 1 September 1914, p. 7.

55. Ibid, p. 7.

56. J.E. Scott, *A Bibliography of the Works of Sir Henry Rider Haggard, 1856–1925*, Bishop's Stortford: Elkin Mathews, 1947, p. 129.

57. *PD,* 13 September 1914, p. 8.

58. Ibid, 18 September 1914, p. 8.

59. Ibid, 4 October 1914, p. 9.

60. Ibid, 23 October 1914, p. 11.

61. *RR*, p. 81.

62. *PD*, 14 October 1914, p. 10.

63. Ibid, 11 November 1914, p. 14.

64. Ibid, 17 October 1914, p. 10.

65. Ibid, 6 November 1914, p. 13.

66. Ibid, 28 October 1914, p. 12.

67. Thomas Henry Hall Caine (1853–1931) was an immensely popular novelist of the time.

68. Scott, *Bibliography*, p. 168. *King Albert's Book* was edited by Hall Caine; among its numerous contributors were Edith Wharton, Jack London, Thomas Hardy, Rudyard Kipling, Henri Bergson, Edward Elgar, Claude Debussy and the Aga Khan.

69. *PD*, 23 October 1914, p. 11.

70. Ibid, 11 November 1914, p. 14.

71. Ibid, 12 November 1914, p. 14.

72. Ibid, 15 November 1914, p. 14.

73. When in London, during the war and after, Haggard stayed either at his club, Windham's, or in furnished rooms and hotels. These include Queen Anne's Mansions in Queen Anne's Gate, south of St James's Park; Hotel York in Earl's Court; Norfolk

Hotel, Harrington Road, in South Kensington, now the Ampersand; and the Garlant in Suffolk Street, off Pall Mall, 'popular with literary people, MPs and the Clergy'. Anne Harcombe and Judy Hickey, 'Haggard's London', *Rider Haggard Society Journal*, no. 118, November 2015, p. 8.

74. *PD*, 16 December 1914, p. 17.

75. Ibid, 31 March 1915, p. 25.

76. The Royal Commonwealth Institute was founded in 1868 as the Colonial Society, the 'royal' prefix was added in 1869 and the Society was renamed the Royal Colonial Institute in 1870. It was subsequently renamed the Royal Empire Society in 1958 and exists today as the Royal Commonwealth Society.

77. *Cloak*, p. 247.

78. *PD*, 23 March 1915, p. 24.

79. Ibid.

80. Ibid. Among stories written by Kipling at this time were 'Mary Postgate' and 'Sea Constables: A Tale of 15'. Haggard was working on *The Ancient Allan*, a drug-induced hallucinatory fantasy with Allan Quatermain and Lady Ragnall tripping back in time to ancient Egypt; it was published in 1920.

81. *PD*, 6 April 1915, p. 25.

82. Ibid, 7 April 1915, p. 25.

83. Ibid, 21 April 1915, p. 26.

84. Ibid, 24 June 1915, p. 32. Rose Hildyard had been living with the Haggards and looking after the children since 1900.

85. Ibid, 22 June 1915, p. 32.

86. Ibid, 28 June 1915, p. 33.

87. Ibid, 5 July 1915, p. 34.

88. Ibid, 12 July 1915, p. 34.

89. Ibid, 25 June 1915, pp. 32–3.

90. Ibid, 19 July 1915, p. 35. Meanwhile the mooted resumption of the Dominions Royal Commission trip to Canada had stalled and, after consultation with the Canadian government and members of the commission, the visit to Canada was postponed indefinitely.

91. . Ibid, p. 35.

92. Ibid, 23 July 1914, p. 35.

93. Ibid.

94. Ibid, 5 October 1915, p. 41. Ella's husband the Reverend Charles Maddison Green died in 1911.

95. Ibid, 29 October 1915, p. 42.

96. Reese, Trevor R., *The History of the Royal Commonwealth Society 1868–1968*, Oxford University Press, 1968, p. 118.

97. *PD*, 7 October 1914, p. 44.

98. Ibid.

99. Ibid, 13 December 1915, p. 45.

100. Ibid, 27 December 1915, p. 45.

101. Ibid.

102. Ibid, 28 December 1915. Kipling recorded his son's death during the battle of Loos in the second of his two-volume history, *The Irish Guards in the Great War: The Second Battalion*, a labour of love 'done with agony and bloody sweat'. Kipling quoted in Andrew Lycett, *Rudyard Kipling*, London: Phoenix, 2000, p. 689.

103. *PD*, 22 December 1915, p. 44.

104. *Cloak*, pp. 247–8.

105. *RR*, p. 142.

106. *PD*, 3 January 1916, p. 49.

107. War Diaries, 11 March 1919, CC.

108. Little is known about Uvedale Corbett. Haggard described him in a letter no longer extant; and in a letter from Louie to HRH she writes: 'We are much amused at the account of your travelling companions and Lilias has dark suspicions of Mr Corbett whom she always thought was a "gay dog"'. Louie to Haggard, 21 March 1916, CC. References to Corbett in later letters indicate Louie thought he was a 'ladies' man'.

109. *PD*, 1 February 1916, p. 51.

110. Quoted in *RR*, p. 92.

29. 'A SECOND ST. PAUL'

1. War Diaries, 11 February 1916, p. 297, CC.

2. Ibid, pp. 299–300.

3. HRH to Louie, 2 March 1916, MC 32/39/31, NRO.

4. War Diaries, p. 300, CC.

5. By the time of Haggard's visit, Hertzog's Afrikaner National Party was the second largest party and its policies, dubbed 'Hertzogism', were 'synonymous with anti-imperialism and anti-British sentiment'. Richard Steyn, *Louis Botha: A Man Apart*, Johannesburg: Jonathan Ball, 2018, p. 173.

6. Ibid, p. 188.

7. Ibid, p. 190.

8. *Cambridge History of the British Empire*, quoted in ibid, p. 235.

9. Ibid, p. 234.

10. War Diaries, 13 March 1916, p. 312, CC.

11. Telegram from BSAC to Haggard, quoted in War Diaries, 28 February 1916, p. 300.

12. War Diaries, 19 February 1916, p. 301, CC.

13. Ibid.

14. Ibid, 29 February 1916, p. 302.

15. Ibid.

16. Ibid, 9 March 1916, p. 309.

17. Ibid, 2 March 1916, p. 303.

18. Ibid, 4 March 1916, p. 306.

19. HRH to Louie, 2 March 1916, MC 32/39/31, NRO.
20. War Diaries, 4 March 1916, p. 306, CC.
21. Ibid, p. 305.
22. Ibid.
23. Ibid.
24. Ibid, 7 March 1916, p. 307.
25. Ibid, pp. 307–8.
26. Ibid, 8 March 1916, p. 308.
27. Ibid, p. 309.
28. Ibid, 9 March 1916, p. 309.
29. Ibid, quoted in entry for 13 March 1916, p. 312.
30. Ibid, p. 313. Haggard was sufficiently encouraged to begin dictating to Corbett a chapter on South Africa for a projected book, 'The Empire and Its Land', which was not completed. A pencilled footnote in the typescript of Haggard's diary states, 'I never wrote this book.'
31. On 13 August 1917, while sailing from London to New York, the *Turakina* was sunk by a German submarine with the loss of two lives.
32. HRH to Louie, 11 March 1916, MC 32/39/34, NRO.
33. War Diaries, 13 March 1916, p. 312.
34. Ibid, 16 March 1916, p. 313.
35. Ibid.
36. Ibid, 19 March 1916, p. 314.
37. *PD*, 19 March 1916, p. 57. It was published posthumously under the latter title in 1929.
38. HRH to Louie, quoted in *Cloak*, pp. 249–50.
39. *PD*, 3 April 1919, p. 57.
40. Ibid, 7 April 1916 p. 57.
41. Ibid, 9 April 1916, p. 58.
42. Ibid, 13 April 1916, p. 58.
43. Louie to HRH, 21 March 1916, CC.
44. Louie to HRH, 29 March 1916, CC.
45. Louie to HRH, 5 April 1916, CC. Will Haggard retired from the diplomatic service in 1914 and was duly knighted.
46. Ibid.
47. Louie to HRH, 16 April 1916, CC.
48. *PD*, 5 June 1916, p. 65.
49. HRH to Lilias, 22 June 1916, CC.
50. *PD*, 26 April, 1916, p. 60.
51. Ibid, 18 May 1916, pp. 62–3.
52. War Diaries, 2 May 1916, CC.
53. Jan Morris, *Farewell the Trumpets: An Imperial Retreat*, London: Faber, 2012, p. 171.
54. HRH to Louie, 22 June 1916, CC.
55. *PD*, 11 June 1916, p. 66.

56. *Cloak*, p. 251.

57. HRH to Lilias, 22 June 1916, CC.

58. War Diaries, 17 June 1916, CC.

59. Arthur Christopher Benson, eldest son of Edward White Benson, Archbishop of Canterbury, and brother of the novelist E.F. Benson (best known for the Mapp and Lucia series of social comedies and his ghost stories) and R.H. Benson, also a writer who became a Roman Catholic priest and Catholic apologist.

60. War Diaries, 14 June 1916, CC. Haggard vaguely recalled meeting Benson at a luncheon. According to David Newsome, Benson knew Haggard through Edmund Gosse and once visited Haggard at Ditchingham while holidaying at Aylsham in Norfolk, this shortly after Haggard had been to Cyprus. In the course of a disquisition about mining on Cyprus, Haggard quoted *The Odyssey* 'with gusto'. Benson 'was assured later' by someone unknown (Gosse?) that Haggard 'was not really a well-informed man'; he just knew how 'to butter his knowledge very thin and make it go a long way'. Quoted in David Newsome, *The Edge of Paradise: A.C. Benson the Diarist*, Chicago: University of Chicago Press, 1980, p. 89.

61. HRH to Louie, 22 June 1916, CC.

62. *PD*, 22 June 1916, p. 67.

63. Ibid, 23 June 1916, p. 68. The reference is to the famous 'Aloha 'Oe' (Farewell to Thee) folk song written by Princess Lili'uokalani in the 1870s. In 1891 she became queen and the last monarch of Hawaii before it became a republic and was subsequently annexed by the United States in 1898.

64. Ibid, 29 June 1916, p. 68.

65. Ibid, p. 69.

66. Ibid, 1 July 1916, p. 69.

67. Ibid, 7 July 1916, p. 70.

68. Ibid, 11 July 1916, p. 71. A 'pightle' is a small piece of land or meadow.

69. Ibid, p. 71n. At a lunch in Calgary, Alberta, Haggard joked that Mount Sir Rider 'would make the best and most enduring of tombstones'.

70. Ibid, 22 July 1916, pp. 72–3.

71. Ibid, p. 73. Roosevelt didn't stand for re-election in 1909 but was persuaded to run for president again in 1912. He survived an assassination attempt during the campaign but lost to Woodrow Wilson.

72. War Diaries, 22 July 1916, CC.

73. PD, 22 July 1916, p. 74.

74. Ibid, 1 August 1916, p. 75.

75. Ibid.

76. Ibid.

77. Ibid.

78. Ibid, 2 August 1916, p. 75. Haggard's doctor and friend Lyne-Stivens had died in 1915, aged 60. 'In spite of his manly figure and fine presence Dr. Stivens had visibly failed since the death of his beloved little daughter two years ago ... His friend and patient, Sir Rider

Haggard, suggests for his epitaph the words "Our Beloved Physician". *British Medical Journal*, 22 May 1915, pp. 914–5.

30. 'ONE OF THE HELLS'

1. *PD*, 16 August 1916, pp. 77–8.
2. Ibid, 18 August 1916, p. 78.
3. Ibid, 24 August 1916, p. 79.
4. Ibid, 18 August 1916, pp. 78–9.
5. Ibid.
6. Ibid, 3 September 1916, p. 80.
7. Ibid, 10 September 1916, p. 81.
8. Ibid, 27 September 1916, p. 84.
9. *The Battle of the Somme*, a War Office-approved documentary filmed by cinematographers Geoffrey Malins and John McDowell.
10. *PD*, 14 October 1916, p. 85.
11. In March 1917 Haggard was elected one of the two vice presidents of the Institute, 'a very nice compliment'. Ibid, 8 March 1917, p. 98.
12. Ibid, 14 November 1916, p. 87.
13. Ibid, 16 November 1916, p. 88.
14. Ibid. St Thomas stood behind Mappin & Webb, 132 Regent Street. The church was demolished during the 1950s.
15. *PD*, 26 December 1916, p. 88.
16. Ibid, 6 January 1917, pp. 93–4. After the war Haggard was instrumental in setting up a committee to organise a memorial for Selous at the Natural History Museum in South Kensington and, together with Roosevelt and Jan Smuts (Selous's commander in East Africa), was a generous subscriber to the memorial, consisting of a bronze statue by William Robert Colton framed within a border and niche of granite from the Matopos Hills, inset in the wall above the north-west staircase of the museum's Central Hall. The inscription describes Selous as 'hunter, naturalist & explorer'. Haggard was present at the unveiling of the memorial at the museum on 10 June 1920.
17. Ibid, 20 January 1917, p. 95.
18. Ibid, 16 February 1917, p. 97. The official sign-off date on the report is 21 February 1916. It was published on 27 March 1916. The complete reports from 1912 to 1917 ran to 24 volumes consisting of 1,919 pages. The report was issued in an edited form (499 pages) in 1918.
19. Ibid, 22 January 1917, p. 95.
20. Ibid, 26 January 1917, p. 96.
21. Ibid, 31 January 1917, p. 96.
22. The Kiplings had spent their honeymoon at Brown's in 1892 and in subsequent years occupied a first-floor suite looking out on Albemarle Street, receiving guests in the large sitting room, where Kipling wrote at a desk by one of the windows. *RR*, p. 95, n. 1.

23. *PD*, 17 March 1917, p. 99.
24. Ibid, 10 March 1917, p. 98.
25. Ibid, 21 March 1917, p. 99.
26. *RR*, p. 94.
27. Ibid, p. 95.
28. *PD*, 31 March 1917, p. 102.
29. *PD*, 15 November 1917, p. 121.
30. Haggard oversaw the furnishing and took occupation on 5 June 1917. In May 1920 it was leased to a Mrs Bentley and then sold to her in May 1922. Anne Harcombe and Judy Hickey, 'Haggard's London', *Rider Haggard Society Journal*, no. 118, November 2015, p. 6.
31. *PD*, 20 April 1917, p. 105.
32. *PD*, 5 June 1917, p. 107. GCMG, Knight Grand Cross in the Most Distinguished Order of Saint Michael and Saint George; CMG, Companion of the same order.
33. Ibid, 7 June 1917, p. 108.
34. Ibid, 11 July 1917, p. 112.
35. Ibid, 11 August 1917, p. 113.
36. Ibid, 8 September 1917, p. 114.
37. See *Cloak*, p. 19.
38. *PD*, 10 September 1917, pp. 114–5. The manuscripts donated to Norwich Castle Museum were minus *Allan Quatermain*, given to Charles Longman, and *Mr. Meeson's Will*, presented to his agent Alexander Watt in recognition of services rendered. The manuscripts are now held by the NRO. The MS of *Allan Quatermain* was kept by Longmans until 1940 'when it was given to the Lord Mayor's Appeal for the Red Cross Fund'. Sotheby's catalogue, 12 February 1951, p. 14. It reappeared briefly in 2000 when it was sold at auction by Sotheby's on 24 February 2000 for £45,500.
39. *PD*, 24 September 1917, p. 116.
40. Ibid, 12 October 1917, p. 117.
41. Ibid, 8 November 1917, p. 121.
42. Greiffenhagen's son and Haggard's godson, Lieutenant Rider Greiffenhagen, died when his submarine was mined and sunk in the North Sea in March 1916. Lagden's son Ronald, a master at Harrow and first-class cricketer for Oxford University, was killed in an attack at St Eloi on 1 March 1915.
43. *PD*, 15 October 1917, p. 118.
44. Ibid, 20 October 1917, p. 119.
45. Ibid, p. 95.
46. Ibid, 7 November 1917, p. 120.
47. Ibid, 29 October 1917, pp. 119–20.
48. Ibid, 19 November 1917, p. 122.
49. Ibid, 11 December 1917, p. 123.
50. One of Cecil Rhodes's sisters – either Louisa or Edith – had lived there. 'Cecil used to stay with her and made a habit of sleeping on the *roof*.' Ibid, 20 April 1918, p. 134.

51. *RR*, p. 97.

52. *PD*, 29 April 1918, p. 134. 2nd Lieutenant Richard Oxley, MC, 13th (Service) Battalion (3rd South Down) Royal Sussex Regiment, killed in action near Wytschaete on 18 April 1918.

53. Ibid.

54. Ibid, 8 January 1918, p. 127.

55. Ibid, 31 January 1918, p. 128.

56. Ibid, 2 February 1918, p. 129.

57. Ibid, 4 February 1918, p. 129.

58. *Love Eternal*, p. 313.

59. Ibid, p. 325.

60. *PD*, 4 April 1918, p. 132.

61. Ibid, 17 April 1918, p. 133.

62. Ibid, 1 May 1918, p. 134.

63. *RR*, p. 98.

64. Ibid, p. 99.

65. Ibid.

66. Ibid, pp. 99–100.

67. Ibid, p. 100.

68. Ibid.

69. Ibid.

70. Ibid, p. 101.

71. Ibid.

72. *PD*, 24 May 1918, p. 138.

73. Ibid, 5 July 1918, p. 141.

74. Ibid, 3 June 1918, p. 139. The guns Haggard heard were those of the Third Battle of the Aisne.

75. Ibid, 30 July 1918, p. 143.

76. *PD*, 4 June 1918, p. 139.

77. Ibid, 17 June 1918, p. 139.

78. Ibid, 4 September 1918, p. 146.

79. Ibid, 24 June 1918, p. 141.

80. HRH to Andrew Haggard, quoted in Victoria Manthorpe, *Children of the Empire: The Victorian Haggards*, London: Gollancz, 1996, p. 223.

81. Ibid, 20 August 1918, p. 144.

82. Ibid.

83. HRH to Ella Maddison Green, quoted in Manthorpe, *Children of the Empire*, p. 224.

84. HRH to Andrew Haggard, quoted in Manthorpe, *Children of the Empire*, p. 224.

85. *PD*, 29 August 1918, pp. 145–6.

86. Ibid, 28 October 1918, p. 149.

87. Ibid, 11 November 1918, p. 150.

88. Ibid.

89. Ibid.
90. Ibid, 15 November 1918, p. 151.
91. Ibid, p. 152. Kipling also thought Haggard's imagination was 'the sign of expression of unusual virility'. Haggard thought this a 'queer theory that may have something in it'. Ibid.
92. Ibid.
93. Ibid, 21 November 1918, p. 153. Earlier in November, while in London to attend a meeting of the Agricultural Relief of Allies Executive Committee, Haggard was appalled at a new poster on display in the streets encouraging the purchase of War Bonds. 'It represents a British soldier realistically driving a bayonet into the stomach of a German, and the legend underneath is "The Last Blow Tells", or something of the sort. Its coarse brutality made me feel sick.' Ibid, 6 November 1918, p. 149.
94. Ibid, 21 November 1918, p. 153.
95. Ibid, 6 December 1918, p. 153.
96. Ibid, 14 December 1918, p. 154.
97. Ibid, 18 December 1918, p. 154.
98. Ibid, 25 December 1918, p. 154.
99. Ibid, 27 December 1918, p. 155.

31. 'I SINK INTO OLD AGE'

1. *RR*, p. 109. At Haggard's investiture at Buckingham Palace, King George V 'remarked upon my living in Norfolk and congratulated me'. Haggard thought the crown and cross pretty but would have been 'more effective if they were somewhat larger'. *PD*, 25 February 1919, p. 162.
2. *PD*, 15 April 1922, p. 239.
3. Quoted in Andrew Lycett, *Rudyard Kipling*, London: Phoenix, 2000, p. 673.
4. *PD*, 4 December 1919, p. 180.
5. Ibid; see also *RR*, p. 110. W.R. Inge, Dean of St Paul's, expressed his fears of the demise of the middle and upper classes, particularly the land-owning aristocracy, in his 1919 essay 'The Future of the English Race'.
6. *RR*, p. 111.
7. Ibid, p. 117. *Allan and the Ice Gods* was conceived on 20 January 1922 at Bateman's, where Haggard and Kipling spent 'a most amusing two hours' hammering out the skeleton plot for a romance ... to deal with the terrible advance of the Ice-Ages upon a little handful of the primitive inhabitants of the earth'. Haggard brought home 'several sheets of manuscript written by him and myself'. As well as a plot outline, the sheets included a sketch by Kipling and lists of characters. The book retained the title *Allan and the Ice Gods* and was published posthumously in 1927. The co-authored outline is given as an appendix in *RR*, p. 184.
8. *PD*, 7 January 1919, p. 159.
9. Ibid, 8 January 1919, p. 159.

10. Ibid, p. 109. Kipling memorialised Roosevelt in the poem 'Great Heart'.

11. Kipling to Haggard, 28 February 1924, in *RR*, p. 138.

12. Samuel Hynes, *A War Imagined: The First World War and English Culture*, London: Bodley Head, 1992, p. 356.

13. *PD*, 12 April 1919, p. 164.

14. Ibid, 28 April 1919, pp. 165–6.

15. Ibid, 14 January 1920, p. 185.

16. Ibid, 22 January 1920, p. 186.

17. Ibid, 30 January 1920, p. 187.

18. Quoted in *RR*, p. 112.

19. Ibid.

20. *PD*, 21 April 1920, pp. 192–3.

21. Ibid, 29 April 1920, p. 194.

22. Ibid, 7 May 1920, p. 196.

23. Ibid, 10 May 1920, p. 196.

24. Ibid.

25. *Daily Chronicle*, 15 September 1924, p. 3 et seq. See also *Daily Mail*, 16 September 1924, p. 3.

26. *PD*, p. 192n.

27. Article headlined 'Race Suicide Peril', *The Times*, reprinted in the *Rider Haggard Society Journal*, no. 129, July 2020, p. 9.

28. Ibid.

29. Ibid, p. 9.

30. *PD*, 16 April 1919, pp. 164–5.

31. Ibid, 8 July 1919, p. 172.

32. Marjorie Harper, *Emigration from Scotland between the Wars*, Manchester: University of Manchester Press, 1998, p. 15.

33. *PD*, 5 February 1919, p. 161.

34. Ibid, 10 February 1922, p. 237.

35. Ibid.

36. Ibid, 27 April 1922, p. 239.

37. *South Africa*, 6 March 1920, http://www.eggsa.org/newspapers/index.php/south-african-magazine/347-south-africa-1920-1-january-march.html, accessed 19 April 2017.

38. *PD*, 6 April 1920, p. 191.

39. Ibid, 21 October 1920, p. 206.

40. Ibid, 6 November 1920, p. 207.

41. Ibid, 11 January 1921, p. 215.

42. Haggard received a copy of the first French translation of *She* in May 1920, noting the 'excitement in France in connection with Benoit's *L'Atlantide*'. He thought the translation 'a mere soulless bald précis of my work, much abbreviated without advertisement thereof, and I am so disgusted I cannot go on reading it.' *PD*, 29 May 1920, p. 198.

43. *PD*, 9 October 1920, pp. 204–5.

44. Ibid, 24 February 1923, p. 254.

45. Ibid, 18 April 1921, p. 219.

46. Ibid, 20 April 1921, p. 219. Also known under the title *A Stronger Passion*. Marie Doro starred as Beatrice.

47. Ibid.

48. Ibid, 12 September 1921, p. 230.

49. Ibid.

50. War Diaries, 12 September 1921, CC.

51. *PD*, 27 July 1923, p. 261. See https://www.youtube.com/watch?v=P4WYnN_IhAs, accessed 15 October 2020. Haggard had been filmed before in January 1916, but the footage is no longer extant.

52. Ibid, 4 June 1919, p. 170.

53. Ibid, 29 July 1919, p. 173.

54. Ibid, 7 July 1919, p. 172.

55. Ibid, 27 September 1919, p. 176.

56. *PD*, 29 October 1919, p. 178.

57. Lodge was a Christian spiritualist and his beliefs grew in parallel with his scientific studies. Like his friend Arthur Conan Doyle, he also lost a son in the war. His attempts to contact him via various mediums was the subject of his book *Raymond, or Life and Death* (1916). Other books on his spiritualist beliefs included *Phantom Walls* (1929) and *The Reality of a Spiritual World* (1930).

58. *PD*, 13 January 1919, p. 160.

59. Ibid, 4 November 1919, pp. 178–9.

60. Ibid, 10 November 1920, p. 208.

61. Ibid, 30 December 1920, p. 211.

62. Quoted in John Senior, 'Spirituality in the Fiction of Henry Rider Haggard', PhD thesis, Rhodes University, 2003, p. 263. Elliott O'Donnell gave an account of the haunting in *Haunted Churches*, London: Quality Press, 1939, pp. 11–2.

63. *PD*, 22 June 1920, p. 198.

64. Ibid, 18 September 1920, p. 202. Walter Besant died in 1901.

65. Ibid, 14 February 1921, p. 217. Anecdotal evidence has Cochrane working for the Rhodes Fruit Farms and inspecting properties run by managers.

66. Ibid, 7 January 1922, p. 235. Richmond was the dedicatee of *The World's Desire*, 'a picturesque figure with his long hair parted in the middle and a large and floppy necktie fastened in a bow; indeed about him was the aestheticism of my early youth; not that he was in any way an aesthete in character, rather the reverse in fact.' Ibid, 14 February 1921, p. 217.

67. Ibid, 1 May 1921, pp. 219–20.

68. Ibid, 1 May 1921, p. 219.

69. Ibid, 31 March 1922, p. 238. In 1932 his widow Lady Louisa Haggard donated a cast

of the bust and seventeen other items connected with her late husband to the Pretoria Publicity Association. Their present whereabouts are unknown.

70. For Haggard on Epstein, see *PD*, 9 April 1917, p. 103.
71. Dedication to *The Brethren*.
72. *PD*, 8 May 1923, p. 258.
73. Ibid, 14 May 1923, pp. 258–9.
74. Ibid, 23 March 1917, pp. 99–100. *Child of the Ocean* by Ronald Ross was published in 1889.
75. Ibid, 7 May 1921, pp. 220–1.
76. Ibid, 21 October 1921, p. 231.
77. Ibid, 1 November 1921, p. 231.
78. Ibid, 5 May 1922, p. 240.
79. Ibid, 22 November 1922, p. 247.
80. Ibid, 13 December 1922, p. 248. Not until 1933 was it discovered Kipling had been suffering from duodenal ulcers for fifteen years. In 1922 Haggard gave Kipling the recipe for making Dr Paget's Jam, a well-known laxative.
81. Ibid, 22 July 1921, p. 226.
82. Ibid, p. 227.
83. Ibid, 22 July 1922, p. 242.
84. Ibid.
85. Ibid, 27 July 1923, p. 261.
86. Ibid, 30 October 1923, p. 263.
87. Ibid, p. 264.
88. Ibid, 1 August 1921, p. 228; Victoria Manthorpe, *Lilias Rider Haggard: Countrywoman*, Cromer: Poppyland, 2015, p. 80.
89. *PD*, 22 June 1922, p. 241.
90. Quoted in *Cloak*, p. 274.
91. *PD*, 21 August 1922, p. 243.
92. Ibid.
93. Ibid, p. 244.
94. Ibid.
95. Ibid, 25 December 1922, p. 249.
96. Ibid, 2 March 1923, p. 254.
97. After serialisation in *Hutchinson's Magazine* from March 1922 to March 1923.
98. *PD*, 8 March 1923, p. 254.
99. Ibid, 10 March 1923, p. 255.
100. Ronald Ross to HRH, [April 1923], copy, CC.
101. *PD*, 20 March 1923, p. 255.
102. Ibid.
103. HRH to Kipling, in *RR*, p. 125.
104. Ibid, pp. 125–6.
105. Quoted in *Cloak*, p. 272.

106. Ibid, p. 273.

107. Ibid.

32. 'OLD PHARAOH'

1. *PD*, 30 November 1922, p. 248. In 1909 after the death of Lord Amherst, Carter became an agent 'placing and purchasing antiquities for private and public interests' (T.G.H. James, *Howard Carter: The Path to Tutankhamun*, London: Tauris, 2001, p. 217) and 'established a flourishing antiquities practice apart from his strictly professional archaeological work' (James, *Howard Carter*, 230). In 1917 Carter brokered the sale of the 'seven large granite statues of the lioness deity Sakhmet (in the Amherst collection) to the Metropolitan Museum of Art' (James, *Howard Carter*, p. 217) and compiled the catalogue for the remaining items of the Amherst Collection auctioned at Sotheby's in 1919.

2. *PD*, 9 February 1923, p. 253.

3. A similar arrangement between *The Times* and the Royal Geographical Society for the 1921 Everest Expedition had been a success.

4. *PD*, 22 March 1923, p. 256.

5. War Diaries, 5 April 1923, CC.

6. *Daily Telegraph* article transcribed in War Diaries, 7 April 1923, CC.

7. Ronald Ross to HRH, [April 1923], transcription, CC.

8. *Cloak*, p. 274.

9. Victoria Manthorpe, *Lilias Rider Haggard: Countrywoman*, Cromer: Poppyland, 2015, p. 83.

10. HRH's diary, quoted in M. Shirley Addy, *Rider Haggard and Egypt*, Accrington, Lancashire: AL Publications, 1998, p. 27.

11. *Cloak*, p. 274. Haggard also contracted with P&O to give four lectures on ancient Egypt to his fellow passengers.

12. Manthorpe, *Lilias*, p. 83.

13. HRH to Louie, 22 January 1924, CC.

14. James, *Howard Carter*, p. 316.

15. HRH's diary, quoted in Addy, *Rider Haggard and Egypt*, p. 27.

16. Ibid.

17. *Cloak*, p. 275.

18. Ibid.

19. HRH to Louie, 4 February 1924, CC.

20. HRH's diary, quoted in Addy, *Rider Haggard and Egypt*, pp. 27–8.

21. Ibid, p. 28.

22. HRH to Louie, 30 January 1924, CC.

23. HRH to Louie, 4 February 1924, CC.

24. HRH's diary, quoted in Addy, *Rider Haggard and Egypt*, pp. 28–9.

25. Ibid, p. 31.

26. Jack's bad language was attributed to his naval background.

27. Manthorpe, *Lilias*, p. 90.

28. HRH to Louie, 14 February 1924, CC.

29. HRH's diary, 20 February 1924, quoted in Addy, *Rider Haggard and Egypt*, p. 31.

30. HRH's diary, 27 February 1924, quoted in Addy, *Rider Haggard and Egypt*, p. 32.

31. Ibid, p. 32.

32. HRH to Louie 25 February 1924, CC. Evelyn Samuel had returned to Cairo and resumed her rows with Joan.

33. HRH's diary, 5 March 1924, quoted in Addy, *Rider Haggard and Egypt*, p. 32.

34. HRH's diary, 23 March 1924, quoted in Addy, *Rider Haggard and Egypt*, p. 34.

35. Ibid.

36. *PD*, 8 April 1924, p. 270.

37. Ibid, 20 June 1924, p. 272.

38. Ibid, 24 July 1924, p. 273.

39. Trevor R. Reese, *The History of the Royal Commonwealth Society, 1868–1968*, Oxford: OUP, 1968, p. 188.

40. *PD*, 23 April 1924, pp. 270–1.

41. Piers Brendon, *Decline and Fall of the British Empire, 1781–1997*, London: Jonathan Cape, 2007, p. 331.

42. Ibid. During the twenty weeks it was open 27 million people came through the gates, more than half of Britain's population.

43. See James, *Howard Carter*, p. 355.

44. *PD*, 29 May 1924, p. 271. Wembley was then the terminus of the London Underground's Metropolitan line.

45. Ibid.

46. Stuart died in London on 8 April 1942. His collection of oral evidence narrowly escaped destruction during the Blitz and after negotiations with his widow was returned to South Africa in 1949. It is now housed in the Campbell Collections of the University of KwaZulu-Natal in Durban. To date, six volumes of the testimonies he collected have been published as *The James Stuart Archive*.

47. *PD*, 23 June 1924, p. 272.

48. Ibid, 7 October 1924, p. 275. The Authors' Club was founded by Walter Besant in 1891.

49. Ibid, 14 October 1924, p. 275.

50. HRH to Louie, 16 October 1924, CC.

51. *PD*, 25 October 1924, p. 276.

52. Ibid.

53. Ibid.

54. Ibid, 6 November 1924, p. 277.

55. Ibid, 29 October 1924, p. 277.

56. Ibid, 29 October 1924, p. 277. William Haggard met Emily Margaret Hancox, known as Nitie, during his posting to Rio de Janeiro in the mid-1880s. They married in 1885.

57. Ibid, 6 November 1924, p. 277.
58. Ibid.
59. Harold Cox and John E. Chandler, *The House of Longman with a Record of Their Bicentenary Celebrations*, London: Longmans, 1925, p. 65.
60. Ibid.
61. *PD*, 6 November 1924, p. 277.
62. Ibid, p. 278.
63. *Cloak*, pp. 277–8.
64. Ibid, p. 278.
65. Ibid.
66. Ibid.
67. *PD*, 27 December 1924, p. 279.
68. HRH to Lucoque, 7 January 1925, Huntington Collection, HM 43545.
69. Ibid.
70. HRH to Lucoque, 8 January 1925, Huntington Collection, HM 43546.
71. HRH to Lucoque, 15 January 1925, Huntington Collection, HM 43547. The film was shot in Berlin during 1925 as a British-German co-production starring Betty Blythe. A title credit reads: 'The sub-titles [inter-titles] for this production were specially written by the late Sir Rider Haggard.'. In November at the age of 38, Lucoque committed suicide when his company went into bankruptcy.
72. *PD*, 16 January 1925, p. 283.
73. Ibid.
74. Ibid.
75. HRH to Louie, 14 October 1924, CC.
76. *PD*, 16 January 1925, pp. 283–4.
77. Ibid, 3 February 1925, p. 284. Arthur had been so moved at the sight of destitute army veterans begging on London streets after the Anglo-Boer War that he and a friend, James Malcolm, co-founded the Veterans Club and Employment Bureau to assist ex-servicemen in finding employment. The organisation is still active as the Victory Services Club.
78. Ibid.
79. *RR*, pp. 129–130.
80. Ibid, pp. 138–40.
81. HRH to Kipling, in *RR*, pp. 141–2.
82. Ibid, p. 143.
83. In his letter of 28 February 1925 Kipling spoke of Haggard's ability to 'inspire affection at short notice'. *RR*, p. 140.
84. *RR*, pp. 143–144.
85. *RR*, p. 146.
86. Haggard thought the ring was from the Amherst collection, but it was the one he bought from a peasant at Thebes in 1887. See Addy, *Rider Haggard and Egypt*, p. 91.
87. *RR*, p. 140.

88. Ibid, p. 147.
89. *PD*, 26 March 1925, p. 284. Haggard's verdict on Curzon: 'To my mind, magnificent as it was and in many ways successful, publicly speaking his career was still a failure. He could never catch the ear of the crowd; his cold and rather lofty manner was against him. In short he had not the art of popularity.'
90. *Cloak*, p. 278.
91. Ibid., pp. 278–9.
92. Kipling to HRH, 5 May 1925, in *RR*, p. 177.
93. *Cloak*, p. 279.
94. *RR*, p. 180.
95. *Cloak*, p. 279.
96. Ibid, Preface by Godfrey Cheyne, p. 21.
97. HRH obituary in *The Times*, 15 May 1925.
98. At the same hour a memorial service was held at St Mary's, Ditchingham.
99. He gave up literature and became a partner in a firm of bill brokers. He died in 1926.
100. Better known under his pseudonym, Anthony Hope, author of *The Prisoner of Zenda* (1894). He founded the Society of Authors' pension scheme.
101. Haggard's brother William died in 1926; Haggard's sister Mary d'Anethan, in 1935; Frederick Jackson, in 1930; Rudyard Kipling, in 1936; Haggard's widow Louisa, in 1943; and Haggard's sister-in-law Agnes (née Barber), map-maker for *King Solomon's Mines* and creator of the sherd of Amenartas for *She*, in 1960 aged 100, the last of her generation.

APPENDIX: MHLOPEKAZI

1. Mhlopekazi is mentioned by his real name in the introduction to *She and Allan*, p. x, and refers to himself using his real name on pp. 42–3.
2. *Natal Witness*, 26 October 1897; transcript in William Lucas, 'Umhlopekazi: A Life Study', 1 January 1898, p. 4, Campbell Collections, MS 52.
3. H.C. Lugg, *Historic Natal and Zululand*, Pietermaritzburg: Shuter and Shooter, 1949, p. 44.
4. *Natal Witness*, 26 October 1897, pp. 3–4.
5. Lucas, 'Umhlopekazi: A Life Study', p. 1.
6. *The Natal Who's Who*, Durban: Natal Who's Who, 1906, p. 119.
7. Lucas, 'Umhlopekazi: A Life Study', p. 1.
8. *Days*, vol. 1, pp. 75–6.
9. On 12 January 1920 Haggard received Mhlopekazi's Victoria Medal, sent to him by S.B. Samuelson, son of the late R.C. Samuelson, former Secretary for Native Affairs in Natal. 'He handed it back to Mr Samuelson a few days before his death' in 1897. 'Evidently he always wore it as I know by the scent. I never thought I should live to smell old Umslopogaas again.' *PD*, 12 January 1920, p. 185.
10. The cemetery no longer exists.

11. Tikuba testimony, in C. de B. Webb and John Wright (eds.), *The James Stuart Archive of Recorded Oral Evidence Relating to the History of the Zulu and Neighbouring Peoples*, 6 vols., Pietermaritzburg: University of KwaZulu-Natal Press, vol. 6, 2014, p. 228.

12. Xaba testimony, ibid, p. 324.

13. Philip Bonner, *Kings, Commoners and Concessionaires: The Evolution and Dissolution of the Nineteenth-Century Swazi State*, Johannesburg: Ravan, 1983, p. 63.

14. Ibid.

15. Ibid, p. 64.

16. Ibid.

17. See E.J. Liebenberg-Barkhuizen, 'The Iconography of the "Indigene" in Mary Stainbank's Sculpture c.1920–1940', PhD thesis, University of South Africa, 2001, p. 28.

BIBLIOGRAPHY

Collections

Bodleian Library, Oxford, United Kingdom
Brenthurst Library, Johannesburg, South Africa
British Library, London, United Kingdom
Campbell Collections, Durban, South Africa
Cheyne Collection, Norfolk, United Kingdom
Columbia University, Rare Book and Manuscript Library, New York, United States
Huntington Collection, San Marino, United States
Lockwood Collection, State University of New York, Buffalo, United States
Cushing Memorial Library & Archives, Texas A&M University, United States
Norfolk Record Office, Norwich, United Kingdom
Peter Smits Collection. Privately held.
Pietermaritzburg Archives Repository, Pietermaritzburg, South Africa
Royal Maritime Museum, Greenwich, United Kingdom
Transvaal Archives Repository, Pretoria, South Africa
University of Cambridge Library, Cambridge, United Kingdom
University of the Witswatersrand, Historical Papers and Research Archive, South Africa.

Websites

http://www.visualhaggard.org
https://literarytourism.co.za
https://www.victorianweb.org
https://en.wikipedia.org

Unpublished Haggard items

HRH, 'Camp Life in Pretoria', Memorandum, MS 251, The Brenthurst Library, Johannesburg.
Lady Haggard's diary, 1880–1881, Cheyne Collection.
HRH's India Diary and War Diaries, Cheyne Collection.

BIBLIOGRAPHY

'Notes on the Family of William Meybohm Rider Haggard (1817–1893) and Ella Haggard (née Doveton) (1819–1889) by Andrew Haggard (1892–1976)', written in 1974 for his cousin Nada Cheyne. Jack Haggard Papers, National Maritime Museum, Greenwich.

Articles by Rider Haggard

HRH, 'Books That Have Influenced Me', *British Weekly*, May 1887.

HRH, 'Childhood Reminiscences: An Unpublished Manuscript', *Columbia Library Columns*, New York, November 1981. The reminiscence is preceded by an introduction, HRH, 'Rider Haggard Looks Back' by Morton N. Cohen.

HRH, 'The Fate of Swaziland', *New Review*, January 1890.

HRH, 'Haggard on the Zulus: The Story of a Rebellious People', *Illustrated London News*, 19 May 1906.

HRH, 'The Hill of Death', *Windsor Magazine*, December 1919.

HRH, 'An Incident of African History', *Windsor Magazine*, 1900.

HRH, 'A Journey through Zululand', *Windsor Magazine*, December 1916.

HRH, 'Lost on the Veld', *Windsor Magazine*, 1903.

HRH, *Memorandum of the Circumstances Connected with the Plot to Murder the Late Melmoth Osborn, Sir Marshall Clarke, and H. Rider Haggard*, privately printed, McLean, VA: Alfred Tella, 2003.

HRH, 'My First Book', *Idler*, April 1893.

HRH, *My Stallion Moresco*, privately printed, McClean, VA: Alfred Tella, 1998.

HRH, 'On Going Back', *Longmans Magazine*, XI, November 1887.

HRH, 'The Transvaal', *Macmillan's Magazine*, May 1877.

HRH, 'A Visit to the Chief Secocoeni', *Gentleman's Magazine*, September 1877.

HRH, 'The Wreck of the Copeland', *Illustrated London News*, 18 August 1888.

HRH, 'A Zulu War Dance', *Gentleman's Magazine*, July 1877.

Norfolk Roll of Honour, 1914–18: List of Men from Norfolk Parishes Who Fell in the Great War, Norfolk News Company, 1920; Gliddon Books, 1988. The Introduction is by HRH.

Rosmarine: A Story of Twenty-Five Years and a Sequel, with a preface by Sir H. Rider Haggard, London: Mowbray, 1913.

Whatmore, D.E. (comp.), *Rider Haggard's Good Deeds*, Pamphlet One: *Deeds for the Church*, Cheltenham: D.E. Whatmore, 1995.

Whatmore, D.E. (comp.), *Rider Haggard's Good Deeds*, Pamphlet Two: *Deeds for Children and Young People*, Cheltenham: D.E. Whatmore, 1996.

Whatmore, D.E. (comp.), *Rider Haggard's Good Deeds*, Pamphlet Three: *Deeds for the Salvation Army*, Cheltenham: D.E. Whatmore, 1996.

Whatmore, D.E. (comp.), *Rider Haggard's Good Deeds*, Pamphlet Four: *Letters to the Right Hon. Lewis Harcourt*, Cheltenham: D.E. Whatmore, 1996.

Wilmot, Theodore, *Monomotapa (Rhodesia), and Its History from the Most Ancient Times to the Present*, with introduction by Rider Haggard, London: Fisher Unwin, 1896.

BIBLIOGRAPHY

Works of H. Rider Haggard
(Editions referred to in the text)

Allan and the Holy Flower, London: Macdonald, 1963.

Allan and the Ice Gods, Polegate: Pulp, 1999.

Allan Quatermain, ed. Dennis Butts, Oxford: OUP, 1995.

Allan's Wife, London: Macdonald, 1963.

The Ancient Allan, London: Cassell, 1920.

The Annotated She: A Critical Edition of H. Rider Haggard's Victorian Romance with Introduction and Notes, ed. Norman Etherington, Bloomington: Indiana University Press, 1991.

Ayesha: The Return of She, London: Macdonald, 1956.

Beatrice, New York: Collier, 1894.

Belshazzar, London: Stanley Paul, 1928.

Benita, London: Macdonald, 1965.

The Best Short Stories of Rider Haggard, ed. Peter Haining, London: Michael Joseph, 1981.

The Brethren, London: Macdonald, 1952.

Cetywayo and His White Neighbours, or, Remarks on Recent Events in Zululand, Natal, and the Transvaal, London: Kegan Paul, 1896.

Child of Storm, London: Macdonald, 1952.

Cleopatra, London: Macdonald, 1958.

Colonel Quaritch, V.C., London: Longmans, 1890.

Dawn, London: Harrap, 1932.

The Days of My Life, 2 vols., London: Longmans, 1926.

Diary of an African Journey, Pietermaritzburg: University of Natal Press, 2000.

Dr. Therne, London: Hodder and Stoughton, 1923.

Elissa; or, The Doom of Zimbabwe, London: Hodder and Stoughton, 1917.

Eric Brighteyes, London: Macdonald, 1963.

Fair Margaret, London: Hutchinson, 1907.

A Farmer's Year, introduction by Ronald Blythe, London: Hutchinson, 1987.

Finished, London: Macdonald, 1962.

A Gardener's Year, London: Longmans, 1905.

The Ghost Kings, London: Cassell, 1926.

Heart of the World, London: Macdonald, 1954.

Heu-Heu, or, The Monster, London: Hutchinson, 1923.

Hunter Quatermain's Story: The Uncollected Adventures of Allan Quatermain, ed. Peter Haining, London: Peter Owen, 2003.

The Ivory Child, London: Macdonald, 1958.

Jess, London: Smith, Elder, 1900.

Joan Haste, London: Longmans, 1897.

King Solomon's Mines, ed. Gerald Monsman, Peterborough: Broadview Press, 2002.

King Solomon's Mines, ed. Denis Butts, Oxford: OUP, 1992.

BIBLIOGRAPHY

The Lady of Blossholme, London: Hodder and Stoughton, 1909.

The Last Boer War, London: Kegan Paul, 1899.

Love Eternal, London: Cassell, 1918.

Lysbeth: A Tale of the Dutch, London: Longmans, 1933.

Maiwa's Revenge, London, Macdonald, 1965.

Mameena and Other Plays: The Complete Dramatic Works of H. Rider Haggard, ed. Stephen Coan and Alfred Tella, Pietermaritzburg: University of KwaZulu-Natal Press, 2007.

Marie, London: Macdonald 1959.

Mary of Marion Isle, London: Andrew Melrose, n.d.

Montezuma's Daughter, London: Macdonald, 1948.

Moon of Israel, London: John Murray, 1918.

Morning Star, London: Cassell, 1912.

Mr. Meeson's Will, London: Longmans, 1897.

Nada the Lily, London: Macdonald, 1949.

Nada the Lily, introduction by Edward Boyd, London: Collins, 1957.

The Pearl Maiden, London: Stacey, 1972.

The People of the Mist, London: Macdonald, 1951.

The Poor and the Land, London: Longmans, 1905.

Queen of the Dawn, London: Hutchinson, 1925.

Queen Sheba's Ring, London: Macdonald, 1958.

Red Eve, London: Hodder and Stoughton, 1911.

Regeneration, London: Longmans, 1910.

Rural Denmark, 2nd edn, London: Longmans, 1913.

Rural England, London: Longmans, 1902; 2nd edn, 1906.

She, introduction by Morton N. Cohen, New York: Collier, 1962.

She, ed. Andrew M. Stauffer, Toronto: Broadview Editions, 2006.

She, ed. Daniel Karlin, Oxford: OUP, 1991.

She and Allan, London: Hutchinson, 1922; London: Macdonald, 1960.

Smith and the Pharaohs and Other Tales, London: Arrowsmith, 1920.

Stella Fregelius, London: Longmans, 1904.

Swallow, London: Longmans, 1899.

The Treasure of the Lake, London: Hutchinson, 1971.

The Wanderer's Necklace, London: Cassell, 1914,

The Way of the Spirit, London: Hutchinson, 1906.

When the World Shook, New York: Ballantine, 1978.

A Winter Pilgrimage, 2 vols., Leipzig: Tauchnitz, 1902.

Wisdom's Daughter, London: Hutchinson, 1924.

The Witch's Head, London: Longmans, 1903.

The Wizard, London: Arrowsmith, 1933.

The World's Desire, London: Macdonald, 1963.

The Yellow God, London: Cassell, 1926.

BIBLIOGRAPHY

Books and articles

Abbot, Claude Colleer (ed.), *Letters of Gerard Manley Hopkins to Robert Bridges*, Oxford: OUP, 1970.

Ackroyd, Peter, *London: The Biography*, London: Chatto and Windus, 2000.

Addy, M. Shirley, *Rider Haggard and Egypt*, Accrington, Lancashire: AL Publications, 1998.

Addy, M. Shirley, 'Rider Haggard's Egyptian Bookplate', *Rider Haggard Society Journal*, no. 141, July 2023.

Allen, Roger, *A Guide to the Non-Fiction of Rider Haggard*, privately published, 1998.

Armstrong, C.S. (ed.), *Under the Parson's Nose: Further Extracts from the Diary of the Revd B.J. Armstrong M.A. (Cantab), Vicar of East Dereham 1850–1888*, Dereham: Larks Press, 1912.

Asche, Oscar, *His Life*, London: Hurst and Blackett, 1929.

Austin, Sue, 'Desire, Fascination and the Other: Some Thoughts on Jung's Interest in Rider Haggard's *She* and on the Nature of Archetypes', *Harvest: International Journal for Jungian Studies*, vol. 50, no. 2, 2004.

Aylward, Alfred, *The Transvaal of Today: War, Witchcraft, Sport and Spoils in South Africa*, Edinburgh: William Blackwood and Sons, 1881.

Barker, Anne, *Life in South Africa*, Philadelphia: Lippincott, 1877; reprint, New York: Negro Universities Press, 1969. English edition: *A Year's Housekeeping in South Africa*, London: Macmillan, 1877.

Batchelor, Stephen, *The Awakening of the West: The Encounter of Buddhism and Western Culture, 543 BCE – 1992*, London: HarperCollins, 1994.

Baxter, David, 'Opposition to Vaccination and Immunisation: The UK Experience; From Smallpox to MMR', *Journal of Vaccines and Vaccination*, vol. 5, 2014, doi:/10.4172/2157-7560.1000254.

Beerbühl, Margrit Schulte, *The Forgotten Majority: German Merchants, Naturalization and Global Trade 1660–1815*, New York: Berghahn, 2015.

Bennett, Ian, *A Rain of Lead: The Siege and Surrender of the British at Potchefstroom 1880–1881*, London: Greenhill, 2001.

Bentley, J.M. and C.G. Griffinhoofe, *Wintering in Egypt: Hints for Invalids and Travellers*, 2nd edn, London: Simpkin, 1895.

Blatchly, John, *A Famous Antient Seed-Plot of Learning: A History of Ipswich School*, Ipswich: Ipswich School, 2003.

Blatchly, John, 'Sir Henry Rider Haggard: Storyteller Supreme', *Old Ipswichian: Journal of the Old Ipswichian Club*, vol. 7, October 2006.

Bond, Brian (ed.), *Victorian Military Campaigns*, London: Hutchinson, 1967.

Bonner, Philip, *Kings, Commoners and Concessionaires: The Evolution and Dissolution of the Nineteenth-Century Swazi State*, Johannesburg: Ravan, 1983.

Bourne, Stephen, *Black in the British Frame: Black People in British Film and Television 1896–1996*, London: Cassell, 1998.

Braddock, Joseph, *Haunted Houses*, London: Batsford, 1956.

BIBLIOGRAPHY

Branford, Jean and William Branford, *A Dictionary of South African English*, Cape Town: OUP, 1991.

Brendon, Piers, *Decline and Fall of the British Empire, 1781–1997*, London: Jonathan Cape, 2007.

Brodie, F.M., *The Devil Drives: A Life of Sir Richard Burton*, London: Eyre and Spottiswoode, 1967.

Brunner, Cornelia, *Anima as Fate*, Dallas, TX: Spring Publications, 1986.

Bullock, Geoff, 'Rider Haggard and Royal Air Force Connections', *RAF Historical Society Journal*, http://www.raf.mod.uk/history/theroyalairforcemotto.cfm.

Bullock, Geoff, 'Rider Haggard's Residences', *Haggard Journal*, no. 119, March 2016.

Bulpin, T.V., *Discovering Southern Africa*, Cape Town: Bulpin, 2001.

Bulpin, T.V., *Lost Trails of the Transvaal*, Cape Town: Bulpin, 1974.

Bulpin, T.V., *To the Banks of the Zambezi*, Cape Town: Books of Africa, 1968.

Carrington, Charles, *Rudyard Kipling: His Life and Work*, London: Macmillan, 1955.

Carton, Benedict, John Laband and Jabulani Sithole (eds.), *Zulu Identities: Being Zulu, Past and Present*, Pietermaritzburg: University of KwaZulu-Natal Press, 2008.

Castle, Ian, *Majuba 1881, The Hill of Destiny*, Osprey, London, 1996.

Chilvers, Hedley A., *The Seven Wonders of Southern Africa*, Johannesburg: SA Railways and Harbours, 1929.

Chrisman, Laura, *Rereading the Imperial Romance: British Imperialism and South African Resistance in Haggard, Schreiner and Plaatje*, Oxford: OUP, 2000.

Coan, Stephen, '*King Solomon's Mines* on Film: Modernity in Reverse', 2020, https://journals.openedition.org/erea/10648.

Cohen, Morton, *Rider Haggard: His Life and Works*, London: Hutchinson, 1960.

Cohen, Morton, *Rudyard Kipling to Rider Haggard: The Record of a Friendship*, New Jersey: Associated University Presses, 1965.

Collier, Joy, *The Purple and the Gold: The Story of Pretoria and Johannesburg*, Cape Town: Longmans, 1965.

Cope, Richard, *Ploughshare of War: The Origins of the Anglo-Zulu War of 1879*, Pietermaritzburg: University of Natal Press, 1999.

Cousins, Mark, *The Story of Film*, London: Pavilion, 2004.

Couzens, Tim, *The New African: A Study of the Life and Works of H.I.E. Dhlomo*, Johannesburg: Ravan Press, 1985.

Couzens, Tim, 'A Tale of Two Mysteries: The Patterson Embassy to Lobengula', *Brenthurst Archive*, vol. 2, no.1, 1995.

Cowley, Cecil, *Schwikkard of Natal and the Old Transvaal*, Cape Town: Struik, 1974.

Cox, Harold and John E. Chandler, *The House of Longman with a Record of Their Bicentenary Celebrations*, London: Longmans, 1925.

Currey, R.N., *Vinnicombe's Trek: Son of Natal, Stepson of Transvaal*, London: James Currey; Portsmouth: Heinemann; Pietermaritzburg: University of Natal Press and Shuter & Shooter, 1989.

BIBLIOGRAPHY

De Kock, W.J. et al. (eds.), *Dictionary of South African Biography*, 5 vols., Pretoria: Nasionale Boekhandel, 1968–87.

Delius, Peter, *The Land Belongs to Us: The Pedi Polity, the Boers and the British in the Nineteenth-Century Transvaal*, Johannesburg: Ravan Press, 1983.

Dixie, Florence, *In the Land of Misfortune*, London: Bentley, 1882.

Doke, C.M. and B.W. Vilakazi, *Zulu–English Dictionary*, Johannesburg: Witwatersrand University Press, 1958.

Dokotum, Okaka Opio, *Hollywood and Africa: Recycling the 'Dark Continent' Myth, 1908–2020*, Grahamstown: NISC, 2020.

Dolman, Frederick, 'Mrs. Alexander's Daughter', *Ladies' Home Journal*, February 1894.

Dominy, Graham, *The Last Outpost on the Zulu Frontiers: Fort Napier and the Imperial Garrison*, Urbana: University of Illinois Press, 2016.

Drazin, Charles, *Mapping the Past: A Search for Five Brothers at the Edge of Empire*, London: Heinemann, 2016.

Duminy, Andrew and Bill Guest (eds.), *Natal and Zululand: From Earliest Times to 1910*, Pietermaritzburg: University of Natal Press and Shuter & Shooter, 1989.

Dunn, John, *Cetywayo and the Three Generals*, ed. D.C.F. Moodie, reprint, privately published, Durban, 2006.

Edel, Leon (ed.), *Henry James Letters*, vol. 3, Cambridge, MA: Harvard University Press, 1980.

Ellis, Peter Beresford, *H. Rider Haggard: A Voice from the Infinite*, London: Routledge 1978.

Ellmann, Richard, *Oscar Wilde*, London: Penguin, 1988.

Emms, M., 'Henry Rider and the Elusive Jess Cottage', *Africana: Yearbook of the Africana Society of Pretoria*, no. 30, 2013.

Etherington, Norman, *Rider Haggard*, Boston: Twayne, 1984.

Etherington, Norman, 'South African Origins of Rider Haggard's Early Romances', *Notes and Queries*, October 1977.

Fawcett, P.H., *Exploration Fawcett*, London: Hutchinson, 1953.

Foster, R.F., *W.B. Yeats: A Life*, vol. 1, *The Apprentice Mage*, Oxford: OUP, 1997.

Franklin, J. Jeffrey, *The Lotus and the Lion: Buddhism and the British Empire*, Ithaca, NY: Cornell University Press, 2008.

Freeman, Mark, *Social Investigation and Rural England 1870–1914*, Woodbridge, Suffolk: Boydell, 2003.

Freud, S., *The Interpretation of Dreams*, London: Penguin, 1992.

Gilderdale, Betty, *The Seven Lives of Lady Barker*, Auckland: Bateman, 1996.

Giliomee, Hermann and Bernard Mbenga, *New History of South Africa*, Cape Town: Tafelberg, 2007.

Gillies, Mary Ann, *The Professional Literary Agent in Britain, 1880–1920*, Toronto: University of Toronto Press, 2007.

Goodman, Ruth, *How to Be a Victorian*, London: Penguin, 2013.

Gordan, John D., 'The Ghost at Brede Place', *Bulletin of the New York Public Library*, December 1952.

Gordon, Ruth E., *Shepstone: The Role of the Family in the History of South Africa, 1820–1900*, Cape Town: Balkema, 1968.

Greaves, Adrian and Ian Knight, *The Who's Who of the Anglo-Zulu War 1879*, 2 vols., Barnsley: Pen and Sword, 2006.

Green, Jeffrey P., *Black Edwardians: Black People in Britain, 1901–1914*, London: Frank Cass, 1998.

Green, Roger Lancelyn, *Andrew Lang*, Leicester: Ward, 1946.

Green, Roger Lancelyn, *Tales of Ancient Egypt*, London: Puffin, 2004.

Greene, Graham, *Collected Essays*, London: Penguin, 1971.

Guy, Jeff, *The Destruction of the Zulu Kingdom: The Civil War in Zululand, 1879–1884*, Pietermaritzburg: University of Natal Press, 1994.

Guy, Jeff, *The Heretic: A Study of the Life of William Colenso, 1814–1883*, Pietermaritzburg and Johannesburg: University of Natal Press and Ravan Press, 1983.

Guy, Jeff, *The Maphumulo Uprising: War, Law and Ritual in the Zulu Rebellion*, Pietermaritzburg: University of KwaZulu-Natal Press, 2005.

Guy, Jeff, *Remembering the Rebellion: The Zulu Uprising of 1906*, Pietermaritzburg: University of KwaZulu-Natal Press, 2006.

Guy, Jeff, *Theophilus Shepstone and the Forging of Natal: African Autonomy and Settler Colonialism in the Making of Traditional Authority*, Pietermaritzburg: University of KwaZulu-Natal Press, 2013.

Haggard, Ella, *Life and Its Author: An Essay in Verse*, London: Longmans, 1890.

Haggard, Lilias Rider, *The Cloak That I Left*, London: Hodder and Stoughton, 1951.

Haggard, Lilias Rider, *Too Late for Tears*, Bungay, Suffolk: Waveney Publications, 1969.

Hamilton, Carolyn, *Terrific Majesty: The Powers of Shaka Zulu and the Limits of Historical Invention*, Cape Town: David Philip, 1998.

Hammond, John Hayes, *The Autobiography of John Hayes Hammond*, vol. 2, New York: Farrar, 1935.

Hapgood, Isabel, 'Count Tolstoy at Home', *Atlantic Monthly*, November 1891.

Harcombe, Anne and Judy Hickey, 'Haggard's London', *Rider Haggard Society Journal*, no. 118, November 2015.

Harding, E.J., *Dominions Diary: The Letters of E.J. Harding, 1913–1916*, ed. Stephen Constantine, Halifax: Ryburn Publishing, 1992.

Hardy, Thomas, *The Collected Letters of Thomas Hardy*, ed. Richard Little Purdy and Michael Millgate, Oxford: Clarendon Press, vols. 1 (1979), 3 (1982) and 4 (1984).

Harman, Claire, *Robert Louis Stevenson: A Biography*, London: Harper, 2006.

Harper, Marjory, *Emigration from Scotland between the Wars*, Manchester: University of Manchester Press, 1998.

Hart-Davis, Rupert (ed.), *Selected Letters of Oscar Wilde*, Oxford: OUP, 1979.

Haw, Simon, *Bearing Witness: The Natal Witness, 1846–1996*, Pietermaritzburg: Natal Witness, 1996.

Herd, Norman, *The Bent Pine: The Trial of Chief Langalibalele*, Johannesburg: Ravan Press, 1976.

BIBLIOGRAPHY

Hickey, Judith, *Journal: Agnes Marion Haggard (née Barber)*, privately published, 2013.

Higgins, D.S., 'Identifying Haggard's Secret Love', *London Magazine*, vol. 26, no. 11, February 1987.

Higgins, D.S. (ed.), *The Private Diaries of Sir H. Rider Haggard*, London: Cassell, 1980.

Higgins, D.S., *Rider Haggard: The Great Storyteller*, London: Cassell, 1981; rev. edn, 2013.

Higgs, Catherine, *Chocolate Islands: Cocoa, Slavery, and Colonial Africa*, Athens: Ohio University Press, 2012.

Hogarth, O.J. and R.L. White, *The Life of Archbishop Carter: 'Eton's Gift to South Africa'*, privately published, 1952.

Hughes, Heather, *First President: A Life of John Dube, Founding President of the ANC*, Johannesburg: Jacana, 2011.

Hultgren, Neil E., 'Haggard Criticism since 1980: Imperial Romance before and after the Postcolonial Turn', Literature Compass, https://doi.org/10.1111/j.1741-4113.2011.00827.x.

Huxley, Elspeth, *Out in the Midday Sun: My Kenya*, London: Chatto, 1985.

Hyde, Montgomery, *Oscar Wilde: A Biography*, London: Methuen, 1975.

Hynes, Samuel, *A War Imagined: The First World War and English Culture*, London: Bodley Head, 1992.

Inwood, Stephen, *A History of London*, London: Macmillan, 1998.

Jackson, Frederick, *Early Days in East Africa*, London: Edward Arnold, 1930.

Jackson, Joseph, 'The Author of the Poem "If I Should Die Tonight"', *Notes and Queries*, vol. 55, no. 2, 1931.

James, T.G.H., *Howard Carter: The Path to Tutankhamun*, London: Tauris, 2001.

Jeal, Tim, *Livingstone*, London: Hutchinson, 1973.

Jebb, Mrs, *A Strange Career: The Life and Adventures of John Gladwyn Jebb*, Edinburgh: Blackwood, 1894.

Jenkins, Roy, *Gladstone*, London: Papermac, 1996.

Jeppe, Fred, *Transvaal Book Almanac and Directory for 1877*, reprint, Pretoria: State Library, 1976.

Johns, Ayresome, *'She' and 'Jess': The Great Plagiarism Debate*, London: Ferret Fantasy privately published, 1997.

Johnson, John J., *Going Forth by Night*, London: Jurassic, 2013.

Jones, Huw M., *A Biographical Register of Swaziland to 1902*, Pietermaritzburg: University of Natal Press, 1993.

Jones, Huw, *The Boiling Cauldron: Utrecht District and the Anglo-Zulu War, 1879*, Bisley, Gloucestershire: Shermershill, 2006.

Jung, C.G., *Memories, Dreams, Reflections*, London: Fontana, 1993.

Katz, Wendy R., *Rider Haggard and the Fiction of Empire*, Cambridge: CUP, 1987.

Kemp, Sandra, Charlotte Mitchell and David Trotter (eds.), *Edwardian Fiction: An Oxford Companion*, Oxford: OUP, 1997.

Kemper, Steve, *A Splendid Savage: The Restless Life of Frederick Russell Burnham*, New York: Norton, 2015.

King, Marina, *Sunrise to Evening Star: My Seventy Years in South Africa*, London: Harrap, 1938.

Kipling, Rudyard, *The Irish Guards in the Great War: The Second Battalion*, reprint, Stroud: History Press, 1997.

Kipling, Rudyard, *Something of Myself*, London: Macmillan, 1981.

Knight, Ian, *The Anatomy of the Zulu Army from Shaka to Cetshwayo, 1818–1879*, London: Greenhill Books, 1995.

Knight, Ian, *Brave Men's Blood: The Epic of the Zulu War, 1879*, London: Greenhill Books, 1990.

Knight, Ian, *Great Zulu Battles*, London: Arms and Armour, 1998.

Knight, Ian, *With His Face to the Foe: The Life and Death of Louis Napoleon, the Prince Imperial, Zululand, 1879*, Stroud: History Press, 2001.

Knight, Ian, *Zulu Rising: The Epic Story of iSandlwana and Rorke's Drift*, London: Macmillan, 2010.

Kollar, Rene, *A Foreign and Wicked Institution? The Campaign against Convents in Victorian England*, Cambridge: James Clarke, 2011.

Koopman, Adrian, *Zulu Names*, Pietermaritzburg: University of Natal Press, 2002.

Kotzé, John, *Biographical Memoirs and Reminiscences*, Cape Town: Maskew Miller, [1934].

Kotzé, John, *Cases Decided in the High Court of the Transvaal Province Reported by J.G. Kotzé, July 1877 to June 1881*, Pretoria: John Keith, 1885.

Krige, E.J. and J.D. Krige, *The Realm of the Rain Queen: A Study of the Pattern of Lovedu Society*, London: OUP, 1943.

Laband, John, *The Eight Zulu Kings: From Shaka to Goodwill Zwelithini*, Johannesburg: Jonathan Ball, 2018.

Laband, John, *Rope of Sand: The Rise and Fall of the Zulu Kingdom in the Nineteenth Century*, Johannesburg: Jonathan Ball, 1995.

Laband, John, *The Transvaal Rebellion: The First Boer War, 1880–1881*, Harlow: Pearson Longman, 2005.

Laband, John, *Zulu Warriors: The Battle for the South African Frontier*, London: Yale University Press, 2014.

Laband, John and Paul Thompson, *The Illustrated Guide to the Anglo-Zulu War*, Pietermaritzburg: University of KwaZulu-Natal Press, 2004.

Lang, Andrew, *New Collected Rhymes*, London: Longmans, 1905.

Lang, Andrew, *The True Story Book*, London: Longmans, 1900.

Lewsen, Phyllis, 'Olive Schreiner: Selected Documents', *Brenthurst Archives*, vol. 1, no. 1, 1994.

Liebenberg-Barkhuizen, Estelle Juliana, 'The Iconography of the "Indigene" in Mary Stainbank's Sculpture c.1920–1940', PhD thesis, University of South Africa, 2001.

Lock, Ron and Peter Quantrill (eds.), *Zulu Frontiersman: Major C.G. Dennison*, London: Frontline Books, 2008.

Longford, Elizabeth, *Jameson's Raid*, Jonathan Ball, Johannesburg, 2012.

BIBLIOGRAPHY

Luckhurst, Roger, *The Mummy's Curse: The True History of a Dark Fantasy*, Oxford: OUP, 2012.

Lugg, H.C., *Historic Natal and Zululand*, Pietermaritzburg: Shuter and Shooter, 1949.

Lycett, Andrew, *Conan Doyle: The Man Who Created Sherlock Holmes*, London: Phoenix, 2008.

Lycett, Andrew, *Rudyard Kipling*, London: Phoenix, 2000.

Mackenzie, W.D., *John Mackenzie: South African Missionary and Statesman*, London: Hodder and Stoughton, 1902.

Mackeurtan, Graham, *The Cradle Days of Natal*, London: Longmans, 1930; reprint, Durban: T.W. Griggs, 1972.

Maddox, Brenda, *George's Ghosts: A New Life of W.B. Yeats*, London: Picador, 2000.

Main, Mike and Tom Huffman, *Palaces of Stone: Uncovering Ancient Southern African Kingdoms*, Cape Town: Struik, 2021.

Manthorpe, Victoria, *Children of the Empire: The Victorian Haggards*, London: Gollancz, 1996.

Manthorpe, Victoria, *Lilias Rider Haggard: Countrywoman*, Cromer: Poppyland, 2015.

Martin, Andrew, *Ghoul Britannia: Notes from a Haunted Isle*, London: Short Books, 2009.

Martin, Bruno and Michael Cottrell (eds.), *The Natal Old Main Line from Durban to Pietermaritzburg*, Montclair: KwaZulu-Natal Railway History Society, 2015.

Martins, Susanna Wade, *Norfolk: A Changing Countryside, 1780–1914*, Chichester: Phillimore, 1988.

Martins, Susanna Wade, *A History of Norfolk*, Chichester: Phillimore, 1997.

Mason, Michael, *The Making of Victorian Sexuality*, Oxford: OUP, 1994.

McClendon, Thomas V., *White Chief, Black Lords: Shepstone and the Colonial State in Natal, South Africa, 1845–1878*, New York: University of Rochester Press, 2010.

McLintock, Anne, *Imperial Leather*, London: Routledge, 1995.

Meredith, Martin, *Diamonds, Gold and War: The Making of South Africa*, London: Simon and Schuster, 2008.

Monsman, Gerald, *Rider Haggard on the Imperial Frontier*, Greensboro, NC: ELT Press, 2006.

Morfey, Wallace Mortimer, 'Guts Sanderson', *The Ipswichian*, 1990.

Morrell, Robert, *From Boys to Gentlemen: Settler Masculinity in Colonial Natal 1880–1920*, Pretoria: University of South Africa, 2001.

Morris, Jan, *Farewell the Trumpets: An Imperial Retreat*, London: Faber, 2012.

Mourby, Adrian, *Rooms with a View: The Secret Life of Great Hotels*, London: Icon, 2017.

The Natal Who's Who, Durban: Natal Who's Who, 1906.

Newsome, David, *The Edge of Paradise: A.C. Benson the Diarist*, Chicago: University of Chicago Press, 1980.

Nixon, John, *The Complete Story of the Transvaal*, reprint, Cape Town: Struik, 1972 [1885].

Nowell-Smith, Simon, *The House of Cassell*, London: Cassell, 1958.

Oates, Frank, *Matabele Land and the Victoria Falls*, ed. C.G. Oates, London: Kegan and Paul, 1881; reprint, Salisbury, Rhodesia: Pioneer Head, 1971.

BIBLIOGRAPHY

O'Brien, Jim, 'Rider Haggard and the Brothers Little', *Rider Haggard Society Journal*, no. 124, November 2017.

O'Donnell, E., *Haunted Churches*, London: Quality Press, 1939.

Otte, T.G., *The Foreign Office Mind: The Making of British Foreign Policy, 1865–1914*, Cambridge: CUP, 2011.

Owen, Alex, *The Darkened Room: Women, Power and Spiritualism in Late Victorian England*, Philadelphia: University of Pennsylvania Press, 1990.

Pakenham, Thomas, *The Boer War*, London: Abacus, 1995.

Pakenham, Thomas, *The Scramble for Africa*, London: Abacus, 2005.

Parris, Matthew, *Great Parliamentary Scandals: Four Centuries of Calumny, Smear and Innuendo*, London: Robson Books, 1997.

Parsons, Neil, *Black and White Bioscope: Making Movies in Africa, 1899–1925*, Pretoria: Protea, 2018.

Pearson, Hesketh, *The Last Actor Managers*, London: White Lion, 1974.

Perry, P.J., *British Agriculture, 1875–1915*, London: Methuen, 1973.

Plaut, Martin, *Promise and Despair: The First Struggle for a Non-Racial South Africa*, Johannesburg: Jacana, 2016.

Pocock, Tom, *Rider Haggard and the Lost Empire*, London: Weidenfeld and Nicholson, 1993.

Pritchett, V.S., 'Haggard Still Riding', *New Statesman*, 27 August 1960.

Reese, Trevor R., *The History of the Royal Commonwealth Society, 1868–1968*, Oxford: OUP, 1968.

Reeves, Richard, *The Sexual Imperative in the Novels of Sir Henry Rider Haggard*, London: Anthem Press, 2018.

Roberts, Andrew, *Salisbury: Victorian Titan*, London: Weidenfeld and Nicholson, 1999.

Roberts, Brian, *Ladies of the Veld*, London: John Murray, 1965.

Robinson, Ronald and John Gallagher, with Alice Denny, *Africa and the Victorians: The Official Mind of Imperialism*, London: Macmillan, 1972.

Rotberg, Robert I., *The Founder*, Johannesburg: Jonathan Ball, 2002.

Rotberg, Robert, *Joseph Thomson and the Exploration of Africa*, London: Chatto and Windus, 1971.

Sandeman, E.F., *Eight Months in an Ox-Waggon*, reprint, Johannesburg: Africana Book Society, 1975 [1880].

Sanderson, John, *Memoranda of a Trading Trip into the Orange River (Sovereignty) Free State, and the Country of the Transvaal Boers*, reprint, Pretoria: State Library, 1981.

Saunders, Christopher, and Southey, Nicholas, *A Dictionary of South African History*, David Philip, Cape Town, 1998.

Schreiner, Olive, *My Other Self: The Letters of Olive Schreiner and Havelock Ellis, 1884–1920*, ed. Yaffa Claire Draznin, New York: Peter Lang, 1992.

Scott, J.E., *A Bibliography of the Works of Sir Henry Rider Haggard, 1856–1925*, Bishop's Stortford: Elkin Mathews, 1947.

Scott, J.E., 'Hatchers-Out of Tales', *New Colophon*, part IV, October 1948; reprint, *Haggard Journal*, no. 64, Easter 2002.

BIBLIOGRAPHY

Selous, Frederick Courtney, *A Hunter's Wanderings in South Africa*, London: Bentley, 1881.

Senior, John, 'Spirituality in the Fiction of Henry Rider Haggard', PhD thesis, Rhodes University, 2003.

Seymour, Miranda, *A Ring of Conspirators: Henry James and His Literary Circle, 1895–1915*, London: Scribner, 2004.

Shephard, Ben, *Kitty and the Prince*, Johannesburg: Jonathan Ball, 2003.

Siemens, Lloyd, *The Critical Reception of Sir Henry Rider Haggard: An Annotated Bibliography 1882–1991*, English Literature in Transition 1880–1920, Special Series no. 5, 1991, Greensboro: University of North Carolina, 1991.

Simpson, Thula, *History of South Africa: From 1902 to the Present*, Johannesburg: Penguin, 2021.

Singleton, Brian, *Oscar Asche: Orientalism, and British Musical Comedy*, Westport, CN: Praeger, 2004.

Spencer, Shelagh O'Byrne, *British Settlers in Natal: A Biographical Register*, vol. 8, Pietermaritzburg: University of KwaZulu-Natal Press, 2016.

Steyn, Richard, *Louis Botha: A Man Apart*, Johannesburg: Jonathan Ball, 2018.

Stiebel, Lindy, *Imagining Africa: Landscape in H. Rider Haggard's African Romances*, Westport: Greenwood Press, 2001.

Stiebel, Lindy, *Lives of Victorian Literary Figures, Part VII , Volume 2, Joseph Conrad, H. Rider Haggard and Rudyard Kipling by their contemporaries*, Routledge, London, 2009.

Struben, H.W., *Recollections and Adventures*, Cape Town: Maskew Miller, 1920.

Stuart, James, *A History of the Zulu Rebellion, 1906*, London: Macmillan, 1913; reprint, New York: Negro Universities Press, 1969.

Sutherland, John, *Lives of the Novelists: A History of Fiction in 294 Lives*, London: Profile, 2013.

Sutherland, John, *The Longman Companion to Victorian Fiction*, Harlow: Longman, 1988.

Swart, Sandra, *Riding High: Horses, Humans and History in South Africa*, Johannesburg: Wits University Press, 2010.

Tabler, Edward C. (ed.), *Trade and Travel in Barotseland: The Diaries of George Westbeech and Captain Norman Macleod*, Berkeley: University of California Press, 1963.

Taylor, Stephen, *The Mighty Nimrod: A Life of Frederick Courtenay Selous, African Hunter and Adventurer, 1851–1917*, London: Collins, 1989.

Theron, Bridget, 'Theophilus Shepstone and the Transvaal Colony, 1877–1879', *Kleio*, no. 34, 2002.

Theron-Bushell, Bridget Mary, 'Puppet on an Imperial String? Owen Lanyon in South Africa, 1875–1880', PhD thesis, University of South Africa, 2002.

Thompson, P.S., *An Historical Atlas of the Zulu Rebellion of 1906*, Howick: Brevitas, 2001.

Thompson, P.S., *The Natal Native Contingent in the Anglo-Zulu War*, Howick: Brevitas, 1997.

Thomson, J.B., *Joseph Thomson: African Explorer*, London: *Sampson Low, 1896.*

Thomson, Joseph, *Through Masai Land*, London: Sampson Low, 1884.

BIBLIOGRAPHY

Thwaite, Ann, *Edmund Gosse: A Literary Landscape, 1849–1928*, London: Secker and Warburg, 1984.

Tomalin, Claire, *Thomas Hardy: The Time-Torn Man*, London: Penguin, 2006.

Torlage, Gilbert, 'Impi Yaba Ntwana: The War of the Children', *Soldiers of the Queen*, no. 74, September 1993.

Trollope, Anthony, *South Africa*, 2 vols., reprint, Manzini: Bok Books, 1987.

Tuchman, Barbara, *The Proud Tower*, London: Papermac, 1997.

Tyrrell, Barbara, *Her African Quest*, Cape Town: Lindlife, 1996.

Uys, C.J., *In the Era of Shepstone*, Lovedale: Lovedale Press, 1933.

Vinson, Steve, 'They-Who-Must-Be-Obeyed: Arsake, Rhadopis and Tabubu; Ihweret and Charikleia', *Comparative Literature Studies*, vol. 45, no. 3, 2008.

Vogel, Joseph O., 'Merensky and Nachtigal in Southern Africa: A Contemporary Source for King Solomon's Mines', *Journal of African Travel Writing*, no. 4, 1998.

Walker, Cheryl (ed.), *Women and Gender in Southern Africa to 1945*, Cape Town: David Philip, 1990.

Waller, Phillip, *Writers, Readers, and Reputations: Literary Life in Britain, 1870–1918*, Oxford: OUP, 2008.

Webb, C. de B. and J.B. Wright (eds.), *The James Stuart Archive of Recorded Oral Evidence Relating to the History of the Zulu and Neighbouring Peoples*, 6 vols., Pietermaritzburg: University of KwaZulu-Natal Press, 1976, 1979, 1982, 1986, 2001, 2014.

Weir, Jennifer and Norman Etherington, 'Shepstone in Love: The Other Victorian in an African Colonial Administrator', in *Orb and Sceptre: Studies on British Imperialism and Its Legacies, in Honour of Norman Etherington*, ed. Peter Limb, Melbourne: Monash University ePress, 2008, DOI: 10.2104/os080002.

Whatmore, Denys Edwin, *H. Rider Haggard: A Bibliography*, London: Mansell, 1987.

Wildenboer, Liezl, 'For a Few Dollars More: Overcharging and Misconduct in the Legal Profession of the Zuid-Afrikaansche Republiek', *De Jure* (Pretoria), vol. 44, no. 2, 2011.

Wildenboer, Liezl, 'The Judicial Officers of the Transvaal High Court, 1877–1881', *Fundmina*, vol. 25, no. 2, 2019.

Wills, W.A. and L.T. Collingridge, *The Downfall of Lobengula*, London: Simpkin, Marshall, Hamilton and Kent, 1894; reprint, Bulawayo: Books of Rhodesia, 1971.

Wilmot, Alexander, *Monomotapa (Rhodesia), Its Monuments, and its History from the most Ancient Times to the present Century*, Fisher Unwin, London, 1896.

Wilson, A.N., *After the Victorians*, London: Arrow, 2006.

Wilson, A.N., *The Elizabethans*, London: Arrow, 2012.

Wilson, A.N., *Victoria*, London: Atlantic, 2015.

Wilson, A.N., *The Victorians*, London: Arrow Books, 2003.

Wilson, Colin, *The Occult*, London: Granada, 1981.

Wolseley, Sir Garnet, *Sir Garnet Wolseley's South African Diaries (Natal), 1875*, ed. Adrian Preston, Cape Town: Balkema, 1971.

Wolseley, Sir Garnet, *Sir Garnet Wolseley's South African Journal, 1879–1880*, ed. Adrian Preston, Cape Town: Balkema, 1973.

BIBLIOGRAPHY

Wood, Arthur J., *Natal Past and Present: A History of the Natal Mounted Police 1874–1894 and the Natal Police 1894–1913*, Ilfracombe: Stockwell, 1961.

Wylie, Dan, *Death and Compassion: The Elephant in Southern African Literature*, Johannesburg: Wits University Press, 2018.

Wylie, Dan, *Myth of Iron: Shaka in History*, Pietermaritzburg: University of KwaZulu-Natal Press, 2006.

Wylie, Dan, *Savage Delight: White Myths of Shaka*, Pietermaritzburg: University of Natal Press, 2000.

Zulli, Tania, *Colonial Transitions: Literature and Culture in the Later Victorian Age*, Bern: Peter Lang, 2011.

Zulli, Tania (ed.), *She: Explorations into a Romance*, Rome: Aracne, 2009.

INDEX

HRH is Henry Rider Haggard. This index is filed word by word

Aagaard (Denmark) 358

Abbey Theatre (Dublin) 355–356

Acours, Edmund (fictional character) 352

Adair, Molly 451

Adams, Charles 400

Adcock, Samuel 20, 246

Addison, Richard 387

African National Congress (ANC) 377, 405

African Review 302, 303–304, 305, 306, 307, 311, 552 n.11, 552 n.23

The After-War Settlement and Employment of Ex-Servicemen (1916) 429–430

Agricultural Show (Pietermaritzburg) 70, 491 n.55

Agricultural Wages Board 437

Aisne (third battle) 440, 594 n.74

Alciphron (Thomas Moore) 259, 260

Alexandra Park (Pietermaritzburg) 389

Allan and the Holy Flower (1915) 364, 411, 569 n.34

Allan and the Ice Gods (1927) 446, 595 n.7

Allan Quatermain (1887) 1, 83, 93, 218, 225–228, 232, 234, 239, 246, 249, 261, 281, 364, 413, 414, 473, 504 n.28, 593 n.38

Allan's Wife (1889) 28, 275–276, 520 n.124

Allison, James 71

Alphonse (fictional character) 226, 227, 228

Alston (fictional character) 125, 204, 205, 505 n.65

Amahagger (fictional people) 237

amakholwa (Christian Africans) 70–71

Amenartas (fictional character) 236, 237, 239, 348

Amery, Leo 449

Amherst Collection 599 n.1

Amor, Nesta (fictional character) 270–271

Amyand family 15–16, 23, 128, 477 n.20

The Ancient Allan (1920) 436, 588 n.80

Anglo-African Writers Club 304–305

Anglo-Boer War (first) 170–174

Anglo-Boer War (second) 323–324, 327–328, 383–384, 385

Anglo-Pedi wars 119–120, 145–146

Anglo-Zulu War 134–138, 144–145, 146

Anti-Bolshevik (later Liberty) League 447–448

Archer, Francis 313

Archer, Francis Bradley 125, 313, 314, 351, 565 n.35

Archer, Geoffrey 313, 555 n.93

Archer, Lily *see* Jackson, Mary Elizabeth (Lilly)

Archer, William 412

Armstrong, Benjamin 17–18, 21, 24

Asche, Lily (née Brayton) 371–372, 412

Asche, Oscar 12, 371–372, 373, 411, 412, 413

Asquith, Herbert H. 361, 568 n.4

Atene (fictional character) 348, 349

L'Atlantide (Pierre Benoit, *Queen of Atlantis*) 450, 451

Authors' Club 600 n.48

Averill, Alfred 426–427

Ayesha (1905) 347–349

Ayesha (fictional character, She-Who-Must-Be-Obeyed) 1, 2, 22, 25, 230, 232, 235, 237, 238, 241, 242, 243, 244, 245, 270, 348–349, 434, 457, 543 n.57

Aylward, Alfred 74, 119, 174, 518 n.57

Ayrton, Edward Russell 370, 571 n.81

Aziel (fictional character) 395

Bailey, Abe 378–379, 574 n.24

Bainbrigge, Philip T. 433, 438, 453

Baines, Thomas 218, 219

Baker, Herbert 378, 579 n.73

Baleka 280

Balestier, Beatty 350

Balfour, Arthur 232, 338, 343, 353

Balfour, Eustace 250

Bara, Theda 586 n.44

Barber, Agnes Marion (Aggie) *see* Haggard, Agnes Marion

Barber, Fairless 149, 522 n.38

Barber, Mabel 149

Barber, Margaret (*pseud.* Michael Fairless) 149, 512 n.23

Barber, Maria 149, 522 n.38

Barber, William 269

Barker, Anne 56–59, 61, 62, 70, 71, 76, 88, 138, 147, 152

Barker, Will 413

Barkly, Henry 46–47, 99, 485 n.9

Barr, Robert 261

Barrie, J.M. (*pseud.* Gavin Ogilvy) 227–228, 243, 274

Bastin (fictional character) 308

Bateman, Alfred 409, 416, 568 n.11, 573 n.6

Bateman's (Sussex) 349–350

Battle of the Somme (film) 432, 592 n.9

Bax-Ironside, Henry 447

Baynes, Joseph 389

Bazett family 477 n.2

Beaconsfield, *Lord* (Benjamin Disraeli) 145

Beatrice (1890) 267–269, 451, 542 n.50; *see also The Stronger Passion*

Beaumont, Wentworth 295

Beaumont, William 45, 52, 53, 54, 71–72, 161, 171, 173, 424

Bechuanaland 393, 579 n.65

Beerbohm, Max 250

Bell, Francis 427

Bell, John Keble (*pseud.* Chicot, Keble Howard) 304, 552 n.20

Bell, Moberly 324, 327

Bell, Robert 115, 120, 502 n.72

Belshazzar (1930) 464, 467

Benson, Arthur Christopher 427, 591 n.59 & n.60

Benson, E.F. & R.H. 591 n.59

Bent, J. Theodore 394, 395, 527 n.77

Bernard, *Mr* 33

Berwick, John *see* Haggard, Agnes Marion

Besant, Walter 233, 241, 250, 251, 283, 307, 531 n.56, 597 n.64, 600 n.48

Bessie (fictional character) 229, 230

Bhambatha Rebellion (1906) 350–351, 365, 366, 402, 565 n.28

Bingham, Effie (fictional character) 267, 268

Bingham, Geoffrey (fictional character) 267, 268, 451

Bingham, Honoria (fictional character) 267, 268

black Britons 412, 585 n.31, 586 n.32

Blackett, Arthur 197

Blackett, Spencer 275, 542 n.51

Blake, Fred John 157, 180, 182

Blake, Isobel (fictional character) 438

Blavatsky, Helena Petrova 234, 348

Blomefield, Catherine (née Arnison) 200, 392

Blomefield, George 20

Blomefield, George (George Mayes) 21, 127, 150, 152, 161, 163, 164, 176, 177, 182, 193, 200, 392

Blowers, Arthur 368

Blythe, Betty 601 n.71

Bob (dog) 337, 338, 359

Boer-Pedi war (first Sekhukhune war) 72, 73–74, 91

Bolton, Thomas 15

Bonar Law, Andrew 418, 419, 433

Booth, William 330, 338, 357, 564 n.87

Borthwick, Alice 252

Botha, Annie 380–381, 422

Botha, Louis 378, 422–423, 574 n.41

Botmar, Vrou (fictional character) 321

Botshabelo (Transvaal) 93, 111, 226, 497 n.61

'Bottles' (rejected book manuscript) 206, 208, 525 n.134

Bousfield, Charlotte 133

Bousfield, Henry Brougham 133, 144, 507 n.4

Bower, Arthur de Courcy 447, 448

Bowles, Thomas Gibson (Jehu Junior) 34–35, 242–243

Bowring, Edgar Rennie 385, 393, 394, 570 n.49, 573 n.6

Boyd, Edward 280

Bozard, Lily (fictional character) 291, 292

Bradenham Hall (Norfolk) 2, 14–15, 18, 22, 187, 198, 276–277, 299, 425–426, 432, 438–439, 440–441, 456–457, 478 n.39 & n.40

Bradstreet, Maud 508 n.22, 518 n.65

Bradstreet, Robert 137, 508 n.22

Brand, Johannes 74, 178

Brayton, Lily see Asche, Lily

Brede Place (Sussex) 355, 566 n.68

Brenon, Herbert 542 n.50

The Brethren (1904) 326

Bridges, Robert 250

Bridgman, Alfred 573 n.6

British Empire 362, 600 n.42

British Empire Exhibition (1924 & 1925) 463–464

British South Africa Company (BSAC) 302, 303, 306, 309, 393, 422

Britten, James 292–293

Brooke, Edward 77, 102, 122

Brooks, Thomas Marwick 63

Broome, Frederick 45, 52, 56–57, 62, 70, 76, 88, 130, 138, 147, 488 n.77, 511 n.6

Browne, Wilfred Gore 382

Bruce, Joseph 585 n.31

Brugsch, Heinrich Karl 252

Brunner, Cornelia 242

Buddhism 234, 235

Budge, Ernest Wallace 354, 538 n.42

Bührmann, Hendrik Theodorus 113

Bulawayo (Rhodesia) 393

Buller, Redvers 176, 323, 327, 385

Bulwer, Henry 2, 11, 40–41, 46–47, 51–52, 53, 58, 59, 63, 64, 65, 67, 69, 75–77, 80, 103, 110, 135, 145, 190, 250, 254, 295, 296, 364, 385

Bulwer, William 150

Burch, Mr 435

Burgers, Mary 108

Burgers, Thomas François 73, 74, 80, 87, 90, 91, 100, 101, 108, 129, 504 n.27

Burnham, Blanche 307, 308, 340

Burnham, Bruce 340

Burnham, Frederick 307, 308, 340, 553 n.47 & n.52

Burnham, Nada 307–308

Burnham, Roderick 340

Buskes, Gerhardus Hendricus 114, 231–232, 531 n.47

Buxton, Sydney Charles 421–422, 424

Caine, Thomas Henry Hall 415–416, 587
  n.67
Caithness, *Lady* (Marie Sinclair) 36, 483
  n.80
Caldwell, Mary Eleanor 250, 254
A Call to Arms: To the Men of East Anglia
  (1914) 414
Calvert, Percy 460, 461
Calvert, Ralph 460, 462
Campbell, Donald 393, 394, 570 n.49, 573
  n.6
Campbell-Bannerman, Henry 353
Canada 410
Cango Caves (South Africa) 381, 526 n.50,
  575 n.50
Cannell, Cameron Corlett 302, 552 n.11
Cape Frontier War (ninth) 134
Capernaum (tortoise) 327
Caresfoot, Angela (fictional character) 43,
  194, 195, 196, 198, 199, 200, 260, 413
Caresfoot, George (fictional character) 20,
  199, 246
Carmichael, J.G.H. 550 n.63
Carnarvon, *Lord* (George Herbert) 50–51,
  56, 73, 74, 75, 93, 99, 110, 122, 134,
  192, 459–460
Carr, Mildred (Muriel, fictional character)
  194, 195, 197, 198–199
Carr, William 417, 468
Carson, Stella (fictional character) 28, 275,
  276, 336
Carter, Hester 407, 424
Carter, Howard 22, 334, 459, 460, 461,
  464, 479 n.79, 561 n.12, 599 n.1
Carter, Samuel 22, 223, 334
Carter, Thomas 584 n.79
Carter, William 407, 424, 584 n.79
Cassell (publisher) 208–210, 525 n.20
Castle, Egerton 250, 453
Caygill, Ranson 340

Celliers, Jan 129
Ceswick, Eva (fictional character) 39, 103,
  124, 125, 127, 204, 205, 234
Cetewayo and his White Neighbours (1882,
  1888; *The Last Boer War*, 1899) 4, 180,
  182–183, 188–192, 202, 282, 323, 390,
  391, 521 n.36
Cetshwayo kaMpande 7–8, 10, 49–50,
  74–75, 77, 100, 110, 115–116, 135,
  145, 146, 181, 182, 189, 190, 191,
  192–193, 201–202, 398–399, 400,
  404, 524 n.105, 581 n.18, 583 n.59
Ceylon 370
Chamberlain, Joseph 309, 310, 322, 323,
  362
Chambers, C. Haddon 263
charity books 336, 415, 562 n.34
Charmion (fictional character) 265
Charrington, Harold 307, 553 n.42
Chelmsford, *Lord* (Frederic Thesiger) 116,
  119, 130, 135, 137, 145
Cheyne, Godfrey (nephew of HRH) 289
Cheyne, Reginald (son-in-law of HRH)
  367, 368, 414–415, 433, 436, 442,
  470–471
Cheyne, Reginald (grandson of HRH)
  368
Cheyne, Rider (grandson of HRH) 368
Child of Storm (1913) 11, 281, 364–365,
  366, 367–368, 371, 397, 403, 572 n.95;
  see also Mameena
Child of the Ocean (Ronald Ross) 454, 598
  n.74
Chris, Edwin 231
Christian, Charles 325
Christian, Gladys (née Jebb) 325, 326
Christian, Percy 325
Christian Africans *see* amakholwa
Church of the Vow (Pietermaritzburg)
  387, 577 n.25
Churchill, Randolph 192
Churchill, Winston 228, 350–351, 361,

424, 449–450, 455–456, 559 n.90, 566
n.68

circulating libraries 233

Clarke, Marshall 77, 91, 93–94, 97, 98,
112, 119, 146, 177, 321, 322, 398, 473,
518 n.76, 581 n.13

Clavering, Eve (fictional character) 352

Cleopatra (1889) 249, 258, 263, 264–266,
276, 354, 541 n.21, 544 n.107

Clifford, Lucy 256, 538 n.63

The Cloak that I Left (Lilias Haggard,
1951) 3, 68, 69

Cloete, Henry (Hendrik) 144, 510 n.82,
513 n.43

Cobalt mine 94, 497 n.66

Cochrane, Arthur C. (Macumazahn) 122,
123–124, 125, 126, 141, 142, 143, 144,
152, 153, 160–162, 163, 164, 170, 171,
176, 177, 178, 180, 182, 193, 200, 211,
311, 312, 328–329, 367, 390, 420,
437–438, 453, 456, 467–468, 508 n.14,
513 n.43, 554 n.74, 597 n.65

Coetzee, D.R.G. 112

Coetzee, Hans (fictional character) 230

Coghill, Nevill 70, 109, 138, 403, 583 n.56

Colenso, Frances (Fanny) 189, 217

Colenso, Harriette 581 n.13

Colenso, John 50, 51, 54, 63, 135, 181–
182, 189, 489 n.16, 490 n.24, 577 n.28

Coley, Ralph (fictional character) 271

Colley, Edith 169, 295

Colley, George Pomeroy 163, 169, 171,
172, 173, 174, 389, 515 n.129

Collingridge, Leonard Thomas 306, 552
n.11

Collins, Robert Martin 371

Collins, Wilkie 233, 241, 531 n.56

*Colonel Quaritch, V.C.: A Tale of Country
Life* (1888) 19, 246–247, 249, 263,
264, 267

Colonial Conference (1907) 344–345

Colton, William Robert 592 n.16

Colvin, Sidney 250

confederation of southern Africa 46,
50–51, 73, 90, 91, 134, 376

Cook, Florence 36, 483 n.92

Cook, Joseph 464

Cooke, George A. 585 n.27

Cooper, Henry William Alexander 130,
133, 506 n.111

Copeland shipwreck 273

Corbett, A.R. Uvedale 420, 423, 424, 429,
589 n.108, 590 n.30

Corelli, Marie 268, 542 n.39, 549 n.30

Cowasjee, Cursetjee 14

Cowley, Richard 71

Cox, William 58, 64, 488 n.85

Crane, Dennis 442

Crane, Stephen 355

Croft, Silas (fictional character) 229, 230

Cromwell, Oliver 356

Cullinan, Thomas 378, 574 n.27

Cunynghame, Arthur 70, 109, 116

Curtis, George (fictional character) 211,
215

Curtis, Henry (fictional character)
211–212, 213, 214, 215, 219, 220, 225,
227, 266

Curzon, George 261, 420, 463, 469, 602
n.89

D'Anethan, Albert (brother-in-law of
HRH) 555 n.89, 558 n.79

Daudet, Alphonse 297

David (dragoman) 326

Dawn (1884, adapted as *Devil Caresfoot*)
2, 39, 43, 127–128, 194–200, 209,
221–222, 246, 260, 263, 264, 267, 321,
354, 413, 475 n.5, 523 n.83

The Days of My Life (1926) 3, 4, 359,
367

De Cordova, Leander 451

De Cressi, Hugh (fictional character) 352

De la Molle, Ida (fictional character) 246

De la Molle, Squire (fictional character) 19, 246

De Villiers, Henry 178

De Villiers, Jacob 390

Deakin, Alfred 345

Deane, Henry Bargrave 207

Defence of the Realm Act (1914) 417

Deirdre of the Sorrows (J.M. Synge) 355–356

Delysia, Alice 413

Denmark 330, 353, 358

Devant, David 412, 585 n.27

Devene, Lady (fictional character) 335

Diary of an African Journey (2000) 4, 190–191, 376

Dick (fictional character) 335

Dick, Grey (fictional character) 352

Dickens, Charles 293

Didlington Hall (Norfolk) 21–22, 334, 479 n.79

Dingane kaSenzangakhona 7, 47, 48, 280, 281, 476 n.3

Dinuzulu ka Cetshwayo 181, 202

Ditchingham House (Norfolk) 153–155, 207, 254, 255, 263, 264, 284, 285, 291, 292–294, 312, 317–318, 331, 352, 425, 426, 431–432, 440, 451, 452, 456, 458, 547 n.45

Dixie, Alexander Beaumont Churchill 179

Dixie, Florence 179, 181–182, 189, 221–222, 268, 519 n.98

Dolman, Frederick 294

Dominions Royal Commission (1914) 4, 218, 361, 363, 366–367, 370–371, 372–373, 377–383, 385–390, 391–392, 409–411, 416, 418, 428, 429, 433, 588 n.90, 592 n.18

Doro, Marie 542 n.50, 597 n.46

Dorothy (fictional character) 204, 205

Douglas, *Captain* 179

Douglas, Alfred 251, 295

Doveton, Bazett (grandfather of HRH) 13, 14

Doveton, Bazett (uncle of HRH) 13

Doveton, Caroline (aunt of HRH) 13, 14

Doveton, Ellen Maria (née Bond, great-grandmother of HRH) 16

Doveton, Sarah (grandmother of HRH) 13, 14

Doveton family 477 n.2

Doyle, Arthur Conan 357, 452, 465, 597 n.57

Dr Therne (1898) 320–321

Drakensberg 64

Du Toit, Michiel 384

Dube, John Langalibalele 4, 283–284, 377, 405–406, 583 n.68

Dunn, John 9, 10–11, 156, 476 n.9

Durban 397, 404

Durnford, Anthony 50, 137, 403, 486 n.24, 508 n.24

Dutt, William 337, 562 n.34

Earle, John 425

East African Committee 463, 465

East Coast (tick) Fever 387, 389, 576 n.16

Edendale (Pietermaritzburg) 71

Edith (fictional character) 335

Edwards, G. Maitland 447, 448

Edwards, H.M. 399, 402

Egypt 251, 460

Einstein, Albert 445

Elissa (fictional character) 395

Elissa, or, the Doom of Zimbabwe (1906) 395, 580 n.81

Elliott, J.M. 168–169, 230

Ellis, Havelock 221–222

Ellison-Macartney, William 425

Elwes, Robert 169, 171, 179, 517 n.38

Emigration Board 433

'The Empire and its Land' (incomplete) 590 n.30

Empire Land Settlement Committee 418, 421–429, 434, 442, 449, 455

Empress Dowager Victoria 277, 296

England, rural 318, 328–330, 338, 353, 556 n.6 & n.7, 557 n.25

The Epicurean (Thomas Moore, 1827) 260

Epstein, Jacob 454

Eric (fictional character) 336

Eric Brighteyes (1891) 273–274, 277, 280, 282, 294, 296, 336

Ernle, *Lord* (Rowland Prothero) 449

Eshowe (Zululand) 398–399, 581 n.9

Essex, Edward 138, 171, 172, 174, 175, 184, 205, 404, 508 n.30

Evans, John 239–240

Evans, Maurice 406

Evening Hours (Anne Barker) 61–63

Everest Expedition (1921) 599 n.3

Every, John (fictional character) 266

evolutionary theory 235

Eyre, Sophie 540 n.4

Fair Margaret (1907) 335

Fairlie, William Frederic 71

Fannin, John Eustace 83

A Farmer's Year (1899) 269, 318–320, 330

Farrer, John 404

Fawcett, Percy Harrison 550 n.63

Ferreira, Ignatius 74, 91, 94, 95, 96, 97, 98, 99, 145, 146, 498 n.90, 511 n.98

Finished (1917) 101, 364, 373, 398, 402, 436, 498 n.92, 504 n.27, 576 n.71, 582 n.39 & n.54

FitzPatrick, Percy 322, 323

Fletcher, Alexander 393

Florent, Napoleon 585 n.31

Flower, Newman 435–436

Fockers, *Dr* 107

Fonseca, Andres de (fictional character) 291

Foote, Francis Barrington 285, 288

Ford, Ellen 107

Ford, Ethel Rider (daughter of HRH and Johanna Ford) 151, 152, 153, 155, 184, 242, 290, 391, 513 n.43

Ford, Johanna Catherine (née Lehmkuhl) 107–108, 109, 137, 152, 153, 160, 215, 229, 242, 258, 259–260, 290, 391

Ford, Lewis Peter 107–108, 109, 110, 112, 113, 114, 118, 130, 152, 160, 176, 392, 503 n.11, 578 n.56

Forster, E.M. 2

Fort Amiel (Newcastle) 162, 169, 516 n.16

Fort Burger 74

Fort Weeber 74, 91, 95, 97, 98, 119

Foster, George Eulas 570 n.49, 573 n.6

Foulata (real and fictional character) 181, 213, 214–215, 220, 281, 414, 529 n.103

Fowle, William & Fanny 159

Fox, Margaret & Kate 35

Frederick III of Germany 231

Fregelius, Stella (fictional character) 314

French, Samuel 250

Frere, Bartle 92–93, 99, 116, 126, 129, 130, 134–135, 136, 139, 141–142, 145, 167, 180, 189–190, 379, 510 n.64

Freud, Sigmund 2, 242, 534 n.31

Freyer, Peter 451

Frontier War (ninth) 116

Fry, *Lieutenant* 141

Fugitives Drift 403–404

Fuller, John Latimer 375, 573 n.7

Fynn, Henry 47, 505 n.66

Fynn, Henry Francis 201

Fynney, Frederick 49, 62, 77, 83, 135, 282

Gabangaye kaPhakade 66, 137

Gagool (Gagaoola, fictional character) 66, 183, 213, 214, 220

Galazi (fictional character) 280, 281

Gandhi, Mohandas 377, 386, 576 n.11

Garcia, Thomas de (fictional character) 291

A Gardener's Year (1905) 331

Garnett, Tom 382, 385, 573 n.6

Garrard, Flo 280

Garsingham (fictional place) 28

Garsington 28, 29, 198

The Ghost (Stephen Crane) 355, 566 n.70

The Ghost Kings (1908) 350

Ghost Mountain (Tshaneni, Zululand) 281, 545 n.17

Gibbs, Lucy 165, 169–170, 179, 184, 187

Gibson, Harriette 398

Gibson, James Young 387, 398, 399, 400, 403, 404

Gideon (interpreter) 94

Gilfillan, Edward 113

Gill, William 307, 553 n.42

Gladstone, Herbert John 380, 406, 427, 574 n.41, 575 n.42

Gladstone, William Ewart 167, 175, 176, 180, 203, 229, 251, 257, 280, 310, 552 n.28

Glynn, *Sergeant* 140–141

Good, John (fictional character) 181, 211, 212–213, 214, 215, 219, 220–221, 225, 227, 246, 266, 281, 414, 529 n.104

Gopal, Daya 368

Gordon, Charles 229

Gosse, Edmund 241, 250, 251, 283, 285, 287, 455, 465, 533 n.26, 591 n.60

Gosse, Philip 285

Gosse, Sylvia 285, 287

Government House (Pietermaritzburg) 52, 53, 55, 59, 70, 487 n.43

iziGqoza 8, 9–10

Graham, Blanche 275

Graham, Henry 28, 29

Granger, Beatrice (fictional character) 267–268, 294, 336, 542 n.33, 597 n.46

Granger, Elizabeth (fictional character) 267

Granger, Reverend (fictional character) 267

Grant, James 252

Graves, Clo 540 n.4

Gray, Robert 487 n.58

Great Trek 322

Great Zimbabwe 217–218, 245, 394–396, 527 n.77

Greenacre, Benjamin 58

Greene, Graham 5

Gregory, Augusta 356

Greiffenhagen, Maurice 293, 315, 436, 453–454

Greiffenhagen, Rider 593 n.42

Grenfell, Bernard Pine 252

Grey, Albert 341–342, 416

Griffiths, William 339

Grimwood, Herbert 412, 585 n.30

Gros, Henri Ferdinand 101, 294

Grossmith, George 554 n.76

Guatemoc (fictional character) 291

Gubbins, Charles O'Grady 175, 179, 162, 518 n.65

Gubbins, Maud (formerly Bradstreet) 175, 518 n.65

Gudmunson, Thorgrimmer 271, 272

Gudruda (fictional character) 273, 274

Guest, Ivor 353, 354

Gunn, Charles Grant Murray Somerset Seymour Stuart 129, 130

Guppy-Volckman, Agnes (Mrs Guppy) 36

Guthrie, Archibald Cowan 455

Gylderstjerne, Anders Pedersen (Andrew Ogard, Agard) 15, 358, 477 n.18

Haggard, Agnes Angela Rider (daughter of HRH) 194, 197, 207, 289, 294, 324, 333, 334, 335, 339, 340, 341, 342, 352, 362, 363, 414, 429, 432, 433, 471

Haggard, Agnes Marion (Aggie, née Barber, sister-in-law, *pseud.* John Berwick) 149, 191, 194, 196, 198, 202, 203, 207, 210,

215, 222, 229, 231, 232, 234, 239, 242, 262, 264, 268, 269, 294, 296, 314, 324, 352, 357, 425, 471, 555 n.101, 565 n.45, 602 n.101

Haggard, Alfred Hinuber (brother of HRH) 17, 29, 32, 33, 299, 303, 304, 426, 552 n.16

Haggard, Alice Geraldine (née Schalch, sister-in-law of HRH) 288

Haggard, Andrew (nephew of HRH) 19, 426

Haggard, Andrew Charles (brother of HRH) 17, 23, 24, 27–28, 29, 32–33, 147, 148, 149, 155, 159–160, 165, 187, 188, 199, 206, 244, 246, 251, 304, 335, 342–343, 428, 454, 479 n.65, 535 n.48, 521 n.6

Haggard, Arthur (brother of HRH) 17, 22, 23, 25, 29, 32, 38, 157, 159, 251, 252, 349, 436, 456, 468, 480 n.80, 601 n.77

Haggard, Arthur (nephew of HRH) 324–326

Haggard, Arthur John Rider (Jock, son of HRH) 179, 180, 187, 197, 207, 225, 285–288, 289, 290, 292, 294, 386, 440, 442, 519 n.104, 548 n.85

Haggard, Bazett Michael (brother of HRH) 17, 29, 32, 33, 41, 157, 158, 283, 304, 352, 546 n.32

Haggard, Caroline (aunt of HRH) 13, 14, 17

Haggard, David (sixteenth century ancestor of HRH) 15

Haggard, Diana (grandchild of HRH) 352

Haggard, Doris Elizabeth Vaughan (née Schuldam) 411, 416, 585 n.23

Haggard, Eleanora Mary (sister of HRH, later Baroness d'Anethan) 17, 25, 29, 32, 81, 103, 124, 149, 150, 153, 154, 157, 204, 555 n.89, 558 n.79

Haggard, Elizabeth (née Meybohm, grandmother of HRH) 16

Haggard, Elizabeth Cecilia (Cissie, sister of HRH, later Western) 17, 29, 140, 160, 515 n.105

Haggard, Ella (later Maddison Green, sister of HRH) 17, 22, 23, 24, 27, 29, 159, 242, 295, 296, 418, 454

Haggard, Ella (née Doveton, mother of HRH) 13–14, 17, 18, 21, 26, 40–42, 81, 103, 142–143, 148, 155–156, 187, 276, 299, 368 , 510 n.64

Haggard, Ellen Maria (cousin of HRH) 17

Haggard, Emily (née Calvert, sister-in-law of HRH) 252

Haggard, Emily (née Chirnside, sister-in-law of HRH) 342

Haggard, Emily Margaret (Nitie, née Hancox, sister-in-law of HRH) 231, 465, 467, 600 n.56

Haggard, Ethel (née Fowler, sister-in-law of HRH) 343, 428, 454

Haggard, Ethel Rider *see* Ford, Ethel Rider

Haggard, Frances (Fanny, aunt of HRH) 16

Haggard, Frances (née Amyand, great-grandmother of HRH) 15–16

Haggard, Geoffrey (nephew of HRH) 460, 461, 462

Haggard, George (nephew of HRH) 411

Haggard, Gerald (nephew of HRH) 578 n.47

Haggard, Godfrey (nephew of HRH) 19

Haggard, Hal (nephew of HRH) 434

Haggard, Henry Rider (HRH)
General
appearance 301, 389, 466–467, 551 n.2
archival papers and memorabilia 435, 593 n.38, 597 n.69
birth 2, 11, 478 n.43
character and self-description 2, 5, 19–20, 42, 80–81, 439, 469
culinary ability 111–112

death 469–471, 602 n.98

family, childhood and youth 13–17, 18–19, 21, 22–26, 27–28, 29–31, 32, 33, 480 n.82

health (physical and mental) 42, 76, 77, 78, 85–86, 91–92, 94–95, 99, 117, 127, 197, 250, 280, 288, 289, 291, 292, 295, 296, 324, 347, 349, 358–359, 360, 361, 363, 363, 417, 421, 425, 426, 428, 429, 431, 432, 435, 437–438, 442, 446, 454–455, 457, 461, 466–467

portrait and bust of 453–454, 467

recognition 361, 428, 432–433, 443, 445, 578 n.50, 591 n.11, 592 n.32, 595 n.1

South Africa (Natal and Transvaal, 1875–1881)

and Amakholwa 70–71

and Anglo-Boer War (first) and Transvaal retrocession 171–173, 175–176, 180, 190, 191

and Anglo-Zulu War 134, 136–137, 142, 189–190

on Bhambatha rebellion 350, 351

and Bartle Frere 141–142

and Boers 89, 90, 92–93, 94, 120, 126, 140–141, 142, 190, 191, 390–391, 422, 423

on Bulwer's staff 45, 51–52, 70, 71, 75–77, 80–81, 85–86, 103, 145

and farming see Hilldrop

government service in Pretoria 104–105, 109, 110–116, 117, 119–121, 123–124, 125–126, 130, 133–134, 138, 139, 140–141, 142–143, 144, 151, 152, 504 n.31

and John Colenso 54, 63

and joint commission to Sekhukhune 91–96, 97–99

lost 64–65, 111, 184

missing notebooks 69, 491 n.47

and Pietermaritzburg 54–55, 59, 145, 167, 168, 169, 184, 218, 245

and Pretoria Horse 138, 139, 140–141

and sangomas 61, 62, 63, 67–68

and Transvaal annexation (12 April 1877) 100, 101–102, 103, 499 n.109

and Transvaal invasion (1876–1877) 77, 78–80, 81–82, 83, 85–90

Weenen trip (1875) 64–70

and Zulu language 65, 68–69

Zulu name (Lundanda uNdand Okalweni) 69, 403, 491 n.51

Literary career (see also individual titles of books)

attitude to writing and writing regime 294, 296–298, 315, 317

Blue Book on land issues 343–344

caricature and parodies of 242–243

characteristics 1–3, 5, 80–81, 255, 388–389

early writing 69–70, 76, 88–89, 91, 147, 152–153, 188, 193–194, 196, 513 n.53, 522 n.48

Egyptian influence on 14, 21, 22, 243–244, 249, 252, 254, 266, 459–460, 535 n.46, n.47 & n.49, 538 n.42, 599 n.11

favourite reading 539 n.64

feminine side 2, 221–222, 242, 534 n.33

on fiction 255–257

and film 413–414, 450, 451–452, 464–465, 467, 586 n.44, 597 n.51, 601 n.71

financial aspects 207, 263–264, 354, 413, 450

humorous writing 285
as a journalist 303–304, 308–309, 311
and morality 335–336
plagiarism 244, 245, 246, 257–261, 450, 539 n.77 & n.80, 541 n.30
popularity and publicity 371, 435
pro bono and charity writing 336–337, 415–416
scholarship about 2, 3–5
and violence 267, 282–283, 291–292, 415

Other involvements
amateur dramatics 122, 157, 514 n.83
clubs 250–251, 304–305, 442, 453, 512 n.16, 587 n.73, 600 n.48
freemasonary 545 n.7
golf 547 n.47, 548 n.85
hunting 19, 55, 59, 110–111, 125, 187, 252, 254, 306, 337–338, 359–360, 454
legal 80–81, 162–163, 188, 200–201, 203, 207, 229, 232, 239, 523 n.62
local affairs and politics 202–203, 293, 302, 310, 311, 312–313, 319, 320, 359, 465, 468, 556 n.22
public service 1, 353–354, 358, 429, 432, 433, 434, 435, 437, 445–446, 449, 463, 465, 468–469
war work 414, 416, 417–418, 419–420

Travel
to Australia and New Zealand 371–373, 424–425, 426–427
to Denmark 358
for Dominions Royal Commission 361–362, 363, 364, 366, 367, 377, 378, 380–383, 385–393, 409–411, 415, 416, 418
to East Africa 407–408
to Egypt, Cyprus and Holy Land 249–250, 251–255, 324–327, 333–335, 362–363, 460–463
for Empire Land Settlement Committee 421–429
to Germany 295–296
to Greece (aborted) 277
to Iceland 271–273
to India and Ceylon 367, 368–370
to Ireland 355–356
to Italy 324
luggage problems 249–250, 253, 334, 339, 368
to Netherlands 317
to North America 284, 285, 286–289, 339–342, 343, 344, 347, 361, 409–411, 428–429, 548 n.78, 562 n.53, 563 n.60
to Rhodesia 392–396
to South Africa 42–43, 45, 46, 47, 51–52, 147, 165, 167, 168, 169–170, 183–185, 187, 375–376, 377–384, 385–392, 397–407, 421–424, 572 n.5
to Zululand 397–404

Opinions. attitudes, beliefs
death, grief and remorse 23–25, 37, 94–95, 184, 285–286, 289–290, 294–295, 325, 334, 360, 432, 548 n.84, 558 n.64, 565 n.43
emigration 449–450
imperialism and indigenous people 1, 4, 190–191, 305, 310, 379, 380–381, 388, 405–406, 408
Jews 198, 327, 445
post-World War I Britain 446–449
religion and spiritual matters 150,

164, 184, 234–235, 359, 369,
427, 429, 439, 452–453, 466
rural issues and farming 317–320,
328–329, 330–331, 338–339,
343–344, 353, 358, 431, 435,
449, 557 n.25, 563 n.70
spiritualism 35–37
women 306, 449, 455
World War I 410–411, 414,
415–418, 421, 426, 433, 436,
440, 441–442, 450, 468

Relationships with
Aggie Barber (later Haggard) 149,
191, 194, 196, 198, 202, 203,
207, 210, 222, 229, 231, 234,
239, 242, 262, 268, 269, 294,
296, 314, 324, 352, 357
father 19, 22, 23, 27, 33, 40, 42,
75, 76, 81, 103–105, 124,
147–149, 150, 153, 182, 188,
287, 296, 299
Johanna Ford 125, 127, 130, 137,
142, 151, 155, 242
Mariana Louisa Margitson (Louie,
later Haggard) 154–158, 163–
164, 194, 242, 249, 252–253,
254–255, 335, 363, 425, 426,
427–428, 469–470
Mary Elizabeth Jackson (Lily,
Lilith, later Archer) 37–39,
40, 41, 43, 103, 124–125,
126–128, 155, 159, 194, 196,
198, 203, 204, 205, 242, 292,
313–314, 351–352, 392, 484
n.105, 555 n.89
mother 14, 21, 26, 40, 41–42, 79,
142–143, 145, 148, 276, 439,
440
Rudyard Kipling 3, 5, 250,
279–280, 282, 320, 331, 336,
340, 349–350, 352, 353, 361,
367–368, 409, 417, 419, 420,

434, 436, 439, 441, 442, 445,
447, 455, 457–458, 464, 468,
469, 470, 545 n.4 & n.7, 560
n.129, 595 n.91 & n.7, 601
n.83
Theophilus Shepstone 4, 11, 76,
98–99, 121, 134, 143, 148,
149–150, 156, 158, 168, 169,
204, 282, 283, 294, 364, 365,
388, 402–403
unknown black woman 125
Haggard, James (uncle of HRH) 14, 16, 17
Haggard, Joan (niece of HRH) 450, 460,
461, 462, 471, 599 n.32
Haggard, John George (Jack, brother of
HRH) 17, 23, 29, 32, 42, 81, 115, 147,
160, 165, 177–178, 179, 180, 181, 182,
184, 187, 193, 197, 199, 200, 202, 203,
215, 220–221, 222, 225, 228, 232, 237,
275, 324, 352, 462, 558 n.57, 565 n.45,
600 n.26
Haggard, Julia (née Barker, later Lofthouse,
sister-in-law of HRH) 32, 149, 283,
352
Haggard, Lance Rider (nephew of HRH)
415, 436, 450
Haggard, Lilias Rider (daughter of HRH)
3, 16, 19, 24, 25, 68, 69, 128, 294, 296,
298, 324, 358, 373, 375, 376, 380, 381,
385, 386, 387, 388, 392, 397, 423,
432, 455, 456, 460, 461, 462, 471,
577 n.19
Haggard, Mariana Louisa (Louie, née
Margitson, wife of HRH) 5, 153,
154–160, 163–164, 168, 169, 170, 176,
178–179, 182, 184, 187, 191, 193–194,
197, 205, 207, 229, 242, 249, 252–253,
254–255, 258, 287, 290, 293, 294–295,
298, 312, 313, 324, 335, 351, 362, 373,
375–376, 380, 381, 385, 386, 387, 388,
392, 397, 429, 431, 432, 442, 450, 451,
452, 455, 456, 463, 465, 469–470, 471,

INDEX

513 n.67, 514 n.68, 519 n.104, 547 n.47, 577 n.19, 597 n.69, 602 n.101

Haggard, Marjorie (Mardie, née Syme, wife of HRH's nephew) 460, 461, 462

Haggard, Mark (nephew of HRH) 411, 414, 585 n.23

Haggard, Mary (née Dixon, sister-in-law of HRH) 148, 159, 160, 165

Haggard, Susan Rebecca (née Barnham, great, great-grandmother of HRH) 15

Haggard, Sybil Dorothy Rider (daughter of HRH, later Cheyne) 202, 207, 289, 294, 324, 367, 368, 414–415, 431, 433, 436, 443, 471, 560 n.125

Haggard, Thomas (nephew of HRH) 352, 471

Haggard, William (grandfather of HRH) 16

Haggard, William Henry (great, great-grandfather of HRH) 15

Haggard, William Henry (great-grandfather of HRH) 15, 17

Haggard, William Henry (Will, brother of HRH) 17, 29, 32, 33, 157, 187, 231, 277, 304, 425, 426, 432, 438–439, 440, 441, 465, 555 n.89, 590 n.45, 600 n.56, 602 n.101

Haggard, William Meybohm Rider (father of HRH) 2, 13, 16, 17, 18, 19, 20–21, 22, 23, 24, 25, 27, 30, 33, 39, 40, 42, 80–81, 103–105, 124, 148, 157, 163, 204, 246, 276, 277, 287, 299

Haggard family 14, 15, 16, 23, 164, 477 n.20

Hall, Reginald 446

Hall, Richard Hicklin 394, 395–396

Halston, Victor 249

Hamilton, Emma 14–15, 25

Hamilton, Frank 154, 155, 156–157, 158

Hamilton, Hannah 154, 157–158, 159

Hamilton, Ian 180, 415

Hamilton, William 159

Hammond, John Hays 341

Hamu kaNzibe 156, 191, 201

Hanbury-Williams, John 447

Hans (fictional character) 364, 569 n.32

Harcourt, Lewis 361, 367, 393, 406, 583 n.68

Hardie, Keir 368, 571 n.69

Harding, Edward 370–371, 372, 375, 378, 410, 411, 433, 435, 578 n.39

Hardinge, Charles 368

Hardinge, Winifred 369

Hardy, Thomas 250, 251, 274, 329–330, 356, 359, 537 n.21

Harmachis (fictional character, Olympus) 265, 266

Harmsworth, Alfred *see* Northcliffe, *Lord*

Harrington, Albert 400

Harris, Frank 267, 541 n.29

Hart-Bennett, Ella (née Tuck) 326, 408, 558 n.79, 584 n.91

Hart-Bennett, Lucy 375

Hart-Bennett, William 326

Hartcup, Jessie 312, 450, 547 n.47

Hartcup, Louisa 159, 312

Hartcup, Lucy 288

Hartcup, William 153, 154, 155, 157–158, 159, 163–164

Hawaii 591 n.63

Hawkins, Anthony Hope 250, 602 n.100

Hawthorne, Julian 340

Haynes, Alfred E. 307

Haynes, H. Manning 451

Hazelhurst, Edward 113

He (Andrew Lang and Walter Herries Pollock) 243, 254, 534 n.41 & n.42, 577 n.36

Heart and Soul (adaptation of *Jess*) 586 n.44

The Heart of the World (1896) 250, 548 n.78

Hector, Annie 297

Hector, Ida 297, 301, 452, 465, 468, 470, 471

Heimann (trader) 112

Helen of Troy 243, 274, 275

Heliodore (fictional character) 358

Henderson, Joseph 77–78, 168

Hendrika (fictional character) 275, 276

Henley, William Ernest 208, 247, 250, 251, 266

Herbert, Robert 151

Hertzog, J.B.M. 422, 423, 589 n.5

Hes (Isis, fictional character) 348

Heu-Heu, or, The Monster (1924) 446, 457

Hicks Beach, Michael 134, 139, 151

Higgins, Edward John 339

Hildyard, Cecil 434

Hildyard, Lily 292, 296

Hildyard, Louisa 158, 180, 514 n.93

Hildyard, Rose 154, 417, 588 n.84

Hilldrop (Newcastle *and* the fictional Mooifontein) 143, 144, 149, 150, 151, 161–162, 163–164, 170, 174–175, 176–177, 178, 179–180, 181, 182, 183, 193, 200, 229, 230, 386, 392, 397, 510 n.73, 579 n.62

Hilton School 491 n.56

Hitchcock, Edward 137, 508 n.22

Hitchcock, Elizabeth (née Osborn) 145, 508 n.22

Hitchcock, Georgina 508 n.22

Hocking, Elizabeth 188, 276, 299, 276, 299, 432, 521 n.11

Holden, Hubert Ashton 30, 32, 239, 263

Holden, Laetitia 30

Hollard, William Emil 126, 130, 505 n.74

Holly, Ludwig Horace (fictional character) 236–237, 238, 240, 348

Holmes, Luna (Lady Ragnall, fictional character) 364, 375, 588 n.80

Holtshausen, J.C. 91, 95, 98

Home, Daniel Dunglas 35

Honham Castle (fictional place) 246

Hood (groom) 159

Hopkins, Gerard Manley 216–217

Horder, Thomas 455

horse sickness 94, 95, 96, 97, 175, 497 n.64

How, Harry 293–294

How, William Walsham 251

Huitzilopochtli (Aztec god) 286, 298, 550 n.61

Hunt, William Holman 287

Hunter, Percy Oxley 437

Huxley, Elspeth, 580 n.90

Hyam, Arthur Preston (fictional character) 43, 194, 195, 196, 198, 199

Hyndeman, *Mrs* (cook) 169, 175

Imperial Hotel (Pietermaritzburg) 386, 576 n.12

inboekselings (apprentices) 501 n.46

Indabezimbi 182–183, 230

India 368–370

Infadoos (fictional character) 212

Inge, W.R. 445, 595 n.5

Ingogo (battle) 172

Inskipp, Frank 393

Ipswich Grammar School 29–32, 239, 337, 533 n.4, 562 n.35

Ireland 229, 355

Isandlwana (battle) 135, 137, 140, 403, 508 n.24, 582 n.54, 583 n.55, n.57 & n.59

Ithobal (fictional character) 395

The Ivory Child (1916, *Lady of the Heavens*) 375, 408

J & R Maxwell (publisher) 264, 269, 275, 542 n.51

Jack (pet rat) 293

Jack the Ripper 546 n.27

Jackson, Charlotte (née Goodricke) 38

Jackson, Frederick 3, 22, 38, 159, 187, 196–197, 202, 203, 221, 237, 275, 293, 304, 313, 471, 480 n.80, 529 n.104, 532 n.88, 551 n.7, 602 n.101

Jackson, Jane (née Outhwaite) 38

Jackson, John 38

Jackson, Mary Elizabeth (Lilly, Lilith, later
Archer) 3, 5, 37–39, 40, 41, 43, 103,
124–125, 126–128, 196–197, 242,
292, 313–314, 351–352, 484 n.105

Jackson, R. 138, 141

Jackson, Thomas 403

Jackson, Tom (fictional character) 523 n.75

Jaffer, Aga Mahomed 13–14

James, Henry 241, 251, 279, 426, 538 n.63

James, James Fencott (Jumbo) 77

Jameson, James Sligo 250

Jameson, Leander Starr 309, 310, 579 n.69

Jameson Raid (1895) 309–310, 311, 322,
378–379

Jeaffreson, John Cordy 195–196, 197,
268–269

Jebb, Bertha 284, 286, 287, 298–299, 432,
547 n.42

Jebb, John Gladwyn 284, 288–289,
298–299

Jehu, James 353

Jeppe, Fred 218

Jeppe, Julius 218, 392

Jeremiah (Sekhukhune's witness) 94

Jess (1887) 113, 228–231, 232, 234, 239,
249, 257–260, 263, 264, 321, 354, 381,
390, 391, 422, 539 n.77, 586 n.44

Jess (fictional character) 229–230, 231,
336

Jesser-Coope, John Charles 393, 579 n.70

Jess's Cottage (fictional place) 230, 390,
391, 578 n.39

Jizika (fictional character) 281

Joan Haste (1895) 269

Job (fictional character) 236–237, 238

Johannesburg 309–310, 391–392

Johnston, Harry 220

Johnstone, William 179

Jones, William West 47, 485 n.14

Jorissen, Eduard Johan 100, 117–118

Joubert, Piet 119, 140, 171, 174

Jung, Carl 2, 242

Just, Hartman 376

Juta, C.J. 110, 113, 114, 120, 121

Kallikrates (fictional character) 236, 237,
238, 348

Kaloons (fictional people) 348

Kelly, Richard 446

Kerr, Charles Henry Malcolm 293, 315,
531 n.36, 556 n.109

Kerr, Robert Malcolm 531 n.36

Kershaw, Ernest (fictional character) 39,
124, 125, 204, 205, 234

Kertész, Mihaly (Michael Curtiz) 465

Kessingland Grange (Suffolk) 314–315,
353, 409, 431, 452, 555 n.102, 556
n.107

Khalifa bin Harub Al-Said 407–408

Khan (fictional character) 348

Khiva (guide, real and fictional character)
131, 212

Kim (Rudyard Kipling) 348

Kimberley 108, 167, 192, 382, 383, 575
n.60

King, Armine Francis 31, 482 n.42

King Albert's Book (edited by Hall Caine,
1914) 415–416, 587 n.68

King Solomon's Mines (1885) 1, 2, 3, 66,
115, 131, 181, 183, 207–217, 218–222,
231, 233, 236, 239, 246, 249, 250, 264,
268, 270, 294, 364, 381, 395, 413, 414,
450, 525 n.8, 527 n.55

King Solomon's Wives (Hyder Ragged
[Henry Chartres Biron], 1887) 534
n.41

The King's Homeland: Sandringham and
North West Norfolk (William A. Dutt)
337

Kinsman, George Whitefield 410

Kipling, Caroline (Carrie, née Balestier)
350, 417

Kipling, John 417, 419, 434

Kipling, Josephine 280, 350

Kipling, Rudyard 531 n.56, 538 n.63, 544 n.89, 560 n.128, 562 n.34, 568 n.2, 588 n.80, 589 n.102, 592 n.22, 602 n.101
  and HRH 3, 5, 250, 279–280, 282, 320, 331, 336, 340, 349–350, 352, 353, 361, 367–368, 409, 417, 419, 420, 434, 436, 439, 441, 442, 445, 447, 455, 457–458, 464, 468, 469, 470, 545 n.4 & n.7, 560 n.128, 595 n.91 & n.7, 598 n.80, 601 n.83

Kismet (Oscar Asche) 372

Kitchener, Horatio Herbert 327, 363, 384, 415, 426–427

Kleyn, Fred 114

Knight, Godfrey (fictional character) 29, 35, 438

Knight, Isobel (fictional character) 29

Knight, Mr (fictional character) 29

Koch, Henry 388

Kôr (fictional place) 237

Kotzé, John 93, 107, 108–109, 110, 111, 112, 113, 114, 118, 120–121, 125, 126, 130, 133, 143, 144, 162, 214, 245, 380, 423, 500 n.14 & n.16

Kotzé, Mary Aurelia (née Bell) 108, 423

Kruger, Gezina (née Du Plessis) 90

Kruger, Maria (née Du Plessis) 90

Kruger, Paul 90, 100, 117–118, 119, 140, 230, 309, 310, 322, 323, 391

Kukuanaland (fictional place) 212, 218

Kungwini (Mzilikazi's homestead) 88

Kuruman (Kruman, Nkulumane) 131, 486 n.21, 507 n.120

KwaGqikazi (Zululand) 201

Kwili kaSitshidi 411–412, 586 n.32

La Monaca, Francesco 454

Lagden, Godfrey 133, 138, 142, 144, 162, 376–377, 417, 436, 471

Lagden, Rebekah Francis (née Bousfield) 133

Lagden, Ronald 593 n.42

Laing's Nek (battle) 171

Lambart, R.H. 168–169, 230

Lang, Andrew 208, 209, 216, 217, 223, 227, 231, 232, 240, 243, 247, 250, 258, 259, 261, 264, 268, 269, 273, 274, 275, 279, 280, 348, 357, 360, 367, 395, 453, 466, 523 n.87, 533 n.15, 577 n.36, 580 n.86

Lang, Leonora 227, 465, 471

Langalibalele kaMtimkhulu 490 n.24

Langalibalele rebellion (1873) 45, 49, 50, 51, 54

Langerman, Jan Willem Stuckeris 570 n.49, 573 n.6

Lanham, Stephen 165, 181, 187, 237

Lankiboy (servant) 91, 93–94, 98

Lanyon, Owen 139, 141, 142, 162, 168, 176, 379

The Last Boer War (1899) *see Cetewayo and his White Neighbours*

Laurier, Wilfred 342

Lehmkuhl, Johanna *see* Ford, Johanna

Lehmkuhl, Josephine (Phinny) 125, 151, 152, 153, 160, 193, 505 n.69

Lekoglane 119

Leney, Frank 435

Levert, A.H. 219

Life and its Author: An Essay in Verse (Ella Haggard) 277, 285

Linton, Eliza Lynn 297

Little, George Leon 529 n.108

Little, James Stanley 221, 258, 263, 471, 529 n.108

Livingstone, David 308

Lloyd George, David 353, 354, 442

Lobengula kaMzilikazi 126, 131, 302, 303, 306, 393, 552 n.16

lobola 387, 576 n.17

Lodge, Oliver 452, 597 n.57

Lofthouse, Samuel 352

Loftie, William John 250, 251, 266, 535 n.49, 541 n.21

log-rolling 243, 534 n.42

Longman, Charles 240, 258, 263, 264, 268, 269, 282, 307, 362, 365, 367, 411, 416, 434, 436, 465–466, 471, 562 n.32, 593 n.38

Longman, Freddie 411, 416, 434

Longman, Harriette 434

Longrigg, John 425, 426

Lorimer, William 568 n.11, 573 n.6

Louis Napoleon (Prince Imperial) 144–145, 192, 366, 510 n.91

Love Eternal (1918) 29, 35, 433, 438

Loveday, Richard Kelsey 138, 144, 513 n.39

Lucas, William 473, 577 n.24

Luck's Farm (fictional place) 113

Lucoque, H. Lisle 413, 414, 425, 467, 451, 601 n.71

Ludlow, Walter 191

Lugard, Frederick 304–305

Lydenburg Volunteer Corps 74

Lyle, Vacy 77, 85, 86, 102

Lyne, Robert 370

Lyne-Strivens, Bertram Herbert 295, 296, 347, 349, 591 n.78

Lysbeth: A Tale of the Dutch (1901) 317

Lyttelton, Alfred 338, 343

MacDonald, George 234

Macfarlane, George 388

Mackenzie, Flossie (fictional character) 226

Mackenzie, James 308, 553 n.56

Mackenzie, John (real and fictional character) 93, 219, 226

Macleod, Norman 71

Macmillan, Alexander 88, 147, 152

Macmillan, Frederick 538 n.63

Macrorie, William K. 50, 51, 54

Maddison Green, Charles (brother-in-law

of HRH) 22, 24, 27, 28, 159, 295, 588 n.94

Magnússon, Eiríki 271

Maguire, James 303

The Mahatma and the Hare: A Dream Story (1911) 359–360

Mahomed (fictional character) 237

Maiwa (fictional character) 266

Maiwa's Revenge, or, the War of the Little Hand (1888) 266

Major Barbara (George Bernard Shaw) 357

Majuba (battle) 173–174, 180, 389

Makurupiji 96, 98

Malaza, Mbekane 120–121, 504 n.28

Malcolm, James 601 n.77

Malins, Geoffrey 592 n.9

Malins, Richard 158

Malvern Farm (Natal) 59

Mameena (fictional character) 281, 368, 412

Mameena (adaptation of *Child of Storm*) 11, 373, 411, 412–413, 585 n.31

Mandhlakazi kaNgini 411–412, 586 n.32

Mandlakazi 201, 202

Manzolwandle ka Cetshwayo (Manzonwandle) 404, 583 n.60

Marais, Marie (fictional character) 364, 391, 569 n.30

Maré, Frederik 114, 502 n.64

Margitson, John & Mary Anna (née Hamilton) 153

Mariannhill 404

Marie (1912) 364, 365, 391, 401

Mark Anthony (in fiction) 265

Marley, John (fictional character) 231

Marville, Reginald (fictional character) 271

Maserumule 119

Maskelyne, John Nevil 412, 585 n.27

Mason, William 15

Maspero, Gaston 363

Masuku (HRH's servant and fictional character) 53, 89–90, 98, 110–111,

113, 136, 171, 172, 183, 204, 205, 206, 294, 386–387, 398, 399, 400, 401, 404, 487 n.53 & n.54, 581 n.15

Matiwane kaMasumpa 401, 582 n.42

Matopos (Rhodesia) 393, 579 n.69

Matravers, William 400, 407

Mauch, Carl 218, 527 n.77

Maurice, Frederick 437

May, Clarence 453, 471

Mazooku, *see* Masuku

Mbilini waSwati 494 n.56

Mbonjana 137

Mbuyazi kaMpande 8, 10, 11

McDowell, John 592 n.9

McIver, David Randall 394

McKenzie, Duncan 350, 565 n.30

Mea (fictional character) 335, 336

Meek's Farm (fictional place) 113–114

Meeson, Eustace (fictional character) 270

Meeson, Mr (fictional character) 269–270

Melvill, Teignmouth 138, 403, 583 n.56

Merensky, Alexander 93, 111, 174, 220, 518 n.56

Meriamun (fictional character) 243

Merriman, John X. 379–380, 422, 423, 574 n.31 & n.41

Mexico 286, 288

Meybohm family 16, 23, 477 n.20

Meyers, R.C.V. 539 n.80

Mhlopekazi (Umslopogaas) 83, 225, 226, 227, 228, 280, 281, 387, 434, 473–474, 509 n.45, 577 n.24, 602 n.1 & n.9

Middelburg Volunteer Corps 74, 95

Milner, Alfred 322, 323, 449

Milner, Frederick & Adelaide 250, 252

missionaries 70–71, 308

Modjadji (Rain Queen of the Lobedu) 245

Mogden, Henry 450

Molyneux, Charles 393–394

Monk, Morris (fictional character) 314

Monk's Acre (fictional place) 29

Montezuma 284

Montezuma's Daughter (1892) 291–292, 298

Moon of Israel (1918, filmed as *Die Slavenkönigin*) 363, 441, 465

Mopo (fictional character) 280, 281

Morcom, Robert 579 n.62

Morcom, William 77, 87, 88, 90, 108, 500 n.16, 579 n.62

Moresco (HRH's horse) 110, 113, 152, 162, 164–165, 175, 390, 456

Morning Star (1910) 354, 363, 535 n.52, 561 n.20; *see also Star of Egypt*

Morris, Augustus 180, 519 n.108

Morris, William 271

Morwamotse 145

Mount Elgon caves (Uganda) 246, 551 n.7

Mount Nelson Hotel (Cape Town) 378, 423, 573 n.21

Mpande kaSenzangakhona 7, 8, 48, 49, 280, 476 n.3

Mr Meeson's Will (1888) 269–270, 586 n.44, 593 n.38

Mrs Keith's Crime (Lucy Clifford, 1885) 256

Msebe (battle) 201

Muir, Percy 535 n.49

Muller, Frank (fictional character) 230, 231

Murgh (fictional character) 352, 353

My Trivial Life and Misfortune (Plain Woman, 1883) 256

Myra; or the Rose of the East: A Tale of the Afghan War (Ella Haggard, 1857) 21

nachtmaal 115

Nada (fictional character) 280–281

Nada the Lily (1892) 83, 280–284, 397, 473, 545 n.14, 546 n.36; *see Umbuso kaShaka*

Nandi 281

Natal Colony 47–48, 49

Natal Government Railways 55–56, 58–59, 167

INDEX

Natal Witness 231, 506 n.95, 518 n.57

National Birth Rate Commission 449

National Propaganda (later Economic League) 446, 448

Natives' Land Act (1913) 405, 406

Ndondakusuka (battle, 1856) 7, 8, 9–11, 12, 213, 397

Nellmapius, Alois 112

Nelson, Horatio 15, 196, 315

Nesmin (Egyptian mummy) 244, 534 n.45, 535 n.48

Nesse, Charles Holder 414

'Nestor Amor or the Coming of the Lady Isis' (unpublished) 270–271, 273

New Republic 202

Newbolt, Henry 465

Niel, John (fictional character) 229–230

Njal's Saga 271, 272, 282

Nojoiani (guide) 97, 98, 498 n.73

Nomaruso (sangoma) 62–63

Nombi (fictional character) 402

Nongoma (Zululand) 400

Norfolk 17, 319, 556 n.6

North Eastern Hospital for Children (later Queen's Hospital for Children) 222–223, 529 n.117

Northcliffe, *Lord* (Alfred Harmsworth) 445, 447–448, 552 n.20

Nourse, Henry 378, 379, 574 n.27

Nozilwane (sangoma) 62, 63

iziNqobo (Crushers) 9, 10

Ntswaneng (Sekhukhuneland) 96, 146

Ntuli, F.L. 283, 284

Nyleptha (fictional character) 227

Oates, Frank 219, 528 n.89 & n.90

Oates, William 219

Oats, Francis 382, 575 n.61

Ochorowitz, Julien 356–357, 567 n.84

Odysseus 243, 274, 275

Ogard, Andrew 358

Olaf Red-Sword (fictional character) 358

Oliphant, Margaret (née Wilson, *pseud.* Mrs Oliphant) 255, 538 n.51

Ollier, Edmund 198

Ondini (battle) 201

O'Neill, Maire 356

O'Reilly, Anna 113, 126

Osborn, Jack 143, 147, 148, 398, 400, 582 n.33

Osborn, Keane 161, 164

Osborn, Melmoth 9, 11, 49, 77, 83, 93–94, 97, 98, 99, 100, 101, 114, 126, 136, 138, 142, 143, 149, 151, 156, 181, 201, 202, 365, 387, 388, 398, 402–403, 473, 499 n.109, 581 n.13

Otomie (fictional character) 291

Outram, Leonard & Thomas (fictional characters) 301 .

Oxley, Percy Hunter 437

Oxley, Richard 594 n.52

Pagadi's Kop (Ntanyana, Natal) 65, 490 n.31

The Palatial (HRH's Pretoria house) 123–124, 143, 152, 161, 162, 163, 390, 578 n.40

Palmer, Edward 307, 553 n.42

Palmer, Gray 126, 131

Paris Commune 484 n.111

Parr, Charles 403

Patterson, Robert 122, 126, 131, 218, 220, 306, 393, 552 n.16

Payn, James 233, 531 n.56

The Pearl Maiden: A Tale of the Fall of Jerusalem (1903) 326

Pearson, Arthur 327, 328

Pearson, Charles 293

Pelham, John 163

penny readings 45, 485 n.2

The People of the Mist (1894) 298, 301–302, 551 n.7

Per ardua ad astra (Outram family motto adopted by the RAF) 301, 302

Petros (Sekhukhune's witness) 94

Phakade kaMacingwane 64, 65, 67, 68, 137, 490 n.24

Phillips, Edward 31

Phillips, Frederick L. 77, 171, 499 n.114, 584 n.75

Phiring (Pedi capital) 95

Pietermaritzburg 52, 54–55, 59, 76, 145, 167, 168, 169, 184, 218, 245, 486 n.37

Pigott, Edward Smyth 295

Pilgrim's Rest (Transvaal) 112

Pillar of Fire (adaptation of *She*) 586 n.44

Pine, Benjamin 41, 45, 51

Pollock, David 389–390, 577 n.36

Pollock, Walter 577 n.36

The Poor and the Land (1905) 344

Porson, Mary (fictional character) 314

Poulett, *Lady* 35

praise-singers 66–67

Preller, Gustav 390–391

Pretoria 86, 88, 89, 122–123, 133, 389

Pretoria Horse 138, 139, 140–141, 508 n.32

Price, Robert 311, 312, 555 n.83

Prince Imperial *see* Louis Napoleon

Prinsloo, Vrou (fictional character) 391

Pritchett, V.S. 2, 242

The Private Diaries of Sir H. Rider Haggard (D.S. Higgins, ed., 1980) 3

Pulleine, Henry 403, 508 n.24

Quaritch, Harold (fictional character) 246

Quatermain, Allan (fictional character, Macumazahn) 5, 11, 28–29, 64, 101, 184, 200, 210–211, 212, 213, 214, 215, 219, 220, 225, 226, 227, 236, 238, 240, 266, 275–276, 280, 281, 307, 364, 371, 397, 434, 481 n.18, 498 n.91, 526 n.30, 545 n.14, 588 n.80

Quatermain, Harry 225, 275

Quatermaine, William & Jayne 29, 211, 481 n.17

The Queen of the Dawn (1925) 252, 464, 470

Queen Sheba's Ring (1910) 111, 553 n.42, 561 n.20

Queen Victoria 192

Ragnall, Lady (fictional character) *see* Holmes, Luna

Ransome, Gilbert 429

Raven, John James 239

Ravenshaw, Bessie 187

Red Eve (1911) 352–353

Red House (Snape, Suffolk) 313, 351

Regeneration (1910) 357

reincarnation 235, 348, 349

Renders, Adam 527 n.77

Retief, Piet 47, 401–402

Rex, Hermann Moritz 578 n.40

Rhodes, Cecil John 302–304, 305, 307, 309, 310, 378, 393, 593 n.50

Rhodesia (Southern Rhodesia) 380, 392–396, 422, 579 n.66, 580 n.90

Richmond, William Blake 453, 597 n.64

Rider Haggard (Norman Etherington, 1984) 3

Rider Haggard: His Life and Works (Morton Cohen, 1960) 2, 3

Rider Haggard: The Great Storyteller (D.S. Higgins, 1981) 3

Rider Haggard and Egypt (Shirley Addy, 1998) 3

Rider Haggard and the Fiction of Empire (Wendy Katz, 1987) 3

Rider Haggard and the Lost Empire (Tom Pocock, 1993) 3

Rider Haggard on the Imperial Frontier (Gerald Monsman, 2006) 4

Rider Haggard Street (Pretoria) 578 n.50

Riennes, Madame (fictional character) 438

Ripley, Blanche (fictional character) 231

Rissik, Johan 101, 391

Robert, John 570 n.49

Roberts, Frederick Sleigh 327

Robinson, Hercules 176, 177, 178, 179, 322

Rodd (fictional character) 498 n.91

Rooi Point farm (Natal) *see* Hilldrop

Roosevelt, Theodore 220, 339–340, 343, 357, 429, 436–437, 446, 591 n.71, 596 n.10

Rorke's Drift (battle) 135–136, 137, 404

Rose, Algernon 471

Rose, Horace 388–389, 577 n.31

Rose, William 347, 540 n.4

Ross, Alexander Galt 250, 251, 271, 272, 273, 471, 543 n.62, 602 n.99

Ross, Robert 543 n.62

Ross, Ronald 349, 454, 457, 460, 466, 564 n.19

Rotenberg, Helena 460, 462

Rowlands, Hugh 119, 120

Royal Agricultural Allies Fund 416

Royal Colonial Institute (later Royal Commonwealth Institute) 416, 418, 429, 432–433, 442, 445, 448, 588 n.76, 592 n.11

Royal Commission on Coast Erosion 353, 354, 358

Rudyard Kipling to Rider Haggard: The Record of a Friendship (Morton Cohen, 1965) 3

Rural Denmark and its Lessons (1911) 358, 568 n.100

Rural England: Being an Account of Agricultural and Social Researches Carried Out in the Years 1901 & 1902 (1902) 328–329, 330–331, 560 n.124

Saduko (fictional character) 412

Saintsbury, George 199, 206, 250, 523 n.87

iSakibuli (Longtailed widow bird) 489 n.10

Sakon (fictional character) 395

Salisbury (Rhodesia) 394

Salisbury, *Lord* (Robert Arthur Talbot Gascoyne-Cecil) 203, 229

Salome (Oscar Wilde, 1893) 295

Salvation Army 330, 338–339, 340, 341, 344, 357

Salvini, Sandro 542 n.50

Samuel, Evelyn 460, 462, 600 n.32

Samuelson, S.B. 602 n.9

Sandeman, Edward 123, 218

Sanderson, 'Guts' 31–32

Sanderson, John 64

Sandringham (Norfolk) 336

Sandys, John Edwin 81

sangomas 61–62, 63, 67–68, 219, 384, 402

Sargeaunt, John 122, 126, 131, 218, 220, 306, 393, 552 n.16

Sargeaunt, William 55–56, 121–122, 139, 148, 541 n.26

Sarhili kaHintsa 115

Saunders, Charles 402

Savile Club (London) 250–251, 453

Schiaparelli, Ernesto 334

Schlesinger, I.W. 413, 451

Schlickman, Conrad von 74, 128

Schreiner, Olive (*pseud.* Ralph Iron) 2, 221–223, 229, 231, 242, 529 n.112, 573 n.17

Schreiner, William 377

Schwikkard, Bernhard Ludwig 82, 83

Schwikkard, Louise Marie Amelia (née Schronn) 82, 83, 171, 172, 176, 179, 180, 519 n.104

Schwikkard, Otto 82, 83, 102, 170–171, 172, 174, 184, 520 n.133

Schwikkard family 144, 161

Scoones, Henrietta 34

Scoones, William Baptiste Wordsworth 33–34

Scott, John 7

Scott, Walter 233

Scudamore, Henry Carter 308

Scudamore, John Charles 393, 579 n.72

Scudamore, Walter 393, 579 n.72

Scudamore, William 163–164, 515 n.131

Scully, William Charles 381–382, 575 n.52

Sekhukhune 91, 92, 94, 96–97, 99, 119, 145, 146, 511 n.98

Sekouili (guide) 97, 98

Selborne, *Lord* (William Waldegrave Palmer) 418

Selous, Frederick Courtney 220, 433, 528 n.96 & n.98, 558 n.55, 592 n.16

The Sexual Imperative in the Novels of Sir Henry Rider Haggard (Richard Reeves, 2018) 4

Shaka kaSenzangakhona 7, 8, 280, 281, 580 n.5

Shangani Patrol 307, 553 n.47

She: A History of Adventure (1887) 1, 2, 3, 218, 226, 231, 232, 234, 235–236, 239–243, 244–245, 246, 249, 250, 254, 257, 259, 260, 261, 263, 268, 269, 283, 293, 294, 348, 354–355, 384, 395, 413, 425, 427, 439, 450, 451, 467, 533 n.14, 535 n.49, 536 n.63, 539 n.77, 540 n.4, 543 n.57, 586 n.44, 596 n.42; *see also* Pillar of Fire

She: Explorations into a Romance (Tania Zulli, ed., 2009) 4

She and Allan (1921) 83, 235, 434, 446, 473, 602 n.1

She-Who-Must-Be-Obeyed (doll) 25; *see also* Ayesha

Shepstone, Arthur 365–366

Shepstone, Averil 387

Shepstone, George 137, 138, 403

Shepstone, Henrique 49, 77, 388

Shepstone, John 49, 135, 142, 168, 201, 387

Shepstone, Offy 142

Shepstone, Percy 387

Shepstone, Theophilus (Somtsewu)
character 486 n.29, 505 n.66, 546 n.35
in fiction 204

and HRH 4, 11, 76, 98–99, 121, 134, 143, 148, 149–150, 156, 158, 168, 169, 204, 282, 283, 294, 364, 365, 388, 402–403

and Natal 48–49, 50, 51, 59, 62, 63–64, 65–68, 75–76, 142, 474, 485 n.19

and Transvaal 75–76, 77, 82–83, 85, 86, 87, 90–93, 100, 101, 102, 109–110, 118, 122, 129, 138, 139, 283, 294, 379, 509 n.44 & n.45

and Zululand 7, 49–50, 115, 135, 192, 193, 282, 283, 387, 402–403

Shiel, Justin 150, 164

Showers, Mary Rosina 36, 483 n.92

Sidney, William 540 n.4

Silvestra, José da (fictional character) 211, 212, 216

Silvestre, José (fictional character) 211

Simpofu (real and fictional character) 401, 582 n.39

Simpson, William 431

Sinclair, John Robert 375, 573 n.6

Sinnett, Alfred Percy 234

smallpox 320, 321

Smartt, Thomas 423

Smith, Harry 48–49

Smith, James 305

Smith, Joseph F. 341

Smith, Josiah (fictional character) 438

Smith and the Pharoahs (1912–1913) 561 n.20

Smithers, Augusta (fictional character) 269–270

Smuts, Jan 378, 422

Society of Authors 233, 464, 562 n.34, 602 n.100

Sohn, Carl Rudolph 192, 522 n.40

Sorais (fictional character) 227

South Africa
indigenous people 379
land 405–406

migrant labour 407

mining 383, 386

strikes (1913–1914) 378, 573 n.22

sugar industry 581 n.6

Union of (1910) 376

and World War I 422

wine industry 574 n.40

South African Native Affairs Commission (1903–1905) 377

Spice (dog) 147, 178, 519 n.92

Spion Kop (battle) 385, 576 n.4

spiritualism 35–37, 483 n.75 & n.89, 597 n.57

Spurgeon, Arthur 435

St Helena 477 n.2

St Mary and All Saints Cathedral (Salisbury, Rhodesia) 394, 579 n.73

St Mary's Church (Ditchingham) 471

St Michael and All Angels Cathedral (Eshowe) 398

St Peter's Cathedral (Pietermaritzburg) 63

St Thomas's Church (London) 433, 453, 471, 592 n.14

Stadsaal caves (Cederberg) 535 n.54

Stainbank, Mary 474

Stalham Bridge (Norfolk, scene of 1895 election riot) 312

Stander, Adriaan 82, 83, 494 n.59

Stanger (KwaDukuza, Natal) 580 n.5

Stanley, Henry Morton 305, 552 n.28

'The Star' (HRH and Charles Montagu Stewart, unpublished) 306, 553 n.38

Star of Egypt (adaptation of *Morning Star*) 356–357

Stead, William Thomas 243, 257, 261, 343, 363, 539 n.68, 563 n.80

Steed, Henry Wickham 447–448

Stella (film) 451

Stella Fregelius: A Tale of Three Destinies (1904) 314, 315, 555 n.100

Stephen, James Kenneth 279

Stevenson, Fanny 546 n.32

Stevenson, R.A.M. 250

Stevenson, Robert Louis 217, 228, 283, 544 n.89, 546 n.32

Stewart, Charles Montagu Duncan (Charles Montague) 71, 76, 119, 195, 306, 511 n.97, 553 n.38

Stopes, Marie 449

The Story of an African Farm (Olive Schreiner, 1883) 222, 229, 256, 539 n.77

A Strange Career: the Life and Adventures of John Gladwyn Jebb ... (Bertha Jebb, 1894) 299

Strong, Stephen (fictional character) 321

The Stronger Passion (film of *Beatrice*) 542 n.50, 597 n.46

Struben, Hendrik Willem 377, 573 n.19

Stuart, Ellen 464

Stuart, James 306, 365–366, 372, 386, 387, 388, 397, 398, 399, 402, 403, 404, 406, 411–412, 474, 464, 570 n.38 & n.40, 600 n.46

Sundays River Settlement (Eastern Cape) 435

Su-Vendi (fictional people) 227, 228

Suzanne (fictional character) 321–322

Swallow: A Tale of the Great Trek (1899) 321–322, 391, 451

Swannhild (fictional character) 336

Swart, Nicolaas 118

Swazi and Swaziland 74, 75, 134, 305–306, 365, 474

Swinburne, John 219

Sydenham, *Lord* (George Clarke) 447

Sykes, Frederick 302

Symons, William Penn 323

Tatlow, Joseph 568 n.11, 573 n.6

Taverner, John 418

Tennyson, Hallam 344, 434

Thacker, Alfred 20–21, 479 n.65

Theosophy 234–235, 348

Therne, James (fictional character) 321

Thesiger, Frederic *see* Chelmsford, *Lord*

Thomas, Evan Morgan 131

Thompson, Charles 272–273

Thomson, Joseph 220, 245, 536 n.63

Thornsett (Budleigh Salterton) 432

three-volume novels 233–234

Through Masai Land (Joseph Thomson, 1885) 245, 246

Thukela River 7, 9, 10–11

Thurston, Herbert 292–293, 323

Thy Rod and Thy Staff (A.C. Benson, 1912) 427

Tibet 348

Tifokati 474

To Hell or Connaught (unpublished play) 356, 357, 409

Tolstoy, Leo 241–242, 534 n.29

Torkington, Charles 193

Townsend, Meredith 543 n.59

Transvaal

    annexation (12 April 1877) 99, 100–102, 117–119, 499 n.109

    convention (1881) 178, 179–180, 322–323

    invasion of (1876–1877) 75, 77–78, 81–83, 85, 86–88, 89 91, 93, 495 n.17

    joint commission to Sekhukhune (1877) 91–96, 97–99, 498 n.73, n.74 & n.75, 498 n.91

    pre-annexation 46, 73

    rebellion and retrocession 140–141, 167–168, 175–176

Treasure Island (Robert Louis Stevenson, 1883) 208, 210, 211, 216

The Treasure of the Lake (1926) 446

Tree, Herbert Beerbohm 357, 567 n.85

Tritton, Edgerton 400

Trollope, Anthony 114

Trübner, Nicolaas 189, 195, 200

Tsate (Pedi stronghold) 74, 91, 94, 95, 96, 97, 119, 120, 145

Tua (fictional character) 354

Tucker, *Mrs* 173, 176

Turquet, André 34

Tutankhamun (tomb) 22, 460, 461, 464

Twala (fictional character) 213, 214

Tyrrell, Barbara 399, 581 n.22

Tyrrell, Harcourt 399

Tyssen-Amherst, Margaret 21, 334

Tyssen-Amherst, Mary Rothes Margaret (later Cecil) 22, 223, 479 n.78 & n.79, 561 n.12

Tyssen-Amherst, William Amherst 21, 22, 334, 479 n.79, 599 n.1

Ullershaw, Rupert (fictional character) 335

Ulu: An African Romance (Joseph Thomson and E. Harris Smith, 1888) 536 n.63

Ulundi (battle) 401, 581 n.23

Umbopa (Ignosi, fictional character) 212, 213, 215

Umbuso kaShaka (In the Realm of Shaka, translation of *Nada the Lily* by F.L. Ntuli, 1930) 283–284

uMgungundhlovu (Zululand) 401, 582 n.41

Umhlangana 281

Umnikwa (real and fictional character) 398, 581 n.19

Umpikanina 400–401

Umslopogaas (fictional character) *see* Mhlopekazi

Unemployed Labour and Reclamation Committee 353–354

Universities Mission to Central Africa 308

uSuthu 8, 9–10

vaccination 320–321

Van Breda, Hendrik 109, 110, 114, 117, 121

Van Deventer, Gerrit 95, 97, 98, 119

Van Eck, *Mr* 114

Van Gorkum, N.J. 91, 95, 97, 98

Ventvögel (guide) 131

Veterans' Club and Employment Bureau (Victory Services Club) 468, 601 n.77

Victoria Club (Pietermaritzburg) 388

Vilakazi, Benedict 284, 546 n.39

Vincent, Edgar (Lord D'Abernon) 366, 371, 373, 377, 378, 385, 409, 418, 433, 435, 570 n.47, 573 n.6

Vincey, Leo (fictional character) 236, 237, 238, 240, 348, 349, 543 n.57

Vincey, M.L. (fictional character) 236

De Volkstem 506 n.95

Vyvyan, Wilmot Lushington 398, 581 n.17

Wakkerstroom 113, 117, 126

Wallace, Alfred Russel 36

Wallop, John Fellowes 303

Walmsley, Hugh Mulleneux 219–220, 528 n.93

Walmsley, Joshua 8–9, 219

Walters, John Cuming 257, 259, 260–261

Wambe (fictional character) 266

Wanderer's Necklace (1914) 358, 373, 409

war dances 67–68, 233, 234, 236

War of the Children (*Impi yabaNtwana*) 7, 11

Ward, Leslie (*pseud.* Spy) 242

Warren, Charles 545 n.27, 553 n.42

Watt, Alexander Pollock 233, 234, 236, 263, 264, 267, 327, 335, 365, 373, 411, 413, 417, 586 n.43, 593 n.38

Watt, Alexander Strahan 471, 586 n.43

Watt, Thomas 423

The Way of the Spirit (1906) 335–336, 561 n.22, 562 n.32, 565 n.35

Weatherley, Frederick Augustus 128, 129–131, 139, 142, 506 n.100 & n.109, 509 n.37 & n.39

Weatherley, Maria Louisa 129

Weatherley, Rupert 129, 130, 139, 509 n.39

Webb, Sidney & Beatrice 465

Weeber, O.C. 492 n.2

Weenen 63

Wells, H.G. 250

Western, Maximilian (brother-in-law of HRH) 149, 252

When the World Shook ('Yva', 1918) 261, 308, 428, 434, 436

White, Etta 40, 115, 147, 199

Whitehead, Percy 78, 94

Wilde, Oscar 223, 251, 295, 540 n.92

Williams, Gussie 416

Williams, John 208–209

Wills, Walter 552 n.11

Wills, William Arthur 302, 303, 304, 306, 309, 311, 312, 552 n.11

Wilson, Allan 307

Wilson, Harry 419

Wilson, James 340

Windham's (London club) 442, 512 n.16, 587 n.73

Wingfield, Thomas (fictional character) 291, 292

A Winter Pilgrimage (1901) 324, 325

Wirgman, Augustus 382

Wisdom's Daughter (1923) 234, 243, 446, 457

The Witch's Head ('Eva', 1884) 39, 53, 124, 125, 127, 203–206, 207, 208, 209, 222, 246, 264, 267, 315, 321, 389, 475 n.5, 486 n.24, 509 n.39, 582 n.54

The Wizard (1896) 308, 554 n.53

Wodehouse, John 312

Wolseley, Garnet 47, 51, 52, 57, 76, 87, 145, 152, 156, 162, 167, 251

Wonderboom (Pretoria) 88, 391, 496 n.30 & n.31

Wonderfontein caves (Transvaal) 115, 214, 526 n.50

Wood, Evelyn 136, 139, 142, 171, 174, 176, 178, 181, 251

Woodroffe, Charles & Marina 59

World War I (1914–1918) 413, 429, 432, 436, 440, 441, 585 n.14, 586 n.38

The World's Desire (HRH and Andrew Lang, 1890) 243, 274–275, 293, 544 n.86 & n.89, 566 n.64, 597 n.66

Wright, Harry 340, 341

Wyckham, Henry 370

Yeats, W.B. 355, 356–357, 567 n.82 & n.84

The Yellow God (1908) 451, 550 n.62

Young, Arthur & Martha 328

Yule, J.S. 302

Zibhebhu kaMapitha 156, 181, 191, 192, 201, 202, 400

Zikali (fictional character) 364, 384, 412, 569 n.31

Zikhali kaMatiwane 569 n.31

Zimboe (fictional place) 395

Zinita (fictional character) 281

Zola, Émile 216, 254, 256

Zulu people and Zululand
annexation and incorporation 202
boundary commission (1878) 134–135
civil wars 521 n.37
dancing 67–68, 233, 234, 236, 399
HRH's travels 397–404
post Anglo-Zulu War settlement 156, 181, 191, 400, 406, 514 n.79
relations with Boers 87, 91, 99–100, 109–110, 134, 202, 492 n.6
royal succession 7–8

Zululand Lands Delimitation Commission (1902–1904) 402